The Individual
and
the Universe

The Individual
—and—
the Universe

An Introduction To Philosophy

Oliver A. Johnson
University of California, Riverside

Holt, Rinehart and Winston
New York   Chicago   San Francisco   Dallas
Montreal   Toronto   London   Sydney

Library of Congress Cataloging in Publication Data

Johnson, Oliver, A.
  The Individual and the Universe

    Includes bibliographies and index.
    1. Philosophy—Introductions. 2. Philosophy—
Addresses, essays, lectures. I. Johnson, Oliver A.
BD21.I52   190   80-27998

ISBN 0-03-056888-9

1 2 3 4   038   9 8 7 6 5 4 3 2 1

PREFACE

In *The Individual and the Universe* I have attempted to accomplish two main objectives: To provide a sourcebook for the introductory course in philosophy that (1) approaches the discipline from a humanistic perspective and at the same time (2) introduces students to the major fields and central issues of our philosophical tradition. I have pursued the first of these objectives by organizing the book around a general theme—the relationship of the individual human being to the forces, both natural and artificial, that surround us all. I develop this theme primarily in my introductory essay as well as in the introductions to the seven Parts into which the book is divided. It is reflected also in the titles I have given to these Parts and to some extent in the reading selections I have chosen for inclusion in the book. Thus the book should prove particularly congenial to teachers who, like myself, believe that a humanistic orientation offers an introduction to philosophy that is not only sound, both pedagogically and intellectually, but of unusual educational value to the kind of students we now find entering our colleges and universities.

I have pursued my second objective by devoting the book entirely to writings that address the central problems in each of the major fields of philosophy which are, with few exceptions, the work of philosophers of acknowledged historical stature. Although the satisfaction of this objective may not in every instance have led to an equal satisfaction of the first, in most cases the two have proved more than merely compatible. Indeed, the history of philosophy gives ample evidence that the greatest thinkers in our tradition made their most significant contributions when they devoted their attention to concerns centering around the individual and his place in the universe. Nevertheless, whether one accepts this conclusion or even finds the approach to philosophy I have adopted here congenial or not, he can find in the book a collection of source documents, covering the main areas and problems of philosophy, sufficiently extensive to provide ample materials for the standard introductory course and sufficiently diverse to generate the kind of controversy that sustains such a course. Teachers, thus, are bound neither by my perspective nor my organization but can pattern a course of their own choosing out of the materials available in the book.

In my various introductions, in addition to offering a humanistic setting for the selections presented, I have endeavored to provide an intellectual and historical context as well, and a survey of the main problems with which they are concerned plus a review of the alternative solutions to these problems that philosophers have offered. Although my aim in doing this has been to help students to understand the selections themselves and thus to get a maximum educational benefit from them, I have kept my introductory materials relatively short. My reasons for doing so are two-fold: To encourage students to concentrate on the selections themselves, which *are* the heart of the book, and to leave the matter of explication and interpretation primarily in the hands of the classroom instructor, where it not only rightly belongs but can most effectively be discharged.

The book contains, in addition to the introductions, other editorial aids that can be of assistance not only to students but to teachers as well. Each selection is followed by a list of study questions. These attempt to focus attention on the main issues raised in the selection and are designed to help students read it with greater understanding as well as to relate the writer's thought to their own lives and concerns. There is also a short bibliography at the end of each selection. The references included in these bibliographies have been carefully chosen for their value in providing students with helpful expositions of and commentaries on the selections.

The Individual and the Universe has been under preparation for several years. During that time many people have given me advice and offered suggestions concerning it. For all this help, some of which is reflected in the finished product, I am deeply grateful. In particular I wish to acknowledge my indebtedness to my colleagues in philosophy at UCR, whose ideas are always good even while almost invariably diverse; to Louis Mink of Wesleyan University, Johannes Morsink of Drew University, Gerald Runkle of Southern Illinois University, and Robert Dewey late of the University of Nebraska, all of whom scrutinized my manuscript thoroughly and, with kindness but without compromise, catalogued its shortcomings; and to David Boynton of Holt, Rinehart and Winston, for his sage advice about book publishing and his conversations on a variety of subjects. Many hands have shared in the typing of the manuscript. I am grateful to all but in particular to those of Clara Dean, which did most of the job, with their justly celebrated speed and accuracy. Finally, my thanks to my wife who, as always, has shouldered the burden of seeing me through another project with a patience and consideration that is beyond recompense.

O.A.J.
November, 1980

CONTENTS

PART III
The Individual and Nature   73

PART IV
The Individual and Society   175

PART VI
The Individual and God   311

The Individual
and
the Universe

Wonders are many, and none is more wonderful than man; the power that crosses the white sea, driven by the stormy south-wind, making a path under surges that threaten to engulf him; and Earth, the eldest of the gods, the immortal, the unwearied, doth he wear, turning the soil with the offspring of horses, as the plows go to and fro from year to year.

And the lighthearted race of birds and the tribes of savage beasts, and the seabrood of the deep, he snares in the meshes of his woven toils, he leads captive, man excellent in wit. And he masters by his arts the beast whose lair is in the wilds, who roams the hills; he tames the horse of shaggy mane, he puts the yoke upon its neck, he tames the tireless mountain bull.

And speech, and wind-swift thought, and all the moods that mold a state, hath he taught himself; and how to flee the arrows of the frost, when 'tis hard lodging under the clear sky, and the arrows of the rushing rain; yea, he hath resource for all; without resource he meets nothing that must come: only against Death shall he call for aid in vain . . .

Sophocles, *Antigone*

The eternal silence of these infinite spaces terrifies me.

Pascal, *Pensées*

INTRODUCTION

What is Philosophy?

I

Most students beginning their first course in philosophy approach the subject with mixed feelings. They don't know just what to expect because they have never studied anything like philosophy before, and they are apprehensive because they have heard that it is hard. But they have registered in the course anyway, partly out of their interest in something new and different and partly because they have got the impression that philosophy is not just another academic subject but actually comes to grips with issues that have real relevance to their lives. To what extent are their apprehensions, as well as their expectations, justified? The first part of the question can be answered quickly; but the second part will take longer. For most students, philosophy is probably more on the hard than the easy side, but it is certainly no harder than many other subjects in the curriculum. In any case, to ask whether a subject is hard is to miss the really pertinent question: Are the results to be gained from studying it worth the effort required? Directing our question to philosophy, we can ask: What value does it have? Before we can answer, we must have some idea of what philosophy is—which in turn necessitates a brief dip into its history.

Philosophy is very old. It had its origins in the Western world among the ancient Greeks, in the centuries before the birth of Christ. Three of the classical Greek philosophers—Socrates, Plato and Aristotle—have had such a profound influence on our civilization that their names, if not their ideas, are familiar to every educated person today. The term "philosophy" itself, which these thinkers originated, results from a combination of two Greek words, one meaning "love" and one meaning "wisdom." Philosophy thus means the love of wisdom, and the philosopher, as a consequence, is a lover of wisdom. The first of these two words hardly requires comment; the meaning of the second, however, is far from evident. What is wisdom? We can say immediately that it includes knowledge as a necessary part. A person is not called wise if he is an ignoramus. But the possession of knowledge in itself does not constitute wisdom; someone who spends his life collecting trivial and worthless facts is usually judged a fool. Wisdom, thus, implies the ability not only to distinguish between what is worth knowing and what is not; but the judgment to concentrate on the former. The wise person devotes his attention to matters of fundamental and perennial significance; he does not dissipate his energies chasing passing fads. He attempts, as the seventeenth-century Dutch philosopher, Spinoza, so aptly put it, to view the universe *sub specie aeternitatis* ("under the aspect of eternity"). Finally, the wise person approaches the issues he is concerned with from a human perspective; he is interested not only in gaining knowledge of the world around him, but particularly, in understanding the place he and others occupy and the roles they play in that world. He values this understanding not simply for its own sake, but equally as much, as a guide for the conduct of his life. Such, then, is a portrait of the philosopher or, at least, of the kind of person the philosopher aspires to be.

Because its goal is wisdom, philosophy stands somewhat apart from most other academic disciplines. Unlike many subjects, which are of interest only to those who are preparing for a specific career, its relevance is universal; for we are all lovers of wisdom—if not actually, at least potentially. To be human is to be naturally concerned with the kind of problems with which philosophers grapple. Like the other animals, all of us are thrown, with neither our knowledge nor consent, into a world in which we must then live. But, unlike the rest, the human animal possesses a unique gift—the power of thought. As a result, we are not confined simply to living in the world; we are able also to understand the world in which we live. Humans (and to some extent even animals) gain pleasure from exercising the capacities they have. Thus, when we are young and agile, we like to run and swim and climb. We also take pleasure, particularly when we gain maturity, in exercising our mental faculties—both in limited ways, as in intellectual games or in mathematics—and in more general ways, as in science; culminating in our pursuit of issues that are universal in their scope, in philosophy. As a thinking being, every individual, and in particular anyone who has sufficient mental gifts to be studying at the college level, has a natural inclination toward philosophy and can find satisfaction in the understanding he gains from it, both of the nature of the universe in which he lives and of his place in that universe. For such persons philosophy can be fun.

II

Because of its breadth, philosophy is concerned with issues that bear relationships to the specific subject matter of every other academic discipline, from art and literature to mathematics. Its closest and most important ties, however, are with the sciences because both share the same primary goal: to understand the nature of the universe. However, the individual sciences are distinguished from philosophy, as well as from each other, because each concentrates on some portion or aspect of the universe: geology, for example, on the earth; biology on living things; psychology on human and animal behavior—and so on. The fact that philosophy does not limit its inquiries, but tries to understand reality as a whole, accounts for one very obvious difference between it and the various sciences—the absence of a philosophy laboratory. To be able to conduct an experiment, an investigator must circumscribe his inquiry sufficiently to allow him to concentrate on some material object he can manipulate with his equipment, subject to tests; or observe through some device such as a telescope or microscope. It is possible to do this with a rock, a piece of living tissue, or even a distant star. But when one is attempting to reach conclusions that apply to the entire universe, including not only the world of physical nature but also the animal kingdom and human beings with their feelings, emotions, and thoughts and even, possibly, supernatural beings; what could the investigator possibly find to examine in his laboratory that would provide him with evidence on which to draw the kind of conclusions he is seeking?

A consequence of the difference between philosophy and science is that philosophical theories, because they cannot be supported by empirical evidence, are much more difficult to defend than scientific theories. This consequence we must accept. It is the result of an intellectual trade-off. The sciences purchase theoretical solidity at the expense of scope; philosophy sacrifices security to gain breadth. This trade-off tends to reveal itself in temperamental differences; scientists lean toward intellectual conservatism whereas philosophers are more prone to speculation. In any case, if we are to understand the universe as clearly and fully as possible, we must have both; so there is plenty of room in the world of the intellect for both scientists and philosophers.

A second difference between science and philosophy should be mentioned; it results from the philosopher's attempt to go beyond the acquisition of knowledge to the attainment of wisdom. A fundamental ideal of scientific inquiry is objectivity. For science this means two things. First, the scientist should never allow extraneous considerations, like personal bias or the demands of religious or political orthodoxy, to influence his judgment or dictate his results; rather he must base his conclusions strictly and solely on the evidence he finds. Second, the scientist does not concern himself with the consequences of his discoveries. Rather, he presents his findings dispassionately; whether the results of what he has found should prove to be helpful or harmful to human welfare does not concern him as scientist. (After World War II a group of atomic scientists banded together in an attempt to have nuclear weapons banned; they did not, however, do this in their role as scientists but as concerned human beings.) With the philosopher the situation is somewhat different and more complex. The ideal of objectivity as the rejection of external bias he shares with the scientist; nothing is more opposed to the spirit of philosophy than prejudice or any type of subjectivity. Free and impartial inquiry is an ideal for which many philosophers have suffered and some have died. The philosopher, however, departs from the scientist on the point of dispassionate objectivity about the consequences of scientific work. If the scientist (or anyone else) makes discoveries that have effects on human welfare, it is the responsibility of the philosopher to assess these and to make recommendations about their development and use on the basis of his assessment. Recent advances in biology, particularly in genetics, have given emphasis to the heavy weight of this responsibility.

III

Philosophy is a large subject matter, so it can be broken down into a number of parts. Of the various different ways of dividing it up, perhaps the most helpful to one who wants to understand what philosophy is all about is to separate it into sub-disciplines that are distinguished from each other by the kind of question they ask. Viewed in this way, philosophy naturally divides into three parts.

(1) *Descriptive philosophy.* The central question of descriptive philosophy is, What is the nature of reality? The descriptive philosopher, thus, attempts to understand the universe, but not in its details; rather his concern is with its most general characteristics. Descriptive philosophy is clearly closely related to science. The relationship between the two might be described by saying that it provides a broad context, or perspective, from which to view the world, within

which the various sciences carry on their special, detailed investigations. Aristotle gave this (central) sub-discipline of philosophy a name, calling it *metaphysics* (literally translated, "the study that comes after the study of nature"). This term is still used by philosophers but unfortunately it has, through the years, developed several misleading and intellectually disrespectable connotations; so it seems better perhaps to replace it. I have chosen "descriptive philosophy" because it seems to me best to describe the aim of philosophers who engage in it.

The primary problem that philosophers concerned with the nature of reality have set themselves is to reach a conclusion concerning the basic material, or stuff, of which the universe is composed. This they call "the problem of substance." Pursuing the issue they have asked themselves such questions as these: Is the universe composed of one basic substance or material? If so, what is it? Or are there two (or more) substances, neither of which is reducible to the other? If so, what are they? Are they related to each other in any way? If so, how? The last question gives rise to another set of issues, which together are known as "the problem of relations." The complexities of this problem are increased by the need to provide an explanation of the relationship between events that succeed each other in time. In our ordinary thought, we single out certain of these events and say that they not only follow other events temporally but are the effects of those earlier events, which are their causes. What is the nature of the connection between such pairs of events, which we call the "cause-effect relationship"? The most difficult of such problems, however, and the one of greatest interest to us, is to give some explanation of the relationship between human beings and the world in which they find themselves. Are we totally immersed in the world, to the extent of being a part of it like everything else, or do we, on the other hand, stand completely outside of it? Or do we, as most people probably think, occupy both positions at once, being in some sense a part of the world but in another sense somehow independent of it? The answer we give to these last questions has important implications for our conception of human nature and thus, indirectly, on the question of the life that is best for us to live. By doing so, it gives rise to problems of value, hence leads to the second subdivision of philosophy.

(2) *Normative philosophy.* The two basic questions asked by normative philosophy are, What is good? and What is bad? What things in life should we seek and what shun? The object of normative philosophy, thus, is not description but evaluation; it is concerned with norms or standards rather than with facts. In its normative aspect, which has the general name *ethics,* philosophy becomes intensely practical in a way in which probably no other discipline does. In saying this, nothing banal is intended, such as that ethics offers psychological counseling or vocational training or similar practical guidance. Its practicality is of a much more fundamental and humanly meaningful kind. In addressing itself to the question, What is the best kind of life that we can live? it faces an issue in which everyone, no matter what his particular interests, has a deep and vital concern. Although we wish to succeed in whatever occupation engages us, most of us would find our success hollow if we had to purchase it at the price of personal misery. Typically, however, we find ourselves so immersed in our immediate affairs and the day-to-day problems of ordinary life that we rarely take the time to disengage ourselves from the here and now to stand back and assess the lives we are leading. The study of normative philosophy gives us an opportunity and an incentive to do that, as well as guidelines to conduct our assessment.

Our search for the good life, however, is not carried on in a social vacuum.

Others around us are seeking the same ends as we, and often their efforts come into conflict with our own. When this happens, how should we react? Are we free to pursue our own interests regardless of the effects that our doing so will have on our fellows, or do we have an obligation to promote their welfare as well as our own? Because of its close relationship to the issue of the best life for ourselves, the question of our duties becomes a matter of interest to normative philosophy. A further, third topic grows out of these two. The existence of multitudes of human beings, with their diverse wants and desires, makes urgent the need for social organization, both to secure cooperative effort for the achievement of ends and to control activities that, if not inhibited, can become mutually destructive. As the primary agency to handle such issues, societies have created the state. But the existence of the state itself leads to further problems. So we can ask, Can the state justify itself? If we answer this question affirmatively, we can then go on to ask, What functions should the state perform? What kind of state succeeds best in performing these functions? What limits, if any, should be placed on the functions the state performs? Such questions are the concern of *political philosophy*.

One other type of normative philosophy needs mention. The values with which it deals are artistic, in the broadest sense. It asks, What is beautiful? and What is ugly? This branch of philosophy is called *aesthetics*.

(3) *Critical philosophy.* Like normative philosophy, critical philosophy engages in assessment, but it is of a different kind. The critical philosopher does not ask, What is good? but What is true? Going further, he asks, How can we determine whether something we believe is true, so constitutes knowledge, or is false, so constitutes error? Critical philosophy deals with these questions in two different ways, so is divided into two parts. The first, *logic*, is concerned with the rules that govern cogent reasoning. The second, *epistemology*, or *theory of knowledge*, is occupied with a cluster of related issues, including such questions as, What do we know? What does it mean to say that we know? How do we go about acquiring knowledge? What, if any, are the limitations on our knowledge?

IV

There are a number of ways of introducing students to the main areas and problems of philosophy that I have just been describing. *The Individual and the Universe* combines two of these. First, this book lets the philosophers speak for themselves. The pages that follow contain selections from the writings of some of the most important and influential thinkers in western history. When you have finished this book, writers like Plato, Descartes, and Kant will be more than just names to you; you will know, from first-hand acquaintance, what they have contributed to our understanding of things. Second, in accord with the view already expressed, that philosophy is not merely another academic subject but is vitally relevant to any thinking being, an attempt has been made to choose writings and to arrange them in a way that will both support and illustrate this conception. Thus, Part I begins the book with an eye-witness account of the last days of one of the most famous philosophers in history, the Athenian Socrates, who devoted his life to philosophy, and finally died for it, because, as he put it, "The unexamined life is not worth living." Part II begins such an examination of life, focusing attention on ourselves. In it a number of writers offer quite different answers to the question, What am I? The focus then shifts from self to world, and, in Parts III through V, attention is given to the relationship between the individual and the three main forces that impinge on his life: first, the world of nature, then other people, or society, and finally the state. In Part VI the discussion centers on a power in the universe that some people believe to exert the most profound of all influences on the lives of humans, and that others believe not even to exist—God. The book ends, in Part VII, with the individual in his role as thinker. Different philosophers express their views on the way in which we gain knowledge of the universe and on the nature of truth.

Philosophy, to be studied for maximum gain, must be read actively rather than passively. This means several things. Mainly it requires the reader himself to engage in the act of philosophizing as he reads. He should analyze the text before him, attempting to determine what conclusion the writer is aiming to establish as well as to sort out the arguments he offers in support of his conclusion. Having done this, the reader is ready to begin the most important part of his task—to examine what he has read critically. Are the author's arguments sound? Do they support the conclusion he draws from them? Has he considered all the possibilities? Answered pertinent objections? And so on. To emphasize the obvious, philosophy is a subject in which speed reading has no place.

To help you get the most possible out of the selections in this book, three aids to your reading have been added. At the end of each selection, you will find a set of study questions. These have been formulated in a way to help you both to focus on the most important points the author makes, and to relate what he says to your own experience. In addition, there are short lists of references for further reading. These have been selected for their value in helping you to understand the problem with which the selection is concerned and in suggesting solutions to it. Finally, each part contains a general introduction that surveys the main issues to be encountered in it, and each selection has a preface giving a brief description of its contents, followed by a biographical sketch of its author. Once you get accustomed to reading philosophically, and even become adept at it, you may well discover, perhaps to your surprise, that it is an exciting intellectual adventure.

Background Readings

Bontempo, C. J., and Odell, S. J., eds. *The Owl of Minerva: Philosophers on Philosophy*. New York: McGraw-Hill, 1975.

Danto, A. C. *What Philosophy Is*. New York: Harper & Row, 1968.

Edwards, P. ed. *The Encyclopedia of Philosophy*. 8 vols. New York: Macmillan, 1967.

Flew, A., ed. *A Dictionary of Philosophy*. New York: St. Martin's, 1979.

Johnstone, H. W., Jr. ed. *What is Philosophy?* New York: Macmillan, 1965.

Moore, G. E. *Some Main Problems of Philosophy*. London: Allen and Unwin, 1953 (Chapter 1).

Newell, R. W. *The Concept of Philosophy*. London: Methuen, 1967.

Perry, R. B. *A Defense of Philosophy*. Cambridge, Mass.: Harvard University Press, 1931.

Rotenstreich, N. *Philosophy: The Concept and Its Manifestations*. Dordrecht, The Netherlands: D. Reidel, 1972 (Part II).

Wheatley, J. *Prolegomena to Philosophy*. Belmont, Calif.: Wadsworth, 1970.

PART I

The Individual as Philosopher

Everyone, the common saying goes, is a philosopher. The remark is unquestionably trite, but it is also true, or very nearly so. Philosophy is, in an essential respect, different from many of the other disciplines that constitute the curriculum of institutions of higher education. One can live a full and satisfying life without the slightest acquaintance with analytic geometry or classical economics, but if one never raises questions about the meaning of life or the individual's place in the universe, he fails to fulfill his nature as a human being. To live an authentic life at the human level, one must, at least occasionally, come to grips with philosophical issues.

What distinguishes the average person from the philosopher, thus, is not that the latter engages in an activity that the former does not, but rather that he engages in the activity in a much more effective way. Nor does the professional philosopher differ from the amateur in his purpose; both have the same goal in view—to understand the world and their place in it. What distinguishes them is that the one usually pursues his goal in a somewhat naive and desultory way, and the other systematically and with sophistication. The aim of philosophical education, therefore, is not to create philosophers but to make better philosophers of persons who already philosophize.

What, then, is required to make a good philosopher? Obviously, more than a modicum of intelligence is necessary. Beyond that, the most important qualities are determination and perseverance. The philosopher must be prepared to devote his life to his task. To justify such a level of devotion, Socrates, one of the most famous philosophers in history, explained, "The unexamined life is not worth living." Because he believed this, Socrates spent his life examining the meaning of life and engaging his fellow Athenians in his quest for understanding. Although his efforts won him a large following, particularly among the youth of Athens, his persistent questioning so disturbed the Athenian establishment that he was finally indicted and brought to trial on a charge of atheism and corruption of the youth. As a measure of his dedication to his philosophic quest, Socrates warned the jurors at his trial that, if they pardoned him on condition that he abandon his way of life, he would disobey their orders; for the pursuit of philosophy was to him more precious than even life itself.

Although Socrates was probably the first and certainly the most famous of all philosophical martyrs, he has not been alone in giving up his life for his beliefs. To mention one other example, the Italian, Giordano Bruno, was burned at the stake in Rome in 1600 for refusing to recant certain views he held that were judged by the church to be heretical. Others, too, have suffered over the ages for holding opinions contrary to some current orthodoxy. During the early modern period, for example, one of the few places in Europe allowing religious dissent was Holland. As a result, philosophers like René Descartes went there to live and write, and many arranged to have books published there that otherwise would never have seen the light of day. Even in our times, persecution of philosophers continues. In several countries, dissident writers have been imprisoned. Their lapse from orthodoxy is no longer religious, of course, but usually political. Lest we succumb to complacency on this score, moreover, we should not forget that during the McCarthy period, only a generation ago, several American philosophers lost their positions because they defended views that were held to be subversive, views that today have become a regular part of the curriculum in most of our better universities.

The first selection in our book gives a picture of the life and career of Socrates, one of the most gifted and dedicated individuals in the history of philosophy, as it unfolds during and after his trial before an Athenian court in 399 B.C.. The son of a stonecutter, Socrates abandoned the family profession to devote his life to philosophy after receiving a command from God to do so. A familiar figure on the streets of Athens, with the exception of military service, he left his native city only once, to attend an athletic event. That his revelation of the ignorance of the high and mighty of Athens should make him the ideal and idol of the city's youth is understandable; that it should engender the bitter enmity of those he unmasked could equally have been predicted. We owe the account we have of Socrates' trial, imprisonment, and death to Plato, the outstanding member of the group of youthful admirers who followed him about Athens, listening to his interrogations of the city fathers. With the exception of the prison conversation between Socrates and Crito, Plato was himself present at the events he describes.

❧ *The Apology*

SCENE—*The Court of Justice*

Socrates. I cannot tell what impression my accusers have made upon you, Athenians: for my own part, I know that they nearly made me forget who I was, so plausible were they; and yet they have scarcely uttered one single word of truth. But of all their many falsehoods, the one which astonished me most, was when they said that I was a clever speaker, and that

Translated by F. J. Church.

you must be careful not to let me mislead you. I thought that it was most impudent of them not to be ashamed to talk in that way; for as soon as I open my mouth the lie will be exposed, and I shall prove that I am not a clever speaker in any way at all: unless, indeed, by a clever speaker they mean a man who speaks the truth. If that is their meaning, I agree with them that I am a much greater orator than they. My accusers, then I repeat, have said little or nothing that is true; but from me you shall hear the whole truth. Certainly you will not hear any elaborate speech, Athenians, dressed up, like theirs, with words and phrases. I will say to you what I have to say, without preparation, and in the words which come first, for I believe that my cause is just; so let none of you expect anything else. Indeed, my friends, it would hardly be seemly for me, at my age, to come before you like a young man with his specious falsehoods. But there is one thing, Athenians, which I do most earnestly beg and entreat of you. Do not be surprised and do not interrupt, if in my defense I speak in the same way that I am accustomed to speak in the marketplace, at the tables of the money changers, where many of you have heard me, and elsewhere. The truth is this. I am more than seventy years old, and this is the first time that I have ever come before a Court of Law; so your manner of speech here is quite strange to me. If I had been really a stranger, you would have forgiven me for speaking in the language and the fashion of my native country: and so now I ask you to grant me what I think I have a right to claim. Never mind the style of my speech—it may be better or it may be worse—give your whole attention to the question, "Is what I say just, or is it not?" That is what makes a good judge, as speaking the truth makes a good advocate.

I have to defend myself, Athenians, first against the old false charges of my old accusers, and then against the later ones of my present accusers. For many men have been accusing me to you, and for very many years, who have not uttered a word of truth: and I fear them more than I fear Anytus and his companions, formidable as they are. But, my friends, those others are still more formidable; for they got hold of most of you when you were children, and they have been more persistent in accusing me with lies, and in trying to persuade you that there is one Socrates, a wise man, who speculates about the heavens, and who examines into all things that are beneath the earth, and who can "make the worse appear the better reason." These men, Athenians, who spread abroad this report,

are the accusers whom I fear; for their hearers think that persons who pursue such inquiries never believe in the gods. And then they are many, and their attacks have been going on for a long time: and they spoke to you when you were at the age most readily to believe them: for you were all young, and many of you were children: and there was no one to answer them when they attacked me. And the most unreasonable thing of all is that commonly I do not even know their names: I cannot tell you who they are, except in the case of the comic poets. But all the rest who have been trying to prejudice you against me, from motives of spite and jealousy, and sometimes, it may be, from conviction, are the enemies whom it is hardest to meet. For I cannot call any one of them forward in Court, to cross-examine him: I have, as it were, simply to fight with shadows in my defense, and to put questions which there is no one to answer. I ask you, therefore, to believe that, as I say, I have been attacked by two classes of accusers—first by Meletus and his friends, and then by those older ones of whom I have spoken. And, with your leave, I will defend myself first against my old enemies; for you heard their accusations first, and they were much more persistent than my present accusers are.

Well, I must make my defense, Athenians, and try in the short time allowed me to remove the prejudice which you have had against me for a long time. I hope that I may manage to do this, if it be good for you and for me, and that my defense may be successful; but I am quite aware of the nature of my task, and I know that it is a difficult one. Be the issue, however, as God wills, I must obey the law, and make my defense.

Let me begin again, then, and see what is the charge which has given rise to the prejudice against me, which was what Meletus relied on when he drew his indictment. What is the calumny which my enemies have been spreading about me? I must assume that they are formally accusing me, and read their indictment. It would run somewhat in this fashion: "Socrates is an evildoer, who meddles with inquiries into things beneath the earth, and in heaven, and who 'makes the worse appear the better reason,' and who teaches others these same things." That is what they say; and in the Comedy of Aristophanes you yourselves saw a man called Socrates swinging round in a basket, and saying that he walked the air, and talking a great deal of nonsense about matters of which I understand nothing, either more or less. I do not mean to disparage that kind of knowledge, if there is any man who possesses it. I trust Meletus may never be able to prosecute me for that. But, the truth is, Athenians, I have nothing to do with these matters, and almost all of you are yourselves my witnesses of this. I beg all of you who have ever heard me converse, and they are many, to inform your neighbors and tell them if any of you have ever heard me conversing about such matters, either more or less. That will show you that the other common stories about me are as false as this one.

But, the fact is, that not one of these stories is true; and if you have heard that I undertake to educate men, and exact money from them for so doing, that is not true either; though I think it would be a fine thing to be able to educate men, as Gorgias of Leontini, and Prodicus of Ceos, and Hippias of Elis do. For each of them, my friends, can go into any city, and persuade the young men to leave the society of their fellow-citizens, with any of whom they might associate for nothing, and to be only too glad to be allowed to pay money for the privilege of associating with themselves. And I believe that there is another wise man from Paros residing in Athens at this moment. I happened to meet Callias, the son of Hipponicus, a man who has spent more money on the Sophists than everyone else put together. So I said to him—he has two sons—"Callias, if your two sons had been foals or calves, we could have hired a trainer for them who would have made them perfect in the excellence which belongs to their nature. He would have been either a groom or a farmer. But whom do

you intend to take to train them, seeing that they are men? Who understands the excellence which belongs to men and to citizens? I suppose that you must have thought of this, because of your sons. Is there such a person," said I, "or not?" "Certainly there is," he replied. "Who is he," said I, "and where does he come from, and what is his fee?" "His name is Evenus, Socrates," he replied: "he comes from Paros, and his fee is five minas." Then I thought that Evenus was a fortunate person if he really understood this art and could teach so cleverly. If I had possessed knowledge of that kind, I should have given myself airs and prided myself on it. But, Athenians, the truth is that I do not possess it.

Perhaps some of you may reply: But, Socrates, what is this pursuit of yours? Whence come these calumnies against you? You must have been engaged in some pursuit out of the common. All these stories and reports of you would never have gone about, if you had not been in some way different from other men. So tell us what your pursuits are, that we may not give our verdict in the dark. I think that that is a fair question, and I will try to explain to you what it is that has raised these calumnies against me, and given me this name. Listen, then: some of you perhaps will think that I am jesting; but I assure you that I will tell you the whole truth. I have gained this name, Athenians, simply by reason of a certain wisdom. But by what kind of wisdom? It is by just that wisdom which is, I believe, possible to men. In that, it may be, I am really wise. But the men of whom I was speaking just now must be wise in a wisdom which is greater than human wisdom, or in some way which I cannot describe, for certainly I know nothing of it myself, and if any man says that I do, he lies and wants to slander me. Do not interrupt me, Athenians, even if you think that I am speaking arrogantly. What I am going to say is not my own: I will tell you who says it, and he is worthy of your credit. I will bring the god of Delphi to be the witness of the fact of my wisdom and of its nature. You remember Chaerephon. From youth upwards he was my comrade; and he went into exile with the people,* and with the people he returned. And you remember, too, Chaerephon's character, how vehement he was in carrying through whatever he took in hand. Once he went to Delphi and ventured to put this question to the oracle—I entreat you again, my friends, not to cry out—he asked if there was any man who was wiser than I: and the priestess answered that there was no man. Chaerephon himself is dead, but his brother here will confirm what I say.

Now see why I tell you this. I am going to explain to you the origin of my unpopularity. When I heard of the oracle I began to reflect: What can God mean by this dark saying? I know very well that I am not wise, even in the smallest degree. Then what can he mean by saying that I am the wisest of men? It cannot be that he is speaking falsely, for he is a god and cannot lie. And for a long time I was at a loss to understand his meaning: then, very reluctantly, I turned to seek for it in this manner. I went to a man who was reputed to be wise, thinking that there, if anywhere, I should prove the answer wrong, and meaning to point out to the oracle its mistake, and to say, "You said that I was the wisest of men, but this man is wiser than I am." So I examined the man—I need not tell you his name, he was a politician—but this was the result, Athenians. When I conversed with him I came to see that, though a great many persons, and most of all he himself, thought that he was wise, yet he was not wise. And then I tried to prove to him that he was not wise, though he fancied that he was: and by so doing I made him, and many of the bystanders, my enemies. So when I went away, I thought to myself, "I am wiser than this man: neither of us probably knows anything that is really good, but he thinks that he has knowledge, when he has not, while I, having no knowledge, do not think that I have. I seem, at any rate, to be a little wiser than he is on

this point: I do not think that I know what I do not know. Next I went to another man who was reputed to be still wiser than the last, with exactly the same result. And there again I made him, and many other men, my enemies.

Then I went on to one man after another, seeing that I was making enemies every day, which caused me much unhappiness and anxiety: still I thought that I must set God's command above everything. So I had to go to every man who seemed to possess any knowledge, and search for the meaning of the oracle: and, Athenians, I must tell you the truth; verily, by the dog of Egypt, this was the result of the search which I made at God's bidding. I found that the men whose reputation for wisdom stood highest were nearly the most lacking in it; while others, who were looked down on as common people, were much better fitted to learn. Now, I must describe to you the wanderings which I undertook, like a series of Heraclean labors, to make full proof of the oracle. After the politicians, I went to the poets, tragic, dithyrambic, and others, thinking that there I should find myself manifestly more ignorant than they. So I took up the poems on which I thought that they had spent most pains, and asked them what they meant, hoping at the same time to learn something from them. I am ashamed to tell you the truth, my friends, but I must say it. Almost any one of the bystanders could have talked about the works of these poets better than the poets themselves. So I soon found that it is not by wisdom that the poets create their works, but by a certain natural power and by inspiration, like soothsayers and prophets, who say many fine things, but who understand nothing of what they say. The poets seemed to me to be in a similar case. And at the same time I perceived that, because of their poetry, they thought that they were the wisest of men in other matters too, which they were not. So I went away again, thinking that I had the same advantage over the poets that I had over the politicians.

Finally, I went to the artisans, for I knew very well that I possessed no knowl-

*At the time of the oligarchy of the Thirty, 404 B.C.—ed.

edge at all, worth speaking of, and I was sure that I should find that they knew many fine things. And in that I was not mistaken. They knew what I did not know, and so far they were wiser than I. But, Athenians, it seemed to me that the skilled artisans made the same mistake as the poets. Each of them believed himself to be extremely wise in matters of the greatest importance, because he was skillful in his own art: and this mistake of theirs threw their real wisdom into the shade. So I asked myself, on behalf of the oracle, whether I would choose to remain as I was, without either their wisdom or their ignorance, or to possess both, as they did. And I made answer to myself and to the oracle that it was better for me to remain as I was.

By reason of this examination, Athenians, I have made many enemies of a very fierce and bitter kind, who have spread abroad a great number of calumnies about me, and people say that I am "a wise man." For the bystanders always think that I am wise myself in any matter wherein I convict another man of ignorance. But, my friends, I believe that only God is really wise: and that by this oracle he meant that men's wisdom is worth little or nothing. I do not think that he meant that Socrates was wise. He only made use of my name, and took me as an example, as though he would say to men, "He among you is the wisest, who, like Socrates, knows that in very truth his wisdom is worth nothing at all." And therefore I still go about testing and examining every man whom I think wise, whether he be a citizen or a stranger, as God has commanded me; and whenever I find that he is not wise, I point out to him on the part of God that he is not wise. And I am so busy in this pursuit that I have never had leisure to take any part worth mentioning in public matters, or to look after my private affairs. I am in very great poverty by reason of my service to God.

And besides this, the young men who follow me about, who are the sons of wealthy persons and have a great deal of spare time, take a natural pleasure in hearing men cross-examined: and they often imitate me among themselves: then they try their hands at cross-examining other people. And, I imagine, they find a great abundance of men who think that they know a great deal, when in fact they know little or nothing. And then the persons who are cross-examined get angry with me instead of with themselves, and say that Socrates is an abominable fellow who corrupts young men. And when they are asked, "Why, what does he do? What does he teach?" they do not know what to say; but, not to seem at a loss, they repeat the stock charges against all philosophers, and allege that he investigates things in the air and under the earth, and that he teaches people to disbelieve in the gods, and "to make the worse appear the better reason." For, I fancy, they would not like to confess the truth, which is that they are shown up as ignorant pretenders to knowledge that they do not possess. And so they have been filling your ears with their bitter calumnies for a long time, for they are zealous and numerous and bitter against me; and they are well disciplined and plausible in speech. On these grounds Meletus and Anytus and Lycon have attacked me. Meletus is indignant with me on the part of the poets, and Anytus on the part of the artisans and politicians, and Lycon on the part of the orators. And so, as I said at the beginning, I shall be surprised if I am able, in the short time allowed me for my defense, to remove from your minds this prejudice which has grown so strong. What I have told you, Athenians, is the truth: I neither conceal, nor do I suppress anything, small or great. And yet I know that it is just this plainness of speech which makes me enemies. But that is only a proof that my words are true, and that the prejudice against me, and the causes of it, are what I have said. And whether you look for them now or hereafter, you will find that they are so.

· · ·

Perhaps someone will say: "Are you not ashamed, Socrates, of following pursuits which are very likely now to cause your death?" I should answer him with justice, and say: "My friend, if you think that a man of any worth at all ought to reckon the chances of life and death when he acts, or that he ought to think of anything but whether he is acting rightly or wrongly, and as a good or a bad man would act, you are grievously mistaken. According to you, the demigods who died at Troy would be men of no great worth, and among them the son of Thetis, who thought nothing of danger when the alternative was disgrace. For when his mother, a goddess, addressed him, as he was burning to slay Hector, I suppose in this fashion, 'My son, if thou avengest the death of thy comrade Patroclus, and slayest Hector, thou wilt die thyself, for fate awaits thee straightway after Hector's death,' he heard what she said, but he scorned danger and death; he feared much more to live a coward, and not to avenge his friend. 'Let me punish the evildoer and straightway die,' he said, 'that I may not remain here by the beaked ships, a scorn of men, encumbering the earth.' " [Homer, *Iliad,* xviii, 96, 98.] Do you suppose that he thought of danger or of death? For this, Athenians, I believe to be the truth. Wherever a man's post is, whether he has chosen it of his own will, or whether he has been placed at it by his commander, there it is his duty to remain and face the danger, without thinking of death, or of any other thing, except dishonor.

When the generals whom you chose to command me, Athenians, placed me at my post at Potidaea, and at Amphipolis, and at Delium, I remained where they placed me, and ran the risk of death, like other men: and it would be very strange conduct on my part if I were to desert my post now from fear of death or of any other thing, when God has commanded me, as I am persuaded that he has done, to spend my life in searching for wisdom, and in examining myself and others. That would indeed be a very strange thing: and then certainly I might with justice be brought to trial for not believing in the gods: for I should be disobeying the oracle, and fearing death, and thinking myself wise, when I was not

wise. For to fear death, my friends, is only to think ourselves wise, without being wise: for it is to think that we know what we do not know. For anything that men can tell, death may be the greatest good that can happen to them: but they fear it as if they knew quite well that it was the greatest of evils. And what is this but that shameful ignorance of thinking that we know what we do not know? In this matter too, my friends, perhaps I am different from the mass of mankind: and if I were to claim to be at all wiser than others, it would be because I do not think that I have any clear knowledge about the other world, when, in fact, I have none. But I do know very well that it is evil and base to do wrong, and to disobey my superior, whether he be man or god. And I will never do what I know to be evil, and shrink in fear from what, for all that I can tell, may be a good. And so, even if you acquit me now, and do not listen to Anytus' argument that, if I am to be acquitted, I ought never to have been brought to trial at all: and that, as it is, you are bound to put me to death, because, as he said, if I escape, all your children will forthwith be utterly corrupted by practicing what Socrates teaches: if you were therefore to say to me, "Socrates, this time we will not listen to Amytus: we will let you go; but on this condition, that you cease from carrying on this search of yours, and from philosophy; if you are found following those pursuits again, you shall die"; I say, if you offered to let me go on these terms, I should reply: "Athenians, I hold you in the highest regard and love; but I will obey God rather than you: and as long as I have breath and strength I will not cease from philosophy, and from exhorting you, and declaring the truth to every one of you whom I meet, saying, as I am wont, 'My excellent friend, you are a citizen of Athens, a city which is very great and very famous for wisdom and power of mind; are you not ashamed of caring so much for the making of money, and for reputation, and for honor? Will you not think or care about wisdom, and truth, and the perfection of your soul?' And if he disputes my words, and says that he does care about these things, I shall not forthwith release him and go away: I shall question him and cross-examine him and test him: and if I think that he has not virtue, though he says that he has, I shall reproach him for setting the lower value on the most important things, and a higher value on those that are of less account. This I shall do to everyone whom I meet, young or old, citizen or stranger: but more especially to the citizens, for they are more nearly akin to me. For, know well, God has commanded me to do so. And I think that no better piece of fortune has ever befallen you in Athens than my service to God. For I spend my whole life in going about and persuading you all to give your first and chiefest care to the perfection of your souls, and not till you have done that to think of your bodies, or your wealth; and telling you that virtue does not come from wealth, but that wealth, and every other good thing which men have, whether in public, or in private, comes from virtue. If then I corrupt the youth by this teaching, the mischief is great: but if any man says that I teach anything else, he speaks falsely. And therefore, Athenians, I say, either listen to Anytus, or do not listen to him: either acquit me, or do not acquit me: but be sure that I shall not alter my way of life; no, not if I have to die for it many times."

Do not interrupt me, Athenians. Remember the request which I made to you, and listen to my words. I think that it will profit you to hear them. I am going to say something more to you, at which you may be inclined to cry out: but do not do that. Be sure that if you put me to death, who am what I have told you that I am, you will do yourselves more harm than me. Meletus and Anytus can do me no harm: that is impossible: for I am sure that God will not allow a good man to be injured by a bad one. They may indeed kill me, or drive me into exile, or deprive me of my civil rights; and perhaps Meletus and others think those things great evils. But I do not think so: I think that it is a much greater evil to do what he is doing now, and to try to put a

man to death unjustly. And now, Athenians, I am not arguing in my own defense at all, as you might expect me to do: I am trying to persuade you not to sin against God, by condemning me, and rejecting his gift to you. For if you put me to death, you will not easily find another man to fill my place. God has sent me to attack the city, as if it were a great and noble horse, to use a quaint simile, which was rather sluggish from its size, and which needed to be aroused by a gadfly; and I think that I am the gadfly that God has sent to the city to attack it; for I never cease from settling upon you, as it were, at every point, and rousing, and exhorting, and reproaching each man of you all day long. You will not easily find any one else, my friends, to fill my place: and if you take my advice, you will spare my life. You are vexed, as drowsy persons are, when they are awakened, and of course, if you listened to Anytus, you could easily kill me with a single blow, and then sleep on undisturbed for the rest of your lives, unless God were to care for you enough to send another man to arouse you. And you may easily see that it is God who has given me to your city: a mere human impulse would never have led me to neglect all my own interests, or to endure seeing my private affairs neglected now for so many years, while it made me busy myself unceasingly in your interests, and go to each man of you by himself, like a father, or an elder brother, trying to persuade him to care for virtue. There would have been a reason for it, if I had gained any advantage by this conduct, or if I had been paid for my exhortations; but you see yourselves that my accusers, though they accuse me of everything else without blushing, have not had the effrontery to say that I ever either exacted or demanded payment. They could bring no evidence of that. And I think that I have sufficient evidence of the truth of what I say in my poverty.

Perhaps it may seem strange to you that, though I am so busy in going about in private with my counsel, yet I do not venture to come forward in the assembly, and take part in the public councils. You have often heard me speak of my reason for this, and in many places: it is that I have a certain divine sign from God, which is the divinity that Meletus has caricatured in his indictment. I have had it from childhood: it is a kind of voice, which whenever I hear it, always turns me back from something which I was going to do, but never urges me to act. It is this which forbids me to take part in politics. And I think that it does well to forbid me. For, Athenians, it is quite certain that if I had attempted to take part in politics, I should have perished at once and long ago, without doing any good either to you or to myself. And do not be vexed with me for telling the truth. There is no man who will preserve his life for long, either in Athens or elsewhere, if he firmly opposes the wishes of the people, and tries to prevent the commission of much injustice and illegality in the State. He who would really fight for justice, must do so as a private man, not in public, if he means to preserve his life, even for a short time.

I will prove to you that this is so by very strong evidence, not by mere words, but by what you value highly, actions. Listen then to what has happened to me, that you may know that there is no man who could make me consent to do wrong from the fear of death: but that I would perish at once rather than give way. What I am going to tell you may be a commonplace in the Courts of Law; nevertheless it is true. The only office that I ever held in the State, Athenians, was that of Senator. When you wished to try the ten generals, who did not rescue their men after the battle of Arginusae, in a body, which was illegal, as you all came to think afterwards, the tribe Antiochis, to which I belong, held the presidency. On that occasion I alone of all the presidents opposed your illegal action, and gave my vote against you. The speakers were ready to suspend me and arrest me; and you were clamoring against me, and crying out to me to submit. But I thought that I ought to face the danger out in the cause of law and justice, rather than join

with you in your unjust proposal, from fear of imprisonment or death. That was before the destruction of the democracy. When the oligarchy came, the Thirty sent for me, with four others, to the Council-Chamber, and ordered us to bring over Leon the Salaminian from Salamis, that they might put him to death. They were in the habit of frequently giving similar orders to many others, wishing to implicate as many men as possible in their crimes. But then I again proved, not by mere words, but by my actions, that, if I may use a vulgar expression, I do not care a straw for death; but that I do care very much indeed about not doing anything against the laws of God or man. That government with all its power did not terrify me into doing anything wrong; but when we left the Council-Chamber, the other four went over to Salamis, and brought Leon across to Athens; and I went away home: and if the rule of the Thirty had not been destroyed soon afterwards, I should very likely have been put to death for what I did then. Many of you will be my witnesses in this matter.

Now do you think that I should have remained alive all these years, if I had taken part in public affairs, and had always maintained the cause of justice like an honest man, and had held it a paramount duty, as it is, to do so? Certainly not, Athenians, nor any other man either. But throughout my whole life, both in private, and in public, whenever I have had to take part in public affairs, you will find that I have never yielded a single point in a question of right and wrong to any man; no, not to those whom my enemies falsely assert to have been my pupils. But I was never any man's teacher. I have never withheld myself from anyone, young or old, who was anxious to hear me converse while I was about my mission; neither do I converse for payment, and refuse to converse without payment: I am ready to ask questions of rich and poor alike, and if any man wishes to answer me, and then listen to what I have to say, he may. And I cannot justly be charged with causing these men to turn out good or bad citizens: for I never either taught, or professed to teach any of them any knowledge whatever. And if any man asserts that he ever learnt or heard any thing from me in private, which every one else did not hear as well as he, be sure that he does not speak the truth.

Why is it, then, that people delight in spending so much time in my company? You have heard why, Athenians. I told you the whole truth when I said that they delight in hearing me examine persons who think that they are wise when they are not wise. It is certainly very amusing to listen to that. And, I say, God had commanded me to examine men in oracles, and in dreams, and in every way in which the divine will was ever declared to man. This is the truth, Athenians, and if it were not the truth, it would be easily refuted. For if it were really the case that I have already corrupted some of the young men, and am now corrupting others, surely some of them, finding as they grew older that I had given them evil counsel in their youth, would have come forward today to accuse me and take their revenge. Certainly I see many of them in Court. Here is Crito, of my own deme and of my own age, the father of Critobulus; here is Lysanias of Sphettus, the father of Aeschinus: here is also Antiphon of Cephisus, the father of Epigenes. Then here are others, whose brothers have spent their time in my company; Nicostratus, the son of Theozotides, and brother of Theodotus—and Theodotus is dead, so he at least cannot entreat his brother to be silent: here is Paralus, the son of Demodocus, and the brother of Theages: here is Adeimantus, the son of Ariston, whose brother is Plato here: and Aeantodorus, whose brother is Aristodorus. And I can name many others to you, some of whom Meletus ought to have called as witnesses in the course of his own speech: but if he forgot to call them then, let him call them now—I will stand aside while he does so—and tell us if he has any such evidence. No, on the contrary, my friends, you will find all these men ready to support me, the corrupter, the injurer of their kindred, as Meletus and Anytus call me. Those of them who have been already corrupted might perhaps have some reason for supporting me: but what reason can their relatives, who are grown up, and who are uncorrupted, have, except the reason of truth and justice, that they know very well that Meletus is a liar, and that I am speaking the truth?

Well, my friends, this, together it may be with other things of the same nature, is pretty much what I have to say in my defense. There may be some one among you who will be vexed when he remembers how, even in a less important trial than this, he prayed and entreated the judges to acquit him with many tears, and brought forward his children and many of his friends and relatives in Court, in order to appeal to your feelings; and then finds that I shall do none of these things, though I am in what he would think the supreme danger. Perhaps he will harden himself against me when he notices this: it may make him angry, and he may give his vote in anger. If it is so with any of you—I do not suppose that it is, but in case it should be so—I think that I should answer him reasonably if I said: "My friend, I have kinsmen too, for, in the words of Homer [*Odyssey,* xix. 163.], 'I am not born of sticks and stones, but of woman.' " And so, Athenians, I have kinsmen, and I have three sons, one of them a lad, and the other two still children. Yet I will not bring any of them forward before you, and implore you to acquit me. And why will I do none of these things? It is not from arrogance, Athenians, nor because I hold you cheap: whether or not I can face death bravely is another question: but for my own credit, and for your credit, and for the credit of our city, I do not think it well, at my age, and with my name, to do anything of that kind. Rightly or wrongly, men have made up their minds that in some way Socrates is different from the mass of mankind. And it will be a shameful thing if those of you who are thought to excel in wisdom, or in bravery, or in any other virtue, are going to act in this fashion. I have often seen men with a reputation behaving in a strange way at their trial, as if they thought it a terrible fate to be killed, and as though they expected to live for ever, if you did not put them to death. Such men seem to me to bring discredit on the city: for any stranger would suppose that the best and most eminent Athenians, who are selected by their fellow-citizens to hold office, and for other honors, are no better than women. Those of you, Athenians, who have any reputation at all, ought not to do these things: and you ought not to allow us to do them: you should show that you will be much more merciless to men who make the city ridiculous by these pitiful pieces of acting, than to men who remain quiet.

But apart from the question of credit, my friends, I do not think that it is right to entreat the judge to acquit us, or to escape condemnation in that way. It is our duty to convince his mind by reason. He does not sit to give away justice to his friends, but to pronounce judgment: and he has sworn not to favor any man whom he would like to favor, but to decide questions according to law. And therefore we ought not to teach you to forswear yourselves; and you ought not to allow yourselves to be taught, for then neither you nor we would be acting righteously. Therefore, Athenians, do not require me to do these things, for I believe them to be neither good nor just nor holy; and, more especially do not ask me to do them today, when Meletus is prosecuting me for impiety. For were I to be successful, and to prevail on you by my prayers to break your oaths, I should be clearly teaching you to believe that there are no gods; and I should be simply accusing myself by my defense of not believing in them. But, Athenians, that is very far from the truth. I do believe in the gods as no one of my accusers believes in them: and to you and to God I commit my cause to be decided as is best for you and for me.

[*He is found guilty by 281 votes to 220.*]

I am not vexed at the verdict which you have given, Athenians, for many reasons. I expected that you would find me guilty; and I am not so much surprised at that, as

at the numbers of the votes. I, certainly, never thought that the majority against me would have been so narrow. But now it seems that if only thirty votes had changed sides, I should have escaped. So I think that I have escaped Meletus, as it is: and not only have I escaped him for it is perfectly clear that if Anytus and Lycon had not come forward to accuse me too, he would not have obtained the fifth part of the votes, and would have had to pay a fine of a thousand drachmas.

So he proposes death as the penalty. Be it so. And what counter-penalty shall I propose to you, Athenians? What I deserve, of course, must I not? What then do I deserve to pay or to suffer for having determined not to spend my life in ease? I neglected the things which most men value, such as wealth, and family interests, and military commands, and popular oratory, and all the political appointments, and clubs, and factions, that there are in Athens; for I thought that I was really too conscientious a man to preserve my life if I engaged in these matters. So I did not go where I should have done no good either to you or to myself. I went instead to each one of you by himself, to do him, as I say, the greatest of services, and strove to persuade him not to think of his affairs, until he had thought of himself, and tried to make himself as perfect and wise as possible; nor to think of the affairs of Athens, until he had thought of Athens herself; and in all cases to bestow his thoughts on things in the same manner. Then what do I deserve for such a life? Something good, Athenians, if I am really to propose what I deserve; and something good which it would be suitable to me to receive. Then what is a suitable reward to be given to a poor benefactor, who requires leisure to exhort you? There is no reward, Athenians, so suitable for him as a public maintenance in the Prytaneum. It is a much more suitable reward for him than for any of you who has won a victory at the Olympic games with his horse or his chariots. Such a man only makes you seem happy, but I make you really happy: and he is not in want, and I am. So if I am to propose the penalty which I really deserve, I propose this, a public maintenance in the Prytaneum.*

Perhaps you think me stubborn and arrogant in what I am saying now, as in what I said about the entreaties and tears. It is not so, Athenians; it is rather that I am convinced that I never wronged any man intentionally, though I cannot persuade you of that, for we have conversed together only a little time. If there were a law at Athens, as there is elsewhere, not to finish a trial of life and death in a single day, I think that I could have convinced you of it: but now it is not easy in so short a time to clear myself of the gross calumnies of my enemies. But when I am convinced that I have never wronged any man, I shall certainly not wrong myself, or admit that I deserve to suffer any evil, or propose any evil for myself as a penalty. Why should I? Lest I should suffer the penalty which Meletus proposes, when I say that I do not know whether it is a good or an evil? Shall I choose instead of it something which I know to be an evil, and propose that as a penalty? Shall I propose imprisonment? And why should I pass the rest of my days in prison, the slave of successive officials? Or shall I propose a fine, with imprisonment until it is paid? I have told you why I will not do that. I should have to remain in prison for I have no money to pay a fine with. Shall I then propose exile? Perhaps you would agree to that. Life would indeed be very dear to me, if I were unreasonable enough to expect that strangers would cheerfully tolerate my discussions and reasonings, when you who are my fellow-citizens cannot endure them, and have found them so burdensome and odious to you, that you are seeking now to be released from them. No, indeed, Athenians, that is not likely. A fine life I should lead for an old man, if I were to withdraw from Athens, and pass the rest of my days in wandering from city to city, and continu-

*I.e., a pension, —ed.

ally being expelled. For I know very well that the young men will listen to me, wherever I go, as they do here; and if I drive them away, they will persuade their elders to expel me: and if I do not drive them away, their fathers and kinsmen will expel me for their sakes.

Perhaps someone will say, "Why cannot you withdraw from Athens, Socrates, and hold your peace?" It is the most difficult thing in the world to make you understand why I cannot do that. If I say that I cannot hold my peace, because that would be to disobey God, you will think that I am not in earnest and will not believe me. And if I tell you that no better thing can happen to a man than to converse every day about virtue and the other matters about which you have heard me conversing and examining myself and others, and that an unexamined life is not worth living, then you will believe me still less. But that is the truth, my friends, though it is not easy to convince you of it. And, what is more, I am not accustomed to think that I deserve any punishment. If I had been rich, I would have proposed as large a fine as I could pay: that would have done me no harm. But I am not rich enough to pay a fine, unless you are willing to fix it at a sum within my means. Perhaps I could pay you a mina: so I propose that. Plato here, Athenians, and Crito, and Critobulus, and Apollodorus bid me propose thirty minas, and they will be sureties for me. So I propose thirty minas. They will be sufficient sureties to you for the money.

[He is condemned to death.]

You have not gained very much time, Athenians, and, as the price of it, you will have an evil name from all who wish to revile the city, and they will cast in your teeth that you put Socrates, a wise man, to death. For they will certainly call me wise, whether I am wise or not, when they want to reproach you. If you would have waited for a little while, your wishes would have been fulfilled in the course of nature; for you see that I am an old man, far advanced in years, and near to death. I am speaking not to all of you, only to those who have voted for my death. And now I am speaking to them still. Perhaps, my friends, you think that I have been defeated because I was wanting in the arguments by which I could have persuaded you to acquit me, if, that is, I had thought it right to do or to say anything to escape punishment. It is not so. I have been defeated because I was wanting, not in arguments, but in overboldness and effrontery: because I would not plead before you as you would have liked to hear me plead, or appeal to you with weeping and wailing, or say and do many other things, which I maintain are unworthy of me, but which you have been accustomed to from other men. But when I was defending myself, I thought that I ought not to do anything unmanly because of the danger which I ran, and I have not changed my mind now. I would very much rather defend myself as I did, and die, than as you would have had me do, and live. Both in a lawsuit, and in war, there are some things which neither I nor any other man may do in order to escape from death. In battle a man often sees that he may at least escape from death by throwing down his arms and falling on his knees before the pursuer to beg for his life. And there are many other ways of avoiding death in every danger, if a man will not scruple to say and to do anything. But, my friends, I think that it is a much harder thing to escape from wickedness than from death; for wickedness is swifter than death. And now I, who am old and slow, have been overtaken by the slower pursuer: and my accusers, who are clever and swift, have been overtaken by the swifter pursuer, which is wickedness. And now I shall go hence, sentenced by you to death; and they will go hence, sentenced by truth to receive the penalty of wickedness and evil. And I abide by this award as well as they. Perhaps it was right for these things to be so: and I think that they are fairly measured.

And now I wish to prophesy to you, Athenians who have condemned me. For I am going to die, and that is the time when men have most prophetic power. And I prophesy to you who have sentenced me to death, that a far severer punishment than you have inflicted on me, will surely overtake you as soon as I am dead. You have done this thing, thinking that you will be relieved from having to give an account of your lives. But I say that the result will be very different from that. There will be more men who will call you to account, whom I have held back, and whom you did not see. And they will be harder masters to you than I have been, for they will be younger, and you will be more angry with them. For if you think that you will restrain men from reproaching you for your evil lives by putting them to death, you are very much mistaken. That way of escape is hardly possible, and it is not a good one. It is much better, and much easier, not to silence reproaches, but to make yourselves as perfect as you can. This is my parting prophecy to you who have condemned me.

With you who have acquitted me I should like to converse touching this thing that has come to pass, while the authorities are busy, and before I go to the place where I have to die. So, I pray you, remain with me until I go hence: there is no reason why we should not converse with each other while it is possible. I wish to explain to you, as my friends, the meaning of what has befallen me. A wonderful thing has happened to me, judges—for you I am right in calling judges. The prophetic sign, which I am wont to receive from the divine voice, has been constantly with me all through my life till now, opposing me in quite small matters if I were not going to act rightly. And now you yourselves see what has happened to me; a thing which might be thought, and which is sometimes actually reckoned, the supreme evil. But the sign of God did not withstand me when I was leaving my house in the morning, nor when I was coming up hither to the Court, nor at any point in my speech, when I was going to say anything; though at other times it has often stopped me in the very act of speaking. But now, in this matter, it has never once withstood me, either in my words or my actions. I will tell you what I believe to be the reason of that. This thing that has come upon me must be a good: and those of us who think that death is an evil must needs be mistaken. I have a clear proof that that is so; for my accustomed sign would certainly have opposed me, if I had not been going to fare well.

And if we reflect in another way we shall see that we may well hope that death is a good. For the state of death is one of two things: either the dead man wholly ceases to be, and loses all sensation; or, according to the common belief, it is a change and a migration of the soul unto another place. And if death is the absence of all sensation, and like the sleep of one whose slumbers are unbroken by any dreams, it will be a wonderful gain. For if a man had to select that night in which he slept so soundly that he did not even see any dreams, and had to compare with it all the other nights and days of his life, and then had to say how many days and nights in his life he had spent better and more pleasantly than this night, I think that a private person, nay, even the great King himself, would find them easy to count, compared with the others. If that is the nature of death, I for one count it a gain. For then it appears that eternity is nothing more than a single night. But if death is a journey to another place, and the common belief be true, that there are all who have died, what good could be greater than this, my judges? Would a journey not be worth taking, at the end of which, in the other world, we should be released from the self-styled judges who are here, and should find the true judges, who are said to sit in judgment below, such as Minos, and Rhadamanthus, and Aeacus, and Triptolemus, and the other demigods who were just in their lives? Or what would you not give to converse with Orpheus and Musaeus and Hesiod and Homer? I am willing to die many times, if this be true. And for my own part I should have a wonderful interest in meeting there Palamedes, and Ajax the son of Telamon, and the other men of old who have died through an unjust judgment, and in comparing my experiences with theirs. That I think would be no small

pleasure. And, above all, I could spend my time in examining those who are there, as I examine men here, and in finding out which of them is wise, and which of them thinks himself wise, when he is not wise. What would we not give, my judges, to be able to examine the leader of the great expedition against Troy, or Odysseus, or Sisyphus, or countless other men and women whom we could name? It would be an infinite happiness to converse with them, and to live with them, and to examine them. Assuredly there they do not put men to death for doing that. For besides the other ways in which they are happier than we are, they are immortal, at least if the common belief is true.

And you too, judges, must face death with a good courage, and believe this as a truth, that no evil can happen to a good man, either in life, or after death. His fortunes are not neglected by the gods; and what has come to me today has not come by chance. I am persuaded that it was better for me to die now, and to be released from trouble: and that was the reason why the sign never turned me back. And so I am hardly angry with my accusers, or with those who have condemned me to die. Yet it was not with this in mind that they accused me and condemned me, but meaning to do me an injury. So far I may find fault with them.

Yet I have one request to make of them. When my sons grow up, visit them with punishment, my friends, and vex them in the same way that I have vexed you, if they seem to you to care for riches, or for any other thing, before virtue; and if they think that they are something, when they are nothing at all, reproach them, as I have reproached you, for not caring for what they should, and for thinking that they are great men when in fact they are worthless. And if you will do this, I myself and my sons will have received our deserts at your hands.

But now the time has come, and we must go hence; I to die, and you to live. Whether life or death is better is known to God, and to God only.

✌ *Crito*

SCENE—*The Prison of Socrates*

Socrates. Why have you come at this hour, Crito? Is it not still early?

Crito. Yes, very early.

Socrates. About what time is it?

Crito. It is just daybreak.

Socrates. I wonder that the jailor was willing to let you in.

Crito. He knows me now, Socrates, I come here so often; and besides, I have done him a service.

Socrates. Have you been here long?

Crito. Yes; some time.

Socrates. Then why did you sit down without speaking? why did you not wake me at once?

Crito. Indeed, Socrates, I wish that I myself were not so sleepless and sorrowful. But I have been wondering to see how sweetly you sleep. And I purposely did not wake you, for I was anxious not to disturb your repose. Often before, all through your life, I have thought that your temper was a happy one; and I think so more than ever now, when I see how easily and calmly you bear the calamity that has come to you.

Socrates. Nay, Crito, it would be absurd if at my age I were angry at having to die.

Crito. Other men as old are overtaken by similar calamities, Socrates; but their age does not save them from being angry with their fate.

Socrates. That is so: but tell me, why are you here so early?

Crito. I am the bearer of bitter news, Socrates: not bitter, it seems, to you, but to me, and to all your friends, both bitter and grievous: and to none of them, I think, is it more grievous than to me.

Translated by F. J. Church.

Socrates. What is it? Has the ship come from Delos, at the arrival of which I am to die?

Crito. No, it has not actually arrived: but I think that it will be here today, from the news which certain persons have brought from Sunium, who left it there. It is clear from their news that it will be here today; and then, Socrates, tomorrow your life will have to end.

Socrates. Well, Crito, may it end fortunately. Be it so, if so the gods will. But I do not think that the ship will be here today.

Crito. Why do you suppose not?

Socrates. I will tell you. I am to die on the day after the ship arrives, am I not?

Crito. That is what the authorities say.

Socrates. Then I do not think that it will come today, but tomorrow. I judge from a certain dream which I saw a little while ago in the night: so it seems to be fortunate that you did not wake me.

Crito. And what was this dream?

Socrates. A fair and comely woman, clad in white garments, seemed to come to me, and call me and say, "O Socrates—
'The third day hence shalt thou fair Phthia reach.' " [Homer, *Illiad,* ix. 363.]

Crito. What a strange dream, Socrates!

Socrates. But its meaning is clear; at least to me, Crito.

Crito. Yes, too clear, it seems. But, O my good Socrates, I beseech you for the last time to listen to me and save yourself. For to me your death will be more than a single disaster; not only shall I lose a friend the like of whom I shall never find again, but many persons who do not know you and me well, will think that I might have saved you if I had been willing to spend money, but that I neglected to do so. And what character could be more disgraceful than the character of caring more for money than for one's friends? The world will never believe that we were anxious to save you, but that you yourself refused to escape.

Socrates. But, my excellent Crito, why should we care so much about the opinion of the world? The best men, of whose opinion it is worth our while to think, will believe that we acted as we really did.

Crito. But you see, Socrates, that it is necessary to care about the opinion of the world too. This very thing that has happened to you proves that the multitude can do a man not the least, but almost the greatest harm, if he be falsely accused to them.

Socrates. I wish that the multitude were able to do a man the greatest harm, Crito, for then they would be able to do him the greatest good too. That would have been well. But, as it is, they can do neither. They cannot make a man either wise or foolish: they act wholly at random.

Crito. Well, be it so. But tell me this, Socrates. You surely are not anxious about me and your other friends, and afraid lest, if you escape, the informers should say that we stole you away, and get us into trouble, and involve us in a great deal of expense, or perhaps in the loss of all our property, and, it may be, bring some other punishment upon us besides? If you have any fear of that kind, dismiss it. For of course we are bound to run those risks, and still greater risks than those if necessary, in saving you. So do not, I beseech you, refuse to listen to me.

Socrates. I am anxious about that, Crito, and about much besides.

Crito. Then have no fear on that score. There are men who, for no very large sum, are ready to bring you out of prison into safety. And then, you know, these informers are cheaply bought, and there would be no need to spend much upon them. My fortune is at your service, and I think that it is sufficient: and if you have any feeling about making use of my money, there are strangers in Athens, whom you know, ready to use theirs; and

one of them, Simmias of Thebes, has actually brought enough for this very purpose. And Cebes and many others are ready too. And therefore, I repeat, do not shrink from saving yourself on that ground. And do not let what you said in the Court, that if you went into exile you would not know what to do with yourself, stand in your way; for there are many places for you to go to, where you will be welcomed. If you choose to go to Thessaly, I have friends there who will make much of you, and shelter you from any annoyance from the people of Thessaly.

And besides, Socrates, I think that you will be doing what is wrong, if you abandon your life when you might preserve it. You are simply playing the game of your enemies; it is exactly the game of those who wanted to destroy you. And what is more, to me you seem to be abandoning your children too: you will leave them to take their chance in life, as far as you are concerned, when you might bring them up and educate them. Most likely their fate will be the usual fate of children who are left orphans. But you ought not to beget children unless you mean to take the trouble of bringing them up and educating them. It seems to me that you are choosing the easy way, and not the way of a good and brave man, as you ought, when you have been talking all your life long of the value that you set upon virtue. For my part, I feel ashamed both for you, and for us who are your friends. Men will think that the whole of this thing which has happened to you—your appearance in court to take your trial, when you need not have appeared at all; the very way in which the trial was conducted; and then lastly this, for the crowning absurdity of the whole affair, is due to our cowardice. It will look as if we had shirked the danger out of miserable cowardice; for we did not save you, and you did not save yourself, when it was quite possible to do so, if we had been good for anything at all. Take care, Socrates, lest these things be not evil only, but also dishonorable to you and to us. Consider then; or rather the time for consideration is past;

we must resolve; and there is only one plan possible. Everything must be done tonight. If we delay any longer, we are lost. O Socrates, I implore you not to refuse to listen to me.

Socrates. My dear Crito, if your anxiety to save me be right, it is most valuable: but if it be not right, its greatness makes it all the more dangerous. We must consider then whether we are to do as you say, or not; for I am still what I always have been, a man who will listen to no voice but the voice of the reasoning which on consideration I find to be truest. I cannot cast aside my former arguments because this misfortune has come to me. They seem to me to be as true as ever they were, and I hold exactly the same ones in honor and esteem as I used to: and if we have no better reasoning to substitute for them, I certainly shall not agree to your proposal, not even though the power of the multitude should scare me with fresh terrors, as children are scared with hobgoblins, and inflict upon us new fines, and imprisonments, and deaths. How then shall we most fitly examine the question? Shall we go back first to what you say about the opinions of men, and ask if we used to be right in thinking that we ought to pay attention to some opinions, and not to others? Used we to be right in saying so before I was condemned to die, and has it now become apparent that we were talking at random, and arguing for the sake of argument, and that it was really nothing but play and nonsense? I am anxious, Crito, to examine our former reasoning with your help, and to see whether my present position will appear to me to have affected its truth in any way, or not; and whether we are to set it aside, or to yield assent to it. Those of us who thought at all seriously, used always to say, I think, exactly what I said just now, namely, that we ought to esteem some of the opinions which men form highly, and not others. Tell me, Crito, if you please, do you not think that they were right? For you, humanly speaking, will not have to die tomorrow, and your judgment will not be biased by that circumstance. Consider then: do you not think it reasonable to say that we should not esteem all the opinions of men, but only some, not the opinions of all men, but only of some men? What do you think? Is not this true?

Crito. It is.

Socrates. And we should esteem the good opinions, and not the worthless ones?

Crito. Yes.

Socrates. But the good opinions are those of the wise, and the worthless ones those of the foolish?

Crito. Of course.

Socrates. And what used we to say about this? Does a man who is in training, and who is in earnest about it, attend to the praise and blame and opinion of all men, or of the one man only who is a doctor or a trainer?

Crito. He attends only to the opinion of the one man.

Socrates. Then he ought to fear the blame and welcome the praise of this one man, not of the many?

Crito. Clearly.

Socrates. Then he must act and exercise, and eat and drink in whatever way the man who is his master, and who understands the matter, bids him; not as others bid him?

Crito. That is so.

Socrates. Good. But if he disobeys this one man, and disregards his opinion and his praise, and esteems instead what the many, who understand nothing of the matter, say, will he not suffer for it?

Crito. Of course he will.

Socrates. And how will he suffer? In what direction, and in what part of himself?

Crito. Of course in his body. That is disabled.

Socrates. You are right. And, Crito, to be brief, is it not the same, in everything?

And, therefore, in questions of right and wrong, and of the base and the honorable, and of good and evil, which we are now considering, ought we to follow the opinion of the many and fear that, or the opinion of the one man who understands these matters (if we can find him), and feel more shame and fear before him than before all other men? For if we do not follow him, we shall cripple and maim that part of us which, we used to say, is improved by right and disabled by wrong. Or is this not so?

Crito. No, Socrates, I agree with you.

Socrates. Now, if, by listening to the opinions of those who do not understand, we disable that part of us which is improved by health and crippled by disease, is our life worth living, when it is crippled? It is the body, is it not?

Crito. Yes.

Socrates. Is life worth living with the body crippled and in a bad state?

Crito. No, certainly not.

Socrates. Then is life worth living when that part of us which is maimed by wrong and benefited by right is crippled? Or do we consider that part of us, whatever it is, which has to do with right and wrong to be of less consequence than our body?

Crito. No, certainly not.

Socrates. But more valuable?

Crito. Yes, much more so.

Socrates. Then, my excellent friend, we must not think so much of what the many will say of us; we must think of what the one man, who understands right and wrong, and of what Truth herself will say of us. And so you are mistaken to begin with, when you invite us to regard the opinion of the multitude concerning the right and the honorable and the good, and their opposites. But, it may be said, the multitude can put us to death?

Crito. Yes, that is evident. That may be said, Socrates.

Socrates. True. But, my excellent friend, to me it appears that the conclusion which we have just reached, is the same as our conclusion of former times. Now consider whether we still hold to the belief, that we should set the highest value, not on living, but on living well?

Crito. Yes, we do.

Socrates. And living well and honorably and rightly mean the same thing: do we hold to that or not?

Crito. We do.

Socrates. Then, starting from these premises, we have to consider whether it is right or not right for me to try to escape from prison, without the consent of the Athenians. If we find that it is right, we will try; if not, we will let it alone. I am afraid that considerations of expense, and of reputation, and of bringing up my children, of which you talk, Crito, are only the reflections of our friends, the many, who lightly put men to death, and who would, if they could, as lightly bring them to life again, without a thought. But reason, which is our guide, shows us that we can have nothing to consider but the question which I asked just now: namely, shall we be doing right if we give money and thanks to the men who are to aid me in escaping, and if we ourselves take our respective parts in my escape? Or shall we in truth be doing wrong, if we do all this? And if we find that we should be doing wrong, then we must not take any account either of death, or of any other evil that may be the consequence of remaining quietly here, but only of doing wrong.

Crito. I think that you are right, Socrates. But what are we to do?

Socrates. Let us consider that together, my good sir, and if you can contradict anything that I say, do so, and I will be convinced: but if you cannot, do not go on repeating to me any longer, my dear friend, that I should escape without the consent of the Athenians. I am very anxious to act with your approval: I do not want you to think me mistaken. But now tell me if you agree with the doctrine from which I start, and try to answer my questions as you think best.

Crito. I will try.

Socrates. Ought we never to do wrong intentionally at all; or may we do wrong in some ways, and not in others? Or, as we have often agreed in former times, is it never either good or honorable to do wrong? Have all our former conclusions been forgotten in these few days? Old men as we were, Crito, did we not see, in days gone by, when we were gravely conversing with each other, that we were no better than children? Or is not what we used to say most assuredly the truth, whether the world agrees with us or not? Is not wrong-doing an evil and a shame to the wrong-doer in every case, whether we incur a heavier or a lighter punishment than death as the consequence of doing right? Do we believe that?

Crito. We do.

Socrates. Then we ought never to do wrong at all?

Crito. Certainly not.

Socrates. Neither, if we ought never to do wrong at all, ought we to repay wrong with wrong, as the world thinks we may?

Crito. Clearly not.

Socrates. Well then, Crito, ought we to do evil to any one?

Crito. Certainly I think not, Socrates.

Socrates. And is it right to repay evil with evil, as the world thinks, or not right?

Crito. Certainly it is not right.

Socrates. For there is no difference, is there, between doing evil to a man, and wronging him?

Crito. True.

Socrates. Then we ought not to repay wrong with wrong or do harm to any man, no matter what we may have suffered from him. And in conceding this, Crito, be careful that you do not concede more than you mean. For I know that only a few men hold, or ever will hold this opinion. And so those who hold it, and those who do not, have no common ground of argument; they can of necessity only look with contempt to each other's belief. Do you therefore consider very carefully whether you agree with me and share my opinion. Are we to start in our inquiry from the doctrine that it is never right either to do wrong, or to repay wrong with wrong, or to avenge ourselves on any man who harms us, by harming him in return? Or do you disagree with me and dissent from my principle? I myself have believed in it for a long time, and I believe in it still. But if you differ in any way, explain to me how. If you still hold to our former opinion, listen to my next point.

Crito. Yes, I hold to it, and I agree with you. Go on.

Socrates. Then, my next point, or rather my next question, is this: Ought a man to perform his just agreements, or may he shuffle out of them?

Crito. He ought to perform them.

Socrates. Then, consider. If I escape without the state's consent, shall I be injuring those whom I ought least to injure, or not? Shall I be abiding by my just agreements or not?

Crito. I cannot answer your question, Socrates. I do not understand it.

Socrates. Consider it in this way. Suppose the laws and the commonwealth were to come and appear to me as I was preparing to run away (if that is the right phrase to describe my escape) and were to ask, "Tell us, Socrates, what have you in your mind to do? What do you mean by trying to escape, but to destroy us the laws, and the whole city, so far as in you lies? Do you think that a state can exist and not be overthrown, in which the decisions of law are of no force, and are disregarded and set at nought by private individuals?" How shall we answer questions like that, Crito? Much might be said, especially by an orator, in defense of the law which makes judicial decisions supreme. Shall I reply, "But the state has injured me: it has decided my cause wrongly." Shall we say that?

Crito. Certainly we will, Socrates.

Socrates. And suppose the laws were to reply, "Was that our agreement? or was it that you would submit to whatever judgments the state should pronounce?" And if we were to wonder at their words, perhaps they would say, "Socrates, wonder not at our words, but answer us; you yourself are accustomed to ask questions and to answer them. What complaint have you against us and the city, that you are trying to destroy us? Are we not, first, your parents? Through us your father took your mother and begat you. Tell us, have you any fault to find with those of us that are the laws of marriage?" "I have none," I should reply. "Or have you any fault to find with those of us that regulate the nurture and education of the child, which you, like others, received? Did not we do well in bidding your father educate you in music and gymnastics?" "You did," I should say. "Well then, since you were brought into the world and nurtured and educated by us, how, in the first place, can you deny that you are our child and our slave, as your fathers were before you? And if this be so, do you think that your rights are on a level with ours? Do you think that you have a right to retaliate upon us if we should try to do anything to you? You had not the same rights that your father had, or that your master would have had, if you had been a slave. You had no right to retaliate upon them if they ill-treated you, or to answer them if they reviled you, or to strike them back if they struck you, or to repay them evil with evil in any way. And do you think that you may retaliate on your country and its laws? If we try to destroy you, because we think it right, will you in return do all that you can to destroy us, the laws, and your country, and say that in so doing you are doing right, you, the man, who in truth thinks so much of virtue? Or are you too wise to see that your country is worthier, and more august, and more sacred, and holier, and held in higher honor both by the gods and

by all men of understanding, than your father and your mother and all your other ancestors; and that it is your bounden duty to reverence it, and to submit to it, and to approach it more humbly than you would approach your father, when it is angry with you; and either to do whatever it bids you to do or to persuade it to excuse you; and to obey in silence if it orders you to endure stripes or imprisonment, or if it send you to battle to be wounded or to die? That is what is your duty. You must not give way, nor retreat, nor desert your post. In war, and in the court of justice, and everywhere, you must do whatever your city and your country bid you do, or you must convince them that their commands are unjust. But it is against the law of God to use violence to your father or to your mother; and much more so is it against the law of God to use violence to your country." What answer shall we make, Crito? Shall we say that the laws speak truly, or not?

Crito. I think that they do.

Socrates. "Then consider, Socrates," perhaps they would say, "if we are right in saying that by attempting to escape you are attempting to injure us. We brought you into the world, we nurtured you, we educated you, we gave you and every other citizen a share of all the good things we could. Yet we proclaim that if any man of the Athenians is dissatisfied with us, he may take his goods and go away whithersoever he pleases: we give that permission to every man who chooses to avail himself of it, so soon as he has reached man's estate, and sees us, the laws, and the administration of our city. No one of us stands in his way or forbids him to take his goods and go wherever he likes, whether it be to an Athenian colony, or to any foreign country, if he is dissatisfied with us and with the city. But we say that every man of you who remains here, seeing how we administer justice, and how we govern the city in other matters, has agreed, by the very fact of remaining here, to do whatsoever we bid him. And, we say, he who disobeys us, does a threefold wrong: he disobeys us who are his parents, and he disobeys us who fostered him, and he disobeys us after he has agreed to obey us, without persuading us that we are wrong. Yet we did not bid him sternly to do whatever we told him. We offered him an alternative; we gave him his choice, either to obey us, or to convince us that we were wrong; but he does neither.

"These are the charges, Socrates, to which we say that you will expose yourself, if you do what you intend; and that not less, but more than other Athenians." And if I were to ask, "And why?" they might retort with justice that I have bound myself by the agreement with them more than other Athenians. They would say, "Socrates, we have very strong evidence that you were satisfied with us and with the city. You would not have been content to stay at home in it more than other Athenians, unless you had been satisfied with it more than they. You never went away from Athens to the festivals, save once to the Isthmian games, nor elsewhere except on military service; you never made other journeys like other men; you had no desire to see other cities or other laws; you were contented with us and our city. So strongly did you prefer us, and agree to be governed by us: and what is more, you begat children in this city, you found it so pleasant. And besides, if you had wished, you might at your trial have offered to go into exile. At that time you could have done with the state's consent, what you are trying now to do without it. But then you gloried in being willing to die. You said that you preferred death to exile. And now you are not ashamed of those words: you do not respect us the laws, for you are trying to destroy us: and you are acting just as a miserable slave would act, trying to run away, and breaking the covenant and agreement which you made to submit to our government. First, therefore, answer this question. Are we right, or are we wrong, in saying that you have agreed not in mere words, but in reality, to live under our government?" What are we to say, Crito? Must we not admit that it is true?

Crito. We must, Socrates.

Socrates. Then they would say, "Are you not breaking your covenants and agreements with us? And you were not led to make them by force or by fraud: you had not to make up your mind in a hurry. You had seventy years in which you might have gone away, if you had been dissatisfied with us, or if the agreement had seemed to you unjust. But you preferred neither Lacedaemon nor Crete, though you are fond of saying that they are well-governed, nor any other state, either of the Hellenes, or the Barbarians. You went away from Athens less than the lame and the blind and the cripple. Clearly you, far more than other Athenians, were satisfied with the city, and also with us who are its laws: for who would be satisfied with a city which had no laws? And now will you not abide by your agreement? If you take our advice, you will, Socrates: then you will not make yourself ridiculous by going away from Athens.

"For consider: what good will you do yourself or your friends by thus transgressing, and breaking your agreement? It is tolerably certain that they, on their part, will at least run the risk of exile, and of losing their civil rights, or of forfeiting their property. For yourself, you might go to one of the neighboring cities, to Thebes or to Megara for instance—for both of them are well-governed—but, Socrates, you will come as an enemy to those commonwealths; and all who care for their city will look askance at you, and think that you are a subverter of law. And you will confirm the judges in their opinion, and make it seem that their verdict was a just one. For a man who is a subverter of law, may well be supposed to be a corrupter of the young and thoughtless. Then will you avoid well-governed states and civilized men? Will life be worth having, if you do? Or will you consort with such men, and converse without shame—about what, Socrates? About the things which you talk of here? Will you tell them that virtue, and justice, and institutions, and law are the most precious things that men can have? And do you not think that that will be a shameful thing in Socrates? You ought to think so. But you will leave these places; you will go to the friends of Crito in Thessaly: for there is most disorder and license: and very likely they will be delighted to hear of the ludicrous way in which you escaped from prison, dressed up in peasant's clothes, or in some other disguise which people put on when they are running away, and with your appearance altered. But will no one say how you, an old man, with probably only a few more years to live, clung so greedily to life that you dared to transgress the highest laws? Perhaps not, if you do not displease them. But if you do, Socrates, you will hear much that will make you blush. You will pass your life as the flatterer and the slave of all men; and what will you be doing but feasting in Thessaly? It will be as if you had made a journey to Thessaly for an entertainment. And where will be all our old sayings about justice and virtue then? But you wish to live for the sake of your children? You want to bring them up and educate them? What? will you take them with you to Thessaly, and bring them up and educate them there? Will you make them strangers to their own country, that you may bestow this benefit on them too? Or supposing that you leave them in Athens, will they be brought up and educated better if you are alive, though you are not with them? Yes; your friends will take care of them. Will your friends take care of them if you make a journey to Thessaly, and not if you make a journey to Hades? You ought not to think that, at least if those who call themselves your friends are good for anything at all.

"No, Socrates, be advised by us who have fostered you. Think neither of children, nor of life, nor of any other thing before justice, that when you come to the other world you may be able to make your defense before the rulers who sit in judgment there. It is clear that neither you nor any of your friends will be happier, or juster, or holier in this life, if you do this thing, nor will you be happier after you are dead. Now you will go away wronged, not by us, the laws, but by men. But if you repay evil with evil, and wrong with wrong in this shameful way, and break your agreements and covenants with us, and injure those whom you should least injure, yourself, and your friends, and your country, and us, and so escape, then we shall be angry with you while you live, and when you die our brethren, the laws in Hades, will not receive you kindly; for they will know that on earth you did all that you could to destroy us. Listen then to us, and let not Crito persuade you to do as he says."

Know well, my dear friend Crito, that this is what I seem to hear, as the worshipers of Cybele seem, in their frenzy, to hear the music of flutes: and the sound of these words rings loudly in my ears, and drowns all other words. And I feel sure that if you try to change my mind you will speak in vain; nevertheless, if you think that you will succeed, say on.

Crito. I can say no more, Socrates.

Socrates. Then let it be, Crito: and let us do as I say, seeing that God so directs us.

✒ Phaedo

When he had finished speaking Crito said, "Be it so, Socrates.* But have you any commands for your friends or for me about your children, or about other things? How shall we serve you best?"

Translated by F. J. Church.

*After rejecting Crito's proposal that he escape from prison, Socrates has spent his last day discussing with friends the question of immortality. —ed.

"Simply by doing what I always tell you, Crito. Take care of your own selves, and you will serve me and mine and yourselves in all that you do, even though you make no promises now. But if you are careless of your own selves, and will not follow the path of life which we have pointed out in our discussions both today and at other times, all your promises now, however profuse and earnest they are, will be of no avail."

"We will do our best," said Crito. "But how shall we bury you?"

"As you please," he answered; "only you must catch me first, and not let me escape you." And then he looked at us with a smile and said, "My friends, I cannot convince Crito that I am the Socrates who has been conversing with you, and arranging his arguments in order. He thinks that I am the body which he will presently see a corpse, and he asks how he is to bury me. All the arguments which I have used to prove that I shall not remain with you after I have drunk the poison, but that I shall go away to the happiness of the blessed, with which I tried to comfort you and myself, have been thrown away on him. Do you therefore be my sureties to him, as he was my surety at the trial, but in a different way. He was surety for me then that I would remain; but you must be my sureties to him that I shall go away when I am dead, and not remain with you: then he will feel my death less; and when he sees my body being burnt or buried, he will not be grieved because he thinks that I am suffering dreadful things: and at my funeral he will not say that it is Socrates whom he is laying out, or bearing to the grave, or burying. For, dear Crito," he continued, "you must know that to use words wrongly is not only a fault in itself; it also creates evil in the soul. You must be of good cheer, and say that you are burying my body: and you must bury it as you please, and as you think right."

With these words he rose and went into another room to bathe himself: Crito went with him and told us to wait. So we waited, talking of the argument, and discussing it, and then again dwelling on the greatness of the calamity which had fallen upon us: it seemed as if we were going to lose a father, and to be orphans for the rest of our life. When he had bathed, and his children had been brought to him—he had two sons quite little, and one grown up—and the women of his family were come, he spoke with them in Crito's presence, and gave them his last commands; then he sent the women and children away, and returned to us. By that time it was near the hour of

sunset, for he had been a long while within. When he came back to us from the bath he sat down, but not much was said after that. Presently the servant of the Eleven came and stood before him and said, "I know that I shall not find you unreasonable like other men, Socrates. They are angry with me and curse me when I bid them drink the poison because the authorities make me do it. But I have found you all along the noblest and gentlest and best man that has ever come here; and now I am sure that you will not be angry with me, but with those who you know are to blame. And so farewell, and try to bear what must be as lightly as you can; you know why I have come." With that he turned away weeping, and went out.

Socrates looked up at him, and replied, "Farewell: I will do as you say." Then he turned to us and said, "How courteous the man is! And the whole time that I have been here, he has constantly come in to see me, and sometimes he has talked to me, and has been the best of men; and now, how generously he weeps for me! Come, Crito, let us obey him: let the poison be brought if it is ready, and if it is not ready, let it be prepared."

Crito replied: "Nay, Socrates, I think that the sun is still upon the hills, it has not set. Besides, I know that other men take the poison quite late, and eat and drink heartily, and even enjoy the company of their chosen friends, after the announcement has been made. So do not hurry; there is still time."

Socrates replied: "And those whom you speak of, Crito, naturally do so; for they think that they will be gainers by so doing. And I naturally shall not do so; for I think that I should gain nothing by drinking the poison a little later, but my own contempt for so greedily saving up a life which is already spent. So do not refuse to do as I say."

Then Crito made a sign to his slave who was standing by; and the slave went out, and after some delay returned with the man who was to give the poison, carrying it prepared in a cup. When Socrates saw him, he asked, "You understand these things, my good sir, what have I to do?"

"You have only to drink this," he replied, "and to walk about until your legs feel heavy, and then lie down; and it will act of itself." With that he handed the cup to Socrates, who took it quite cheerfully, without trembling, and without any change of color or of feature, and looked up at the man with that fixed glance of his, and asked, "What say you to making a libation from this draught? May I, or not?" "We only prepare so much as we think sufficient, Socrates," he answered. "I understand," said Socrates. "But I suppose that I may, and must, pray to the gods that my journey hence may be prosperous: that is my prayer; be it so." With these words he put the cup to his lips and drank the poison quite calmly and cheerfully. Till then most of us had been able to control our grief fairly well; but when we saw him drinking, and then the poison finished, we could do so no longer: my tears came fast in spite of myself, and I covered my face and wept for myself: it was not for him, but at my own misfortune in losing such a friend. Even before that Crito had been unable to restrain his tears, and had gone away; and Apollodorus, who had never once ceased weeping the whole time, burst into a loud cry, and made us one and all break down by his sobbing and grief, except only Socrates himself. "What are you doing, my friends?" he exclaimed. "I sent away the women chiefly in order that they might not offend in this way; for I have heard that a man should die in silence. So calm yourselves and bear up." When we heard that we were ashamed, and we ceased from weeping. But he walked about, until he said that his legs were getting heavy, and then he lay down on his back, as he was told.

And the man who gave the poison began to examine his feet and legs, from time to time: then he pressed his foot hard, and asked if there was any feeling in it; and Socrates said, "No" and then his legs, and so higher and higher, and showed us that he was cold and stiff. And Socrates felt himelf, and said that when it came to his heart, he should be gone. He was already growing cold about the groin, when he uncovered his face, which had been covered, and spoke for the last time. "Crito," he said, "I owe a cock to Asclepius; do not forget to pay it." "It shall be done," replied Crito. "Is there anything else that you wish?" He made no answer to this question; but after a short interval there was a movement, and the man uncovered him, and his eyes were fixed. Then Crito closed his mouth and his eyes.

Such was the end of our friend, a man, I think, who was the wisest and justest, and the best man that I have ever known.

STUDY QUESTIONS

1. What did Socrates do that led many prominent Athenians to conclude that he was a dangerous man who had to die?

2. Do you find Socrates' arguments that death is not an evil at all convincing? Explain.

3. What have you learned about justice in ancient Athens from the account of Socrates' trial?

4. State in your own words the reasons Socrates gave for refusing to escape from prison. Do you think his reasons were good? Imagine yourself placed in the same situation. What would you have done? Why?

For Further Reading

Guardini, R. *The Death of Socrates*. New York: Sheed and Ward, 1948.

Gulley, N. *The Philosophy of Socrates*. London: Macmillan, 1968.

Guthrie, W. K. C. *Socrates*. London: Cambridge University Press, 1971.

Plato. *Euthyphro*.

Santas, G. *Socrates*. Boston: Routledge & Kegan Paul, 1978.

Taylor, A. E. *Socrates*. New York: Appleton, 1933 (esp. Chapters 3 and 4).

Vlastos, G. ed. *The Philosophy of Socrates*. New York: Doubleday, 1971.

PART II

——⊲⊳——

What Am I?

High on a rugged crag overlooking the Gulf of Corinth stand the ruins of an ancient Greek temple. Here for centuries during classical times sat the priestesses of the oracle of Delphi, in mystical trances offering their advice regarding the future to individuals and states alike. Inscribed on the wall of the temple were the words "Know thyself."

Like most of the advice given by the Delphian oracle to petitioners, the admonition "Know thyself" is ambiguous, being open to a variety of interpretations. The most obvious reading of it is psychological. The inquirer is urged to focus his attention on his own inner self to become more aware of the kind of person he is. But there are other, and broader, interpretations of the admonition, and it is these that are of most interest to philosophers. To know oneself, for example, is to know what kind of being one is, so philosophers have asked themselves the questions: What does it mean to be human? How do human beings differ from other kinds of beings? Are we unique and distinct from everything else in the universe, or are we much like the other beings that surround us?

One way to seek an answer to these questions is through an inquiry into our origins. The ancient Hebrew account of creation, in which God forms man and woman in an image of himself, offered an explanation of the distinctively human characteristics, particularly our capacity for distinguishing between good and evil, that seemed to set us apart from the animals. It appealed as well to the human feeling of uniqueness and superiority. For such reasons, and also because it appeared in ancient writings that came to be regarded with veneration as the Holy Book, this view was generally accepted in the West for nearly two thousand years. The rise of modern science, however, brought questions. First, geologists, through their study, particularly of rock formations, came to the conclusion that the earth, rather than having been created only a few thousand years ago, as the biblical account described, must have existed for untold millions of years. Added to this came an accumulation of evidence establishing that, at a time far earlier than that at which Adam and Eve were said to have been placed in the Garden of

Eden, the earth was inhabited by beings that could only be described as human. These scientific conclusions, with the increasing masses of data that were gathered in their support, prepared the way for an alternative explanation of the origins of humanity, one which was naturalistic rather than supernaturalistic. This account was supplied about a hundred years ago by Charles Darwin with his theory of organic evolution, in which the human race is said to have descended, over a vast period of time, from animal ancestors.

Although the theory of evolution has profoundly altered our conception of ourselves, its consequences have, on occasion, been exaggerated. Sometimes we hear the argument that, since we are descended from animals, we really are no more than animals ourselves, our so-called human attributes being nothing more than a thin veneer that easily rubs off. To reason in this way, however, is to commit the genetic fallacy by assuming that an account of our genesis, or origin, in itself provides a description of the kind of beings we now are. It is like arguing that, because all Americans can trace their ancestry back to people who were immigrants to this country, we are all really foreigners. If we are to understand human nature as it now is, we must concentrate on the human beings of today, not on their remote ancestors. Philosophers and others who have done this have offered a number of different descriptions of the kind of beings we are. A few of these descriptions can be found in the selections that follow.

The question, What am I? can be asked in quite another way as well. One asking it is not concerned about human beings in general and the ways in which their nature differs from that of other things but rather about his own individual self. He wants to know just what kind of thing he is. An obvious answer to such a question is that the individual is a physical body, which he can see, feel, and so on. Although some philosophers have accepted this answer, most have not. It seems to them that a distinction can be made between a person and his physical body. They want to say, I am not a body; rather I *have* a body. What, then, is this "I" that has a body? This question has been answered in a number of ways. Those writing from a traditional religious perspective usually have said, I am a soul. The seventeenth-century French philosopher, René Descartes, in his famous self-description, wrote, "I am, precisely speaking, only a thinking thing, that is, a mind." Others in search of a neutral term, have concluded, I am a self. The last answer has become embedded in our language. When I speak of *me*, the word I use to refer to me is "myself." Here, however, a problem seems to arise. Is it correct to say that I *am* a self or should we not really say (as we did about one's body), I *have* a self? To speak of my having a self, however, raises a further difficulty. If I say, I have a self, can I mean that this self I possess is *myself*? If so, what is the being (referred to in the last sentence by the word "I") that possesses this self? Surely it is and must be my true self. If that is so, we must conclude that a self is not something we can possess, like a body, but is rather something that we must *be*.

If an individual's self is what he is, or his real, most intimate being, it would seem to follow that it is the thing he knows best. Self-knowledge should be the most direct and thus the easiest of all knowledge to obtain. Such an optimistic view has been challenged by the great Scottish philosopher, David Hume, who claims that self-knowledge, rather than being easy, is impossible. In two of the selections that follow, Hume first offers his reasons for his unusual view and then his fellow Scot, Thomas Reid, gives arguments against Hume's sceptical conclusion.

Whatever our nature as human beings may be, we all live in a world. A crucial difference between us and the other animals lies in the fact that, because we possess intelligence, we can assess our surroundings and make judgments of value about the situation in which we find ourselves. Those who have done so often describe the conclusions they reach by the phrase "the human condition." In their assessments of the human condition, most writers have spoken in negative tones. Although they generally emphasize the need to improve our situation, they are by no means in agreement about how this should be done. Many believe that the matter is out of our control; either the human condition is irretrievable or, if it is to be salvaged, the work must be accomplished by higher hands. Others, however, are more optimistic, arguing that we can work our own salvation. Among the latter is Plato, whose "Allegory of the Cave"—one of the most famous depictions of the human condition in Western literature—concludes Part II.

Background Readings

Bronowski, J. *The Identity of Man.* rev. ed. Garden City, N.Y.: Doubleday, 1971.
Cassirer, E. *An Essay on Man.* New Haven, Conn.: Yale University Press, 1944.
Charon, J. E. *Man in Search of Himself.* New York: Walker, 1967.
Fromm, E. and Xirau, R., eds. *The Nature of Man.* New York: Macmillan, 1968.
Heschel, A. J. *Whos Is Man?* Palo Alto, Calif.: Stanford University Press, 1965.
Hocking, W. E. *What Man Can Make of Man.* New York: Harper & Row, 1942.
Morris, C. *The Open Self.* New York: Prentice-Hall, 1948.
Rhinelander, P. *Is Man Incomprehensible to Man?* San Francisco: W. H. Freeman, 1973.

THE BIBLE: THE IMAGE OF GOD

The author of the story of creation, as it appears in the first chapters of Genesis, is unknown. Indeed, it may well have had no single author but was the result of an oral tradition handed down through the generations. Biblical scholars believe that the account, as we now have it, took its final form during the fifth century B.C.

✢ *Genesis*

In the beginning God created the heaven and the earth. And the earth was without form, and void, and darkness was upon the face of the deep. And the Spirit of God moved upon the face of the waters. And God said, Let there be light: and there was light. And God saw the light, that it was good: and God divided the light from the darkness. And God called the light Day,

The selection is from Chapters 1 and 2 of the King James version.

and the darkness he called Night. And the evening and the morning were the first day. And God said, Let there be a firmament in the midst of the waters, and let it divide the waters from the waters. And God made the firmament, and divided the waters which were under the firmament from the waters which were above the firmament: and it was so. And God called the firmament Heaven. And the evening and the morning were the second day. And God said, Let the waters under the heaven be gathered together unto one place, and let the dry land appear: and it was so. And God called the dry land Earth; and the gathering together of the waters called he Seas: And God saw that it was good. And God said, Let the earth bring forth grass, the herb yielding seed, and the fruit tree yielding fruit after his kind, whose seed is in itself, upon the earth: and it was so. And the earth brought forth grass, and herb yielding seed after his kind, and the tree yielding fruit, whose seed was in itself, after his kind: and God saw that it was good. And the evening and the morning were the third day. And God said, Let there be lights in the firmament of the heaven to divide the day from the night; and let them be for signs, and for seasons, and for days, and years: And let them be for lights in the firmament of the heaven to give light upon the earth: and it was so. And God made two great lights; the greater light to rule the day, and the lesser light to rule the night: he made the stars also. And God set them in the firmament of the heaven to give light upon the earth, and to rule over the day and over the night, and to divide the light from the darkness: and God saw that it was good. And the evening and the morning were the fourth day. And God said, Let the waters bring forth abundantly the moving creature that hath life, and fowl that may fly above the earth in the open firmament of heaven. And God created great whales, and every living creature that moveth, which the waters brought forth abundantly, after their kind, and every winged fowl after his kind: and God saw that it was good. And God blessed them, saying, Be fruitful, and multiply, and fill the waters in the seas, and let fowl multiply in the earth. And the evening and the morning were the fifth day. And God said, Let the earth bring forth the living creature after his kind, cattle, and creeping thing, and beast of the earth after his kind: and it was so. And God made the beast of the earth after his kind, and cattle after their kind, and every thing that creepeth upon the earth after his kind: and God saw that it was good. And God said, Let us make man in

our image, after our likeness: and let them have dominion over the fish of the sea, and over the fowl of the air, and over the cattle, and over all the earth, and over every creeping thing that creepeth upon the earth. So God created man in his own image, in the image of God created he him; male and female created he them. And God blessed them, and God said unto them, Be fruitful, and multiply, and replenish the earth, and subdue it: and have dominion over the fish of the sea, and over the fowl of the air, and over every living thing that moveth upon the earth. And God said, Behold, I have given you every herb bearing seed, which is upon the face of all the earth, and every tree, in the which is the fruit of a tree yielding seed; to you it shall be for meat. And to every beast of the earth, and to every fowl of the air, and to every thing that creepeth upon the earth, wherein there is life, I have given every green herb for meat: and it was so. And God saw every thing that he had made, and, behold, it was very good. And the evening and the morning were the sixth day.

Thus the heavens and the earth were finished, and all the host of them. And on the seventh day God ended his work which he had made; and he rested on the seventh day from all his work which he had made. And God blessed the seventh day, and sanctified it: because that in it he had rested from all his work which God created and made. These are the generations of the heavens and of the earth when they were created, in the day that the LORD God made the earth and the heavens, And every plant of the field before it was in the earth, and every herb of the field before it grew: for the LORD God had not caused it to rain upon the earth, and there was not a man to till the ground. But there went up a mist from the earth, and watered the whole face of the ground. And the LORD God formed man of the dust of the ground, and breathed into his nostrils the breath of life; and man became a living soul. And the LORD God planted a garden eastward in Eden; and there he put the man whom he had formed. And out of the ground made the LORD God to grow every tree that is pleasant to the sight, and good for food; the tree of life also in the midst of the garden, and the tree of knowledge of good and evil.

• • •

And the LORD God took the man, and put him into the garden of Eden to dress it and to keep it. And the LORD God commanded the man, saying, Of every tree of the garden thou mayest freely eat: But of the tree of the knowledge of good and evil, thou shalt not eat of it: for in the day that thou eatest thereof thou shalt surely die. And the LORD God said, It is not good that the man should be alone; I will make him a help meet for him. And out of the ground the LORD God formed every beast of the field, and every fowl of the air; and brought them unto Adam to see what he would call them: and whatsoever Adam called every living creature, that was the name thereof. And Adam gave names to all cattle, and to the fowl of the air, and to every beast of the field; but for Adam there was not found a help meet for him. And

the LORD God caused a deep sleep to fall upon Adam, and he slept; and he took one of his ribs, and closed up the flesh instead thereof. And the rib, which the LORD God had taken from man, made he a woman, and brought her unto the man. And Adam said, This is now bone of my bones, and flesh of my flesh: she shall be called Woman, because she was taken out of man. Therefore shall a man leave his father and his mother, and shall cleave unto his wife: and they shall be one flesh. And they were both naked, the man and his wife, and were not ashamed.

STUDY QUESTIONS

1. Can the account in *Genesis* be taken literally as a description of the creation of things? Explain.
2. *Genesis* contains two different accounts of the creation of man and woman, somewhat different from each other. What do you think is the explanation of this?
3. What is the significance of God's forbidding Adam to eat the fruit of the tree of the knowledge of good and evil?

DARWIN: A PRODUCT OF EVOLUTION

The human self-image received its greatest shock in history just over a century ago with the publication of Charles Darwin's two epochal books, *The Origin of Species* (1859) and *The Descent of Man* (1871). Before Darwin, the orthodox version of human creation, at least from the advent of Christianity, had been the account found in *Genesis*. Darwin's work changed all that. Although his conception of the human race as being descended from lower forms of animal life was contested, sometimes bitterly, for decades, it is now part of the accepted body of scientific knowledge. The most significant issue raised by the theory of evolution is not, as most of its critics believed, one of fact but one of value. Is the fact that we have evolved from lower forms of life demeaning to human worth and dignity? Or, on the contrary, is it something in which we take legitimate pride? Or, finally, is it something we ought to disregard in our assessment of human nature as we actually find it to be?

When Charles Darwin (1809–1882) entered college he had no intention of becoming a scientist. His original plan was to become a doctor, so he enrolled in Edinburgh University to study medicine. Soon finding that he was unsuited for the medical profession, he transferred to Cambridge University to study for the ministry. While at Cambridge he became increasingly interested in science; so, on graduation, instead of occupying a pulpit he set sail as naturalist aboard the ship *Beagle* on a five-year expedition to the South Seas. The observations of life he made on this long cruise supplied him with data on which he later built his theory of organic evolution. Soon after his return, he settled in the village of Down, near London, where he conducted many important scientific experiments. Darwin's home in Down remains open today as a museum.

✌ *The Descent of Man*

General Summary and Conclusion

Main conclusion that man is descended from some lower form—Manner of development—Genealogy of man—Intellectual and moral faculties—Sexual selection—Concluding remarks.

A brief summary will be sufficient to recall to the reader's mind the more salient points in this work. Many of the views which have been advanced are highly speculative, and some no doubt will prove erroneous; but I have in every case given the reasons which have led me to one view rather than to another. It seemed worthwhile to try how far the principle of evolution would throw light on some of the more complex prob-

First published in 1871.

lems in the natural history of man. False facts are highly injurious to the progress of science, for they often endure long; but false views, if supported by some evidence, do little harm, for every one takes a salutary pleasure in proving their falseness; and when this is done, one path towards error is closed and the road to truth is often at the same time opened.

The main conclusion here arrived at, and now held by many naturalists who are well competent to form a sound judgment, is that man is descended from some less highly organised form. The grounds upon which this conclusion rests will never be shaken, for the close similarity between man and the lower animals in embryonic development, as well as in innumerable points of structure and constitution, both of high and of the most trifling importance,—the rudiments which he retains, and the abnormal reversions to which he is occasionally liable,—are facts which cannot be disputed. They have long been known, but until recently they told us nothing with respect to the origin of man. Now when viewed by the light of our knowledge of the whole organic world, their meaning is unmistakable. The great principle of evolution stands up clear and firm, when these groups of facts are considered in connection with others such as the mutual affinities of the members of the same group, their geographical distribution in past and present times, and their geological succession. It is incredible that all these facts should speak falsely. He who is not content to look, like a savage, at the phenomena of nature as disconnected, cannot any longer believe that man is the work of a separate act of creation. He will be forced to admit that the close resemblance of the embryo of man to that, for instance, of a dog—the construction of his skull, limbs and whole frame on the same plan with that of other mammals, independently of the uses to which the parts may be put—the occasional re-appearance of various structures, for instance of several muscles, which man does not normally possess, but which are common to the Quadrumana—and a crowd of analogous facts—all point in the plainest manner to the conclusion that man is the co-descendant with other mammals of a common progenitor.

We have seen that man incessantly presents individual differences in all parts of his body and in his mental faculties. These differences or variations seem to be induced by the same general causes, and to obey the same laws as with the lower animals. In both cases similar laws of inheritance prevail. Man tends to increase at a greater rate than his means of subsistence; consequently he is occasionally subjected to a severe struggle for existence, and natural selection will have effected whatever lies within its scope. A succession of strongly-marked variations of a similar nature is by

no means requisite; slight fluctuating differences in the individual suffice for the work of natural selection; not that we have any reason to suppose that in the same species, all parts of the organization tend to vary to the same degree. We may feel assured that the inherited effects of the long-continued use or disuse of parts will have done much in the same direction with natural selection. Modifications formerly of importance, though no longer of any special use, are long-inherited. When one part is modified, other parts change through the principle of correlation, of which we have instances in many curious cases of correlated monstrosities. Something may be attributed to the direct and definite action of the surrounding conditions of life, such as abundant food, heat or moisture; and lastly, many characters of slight physiological importance, some indeed of considerable importance, have been gained through sexual selection.

No doubt man, as well as every other animal, presents structures, which seem to our limited knowledge, not to be now of any service to him, nor to have been so formerly, either for the general conditions of life, or in the relations of one sex to the other. Such structures cannot be accounted for by any form of selection, or by the inherited effects of the use and disuse of parts. We know, however, that many strange and strongly-marked peculiarities of structure occasionally appear in our domesticated productions, and if their unknown causes were to act more uniformly, they would probably become common to all the individuals of the species. We may hope hereafter to understand something about the causes of such occasional modifications, especially through the study of monstrosities: hence the labours of experimentalists, such as those of M. Camille Dareste, are full of promise for the future. In general we can only say that the cause of each slight variation and of each monstrosity lies much more in the constitution of the organism, than in the nature of the surrounding conditions; though new and changed conditions certainly play an important part in exciting organic changes of many kinds.

Through the means just specified, aided perhaps by others as yet undiscovered, man has been raised to his present state. But since he attained to the rank of manhood, he has diverged into distinct races, or as they may be more fitly called, sub-species. Some of these, such as the Negro and European, are so distinct that, if specimens had been brought to a naturalist without any further information, they would undoubtedly have been considered by him as good and true species. Nevertheless all the races agree in so many unimportant details of structure and in so many mental peculiarities, that these can be accounted for only by inheritance from a common progenitor; and a progenitor thus characterised would probably deserve to rank as man.

It must not be supposed that the divergence of each race from the other races, and of all from a common stock, can be traced back to any one pair of progenitors. On the contrary, at every stage in the process of modification, all the individuals which were in any way better fitted for their conditions of life, though in different degrees, would have survived in greater numbers than the less well-fitted. The process would have been like that followed by man, when he does not intentionally select particular individuals, but breeds from all the superior individuals, and neglects the inferior. He thus slowly but surely modifies his stock, and unconsciously forms a new strain. So with respect to modifications acquired independently of selection, and due to variations arising from the nature of the organism and the action of the surrounding conditions, or from changed habits of life, no single pair will have been modified much more than the other pairs inhabiting the same country, for all will have been continually blended through free intercrossing.

By considering the embryological structure of man,—the homologies which he presents with the lower animals—the rudiments which he retains,—and the rever-sions to which he is liable, we can partly recall in imagination the former condition of our early progenitors; and can approximately place them in their proper place in the zoological series. We thus learn that man is descended from a hairy, tailed quadruped, probably arboreal in its habits, and an inhabitant of the Old World. This creature, if its whole structure had been examined by a naturalist, would have been classed amongst the Quadrumana, as surely as the still more ancient progenitor of the Old and New World monkeys. The Quadrumana and all the higher mammals are probably derived from an ancient marsupial animal, and this through a long line of diversified forms, from some amphibian-like creature, and this again from some fish-like animal. In the dim obscurity of the past we can see that the early progenitor of all the Vertebrata must have been an acquatic animal, provided with branchiæ, with the two sexes united in the same individual, and with the most important organs of the body (such as the brain and heart) imperfectly or not at all developed. This animal seems to have been more like the larvæ of the existing marine Ascidians than any other known form.

The high standard of our intellectual powers and moral disposition is the greatest difficulty which presents itself, after we have been driven to this conclusion on the origin of man. But every one who admits the principle of evolution, must see that the mental powers of the higher animals, which are the same in kind with those of man, though so different in degree, are capable of advancement. Thus the interval between the mental powers of one of the higher apes and of a fish, or between those of an ant and scale-insect, is immense; yet their development does not offer any special difficulty; for with our domesticated animals, the mental faculties are certainly variable, and the variations are inherited. No one doubts that they are of the utmost importance to animals in a state of nature. Therefore the conditions are favorable for their development through natural selection. The same conclusion may be extended to man; the intellect must have been all-important to him, even at a very remote period, as enabling him to invent and use language, to make weapons, tools, traps, etc., whereby with the aid of his social habits, he long ago became the most dominant of all living creatures.

A great stride in the development of the intellect will have followed, as soon as the half-art and half-instinct of language came into use; for the continued use of language will have reacted on the brain and produced an inherited effect; and this again will have reacted on the improvement of language. As Mr. Chauncey Wright has well remarked, the largeness of the brain in man relatively to his body, compared with the lower animals, may be attributed in chief part to the early use of some simple form of language—that wonderful engine which affixes signs to all sorts of objects and qualities, and excites trains of thought which would never arise from the mere impression of the senses, or if they did arise could not be followed out. The higher intellectual powers of man, such as those of ratiocination, abstraction, self-consciousness, etc., probably follow from the continued improvement and exercise of the other mental faculties.

The development of the moral qualities is a more interesting problem. The foundation lies in the social instincts, including under this term the family ties. These instincts are highly complex, and in the case of the lower animals give special tendencies towards certain definite actions; but the more important elements are love, and the distinct emotion of sympathy. Animals endowed with the social instincts take pleasure in one another's company, warn one another of danger, defend and aid one another in many ways. These instincts do not extend to all the individuals of the species, but only to those of the same community. As they are highly beneficial to the species, they have in all probability been acquired through natural selection.

A moral being is one who is capable of reflecting on his past actions and their motives—of approving of some and disapproving of others; and the fact that man is the one being who certainly deserves this designation, is the greatest of all distinctions between him and the lower animals. But in the fourth chapter I have endeavored to show that the moral sense follows, firstly, from the enduring and ever-present nature of the social instincts; secondly, from man's appreciation of the approbation and disapprobation of his fellows; and thirdly, from the high activity of his mental faculties, with past impressions extremely vivid; and in these latter respects he differs from the lower animals. Owing to this condition of mind, man cannot avoid looking both backwards and forwards, and comparing past impressions. Hence after some temporary desire or passion has mastered his social instincts, he reflects and compares the now weakened impression of such past impulses with the ever-present social instincts; and he then feels that sense of dissatisfaction which all unsatisfied instincts leave behind them, he therefore resolves to act differently for the future—and this is conscience. Any instinct, permanently stronger or more enduring than another, gives rise to a feeling which we express by saying that it ought to be obeyed. A pointer dog, if able to reflect on his past conduct, would say to himself, I ought (as indeed we say of him) to have pointed at that hare and not have yielded to the passing temptation of hunting it.

Social animals are impelled partly by a wish to aid the members of their community in a general manner, but more commonly to perform certain definite actions. Man is impelled by the same general wish to aid his fellows; but has few or no special instincts. He differs also from the lower animals in the power of expressing his desires by words, which thus become a guide to the aid required and bestowed. The motive to give aid is likewise much modified in man: it no longer consists solely of a blind instinctive impulse, but is much influenced by the praise or blame of his fellows. The appreciation and the bestowal of praise and blame both rest on sympathy; and this emotion, as we have seen, is one of the most important elements of the social instincts. Sympathy, though gained as an instinct, is also much strengthened by exercise or habit. As all men desire their own happiness, praise or blame is bestowed on actions and motives, according as they lead to this end; and as happiness is an essential part of the general good, the greatest-happiness principle indirectly serves as a nearly safe standard of right and wrong. As the reasoning powers advance and experience is gained, the remoter effects of certain lines of conduct on the character of the individual, and on the general good, are perceived; and then the self-regarding virtues come within the scope of public opinion, and receive praise, and their opposites blame. But with the less civilized nations reason often errs, and many bad customs and base superstitions come within the same scope, and are then esteemed as high virtues, and their breach as heavy crimes.

The moral faculties are generally and justly esteemed as of higher value than the intellectual powers. But we should bear in mind that the activity of the mind in vividly recalling past impressions is one of the fundamental though secondary bases of conscience. This affords the strongest argument for educating and stimulating in all possible ways the intellectual faculties of every human being. No doubt a man with a torpid mind, if his social affections and sympathies are well developed, will be led to good actions, and may have a fairly sensitive conscience. But whatever renders the imagination more vivid and strengthens the habit of recalling and comparing past impressions, will make the conscience more sensitive, and may even somewhat compensate for weak social affections and sympathies.

The moral nature of man has reached its present standard, partly through the advancement of his reasoning powers and consequently of a just public opinion, but especially from his sympathies having been rendered more tender and widely diffused through the effects of habit, example, in-

struction, and reflection. It is not improbable that after long practice virtuous tendencies may be inherited. With the more civilized races, the conviction of the existence of an all-seeing Deity has had a potent influence on the advance of morality. Ultimately man does not accept the praise or blame of his fellows as his sole guide, though few escape this influence, but his habitual convictions, controlled by reason, afford him the safest rule. His conscience then becomes the supreme judge and monitor. Nevertheless the first foundation or origin of the moral sense lies in the social instincts, including sympathy; and these instincts no doubt were primarily gained, as in the case of the lower animals, through natural selection.

The belief in God has often been advanced as not only the greatest, but the most complete of all the distinctions between man and the lower animals. It is however impossible, as we have seen, to maintain that this belief is innate or instinctive in man. On the other hand a belief in all-pervading spiritual agencies seems to be universal; and apparently follows from a considerable advance in man's reason, and from a still greater advance in his faculties of imagination, curiosity and wonder. I am aware that the assumed instinctive belief in God has been used by many persons as an argument for His existence. But this is a rash argument, as we should thus be compelled to believe in the existence of many cruel and malignant spirits, only a little more powerful than man; for the belief in them is far more general than in a beneficent Deity. The idea of a universal and beneficent Creator does not seem to arise in the mind of man, until he has been elevated by long-continued culture.

He who believes in the advancement of man from some low organized form, will naturally ask how does this bear on the belief in the immortality of the soul. The barbarous races of man, as Sir J. Lubbock has shown, possess no clear belief of this kind: but arguments derived from the primeval beliefs of savages are, as we have just seen, of little or no avail. Few persons feel any anxiety from the impossibility of determining at what precise period in the development of the individual, from the first trace of a minute germinal vesicle, man becomes an immortal being; and there is no greater cause for anxiety because the period cannot possibly be determined in the gradually ascending organic scale.

I am aware that the conclusions arrived at in this work will be denounced by some as highly irreligious; but he who denounces them is bound to show why it is more irreligious to explain the origin of man as a distinct species by descent from some lower form, through the laws of variation and natural selection, than to explain the birth of the individual through the laws of ordinary reproduction. The birth both of the species and of the individual are equally parts of that grand sequence of events, which our minds refuse to accept as the result of blind chance. The understanding revolts at such a conclusion, whether or not we are able to believe that every slight variation of structure,—the union of each pair in marriage,—the dissemination of each seed,—and other such events, have all been ordained for some special purpose.

Sexual selection has been treated at great length in this work; for, as I have attempted to show, it has played an important part in the history of the organic world. I am aware that much remains doubtful, but I have endeavored to give a fair view of the whole case. In the lower divisions of the animal kingdom, sexual selection seems to have done nothing: such animals are often affixed for life to the same spot, or have the sexes combined in the same individual, or what is still more important, their perceptive and intellectual faculties are not sufficiently advanced to allow of the feelings of love and jealousy, or of the exertion of choice. When, however, we come to the Arthropoda and Vertebrata, even to the lowest classes in these two great Sub-Kingdoms, sexual selection has effected much.

In the several great classes of the animal kingdom—in mammals, birds, reptiles, fishes, insects, and even crustaceans,—the differences between the sexes follow nearly the same rules. The males are almost always the wooers; and they alone are armed with special weapons for fighting with their rivals. They are generally stronger and larger than the females, and are endowed with the requisite qualities of courage and pugnacity. They are provided, either exclusively or in a much higher degree than the females, with organs for vocal or instrumental music, and with odoriferous glands. They are ornamented with infinitely diversified appendages, and with the most brilliant or conspicuous colours, often arranged in elegant patterns, whilst the females are unadorned. When the sexes differ in more important structures, it is the male which is provided with special sense-organs for discovering the female, with locomotive organs for reaching her, and often with prehensile organs for holding her. These various structures for charming or securing the female are often developed in the male during only part of the year, namely the breeding-season. They have in many cases been more or less transferred to the females; and in the latter case they often appear in her as mere rudiments. They are lost or never gained by the males after emasculation. Generally they are not developed in the male during early youth, but appear a short time before the age for reproduction. Hence in most cases the young of both sexes resemble each other; and the female somewhat resembles her young offspring throughout life. In almost every great class a few anomalous cases occur, where there has been an almost complete transposition of the characters proper to the two sexes; the females assuming characters which properly belong to the males. This surprising uniformity in the laws regulating the differences between the sexes in so many and such widely separated classes, is intelligible if we admit the action of one common cause, namely sexual selection.

Sexual selection depends on the success of certain individuals over others of the same sex, in relation to the propagation of the species; whilst natural selection depends on the success of both sexes, at all ages, in relation to the general conditions of life. The sexual struggle is of two kinds; in the one it is between the individuals of the same sex, generally the males, in order to drive away or kill their rivals, the females remaining passive; whilst in the other, the struggle is likewise between the individuals of the same sex, in order to excite or charm those of the opposite sex, generally the females, which no longer remain passive, but select the more agreeable partners. This latter kind of selection is closely analogous to that which man unintentionally, yet effectually, brings to bear on his domesticated productions, when he preserves during a long period the most pleasing or useful individuals, without any wish to modify the breed.

The laws of inheritance determine whether characters gained through sexual selection by either sex shall be transmitted to the same sex, or to both; as well as the age at which they shall be developed. It appears that variations arising late in life are commonly transmitted to one and the same sex. Variability is the necessary basis for the action of selection, and is wholly independent of it. It follows from this, that variations of the same general nature have often been taken advantage of and accumulated through sexual selection in relation to the propagation of the species, as well as through natural selection in relation to the general purposes of life. Hence secondary sexual characters, when equally transmitted to both sexes can be distinguished from ordinary specific characters only by the light of analogy. The modifications acquired through sexual selection are often so strongly pronounced that the two sexes have frequently been ranked as distinct species, or even as distinct genera. Such strongly-marked differences must be in some manner highly important; and we know that they have been acquired in some instances at the cost not only of inconvenience, but of exposure to actual danger.

The belief in the power of sexual selection rests chiefly on the following considerations. Certain characters are confined to one sex; and this alone renders it probable that in most cases they are connected with the act of reproduction. In innumerable instances these characters are fully developed only at maturity, and often during only a part of the year, which is always the breeding-season. The males (passing over a few exceptional cases) are the more active in courtship; they are the better armed, and are rendered the more attractive in various ways. It is to be especially observed that the males display their attractions with elaborate care in the presence of the females; and that they rarely or never display them excepting during the season of love. It is incredible that all this should be purposeless. Lastly we have distinct evidence with some quadrupeds and birds, that the individuals of one sex are capable of feeling a strong antipathy or preference for certain individuals of the other sex.

Bearing in mind these facts, and the marked results of man's unconscious selection, when applied to domesticated animals and cultivated plants, it seems to me almost certain that if the individuals of one sex were during a long series of generations to prefer pairing with certain individuals of the other sex, characterised in some peculiar manner, the offspring would slowly but surely become modified in this same manner. I have not attempted to conceal that, excepting when the males are more numerous than the females, or when polygamy prevails, it is doubtful how the more attractive males succeed in leaving a larger number of offspring to inherit their superiority in ornaments or other charms than the less attractive males; but I have shown that this would probably follow from the females,—especially the more vigorous ones, which would be the first to breed,—preferring not only the more attractive but at the same time the more vigorous and victorious males.

Although we have some positive evidence that birds appreciate bright and beautiful objects, as with the bower-birds of Australia, and although they certainly appreciate the power of song, yet I fully admit that it is astonishing that the females of many birds and some mammals should be endowed with sufficient taste to appreciate ornaments, which we have reason to attribute to sexual selection; and this is even more astonishing in the case of reptiles, fish, and insects. But we really know little about the minds of the lower animals. It cannot be supposed, for instance, that male birds of paradise or peacocks should take such pains in erecting, spreading, and vibrating their beautiful plumes before the females for no purpose. We should remember the fact given on excellent authority in a former chapter, that several peahens, when debarred from an admired male, remained widows during a whole season rather than pair with another bird.

Nevertheless I know of no fact in natural history more wonderful than that the female Argus pheasant should appreciate the exquisite shading of the ball-and-socket ornaments and the elegant patterns on the wing-feathers of the male. He who thinks that the male was created as he now exists must admit that the great plumes, which prevent the wings from being used for flight, and which are displayed during courtship and at no other time in a manner quite peculiar to this one species, were given to him as an ornament. If so, he must likewise admit that the female was created and endowed with the capacity of appreciating such ornaments. I differ only in the conviction that the male Argus pheasant acquired his beauty gradually, through the preference of the females during many generations for the more highly ornamented males; the aesthetic capacity of the females having been advanced through exercise or habit, just as our own taste is gradually improved. In the male through the fortunate chance of a few feathers being left unchanged, we can distinctly trace how simple spots with a little fulvous shading on one side may have been developed by small steps into the wonderful ball-and-socket ornaments; and it is probable that they were actually thus developed.

Everyone who admits the principle of evolution, and yet feels great difficulty in admitting that female mammals, birds, reptiles, and fish, could have acquired the high taste implied by the beauty of the males, and which generally coincides with our own standard, should reflect that the nerve-cells of the brain in the highest as well as in the lower members of the Vertebrate series, are derived from those of the common progenitor of this great Kingdom. For we can thus see how it has come to pass that certain mental faculties, in various and widely distinct groups of animals, have been developed in nearly the same manner and to nearly the same degree.

The reader who has taken the trouble to go through the several chapters devoted to sexual selection, will be able to judge how far the conclusions at which I have arrived are supported by sufficient evidence. If he accepts these conclusions he may, I think, safely extend them to mankind; but it would be superfluous here to repeat what I have so lately said on the manner in which sexual selection apparently has acted on man, both on the male and female side, causing the two sexes to differ in body and mind, and the several races to differ from each other in various characters, as well as from their ancient and lowly-organised progenitors.

He who admits the principle of sexual selection will be led to the remarkable conclusion that the nervous system not only regulates most of the existing functions of the body, but has indirectly influenced the progressive development of various bodily structures and of certain mental qualities. Courage, pugnacity, perseverance, strength and size of body, weapons of all kinds, musical organs, both vocal and instrumental, bright colours and ornamental appendages, have all been indirectly gained by the one sex or the other, through the exertion of choice, the influence of love and jealousy, and the appreciation of the beautiful in sound, colour or form; and these powers of the mind manifestly depend on the development of the brain.

Man scans with scrupulous care the character and pedigree of his horses, cattle, and dogs before he matches them; but when he comes to his own marriage he rarely, or never, takes any such care. He is impelled by nearly the same motives as the lower animals, when they are left to their own free choice, though he is in so far superior to them that he highly values mental charms and virtues. On the other hand he is strongly attracted by mere wealth or rank. Yet he might by selection do something not only for the bodily constitution and frame of his offspring, but for their intellectual and moral qualities. Both sexes ought to refrain from marriage if they are in any marked degree inferior in body or mind; but such hopes are Utopian and will never be even partially realised until the laws of inheritance are thoroughly known. Everyone does good service, who aids towards this end. When the principles of breeding and inheritance are better understood, we shall not hear ignorant members of our legislature rejecting with scorn a plan for ascertaining whether or not consanguineous marriages are injurious to man.

The advancement of the welfare of mankind is a most intricate problem: all ought to refrain from marriage who cannot avoid abject poverty for their children; for poverty is not only a great evil, but tends to its own increase by leading to recklessness in marriage. On the other hand, as Mr. Galton has remarked, if the prudent avoid marriage, whilst the reckless marry, the inferior members tend to supplant the better members of society. Man, like every other animal, has no doubt advanced to his present high condition through a struggle for existence consequent on his rapid multiplication; and if he is to advance still higher, it is to be feared that he must remain subject to a severe struggle. Otherwise he would sink into indolence, and the more gifted men would not be more successful in the battle of life than the less gifted. Hence our natural rate of increase, though leading to many and obvious evils, must not be greatly diminished by any means. There should be open competition for all men; and the most able should not be prevented by laws or customs from

succeeding best and rearing the largest number of offspring. Important as the struggle for existence has been and even still is, yet as far as the highest part of man's nature is concerned there are other agencies more important. For the moral qualities are advanced, either directly or indirectly, much more through the effects of habit, the reasoning powers, instruction, religion, etc., than through natural selection; though to this latter agency may be safely attributed the social instincts, which afforded the basis for the development of the moral sense.

The main conclusion arrived at in this work, namely that man is descended from some lowly organized form, will, I regret to think, be highly distasteful to many. But there can hardly be a doubt that we are descended from barbarians. The astonishment which I felt on first seeing a party of Feugians on a wild and broken shore will never be forgotten by me, for the reflection at once rushed into my mind—such were our ancestors. These men were absolutely naked and bedaubed with paint, their long hair was tangled, their mouths frothed with excitement, and their expression was wild, startled, and distrustful. They possessed hardly any arts, and like wild animals lived on what they could catch; they had no government, and were merciless to every one not of their own small tribe. He who has seen a savage in his native land will not feel much shame, if forced to acknowledge that the blood of some more humble creatures flows in his veins. For my own part I would as soon be descended from that heroic little monkey, who braved his dreaded enemy in order to save the life of his keeper, or from that old baboon, who descending from the mountains, carried away in triumph his young comrade from a crowd of astonished dogs—as from a savage who delights to torture his enemies, offers up bloody sacrifices, practises infanticide without remorse, treats his wives like slaves, knows no decency, and is haunted by the grossest superstitions.

Man may be excused for feeling some

pride at having risen, though not through his own exertions, to the very summit of the organic scale; and the fact of his having thus risen, instead of having been aboriginally placed there, may give him hope for a still higher destiny in the distant future. But we are not here concerned with hopes or fears, only with the truth as far as our reason permits us to discover it; and I have given the evidence to the best of my ability. We must, however, acknowledge, as it seems to me, that man with all his noble qualities, with sympathy which feels for the most debased, with benevolence which extends not only to other men but to the humblest living creature, with his god-like intellect which has penetrated into the movements and constitution of the solar system—with all these exalted powers—Man still bears in his bodily frame the indelible stamp of his lowly origin.

STUDY QUESTIONS

1. What is meant by the phrase "the evolution of man"? What is the evidence in support of such evolution? How strong is it?

2. What does Darwin mean by natural selection? Sexual selection?

3. What, according to Darwin, is the greatest distinction between man and the lower animals? Do you think he is right?

4. Darwin's argument is based on the assumption that our views about the origin and development of the human species should be based solely on scientific evidence. Do you agree with this assumption? If not, why not?

For Further Reading

Bronowski, J. *The Ascent of Man.* Boston: Little, Brown, 1973 (Chapter 9).

Dewey, J. *The Influence of Darwin on Philosophy.* New York: Peter Smith, 1951 (Chapter 1).

Huxley, T. H. *Evolution and Ethics and Other Essays.* London: Macmillan, 1901 (Chapters 1 and 2).

Simpson, G. G. *The Meaning of Evolution.* New Haven, Conn.: Yale University Press, 1951.

Wallace, A. R. *Darwinism.* London: Macmillan, 1890 (esp. Chapter 15).

LA METTRIE: A MACHINE

During the Industrial Revolution of the eighteenth century, machines, of ever-increasing complexity, came to play a dominant role in the civilization of the West. It was, perhaps, inevitable that an analogy should be drawn between these machines and the beings who created them. The fullest development of this analogy occurs in La Mettrie's book, *Man A Machine (L'Homme Machine)* first published in 1747. Although the human body can, without undue strain, be regarded as a living machine, the analogy becomes considerably more tenuous when we consider the human mind. The problem might be put in the following terms: Suppose we could construct a robot (i.e., a machine) capable of performing all of the activities that ordinary humans do, but lacking any conscious experience. Would we be willing to call such a robot a human being? And on what grounds would we make our decision?

Julien Offray de La Mettrie was born in Brittany in 1709, of a wealthy family. After his early schooling, he went first to Paris and later to Reims and Leiden to complete his education. While still a student, he wrote his first treatise which, oddly enough, was on religion. Soon after finishing medical school he became a military doctor and spent some time as a physician with the French army. Meanwhile, he began to write satires directed mainly against the medical profession and the clergy. As a result he gained numerous enemies and was forced to move from France to what is now Belgium, and then to Holland, and finally to Prussia to join the court of the eminent eighteenth-century patron of the intellect, Frederick the Great. La Mettrie died suddenly in 1751, after consuming a prodigious amount of *pâté de faison aux truffes* (pheasant paté with truffles).

✌ *Man A Machine*

The human body is a machine which winds its own springs. It is the living image of perpetual movement. Nourishment keeps up the movements which fever excites. Without food, the soul pines away, goes mad, and dies exhausted. The soul is a taper whose light flares up the moment before it goes out. But nourish the body, pour into its veins life-giving juices and strong liquors, and then the soul grows strong like them, as if arming itself with a proud courage, and the soldier whom water would have made flee, grows bold and runs joyously to death to the sound of drums. Thus a hot drink sets into stormy movement the blood which a cold drink would have calmed.

What power there is in a meal! Joy revives in a sad heart, and infects the souls of comrades, who express their delight in the friendly songs in which the Frenchman excels. The melancholy man alone is dejected, and the studious man is equally out of place in such company.

Raw meat makes animals fierce, and it would have the same effect on man. This is so true that the English who eat meat red and bloody, and not as well done as ours, seem to share more or less in the savagery due to this kind of food, and to other causes which can be rendered ineffective by education only. This savagery creates in the soul, pride, hatred, scorn of other nations, indocility and other sentiments which

First published in French in 1748. Translated by B. G. Bussey; revised by M. W. Calkins.

degrade the character, just as heavy food makes a dull and heavy mind whose usual traits are laziness and indolence.

• • •

Words, languages, laws, sciences, and the fine arts have come, and by them finally the rough diamond of our mind has been polished. Man has been trained in the same way as animals. He has become an author, as they became beasts of burden. A geometrician has learned to perform the most difficult demonstrations and calculations, as a monkey has learned to take his little hat off and on, and to mount his tame dog. All has been accomplished through signs, every species has learned what it could understand, and in this way men have acquired symbolic knowledge, still so called by our German philosophers.

Nothing, as any one can see, is so simple as the mechanism of our education. Everything may be reduced to sounds or words that pass from the mouth of one through the ears of another into his brain. At the same moment, he perceives through his eyes the shape of the bodies of which these words are the arbitrary signs.

But who was the first to speak? Who was the first teacher of the human race? Who invented the means of utilizing the plasticity of our organism? I can not answer: the names of these first splendid geniuses have been lost in the night of time. But art is the child of nature, so nature must have long preceded it.

We must think that the men who were the most highly organized, those on whom nature had lavished her richest gifts, taught the others. They could not have heard a new sound for instance, nor experienced new sensations, nor been struck by all the varied and beautiful objects that compose the ravishing spectacle of nature without finding themselves in the state of mind of the deaf man of Chartres, whose experience was first related by the great Fontenelle, when, at forty years, he heard for the first time, the astonishing sound of bells.

Would it be absurd to conclude from this that the first mortals tried after the manner of this deaf man, or like animals and like mutes (another kind of animals), to express their new feelings by motions depending on the nature of their imagination, and therefore afterwards by spontaneous sounds, distinctive of each animal, as the natural expression of their surprise, their joy, their ecstasies and their needs? For doubtless those whom nature endowed with finer feeling had also greater facility in expression.

That is the way in which, I think, men have used their feeling and their instinct to gain intelligence and then have employed their intelligence to gain knowledge. Those are the ways, so far as I can understand them, in which men have filled the brain with the ideas, for the reception of which nature made it. Nature and man have helped each other; and the smallest beginnings have, little by little, increased, until everything in the universe could be as easily described as a circle.

As a violin string or a harpsichord key vibrates and gives forth sound, so the cerebral fibres, struck by waves of sound, are stimulated to render or repeat the words that strike them. And as the structure of the brain is such that when eyes well formed for seeing, have once perceived the image of objects, the brain can not help seeing their images and their differences, as when the signs of these differences have been traced or imprinted in the brain, the soul necessarily examines their relations— an examination that would have been impossible without the discovery of signs or the invention of language. At the time when the universe was almost dumb, the soul's attitude toward all objects was that of a man without any idea of proportion toward a picture or a piece of sculpture, in which he could distinguish nothing; or the soul was like a little child (for the soul was then in its infancy) who, holding in his hand small bits of straw or wood, sees them in a vague and superficial way without being able to count or distinguish them. But let some one attach a kind of banner, or standard, to this bit of wood (which perhaps is called a mast), and another banner to another similar object; let the first be known by the symbol 1, and the second by the symbol or number 2, then the child will be able to count the objects, and in this way he will learn all of arithmetic. As soon as one figure seems equal to another in its numerical sign, he will decide without difficulty that they are two different bodies, that 1 + 1 make 2, and 2 + 2 make 4, etc.

This real or apparent likeness of figures is the fundamental basis of all truths and of all we know. Among these sciences, evidently those whose signs are less simple and less sensible are harder to understand than the others, because more talent is required to comprehend and combine the immense number of words by which such sciences express the truths in their province. On the other hand, the sciences that are expressed by numbers or by other small signs, are easily learned; and without doubt this facility rather than its demonstrability is what has made the fortune of algebra.

All this knowledge, with which vanity fills the balloon-like brains of our proud pedants, is therefore but a huge mass of words and figures, which form in the brain all the marks by which we distinguish and recall objects. All our ideas are awakened after the fashion in which the gardener who knows plants recalls all stages of their growth at sight of them. These words and the objects designated by them are so connected in the brain that it is comparatively rare to imagine a thing without the name or sign that is attached to it.

• • •

Since all the faculties of the soul depend to such a degree on the proper organization of the brain and of the whole body, that apparently they are but this organization itself, the soul is clearly an enlightened machine. For finally, even if man alone had received a share of natural law, would he be any less a machine for that? A few more wheels, a few more springs than in the most perfect animals, the brain proportionally

nearer the heart and for this very reason receiving more blood—any one of a number of unknown causes might always produce this delicate conscience so easily wounded, this remorse which is no more foreign to matter than to thought, and in a word all the differences that are supposed to exist here. Could the organism then suffice for everything? Once more, yes; since thought visibly develops with our organs, why should not the matter of which they are composed be susceptible of remorse also, when once it has acquired, with time, the faculty of feeling?

The soul is therefore but an empty word, of which no one has any idea, and which an enlightened man should use only to signify the part in us that thinks. Given the least principle of motion, animated bodies will have all that is necessary for moving, feeling, thinking, repeating, or in a word for conducting themselves in the physical realm, and in the moral realm which depends upon it.

• • •

Let us now go into some detail concerning these springs of the human machine. All the vital, animal, natural, and automatic motions are carried on by their action. Is it not in a purely mechanical way that the body shrinks back when it is struck with terror at the sight of an unforeseen precipice, that the eyelids are lowered at the menace of a blow, as some have remarked, and that the pupil contracts in broad daylight to save the retina, and dilates to see objects in darkness? Is it not by mechanical means that the pores of the skin close in winter so that the cold can not penetrate to the interior of the blood vessels, and that the stomach vomits when it is irritated by poison, by a certain quantity of opium and by all emetics, etc.? that the heart, the arteries and the muscles contract in sleep as well as in waking hours, that the lungs serve as bellows continually in exercise, . . . that the heart contracts more strongly than any other muscle? . . . .

I shall not go into any more detail concerning all these little subordinate forces, well known to all. But there is another more subtle and marvelous force, which animates them all; it is the source of all our feelings, of all our pleasures, of all our passions, and of all our thoughts: for the brain has its muscles for thinking, as the legs have muscles for walking. I wish to speak of this impetuous principle that Hippocrates calls 'ενορμών (soul). This principle exists and has its seat in the brain at the origin of the nerves, by which it exercises its control over all the rest of the body. By this fact is explained all that can be explained, even to the surprising effects of maladies of the imagination. . . .

Look at the portrait of the famous Pope* who is, to say the least, the Voltaire of the English. The effort, the energy of his genius are imprinted upon his countenance. It is convlused. His eyes protrude from their sockets, the eyebrows are raised with the muscles of the forehead. Why? Because the brain is in travail and all the body must share in such a laborious deliverance. If there were not an internal cord which pulled the external ones, whence would come all these phenomena? To admit a soul as explanation of them, is to be reduced to explaining phenomena by the operations of the Holy Spirit.

In fact, if what thinks in my brain is not a part of this organ and therefore of the whole body, why does my blood boil, and the fever of my mind pass into my veins, when lying quietly in bed, I am forming the plan of some work or carrying on an abstract calculation? Put this question to men of imagination, to great poets, to men who are enraptured by the felicitous expression of sentiment, and transported by an exquisite fancy or by the charms of nature, of truth, or of virtue! By their enthusiasm, by what they will tell you they have experienced, you will judge the cause by its effects: by that harmony which Borelli, a mere anatomist, understood better than all the Leibnizians, you will comprehend the material unity of man. In

*[Alexander Pope, English poet—ed.]

short, if the nerve-tension which causes pain occasions also the fever by which the distracted mind loses its will-power, and if, conversely, the mind too much excited, disturbs the body (and kindles that inner fire which killed Bayle while he was still so young); if an agitation rouses my desire and my ardent wish for what, a moment ago, I cared nothing about, and if in their turn certain brain impressions excite the same longing and the same desires, then why should we regard as double what is manifestly one being? In vain you fall back on the power of the will, since for one order that the will gives, it bows a hundred times to the yoke. And what wonder that in health the body obeys, since a torrent of blood and of animal spirits forces its obedience, and since the will has as ministers an invisible legion of fluids swifter than lightning and ever ready to do its bidding! But as the power of the will is exercised by means of the nerves, it is likewise limited by them.

• • •

Is more needed . . . to prove that man is but an animal, or a collection of springs which wind each other up, without our being able to tell at what point in this human circle, nature has begun? If these springs differ among themselves, these differences consist only in their position and in their degrees of strength, and never in their nature; wherefore the soul is but a principle of motion or a material and sensible part of the brain, which can be regarded, without fear of error, as the mainspring of the whole machine, having a visible influence on all the parts. The soul seems even to have been made for the brain, so that all the other parts of the system are but a kind of emanation from the brain.

• • •

The human body is a watch, a large watch constructed with such skill and ingenuity, that if the wheel which marks the seconds happens to stop, the minute wheel turns and keeps on going its round, and in the same way the quarter-hour wheel, and all the others go on running when the first wheels have stopped because rusty or, for any reason, out of order. Is it not for a similar reason that the stoppage of a few blood vessels is not enough to destroy or suspend the strength of the movement which is in the heart as in the mainspring of the machine; since, on the contrary, the fluids whose volume is diminished, having a shorter road to travel, cover the ground more quickly, borne on as by a fresh current which the energy of the heart increases in proportion to the resistance it encounters at the ends of the blood-vessels? And is not this the reason why the loss of sight (caused by the compression of the optic nerve and by its ceasing to convey the images of objects) no more hinders hearing, than the loss of hearing (caused by obstruction of the functions of the auditory nerve) implies the loss of sight? In the same way, finally, does not one man hear (except immediately after the attack) without being able to say that he hears, while another who hears nothing, but whose lingual nerves are uninjured in the brain, mechanically tells of all the dreams which pass through his mind? These phenomena do not surprise enlightened physicians at all. They know what to think about man's nature, and (more accurately to express myself in passing) of two physicians, the better one and the one who deserves more confidence is always, in my opinion, the one who is more versed in the physique or mechanism of the human body, and who, leaving aside the soul and all the anxieties which this chimera gives to fools and to ignorant men, is seriously occupied only in pure naturalism.

• • •

To be a machine, to feel, to think, to know how to distinguish good from bad, as well as blue from yellow, in a word, to be born with an intelligence and a sure moral instinct, and to be but an animal, are therefore characters which are no more con-tradictory, than to be an ape or a parrot and to be able to give oneself pleasure . . . I believe that thought is so little incompatible with organized matter, that it seems to be one of its properties on a par with electricity, the faculty of motion, impenetrability, extension, etc.

Do you ask for further observations? Here are some which are incontestable and which all prove that man resembles animals perfectly, in his origin as well as in all the points in which we have thought it essential to make the comparison. . . .

Let us observe man both in and out of his shell, let us examine young embryos of four, six, eight or fifteen days with a microscope; after that time our eyes are sufficient. What do we see? The head alone; a little round egg with two black points which mark the eyes. Before that, everything is formless, and one sees only a medullary pulp, which is the brain, in which are formed first the roots of the nerves, that is, the principle of feeling, and the heart, which already within this substance has the power of beating itself; it is the *punctum saliens* of Malpighi, which perhaps already owes a part of its excitability to the influences of the nerves. Then little by little, one sees the head lengthen from the neck, which, in dilating, forms first the thorax inside which the heart has already sunk, there to become stationary; below that is the abdomen which is divided by a partition (the diaphragm). One of these enlargements of the body forms the arms, the hands, the fingers, the nails, and the hair; the other forms the thighs, the legs, the feet, etc., which differ only in their observed situation, and which constitute the support and the balancing pole of the body. The whole process is a strange sort of growth, like that of plants. On the tops of our heads is hair in place of which the plants have leaves and flowers: everywhere is shown the same luxury of nature, and finally the directing principle of plants is placed where we have our soul, that other quintessence of man.

Such is the uniformity of nature, which we are beginning to realize; and the analogy of the animal with the vegetable kingdom, of man with plant. Perhaps there even are animal plants, which in vegetating, either fight as polyps do, or perform other functions characteristic of animals . . . .

We are veritable moles in the field of nature; we achieve little more than the mole's journey and it is our pride which prescribes limits to the limitless. We are in the position of a watch that should say (a writer of fables would make the watch a hero in a silly tale): "I was never made by that fool of a workman. I who divide time, who mark so exactly the course of the sun, who repeat aloud the hours which I mark! No! that is impossible!" In the same way, we disdain, ungrateful wretches that we are, this common mother of all kingdoms, as the chemists say. We imagine, or rather we infer, a cause superior to that to which we owe all, and which truly has wrought all things in an inconceivable fashion. No; matter contains nothing base, except to the vulgar eyes which do not recognize her in her most splendid works; and nature is no stupid workman. She creates millions of men, with a facility and a pleasure more intense than the effort of a watchmaker in making the most complicated watch. Her power shines forth equally in creating the lowliest insect and in creating the most highly developed man; the animal kingdom costs her no more than the vegetable, and the most splendid genius no more than a blade of wheat. Let us then judge by what we see of that which is hidden from the curiosity of our eyes and of our investigations, and let us not imagine anything beyond. Let us observe the ape, the beaver, the elephant, etc., in their operations. If it is clear that these activities can not be performed without intelligence, why refuse intelligence to these animals? And if you grant them a soul, you are lost, you fanatics! You will in vain say that you assert nothing about the nature of the animal soul and that you deny its immortality. Who does not see that this is a gratuitous assertion; who does not see that the soul of an animal must be either mortal or immortal,

whichever ours is, and that it must therefore undergo the same fate as ours, whatever that may be, and that thus in admitting that animals have souls, you fall into Scylla in the effort to avoid Charybdis?

Break the chain of your prejudices, arm yourselves with the torch of experience, and you will render to nature the honor she deserves, instead of inferring anything to her disadvantage, from the ignorance in which she has left you. Only open wide your eyes, only disregard what you can not understand, and you will see that the ploughsman whose intelligence and ideas extend no further than the bounds of his furrow, does not differ essentially from the greatest genius—a truth which the dissection of Descartes' and of Newton's brains would have proved; you will be persuaded that the imbecile and the fool are animals with human faces, as the intelligent ape is a little man in another shape; in short, you will learn that since everything depends absolutely on difference of organization, a well constructed animal which has studied astronomy, can predict an eclipse, as it can predict recovery or death when it has used its genius and its clearness of vision, for a time, in the school of Hippocrates and at the bedside of the sick. By this line of observations and truths, we come to connect the admirable power of thought with matter, without being able to see the links, because the subject of this attribute is essentially unknown to us.

Let us not say that every machine or every animal perishes altogether or assumes another form after death, for we know absolutely nothing about the subject. On the other hand, to assert that an immortal machine is a chimera or a logical fiction, is to reason as absurdly as caterpillars would reason if, seeing the cast-off skins of their fellow-caterpillars, they should bitterly deplore the fate of their species, which to them would seem to come to nothing. The soul of these insects (for each animal has his own) is too limited to comprehend the metamorphoses of nature. Never one of the most skilful among them could have imagined that it was destined to become a butterfly. It is the same with us. What more do we know of our destiny than of our origin? Let us then submit to an invincible ignorance on which our happiness depends.

He who so thinks will be wise, just, tranquil about his fate, and therefore happy. He will await death without either fear or desire, and will cherish life (hardly understanding how disgust can corrupt a heart in this place of many delights); he will be filled with reverence, gratitude, affection, and tenderness for nature, in proportion to his feeling of the benefits he has received from nature; he will be happy, in short, in feeling nature, and in being present at the enchanting spectacle of the universe, and he will surely never destroy nature either in himself or in others. More than that! Full of humanity, this man will love human character even in his enemies. Judge how he will treat others. He will pity the wicked without hating them; in his eyes, they will be but mis-made men. But in pradoning the faults of the structure of mind and body, he will none the less admire the beauties and the virtues of both. Those whom nature shall have favored will seem to him to deserve more respect than those whom she has treated in step-motherly fashion. Thus, as we have seen, natural gifts, the source of all acquirements, gain from the lips and heart of the materialist, the homage which every other thinker unjustly refused them. In short,

the materialist, convinced, in spite of the protests of his vanity, that he is but a machine or an animal, will not maltreat his kind, for he will know too well the nature of those actions, whose humanity is always in proportion to the degree of the analogy proved above between human beings and animals, and following the natural law given to all animals, he will not wish to do to others what he would not wish them to do to him.

Let us conclude boldly that man is a machine, and that in the whole universe there is but a single substance differently modified.

STUDY QUESTIONS

1. What does La Mettrie mean by the statement, "Art is the child of nature"?
2. What does La Mettrie mean by the human soul? How is it related to our body?
3. What role does will play in La Mettrie's account of human nature? Do you think he allows it to have as much impact on action as our experience indicates it has?
4. Do you think La Mettrie's willingness to allow the possibility of immortality is consistent with his account of human nature?
5. Do you believe that anything important in human nature is lost by the identification of human beings with animals or machines? If so, what?

For Further Reading

Anderson, A. R. ed. *Minds and Machines*. Englewood Cliffs, N.J.: Prentice-Hall, 1964.

Asimov, I. *I, Robot*. New York: Doubleday, 1963.

Hook, S., ed. *Dimensions of Mind*. New York University Press, 1960 (Part II).

Sluckin, W. *Minds and Machines*. London: Penguin, 1954.

Türing, A. M. "Computing Machinery and Intelligence," *Mind* 59 (1950), 433–60.

FREUD: EGO, SUPER-EGO, AND ID

To say that Freud has had a significant impact on modern life as well as psychology is to state a truism. Besides creating the science and practice of psychoanalysis, his work has had the more general result of making most of us considerably more interested in our own psyches—particularly their hidden, erotic sides—than we would otherwise have been. But his work has also affected our understanding of ourselves in a philosophical way, by offering us a much richer conception of human nature than we had previously had. Although Freud was certainly not the first to recognize that the human psyche has complex and hidden depths, he, more than anyone else, set about to understand these levels of unconsciousness, relate them to our conscious thoughts and behavior, and develop techniques of therapy to help those whose psyches were in serious disarray.

Although he was born in what is now Czechoslovakia, Sigmund Freud (1856–1939) lived almost his entire life in Vienna. At the University of Vienna he studied medicine and began his career by specializing in neurology. His interest in psychology led him to collaborate with the Viennese physician Josef Breuer in a study of hysteria. The two treated the disease by the method of hypnosis. Later Freud shifted from this method to that of free association, thus laying the foundations for the science and practice of psychiatry. Freud's views were at first opposed by the European medical profession, but his popularity in America gradually led to the acceptance of psychiatry as a respectable science and psycho-analysis as an effective method of medical treatment.

✬ The Ego and The Id

I
Consciousness and What Is Unconscious

• • •

The division of the psychical into what is conscious and what is unconscious is the fundamental premise of psycho-analysis; and it alone makes it possible for psycho-analysis to understand the pathological processes in mental life, which are as common as they are important, and to find a

Reprinted from *The Ego and the Id* by Sigmund Freud. Translated by Joan Riviere, Revised and Edited by James Strachey. Used by permission of W. W. Norton & Company, Inc. Copyright © 1960 by James Strachey. Also used by permission of Sigmund Freud Copyrights Ltd., The Institute of Psycho-Analysis, and The Hogarth Press Ltd.

place for them in the framework of science. To put it once more, in a different way: psycho-analysis cannot situate the essence of the psychical in consciousness, but is obliged to regard consciousness as a quality of the psychical, which may be present in addition to other qualities or may be absent.

If I could suppose that everyone interested in psychology would read this book, I should also be prepared to find that at this point some of my readers would already stop short and would go no further; for here we have the first shibboleth of psycho-analysis. To most people who have been educated in philosophy the idea of anything psychical which is not also conscious is so inconceivable that it seems to them absurd and refutable simply by logic. I believe this is only because they have never studied the relevant phenomena of hypnosis and dreams, which—quite apart from pathological manifestations— necessitate this view. Their psychology of consciousness is incapable of solving the problems of dreams and hypnosis.

'Being conscious' is in the first place a purely descriptive term, resting on perception of the most immediate and certain character. Experience goes on to show that a psychical element (for instance, an idea) is not as a rule conscious for a protracted length of time. On the contrary, a state of consciousness is characteristically very transitory; an idea that is conscious now is no longer so a moment later, although it can become so again under certain conditions that are easily brought about. In the interval the idea was—we do not know what. We can say that it was *latent*, and by this we mean that it was *capable of becoming conscious* at any time. Or, if we say that it was *unconscious*, we shall also be giving a correct description of it. Here 'unconscious' coincides with 'latent and capable of becoming conscious'. The philosophers would no doubt object: 'No, the term "unconscious" is not applicable here; so long as the idea was in a state of latency it was not anything psychical at all.' To contradict them at this point would lead to nothing more profitable than a verbal dispute.

But we have arrived at the term or concept of the unconscious along another path, by considering certain experiences in which mental *dynamics* play a part. We have found—that is, we have been obliged to assume—that very powerful mental processes or ideas exist (and here a quantitative or *economic* factor comes into question for the first time) which can produce all the effects in mental life that ordinary ideas do (including effects that can in their turn become conscious as ideas), though they themselves do not become conscious. It is unnecessary to repeat in detail here what has been explained so often before. It is enough to say that at this point psychoanalytic theory steps in and asserts that the reason why such ideas cannot become conscious is that a certain force opposes them, that otherwise they could become con-

scious, and that it would then be apparent how little they differ from other elements which are admittedly psychical. The fact that in the technqiue of psycho-analysis a means has been found by which the opposing force can be removed and the ideas in question made conscious renders this theory irrefutable. The state in which the ideas existed before being made conscious is called by us *repression*, and we assert that the force which instituted the repression and maintains it is perceived as *resistance* during the work of analysis.

Thus we obtain our concept of the unconscious from the theory of repression. The repressed is the prototype of the unconscious for us. We see, however, that we have two kinds of unconscious—the one which is latent but capable of becoming conscious, and the one which is repressed and is not, in itself and without more ado, capable of becoming conscious. This piece of insight into psychical dynamics cannot fail to affect terminology and description. The latent, which is unconscious only descriptively, not in the dynamic sense, we call *preconscious*; we restrict the term *unconscious* to the dynamically unconscious repressed; so that now we have three terms, conscious (*Cs.*) preconscious (*Pcs.*), and unconscious (*Ucs.*), whose sense is no longer purely descriptive. The *Pcs.* is presumably a great deal closer to the *Cs.* than is the *Ucs.*, and since we have called the *Ucs.* psychical we shall with even less hesitation call the latent *Pcs.* psychical.

• • •

II
The Ego and the Id

• • •

Now I think we shall gain a great deal by following the suggestion of a writer who, from personal motives, vainly asserts that he has nothing to do with the rigours of pure science. I am speaking of Georg Groddeck, who is never tired of insisting that what we call our ego behaves essentially passively in life, and that, as he expresses it, we are 'lived' by unknown and uncontrollable forces. We have all had impressions of the same kind, even though they may not have overwhelmed us to the exclusion of all others, and we need feel no hesitation in finding a place for Groddeck's discovery in the structure of science. I propose to take it into account by calling the entity which starts out from the system *Pcpt.* [perception] and begins by being *Pcs.* the 'ego', and by following Groddeck in calling the other part of the mind, into which this entity extends and which behaves as though it were *Ucs.*, the 'id'.

We shall soon see whether we can derive any advantage from this view for purposes either of description or of understanding. We shall now look upon an individual as a psychical id, unknown and unconscious, upon whose surface rests the ego, developed from its nucleus the *Pcpt.* system. If we make an effort to represent this pictorially, we may add that the ego does not completely envelop the id, but only does so to the extent to which the system *Pcpt.* forms its [the ego's] surface, more or less as the germinal disc rests upon the ovum. The ego is not sharply separated from the id; its lower portion merges into it.

But the repressed merges into the id as well, and is merely a part of it. The repressed is only cut off sharply from the ego by the resistances of repression; it can communicate with the ego through the id. We at once realize that almost all the lines of demarcation we have drawn at the instigation of pathology relate only to the superficial strata of the mental apparatus—the only ones known to us. . . .

It is easy to see that the ego is that part of the id which has been modified by the direct influence of the external world through the medium of the *Pcpt.-Cs.*; in a sense it is an extension of the surface . . . differentiation. Moreover, the ego seeks to bring the influence of the external world to bear upon the id and its tendencies, and endeavours to substitute the reality principle for the pleasure principle which reigns unrestrictedly in the id. For the ego, perception plays the part which in the id falls to instinct. The ego represents what may be called reason and common sense, in contrast to the id, which contains the passions. All this falls into line with popular distinctions which we are all familiar with; at the same time, however, it is only to be regarded as holding good on the average or 'ideally'.

The functional importance of the ego is manifested in the fact that normally control over the approaches to motility devolves upon it. Thus in its relation to the id it is like a man on horseback, who has to hold in check the superior strength of the horse; with this difference, that the rider tries to do so with his own strength while the ego uses borrowed forces. The analogy may be carried a little further. Often a rider, if he is not to be parted from his horse, is obliged to guide it where it wants to go, so in the same way the ego is in the habit of transforming the id's will into action as if it were its own.

• • •

The relation of the ego to consciousness has been entered into repeatedly; yet there are some important facts in this connection which remain to be described here. Accustomed as we are to taking our social or ethical scale of values along with us wherever we go, we feel no surprise at hearing that the scene of the activities of the lower passions is in the unconscious; we expect, moreover, that the higher any mental function ranks in our scale of values the more easily it will find access to consciousness assured to it. Here, however, psycho-analytic experience disappoints us. On the one hand, we have evidence that even subtle and difficult intellectual operations which ordinarily require strenuous reflection can equally be carried out preconsciously and without coming into consciousness. Instances of this are quite incontestable; they may occur, for example, during the state of sleep, as is shown when someone finds, immediately after waking, that he knows the solution to a difficult mathematical or other problem with which he had been wrestling in vain the day before.

• • •

III
The Ego and the Super-Ego (Ego Ideal)

If the ego were merely the part of the id modified by the influence of the perceptual system, the representative in the mind of the real external world, we should have a simple state of things to deal with. But there is a further complication.

The considerations that led us to assume the existence of a grade in the ego, a differentiation within the ego, which may be called the 'ego ideal' or 'super-ego', have been stated elsewhere. They still hold good. The fact that this part of the ego is less firmly connected with consciousness is the novelty which calls for explanation.

• • •

The whole subject, however, is so complicated that it will be necessary to go into it in greater detail. The intricacy of the problem is due to two factors: the triangular character of the Oedipus situation and the constitutional bisexuality of each individual.

In its simplified form the case of a male child may be described as follows. At a very early age the little boy develops an object-cathexis for his mother, which originally related to the mother's breast and is the prototype of an object-choice on the anaclitic model; the boy deals with his father by identifying himself with him. For a time these two relationships proceed side by side, until the boy's sexual wishes in regard to his mother become more intense and his father is perceived as an obstacle to them; from this the Oedipus complex originates. His identification with his father then takes on a hostile colouring and changes into a wish to get rid of his father in order to take his place with his mother. Henceforward his relation to his father is ambivalent; it seems as if the ambivalence inherent in the identification from the beginning had become manifest. An ambivalent attitude to his father and an object-relation of a solely affectionate kind to his mother make up the content of the simple positive Oedipus complex in a boy.

Along with the demolition of the Oedipus complex, the boy's object-cathexis of his mother must be given up. Its place may be filled by one of two things: either an identification with his mother or an intensification of his identification with his father. We are accustomed to regard the latter outcome as more normal; it permits the affectionate relation to the mother to be in a measure retained. In this way the dissolution of the Oedipus complex would consolidate the masculinity in a boy's character. In a precisely analogous way, the outcome of the Oedipus attitude in a little girl may be an intensification of her identification with her mother (or the setting up of such an identification for the first time)—a result which will fix the child's feminine character.

These identifications are not what we should have expected, since they do not introduce the abandoned object into the ego; but this alternative outcome may also occur, and is easier to observe in girls than in boys. Analysis very often shows that a little girl, after she has had to relinquish her father as a love-object, will bring her masculinity into prominence and identify herself with her father (that is, with the object which has been lost), instead of her mother. This will clearly depend on whether the masculinity in her disposition—whatever that may consist in—is strong enough.

It would appear, therefore, that in both sexes the relative strength of the masculine and feminine sexual dispositions is what determines whether the outcome of the Oedipus situation shall be an identification with the father or with the mother. This is one of the ways in which bisexuality takes a hand in the subsequent vicissitudes of the

Oedipus complex. The other way is even more important. For one gets an impression that the simple Oedipus complex is by no means its commonest form, but rather represents a simplification or schematization which, to be sure, is often enough justified for practical purposes. Closer study usually discloses the more complete Oedipus complex, which is twofold, positive and negative, and is due to the bisexuality originally present in children: that is to say, a boy has not merely an ambivalent attitude towards his father and an affectionate object-choice towards his mother, but at the same time he also behaves like a girl and displays an affectionate feminine attitude to his father and a corresponding jealousy and hostility towards his mother. It is this complicating element introduced by bisexuality that makes it so difficult to obtain a clear view of the facts in connection with the earliest object-choices and identifications, and still more difficult to describe them intelligibly. It may even be that the ambivalence displayed in the relations to the parents should be attributed entirely to bisexuality and that it is not, as I have represented above, developed out of identification in consequence of rivalry.

In my opinion it is advisable in general, and quite especially where neurotics are concerned, to assume the existence of the complete Oedipus complex. Analytic experience then shows that in a number of cases one or the other constituent disappears, except for barely distinguishable traces; so that the result is a series with the normal positive Oedipus complex at one end and the inverted negative one at the other, while its intermediate members exhibit the complete form with one or other of its two components preponderating. At the dissolution of the Oedipus complex the four trends of which it consists will group themselves in such a way as to produce a father-identification and a mother-identification. The father-identification will preserve the object-relation to the mother which belonged to the positive complex and will at the same time replace the object-relation to the father which belonged to the inverted complex: and the same will be true, *mutatus mutandis,* of the mother-identification. The relative intensity of the two identifications in any individual will reflect the preponderance in him of one or other of the two sexual dispositions.

The broad general outcome of the sexual phase dominated by the Oedipus complex may, therefore, be taken to be the forming of a precipitate in the ego, consisting of these two identifications in some way united with each other. This modification of the ego retains its special position; it confronts the other contents of the ego as an ego ideal or super-ego.

The super-ego is, however, not simply a residue of the earliest object-choices of the id; it also represents an energetic reaction-formation against those choices. Its relation to the ego is not exhausted by the precept: 'You *ought to be* like this (like your father),' It also comprises the prohibition: 'You *may not be* like this (like your father)—that is, you may not do all that he does; some things are his prerogative.' This double aspect of the ego ideal derives from the fact that the ego ideal had the task of repressing the Oedipus complex; indeed, it is to that revolutionary event that it owes its existence. Clearly the repression of the Oedipus complex was no easy task. The child's parents, and especially his father, were perceived as the obstacle to a realization of his Oedipus wishes; so his infantile ego fortified itself for the carrying out of the repression by erecting this same obstacle within itself. It borrowed strength to do this, so to speak, from the father, and this loan was an extraordinarily momentous act. The super-ego retains the character of the father, while the more powerful the Oedipus complex was and the more rapidly it succumbed to repression (under the influence of authority, religious teaching, schooling and reading), the stricter will be the domination of the super-ego over the ego later on—in the form of conscience or perhaps of an unconscious sense of guilt.

Psycho-analysis has been reproached time after time with ignoring the higher, moral, supra-personal side of human nature. The reproach is doubly unjust, both historically and methodologically. For, in the first place, we have from the very beginning attributed the function of instigating repression to the moral and aesthetic trends in the ego, and secondly, there has been a general refusal to recognize that psycho-analytic research could not, like a philosophical system, produce a complete and ready-made theoretical structure, but had to find its way step by step along the path towards understanding the intricacies of the mind by making an analytic dissection of both normal and abnormal phenomena. So long as we had to concern ourselves with the study of what is repressed in mental life, there was no need for us to share in any agitated apprehensions as to the whereabouts of the higher side of man. But now that we have embarked upon the analysis of the ego we can give an answer to all those whose moral sense has been shocked and who have complained that there must surely be a higher nature in man: 'Very true,' we can say, 'and here we have that higher nature, in this ego ideal of super-ego, the representative of our relation to our parents. When we were little children we knew these higher natures, we admired them and feared them; and later we took them into ourselves.'

STUDY QUESTIONS

1. What does Freud mean by the "unconscious"? How important is it? How is it related to repression?
2. Distinguish between "ego," "super-ego," and "id" in Freud's thought.
3. What is the "Oedipus complex"? What are its usual outcomes? How is it related to the super-ego?
4. How do our moral attitudes originate, according to Freud? Does their manner of origination affect their validity?

For Further Reading

Freud, S. *Civilization and Its Discontents.* New York: Norton, 1961.

―――. *Psychopathology of Everyday Life.* London: Ernest Benn, 1914.

Miller, J. ed. *Freud: The Man, His World, His Influence.* London: Weidenfeld and Nicolson, 1972, (esp. Chapters 5 and 11).

Nye, R. D. *Three Views of Man.* Monterey: Brooks/Cole, 1975 (Chapter 1).

Philp, H. L. *Freud and Religious Belief.* London: Rockliff, 1956.

Ricoeur, P. *Freud and Philosophy.* New Haven, Conn.: Yale University Press, 1970 (Book III).

Rosenfield, I. *Freud: Character and Consciousness.* New York: University Books, 1970.

SARTRE: A SELF-CREATOR

Most of us believe in human nature. We believe that individuals, although they may differ from each other in a variety of surface respects, are fundamentally alike. We share a nature that makes us human, setting us apart from all other members of the animal kingdom. Sartre rejects this traditional view, arguing that it is a holdover from our orthodox religious belief in God, as creator of man in his own image. In Sartre's view, each individual starts out afresh, with no prescribed nature at all. Thus, what we become is what we make of ourselves. Such a view has a number of important consequences for human life, which Sartre discusses in the selection that follows.

Jean-Paul Sartre was born in Paris in 1905. After completing his schooling at the Ecole Normale Supérieure and teaching for some years, he went to Berlin to study German philosophy. From this visit he developed his own version of the philosophy of existentialism, which he presented not only in philosophical treatises but also in numerous novels and plays. During World War II he served in the French underground and after the liberation he became active in politics, generally espousing left-wing causes. In 1964 he was awarded the Nobel prize for literature, but he refused to accept it. Sartre died in 1980.

Existentialism

What is meant by the term existentialism? Most people who use the word would be rather embarrassed if they had to explain it, since, now the word is all the rage, even the work of a musician or painter is being called existentialist. A gossip columnist in *Clartés* signs himself *The Existentialist,* so that by this time the word has been so stretched and has taken on so broad a meaning, that it no longer means anything at all. It seems that for want of an advance-guard doctrine analogous to surrealism, the kind of people who are eager for scandal and flurry turn to this philosophy which in other respects does not at all serve their purposes in this sphere.

Actually, it is the least scandalous, the most austere of doctrines. It is intended strictly for specialists and philosophers. Yet it can be defined easily. What complicates matters is that there are two kinds of existentialist; first, those who are Christian, among whom I would include Jaspers and Gabriel Marcel; both Catholic; and on the other hand the atheistic existentialists, among whom I class Heidegger, and then the French existentialists and myself. What they have in common is that they think that existence precedes essence, or, if you prefer, that subjectivity must be the starting point.

Just what does that mean? Let us consider some object that is manufactured, for example, a book or a paper-cutter: here is an object which has been made by an artisan whose inspiration came from a concept. He referred to the concept of what a paper-cutter is and likewise to a known method of production, which is part of the concept, something which is, by and large, a routine. Thus, the paper-cutter is at once an object produced in a certain way, and, on the other hand, one having a specific use; and one can not postulate a man who produces a paper-cutter but does not know what it is used for. Therefore, let us say that, for the paper-cutter, essence—that is, the ensemble of both the production

Translated by Bernard Frechtman. *Existentialism* was originally delivered as a lecture.

routines and the properties which enable it to be both produced and defined—precedes existence. Thus, the presence of the paper-cutter or book in front of me is determined. Therefore, we have here a technical view of the world whereby it can be said that production precedes existence.

When we conceive God as the Creator, He is generally thought of as a superior sort of artisan. Whatever doctrine we may be considering, whether one like that of Descartes or that of Leibnitz, we always grant that will more or less follows understanding or, at the very least, accompanies it, and that when God creates He knows exactly what He is creating. Thus, the concept of man in the mind of God is comparable to the concept of paper-cutter in the mind of the manufacturer, and, following certain techniques and a conception, God produces man, just as the artisan, following a definition and a technique, makes a paper-cutter. Thus, the individual man is the realization of a certain concept in the divine intelligence.

In the eighteenth century, the atheism of the *philosophes* discarded the idea of God, but not so much for the notion that essence precedes existence. To a certain extent, this idea is found everywhere; we find it in Diderot, in Voltaire, and even in Kant. Man has a human nature; this human nature, which is the concept of the human, is found in all men, which means that each man is a particular example of a universal concept, man. In Kant, the result of this universality is that the wild-man, the natural man, as well as the bourgeois, are circumscribed by the same definition and have the same basic qualities. Thus, here too the essence of man precedes the historical existence that we find in nature.

Atheistic existentialism, which I represent, is more coherent. It states that if God does not exist, there is at least one being in whom existence precedes essence, a being who exists before he can be defined by any concept, and that this being is man, or, as Heidegger says, human reality. What is meant here by saying that existence precedes essence? It means that, first of all,

man exists, turns up, appears on the scene, and, only afterwards, defines himself. If man, as the existentialist conceives him, is indefinable, it is because at first he is nothing. Only afterward will he be something, and he himself will have made what he will be. Thus, there is no human nature, since there is no God to conceive it. Not only is man what he conceives himself to be, but he is also only what he wills himself to be after this thrust toward existence.

Man is nothing else but what he makes of himself. Such is the first principle of existentialism. It is also what is called subjectivity, the name we are labeled with when charges are brought against us. But what do we mean by this, if not that man has a greater dignity than a stone or table? For we mean that man first exists, that is, that man first of all is the being who hurls himself toward a future and who is conscious of imagining himself as being in the future. Man is at the start a plan which is aware of itself, rather than a patch of moss, a piece of garbage, or a cauliflower; nothing exists prior to this plan; there is nothing in heaven; man will be what he will have planned to be. Not what he will want to be. Because by the word "will" we generally mean a conscious decision, which is subsequent to what we have already made of ourselves. I may want to belong to a political party, write a book, get married; but all that is only a manifestation of an earlier, more spontaneous choice that is called "will." But if existence really does precede essence, man is responsible for what he is. Thus, existentialism's first move is to make every man aware of what he is and to make the full responsibility of his existence rest on him. And when we say that a man is responsible for himself, we do not only mean that he is responsible for his own individuality, but that he is responsible for all men.

• • •

Thus, our responsibility is much greater than we might have supposed, because it involves all mankind. If I am a workingman and choose to join a Christian trade-union rather than be a communist, and if by being a member I want to show that the best thing for man is resignation, that the kingdom of man is not of this world, I am not only involving my own case—I want to be resigned for everyone. As a result, my action has involved all humanity. To take a more individual matter, if I want to marry, to have children; even if this marriage depends solely on my own circumstances or passion or wish, I am involving all humanity in monogamy and not merely myself. Therefore, I am responsible for myself and for everyone else. I am creating a certain image of man of my own choosing. In choosing myself, I choose man.

• • •

If existence really does precede essence, there is no explaining things away by reference to a fixed and given human nature. In other words, there is no determinism, man is free, man is freedom. On the other hand, if God does not exist, we find no values or commands to turn to which legitimize our conduct. So, in the bright realm of values, we have no excuse behind us, nor justification before us. We are alone, with no excuses.

That is the idea I shall try to convey when I say that man is condemned to be free. Condemned, because he did not create himself, yet, in other respects is free; because, once thrown into the world, he is

responsible for everything he does. The existentialist does not believe in the power of passion. He will never agree that a sweeping passion is a ravaging torrent which fatally leads a man to certain acts and is therefore an excuse. He thinks that man is responsible for his passion.

The existentialist does not think that man is going to help himself by finding in the world some omen by which to orient himself. Because he thinks that man will interpret the omen to suit himself. Therefore, he thinks that man, with no support and no aid, is condemned every moment to invent man. Ponge, in a very fine article, has said, "Man is the future of man." That's exactly it.

STUDY QUESTIONS

1. What do you think Sartre means by the phrase "existence precedes essence"? What does it have to do with human nature?
2. Do you think Sartre is right in his view that, if God does not exist, there is no such thing as human nature?
3. What, for Sartre, is the relationship between human subjectivity and human dignity?
4. What does Sartre mean by his view that we are "condemned to be free"? Do you agree with him in his conception of the individual's responsibilities?

For Further Reading

Barnes, H. E. *An Existentialist Ethics*. New York: Knopf, 1967 (Chapters 1 and 2).

Barrett, W. *Irrational Man: A Study in Existential Philosophy*. Garden City, N.Y.: Doubleday, 1958 (Chapter 10).

Blackham, H. J. *Six Existentialist Thinkers*. New York: Macmillan, 1952 (Chapter 6).

Grene, M. *Introduction to Existentialism*. Chicago: University of Chicago Press, 1959 (esp. Chapters 3 and 4).

Harper, R. *Existentialism: A Theory of Man*. Cambridge, Mass.: Harvard University Press, 1958.

Warnock, M. *Existentialism*. London: Oxford University Press, 1970 (Chapters 5 and 6).

HUME: NOTHING

Nothing can be closer to us than our self. It is what we are. It should, as a result, be the thing best known to us. Although we may, and probably do, believe this, David Hume has offered strong measures for doubting it. If we are to know our self, he asks, how do we go about doing so? In his opinion, only one way is possible: to observe our self, by the method of introspection. (We can observe our own physical body by our external senses, but this is not the *self* we are seeking.) When, however, we attempt to make our self the object of our introspective scrutiny, we find our efforts ending in frustration. We cannot locate and observe any entity that we can identify as our self. So, Hume concludes, we must admit that we cannot know our self; indeed, we can produce no good reasons for believing that any such self really exists.

David Hume (1711−1776), the most important philosopher in the English language, lived a varied life. Born in Edinburgh, into a somewhat impoverished family, he was forced to work for a living. For a time he served as companion to a mad nobleman. Later he became secretary to the general of a military expedition to Canada which missed its objective and instead made an abortive attack on France. Then he became a librarian in Edinburgh but was discharged for stacking the shelves with obscene books. Late in life he served in the British embassy in Paris where he was lionized by French society. He completed his greatest work in philosophy, the monumental *Treatise of Human Nature*, at the astonishing age of twenty-six.

🌿 *A Treatise of Human Nature*

Of Personal Identity.

There are some philosophers, who imagine we are every moment intimately conscious of what we call our SELF; that we feel its existence and its continuance in existence; and are certain, beyond the evidence of a demonstration, both of its perfect identity and simplicity. The strongest sensation, the most violent passion, say they, instead of distracting us from this view, only fix it more intensely, and make us consider their influence on *self* either by their pain or pleasure. To attempt a farther proof of this were to weaken its evidence; since no proof can be deriv'd from any fact, of which we are so intimately conscious; nor is there any thing, of which we can be certain, if we doubt of this.

Unluckily all these positive assertions

First published in 1739. The selection is from Book I, Part IV, §6.

are contrary to that very experience, which is pleaded for them, nor have we any idea of *self*, after the manner it is here explain'd. For from what impression cou'd this idea be deriv'd? This question 'tis impossible to answer without a manifest contradiction and absurdity; and yet 'tis a question, which must necessarily be answer'd, if we wou'd have the idea of self pass for clear and intelligible. It must be some one impression, that gives rise to every real idea. But self or person is not any one impression, but that to which our several impressions and ideas are suppos'd to have a reference. If any impression gives rise to the idea of self, that impression must continue invariably the same, thro' the whole course of our lives; since self is suppos'd to exist after that manner. But there is no impression constant and invariable. Pain and pleasure, grief and joy, passions and sensations succeed each other, and never all exist at the same time. It cannot, therefore, be from any of these impressions, or from any other, that the idea of self is deriv'd; and consequently there is no such idea.

But farther, what must become of all our particular perceptions upon this hypothesis? All these are different, and distinguishable, and separable from each other, and may be separately consider'd, and may exist separately, and have no need of any thing to support their existence. After what manner, therefore, do they belong to self; and how are they connected with it? For my part, when I enter most intimately into what I call *myself*, I always stumble on some particular perception or other, of heat or cold, light or shade, love or hatred, pain or pleasure. I never can catch *myself* at any time without a perception, and never can observe any thing but the perception. When my perceptions are remov'd for any time, as by sound sleep; so long am I insensible of *myself*, and may truly be said not to exist. And were all my perceptions remov'd by death, and cou'd I neither think, nor feel, nor see, nor love, nor hate after the dissolution of my body, I shou'd be entirely annihilated, nor do I conceive what is farther requisite to make me a perfect non-entity. If any one upon serious and unprejudic'd reflexion, thinks he has a different notion of *himself*, I must confess I can reason no longer with him. All I can allow him is, that he may be in the right as well as I, and that we are essentially different in this particular. He may, perhaps, perceive something simple and continu'd, which he calls *himself*; tho' I am certain there is no such principle in me.

But setting aside some metaphysicians of this kind, I may venture to affirm of the rest of mankind, that they are nothing but a bundle or collection of different percep-

tions, which succeed each other with an inconceivable rapidity, and are in a perpetual flux and movement. Our eyes cannot turn in their sockets without varying our perceptions. Our thought is still more variable than our sight; and all our other senses and faculties contribute to this change; nor is there any single power of the soul, which remains unalterably the same, perhaps for one moment. The mind is a kind of theatre, where several perceptions successively make their appearance; pass, re-pass, glide away, and mingle in an infinite variety of postures and situations. There is properly no *simplicity* in it at one time, nor *identity* in difference: whatever natural propension we may have to imagine that simplicity and identity. The comparison of the theatre must not mislead us. They are the successive perceptions only, that constitute the mind; nor have we the most distant notion of the place, where these scenes are represented, or of the materials, of which it is compos'd.

STUDY QUESTIONS

1. Do you have a self? How do you know that you do? Is the self you know your real self? If so, who does the knowing?
2. On what grounds does Hume deny the possibility of one's knowing oneself?
3. Do you agree with Hume that one ceases to exist when he is in a deep sleep? Why or why not?
4. If, as Hume says, Hume's self is nothing but a bundle of perceptions, how could this bundle of perceptions know that it is nothing but a bundle of perceptions?
5. In what senses, if any, do you think you are the same self you were ten years ago?

For Further Reading appears on page 68.

REID: ONE WHO REMEMBERS

Since the time of David Hume, philosophers have devoted much attention to the problem of self-knowledge. One of the first of those who attempted to allay the doubts Hume had raised about the possibility of our knowing our self was his Scottish contemporary, Thomas Reid. According to Reid, the clue both to self-knowledge and self-identity lies in memory. Each one of us is a self or person that exists as an identifiable entity throughout life; we know this to be true because at any given time in our life we can remember our past, as the past we ourself experienced. If we agree with Reid that we do know that we are one self that persists through time because we remember our past, we might ask this further, speculative question: Suppose we had no memory, or only an extremely episodic one. Would we be able to recognize that we had a self? Would we really have such a self?

Next to David Hume, Thomas Reid (1710–1796) is the most famous of Scottish philosophers. Not only were the two contemporaries, but Reid devoted a good part of his energies to the refutation of Hume's ideas, arguing that Humean scepticism could be answered by a philosophy of "common sense." Reid began his career as a clergyman but later moved into the academic world. In 1763 he was appointed professor of moral philosophy at the University of Glasgow, replacing the renowned economist Adam Smith. At Glasgow he gained the reputation of being a dull but clear lecturer.

✍ Essays on the Intellectual Powers of Man

Of the Nature and Origin of Our Notion of Personal Identity.

I. *Of Identity in General*. The conviction which every man has of his identity, as far back as his memory reaches, needs no aid of philosophy to strengthen it; and no philosophy can weaken it, without first producing some degree of insanity.

The philosopher, however, may very properly consider this conviction as a phenomenon of human nature worthy of his attention. If he can discover its cause, an addition is made to his stock of knowledge; if not, it must be held as a part of our original constitution, or an effect of that constitution produced in a manner unknown to us.

That we may form as distinct a notion as we are able of this phenomenon of the

First published in 1785. The selection is from Essay III, Chapter III.

human mind, it is proper to consider what is meant by identity in general, what by our own personal identity, and how we are led into that invincible belief and conviction which every man has of his own personal identity, as far as his memory reaches.

Identity in general I take to be a relation between a thing which is known to exist at one time, and a thing which is known to have existed at another time. If you ask whether they are one and the same, or two different things, every man of common sense understands the meaning of your question perfectly. Whence we may infer with certainty, that every man of common sense had a clear and distinct notion of identity.

If you ask a definition of identity, I confess I can give none; it is too simple a notion to admit of logical definition: I can say it is a relation, but I cannot find words to express the specific difference between this and other relations, though I am in no danger of confounding it with any other. I can say that diversity is a contrary relation, and that similitude and dissimilitude are another couple of contrary relations, which every man easily distinguishes in his conception from identity and diversity.

I see evidently that identity supposes *an uninterrupted continuance of existence*. That which has ceased to exist cannot be the same with that which afterwards begins to exist; for this would be to suppose a being to exist after it ceased to exist, and to have had existence before it was produced, which are manifest contradictions. Continued uninterrupted existence is therefore necessarily implied in identity. Hence we may infer, that identity cannot, in its proper sense, be applied to our pains, our pleasures, our thoughts, or any operation of our minds. The pain felt this day is not the same individual pain which I felt yesterday, though they be be *similar* in kind and degree, and have the same cause. The same may be said of every feeling, and of every operation of mind. They are all successive in their nature, like time itself, no two moments of which can be the same moment. It is otherwise with the parts of absolute space. They always are, and were, and will be the same. So far, I think, we proceed upon clear ground in fixing the notion of identity in general.

II. *Nature and Origin of our Idea of Personal Identity.* It is perhaps more difficult to ascertain with precision the meaning of *personality*; but it is not necessary in the present subject: it is sufficient for our purpose to observe that all mankind place their personality in something that *cannot be divided, or consist of parts*. A part of a person is a manifest absurdity. When a man loses his estate, his health, his strength, he is still the same person, and has lost nothing of his personality. If he has a leg or an arm cut off, he is the same person as he was before. The amputated member is no part of his person, otherwise it would have a right to a part of his estate, and be liable for a part of his engagements. It would be entitled to a share of his merit and demerit, which is

manifestly absurd. A person is something indivisible, and is what Leibniz calls a *monad*.

My personal identity, therefore, implies the continued existence of that indivisible thing which I call *myself*. Whatever this self may be, it is something which thinks, and deliberates, and resolves, and acts, and suffers. I am not thought, I am not action, I am not feeling; I am something that thinks, and acts, and suffers. My thoughts, and actions, and feelings, change every moment; they have no continued, but a successive, existence; but that *self*, or *I*, to which they belong, is permanent, and has the same relation to all the succeeding thoughts, actions, and feelings which I call mine.

Such are the notions that I have of my personal identity. But perhaps it may be said, this may all be fancy without reality. How do you know,—what evidence have you,—that there is such a permanent self which has a claim to all the thoughts, actions, and feelings which you call yours?

To this I answer, that the proper evidence I have of all this is *remembrance*. I remember that twenty years ago I conversed with such a person; I remember several things that passed in that conversation: my memory testifies, not only that this was done, but that it was done by me who now remember it. If it was done by me, I must have existed at that time, and continued to exist from that time to the present: if the identical person whom I call myself had not a part in that conversation, my memory is fallacious; it gives a distinct and positive testimony of what is not true. Every man in his senses believes what he distinctly remembers, and every thing he remembers convinces him that he existed at the time remembered.

Although memory gives the most irresistible evidence of my being the identical person that did such a thing, at such a time, I may have other good evidence of things which befell me, and which I do not remember: I know who bare me, and suckled me, but I do not remember these events.

It may here be observed, (though the

observation would have been unnecessary, if some great philosophers had not contradicted it) that it is not my remembering any action of mine that *makes* me to be the person who did it. This remembrance makes me to *know* assuredly that I did it; *but I might have done it, though I did not remember it.* That relation to me, which is expressed by saying that *I did it*, would be the same, though I had not the least remembrance of it. To say that my remembering that I did such a thing, or, as some choose to express it, my being conscious that I did it, makes me to have done it, appears to me as great an absurdity as it would be to say, that my belief that the world was created made it to be created.

When we pass judgment on the identity of other persons than ourselves, we proceed upon other grounds, and determine from a variety of circumstances, which sometimes produce the firmest assurance, and sometimes leave room for doubt. The identity of persons has often furnished matter of serious litigation before tribunals of justice. But no man of a sound mind ever doubted his own identity, as far as he distinctly remembered.

The identity of a person is a perfect identity: wherever it is real, it admits of no degrees; and it is impossible that a person should be in part the same, and in part different; because a person is a *monad*, and is not divisible into parts. The evidence of identity in other persons than ourselves does indeed admit of all degrees, from what we account certainty, to the least degree of probability. But still it is true, that the same person is perfectly the same, and cannot be so in part, or in some degree only.

For this cause, I have first considered personal identity, as that which is perfect in its kind, and the natural measure of that which is imperfect.

We probably at first derive our notion of identity from that natural conviction which every man has from the dawn of reason of *his own* identity and continued existence. The operations of our minds are all successive, and have no continued exis-

tence. But the thinking being has a continued existence, and we have an invincible belief, that it remains the same when all its thoughts and operations change.

Our judgments of the identity of objects of sense seem to be formed much upon the same grounds as our judgments of the identity of *other persons* than ourselves. Wherever we observe great *similarity*, we are apt to presume identity, if no reason appears to the contrary. Two objects ever so like, when they are perceived at the same time, cannot be the same; but if they are presented to our senses at different times, we are apt to think them the same, merely from their similarity.

Whether this be a natural prejudice, or from whatever cause it proceeds, it certainly appears in children from infancy; and when we grow up, it is confirmed in most instances by experience: for we rarely find two individuals of the same species that are not distinguishable by obvious differences. A man challenges a thief whom he finds in possession of his horse or his watch, only on similarity. When the watchmaker swears that he sold this watch to such a person, his testimony is grounded on similarity. The testimony of witnesses to the identity of a person is commonly grounded on no other evidence.

Thus it appears, that the evidence we have of our own identity, as far back as we remember, is totally of a different kind from the evidence we have of the identity of other persons, or of objects of sense. The first is grounded on *memory*, and gives undoubted certainty. The last is grounded on *similarity*, and on other circumstances, which in many cases are not so decisive as to leave no room for doubt.

It may likewise be observed, that the identity of *objects of sense* is never perfect. All bodies, as they consist of innumerable parts that may be disjoined from them by a great variety of causes, are subject to continual changes of their substance, increasing, diminishing, changing insensibly. When such alterations are gradual, because language could not afford a different name for every different state of such a changeable being, it retains the same name, and is considered as the same thing. Thus we say of an old regiment, that it did such a thing a century ago, though there now is not a man alive who then belonged to it. We say a tree is the same in the seed-bed and in the forest. A ship of war, which has successively changed her anchors, her tackle, her sails, her masts, her planks, and her timbers, while she keeps the same name, is the same.

The identity, therefore, which we ascribe to bodies, whether natural or artificial, is not perfect identity; it is rather something which, for the conveniency of speech, we call identity. It admits of a great change of the subject, providing the change be *gradual*; sometimes, even of a total change. And the changes which in common language are made consistent with identity differ from those that are thought to destroy it, not in *kind*, but in *number* and *degree*. It has no fixed nature when applied to bodies; and questions about the identity of a body are very often questions about words. But identity, when applied to persons, has no ambiguity, and admits not of degrees, or of more and less. It is the foundation of all rights and obligations, and of all accountableness; and the notion of it is fixed and precise.

STUDY QUESTIONS

1. Do you agree with Reid that identity "supposes an uninterrupted continuance of existence"? Is the victim of amnesia the same person after he recovers, or someone else?
2. What is the relationship between memory and selfhood? How important is it?
3. Can we know that certain things happen to us, even if we do not remember them? How would we know this?
4. Do you agree with Reid that to doubt of one's own identity is a mark of insanity?
5. Can you be the same self you were ten years ago and still be quite different from that self? If so, in what sense are you the same self?

For Further Reading

Ayer, A. J. *The Concept of a Person and Other Essays*. London: Macmillan, 1963 (Chapter 4).

Broad, C. D. *The Mind and Its Place in Nature*. London: Routledge & Kegan Paul, 1925 (Chapter 13).

James, W. *Psychology*. New York: Holt, 1892 (Chapter 12).

Penelhum, T. "Hume on Personal Identity." *The Philosophical Review* 64 (1955), 571−89.

Shoemaker, S. *Self-Knowledge and Self-Identity*. Ithaca: Cornell University Press, 1963.

Vesey, G. N. A. *Personal Identity*. London: Macmillan, 1974.

Williams, B. A. O. "Personal Identity and Individuation." *Proceedings of the Aristotelian Society* 57 (1956−57), 229−52.

PLATO: THE HUMAN CONDITION

Much has been written about "the human condition," most of it negative. Indeed, the very phrase itself is negative, for the idea of being in a "condition" indicates that something is wrong. Many descriptions have been offered of this condition and many suggestions made about how we can escape from it. In the Western tradition, these have usually been couched in religious terms; our condition is the result of sin and our escape achieved through salvation. In his famous account of the human condition, however, Plato adopts a different perspective. The basic human problem he believes to be intellectual. The unfortunate condition we find ourselves in results from our failure to comprehend the true nature of things because our intellectual vision is limited to appearances, hence never comes into contact with reality. The philosopher, who can escape from his bondage to appearances and confront the real world, has a unique and heavy obligation—to get others to follow his lead and share with him the vision of reality he has had.

Among the coterie of Socrates' youthful followers, the most talented by far was Plato (427–347 B.C.). The scion of a wealthy and noble Athenian family, Plato was preparing for a career in politics when the trial and execution of Socrates caused him to abandon his plans to devote his life to the Socratic search for wisdom. He retired to the outskirts of Athens where he set up a school of philosophy, spending his life teaching and writing. Plato's school, The Academy, was the first university in Western history. It remained in existence for over nine hundred years, until closed by the Emperor Justinian in A.D. 529. With the possible exception of his pupil, Aristotle, Plato is the most influential thinker in Western history.

The selection that follows is taken from his most famous work, *The Republic*.

℣ *The Republic*

Book VII

Next, said I [Socrates] here is a parable to illustrate the degree in which our nature may be enlightened or unenlightened. Imagine the condition of men living in a sort of cavernous chamber underground, with an entrance open to the light and a long passage all down the cave. Here they have been from childhood, chained by the leg and also by the neck, so that they cannot move and can see only what is in front of them, because the chains will not let them turn their heads. At some distance higher up is the light of a fire burning behind them; and between the prisoners and the fire is a track with a parapet built along it, like the screen at a puppet-show, which hides the performers while they show their puppets over the top.

I see, said he.

Now behind this parapet imagine persons carrying along various artificial objects, including figures of men and animals in wood or stone or other materials, which project above the parapet. Naturally, some

*From *The Republic of Plato* translated by F. M. Cornford and published by Oxford University Press (1941). Reprinted by permission of Oxford University Press.

of these persons will be talking, others silent.*

It is a strange picture, he said, and a strange sort of prisoners.

Like ourselves, I replied; for in the first place prisoners so confined would have seen nothing of themselves or of one another, except the shadows thrown by the fire-light on the wall of the Cave facing them, would they?

Not if all their lives they had been prevented from moving their heads.

And they would have seen as little of the objects carried past.

Of course.

Now, if they could talk to one another, would they not suppose that their words referred only to those passing shadows which they saw?

Necessarily.

And suppose their prison had an echo from the wall facing them? When one of the people crossing behind them spoke, they could only suppose that the sound came from the shadow passing before their eyes.

No doubt.

In every way, then, such prisoners would recognize as reality nothing but the shadows of those artificial objects.

Inevitably.

Now consider what would happen if their release from the chains and the healing of their unwisdom should come about in this way. Suppose one of them set free and forced suddenly to stand up, turn his head, and walk with eyes lifted to the light;

*A modern Plato would compare his Cave to an underground cinema, where the audience watch the play of shadows thrown by the film passing before a light at their backs. The film itself is only an image of "real" things and events in the world outside the cinema. For the film, Plato has to substitute the clumsier apparatus of a procession of artificial objects carried on their heads by persons who are merely part of the machinery, providing for the movement of the objects and the sounds whose echo the prisoners hear. The parapet prevents these persons' shadows from being cast on the wall of the Cave. —Tr.

all these movements would be painful, and he would be too dazzled to make out the objects whose shadows he had been used to see. What do you think he would say, if someone told him that what he had formerly seen was meaningless illusion, but now, being somewhat nearer to reality and turned towards more real objects, he was getting a truer view? Suppose further that he were shown the various objects being carried by and were made to say, in reply to questions, what each of them was. Would he not be perplexed and believe the objects now shown him to be not so real as what he formerly saw?

Yes, not nearly so real.

And if he were forced to look at the fire-light itself, would not his eyes ache, so that he would try to escape and turn back to the things which he could see distinctly, convinced that they really were clearer than these other objects now being shown to him?

Yes.

And suppose someone were to drag him away forcibly up the steep and rugged ascent and not let him go until he had hauled him out into the sunlight, would he not suffer pain and vexation at such treatment, and, when he had come out into the light, find his eyes so full of its radiance that he could not see a single one of the things that he was now told were real?

Certainly he would not see them all at once.

He would need, then, to grow accustomed before he could see things in that upper world. At first it would be easiest to make out shadows, and then the images of men and things reflected in water, and later on the things themselves. After that, it would be easier to watch the heavenly bodies and the sky itself by night, looking at the light of the moon and stars rather than the Sun and the Sun's light in the day-time.

Yes, surely.

Last of all, he would be able to look at the Sun and contemplate its nature, not as it appears when reflected in water or any alien medium, but as it is in itself in its own domain.

No doubt.

And now he would begin to draw the conclusions that it is the Sun that produces the seasons and the course of the year and controls everything in the visible world, and moreover is in a way the cause of all that he and his companions used to see.

Clearly he would come at last to that conclusion.

Then if he called to mind his fellow prisoners and what passed for wisdom in his former dwelling-place, he would surely think himself happy in the change and be sorry for them. They may have had a practice of honouring and commending one another, with prizes for the man who had the keenest eye for the passing shadows and the best memory for the order in which they followed or accompanied one another, so that he could make a good guess as to which was going to come next. Would our released prisoner be likely to covet those prizes or to envy the men exalted to honour and power in the Cave? Would he not feel like Homer's Achilles, that he would far sooner "be on earth as a hired servant in the house of a landless man" or endure anything rather than go back to his old beliefs and live in the old way?

Yes, he would prefer any fate to such a life.

Now imagine what would happen if he went down again to take his former seat in the Cave. Coming suddenly out of the sunlight, his eyes would be filled with darkness. He might be required once more to deliver his opinion on those shadows, in competition with the prisoners who had never been released, while his eyesight was still dim and unsteady; and it might take some time to become used to the darkness. They would laugh at him and say that he had gone up only to come back with his sight ruined; it was worth no one's while even to attempt the ascent. If they could lay hands on the man who was trying to set them free and lead them up, they would kill him.*

*An allusion to the fate of Socrates. —Tr.

Yes, the would.

Every feature in this parable, my dear Glaucon, is meant to fit our earlier analysis. The prison dwelling corresponds to the region revealed to us through the sense of sight, and the fire-light within it to the power of the Sun. The ascent to see the things in the upper world you may take as standing for the upward journey of the soul into the region of the intelligible; then you will be in possession of what I surmise, since that is what you wish to be told. Heaven knows whether it is true; but this, at any rate, is how it appears to me. In the world of knowledge, the last thing to be perceived and only with great difficulty is the essential Form of Goodness. Once it is perceived, the conclusion must follow that, for all things, this is the cause of whatever is right and good; in the visible world it gives birth to light and to the lord of light, while it is itself sovereign in the intelligible world and the parent of intelligence and truth. Without having had a vision of this Form no one can act with wisdom in his own life or in matters of state.

So far as I can understand, I share your belief.

Then you may also agree that it is no wonder if those who have reached this height are reluctant to manage the affairs of men. Their souls long to spend all their time in that upper world—naturally enough, if here once more our parable holds true. Nor, again, is it at all strange that one who comes from the contemplation of divine things to the miseries of human life should appear awkward and ridiculous when, with eyes still dazed and not yet accustomed to the darkness, he is compelled, in a law-court or elsewhere, to dispute about the shadows of justice or the images that cast those shadows, and to wrangle over the notions of what is right in the minds of men who have never beheld Justice itself.

It is not at all strange.

No; a sensible man will remember that the eyes may be confused in two ways—by a change from light to darkness or from darkness to light; and he will recognize that the same thing happens to the soul. When he sees it troubled and unable to discern anything clearly, instead of laughing thoughtlessly, he will ask whether, coming from a brighter existence, its unaccustomed vision is obscured by the darkness, in which case he will think its condition enviable and its life a happy one; or whether, emerging from the depths of ignorance, it is dazzled by excess of light. If so, he will rather feel sorry for it; or, if he were inclined to laugh, that would be less ridiculous than to laugh at the soul which has come down from the light.

That is a fair statement.

If this is true, then, we must conclude that education is not what it is said to be by some, who profess to put knowledge into a soul which does not possess it, as if they could put sight into blind eyes. On the contrary, our own account signifies that the soul of every man does possess the power of learning the truth and the organ to see it with; and that, just as one might have to turn the whole body round in order that the eye should see light instead of dark-

ness, so the entire soul must be turned away from this changing world, until its eye can bear to contemplate reality and that supreme splendour which we have called the Good. Hence there may well be an art whose aim would be to effect this very thing, the conversion of the soul, in the readiest way; not to put the power of sight into the soul's eye, which already has it, but to ensure that, instead of looking in the wrong direction, it is turned the way it ought to be.

STUDY QUESTIONS

1. What, for Plato, is the role of philosophy in human life?
2. What does Plato mean by the Form of Goodness? How is it related to the rest of the world? Would you call Plato an optimist or a pessimist?
3. What is Plato's theory of education? Do you think it is sound?
4. Do you think there is any validity in Plato's description of the human condition?

For Further Reading

Gould, T. *Platonic Love.* New York: Free Press, 1963 (Chapter 5).

Hall, R. W. *Plato and the Individual.* The Hague: Martinus Nijhoff, 1963 (esp. Chapter 1).

Rankin, H. D. *Plato and the Individual.* London: Methuen, 1964.

Raven, J. E. *Plato's Thought in the Making.* Cambridge: At the University Press, 1965 (pp. 164–87).

Wild, J. *Plato's Theory of Man.* Cambridge, Mass.: Harvard University Press, 1946 (Chapter 5).

PART III

The Individual and Nature

Of all the things that surround us, the most pervasive is physical nature. No matter which way we turn, we find ourselves confronted by physical objects. They surround us on every side, from the ground beneath our feet, to the mountains that hedge us in, to the starry heavens that recede into infinite space above our heads. The immensity of the universe fills most of us with awe and some even with terror; nevertheless, it is something that we have found ourselves able to comprehend and to some extent to control.

From the earliest records we have of their thought, philosophers have concerned themselves with understanding nature. Three questions have occupied most of their attention: What is the natural world composed of? How does it operate? What place do human beings occupy in it?

Philosophy in the western world had its origin when a Greek named Thales, who lived in Asia Minor in the sixth century B.C., offered an answer to the first of these questions. According to Thales, everything ultimately is composed of water. This theory may seem naive to us today, but we must remember that it was the first attempt—of which we have any record—in which a thinker tried to reduce the apparently endless variety of the world around us to a single natural element. Thales was soon followed by other thinkers who offered different explanations of things. One said that the ultimate substance of which everything is composed is fire, another that it is air, and another earth. Like the original view of Thales, each of them appeals to an element we can perceive to be of great importance to the world. Yet all suffer from the same defect; each is too limited in its scope to account for everything. How, for example, can water be derived from fire, or earth from air? Their importance remains, however, as the first attempts to understand nature in its own terms.

By the fifth century B.C., philosophers had recognized that, if they were to succeed in accounting for the diversity of things, they would have to produce a theory of substance that was completely general. The result was atomism, or atomistic materialism, a theory first developed by two thinkers, Leucippus (fifth century) and Democritus (c. 460-c. 370). This theory of the nature of things,

73

which is described in the first selection that follows, has ever since remained the accepted explanation of the physical world, being held, in a somewhat more sophisticated form, by scientists of our own day. Besides being completely general, the atomistic theory is exceptionally simple. To explain everything, it makes three basic assumptions: The universe is composed of (1) atoms (2) that are in motion (3) in empty space. The atoms, which are eternal and indestructible, have no qualities, like color or odor, and are too small ever to be observed. However, they differ from each other in size and shape. As they move through empty space they collide with each other, and because of their irregular shapes, sometimes cling together. Thus larger bodies are gradually formed and eventually the world in all its marvelous variety.

The atomistic theory gives an answer not only to the first question we raised (What is the natural world composed of?) but to the second as well (How does it operate?) Physical events occur because, first the atoms, and then later the larger, visible bodies made up of them come into collision with each other. This conception of physical action has come to be known as the mechanical theory of causation or, for short, as mechanism. One of the consequences of the mechanical theory of causation is determinism. If the movements of all physical bodies are the effects of the actions of other physical bodies impinging on them, there can be no such thing as a random event. Rather, whatever happens in the world does so of necessity. Each event throughout history is linked to all others in a gigantic network bound together by vast interlocking chains of causes and effects. Such a conception of the connections among things has two important consequences, one theoretical and the other practical. On the theoretical side, the assumption that everything that happens is the result of mechanical causes provides a strong foundation in terms of which we can understand nature. By observation, the maintenance of records, and calculations, scientists are able to formulate generalizations describing great classes of events, often in terms of simple formulas that can be stated in mathematical terms. Thus are generated "laws of nature." Such laws, or descriptive generalizations, form the basis of our scientific understanding of the world. On the practical side, our recognition that nature operates by settled and unchanging laws which we can understand allows us to order our own lives rationally. We can, for example, make plans for the future. If we are farmers, we can know that, although the weather is unpredictable in its details, it conforms to certain general patterns, in which winter, say, must eventually be followed by spring. Thus, we can know when to plant and when to reap. Furthermore, our mastery of the laws that govern the workings of nature gives us power to use its forces and control its actions. As a result we can grow crops in land once desert and harvest oil from beneath the sea.

In our account so far, we have spoken only of physical nature, not yet considering the question, What place do human beings occupy in the world? Each of us, because we possess a body, can be viewed, like everything else, as a material object whose actions are determined by the same mechanical laws that apply everywhere else. We are, thus, an integral part of nature, as much so as a stone or a tree. If this were the whole truth about us, however, I should not be writing these words or you reading them. People, although they are physical objects, are somehow much more than just that. To note one difference: every physical thing has a space-time location from which it cannot escape. It must always exist in the present and in one single place at any given time. This holds true of human bodies, as well, but not of human minds. In imagination I can picture myself basking in the sun on a South Sea island. Although my body is seated before my desk, my mind is far away. Or I can in memory return to scenes of my childhood or, in anticipation, picture events in the future.

The possibilities I have just described, plus many others of a similar kind, raise serious questions about the extent to which the individual is immersed in nature. Although we all have physical bodies, there seems to be another part of us that makes us aliens in the natural world, governed by its laws of space, time, and mechanical causation. But if we are not fully natural beings in the sense that trees and stones are, what kind of beings are we and how are we related to the rest of the world? About such questions philosophers throughout history have disagreed. One tradition, the materialism stemming from Leucippus and Democritus, maintains that the peculiarities of human nature that I have just mentioned are only apparent deviations from nature; in reality nothing exists, including human minds, that cannot be ultimately reduced to matter in motion. Another tradition, however, takes the exactly opposite position. Convinced of the reality of human minds and the conscious experiences we have, philosophers of this persuasion believe it possible to reduce physical nature to the content of our experience. Thus they see no reason for even postulating the existence of a physical world independent of us. These are the idealists, represented in the selections that follow by George Berkeley. Many other philosophers, however, believe they must acknowledge the existence of both minds and matter. These, the dualists, are then left with the problem of trying to understand how the two can be related to each other. In the selection from his writings that follows, René Descartes offers a solution to that problem.

If one accepts the view that minds exist and are somehow different from the natural world, certain other possibilities and questions emerge. Such minds, since they are nonphysical, presumably are free of the bonds of mechanistic causation. Are they free of causation altogether? Or are they bound by a different form of causation? Questions such as these have given rise to the controversy between free will and determinism. This issue is particularly important for human life because of the implications it has for morality, in particular, for the responsibilities we bear for the acts we do. In the selections that follow, spokesmen for both sides of the issue state their case.

Finally, dualism raises a problem about the life of the mind. A person's body, like other living things, has a natural life span. Death brings its destruction. But what of our mind? If it is not identical with our body, is it separable from it, particularly to the extent of being able to continue its existence after the death of the body? This, the problem of immortality, is debated in the final two sections of this part.

Background Readings

Adams, G. P. *Man and Metaphysics*. New York: Columbia University Press, 1948.

Parker, D. H. *The Self and Nature*. Cambridge, Mass.: Harvard University Press, 1917.

Pears, D. F., ed. *The Nature of Metaphysics*. London: Methuen, 1957.

Sprague, E. *Metaphysical Thinking*. New York: Oxford University Press, 1978.

Taylor, A. E. *Elements of Metaphysics*. 6th ed. London: Methuen, 1921.

Taylor, R. *Metaphysics*. rev. ed. Englewood Cliffs, N.J.: Prentice-Hall, 1974.

Whiteley, C. H. *An Introduction to Metaphysics*. London: Methuen, 1950.

LUCRETIUS: MATERIALISM

Lucretius is famous for two things. His work *De Rerum Natura (On the Nature of Things)* is at once a great poem and the statement and defense of a major theory of metaphysics. In it he expounds in lyrical verses the philosophy of atomistic materialism. (Although Lucretius, at the beginning of his poem, credits the Greek philosopher, Epicurus, with originating the theory, it actually began with the earlier Greek thinkers, Leucippus and Democritus.) Lucretius is concerned not only to elucidate how all the objects and events that make up the world we live in can be explained through an appeal to atoms in motion but also, and especially, to show the consequences such a conception of reality has for human life. He believes that much of the suffering human beings endure results from the terror aroused in their minds by religious superstition. To counteract such influences, he thinks it necessary to convince his readers that they are simply parts of a material world, existing as individual entities for a few years, then disintegrating to return to the whole from which they originally sprang and out of which new individuals will be formed. Although translated in a prose style, the selection that follows retains much of the poetic quality of the Lucretian original.

Very little is known of the life of Lucretius (c. 95-55 B.C.). His full name was Titus Lucretius Carus and, according to his own statement, he was a Roman by birth. According to tradition, he committed suicide after being driven mad by a love potion; that this account of his death is correct, however, must be considered dubious.

℣ *De Rerum Natura*

Book I

O bountiful Venus, mother of the race of Aeneas, delight of gods and men, who, beneath the gliding constellations of heaven, fillest with life the ship-bearing sea and the fruit-producing earth; since by thy influence every kind of living creature is conceived, and springing forth, hails the light of the sun. Thee, O goddess, thee the winds flee; before thee, and thy approach, the clouds of heaven disperse; for thee the variegated earth puts forth her fragrant flowers; on thee the waters of ocean smile, and the calmed heaven beams with effulgent light. For, as soon as the vernal face of day is unveiled, and the genial gale of Favonius exerts its power unconfined, the birds of the air first, O goddess, testify of

The translation is by J. S. Watson and is taken from Books I–III.

thee and thy coming, smitten in heart by thy influence. Next, the wild herds bound over the joyous pastures, and swim across the rapid streams. So all kinds of living creatures, captivated by thy charms and thy allurements, eagerly follow thee whithersoever thou proceedest to lead them. In fine, throughout seas, and mountains, and whelming rivers, and the leafy abodes of birds, and verdant plains, thou, infusing balmy love into the breasts of all, causest them eagerly to propagate their races after their kind.

Since thou alone dost govern all things in nature, neither does any thing without thee spring into the ethereal realms of light, nor any thing become gladsome or lovely; I desire thee to be my associate in this my song, which I am essaying to compose on the NATURE OF THINGS, for the instruction of my friend Memmius, whom thou, O goddess, hast willed at all times to excel, graced with every gift. The more therefore do thou, O goddess, bestow on my words an immortal charm.

• • •

When the life of men lay foully grovelling before our eyes, crushed beneath the weight of a religion, who displayed her head from the regions of the sky, lowering over mortals with terrible aspect, a man of Greece* was the first that dared to raise mortal eyes against her, and first to make a stand against her. Him neither tales of gods, nor thunderbolts, nor heaven itself with its threatening roar, repressed, but roused the more the active energy of his soul, so that he should desire to be the first to break the close bars of nature's portals. Accordingly the vivid force of his intellect prevailed, and proceeded far beyond the flaming battlements of the world, and in mind and thought traversed the whole immensity of space; hence triumphant, he declares to us what can arise into being, and what can not; in fine, in what way the powers of all things are limited, and a deeply-fixed boundary assigned to each. By which means religion, brought down under our feet, is bruised in turn; and his victory sets us on a level with heaven.

• • •

Wherefore with reason then, not only an inquiry concerning celestial affairs is to be accurately made by us, (as by what means the courses of the sun and moon are affected, and by what influence all things individually are directed upon the earth,) but especially also we must consider, with scrutinizing examination, of what the soul and the nature of the mind consist, and what it is, which, haunting us, sometimes when awake, and sometimes when overcome by disease or buried in sleep, terrifies the mind; so that we seem to behold and to hear speaking before us, those whose

*Epicurus—ed.

bones, after death is passed, the earth embraces.

Nor does it escape my consideration, that it is difficult to explain in Latin verse the profound discoveries of the Greeks, especially since we must treat of much in novel words, on account of the poverty of our language, and the novelty of the subjects. But yet thy virtues, and the expected pleasure of thy sweet friendship, prompt me to endure any labour whatsoever, and induce me to out-watch the clear cold nights, weighing with what words, with what possible verse, I may succeed in displaying to thy mind those clear lights, by which thou mayest be able to gain a thorough insight into these abstruse subjects.

This terror and darkness of the mind, therefore, it is not the rays of the sun, or the bright shafts of day, that must dispel, but the reason and the contemplation of nature; of which our first principle shall hence take its commencement, THAT NOTHING IS EVER DIVINELY GENERATED FROM NOTHING. For thus it is that fear restrains all men, because they observe many things effected on the earth, and in heaven, of which effects they can by no means see the causes, and therefore think that they are wrought by a divine power. For which reasons, when we shall have clearly seen that NOTHING CAN BE PRODUCED FROM NOTHING, we shall then have a more accurate perception of that of which we are in search, and shall understand whence each individual thing is generated, and how all things are done without the agency of the gods.

For if things came forth from nothing, every kind of thing might be produced from all things; nothing would require seed. In the first place, men might spring from the sea; the scaly tribe, and birds, might spring from the earth; herds and other cattle, might burst from the sky; the cultivated fields, as well as the deserts, might contain every kind of wild animal without any settled law of production: nor would the same fruits be constant to the same trees, but would be changed; and all trees might bear all kinds of fruit. Since, when there should not be generative elements for each production, how could a certain parent-producer remain invariable for all individual things? But now, because all things are severally produced from certain seeds, each is produced, and comes forth into the regions of light, from that spot in which the matter, and first elements of each, subsist. And for this cause all things cannot be produced from all, inasmuch as there are distinct and peculiar faculties in certain substances.

Besides, why do we see the rose put forth in spring, corn in summer heat, and vines under the influence of autumn, if it be not because, when the determinate seeds of things have united together at their proper time, whatever is produced appears while the seasons are favourable, and while the vigorous earth securely brings forth her tender productions into the regions of light. But if these were generated from nothing, they might arise suddenly at indefinite periods, and at unsuitable seasons of the year, inasmuch as there would be no original elements, which might be restrained from a generative combination at any season, however inconvenient.

Nor, moreover, would there be need of time for the coming together of seed for the growth of things, if they could grow out of nothing. For young men might on a sudden be formed from puny infants, and groves, springing up unexpectedly, might dart forth from the earth; of which things it is plain that none happen, since all things grow gradually, as is fitting, from unvarying atoms, and, as they grow, preserve their kind, so that you may understand that all things individually are enlarged and nourished from their own specific matter.

Add to this, that the earth cannot furnish her cheering fruits without certain rains in the year; nor, moreover, can the nature of animals, if kept from food, propagate their kind, and sustain life; so that you may rather deem that many elements are common to many things, (as we see letters common to many words) than that any

thing can exist without its proper elements.

Still further, why could not nature produce men of such a size that they might ford the sea on foot, and rend great mountains with their hands, and outlast in existence many ages of human life, if it be not because certain matter has been assigned for producing certain things, from which matter it is fixed what can or cannot arise? It must be admitted therefore, that nothing can be made from nothing, since things have need of seed, from which all individually being produced, may be brought forth into the gentle air of heaven.

Lastly, since we observe that cultivated places excel the uncultivated, and yield to our hands better fruits, we may see that there are in the ground the primitive elements of things, which we, in turning the fertile glebe with the ploughshare, and subjugating the soil of the earth, force into birth. But were there no such seeds, you might see things severally grow up and become much better of their own accord without our labour.

Add, too, that nature resolves each thing into its own constituent elements, and DOES NOT REDUCE ANY THING TO NOTHING.

For if any thing were perishable in all its parts, every thing might then dissolve, being snatched suddenly from before our eyes; for there would be no need of force to produce a separation of its parts, and break their connexion. Whereas now, since all things individually consist of eternal seed, nature does not suffer the destruction of any thing to be seen, until such power assail them as to sever them with a blow, or penetrate inwardly through the vacant spaces, and dissolve the parts.

Besides, if time utterly destroys whatever things it removes through length of age, consuming all their constituent matter, whence does Venus restore to the light of life the race of animals according to their kinds? Whence does the variegated earth nourish and develop them, when restored, affording them sustenances according to their kinds? Whence do pure fountains, and eternal rivers flowing from afar, supply the sea? Whence does the æther feed the stars? For infinite time already past, and length of days, ought to have consumed all things which are of mortal consistence: but if those elements, of which this sum of things consists and is renewed, have existed through that long space, and that past duration of time, they are assuredly endowed with an immortal nature. Things therefore cannot return to nothing.

Further, the same force and cause might destroy all things indiscriminately, unless an eternal matter held them more or less bound by mutual connexion. For a mere touch, indeed, would be a sufficient cause of destruction, supposing that there were no parts of eternal consistence, but all perishable, the union of which any force might dissolve. But now, because various connexions of elements unite together, and matter is eternal, things continue of unimpaired consistence, until some force of sufficient strength be found to assail them, proportioned to the texture of each. No thing, therefore, relapses into nonexistence, but all things at dissolution return to the first principles of matter.

Lastly, you may say, perhaps, the showers of rain perish, when Father Aether has poured them down into the lap of Mother Earth. But it is not so; for hence the smiling fruits arise, and the branches become verdant on the trees; the trees themselves increase, and are weighed down with produce. Hence, moreover, is nourished the race of man, and that of beasts; hence we see joyous cities abound with youth, and the leafy woods resound on every side with newly-fledged birds; hence the weary cattle, sleek in the rich pastures, repose their bodies, and the white milky liquor flows from their distended udders; hence the new offspring gambol sportive, with tottering limbs, over the tender grass, their youthful hearts exhilarated with pure milk. Things, therefore, do not utterly perish, which seem to do so, since Nature recruits one thing from another, nor suffers any thing to be produced, unless its production be furthered by the death of another.

Attend, now, further: since I have shown that things cannot be produced from nothing, and also that, when produced, they cannot return to nothing, yet, lest haply thou shouldst begin to distrust my words, because the primary particles of things cannot be discerned by the eye, hear, in addition, what substances thou thyself must necessarily confess to exist, although impossible to be seen.

In the first place, the force of the wind, when excited, lashes the sea, agitates the tall ships, and scatters the clouds; at times, sweeping over the earth with an impetuous hurricane, it strews the plains with huge trees, and harasses the mountain-tops with forest-rending blasts; so violently does the deep chafe with fierce roar and rage with menacing murmur. The winds, then, are invisible bodies, which sweep the sea, the land, the clouds of heaven, and, agitating them, carry them along with a sudden tornado. Not otherwise do they rush forth, and spread destruction, than as when a body of liquid water is borne along in an overwhelming stream, which a vast torrent from the lofty mountains swells with large rain-floods, dashing together fragments of woods and entire groves; nor can the strong bridges sustain the sudden force of the sweeping water, with such overwhelming violence does the river, turbid with copious rain, rush against the opposing mounds; it scatters ruin with a mighty uproar, and rolls huge rocks under its waters; it rushes on triumphant wheresoever any thing opposes its waves. Thus, therefore, must the blasts of the wind also be borne along; which (when, like a mighty flood, they have bent their force in any direction) drive all things before them, and overthrow them with repeated assaults, and sometimes catch them up in a writhing vortex and rapidly bear them off in a whirling hurricane. Wherefore, I repeat, the winds are substances, though invisible, since in their effects, and modes of operation, they are found to rival mighty rivers, which are of manifest bodily substance.

Moreover we perceive various odours of objects, and yet never see them approaching our nostrils. Nor do we behold violent heat, or distinguish cold with our eyes; nor are we in the habit of viewing sounds; all which things, however, must of necessity consist of a corporeal nature, since they have the power of striking the senses: FOR NOTHING, EXCEPT BODILY SUBSTANCE, CAN TOUCH OR BE TOUCHED.

Further, garments, when suspended upon a shore on which waves are broken, grow moist; the same, when spread out in the sun, become dry; yet neither has it been observed how the moisture of the water settled in them, nor, on the other hand, how it escaped under the influences of the heat. The moisture, therefore, is dispersed into minute particles, which our eyes can by no means perceive.

Besides, in the course of many revolutions of the sun, a ring upon the finger is made somewhat thinner by wearing it; the fall of the drop from the eaves hollows a stone; the crooked share of the plough, though made of iron, imperceptibly decreases in the fields; even the stone pavements of the streets we see worn by the feet of the multitude; and the brazen statues, which stand near the gates, show their right hands made smaller by the touch of people frequently saluting them, and passing by. These objects, therefore, after they have been worn, we observe to become diminished; but what particles take their departure on each particular occasion, jealous nature has withheld from us the faculty of seeing.

Lastly, whatever substances time and nature add little by little to objects, obliging them to increase gradually, those substances no acuteness of vision, however earnestly exerted, can perceive; no, moreover, whatever substances waste away through age and decay; nor can you discern what the rocks, which overhang the sea, and are eaten by the corroding salt of the ocean, lose every time that they are washed by the waves. Nature, therefore, carries on her operations by imperceptible particles.

Nor, however, are all things held enclosed by corporeal substance; for there is a void in things; a truth which it will be useful for you, in reference to many points, to know; and which will prevent you from wandering in doubt, and from perpetually inquiring about the entire of things, and from being distrustful of my words. Wherefore, I say, there is space INTANGIBLE, EMPTY, and VACANT. If this were not the case, things could by no means be moved; for that which is the quality of body, namely, to obstruct and to oppose, would be present at all times, and would be exerted against all bodies; nothing, therefore, would be able to move forward, since nothing would begin to give way. But now, throughout the sea and land and heights of heaven, we see many things moved before our eyes in various ways and by various means, which, if there were no void, would not so much want their active motion, as being deprived of it, as they would, properly speaking, never by any means have been produced at all; since matter, crowded together on all sides, would have remained at rest, and have been unable to act.

Besides, although some things may be regarded as solid, yet you may, for the following reasons, perceive them to be of a porous consistence. In rocks and caves, the liquid moisture of the waters penetrates their substance, and all parts weep, as it were, with abundant drops; food distributes itself through the whole of the body in animals; the groves increase, and yield their fruits in their season, because nourishment is diffused through the whole of the trees, even from the lowest roots, over all the trunks and branches; voices pass through the walls, and fly across the closed apartments of houses; keen frost penetrates to the very marrow of our bones; which kind of effects, unless there were void spaces in bodies, where the several particles might pass, you would never by any means observe to take place.

Lastly, why do we see some things exceed other things in weight, though of no greater shape and bulk? For, if there is just as much substance in a ball of wool as there is in a ball of lead, it is natural that they should weigh the same, since it is the property of all bodily substance to press everything downwards; but the nature of a void, on the contrary, continues without weight. That body, therefore, which is equally large with another, and is evidently lighter, shows plainly that it contains a greater portion of vacuity. But the heavier body, on the other hand, indicates that there is in it more material substance, and that it comprises much less empty space.

That, therefore, which we are now, by the aid of searching argument, investigating, that, namely, which we call void; is doubtless mixed among material substances.

• • •

But since I have taught that atoms of matter, entirely solid, pass-to-and-fro perpetually, unwasted through all time; come now, and let us unravel whether there be any limit to their aggregate, or not; also, let us look into that which has been found to be vacancy, or the room and space in which things severally are done, and learn whether the whole is entirely limited, or extends unbounded and unfathomably profound.

All that exists, therefore, I affirm, is bounded in no direction; for, if it were bounded, it must have some extremity; but it appears that there cannot be an extremity of anything, unless there be something beyond, which may limit it; so that there may appear to be some line farther than which this faculty of our senses cannot extend. Now, since it must be confessed that there is nothing beyond the WHOLE, the whole has no extremity; nor does it matter at what part of it you stand, with a view to being distant from its boundary; inasmuch as, whatever place any one occupies, he leaves the WHOLE just as much boundless in every direction.

Besides, if all space which is, be supposed to be bounded, and if any one should go forward as far as possible, even to what he thinks its extreme limits, and should throw, or attempt to throw, a flying

dart, whether would you have that dart, hurled with vigorous strength, go on in the direction in which it may have been propelled, and fly far forwards, or do you rather prefer to think that something would have power to hinder and stop it? For one of the two alternatives you must of necessity admit and adopt; of which alternatives either cuts off escape from you, and compels you to grant that the WHOLE extends without limit. Since whether there is anything to stop the javelin, and to cause that it may not go on in the direction in which it was aimed, and fix itself at the destined termination of its flight, or whether it is borne onwards beyond the supposed limit, it evidently did not begin its flight from a boundary of the WHOLE. In this manner I will go on with you, and wheresoever you shall fix the extreme margin of space, I will ask you what then would be the case with the javelin. The case will be, that a limit can no where exist; and that room for the flight of the javelin will still extend its flight.

• • •

Book II

• • •

Attend now, therefore, and I will explain to thee by what motions the generative bodies of matter produce various things, and resolve them when produced; and by what force they are thus compelled to act, and what activity has been communicated to them for passing through the mighty void of space. Do thou remember to give thyself wholly to my words.

For, assuredly, matter does not constantly cohere as being closely condensed in itself, since we see every object diminished, and perceive that all things flow away, as it were, through length of time, and that age withdraws them from our eyes; while, nevertheless, the sum of all seems to remain undecayed. And this happens for this reason, that the particles of matter which depart from each object, lessen the object from which they depart, and endow with increase the object or objects to which they have transferred themselves; and oblige the former to decay, but the latter, on the contrary, to flourish. Nor do they continue always in the place to which they have gone; and thus the sum of things is perpetually renewed, and the races of mortal men subsist by change and transference from one to the other. Some nations increase, others are diminished, and, in a short space of time, the tribes of living creatures are changed by successive generations, and, like the racers, deliver the torch of life from hand to hand.

If you think that the elemental atoms of things can remain at rest, and can, by remaining at rest, generate fresh motions of things, you stray with a wide deviation from true reason. For, since the primary-particles of all things wander through the void of space, they must necessarily be all carried forwards by their own gravity, or, as it may chance, by the force of another body; for when, being often moved, they, meeting, have struck against one another, it happens that they suddenly start asunder in different directions; since neither is it to be wondered at that bodies should do so, which are of the utmost hardness, and of solid weight; nor, it is to be observed, does any thing behind oppose their motion. And that you may the more clearly understand that all the atoms of matter are tossed about and kept in motion, remember that in the sum of the whole, or in the entire universe, there is no lowest place; nor has it any point where the primary atoms may make a stand; since space is without bound and limit, and shows of itself, by many indications, that it extends around infinite in every direction. And this has been proved by indisputable argument.

Which immensity of space being admitted, there was evidently allowed no rest to the primary atoms passing through the void profound; but rather, driven by perpetual and constant motion, part, when struck by other atoms, rebound to a great distance, and part also, when struck, rebounding only to short distances, are caught and intertwined, as it were, by the stroke of the particles that come in contact with them. And whatsoever particles being brought together in a more close congeries, rebound only to small distances, as being involved by their own entangling shapes, these form the strong substance of rock, and the rigid consistence of iron, and a few other things of their kind, and of similar hardness. Other particles again, which wander through the vast void of space, fly, when struck, far off, and rebound away to great distances; these supply to us the thin air and radiant light of the sun.

And many atoms besides wander through the great void, which are rejected by combination of bodies, and have nowhere been able, admitted into union, to associate their motions with other atoms. Of which circumstance, as I conceive, an example and image is, from time to time, moving and present before our eyes. For, behold, whensoever the beams of the sun pour themselves through a chink into the dark parts of houses, you will see, in the light of the rays, many minute particles throughout the open space, mingled together in many ways, and, as it were, in perpetual conflict, exhibiting battles and fights, contending in companies, nor allowing any pause to their strife, being agitated by frequent concussions and separations; so that you may conjecture, from this spectacle, what it is for the primary-particles of things to be perpetually tossed about in the great void. Assuredly a small thing may give an example, and traces leading to the knowledge of great things. On this account it is more fitting that you should give your attention to these motes which seem to confuse one another in the rays of the sun; because such disorders signify that there secretly exist tendencies to motion also in the principles of matter, though latent and unapparent to our senses. For you will see there, among those atoms in the sun-beam, many, struck with imperceptible forces, change their course, and turn back, being repelled sometimes this way, and sometimes that, everywhere, and all directions. And doubtless this errant-motion in all these atoms proceeds from the primary elements of matter; for the first primordial atoms of things are moved of themselves; and then those bodies which are of light texture, and are, as it were, nearest to the nature of the primary elements, being urged by secret impulses of those elements, are put into motion, and these latter themselves, moreover, agitate others which are somewhat larger. Thus motion ascends from the first principles, and spreads forth by degrees so as to be apparent to our senses, and so that those atoms are moved before us, which we can see in the light of the sun; though it is not clearly evident by what impulses they are thus moved.

• • •

In reference to these subjects, also, we wish you to understand this; that the particles-of-matter, when they are borne downwards straight through the void of space, do for the most part, by their own weights, at some time, though at no fixed and determinate time, and at some points, though at no fixed and determinate points, turn aside from the right line, but only so far as you can call the least possible deviation.

But unless the atoms were accustomed to decline from the right line, they would all fall straight down, through the void profound, like drops of rain through the air; nor would there have been any contact produced, or any collision generated among the primary-elements; and thus nature would never have produced any thing.

But if, perchance, any one believes that the heavier bodies, as being borne, more swiftly, straight through the void of space, might fall from above on the lighter ones, and thus produce concussions, which might give rise to generative movements, he deviates and departs far from just reasoning. For whatsoever bodies fall downwards through the water and the air, they, of necessity, must quicken their motions according to their weights, inasmuch as the dense consistence of water, and the subtle substance of the air, cannot equally retard every body, but yield sooner to the heavier bodies, being overcome by them. But, on the contrary, a pure vacuum can afford no

resistance to anything, in place, or at any time, but must constantly allow it the free passage which its nature requires. For which reason all bodies, when put into motion, must be equally borne onwards, though not of equal weights, through the unresisting void. The heavier atoms will, therefore, never be able to fall from above on the lighter, nor, of themselves, produce concussions which may vary the motions by which nature performs her operations.

For which cause, it must again and again be acknowledged that atoms decline a little from the straight course, though it need not be admitted that they decline more than the least possible space.

• • •

Book III

• • •

And since I have shown of what kind the primordial atoms of all things are, and how, differing in their various forms, and actuated by motion from all eternity, they fly through the void of space of their own accord; and since I have also demonstrated by what means all individual things may be produced from them; the nature of the mind and of the soul now seems, next to these subjects, proper to be illustrated in my verses; and there must be driven utterly from our minds that fear of Acheron, which disturbs human life from its very foundation, suffusing all things with the blackness of death, nor allows any pleasure to be pure and uncontaminated.

• • •

This same course of reasoning teaches us that the nature or substance of the mind and soul is corporeal; for when this nature or substance is seen to impel the limbs, to rouse the body from sleep, and to change the countenance, and to guide and turn about the whole man;—of which effects we see that none can be produced without touch, and that touch, moreover, cannot take place without body;—must we not admit that the mind and soul are of a corporeal nature?

Besides, you see that the mind suffers with the body, and sympathizes for us with the body. Thus, if the violent force of a dart, driven into the body, the bones and nerves being divided, does not hurt the life itself, yet there follows a languor, and a kind of agreeable inclination to sink to the ground, and when we are on the ground, a perturbation and giddiness which is produced in the mind, and sometimes, as it were, in irresolute desire to rise. It therefore necessarily follows that the nature of the mind is corporeal, since it is made to suffer by corporeal weapons and violence.

I shall now proceed to give you a demonstration, in plain words, of what substance this mind is, and of what it consists.

In the first place, I say that it is extremely subtle, and is formed of very minute atoms. And you may, if you please, give me your attention, in order that you may understand clearly that this is so, from the following arguments. Nothing is seen to be done in so swift a way, as if the mind proposes it to be done, and itself undertakes it. The mind, therefore, impels itself more speedily than any thing, among all those of which the nature is manifestly seen before our eyes. But that which is so exceedingly active, must consist of atoms exquisitely round and exquisitely minute; that they may be moved, when acted on, by a slight impulse. For water is moved, and flows, with so trifling a force as we see act upon it, inasmuch as it is composed of voluble and small particles. But the substance of honey, on the other hand, is more dense, and its fluid is sluggish, and its movement more tardy; for its whole mass of material-particles clings more closely together; because, as is evident, it consists of atoms neither so smooth, nor so small and round. For a gentle and light breeze can make a tall heap of poppy-seed waste away, from the top to the bottom, before your eyes; but, on the contrary, can have no such effect upon a heap of stones and darts; particles therefore, according as they are most diminutive and most smooth, have also the

greatest facility of motion. But, on the other hand, whatever particles are found of a greater weight, and rougher surface, are so much the more fixed and difficult to move.

Since, therefore, the nature of the mind has been found preminently active, it must of necessity consist of particles exceedingly diminutive, and smooth and round. Which point, being thus known to you, my excellent friend, will be found useful, and be of advantage, in many of your future inquiries.

This fact also indicates the nature of the soul, and shows of how subtle a texture it consists, and in how small a space it would contain itself, if it could be condensed; because, when the tranquil repose of death has taken possession of a man, and the substance of the mind and the soul has departed, you can there perceive nothing detracted as to appearance, nothing as to weight, from the whole body. Death leaves all things entire, except vital sense and quickening heat.

It must therefore necessarily be the case, that the whole soul consists of extremely small seminal atoms, connected and diffused throughout the veins, the viscera, and the nerves; inasmuch as, when the whole of it has departed from the whole of the body, the extreme outline of the members still shows itself unaltered, nor is an atom of weight withdrawn; just as is the case when the aroma of wine has flown off, or when the sweet odour of ointment has passed away into the air, or when the flavour has departed from any savoury substance; for still the substance itself does not, on that account, appear diminished to the eye, nor does anything seem to have been deducted from the weight; evidently because many and minute atoms compose the flavour and odour throughout the whole constitution of bodies.

Wherefore again and again I say, you may feel assured that the nature or substance of the mind and soul is produced from exquisitely small seminal atoms, since, when it escapes from the body, it carries away no weight with it.

Again, neither can a tree exist in the sky, nor clouds in the deep sea; nor can fish live in the fields; nor blood be in wood, nor liquid in stones. It is fixed and arranged where everything may grow and subsist; thus the nature or substance of the mind cannot spring up alone without the body, or exist apart from the nerves and the blood. Whereas if this could happen, the power of the mind might at time rather arise in the head or the shoulders, or the bottom of the heels, and might rather accustom itself to grow in any place, than to remain in the same man and in the same receptacle. But since it seems fixed and appointed also in our own body, where the soul and the mind may subsist and grow up by themselves, it is so much the more to be denied that they can endure and be produced out of the entire body. For which reason, when the body has perished, you must necessarily admit that the soul, which is diffused throughout the body, has perished with it.

Besides, to join the mortal to the immortal, and to suppose that they can sympathize together, and perform mutual operations, is to think absurdly; for what can be conceived more at variance with reason, or more inconsistent and irreconcilable in itself, than that which is mortal, joined to that which is imperishable and eternal, should submit to endure violent storms and troubles in combination with it?

Further, whatsoever bodies remain eternal, must either, as being of a solid consistence, repel blows, and suffer nothing to penetrate them, that can disunite their compact parts within; (such as are primary-articles of matter, the nature of which we have shown above;) or they must be able to endure throughout all time, because they are free from blows, or unsusceptible of them; (as is a vacuum, which remains intangible, and suffers nothing from a stroke;) or they must be indestructible for this reason, that there is no sufficiency of space round about, into which their constituent substances may, as it were, separate and be dissolved; (as the entire universe is eternal, inasmuch as there is neither any space without it into which its

parts may disperse; nor are there any bodies which may fall upon it, and break it to pieces by a violent concussion:) but, as I have shown, neither is the nature of the soul of a solid consistence, since with all compound bodies vacuum is mixed; nor is it like a vacuum itself; nor, again, are bodies wanting, which, rising fortuitously from the infinite of things, may overturn this frame of the mind with a violent tempest, or bring upon it some other kind of disaster and danger; nor, moreover, is vastness and profundity of space wanting, into which the substance of the soul may be dispersed, or may otherwise perish and be overwhelmed by any other kind of force. The gate of death, therefore, is not shut against the mind and soul.

But if perchance the soul, in the opinion of any, is to be accounted immortal the more on this account, that it is kept fortified by things preservative of life; or because objects adverse to its safety do not all approach it; or because those that do approach, being by some means diverted, retreat before we can perceive what injury they inflict; the notion of those who think thus is evidently far removed from just reasoning. For besides that it sickens from diseases of the body, there often happens something to trouble it concerning future events, and keep it disquieted in fear, and harass it with cares; while remorse for faults, from past acts wickedly and foolishly committed, torments and distresses it. Join to these afflictions the insanity peculiar to the mind, and the oblivion of all things; and add, besides, that it is often sunk into the black waves of lethargy.

Death, therefore, is nothing, nor at all concerns us, since the nature or substance of the soul is to be accounted mortal. And as, in past time, we felt no anxiety, when the Carthaginians gathered on all sides to fight with our forefathers, and when all things under the lofty air of heaven, shaken with the dismaying tumult of war, trembled with dread; and men were uncertain to the sway of which power everything human, by land and by sea, was to fall; so, when we shall cease to be, when there shall be a separation of the body and soul of which we are conjointly composed, it is certain that to us, who shall not then exist, nothing will by any possibility happen, or excite our feeling, not even if the earth shall be mingled with the sea, and the sea with the heaven.

And even if the substance of the mind, and the powers of the soul, after they have been separated from our body, still retain their faculties, it is nothing to us, who subsist only as being conjointly constituted by an arrangement and union of body and soul together. Nor, if time should collect our material atoms after death, and restore them again as they are now placed, and the light of life should be given back to us, would it yet at all concern us that this were done, when the recollection of our existence has once been interrupted. And it is now of no importance to us, in regard to ourselves what we were before; nor does any solicitude affect us in reference to those whom a new age shall produce from our matter, should it again be brought together as it is at present. For when you consider the whole past space of infinite time, and reflect how various are the motions of matter, you may easily believe that our atoms have often been placed in the same order as that in which they now are.

Yet we cannot revive that time in our memory; for a pause of life has been thrown between, and all the motions of our atoms have wandered hither and thither, far away from sentient movements. For he, among men now living, to whom misery and pain are to happen after his death, must himself exist again, in his own identity, at that very time on which the evil which he is to suffer may have power to fall; but since death, which interrupts all consciousness, and prevents all memory of the past, precludes the possibility of this; and since the circumstance of having previously existed, prohibits him who lived before, and with whom these calamities which we suffer might be associated, from existing a second time, (with any recollection of his other life), as the same combination of atoms of which we now consist, we may be assured that in death there is nothing to be dreaded by us; that he who does not exist, cannot become miserable; and that it makes not the least difference to a man, when immortal death has ended his mortal life, that he was ever born at all.

STUDY QUESTIONS

1. Why does Lucretius believe that atoms are eternal? How does he account for the destruction of physical bodies?
2. Do you find Lucretius' argument to prove that the universe is infinite convincing? Explain?
3. Explain what Lucretius means by the swerve of atoms. Why does he believe it must take place? Do you think that the occurrence of such swerves is consistent with the rest of his theory?
4. On what grounds does Lucretius deny personal immortality? Is there any sense in which he acknowledges the possibility of immortality?
5. Would you describe Lucretius' view of human life and our place in the universe as optimistic or pessimistic? Why?

For Further Reading

Lange, F. A. *The History of Materialism.* London: Routledge & Kegan Paul, 1877 (esp. Book, I, I §, Chapter 5).

O'Conner, J., ed. *Modern Materialism.* New York: Harcourt, 1969.

Rosenthal, D. M., ed. *Materialism and the Mind-Body Problem.* Englewood Cliffs, N.J.: Prentice-Hall, 1971.

Santayana, G. "Lucretius." In *Three Philosophical Poets.* Cambridge, Mass.: Harvard University Press, 1919.

Shaffer, J. "Could Mental States Be Brain Processes?" *The Journal of Philosophy* 58, (1961). 813–22.

Winspear, A. D. *Lucretius and Scientific Thought.* Montreal: Harvest House, 1963.

BERKELEY: IDEALISM

Many philosophers throughout history have been struck with the pervasiveness of the physical world and have attempted to explain everything in its terms. These are the materialists. Others, however, have visualized reality in quite another way. What has most impressed them is the reality of persons and the various experiences that persons have. These are the idealists. (The word is not derived from "ideal" but rather from "idea"; thus, strictly speaking, the idealists should be called "ideaists.") The materialists immerse persons in nature by making them a part of it; the idealists turn the tables, immersing nature in persons by reducing the natural world to the experiences that individuals have. For the idealists, thus, reality is made up of persons or selves and their experiences; the material world, as we ordinarily think of it, has no real existence whatsoever.

George Berkeley (1683–1753) was a native of Ireland. He studied at Trinity College, Dublin, and subsequently taught there. He became interested in philosophy early in life, completing his three most important philosophical works before the age of twenty-eight. A later interest was in education. He proposed establishing a college in Bermuda to train clergymen for the American colonies. In pursuit of this project he journeyed to the New World, living for three years in Rhode Island. But Parliament failed to vote funds for the college, so Berkeley returned home disappointed. He did, however, donate a library to the new college in New Haven, Connecticut, that was to become Yale University. In appreciation, two centuries later, Yale named one of its colleges after him. In 1734 Berkeley was appointed bishop of Cloyne, an Anglican diocese in southern Ireland.

✣ *Three Dialogues Between Hylas and Philonous*

The First Dialogue

Philonous. Good morning Hylas. I did not expect to find you abroad so early.

Hylas. It is indeed something unusual; but my thoughts were so taken up with a subject I was discoursing of last night, that finding I could not sleep, I resolved to rise and take a turn in the garden.

Philonous. It happened well, to let you see what innocent and agreeable pleasures you lose every morning. Can there be a pleasanter time of the day, or a more delightful season of the year? That purple sky, those wild but sweet notes of birds, the fragrant bloom upon the trees and flowers, the gentle influence of the rising sun, these and a thousand nameless beauties of nature inspire the soul with secret transports; its faculties too being at this time fresh and lively, are fit for these meditations, which the solitude of a garden and tranquillity of the morning naturally dispose us to. But I am afraid I interrupt your thoughts: for you seemed very intent on something.

Hylas. It is true, I was, and shall be obliged to you if you will permit me to go on in the same vein; not that I would by any means deprive myself of your company, for my thoughts always flow more easily in conversation with a friend, than when I am alone: but my request is, that you would suffer me to impart my reflections to you.

Philonous. With all my heart, it is what I should have requested myself if you had not prevented me.

First published in 1713.

Hylas. I was considering the odd fate of those men who have in all ages, through an affectation of being distinguished from the vulgar, or some unaccountable turn of thought, pretended either to believe nothing at all or to believe the most extravagant things in the world. This however might be borne, if their paradoxes and skepticism did not draw after them some consequences of general disadvantage to mankind. But the mischief lieth here; that when men of less leisure see them who are supposed to have spent their whole time in the pursuits of knowledge professing an entire ignorance of all things, or advancing such notions as are repugnant to plain and commonly-received principles, they will be tempted to entertain suspicions concerning the most important truths, which they had hitherto held sacred and unquestionable.

Philonous. I entirely agree with you, as to the ill tendency of the affected doubts of some philosophers, and fantastical conceits of others. I am even so far gone of late in this way of thinking, that I have quitted several of the sublime notions I had got in their schools for vulgar opinions. And I give it you on my word, since this revolt from metaphysical notions, to the plain dictates of nature and common sense, I find my understanding strangely enlightened, so that I can now easily comprehend a great many things which before were all mystery and riddle.

Hylas. I am glad to find there was nothing in the accounts I heard of you.

Philonous. Pray, what were those?

Hylas. You were represented in last night's conversation, as one who maintained the most extravagant opinion that ever entered into the mind of man, to wit, that there is no such thing as *material substance* in the world.

Philonous. That there is no such thing as what philosophers call *material substance*, I am seriously persuaded: but, if I were made to see anything absurd or skeptical in this, I should then have the same reason to renounce this that I imagine I have now to reject the contrary opinion.

Hylas. What! can anything be more fantastical, more repugnant to common sense, or a more manifest piece of Skepticism, than to believe there is no such thing as *matter*?

Philonous. Softly, good Hylas. What if it should prove, that you, who hold there is, are, by virtue of that opinion, a greater skeptic, and maintain more paradoxes and repugnances to common sense, than I who believe no such thing?

Hylas. You may as soon persuade me, the part is greater than the whole, as that, in order to avoid absurdity and Skepticism, I should ever be obliged to give up my opinion in this point.

Philonous. Well then, are you content to admit that opinion for true, which, upon examination, shall appear most agreeable to common sense, and remote from Skepticism?

Hylas. With all my heart. Since you are for raising disputes about the plainest things in nature, I am content for once to hear what you have to say.

Philonous. Pray, Hylas, what do you mean by a *skeptic*?

Hylas. I mean what all men mean, one that doubts of everything.

Philonous. He then who entertains no doubt concerning some particular point, with regard to that point cannot be thought a skeptic.

Hylas. I agree with you.

Philonous. Whether does doubting consist in embracing the affirmative or negative side of a question?

Hylas. In neither; for whoever understands English cannot but know that *doubting* signifies a suspense between both.

Philonous. He then that denieth any point, can no more be said to doubt of it, than he who affirmeth it with the same degree of assurance.

Hylas. True.

Philonous. And, consequently, for such his denial is no more to be esteemed a skeptic than the other.

Hylas. I acknowledge it.

Philonous. How cometh it to pass then, Hylas, that you pronounce me a *skeptic*, because I deny what you affirm, to wit, the existence of Matter? Since, for aught you can tell, I am as peremptory in my denial, as you in your affirmation.

Hylas. Hold, Philonous, I have been a little out in my definition; but every false step a man makes in discourse is not to be insisted on. I said indeed that a *skeptic* was one who doubted of everything; but I should have added, or who denies the reality and truth of things.

Philonous. What things? Do you mean the principles and theorems of sciences? But these you know are universal intellectual notions, and consequently independent of Matter; the denial therefore of this doth not imply the denying them.

Hylas. I grant it. But are there no other things? What think you of distrusting the senses, of denying the real existence of sensible things, or pretending to know nothing of them. Is not this sufficient to denominate a man a *skeptic*?

Philonous. Shall we therefore examine which of us it is that denies the reality of sensible things, or professes the greatest ignorance of them; since, if I take you rightly, he is to be esteemed the greatest *skeptic*?

Hylas. That is what I desire.

Philonous. What mean you by Sensible Things?

Hylas. Those things which are perceived by the senses. Can you imagine that I mean anything else?

Philonous. Pardon me, Hylas, if I am desirous clearly to apprehend your notions, since this may much shorten our inquiry. Suffer me then to ask you this farther question. Are those things only perceived by the senses which are perceived immediately? Or, may those things properly be said to be *sensible* which are perceived mediately, or not without the intervention of others?

Hylas. I do not sufficiently understand you.

Philonous. In reading a book, what I immediately perceive are the letters, but mediately, or by means of these, are suggested to my mind the notions of God, virtue, truth, etc. Now, that the letters are truly sensible things, or perceived by sense, there is no doubt: but I would know whether you take the things suggested by them to be so too.

Hylas. No, certainly; it were absurd to think *God* or *virtue* sensible things, though they may be signified and suggested to the mind by sensible marks, with which they have an arbitrary connection.

Philonous. It seems then, that by *sensible things* you mean those only which can be perceived *immediately* by sense?

Hylas. Right.

Philonous. Doth it not follow from this, that though I see one part of the sky red, and another blue, and that my reason doth thence evidently conclude there must be some cause of that diversity of colors, yet that cause cannot be said to be a sensible thing, or perceived by the sense of seeing?

Hylas. It doth.

Philonous. In like manner, though I hear variety of sounds, yet I cannot be said to hear the causes of those sounds?

Hylas. You cannot.

Philonous. And when by my touch I perceive a thing to be hot and heavy, I cannot say, with any truth or propriety, that I feel the cause of its heat or weight?

Hylas. To prevent any more questions of this kind, I tell you once for all, that by *sensible things* I mean those only which are perceived by sense, and that in truth the senses perceive nothing which they do not perceive immediately: for they make no inferences. The deducing therefore of causes or occasions from effects and appearances, which alone are perceived by sense, entirely relates to reason.

Philonous. This point then is agreed between us—that *sensible things are those only which are immediately perceived by sense.* You will farther inform me, whether we immediately perceive by sight anything beside light, and colors, and figures; or by hearing, anything but sounds; by the palate, anything beside tastes; by the smell, beside odors; or by the touch, more than tangible qualities.

Hylas. We do not.

Philonous. It seems therefore, that if you take away all sensible qualities, there remains nothing sensible?

Hylas. I grant it.

Philonous. Sensible things therefore are nothing else but so many sensible qualities, or combinations of sensible qualities?

Hylas. Nothing else.

Philonous. Heat is then a sensible thing?

Hylas. Certainly.

Philonous. Doth the reality of sensible things consist in being perceived? or, is it something distinct from their being perceived, and that bears no relation to the mind?

Hylas. To *exist* is one thing, and to be *perceived* is another.

Philonous. I speak with regard to sensible things only: and of these I ask, whether by their real existence you mean a subsistence exterior to the mind, and distinct from their being perceived?

Hylas. I mean a real absolute being, distinct from, and without any relation to their being perceived.

Philonous. Heat therefore, if it be allowed a real being, must exist without the mind?

Hylas. It must.

Philonous. Tell me, Hylas, is this real existence equally compatible to all degrees of heat, which we perceive; or is there any reason why we should attribute it to some, and deny it to others? and if there be, pray let me know that reason.

Hylas. Whatever degree of heat we perceive by sense, we may be sure the same exists in the object that occasions it.

Philonous. What! the greatest as well as the least?

Hylas. I tell you, the reason is plainly the same in respect of both: they are both perceived by sense; nay, the greater degree of heat is more sensibly perceived; and consequently, if there is any difference, we are more certain of its real existence than we can be of the reality of a lesser degree.

Philonous. But is not the most vehement and intense degree of heat a very great pain?

Hylas. No one can deny it.

Philonous. And is any unperceiving thing capable of pain or pleasure?

Hylas. No, certainly.

Philonous. Is your material substance a sensless being, or a being endowed with sense and perception?

Hylas. It is senseless without doubt.

Philonous. It cannot therefore be the subject of pain?

Hylas. By no means.

Philonous. Nor consequently of the greatest heat perceived by sense, since you acknowledge this to be no small pain?

Hylas. I grant it.

Philonous. What shall we say then of your external object; is it a material substance, or no?

Hylas. It is a material substance with the sensible qualities inhering in it.

Philonous. How then can a great heat exist in it, since you own it cannot in a material substance? I desire you would clear this point.

Hylas. Hold, Philonous, I fear I was out in yielding intense heat to be a pain. It should seem rather, that pain is something distinct from heat, and the consequence or effect of it.

Philonous. Upon putting your hand near the fire, do you perceive one simple uniform sensation, or two distinct sensations?

Hylas. But one simple sensation.

Philonous. Is not the heat immediately perceived?

Hylas. It is.

Philonous. And the pain?

Hylas. True.

Philonous. Seeing therefore they are both immediately perceived at the same time, and the fire affects you only with one simple, or uncompounded idea, it follows that this same simple idea is both the intense heat immediately perceived, and the pain; and, consequently, that the intense heat immediately perceived, is nothing distinct from a particular sort of pain.

Hylas. It seems so.

Philonous. Again, try in your thoughts, Hylas, if you can conceive a vehement sensation to be without pain or pleasure.

Hylas. I cannot.

Philonous. Or can you frame to yourself an idea of sensible pain or pleasure, in general abstracted from every particular idea of heat, cold, tastes, smells? etc.

Hylas. I do not find that I can.

Philonous. Doth it not therefore follow, that sensible pain is nothing distinct from those sensations or ideas—in an intense degree?

Hylas. It is undeniable; and, to speak the truth, I begin to suspect a very great heat cannot exist but in a mind perceiving it.

Philonous. What! are you then in that *skeptical* state of suspense, between affirming and denying?

Hylas. I think I may be positive in the point. A very violent and painful heat cannot exist without the mind.

Philonous. It hath not therefore, according to you, any real being?

Hylas. I own it.

Philonous. It is therefore certain, that there is no body in nature really hot?

Hylas. I have not denied there is any real heat in bodies. I only say, there is no such thing as an intense real heat.

Philonous. But, did you not say before that all degrees of heat were equally real; or, if there was any difference, that the greater were more undoubtedly real than the lesser?

Hylas. True: but it was because I did not then consider the ground there is for distinguishing between them, which I now plainly see. And it is this:—because intense heat is nothing else but a particular kind of painful sensation; and pain cannot exist but in a perceiving being; it follows that no intense heat can really exist in an unperceiving corporeal substance. But this is no reason why we should deny heat in an inferior degree to exist in such a substance.

Philonous. But how shall we be able to discern those degrees of heat which exist only in the mind from those which exist without it?

Hylas. That is no difficult matter. You know the least pain cannot exist unperceived; whatever, therefore, degree of heat is a pain exists only in the mind. But, as for all other degrees of heat, nothing obliges us to think the same of them.

Philonous. I think you granted before

that no unperceiving being was capable of pleasure, any more than of pain.

Hylas.   I did.

Philonous.   And is not warmth, or a more gentle degree of heat than what causes uneasiness, a pleasure?

Hylas.   What then?

Philonous.   Consequently, it cannot exist without the mind in an unperceiving substance, or body.

Hylas.   So it seems.

Philonous.   Since, therefore, as well those degrees of heat that are not painful, as those that are, can exist only in a thinking substance; may we not conclude that external bodies are absolutely incapable of any degree of heat whatsoever?

Hylas.   On second thoughts, I do not think it is so evident that warmth is a pleasure, as that a great degree of heat is a pain.

Philonous.   I do not pretend that warmth is as great a pleasure as heat is a pain. But, if you grant it to be even a small pleasure, it serves to make good my conclusion.

Hylas.   I could rather call it an *indolence*. It seems to be nothing more than a privation of both pain and pleasure. And that such a quality or state as this may agree to an unthinking substance, I hope you will not deny.

Philonous.   If you are resolved to maintain that warmth, or a gentle degree of heat, is no pleasure, I know not how to convince you otherwise, than by appealing to your own sense. But what think you of cold?

Hylas.   The same that I do of heat. An intense degree of cold is a pain; for to feel a very great cold, is to perceive a great uneasiness: it cannot therefore exist without the mind; but a lesser degree of cold may, as well as a lesser degree of heat.

Philonous.   Those bodies, therefore, upon whose application to our own, we perceive a moderate degree of heat, must be concluded to have a moderate degree of heat or warmth in them; and those, upon whose application we feel a like degree of cold, must be thought to have cold in them.

Hylas.   They must.

Philonous.   Can any doctrine be true that necessarily leads a man into an absurdity?

Hylas.   Without doubt it cannot.

Philonous.   Is it not an absurdity to think that the same thing should be at the same time both cold and warm?

Hylas.   It is.

Philonous.   Suppose now one of your hands hot, and the other cold, and that they are both at once put into the same vessel of water, in an intermediate state; will not the water seem cold to one hand, and warm to the other?

Hylas.   It will.

Philonous.   Ought we not therefore, by our principles, to conclude it is really both cold and warm at the same time, that is, according to your own concession, to believe an absurdity?

Hylas.   I confess it seems so.

Philonous.   Consequently, the principles themselves are false, since you have granted that no true principle leads to an absurdity.

• • •

Philonous.   Then as to *sounds,* what must we think of them: are they accidents really inherent in external bodies, or not?

Hylas.   That they inhere not in the sonorous bodies is plain from hence; because a bell struck in the exhausted receiver of an air-pump sends forth no sound. The air, therefore, must be thought the subject of sound.

Philonous.   What reason is there for that, Hylas?

Hylas. Because, when any motion is raised in the air, we perceive a sound greater or lesser, according to the air's motion; but without some motion in the air, we never hear any sound at all.

Philonous. And granting that we never hear a sound but when some motion is produced in the air, yet I do not see how you can infer from thence, that the sound itself is in the air.

Hylas. It is this very motion in the external air that produces in the mind the sensation of *sound*. For, striking on the drum of the ear, it causeth a vibration, which by the auditory nerves being communicated to the brain, the soul is thereupon affected with the sensation called *sound*.

Philonous. What! is sound then a sensation?

Hylas. I tell you, as perceived by us, it is a particular sensation in the mind.

Philonous. And can any sensation exist without the mind?

Hylas. No, certainly.

Philonous. How then can sound, being a sensation, exist in the air, if by the *air* you mean a senselss substance existing without the mind?

Hylas. You must distinguish, Philonous, between sound as it is perceived by us, and as it is in itself; or (which is the same thing) between the sound we immediately perceive, and that which exists without us. The former, indeed, is a particular kind of sensation, but the latter is merely a vibrative or undulatory motion in the air.

Philonous. I thought I had already obviated that distinction, by the answer I gave when you were applying it in a like case before. But, to say no more of that, are you sure then that sound is really nothing but motion?

Hylas. I am.

Philonous. Whatever therefore agrees to real sound, may with truth be attributed to motion?

Hylas. It may.

Philonous. It is then good sense to speak of *motion* as of a thing that is *loud, sweet, acute,* or *grave*.

Hylas. I see you are resolved not to understand me. Is it not evident those accidents or modes belong only to sensible sound, or *sound* in the common acceptation of the word, but not to *sound* in the real and philosophic sense; which, as I just now told you, is nothing but a certain motion of the air?

Philonous. It seems then there are two sorts of sound—the one vulgar, or that which is heard, the other philosophical and real?

Hylas. Even so.

Philonous. And the latter consists in motion?

Hylas. I told you so before.

Philonous. Tell me, Hylas, to which of the senses, think you, the idea of motion belongs? to the hearing?

Hylas. No, certainly; but to the sight and touch.

Philonous. It should follow then, that, according to you, real sounds may possibly be *seen* or *felt*, but never *heard*.

Hylas. Look you, Philonous, you may, if you please, make a jest of my opinion, but that will not alter the truth of things. I own, indeed, the inferences you draw me into, sound something oddly; but common language, you know, is framed by, and for the use of the vulgar: we must not therefore wonder, if expressions adapted to exact philosophic notions seem uncouth and out of the way.

Philonous. Is it come to that? I assure you, I imagine myself to have gained no small point, since you make so light of departing from common phrases and opinions; it being a main part of our inquiry, to examine whose notions are widest of the common road, and most repugnant to the general sense of the world. But, can you think it no more than a philosophical paradox, to say that *real sounds are never heard*, and that the idea of them is obtained by some other sense? And is there nothing in this contrary to nature and the truth of things?

Hylas. To deal ingenuously, I do not like it. And, after the concessions already made, I had as well grant that sounds too have no real being without the mind.

Philonous. And I hope you will make no difficulty to acknowledge the same of *colors*.

Hylas. Pardon me: the case of colors is very different. Can anything be plainer than that we see them on the objects?

Philonous. The objects you speak of are, I suppose, corporeal substances existing without the mind?

Hylas. They are.

Philonous. And have true and real colors inhering in them?

Hylas. Each visible object hath that color which we see in it.

Philonous. How! is there anything visible but what we perceive by sight?

Hylas. There is not.

Philonous. And, do we perceive anything by sense which we do not perceive immediately?

Hylas. How often must I be obliged to repeat the same thing? I tell you, we do not.

Philonous. Have patience, good Hylas; and tell me once more, whether there is anything immediately perceived by the senses, except sensible qualities. I know you asserted there was not; but I would now be informed, whether you still persist in the same opinion.

Hylas. I do.

Philonous. Pray, is your corporeal substance either a sensible quality, or made up of sensible qualities?

Hylas. What a question that is! who ever thought it was?

Philonous. My reason for asking was, because in saying, *each visible object hath that color which we see in it*, you make visible objects to be corporeal substances; which implies either that corporeal substances are sensible qualities, or else that there is something beside sensible qualities perceived by sight: but, as this point was formerly agreed between us, and is still maintained by you, it is a clear consequence, that your corporeal substance is nothing distinct from sensible qualities.

Hylas. You may draw as many absurd consequences as you please, and endeavour to perplex the plainest things; but you shall never persuade me out of my senses. I clearly understand my own meaning.

Philonous. I wish you would make me understand it too. But, since you are unwilling to have your notion of corporeal substance examined, I shall urge that point no farther. Only be pleased to let me know whether the same colors which we see exist in external bodies, or some other.

Hylas. The very same.

Philonous. What! are then the beautiful red and purple we see on yonder clouds really in them? Or do you imagine they have in themselves any other form than that of a dark mist or vapor?

Hylas. I must own, Philonous, those colors are not really in the clouds as they seem to be at this distance. They are only apparent colors.

Philonous. Apparent call you them? how shall we distinguish these apparent colors from real?

Hylas. Very easily. Those are to be thought apparent which, appearing only at a distance, vanish upon a nearer approach.

Philonous. And those, I suppose, are to be thought real which are discovered by the most near and exact survey.

Hylas. Right.

Philonous. Is the nearest and exactest survey made by the help of a microscope, or by the naked eye?

Hylas. By a microscope, doubtless.

Philonous. But a microscope often discovers colors in an object different from those perceived by the unassisted sight. And, in case we had microscopes magnifying to any assigned degree, it is certain that no object whatsoever, viewed through them, would appear in the same color which it exhibits to the naked eye.

Hylas. And what will you conclude from all this? You cannot argue that there are really and naturally no colors on objects: because by artificial managements they may be altered, or made to vanish.

Philonous. I think it may evidently be concluded from your own concessions, that all the colors we see with our naked eyes are only apparent as those on the clouds, since they vanish upon a more close and accurate inspection which is afforded us by a microscope. Then, as to what you say by way of prevention: I ask you whether the real and natural state of an object is better discovered by a very sharp and piercing sight, or by one which is less sharp?

Hylas. By the former without doubt.

Philonous. Is it not plain from *Dioptrics* that microscopes make the sight more penetrating, and represent objects as they would appear to the eye in case it were naturally endowed with a most exquisite sharpness?

Hylas. It is.

Philonous. Consequently the microscopical representation is to be thought that which best sets forth the real nature of the thing, or what it is in itself. The colors, therefore, by it perceived are more genuine and real than those perceived otherwise.

Hylas. I confess there is something in what you say.

Philonous. Besides, it is not only possible but manifest, that there actually are animals whose eyes are by nature framed to perceive those things which by reason of their minuteness escape our sight. What think you of those inconceivably small animals perceived by glasses? must we suppose they are all stark blind? Or, in case they see, can it be imagined their sight hath not the same use in preserving their bodies from injuries, which appears in that of all other animals? And if it hath, is it not evident they must see particles less than their own bodies, which will present them with a far different view in each object from that which strikes our senses? Even our own eyes do not always represent objects to us after the same manner. In the *jaundice* every one knows that all things seem yellow. Is it not therefore highly probable those animals in whose eyes we discern a very different texture from that of ours, and whose bodies abound with different humors, do not see the same colors in every object that we do? From all which, should it not seem to follow that all colors are equally apparent, and that none of those which we perceive are really inherent in any outward object?

Hylas. It should.

Philonous. The point will be past all doubt, if you consider that, in case colors were real properties or affections inherent in external bodies, they could admit of no alteration without some change wrought in the very bodies themselves: but, is it not evident from what hath been said that, upon the use of microscopes, upon a change happening in the humors of the eye, or a variation of distance, without any manner of real alteration in the thing itself, the colors of any object are either changed, or totally disappear? Nay, all other circumstances remaining the same, change but the situation of some objects, and they shall present different colors to the eye. The same thing happens upon viewing an object in various degrees of light. And what is more known than that the same bodies appear differently colored by candlelight from what they do in the open day? Add to these the experiment of a prism which, separating the heterogeneous rays of light, alters the color of any object, and will cause the whitest to appear of a deep blue or red to the naked eye. And now tell me whether you are still of opinion that every body hath its true real color inhering in it; and, if you think it hath, I would fain know farther from you, what certain distance and position of the object, what peculiar texture and formation of the eye, what degree or kind of light is necessary for ascertaining that true color, and distinguishing it from apparent ones.

• • •

Hylas. I frankly own, Philonous, that it is in vain to stand out any longer. Colors, sounds, tastes, in a word all those termed *secondary qualities*, have certainly no existence without the mind. But, by this acknowledgment I must not be supposed to derogate anything from the reality of Matter or external objects; seeing it is no more than several philosophers maintain, who nevertheless are the farthest imaginable from denying Matter. For the clearer understanding of this, you must know sensible qualities are by philosophers divided into *primary* and *secondary*. The former are Extension, Figure, Solidity, Gravity, Motion, and Rest. And these they hold exist really in bodies. The latter are those above enumerated; or briefly, all sensible qualities beside the primary, which they assert are only so many sensations or ideas existing nowhere but in the mind. But all this, I doubt not, you are apprised of. For my part, I have been a long time sensible there was such an opinion current among philosophers, but was never thoroughly convinced of its truth until now.

Philonous. You are still then of opinion that *extension* and *figures* are inherent in external unthinking substances?

Hylas. I am.

Philonous. But what if the same arguments which are brought against secondary qualities will hold good against these also?

Hylas. Why then I shall be obliged to think, they too exist only in the mind.

Philonous. Is it your opinion the very figure and extension which you perceive by

sense exist in the outward object or material substance?

Hylas. It is.

Philonous. Have all other animals as good grounds to think the same of the figure and extension which they see and feel?

Hylas. Without doubt, if they have any thought at all.

Philonous. Answer me, Hylas. Think you the senses were bestowed upon all animals for their preservation and well-being in life? or were they given to men alone for this end?

Hylas. I make no question but they have the same use in all other animals.

Philonous. If so, is it not necessary they should be enabled by them to perceive their own limbs, and those bodies which are capable of harming them?

Hylas. Certainly.

Philonous. A mite therefore must be supposed to see his own foot, and things equal or even less than it, as bodies of some considerable dimension; though at the same time they appear to you scarce discernible, or at best as so many visible points?

Hylas. I cannot deny it.

Philonous. And to creatures less than the mite they will seem yet larger?

Hylas. They will.

Philonous. Insomuch that what you can hardly discern will to another extremely minute animal appear as some huge mountain?

Hylas. All this I grant.

Philonous. Can one and the same thing be at the same time in itself of different dimensions?

Hylas. That were absurd to imagine.

Philonous. But, from what you have laid down it follows that both the extension by you perceived, and that perceived by the mite itself, as likewise all those perceived by lesser animals, are each of them the true extension of the mite's foot; that is to say, by your own principles you are led into an absurdity.

• • •

Hylas. I acknowledge, Philonous, that, upon a fair observation of what passes in my mind, I can discover nothing else but that I am a thinking being, affected with variety of sensations; neither is it possible to conceive how a sensation should exist in an unperceiving substance. But then, on the other hand, when I look on sensible things in a different view, considering them as so many modes and qualities, I find it necessary to suppose a material *substratum*, without which they cannot be conceived to exist.

Philonous. *Material substratum* call you it? Pray, by which of your senses came you acquainted with that being?

Hylas. It is not itself sensible; its modes and qualities only being perceived by the senses.

Philonous. I presume then it was by reflection and reason you obtained the idea of it?

Hylas. I do not pretend to any proper positive idea of it. However, I conclude it exists, because qualities cannot be conceived to exist without a support.

Philonous. It seems then you have only a relative notion of it, or that you conceive it not otherwise than by conceiving the relation it bears to sensible qualities?

Hylas. Right.

Philonous. Be pleased therefore to let me know wherein that relation consists.

Hylas. Is it not sufficiently expressed in the term *substratum* or *substance*?

Philonous. If so, the word *substratum* should import that it is spread under the sensible qualities or accidents?

Hylas. True.

Philonous. And consequently under extension?

Hylas. I own it.

Philonous. It is therefore somewhat in its own nature entirely distinct from extension?

Hylas. I tell you, extension is only a mode, and Matter is something that supports modes. And is it not evident the thing supported is different from the thing supporting?

Philonous. So that something distinct from, and exclusive of, extension is supposed to be the *substratum* of extension?

Hylas. Just so.

Philonous. Answer me, Hylas. Can a thing be spread without extension? or is not the idea of extension necessarily included in *spreading*?

Hylas. It is.

Philonous. Whatsoever therefore you suppose spread under anything must have in itself an extension distinct from the extension of that thing under which it is spread?

Hylas. It must.

Philonous. Consequently, every corporeal substance being the *substratum* of extension must have in itself another extension, by which it is qualified to be a *substratum*, and so on to infinity? And I ask whether this be not absurd in itself, and repugnant to what you granted just now, to wit, that the *substratum* was something distinct from and exclusive of extension?

Hylas. Aye, but Philonous, you take me wrong. I do not mean that Matter is *spread* in a gross literal sense under extension. The word *substratum* is used only to express in general the same thing with *substance*.

Philonous. Well then, let us examine the relation implied in the term *substance*. Is it not that it stands under accidents?

Hylas. The very same.

Philonous. But, that one thing may stand under or support another, must it not be extended?

Hylas. It must.

Philonous. Is not therefore this supposition liable to the same absurdity with the former?

Hylas. You still take things in a strict literal sense; that is not fair, Philonous.

Philonous. I am not for imposing any sense on your words: you are at liberty to explain them as you please. Only, I beseech you, make me understand something by them. You tell me Matter supports or stands under accidents. How! is it as your legs support your body?

Hylas. No; that is the literal sense.

Philonous. Pray let me know any sense, literal or not literal, that you understand it in . . . . How long must I wait for an answer, Hylas?

Hylas. I declare I know not what to say. I once thought I understood well enough what was meant by Matter's supporting accidents. But now, the more I think on it the less can I comprehend it; in short I find that I know nothing of it.

Philonous. It seems then you have no idea at all, neither relative nor positive, of Matter; you know neither what it is in itself, nor what relation it bears to accidents.

Hylas. I acknowledge it.

• • •

Hylas. To speak the truth, Philonous, I think there are two kinds of objects: the one perceived immediately, which are likewise called *ideas*; the other are real things or external objects perceived by the mediation of ideas, which are their images and representations. Now, I own ideas do not exist without the mind; but the latter sort of objects do. I am sorry I did not think of this distinction sooner; it would probably have cut short your discourse.

Philonous. Are those external objects perceived by sense, or by some other faculty?

Hylas. They are perceived by sense.

Philonous. How! is there anything perceived by sense which is not immediately perceived?

Hylas. Yes, Philonous, in some sort there is. For example, when I look on a picture or statue of Julius Cæsar, I may be said after a manner to perceive him (though not immediately) by my senses.

Philonous. It seems then you will have our ideas, which alone are immediately perceived, to be pictures of external things: and that these also are perceived by sense, inasmuch as they have a conformity or resemblance to our ideas?

Hylas. That is my meaning.

Philonous. And, in the same way that Julius Cæsar, in himself invisible, is nevertheless perceived by sight; real things, in themselves imperceptible, are perceived by sense.

Hylas. In the very same.

Philonous. Tell me, Hylas, when you behold the picture of Julius Cæsar, do you see with your eyes any more than some colors and figures, with a certain symmetry and composition of the whole?

Hylas. Nothing else.

Philonous. And would not a man who had never known anything of Julius Cæsar see as much?

Hylas. He would.

Philonous. Consequently he hath his sight, and the use of it, in as perfect a degree as you?

Hylas. I agree with you.

Philonous. Whence comes it then that your thoughts are directed to the Roman emperor, and his are not? This cannot proceed from the sensations or ideas of sense by you then perceived; since you acknowledge you have no advantage over him in that respect. It should seem therefore to proceed from reason and memory: should it not?

Hylas. It should.

Philonous. Consequently, it will not follow from that instance that anything is perceived by sense which is not immediately perceived. Though I grant we may, in one acceptation, be said to perceive sensible things mediately by sense—that is, when, from a frequently perceived connection, the immediate perception of ideas by one sense suggests to the mind others, perhaps belonging to another sense, which are wont to be connected with them. For instance, when I hear a coach drive along the streets, immediately I perceive only the sound; but, from the experience I have had that such a sound is connected with a coach, I am said to hear the coach. It is nevertheless evident that, in truth and strictness, nothing can be *heard* but *sound*; and the coach is not then properly perceived by sense, but suggested from experience. So likewise when we are said to see a red-hot bar of iron; the solidity and heat of the iron are not the object of sight, but suggested to the imagination by the color and figure which are properly perceived by that sense. In short, those things alone are actually and strictly perceived by any sense, which would have been perceived in case that same sense had then been first conferred on us. As for other things, it is plain they are only suggested to the mind by experience, grounded on former perceptions. But, to return to your comparison of Cæsar's picture, it is plain, if you keep to that, you must hold the real things or archetypes of our ideas are not perceived by sense, but by some internal faculty of the soul, as reason or memory. I would therefore fain know what arguments you can draw from reason for the existence of what you call *real things* or *material objects.* Or, whether you remember to have seen them formerly as they are in themselves; or, if you have heard or read of any one that did.

Hylas. I see, Philonous, you are disposed to raillery; but that will never convince me.

Philonous. My aim is only to learn from you the way to come at the knowledge of *material beings.* Whatever we perceive is perceived immediately or mediately: by sense; or by reason and reflection. But, as you have excluded sense, pray show me what reason you have to believe their existence; or what *medium* you can possibly make use of to prove it, either to mine or your own understanding.

Hylas. To deal ingenuously, Philonous, now I consider the point, I do not find I can give you any good reason for it. But, this much seems pretty plain, that it is at least possible such things may really exist. And, as long as there is no absurdity in supposing them, I am resolved to believe as I did, till you bring good reasons to the contrary.

Philonous. What! is it come to this, that you only believe the existence of material objects, and that your belief is founded barely on the possibility of its being true? Then you will have me bring reasons against it: though another would think it reasonable the proof should lie on him who holds the affirmative. And, after all, this very point which you are now resolved to maintain, without any reason, is in effect what you have more than once during this discourse seen good reason to give up. But, to pass over all this; if I understand you rightly, you say our ideas do not exist without the mind; but they are copies, images, or representations, of certain originals that do?

Hylas. You take me right.

Philonous. They are then like external things?

Hylas. They are.

Philonous. Have those things a stable and permanent nature, independent of our senses; or are they in a perpetual change, upon our producing any motions in our bodies, suspending, exerting, or altering, our faculties of organs of sense?

Hylas. Real things, it is plain, have a fixed and real nature, which remains the same notwithstanding any change in our senses, or in the posture and motion of our bodies; which indeed may affect the ideas in our minds, but it were absurd to think they had the same effect on things existing without the mind.

Philonous. How then is it possible that things perpetually fleeting and variable as our ideas should be copies or images of anything fixed and constant? Or, in other words, since all sensible qualities, as size, figure, color, etc., that is, our ideas, are continually changing upon every alteration in the distance, medium, or instruments of sensation; how can any determinate material objects be properly represented or painted forth by several distinct things, each of which is so different from and unlike the rest? Or, if you say it resembles some one only of our ideas, how shall we be able to distinguish the true copy from all the false ones?

Hylas. I profess, Philonous, I am at a loss. I know not what to say to this.

Philonous. But neither is this all. Which are material objects in themselves—perceptible or imperceptible?

Hylas. Properly and immediately nothing can be perceived but ideas. All material things, therefore, are in themselves insensible, and to be perceived only by our ideas.

Philonous. Ideas then are sensible, and their archetypes or originals insensible?

Hylas. Right.

Philonous. But how can that which is sensible be like that which is insensible? Can a real thing, in itself *invisible*, be like a *color*; or a real thing, which is not *audible*, be like a *sound*? In a word, can anything be like a sensation or idea, but another sensation or idea?

Hylas. I must own, I think not.

Philonous. Is it possible there should be any doubt on the point? Do you not perfectly know your own ideas?

Hylas. I know them perfectly; since what I do not perceive or know can be no part of my idea.

Philonous. Consider, therefore, and examine them, and then tell me if there be anything in them which can exist without the mind? or if you can conceive anything like them existing without the mind?

Hylas. Upon inquiry, I find it is impossible for me to conceive or understand how anything but an idea can be like an idea. And it is most evident that *no idea can exist without the mind.*

Philonous. You are therefore, by our principles, forced to deny the reality of sensible things; since you made it to consist in an absolute existence exterior to the mind. That is to say, you are a downright skeptic. So I have gained my point, which was to show your principles led to Skepticism.

Hylas. For the present I am, if not entirely convinced, at least silenced.

STUDY QUESTIONS

1. What does Philonous mean when he says that a belief in the existence of matter leads to skepticism? What reasons does he give for saying this?
2. What does Philonous mean by "sensible things" or "sensible qualities"? What reasons does he give for claiming that such things can have no existence independent of a mind that perceives them? Do you find his view acceptable? Why or why not?
3. What is the difference between primary and secondary qualities? Do you think Philonous is right in concluding that primary qualities, as well as secondary, have no existence independent of mind? What, then, becomes of space?
4. If you became convinced that Berkeley

is right in his denial of the existence of matter, do you think you would change the way you lived? If so, how?

5. Berkeley claims that his position is the same as the common-sense view of the world. Do you agree? Explain.

For Further Reading

Bennett, J. F. *Locke, Berkeley, Hume.* Oxford: Clarendon Press, 1971 (Chapter 6).

Berkeley, G. *The Principles of Human Knowledge.*

Bracken, H. M. *Berkeley.* London:Macmillan, 1974.

Ewing, A.C. *Idealism.* London: Methuen, 1934 (Chapter 2).

Moore, G. E. "The Refutation of Idealism." In *Philosophical Studies.* London: Kegan & Paul, 1922 (Chapter 1).

Pitcher, G. *Berkeley.* Boston: Routledge & Kegan Paul, 1977.

Steinkraus, W. E., ed. *New Studies in Berkeley's Philosophy.* New York: Holt, Rinehart and Winston, 1966.

Warnock, J. G. *Berkeley.* Baltimore: Penguin, 1953.

DESCARTES: DUALISM

Although some philosophers believe that human beings are just a part of material nature, and others consider nature to be no more than the experiences of humans, most philosophers share the view that we are a part of nature yet somehow at the same time stand outside of nature. These are the dualists. According to the dualistic view of reality, the universe can be divided into two kinds of things. On the one side are physical bodies, whose chief characteristic is that they occupy space. Included in this part of the universe are the bodies of human individuals. On the other side are minds. Minds are nonphysical so do not occupy space; their chief characteristic is that they are conscious. They think, will, desire, feel, and so on. Since every living human individual is a combination of a mind and a body, one might ask: which of the two is primary and which secondary? To this question some dualists would answer that neither takes precedence because both are essential to the complete person. Others, however, would put mind first, saying that a human being is a mind that possesses a body, thus leaving open the possibility that an individual could continue to exist even though he had no body.

René Descartes (1596–1650) is often called "the father of modern philosophy." He made the first decisive break with the medieval world view and raised the basic issues with which philosophers have been wrestling ever since. A native of Brittany in Western France, Descartes moved to Holland in 1628, where he spent the next twenty years enjoying a quiet life of meditation and writing. In 1649 he accepted the invitation of Queen Christina of Sweden to become court philosopher. On his arrival in Stockholm he discovered, to his dismay, that the queen wished to discuss philosophy every morning at five. Descartes, who had throughout his life risen at noon, was unable to stand such rigors; he contracted pneumonia and died during his first winter there.

Meditations on the First Philosophy

Meditation VI

Of the Existence of Material Things, and of the Real Distinction between the Soul and Body of Man

Nothing further now remains but to inquire whether material things exist. And certainly I at least know that these may exist in so far as they are considered as the objects of pure mathematics, since in this aspect I perceive them clearly and distinctly. For there is no doubt that God possesses the power to produce everything that I am capable of perceiving with distinctness, and I have never deemed that anything was impossible for Him, unless I found a contradiction in attempting to conceive it clearly. Further, the faculty of imagination which I possess, and of which, experience tells me, I make use when I apply myself to the consideration of material things, is capable of persuading me of their existence; for when I attentively consider what imagination is, I find that it is nothing but a certain application of the faculty of knowledge to the body which is immediately present to it, and which therefore exists.

And to render this quite clear, I remark in the first place the difference that exists between the imagination and pure intellection or conception. For example, when I imagine a triangle, I do not conceive it only as a figure comprehended by three lines, but I also apprehend these three lines as present by the power and inward vision of my mind, and this is what I call imagining. But if I desire to think of a chiliagon, I certainly conceive truly that it is a figure composed of a thousand sides, just as easily as I conceive of a triangle that it is a figure of three sides only; but I cannot in any way imagine the thousand sides of a chiliagon as I do the three sides of a triangle, nor do I, so to speak, regard them as present with the eyes of my mind. And although in accordance with the habit I have formed of always employing the aid of my imagination when I think of corporeal things, it may happen that in imagining a chiliagon I confusedly represent to myself some figure, yet it is very evident that this figure is not a chiliagon, since it in no way differs from that which I represent to myself when I think of a myriagon or any other many-sided figure; nor does it serve my purpose in discovering the properties which go to form the distinction between a chiliagon and other polygons. But if the question turns upon a pentagon, it is quite true that I can conceive its figure as well as that of a chiliagon without the help of my imagination; but I can also imagine it by applying the attention of my mind to each of its five sides, and at the same time to the space which they enclose. And thus I clearly recognise that I have need of a particular effort of mind in order to effect the act of imagination, such as I do not require in order to understand, and this particular effort of mind clearly manifests the difference which exists between imagination and pure intellection.

I remark besides that this power of imagination which is in one, inasmuch as it differs from the power of understanding, is in no wise a necessary element in my nature, or in my essence, that is to say, in the essence of my mind; for although I did not possess it I should doubtless ever remain the same as I now am, from which it appears that we might conclude that it depends on something which differs from me. And I easily conceive that if some body exists with which my mind is conjoined and united in such a way that it can apply itself to consider it when it pleases, it may be that by this means it can imagine corporeal objects; so that this mode of thinking differs from pure intellection only inasmuch

Reprinted from *The Philosophical Works of Descartes*, translated by E. S. Haldane and G. R. T. Ross, Vol. 1, with permission of the publisher, Cambridge University Press.

as mind in its intellectual activity in some manner turns on itself, and considers some of the ideas which it possesses in itself; while in imagining it turns towards the body, and there beholds in it something conformable to the idea which it has either conceived of itself or perceived by the senses. I easily understand, I say, that the imagination could be thus constituted if it is true that body exists; and because I can discover no other convenient mode of explaining it, I conjecture with probability that body does exist; but this is only with probability, and although I examine all things with care, I nevertheless do not find that from this distinct idea of corporeal nature, which I have in my imagination, I can derive any argument from which there will necessarily be deduced the existence of body.

But I am in the habit of imagining many other things besides this corporeal nature which is the object of pure mathematics, to wit, colors, sounds, scents, pain, and other such things, although less distinctly. And inasmuch as I perceive these things much better through the senses by the medium of which, and by the memory, they seem to have reached my imagination, I believe that, in order to examine them more conveniently, it is right that I should at the same time investigate the nature of sense perception, and that I should see if from the ideas which I apprehend by this mode of thought, which I call feeling, I cannot derive some certain proof of the existence of corporeal objects.

And first of all I shall recall to my memory those matters which I hitherto held to be true, as having perceived them through the senses, and the foundations on which my belief has rested; in the next place I shall examine the reasons which have since obliged me to place them in doubt; in the last place I shall consider which of them I must now believe.

First of all, then, I perceived that I had a head, hands, feet, and all other members of which this body—which I considered as a part, or possibly even as the whole, of myself—is composed. Further I was sensi-ble that this body was placed amidst many others, from which it was capable of being affected in many different ways, beneficial and hurtful, and I remarked that a certain feeling of pleasure accompanied those that were beneficial, and pain those which were harmful. And in addition to this pleasure and pain, I also experienced hunger, thirst, and other similar appetites, as also certain corporeal inclinations towards joy, sadness, anger, and other similar passions. And outside myself, in addition to extension, figure, and motions of bodies, I remarked in them hardness, heat, and all other tactile qualities, and, further, light and color, and scents and sounds, the variety of which gave me the means of distinguishing the sky, the earth, the sea, and generally all the other bodies, one from the other. And certainly, considering the ideas of all these qualities which presented themselves to my mind, and which alone I perceived properly or immediately, it was not without reason that I believed myself to perceive objects quite different from my thought, to wit, bodies from which those ideas proceeded; for I found by experience that these ideas presented themselves to me without my consent being requisite, so that I could not perceive any object, however desirous I might be, unless it were present to the organs of sense; and it was not in my power not to perceive it, when it was present. And because the ideas which I received through the senses were much more lively, more clear, and even, in their own way, more distinct than any of those which I could of myself frame in meditation, or than those I found impressed on my memory, it appeared as though they could not have proceeded from my mind, so that they must necessarily have been produced in me by some other things. And having no knowledge of those objects excepting the knowledge which the ideas themselves gave me, nothing was more likely to occur to my mind than that the objects were similar to the ideas which were caused. And because I likewise remembered that I had formerly made use of my senses rather than my reason, and recognized that the ideas which I formed of myself were not so distinct as those which I perceived through the senses, and that they were most frequently even composed of portions of these last, I persuaded myself easily that I had no idea in my mind which had not formerly come to me through the senses. Nor was it without some reason that I believed that this body (which by a certain special right I call my own) belonged to me more properly and more strictly than any other; for in fact I could never be separated from it as from other bodies; I experienced in it and on account of it all my appetites and affections, and finally I was touched by the feeling of pain and the titillation of pleasure in its parts, and not in the parts of other bodies which were separated from it. But when I inquired, why, from some, I know not what, painful sensation, there follows sadness of mind, and from the pleasurable sensation there arises joy, or why this mysterious pinching of the stomach which I call hunger causes me to desire to eat, and dryness of throat causes a desire to drink, and so on, I could give no reason excepting that nature taught me so; for there is certainly no affinity (that I at least can understand) between the craving of the stomach and the desire to eat, any more than between the perception of whatever causes pain and the thought of sadness which arises from this perception. And in the same way it appeared to me that I had learned from nature all the other judgments which I formed regarding the objects of my senses, since I remarked that these judgments were formed in me before I had the leisure to weigh and consider any reasons which might oblige me to make them.

But afterwards many experiences little by little destroyed all the faith which I had rested in my senses; for I from time to time observed that those towers which from afar appeared to me to be round, more closely observed seemed square, and that colossal statues raised on the summit of these towers, appeared as quite tiny statues when viewed from the bottom; and so in an infinitude of other cases I found error in judgments founded on the external senses. And not only in those founded on the external senses, but even in those founded on the internal as well; for is there anything more intimate or more internal than pain? And yet I have learned from some persons whose arms or legs have been cut off, that they sometimes seemed to feel pain in the part which had been amputated, which made me think that I could not be quite certain that it was a certain member which pained me, even although I felt pain in it. And to those grounds of doubt I have lately added two others, which are very general; the first is that I never have believed myself to feel anything in waking moments which I cannot also sometimes believe myself to feel when I sleep, and as I do not think that these things which I seem to feel in sleep, proceed from objects outside of me, I do not see any reason why I should have this belief regarding objects which I seem to perceive while awake. The other was that being still ignorant, or rather supposing myself to be ignorant of the author of my being, I saw nothing to prevent me from having been so constituted by nature that I might be deceived even in matters which seemed to me to be most certain. And as to the grounds on which I was formerly persuaded of the truth of sensible objects, I had not much trouble in replying to them. For since nature seemed to cause me to lean towards many things from which reason repelled me, I did not believe that I should trust much to the teachings of nature. And although the ideas which I receive by the senses do not depend on my will, I did not think that one should for that reason conclude that they proceeded from things different from myself, since possibly some faculty might be discovered in me—though hitherto unknown to me—which produced them.

But now that I begin to know myself better, and to discover more clearly the author of my being, I do not in truth think that I should rashly admit all the matters which the senses seem to teach us, but, on the other hand, I do not think that I should doubt them all universally.

And first of all, because I know that all things which I apprehend clearly and distinctly can be created by God as I apprehend them, it suffices that I am able to apprehend one thing apart from another clearly and distinctly in order to be certain that the one is different from the other, since they may be made to exist in separation at least by the omnipotence of God; and it does not signify by what power this separation is made in order to compel me to judge them to be different: and, therefore, just because I know certainly that I exist, and that meanwhile I do not remark that any other thing necessarily pertains to my nature or essence, excepting that I am a thinking thing, I rightly conclude that my essence consists solely in the fact that I am a thinking thing or a substance whose whole essence or nature is to think. And although possibly (or rather certainly, as I shall say in a moment) I possess a body with which I am very intimately conjoined, yet because, on the one side, I have a clear and distinct idea of myself inasmuch as I am only a thinking and unextended thing, and as, on the other, I possess a distinct idea of body, inasmuch as it is only an extended and unthinking thing, it is certain that this *I* (this is to say, my soul by which I am what I am), is entirely and absolutely distinct from my body, and can exist without it.

I further find in myself faculties employing modes of thinking peculiar to themselves, to wit, the faculties of imagination and feeling, without which I can easily conceive myself clearly and distinctly as a complete being; while, on the other hand, they cannot be so conceived apart from me, that is without an intelligent substance in which they reside, for in the notion we have of these faculties, or, to use the language of the Schools, in their formal concept, some kind of intellection is comprised, from which I infer that they are distinct from me as its modes are from a thing. I observe also in me some other faculties, such as that of change of position, the assumption of different figures and such like, which cannot be conceived, any more than can the preceding, apart from some substance to

which they are attached, and consequently cannot exist without it; but it is very clear that these faculties, if it be true that they exist, must be attached to some corporeal or extended substance, and not to an intelligent substance, since in the clear and distinct conception of these there is some sort of extension found to be present, but no intellection at all. There is certainly further in me a certain passive faculty of perception, that is, of receiving and recognizing the ideas of sensible things, but this would be useless to me and I could in no way avail myself of it, if there were not either in me or in some other thing another active faculty capable of forming and producing these ideas. But this active faculty cannot exist in me inasmuch as I am a thing that thinks, seeing that it does not presuppose thought, and also that those ideas are often produced in me without my contributing in any way to the same, and often even against my will; it is thus necessarily the case that the faculty resides in some substance different from me in which all the reality which is objectively in the ideas that are produced by this faculty is formally or eminently contained, as I remarked before. And this substance is either a body, that is, a corporeal nature in which there is contained formally and really all that which is objectively and by representation in those ideas, or it is God Himself, or some other creature more noble than body in which that same is contained eminently. But, since God is no deceiver, it is very manifest that He does not communicate to me these ideas immediately and by Himself, nor yet by the intervention of some creature in which their reality is not formally, but only eminently, contained. For since He has given me no faculty to recognize that this is the case, but, on the other hand, a very great inclination to believe that they are conveyed to me by corporeal objects, I do not see how He could be defended from the accusation of deceit if these ideas were produced by causes other than corporeal objects. Hence we must allow that corporeal things exist. However, they are perhaps not exactly what we perceive by the senses, since this comprehension by the senses is in many instances very obscure and confused; but we must at least admit that all things which I conceive in them clearly and distinctly, that is to say, all things which, speaking generally, are comprehended in the object of pure mathematics, are truly to be recognized as external objects.

As to other things, however, which are either particular only, as, for example, that the sun is of such and such a figure, etc., or which are less clearly and distinctly conceived, such as light, sound, pain and the like, it is certain that although they are very dubious and uncertain, yet on the sole ground that God is not a deceiver, and that consequently He has not permitted any falsity to exist in my opinion which He has not likewise given me the faculty of correcting, I may assuredly hope to conclude that I have within me the means of arriving at the truth even here. And first of all there is no doubt that in all things which nature teaches me there is some truth contained; for by nature, considered in general, I now understand no other thing than either God Himself or else the order and disposition which God has established in created things; and by my nature in particular I understand no other thing than the complexus of all the things which God has given me.

But there is nothing which this nature teaches me more expressly than that I have a body which is adversely affected when I feel pain, which has need of food or drink when I experience the feelings of hunger and thirst, and so on; nor can I doubt there being some truth in all this.

Nature also teaches me by these sensations of pain, hunger, thirst, etc., that I am not only lodged in my body as a pilot in a vessel, but that I am very closely united to it, and so to speak so intermingled with it that I seem to compose with it one whole. For if that were not the case, when my body is hurt, I, who am merely a thinking thing, should not feel pain, for I should perceive this wound by the understanding only, just as the sailor perceives by sight when some-

thing is damaged in his vessel; and when my body has need of drink or food, I should clearly understand the fact without being warned of it by confused feelings of hunger and thirst. For all these sensations of hunger, thirst, pain, etc., are in truth none other than certain confused modes of thought which are produced by the union and apparent intermingling of mind and body.

Moreover, nature teaches me that many other bodies exist around mine, of which some are to be avoided, and others sought after. And certainly from the fact that I am sensible of different sorts of colors, sounds, scents, tastes, heat, hardness, etc., I very easily conclude that there are, in the bodies from which all these diverse sense-perceptions proceed, certain variations which answer to them, although possibly these are not really at all similar to them. And also from the fact that amongst these different sense-perceptions some are very agreeable to me and others disagreeable, it is quite certain that my body (or rather myself in my entirety, inasmuch as I am formed of body and soul) may receive different impressions, agreeable and disagreeable, from the other bodies which surround it.

But there are many other things which nature seems to have taught me, but which at the same time I have never really received from her, but which have been brought about in my mind by a certain habit which I have of forming inconsiderate judgments on things; and thus it may easily happen that these judgments contain some error. Take, for example, the opinion which I hold that all space in which there is nothing that affects my senses is void; that in a body which is warm there is something entirely similar to the idea of heat which is in me; that in a white or green body there is the same whiteness or greenness that I perceive; that in a bitter or sweet body there is the same taste, and so on in other instances; that the stars, the towers, and all other distant bodies are of the same figure and size as they appear from far off to our eyes, etc. But in order that in this there should be nothing which I do not conceive distinctly, I should define exactly what I really understand when I say that I am taught somewhat by nature. For here I take nature in a more limited signification than when I term it the sum of all the things given me by God, since in this sum many things are comprehended which only pertain to mind (and to these I do not refer in speaking of nature), such as the notion which I have of the fact that what has once been done cannot ever be undone, and an infinitude of such things which I know by the light of nature without the help of the body; and seeing that it comprehends many other matters besides which only pertain to body, and are no longer here contained under the name of nature, such as the quality of weight which it possesses and the like, with which I also do not deal; for in talking of nature I only treat of those things given by God to me as a being composed of mind and body. But the nature here described truly teaches me to flee from things which cause the sensation of pain, and seek after the things which communicate to me the sentiment of pleasure and so forth; but I do not see that beyond this it teaches me that from those diverse sense perceptions we should ever form any conclusion regarding things outside of us, without having mentally examined them beforehand. For it seems to me that it is mind alone, and not mind and body in conjunction, that is requisite to a knowledge of the truth in regard to such things. Thus, although a star makes no larger an impression on my eye than the flame of a little candle there is yet in me no real or positive propensity impelling me to believe that it is not greater than the flame; but I have judged it to be so from my earliest years, without any rational foundation. And although in approaching fire I feel heat, and in approaching it a little too near I even feel pain, there is at the same time no reason in this which could persuade me that there is in the fire something resembling this heat any more than there is in it something resembling the pain; all that I have any reason to believe from this is, that there is something in it,

whatever it may be, which excites in me these sensations of heat or of pain. So also, although there are spaces in which I find nothing which excites my senses, I must not from that conclude that these spaces contain no body; for I see in this, as in other similar things, that I have been in the habit of perverting the order of nature, because these perceptions of sense having been placed within me by nature merely for the purpose of signifying to my mind what things are beneficial or hurtful to the composite whole of which it forms a part, and being up to that point sufficiently clear and distinct, I yet avail myself of them as though they were absolute rules by which I might immediately determine the essence of the bodies which are outside me, as to which, in fact, they can teach me nothing but what is most obscure and confused.

But I have already sufficiently considered how, notwithstanding the supreme goodness of God, falsity enters into the judgments I make. Only here a new difficulty is presented—one respecting those things the pursuit or avoidance of which is taught me by nature, and also respecting the internal sensations which I possess, and in which I seem to have sometimes detected error and thus to be directly deceived by my own nature. To take an example, the agreeable taste of some food in which poison has been intermingled may induce me to partake of the poison, and thus deceive me. It is true, at the same time, that in this case nature may be excused, for it only induces me to desire food in which I find a pleasant taste, and not to desire the poison which is unknown to it; and thus I can infer nothing from this fact, except that my nature is not omniscient, at which there is certainly no reason to be astonished, since man, being finite in nature, can only have knowledge the perfectness of which is limited.

But we not unfrequently deceive ourselves even in those things to which we are directly impelled by nature, as happens with those who when they are sick desire to drink or eat things hurtful to them. It will perhaps be said here that the cause of their deceptiveness is that their nature is corrupt, but that does not remove the difficulty, because a sick man is none the less truly God's creature than he who is in health; and it is therefore as repugnant to God's goodness for the one to have a deceitful nature as it is for the other. And as a clock composed of wheels and counter-weights no less exactly observes the laws of nature when it is badly made, and does not show the time properly, than when it entirely satisfies the wishes of its maker, and as, if I consider the body of a man as being a sort of machine so built up and composed of nerves, muscles, veins, blood and skin, that though there were no mind in it at all, it would not cease to have the same motions as at present, exception being made of those movements which are due to the direction of the will, and in consequence depend upon the mind as opposed to those which operate by the disposition of its organs, I easily recognize that it would be as natural to this body, supposing it to be, for example, dropsical, to suffer the parchedness of the throat which usually signifies to the mind the feeling of thirst, and to be disposed by this parched feeling to move the nerves and other parts in the way requisite for drinking, and thus to augment its malady and do harm to itself, as it is natural to it, when it has no indisposition, to be impelled to drink for its good by a similar cause. And although, considering the use to which the clock has been destined by its maker, I may say that it deflects from the order of its nature when it does not indicate the hours correctly; and as, in the same way, considering the machine of the human body as having been formed by God in order to have in itself all the movements usually manifested there, I have reason for thinking that it does not follow the order of nature when, if the throat is dry, drinking does harm to the conservation of health, nevertheless I recognize at the same time that this last mode of explaining nature is very different from the other. For this is but a purely verbal characterization depending entirely on my

thought, which compares a sick man and a badly-constructed clock with the idea which I have of a healthy man and a well-made clock, and it is hence extrinsic to the things to which it is applied; but according to the other interpretation of the term *nature* I understand something which is truly found in things and which is therefore not without some truth.

But certainly although in regard to the dropsical body it is only so to speak to apply an extrinsic term when we say that its nature is corrupted, inasmuch as apart from the need to drink, the throat is parched; yet in regard to the composite whole, that is to say, to the mind or soul united to this body, it is not a purely verbal predicate, but a real error of nature, for it to have thirst when drinking would be hurtful lo it. And thus it still remains to inquire how the goodness of God does not prevent the nature of man so regarded from being fallacious.

In order to begin this examination, then, I here say, in the first place, that there is a great difference between mind and body, inasmuch as body is by nature always divisible, and the mind is entirely indivisible. For, as a matter of fact, when I consider the mind, that is to say, myself inasmuch as I am only a thinking thing, I cannot distinguish in myself any parts, but apprehend myself to be clearly one and entire; and although the whole mind seems to be united to the whole body, yet if a foot, or an arm, or some other part, is separated from my body, I am aware that nothing has been taken away from my mind. And the faculties of willing, feeling, conceiving, etc., cannot be properly speaking said to be its parts, for it is one and the same mind which employs itself in willing and in feeling and understanding. But it is quite otherwise with corporeal or extended objects, for there is not one of these imaginable by me which my mind cannot easily divide into parts, and which consequently I do not recognize as being divisible; this would be sufficient to teach me that the mind or soul of man is entirely different from the body, if I had not already learned it from other sources.

I further notice that the mind does not receive the impressions from all parts of the body immediately, but only from the brain, or perhaps even from one of its smallest parts, to wit, from that in which the common sense is said to reside, which, whenever it is disposed in the same particular way, conveys the same thing to the mind, although meanwhile the other portions of the body may be differently disposed, as is testified by innumerable experiments which it is unnecessary here to recount.

I notice, also, that the nature of body is such that none of its parts can be moved by another part a little way off which cannot also be moved in the same way by each one of the parts which are between the two, although this more remote part does not act at all. As, for example, in the cord ABCD which is in tension, if we pull the last part D, the first part A will not be moved in any way differently from what would be the case if one of the intervening parts B or C were pulled, and the last part D were to remain unmoved. And in the same way, when I feel pain in my foot, my knowledge of physics teaches me that this sensation is communicated by means of nerves dispersed through the foot, which, being extended like cords from there to the brain, when they are contracted in the foot, at the same time contract the inmost portions of the brain which is their extremity and place of origin, and then excite a certain movement which nature has established in order to cause the mind to be affected by a sensation of pain represented as existing in the foot. But because these nerves must pass through the tibia, the thigh, the loins, the back, and the neck, in order to reach from the leg to the brain, it may happen that although their extremities which are in the foot are not affected, but only certain ones of their intervening parts, this action will excite the same movement in the brain that might have been excited there by a hurt received in the foot, in consequence of

which the mind will necessarily feel in the foot the same pain as if it had received a hurt. And the same holds good of all the other perceptions of our senses.

I notice finally that since each of the movements which are in the portion of the brain by which the mind is immediately affected brings about one particular sensation only, we cannot under the circumstances imagine anything more likely than that this movement, amongst all the sensations which it is capable of impressing on it, causes mind to be affected by that one which is best-fitted and most generally useful for the conservation of the human body when it is in health. But experience makes us aware that all the feelings with which nature inspires us are such as I have just spoken of; and there is therefore nothing in them which does not give testimony to the power and goodness of the God who has produced them. Thus, for example, when the nerves which are in the feet are violently or more than usually moved, their movement, passing through the medulla of the spine to the inmost parts of the brain, gives a sign to the mind which makes it feel somewhat, to wit, pain, as though in the foot, by which the mind is excited to do its utmost to remove the cause of the evil as dangerous and hurtful to the foot. It is true that God could have constituted the nature of man in such a way that this same movement in the brain would have conveyed something quite different to the mind; for example, it might have produced consciousness of itself either in so far as it is in the brain, or as it is in the foot, or as it is in some other place between the foot and the brain, or it might finally have produced consciousness of anything else whatsoever; but none of all this would have contributed so well to the conservation of the body. Similarly, when we desire to drink, a certain dryness of the throat is produced which moves its nerves, and by their means the internal portions of the brain; and this movement causes in the mind the sensation of thirst, because in this case there is nothing more useful to us than to become aware that we have need to drink for the conservation of our health; and the same holds good in other instances.

From this it is quite clear that, notwithstanding the supreme goodness of God, the nature of man, inasmuch as it is composed of mind and body, cannot be otherwise than sometimes a source of deception. For if there is any cause which excites, not in the foot but in some part of the nerves which are extended between the foot and the brain, or even in the brain itself, the same movement which usually is produced when the foot is detrimentally affected, pain will be experienced as though it were in the foot, and the sense will thus naturally be deceived; for since the same movement in the brain is capable of causing but one sensation in the mind, and this sensation is much more frequently excited by a cause which hurts the foot than by another existing in some other quarter, it is reasonable that it should convey to the mind pain in the foot rather than in any other part of the body. And although the parchedness of the throat does not always proceed, as it usually does, from the fact that drinking is necessary for the health of the body, but sometimes comes from a quite different cause, as is the case with dropsical patients, it is yet much better that it should mislead on this occasion than if, on the other hand, it were always to deceive us when the body is in good health; and so on in similar cases.

And certainly this consideration is of great service to me, not only in enabling me to recognize all the errors to which my nature is subject, but also in enabling me to avoid them or to correct them more easily. For knowing that all my senses more frequently indicate to me truth than falsehood respecting the things which concern that which is beneficial to the body, and being able almost always to avail myself of many of them in order to examine one particular thing, and, besides that, being able to make use of my memory in order to connect the present with the past, and of my un-derstanding which already has discovered all the causes of my errors, I ought no longer to fear that falsity may be found in matters every day presented to me by my senses. And I ought to set aside all the doubts of these past days as hyperbolical and ridiculous, particularly that very common uncertainty respecting sleep, which I could not distinguish from the waking state; for at present I find a very notable difference between the two, inasmuch as our memory can never connect our dreams one with the other, or with the whole course of our lives, as it unites events which happen to us while we are awake. And, as a matter of fact if someone, while I was awake, quite suddenly appeared to me and disappeared as fast as do the images which I see in sleep, so that I could not know from whence the form came nor whither it went, it would not be without reason that I should deem it a specter or a phantom formed by my brain and similar to those which I form in sleep, rather than a real man. But when I perceive things as to which I know distinctly both the place from which they proceed, and that in which they are, and the time at which they appeared to me; and when, without any interruption, I can connect the perceptions which I have of them with the whole course of my life, I am perfectly assured that these perceptions occur while I am waking and not during sleep, and I ought in no wise to doubt the truth of such matters, if, after having called up all my senses, my memory, and my understanding, to examine them, nothing is brought to evidence by any one of them which is repugnant to what is set forth by the others. For because God is in no wise a deceiver, it follows that I am not deceived in this. But because the exigencies of action often oblige us to make up our minds before having leisure to examine matters carefully, we must confess that the life of man is very frequently subject to error in respect to individual objects, and we must in the end acknowledge the infirmity of our nature.

❦ The Passions of the Soul

That the Soul is United to All the Portions of the Body Conjointly

But in order to understand all these things more perfectly, we must know that the soul is really joined to the whole body, and that we cannot, properly speaking, say that it exists in any one of its parts to the exclusion of the others, because it is one and in some manner indivisible, owing to the disposition of its organs, which are so related to one another that when any one of them is removed, that renders the whole body defective; and because it is of a nature which has no relation to extension, nor dimensions, nor other properties of the matter of which the body is composed, but only to the whole conglomerate of its organs, as appears from the fact that we could not in any way conceive of the half or the third of a soul, nor of the space it occupies, and because it does not become smaller owing to the cutting off of some portion of the body, but separates itself from it entirely when the union of its assembled organs is dissolved.

That There Is a Small Gland in the Brain in Which the Soul Exercises Its Functions More Particularly than in the Other Parts

It is likewise necessary to know that although the soul is joined to the whole body, there is yet in that a certain part in which it exercises its functions more particularly than in all the others; and it is usually believed that this part is the brain, or possibly the heart: the brain, because it is with it that the organs of sense are connected, and the heart because it is apparently in it that we experience the passions. But, in examining the matter with care, it seems as though I had clearly ascertained that the part of the body in which the soul exercises its functions immediately is in nowise the heart, nor the whole of the brain, but merely the most inward of all its parts, to wit, a certain very small gland which is situated in the middle of its substance,* and so suspended above the duct whereby the animal spirits in its anterior cavities have communication with those in the posterior, that the slightest movements which take place in it may alter very greatly the course of these spirits; and reciprocally that the smallest changes which occur in the course of the spirits may do much to change the movements of this gland.

How We Know That This Gland Is the Main Seat of the Soul

The reason which persuades me that the soul cannot have any other seat in all the body than this gland wherein to exercise its functions immediately, is that I reflect that the other parts of our brain are all of them double, just as we have two eyes, two hands, two ears, and finally all the organs of our outside senses are double; and inasmuch as we have but one solitary and simple thought of one particular thing at one and the same moment, it must necessarily be the case that there must somewhere be a place where the two images which come to us by the two eyes, where the two other impressions which proceed from a single object by means of the double organs of the other senses, can unite before arriving at the soul, in order that they may not represent to it two objects instead of one. And it is easy to apprehend how these images or other impressions might unite in this gland by the intermission of the spirits which fill the cavities of the brain; but there is no other place in the body where they can be thus united unless they are so in this gland.

· · ·

Translated by E. S. Haldane and G. R. T. Ross.

*The pineal gland. —Ed.

How the Soul and the Body Act on One Another

Let us then conceive here that the soul has its principal seat in the little gland which exists in the middle of the brain, from whence it radiates forth through all the remainder of the body by means of the animal spirits, nerves, and even the blood, which, participating in the impressions of the spirits, can carry them by the arteries into all the members. And recollecting what has been said above about the machine of our body, i.e., that the little filaments of our nerves are so distributed in all its parts, that on the occasion of the diverse movements which are there excited by sensible objects, they open in diverse ways the pores of the brain, which causes the animal spirits contained in these cavities to enter in diverse ways into the muscles, by which means they can move the members in all the different ways in which they are capable of being moved; and also that all the other causes which are capable of moving the spirits in diverse ways suffice to conduct them into diverse muscles; let us here add that the small gland which is the main seat of the soul is so suspended between the cavities which contain the spirits that it can be moved by them in as many different ways as there are sensible diversities in the object, but that it may also be moved in diverse ways by the soul, whose nature is such that it receives in itself as many diverse impressions, that is to say, that it possesses as many diverse perceptions as there are diverse movements in this gland. Reciprocally, likewise, the machine of the body is so formed that from the simple fact that this gland is diversely moved by the soul, or by such other cause, whatever it is, it thrusts the spirits which surround it towards the pores of the brain, which conduct them by the nerves into the muscles, by which means it causes them to move the limbs.

STUDY QUESTIONS

1. How does Descartes distinguish between imagination and intellection? Which does he believe the more powerful? Do you agree?

2. Why does Descartes believe that his mind, or soul, is entirely distinct from his body?

3. What role does God perform in Descartes' argument to prove the existence of body? Do you find his argument convincing?

4. Having claimed that mind (soul) and body are entirely distinct from each other, Descartes goes on to say that they are "intermingled," and affect each other causally. How does he explain the connection between the two? Do you see any problems in his explanation?

5. Most people are, like Descartes, mind-body dualists. Do you consider yourself to be one? Why or why not?

For Further Reading

Ducasse, C. J. "In Defense of Dualism." In *Dimensions of Mind*, ed. S. Hook. New York: New York University Press, 1960 (Chapter 8).

Hooker, M., ed. *Descartes*. Baltimore: The Johns Hopkins University Press, 1978 (pp. 197–211 and 223–33).

Lovejoy, A. O. *The Revolt Against Dualism*. New York: Norton, 1930 (esp. Chapter 1).

Russell, B. *Religion and Science*. London: Oxford University Press, 1935 (Chapter 5).

Smith, N. K. *Studies in the Cartesian Philosophy*. New York: Russell and Russell, 1962 (Chapter 3).

Wilson, M. D. *Descartes*. London: Routledge & Kegan Paul, 1978 (Chapters 2 and 6).

BROAD: THE MIND-BODY PROBLEM

If a thorn pricks my finger, I will feel pain; if I decide to finish writing this sentence, my fingers will move. In both of these instances a cause-effect relationship is being described. In the first, the pricking is the cause and the pain the effect; in the second, the decision is the cause and the finger movements the effect. But these two cause-effect relationships are extraordinary and, many philosophers believe, inexplicable. Their peculiarity lies in the fact that in the first the cause is an event in the material world and the effect an event in the mental world and in the second the situation is reversed. How can such causation occur? If minds are nonphysical and bodies nonmental, how can either function as causes that have effects in the other? These questions constitute the mind-body problem. Philosophers have developed a number of different theories to resolve it. The most widely accepted of these is called interactionism; it is defended by Broad in the selection that follows. Critics of interactionism argue that it does not solve, but merely states, the mind-body problem.

Charlie Dunbar Broad (1887–1971) was born in London and educated at Dulwich College and later at Cambridge University. After teaching for ten years at St. Andrews University in Scotland and briefly at the University of Bristol, he returned to Cambridge where he taught for the remainder of his career and lived in Trinity College in an apartment once occupied by Isaac Newton. In addition to philosophy, Broad had a deep interest in psychical research—serving as president of the British Society for Psychical Research—and in Sweden, its land and its people.

℣ *The Mind and Its Place in Nature*

Chapter III
The Traditional Problem of Body and Mind

In the last chapter we considered organisms simply as complicated material systems which behave in certain characteristic ways. We did not consider the fact that some organisms are animated by minds, and that all the minds of whose existence we are certain animate organisms. And we did not deal with those features in the behavior of certain organisms which are commonly supposed to be due to the mind which animates the organism. It is such facts as these, and certain problems to

C. D. Broad, *The Mind and Its Place in Nature* (London: Routledge & Kegan Paul Ltd., 1925), pp. 95–121. Used with permission of Routledge & Kegan Paul Ltd. and Humanities Press, Inc. New York.

which they have given rise, which I mean to discuss in the present chapter. There is a question which has been argued about for some centuries now under the name of "interaction"; this is the question whether minds really do act on the organisms which they animate, and whether organisms really do act on the minds which animate them. (I must point out at once that I imply no particular theory of mind or body by the word "to animate." I use it as a perfectly neutral name to express the fact that a certain mind is connected in some peculiarly intimate way with a certain body, and, under normal conditions with no other body. This is a fact even on a purely behavioristic theory of mind; on such a view to say that the mind M animates the body B would mean that the body B, in so far as it behaves in certain ways, *is* the mind M. A body which did not act in these ways would be said not to be animated by a mind. And a different body B', which acted in the same general way as B, would be said to be animated by a different mind M').

The problem of interaction is generally discussed at the level of enlightened common sense; where it is assumed that we know pretty well what we mean by "mind," by "matter," and by "causation." Obviously, no solution which is reached at that level can claim to be ultimate. If what we call "matter" should turn out to be a collection of spirits of low intelligence, as Leibniz thought, the argument that mind and body are so unlike that their interaction is impossible would become irrelevant. Again, if causation be nothing but regular sequence and concomitance, as some philosophers have held, it is ridiculous to regard psycho-neural parallelism and interaction as mutually exclusive alternatives. For interaction will mean no more than parallelism, and parallelism will mean no less than interaction. Nevertheless I am going to discuss the arguments here at the common-sense level, because they are so incredibly bad, and yet have imposed upon so many learned men.

We start then by assuming a developed mind and a developed organism as two distinct things, and by admitting that the two are now intimately connected in some way or other which I express by saying that "this mind *animates* this organism." We assume that bodies are very much as enlightened common sense believes them to be; and that, even if we cannot define "causation," we have some means of recognizing when it is present and when it is absent. The question then is: "Does a mind ever act on the body which it animates, and does a body ever act on the mind which animates it?" The answer which common sense would give to both questions is: "Yes, certainly." On the face of it, my body acts on my mind whenever a pin is stuck into the former and a painful sensation thereupon arises in the latter. And, on the face of it, my mind acts on my body whenever a desire to move my arm arises in the former and is followed by this movement in the

latter. Let us call this common-sense view "two-sided interaction." Although it seems so obvious, it has been denied by probably a majority of philosophers and a majority of physiologists. So the question is: "Why should so many distinguished men, who have studied the subject, have denied the apparently obvious fact of two-sided interaction?"

The arguments against two-sided interaction fall into two sets: philosophical and scientific. We will take the philosophical arguments first; for we shall find that the professedly scientific arguments come back in the end to the principles or prejudices which are made explicit in the philosophical arguments.

Philosophical Arguments Against Two-Sided Interaction

No one can deny that there is a close correlation between certain bodily events and certain mental events, and conversely. Therefore anyone who denies that there is action of mind on body and of body on mind must presumably hold (a) that concomitant variation is not an adequate criterion of causal connection, and (b) that the other feature which is essential for causal connection is absent in the case of body and mind. Now, the common philosophical argument is that minds and mental states are so extremely unlike bodies and bodily states that it is inconceivable that the two should be causally connected. It is certainly true that, if minds and mental events are just what they seem to be to introspection and nothing more, and if bodies and bodily events are just what enlightened common sense thinks them to be and nothing more, the two *are* extremely unlike. And this fact is supposed to show that, however closely correlated certain pairs of events in mind and body respectively may be, they cannot be causally connected.

Evidently the assumption at the back of this argument is that concomitant variation, together with a high enough degree of likeness, is an adequate test for causation; but that no amount of concomitant variation can establish causation in the absence of a high enough degree of likeness. Now I am inclined to admit part of this assumption. I think it is practically certain that causation does not simply *mean* concomitant variation. (And, if it did, *cadit quaestio*). Hence the existence of the latter is not *ipso facto* a proof of the presence of the former. Again, I think it is almost certain that concomitant variation between *A* and *B* is not in fact a sufficient sign of the presence of a *direct* causal relation between the two. (I think it may perhaps be a sufficient sign of *either* a direct causal relation between *A* and *B* *or* of several causal relations which indirectly unite *A* and *B* through the medium of other terms *C, D,* etc.). So far, I agree with the assumptions of the argument. But I cannot see the least reason to think that the other characteristic, which must be added to concomitant variation before we can be sure that *A* and *B* are causally connected, is a high degree of likeness between the two. One would like to know just how unlike two events may be before it becomes impossible to admit the existence of a causal relation between them. No one hesitates to hold that draughts and colds in the head are causally connected, although the two are extremely unlike each other. If the unlikeness of draughts and colds in the head does not prevent one from admitting a causal connection between the two, why should the unlikeness of volitions and voluntary movements prevent one from holding that they are causally connected? To sum up. I am willing to admit that an adequate criterion of causal connection needs some other relation between a pair of events beside concomitant variation; but I do not believe for a moment that this other relation is that of qualitative likeness.

This brings us to a rather more refined form of the argument against interaction. It is said that, whenever we admit the existence of a causal relation between two events, these two events (to put it crudely) must also form parts of a single substantial whole. *E.g.*, all physical events are spatially related and form one great extended whole. And the mental events which would commonly be admitted to be causally connected are always events in a single mind. A mind is a substantial whole of a peculiar kind, too. Now it is said that between bodily events and mental events there are no relations such as those which unite physical events in different parts of the same space or mental events in the history of the same mind. In the absence of such relations, binding mind and body into a single substantial whole, we cannot admit that bodily and mental events can be causally connected with each other, no matter how closely correlated their variations may be.

This is a much better argument than the argument about qualitative likeness and unlikeness. If we accept the premise that causal relations can subsist only between terms which form parts of a single substantial whole must we deny that mental and bodily events can be causally connected? I do not think that we need.

(1) It is of course perfectly true that an organism and the mind which animates it do not form a physical whole, and that they do not form a mental whole; and these, no doubt, are the two kinds of substantial whole with which we are most familiar. But it does not follow that a mind and its organism do not form a substantial whole of *some* kind. There, plainly, is the extraordinary intimate union between the two which I have called "animation" of the one by the other. Even if the mind be just what it seems to introspection, and the body be just what it seems to perception aided by the more precise methods of science, this seems to me to be enough to make a mind and its body a substantial whole. Even so extreme a dualist about Mind and Matter as Descartes occasionally suggests that a mind and its body together form a quasi-substance; and, although we may quarrel with the language of the very numerous philosophers who have said that the mind is "the form" of its body, we must admit that such language would never have seemed plausible unless a mind and its body together had formed something very much like a single substantial whole.

(2) We must, moreover, admit the pos-

sibility that minds and mental events have properties and relations which do not reveal themselves to introspection, and that bodies and bodily events may have properties and relations which do not reveal themselves to perception or to physical and chemical experiment. In virtue of these properties and relations the two together may well form a single substantial whole of the kind which is alleged to be needed for causal interaction. Thus, if we accept the premise of the argument, we have no right to assert that mind and body *cannot* interact; but only the much more modest proposition that introspection and perception do not suffice to assure us that mind and body are so interrelated that they *can* interact.

(3) We must further remember that the two-sided interactionist is under no obligation to hold that the *complete* conditions of any mental event are bodily, or that the complete conditions of any bodily event are mental. He needs only to assert that some mental events include certain bodily events among their necessary conditions, and that some bodily events include certain mental events among their necessary conditions. If I am paralyzed, my volition may not move my arm; and, if I am hypnotized or intensely interested or frightened, a wound may not produce a painful sensation. Now, if the complete cause and the complete effect in all interaction include both a bodily and a mental factor, the two wholes will be related by the fact that the mental constituents belong to a single mind, that the bodily constituents belong to a single body, and that this mind animates this body. This amount of connection should surely be enough to allow of causal interaction.

This will be the most appropriate place to deal with the contention that, in voluntary action, and there only, we are immediately acquainted with an instance of causal connection. If this be true the controversy is of course settled at once in favor of the interactionist. It is generally supposed that this view was refuted once and for all by Mr. Hume in his *Enquiry concerning Human Understanding* (Sec. 7, Part I). I should not care to assert that the doctrine in question is true; but I do think that it is plausible, and I am quite sure that Mr. Hume's arguments do not refute it. Mr. Hume uses three closely connected arguments.

(1) The connection between a successful volition and the resulting bodily movement is as mysterious and as little self-evident as the connection between any other event and its effect.

(2) We have to learn from experience which of our volitions will be effective and which will not. *e.g.*, we do not know, until we have tried, that we can voluntarily move our arms and cannot voluntarily move our livers. And again, if a man were suddenly paralyzed, he would still expect to be able to move his arm voluntarily, and would be surprised when he found that it kept still in spite of his volition.

(3) We have discovered that the immediate consequence of a volition is a change in our nerves and muscles, which most people know nothing about; and is not the movement of a limb, which most people believe to be its immediate and necessary consequence.

The second and third arguments are valid only against the contention that we know immediately that a volition to make a certain movement is the *sufficient* condition for the happening of that movement. They are quite irrelevant to the contention that we know immediately that the volition is a *necessary* condition for the happening of just that movement at just that time. No doubt many other conditions are also necessary, *e.g.*, that our nerves and muscles shall be in the right state; and these other necessary conditions can be discovered only by special investigation. Since our volitions to move our limbs are in fact followed in the vast majority of cases by the willed movement, and since the other necessary conditions are not very obvious, it is natural enough that we should think that we know immediately that our volition is the *sufficient* condition of the movement of our limbs. If we think so, we are certainly wrong; and Mr. Hume's arguments prove that we are. But they prove nothing else. It does not follow that we are wrong in thinking that we know, without having to wait for the result, that the volition is a *necessary* condition of the movement.

It remains to consider the first argument. Is the connection between cause and effect as mysterious and as little self-evident in the case of the voluntary production of bodily movement as in all other cases? If so, we must hold that the first time a baby wills to move its hand it is just as much surprised to find its hand moving as it would be to find its leg moving or its nurse bursting into flames. I do not profess to know anything about the infant mind; but it seems to me that this is a wildly paradoxical consequence, for which there is no evidence or likelihood. But there is no need to leave the matter there. It is perfectly plain that, in the case of volition and voluntary movement, there *is* a connection between the cause and the effect which is not present in other cases of causation, and which does make it plausible to hold that in this one case the nature of the effect can be foreseen by merely reflecting on the nature of the cause. The peculiarity of a volition as a cause-factor is that it involves as an essential part of it the idea of the effect. To say that a person has a volition to move his arm involves saying that he has an idea of his arm (and not of his leg or his liver) and an idea of the position in which he wants his arm to be. It is simply silly in view of this fact to say that there is no closer connection between the desire to move my arm and the movement of my arm than there is between this desire and the movement of my leg or my liver. We cannot detect any analogous connection between cause and effect in causal transactions which we view wholly from outside, such as the movement of a billiard-ball by a cue. It is therefore by no means unreasonable to suggest that, in the one case of our own voluntary movements, we can see without waiting for the result that such and such a volition is a necessary condition of such and such a bodily movement.

It seems to me then that Mr. Hume's arguments on this point are absolutely irrelevant, and that it may very well be true that in volition we positively know that our desire for such and such a bodily movement is a necessary (though not a sufficient) condition of the happening of just that movement at just that time. On the whole, then, I conclude that the philosophical arguments certainly do not disprove two-sided interaction, and that they do not even raise any strong presumption against it. And, while I am not prepared definitely to commit myself to the view that, in voluntary movement, we positively *know* that the mind acts on the body, I do think that this opinion is quite plausible when properly stated and that the arguments which have been brought against it are worthless. I pass therefore to the scientific arguments.

Scientific Arguments Against Two-Sided Interaction

There are, so far as I know, two of these. One is supposed to be based on the physical principle of the Conservation of Energy, and on certain experiments which have been made on human bodies. The other is based on the close analogy which is said to exist between the structures of the physiological mechanism of reflex action and that of voluntary action. I will take them in turn.

(1) *The Argument from Energy.* It will first be needful to state clearly what is asserted by the principle of the Conservation of Energy. It is found that, if we take certain material systems, *e.g.,* a gun, a cartridge, and a bullet, there is a certain magnitude which keeps approximately constant throughout all their changes. This is called "energy." When the gun has not been fired it and the bullet have no motion, but the explosive in the cartridge has great chemical energy. When it has been fired the bullet is moving very fast and has great energy of movement. The gun, though not moving fast in its recoil, has also great energy of movement because it is very massive. The gases produced by the explo-

sion have some energy of movement and some heat-energy, but much less chemical energy than the unexploded charge had. These various kinds of energy can be measured in common units according to certain conventions. To an innocent mind there seems to be a good deal of "cooking" at this stage, *i.e.*, the conventions seem to be chosen and various kinds and amounts of concealed energy seem to be postulated in order to make the principle come out right at the end. I do not propose to go into this in detail, for two reasons. In the first place, I think that the conventions adopted and the postulates made, though somewhat suggestive of the fraudulent company-promoter, can be justified by their coherence with certain experimental facts, and that they are not simply made *ad hoc*. Secondly, I shall show that the Conservation of Energy is absolutely irrelevant to the question at issue, so that it would be waste of time to treat it too seriously in the present connection. Now, it is found that the total energy of all kinds in this system, when measured according to these conventions, is approximately the same in amount, though very differently distributed, after the explosion and before it. If we had confined our attention to a part of this system and *its* energy this would not have been true. The bullet, *e.g.*, had no energy at all before the explosion and a great deal afterwards. A system like the bullet, the gun, and the charge, is called a "conservative system"; the bullet alone, or the gun and the charge, would be called "non-conservative systems." A conservative system might therefore be defined as one whose total energy is redistributed, but not altered in amount, by changes that happen within it. Of course, a given system might be conservative for some kinds of change and not for others.

So far we have merely defined a "conservative system," and admitted that there are systems which, for some kinds of change at any rate, answer approximately to our definition. We can now state the principle of the Conservation of Energy in terms of the conceptions just defined. The principle asserts that every material system is either itself conservative, or, if not, is part of a larger material system which is conservative. We may take it that there is good inductive evidence for this proposition.

The next thing to consider is the experiments on the human body. These tend to prove that a living body, with the air that it breathes and the food that it eats, forms a conservative system to a high degree of approximation. We can measure the chemical energy of the food given to a man, and that which enters his body in the form of oxygen breathed in. We can also, with suitable apparatus, collect, measure, and analyze the air breathed out, and thus find its chemical energy. Similarly, we can find the energy given out in bodily movement, in heat, and in excretion. It is alleged that, on the average, whatever the man may do, the energy of his bodily movements is exactly accounted for by the energy given to him in the form of food and of oxygen. If you take the energy put in food and oxygen, and subtract the energy given out in waste products, the balance is almost exactly equal to the energy put out in bodily movements. Such slight differences as are found are as often on one side as on the other, and are therefore probably due to unavoidable experimental errors. I do not propose to criticize the interpretation of these experiments in detail, because, as I shall show soon, they are completely irrelevant to the problem of whether mind and body interact. But there is just one point that I will make before passing on. It is perfectly clear that such experiments can tell us only what happens on the average over a long time. To know whether the balance was accurately kept at every moment we should have to kill the patient at each moment and analyze his body so as to find out the energy present then in the form of stored-up products. Obviously, we cannot keep on killing the patient in order to analyze him, and then reviving him in order to go on with the experiment. Thus it would seem that the results of the experiment are perfectly compatible with the presence of quite large excesses or defects in the total bodily energy at certain moments, provided that these average out over longer periods. However, I do not want to press this criticism; I am quite ready to accept, for our present purpose, the traditional interpretation which has been put on the experiments.

We now understand the physical principle and the experimental facts. The two together are generally supposed to prove that mind and body cannot interact. What precisely is the argument, and is it valid? I imagine that the argument, when fully stated, would run somewhat as follows: "I will to move my arm, and it moves. If the volition has anything to do with causing the movement we might expect energy to flow from my mind to my body. Thus the energy of my body ought to receive a measurable increase, not accounted for by the food that I eat and the oxygen that I breathe. But no such physically unaccountable increases of bodily energy are found. Again, I tread on a tin-tack, and a painful sensation arises in my mind. If treading on the tack has anything to do with causing the sensation we might expect energy to flow from my body to my mind. Such energy would cease to be measurable. Thus there ought to be a noticeable decrease in my bodily energy, not balanced by increases anywhere in the physical system. But such unbalanced decreases of bodily energy are not found." So it is concluded that the volition has nothing to do with causing my arm to move, and that treading on the tack has nothing to do with causing the painful sensation.

Is this argument valid? In the first place it is important to notice that the conclusion does not follow from the Conservation of Energy and the experimental facts alone. The real premise is a tacitly assumed proposition about causation; viz., that, if a change in A has anything to do with causing a change in B, energy must leave A and flow into B. This is neither asserted nor entailed by the Conservation of Energy. What *it* says is that, *if* energy leaves A, it must appear in something else, say B; so that A and B together form a conservative system. Since the Conservation of Engergy is not itself the premise for the argument against interaction, and since it does not entail that premise, the evidence for the Conservation of Energy is not evidence against interaction. Is there any independent evidence for the premise? We may admit that it *is* true of many, though not of all, transactions within the physical realm. But there are cases where it is not true even of purely physical transactions; and, even if it were always true in the physical realm, it would not follow that it must also be true of trans-physical causation. Take the case of a weight swinging at the end of a string hung from a fixed point. The total energy of the weight is the same at all positions in its course. It is thus a conservative system. But at every moment the direction and velocity of the weight's motion are different, and the proportion between its kinetic and its potential energy is constantly changing. These changes are caused by the pull of the string, which acts in a different direction at each different moment. The string makes no difference to the total energy of the weight; but it make all the difference in the world to the particular way in which the weight moves and the particular way in which the energy is distributed between the potential and the kinetic forms. This is evident when we remember that the weight would begin to move in an utterly different course if at any moment the string were cut.

Here, then, we have a clear case even in the physical realm where a system is conservative but is continually acted on by something which affects its movement and the distribution of its total energy. Why should not the mind act on the body in this way? If you say that you can see how a string can affect the movement of a weight, but cannot see how a volition could affect the movement of a material particle, you have deserted the scientific argument and have gone back to one of the philosophical arguments. Your real difficulty is either that volitions are so very unlike movements, or that the volition is in your mind whilst the movement belongs to the physical realm. And we have seen how little weight can be attached to these objections.

The fact is that, even in purely physical systems, the Conservation of Energy does not explain what changes will happen or when they will happen. It merely imposes a very general limiting condition on the changes that are possible. The fact that the system composed of bullet, charge, and gun, in our earlier example, is conservative does not tell us that the gun ever will be fired, or when it will be fired if at all, or what will cause it to go off, or what forms of energy will appear if and when it does go off. The change in this case is determined by pulling the trigger. Likewise, the mere fact that the human body and its neighborhood form a conservative system does not explain any particular bodily movement; it does not explain why I ever move at all, or why I sometimes write, sometimes walk, and sometimes swim. To explain the happening of these particular movements at certain times it seems to be essential to take into account the volitions which happen from time to time in my mind; just as it is essential to take the string into account to explain the particular behavior of the weight, and to take the trigger into account to explain the going off of the gun at a certain moment. The difference between the gun-system and the body-system is that a little energy does flow into the former when the trigger is pulled, whilst it is alleged that none does so when a volition starts a bodily movement. But there is not even this amount of difference between the body-system and the swinging weight.

Thus the argument from energy has no tendency to disprove two-sided interaction. It has gained a spurious authority from the august name of the Conservation of Energy. But this impressive principle proves to have nothing to do with the case. And the real premise of the argument is not self-evident, and is not universally true even in purely intra-physical transactions. In the end this scientific argument has to lean on the old philosophic arguments; and we have seen that these are but bruised reeds. Nevertheless, the facts brought forward by the argument from energy do throw some light on the *nature* of the interaction between mind and body, assuming this to happen. They do suggest that all the energy of our bodily actions comes out of and goes back into the physical world, and that minds neither add energy to nor abstract it from the latter. What they do, if they do anything, is to determine that at a given moment so much energy shall change from the chemical form to the form of bodily movement; and they determine this, so far as we can see, without altering the total amount of energy in the physical world.

(2) *The Argument from the Structure of the Nervous System.* There are purely reflex actions, like sneezing and blinking, in which there is no reason to suppose that the mind plays any essential part. Now we know the nervous structure which is used in such acts as these. A stimulus is given to the outer end of an afferent nerve; some change or other runs up this nerve, crosses a synapsis between this and an afferent nerve, travels down the latter to a muscle, causes the muscle to contract, and so produces a bodily movement. There seems no reason to believe that the mind plays any essential part in this process. The process may be irreducibly vital, and not merely physico-chemical; but there seems no need to assume anything more than this. Now it is said that the whole nervous system is simply an immense complication of interconnected nervous arcs. The result is that a change which travels inwards has an immense number of alternative paths by which it may travel outwards. Thus the reaction to a given stimulus is no longer one definite movement, as in the simple reflex. Almost any movement may follow any stimulus according to the path which the afferent disturbance happens to take. This path will depend on the relative resistance of the various synapses at the time. Now, a variable response to the same stimulus is characteristic of deliberate, as opposed to reflex, action.

These are the facts. The argument based on them runs as follows. It is admitted that the mind has nothing to do with the causation of purely reflex actions. But the nervous structure and the nervous processes involved in deliberate action do not differ in kind from those involved in reflex action; they differ only in degrees of complexity. The variability which characterizes deliberate action is fully explained by the variety of alternative paths and the variable resistances of the synapses. So it is unreasonable to suppose that the mind has any more to do with causing deliberate actions than it has to do with causing reflex actions.

I think that this argument is invalid. In the first place, I am pretty sure that the persons who use it have before their imagination a kind of picture of how mind and body must interact if they interact at all. They find that the facts do not answer to this picture, and so they conclude that there is no interaction. The picture is of the following kind. They think of the mind as sitting somewhere in a hole in the brain, surrounded by telephones. And they think of the afferent disturbance as coming to an end at one of these telephones and there affecting the mind. The mind is then supposed to respond by sending an afferent impulse down another of these telephones. As no such hole, with afferent nerves stopping at its walls and afferent nerves starting from them, can be found, they conclude that the mind can play no part in the transaction. But another alternative is that this picutre of how the mind must act, if it acts at all, is wrong. To put it shortly, the mistake is to confuse a gap in an explanation with a spatio-temporal gap, and to argue from the absence of the latter to the absence of the former.

The interactionist's contention is simply that there is a gap in any purely physiological explanation of deliberate action; *i.e.*, that all such explanations fail to account completely for the facts because they leave out one necessary condition. It does not follow in the least that there must be a spatio-temporal breach of continuity in the physiological conditions, and that the missing condition must fill this gap in the way in which the movement of a wire fills the spatio-temporal interval between the pulling of a bell-handle and the ringing of a distant bell. To assume this is to make the mind a kind of physical object, and to make its action a kind of mechanical action. Really, the mind and its actions are not literally in space at all, and the time which is occupied by the mental event is no doubt *also* occupied by some part of the physiological process. Thus I am inclined to think that much of the force which this argument actually exercises on many people is simply due to the presupposition about the *modus operandi* of interaction, and that it is greatly weakened when this presupposition is shown to be a mere prejudice due to our limited power of envisaging unfamiliar alternative possibilities.

We can, however, make more detailed objections to the argument than this. There is a clear introspective difference between the mental accompaniment of voluntary action and that of reflex action. What goes on in our minds when we decide with difficulty to get out of a hot bath on a cold morning is obviously extremely different from what goes on in our minds when we sniff pepper and sneeze. And the difference is qualitative; it is not a mere difference of complexity. This difference has to be explained somehow; and the theory under discussion gives no plausible explanation of it. The ordinary view that, in the latter case, the mind is not acting on the body at all; whilst, in the former, it is acting on the body in a specific way, does at least make the introspective difference between the two intelligible.

Again, whilst it is true that deliberate action differs from reflex action in its greater variability of response to the same stimulus, this is certainly not the whole or the most important part of the difference between them. The really important difference is that, in deliberate action, the response is varied *appropriately* to meet the special circumstances which are supposed to exist at the tine or are expected to arise later; whilst reflex action is not varied in this way, but is blind and almost mechanical. The complexity of the nervous system explains the *possibility* of variation; it does not in the least explain why the alternative which actually takes place should as a rule be appropriate and not merely haphazard. And so again it seems as if some factor were in operation in deliberate action which is not present in reflex action; and it is reasonable to suppose that this factor is the volition in the mind.

It seems to me that this second scientific argument has no tendency to disprove interaction; but that the facts which it brings forward do tend to suggest the particular form which interaction probably takes if it happens at all. They suggest that what the mind does to the body in voluntary action, if it does anything, is to lower the resistance of certain synapses and to raise that of others. The result is that the nervous current follows such a course as to produce the particular movement which the mind judges to be appropriate at the time. On such a view the difference between reflex, habitual, and deliberate actions for the present purpose becomes fairly plain. In pure reflexes the mind cannot voluntarily affect the resistance of the snyapses concerned, and so the action takes place in spite of it. In habitual action it deliberately refrains from interfering with the resistance of the synapses, and so the action goes on like a complicated reflex. But it *can* affect these resistances if it wishes, though often only with difficulty; and it is ready to do so if it judges this to be expedient. Finally, it may lose the power altogether. This would be what happens when a person becomes a slave to some habit, such as drug-taking.

I conclude that, at the level of enlightened common sense at which the ordinary discussion of interaction moves, no good reason has been produced for doubting that the mind acts on the body in volition, and that the body acts on the mind in sensation. The philosophic arguments are quite inconclusive; and the scientific arguments, when properly understood, are quite compatible with two-sided interaction. At most they suggest certain conclusions as to the form which interaction probably takes if it happens at all.

Difficulties in the Denial of Interaction

I propose now to consider some of the difficulties which would attend the denial of interaction, still keeping the discussion at the same common-sense level. If a man denies the action of body on mind he is at once in trouble over the causation of new sensations. Suppose that I suddenly tread on an unsuspected tin-tack. A new sensation suddenly comes into my mind. This is an event, and it presumably has some cause. Now, however carefully I introspect and retrospect, I can find no other mental event which is adequate to account for the fact that just that sensation has arisen at just that moment. If I reject the common-sense view that treading on the tack is an essential part of the cause of the sensation, I must suppose either that it is uncaused, or that it is caused by other events in my mind which I cannot discover by introspection or retrospection, or that it is caused telepathically by other finite minds or by God. Now inquiry of my neighbors would show that it is not caused telepathically by any event in their minds which they can introspect or remember. Thus anyone who denies the action of body on mind, and admits that sensations have causes, must postulate either (a) immense numbers of unobservable states in his own mind; or (b) as many unobservable states in his neighbors' minds, together with telepathic action; or (c) some non-human spirit together with telepathic action. I must confess that the difficulties which have been alleged against the action of body on mind seem to be mild compared with those of the alternative hypotheses which are involved in the denial of such action.

The difficulties which are involved in the denial of the action of mind on body are at first sight equally great; but I do not think that they turn out to be so serious as those which are involved in denying the action of body on mind. The *prima facie* difficulty is this. The world contains many obviously artificial objects, such as books, bridges, clothes, etc. We know that, if we go far enough back in the history of their production, we always do in fact come on the actions of some human body. And the minds connected with these bodies did design the objects in question, did will to produce them, and did believe that they were initiating and guiding the physical process by means of these designs and volitions. If it be true that the mind does not act on the body, it follows that the designs and volitions in the agents' minds did not in fact play any part in the production of books, bridges, clothes, etc. This appears highly paradoxical. And it is an easy step from it to say that anyone who denies the action of mind on body must admit that books, bridges, and other such objects *could* have been produced even though there had been no minds, no thought of these objects, and no desire for them. This consequence seems manifestly absurd to common sense, and it might be argued that it reflects its absurdity back on the theory which entails it.

The man who denies that mind can act on body might deal with this difficulty in two ways: (1) He might deny that the conclusion *is* intrinsically absurd. He might say that human bodies are extraordinarily complex physical objects, which probably obey irreducible laws of their own, and that we really do not know enough about them to set limits to what their unaided powers could accomplish. This is the line which Spinoza took. The conclusion, it would be argued, *seems* absurd only because the state of affairs which it contemplates is so very unfamiliar. We find it difficult to imagine a body like ours without a mind like ours; but, if we could get over this defect in our powers of imagination, we might have no difficulty in admitting that such a body could do all the things which our bodies do. I think it must be admitted that the difficulty is not so great as that which is involved in denying the action of body on mind. There we had to postulate *ad hoc* utterly unfamiliar entities and modes of action; here it is not certain that we should have to do this.

(2) The other line of argument would be to say that the alleged consequence does not necessarily follow from denying the action of mind on body. I assume that both

parties admit that causation is something more than mere *de facto* regularity of sequence and concomitance. If they do not, of course the whole controversy betweeen them becomes futile; for there will certainly be causation between mind and body and between body and mind, in the only sense in which there is causation anywhere. This being presupposed, the following kind of answer is logically possible. When I say that B could not have happened unless A had happened, there are two alternative possibilities. (a) A may itself be an indispensable link in any chain of causes which ends up with B. (b) A may not itself be a link in any chain of causation which ends up with B. But there may be an indispensable link a in any such chain of causation, and A may be a necessary accompaniment or sequent of a. These two possibilities may be illustrated by diagrams. (a) is represented by the figure below:—

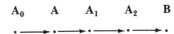

The two forms of (b) are represented by the two figures below:—

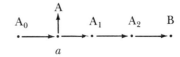

and

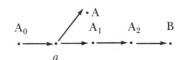

Evidently, if B cannot happen unless a precedes, and if a cannot happen without A accompanying or immediately following it, B will not be able to happen unless A precedes it. And yet A will have had no part in causing B. It will be noticed that, on this view, a has a complex effect AA_1, of which a certain part, viz., A_1 is sufficient by itself to produce A_2 and ultimately B. Let us apply this abstract possibility to our present problem. Suppose that B is some artificial object, like a book or a bridge. If we admit that this could not have come into existence unless a certain design and volition had existed in a certain mind, we could interpret the facts in two ways. (*a*) We could hold that the design and volition are themselves an indispensable link in the chain of causation which ends in the production of a bridge or a book. This is the common view, and it requires us to admit the action of mind on body. (*b*) We might hold that the design and the volition are not themselves a link in the chain of causation which ends in the production of the artificial object; but that they are a necessary accompaniment or sequent of something which *is* an indispensable link in this chain of causation. On this view the chain consists wholly of physical events; but one of these physical events (viz., some event in the brain) has a complex consequent. One part of this consequent is purely physical, and leads by purely physical causation to the ultimate production of a bridge or a book. The other is purely mental, and consists of a certain design and volition in the mind which animates the human body concerned. If this has any consequences they are purely mental. Each part of this complex consequent follows with equal necessity; this particular brain-state could no more have existed without such and such a mental state accompanying or following it than it could have existed without such and such a bodily movement following it. If we are willing to take some such view as this, we can admit that certain objects could not have existed unless there had been designs of them and desires for them; and yet we could consistently deny that these desires and designs have any effect on the movements of our bodies.

It seems to me then that the doctrine which I will call "one-sided action of body on mind" is logically possible; *i.e.*, a theory which accepts the action of body on mind but denies the action of mind on body. But I do not see the least reason to accept it,

since I see no reason to deny that mind acts on body in volition. One-sided action has, I think, generally been held in the special form called "Epiphenomenalism." I take this doctrine to consist of the following four propositions: (1) Certain bodily events cause certain mental events. (2) No mental event plays any part in the causation of any bodily event. (3) No mental event plays any part in the causation of any other mental event. Consequently (4) all mental events are caused by bodily events, and by them only. Thus Epiphenomenalism is just one-sided action of body on mind, together with a special theory about the nature and structure of mind. This special theory does not call for discussion here, where I am dealing only with the relations between minds and bodies, and am not concerned with a detailed analysis of mind. In a later chapter we shall have to consider the special features of Epiphenomenalism.

Arguments in Favor of Interaction

The only arguments *for* one-sided action of body on mind or for parallelism are the arguments *against* two-sided interaction; and these, as we have seen, are worthless. Are there any arguments in favor of two-sided interaction? I have incidentally given two which seem to me to have considerable weight. In favor of the action of mind on body is the fact that we seem to be immediately aware of a causal relation when we voluntarily try to produce a bodily movement, and that the arguments to show that this cannot be true are invalid. In favor of the action of body on mind are the insuperable difficulties which I have pointed out in accounting for the happening of new sensations on any other hypothesis. There are, however, two other arguments which have often been thought to prove the action of mind on body. These are (1) an evolutionary argument, first used, I believe, by William James; and (2) the famous "telegram argument." They both seem to me to be quite obviously invalid.

(1) The evolutionary argument runs as follows: It is a fact, which is admitted by

persons who deny two-sided interaction, that minds increase in complexity and power with the growth in complexity of the brain and nervous system. Now, if the mind makes no difference to the actions of the body, this development of the mental side is quite unintelligible from the point of view of natural selection. Let us imagine two animals whose brains and nervous systems were of the same degree of complexity; and suppose, if possible, that one had a mind and the other had none. If the mind makes no difference to the behavior of the body the chance of survival and of leaving descendants will clearly be the same for the two animals. Therefore natural selection will have no tendency to favor the evolution of mind which has actually taken place. I do not think that there is anything in this argument. Natural selection is a purely negative process; it simply tends to eliminate individuals and species which have variations unfavorable to survival. Now, by hypothesis, the possession of a mind is not *unfavorable* to survival; it simply makes no difference. Now it may be that the existence of a mind of such and such a kind is an inevitable consequence of the existence of a brain and nervous system of such and such a degree of complexity. Indeed, we have seen that some such view is essential if the opponent of two-sided interaction is to answer the common-sense objection that artificial objects could not have existed unless there had been a mind which designed and desired them. On this hypothesis, there is no need to invoke natural selection twice over, once to explain the evolution of the brain and nervous system, and once to explain the evolution of the mind. If natural selection will account for the evolution of the brain and nervous system, the evolution of the mind will follow inevitably, even though it adds nothing to the survival-value of the organism. The plain fact is that natural selection does not account for the origin or for the growth in complexity of anything whatever; and therefore it is no objection to any particular theory of the relations of mind and body that, if it were true, natural selection would

not explain the origin and development of mind.

(2) The "telegram argument" is as follows: Suppose there were two telegrams, one saying "Our son has been killed," and the other saying: "Your son has been killed." And suppose that one or other of them was delivered to a parent whose son was away from home. As physical stimuli they are obviously extremely alike, since they differ only in the fact that the letter "Y" is present in one and absent in the other. Yet we know that the reaction of the person who received the telegram might be very different according to which one he received. This is supposed to show that the reactions of the body cannot be wholly accounted for by bodily causes, and that the mind must intervene causally in some cases. Now, I have very little doubt that the mind does play a part in determining the action of the recipient of the telegram; but I do not see why this argument should prove it to a person who doubted or denied it. If two very similar stimuli are followed by two very different results, we are no doubt justified in concluding that these stimuli are not the complete causes of the reactions which follow them. But of course it would be admitted by everyone that the receipt of the telegram is not the complete cause of the recipient's reaction. We all know that his brain and nervous system play an essential part in any reaction that he may make to the stimulus. The question then is whether the minute structure of his brain and nervous system, including in this the supposed traces left by past stimuli and past reactions, is not enough to account for the great difference in his behavior on receiving two very similar stimuli. Two keys may be very much alike, but one may fit a certain lock and the other may not. And, if the lock be connected with the trigger of a loaded gun, the results of "stimulating" the system with one or other of the two keys will be extremely different. We know that the brain and nervous system are very complex, and we commonly suppose that they contain more or less permanent traces and linkages due to past stimuli and reac-

tions. If this be granted, it is obvious that two very similar stimuli may produce very different results, simply because one fits in with the internal structure of the brain and nervous system whilst the other does not. And I do not see how we can be sure that anything more is needed to account for the mere difference of reaction adduced by the "telegram argument."

STUDY QUESTIONS

1. State the mind-body problem in your own words. Is it a problem for a materialist? An idealist?

2. What does Broad mean by "two-sided interaction"? What are the main objections to it? Do you think Broad is successful in answering these objections?
3. Explain what is meant by "epiphenomenalism." Do you think it offers as good an explanation of the relationship between mind and body as two-sided interactionism does?
4. Do you think Broad answers the "telegram argument" successfully?

For Further Reading

Campbell, K. *Body and Mind.* Garden City, N.Y.: Doubleday, 1970.

Feigl, H. *The "Mental" and the "Physical."* Minneapolis: University of Minnesota Press, 1967.

Laird, J. *Our Minds and Their Bodies.* London: Oxford University Press, 1925.

Pratt, J. B. *Matter and Spirit.* New York: Macmillan, 1926.

Shaffer, J. A. *Philosophy of Mind.* Englewood Cliffs, N.J.: Prentice-Hall, 1968 (esp. Chapters 3 and 4).

Vesey, G. N. A., ed. *Body and Mind.* London: Allen and Unwin, 1964.

EWING: CAUSATION

Picture a billiard ball rolling across a table, striking another ball, and the second ball then rolling into a corner pocket. If you were asked, Why did the second ball suddenly start moving in the way that it did? you would probably reply that its motion was caused by the impact of the first ball on it. Given the way in which the first ball struck it, it had to roll into the corner pocket. This billiard ball example offers a paradigm case of a cause-effect relationship. Nevertheless, it gives rise to a number of perplexing philosophical questions. As we watch the billiard table, although we see the motion of the balls and are prepared to claim that the second ball must move as it does, we never actually observe what we call the cause-effect connection between the two balls. This lack of observation leads some philosophers to ask: Does the second ball really have to roll into the corner pocket? If so, why? Questions like these raise doubts about the entire cause-effect relationship. Is the connection between a cause and its effect a necessary one? If not, what exactly is it? To this question philosophers have given a number of different answers. The most important of these are discussed in the selection that follows.

Alfred Cyril Ewing (1899–1973) received both his undergraduate and graduate education at Oxford University. For most of his career he taught at Cambridge University, although he made several trips to the United States where he visited a number of leading universities. Ewing's writings encompass a wide variety of philosophical topics.

✌ *The Fundamental Questions of Philosophy*

Chapter Eight
Cause

Importance of Concept

A conception which has played a very great part both in science and philosophy is that of cause. It is indeed sometimes said that science nowadays is able to dispense with cause, but what the people who say this have in view is some metaphysical conception of cause with which they do not agree. In one sense at least science cannot possibly dispense with cause, neither can the practical man. It is essential both to science and to practice that we should be able to go beyond what has actually been observed and make inferences from it, whether in the form of generalizations as to what usually happens or predictions as to particular facts. Now, whatever else the concept of cause involves, it involves this, that we can pass from what has happened in observed cases to what is likely to happen in cases which have not been observed, and this is absolutely necessary if we are to have any science at all or if we are to take any sensible practical steps. This has always been a difficulty for the empiricist: it cannot possibly be a merely empirical matter to predict, as science does, for we have not empirically observed the future which we predict. Not that the topic is without difficulties for the rationalist also, as we shall see shortly. However in modern philosophy it was hardly questioned till the time of Hume that we knew *a priori* the principle that every change had a cause (with the possible exception of those involving 'free will') ... and that this principle was a necessary presupposition of science. Even Hume did not, as he is often supposed to have done, reject it, but merely raised philosophical difficulties which he thought made it impossible to justify or defend it. The minimum sense of the principle of causation which must be accepted if we are to have science is then that the repeated occurrence of a certain kind of event under certain conditions is generally evidence which makes it likely that similar events will repeat themselves under similar conditions. Without assuming this much we can never make any scientific predictions whatever or pass from the observed to the unobserved.

Regularity Theory

Let us now consider philosophical theories of what the nature of causation is or, if you prefer to put it that way, what is meant by the term 'cause'. The philosopher who is inclined to be an empiricist will be likely to adopt a view on this topic which identifies or approximates to identifying causation with regular sequence, since regular sequence is something that can be observed empirically. He will indeed have to assume one principle which he cannot justify empirically, namely, that what has succeeded a certain kind of event regularly in the past is also likely to do so in the future, but the regular sequence or 'regularity' view at any rate makes the minimum concessions to the non-empiricist. 'A causes B', if A and B stand for classes of events, will then mean that B usually or always follows A. This view is by no means identical with the common-sense view of cause, as is shown by the fact that, if it were true, there would be no more special connection between the striking of a match and the flame which followed it than between the striking of the match and an earthquake which might also occur just afterwards. It would merely be that the striking of a match is usually followed by a flame and not usually followed by earthquakes, and that would be all. We could not then say that the striking *made* the flame follow. All intrinsic necessary connection between cause and effect, all active power on the part of the cause is denied. On this view to give a cause is *toto genere* different from giving a reason, it does not in the least help to explain why the effect happened, it only tells us what pre-

Reprinted with permission of Macmillan Publishing Co., Inc. and Routledge & Kegan Paul Ltd. from *The Fundamental Questions of Philosophy* by A. C. Ewing, New York, 1951.

ceded the effect. So it is clear that the regularity view stands in very sharp contrast to the common-sense view of causation, though this does not necessarily refute the regularity view . Despite this the latter theory, or something very like it, is distinctly popular today. It agrees well with the modern empiricist trend, since it makes causation something that can be empirically observed and goes as far as one can towards eliminating the *a priori*. And it is in accord with one fact about causation. Whether causation is merely regular sequence or not, it is clear that at least in the physical world we cannot see any intelligible connection between cause and effect which explains why the latter must occur if the former does so. The chemist may bring propositions such as that wood burns under more general principles about the nature of matter from which they could be deduced, but these more general propositions themselves are not of such a kind that we can see at all why they should be true, we only find that empirically in fact they are true.

But there are other respects in which the theory is less plausible. First, it presents serious difficulties when we start talking about the causation of single events. 'I caused the flame by striking the match' might be interpreted as meaning: 'Striking a match by me was followed by a flame, and an event of the second class usually does follow an event of the first.' But what about events the causation of which is much more complex such as wars and economic depressions? Nobody has succeeded in discovering a really satisfactory formulation of statements about the causes of these in terms of the regularity view. If we say that Hitler's invasion of Poland caused the second world war to break out when it did we no doubt mean that the war followed it, but the rest of what we mean is not that wars always or usually follow invasions of Poland, it is something much more specific.

Another difficulty about the regularity view is that there are cases of regular sequence which nobody would call cases of causation. For instance, the sounding of a hooter at 8 A.M. in London is regularly followed not only by men going to work at that factory in London but by men going to work at a factory in Manchester which also opens at 8 A.M. Yet everybody would say that, while the arrivals at the factory in London were caused by the hooter in that factory, the arrivals at Manchester were not.

These difficulties might possibly be met by minor amendments of the theory, others are more serious. The theory seems particularly inapplicable in the case of psychology. For instance, when I believe something for a reason, surely my mental state is really determined by the apprehension of the reason and is not merely one of a class of mental states which usually follow the apprehension of similar reasons. If that is all, the belief is not reasonable; for it to be reasonable it must not merely follow on the apprehension of the reason but be determined by the intrinsic character of the reason. Again it is surely incredible that, when I will an action, the action is not determined by my will, or that to say it is 'determined' here merely means something like 'it is a kind of action which follows most or all states of mind like my own at the time in certain specific respects'. Again for memory to be possible one would think that my present state of consciousness must be genuinely determined by, not merely follow on, the past event remembered. There can be no trusting my memory of yesterday's events if it was not really determined by the events said to have been remembered.

Entailment Theory

All this should make one hesitate very much before accepting the regularity theory merely because it is the simplest and keeps closest to what is empirically observed. It seems that besides regularity we must introduce the notion of determination and necessity. There is a sense, it seems, in which the effect not merely does but must follow the cause, and this depends on the specific nature of the cause as such. Can we say anything more to make clearer what it is in which this necessity consists? There is another case of necessity, a clear one, which it is tempting and, I think reasonable, to take as at least an analogy. That is the necessity underlying valid inference. Where a conclusion follows logically from a premise, this must be because the fact expressed by the premise is so connected with the fact expressed by the conclusion that the former could not possibly occur without the latter occurring. This is logical necessity. The theory according to which the connection between cause and effect is the same as or very like that of logical necessity may be called the rationalist or the entailment theory of causation ('entailment' being the relation between the premises and the conclusion in an argument where the latter follows necessarily from the former or between the objective fact expressed by the premises and by the conclusion).

The entailment theory is a theory of philosophers, but it certainly is more closely akin to the common-sense view than is a purely regularity theory, and though one should not say that causation is just entailment, there is a good case for saying that it involves the entailment relation or else something very similar. It is also true of course that an effect does follow regularly its cause; the regularity theory is not mistaken in what it asserts but only in what it denies. The entailment theory was almost universal among philosophers till the nineteenth century (though they did not use that name). The first leading philosopher to question it was David Hume (1711–1776), and at the time his views found little favour, though today the regularity theory is the one most commonly advocated.

However, it seems to me that there are two strong arguments for the entailment theory. These may be added to the arguments already given against the regularity theory, which did not by themselves suggest another theory to put in its place. The first is that we can after all make legitimate inferences from cause to effect. How could we do this if the cause did not in

a very important sense entail the effect? The relation need not be exactly the same as the entailment which occurs in formal logical reasoning, but it must at least be analogous to it in the important respect that it justifies the conclusion. It would be a very odd kind of inference in which we were allowed to draw conclusions from premises which in no way entailed their conclusions. This argument gives the main, though usually unexpressed, reason why philosophers have so often believed in the rationalist (or entailment) theory of causation. I do not of course in using this argument mean to imply that a person must consciously assume the entailment theory before he can see that a particular induction is justified, only that the theory is logically presupposed if induction is to be justified. We do not know the ultimate logical presuppositions of our thinking, at any rate till we become philosophers.

The second argument is as follows. The occurrence of regularities is in any case a fact of experience. For instance, whenever solid objects are left unattached in mid-air they fall to the ground (with certain reservations to cover aeroplanes, etc.). Now, if it were not explained in any way, it would be an incredible coincidence that this should happen so constantly. It would be like having all the trumps in one hand at bridge several times running, or more improbable even than this. But what explanation could there be except that the nature of the bodies or the nature of the physical universe as a whole somehow entailed their moving in that way? If causation merely means regular sequence, to say that A causes B gives no explanation of the regular sequence of B on A, it merely affirms that B thus succeeds. Only if the cause is a *reason* for the effect, will it explain why this repeated regularity occurs, and the facts surely cry out for an explanation, since the alternative is to leave it as a mere coincidence which would be incredibly unlikely. But how can the cause be a reason for the effect if its nature does not somehow involve the effect? In that case the latter will logically follow from, i.e., be entailed by the former, or at least the relation will be very closely analogous to that of logical entailment.*

The following are the main objections brought against the entailment theory. (1) We cannot see any logical connection between cause and effect. This must be admitted as regards the physical world at least. We do not see any ultimate reason why water and not oil should put out a fire or why we should be nourished by bread and not by stones. No doubt a scientist could in a sense give reasons for these laws by explaining, e.g. that stones are too hard to digest and that bread contains nitrogenous matter in an organized form in which it is not present in stones; but the reasons of the scientist only amount either to interpolating intermediate causes so that he explains how A causes B by pointing to an intermediate link C, i.e. something which appears between A and B or to showing that the generalization to be explained is just an instance of a wider generalization itself founded on experience, e.g. that no animals can extract nutriment direct from inorganic matter. In neither case does he tell us anything which amounts to more than a statement that events of a certain kind occur under certain circumstances; he does not explain why they occur. This is made clearer by comparing the conclusions of other sciences with those of mathematics. In the latter alone do we see not merely as an empirical fact that the conclusion is true but why it must be true. No causal law about the physical world even appears to us as logically necessary like the laws of mathematics; we cannot prove any such law *a priori*, but only establish it as an empirical generalization. However the fact that we cannot see any necessary *a priori*

*Some people prefer not to use the term 'entail' of the connection between facts but only of the connection between propositions, but we cannot avoid admitting that, if two true propositions are necessarily connected, the facts for which they stand must also be necessarily connected. Whether we are to call this necessary connection between facts 'entailment' or not seems to me only a verbal question.

connection behind causal laws is no proof that there is not any. Till comparatively recently most of the logically necessary connections of mathematics had not been discovered by any human being, but they no doubt held all the same in prehistoric days as much as today. We cannot set limits to what is in nature by our ignorance. It would be very different if we were not only unable to see any necessary connection between cause and effect but were able to see positively that there is no such connection. Some philosophers think that they can see this, and if so they are justified in ruling out the entailment theory, but in the absence of this positive insight the negative argument is only of light weight.

(2) The relation between cause and effect is in one respect at least different from that holding in any generally recognized case of necessary connection, i.e. cause and effect are not, normally at least, simultaneous, but occur at different times. This of course again does not prove that necessary causal connection cannot occur, but only somewhat lessens the plausibility of the contention that it does. But if there are good positive reasons to suppose it occurs, the fact that it is unlike what happens in other cases is no adequate ground for rejecting the reasons in question.

(3) It is objected that in cases of *a priori* reasoning we attain certainty, but in cases of causal reasoning only probability. This may, however, be explained compatibly with the entailment theory. In the first place we never know the whole cause. What common sense calls the cause is only the most striking part of a vast complex of conditions all of which are relevant to the exact manner in which the effect occurs. But, even if the whole cause entails the whole effect, this gives no reason to suppose that a part of it, which is all we know, will do so. The best we can do is to conclude on the ground of previous experience that the factors in the cause of which we are not aware are unlikely to be of such a kind as to counteract the others and prevent the occurrence of something like the expected effect. Secondly, since we cannot see the

necessary connection directly even if it is there, we are in any case bound to proceed by employing the recognized methods of induction, which can logically only yield probability not certainty. For in the absence of direct insight into it, we can only arrive at conclusions as to when it occurs indirectly by considering what regularities normally occur and inferring from those what are most likely to be the laws underlying them, as on any other view of causation.

The entailment theory is of course incompatible with the view which we earlier rejected that all logically necessary propositions are verbal or analytic in a sense which would make what is entailed part of what entails. Since the effect is a different event from and not part of the cause, the two cannot be necessarily connected unless some propositions not analytic in this sense are *a priori*. Propositions about causation may be analytic in some cases, where something has been defined in terms of its causal properties, but this cannot always be so. If we define a species of thing in terms of one causal property, it will be a synthetic proposition that members of the species have any other causal property they may possess.

So far I have spoken as if it were common ground that we could never have insight into causal entailments, but I should not be ready to admit this. It seems to me true of the physical world, not of the world of psychology. Our insight that the death of a beloved person will tend to cause grief or that insults will tend to cause annoyance does not seem to be based merely on experience. We seem also to see *a priori* that the cause will tend to produce these effects. There is surely something in the thwarting of a desire which entails a tendency to produce pain. Even apart from experience it would not be as reasonable to expect that the death of a beloved person would cause the lover to jump from joy. We must indeed admit that we can at the best only see a causal *tendency* in these cases. If A loves B now, it is not certain that he will grieve if B dies, for by the time this has happened he may have gone mad or quarrelled with B so

violently as to rejoice at his death. But we can see, it seems, that the nature of love is such as to tend strongly in the direction mentioned and not in the opposite one. That we can only say what its tendency is and not predict with certainty that this will be fulfilled on a given occasion is presumably because the situation is always very complex and we cannot know that there will not be factors which counteract the tendency in question. It may further be argued that we can easily explain why we should not see entailments in the physical world even if they are really there. For, firstly it is generally held that the internal nature of matter is quite unknown to us, and how can we tell whether what is quite unknown to us does or does not entail something? In psychology alone are we immediately aware of the internal nature of the object with which we are dealing, namely mind, and here we can reasonably claim to see that certain causal entailments hold, as we have just noted. Secondly, we never are in a position to give the whole cause, and it would be the whole cause that entailed the effect, not a part of it. Incidentally it is not necessary to the entailment theory to suppose that there are any causal laws which by themselves would be self-evident even to God. It may be that any causal law depends for its evidence on the whole system to which it belongs, as many have argued to be the case even with the *a priori* propositions of mathematics. It may be that water would not freeze in the way it does in a universe where the chemical constitution of water was the same but the general world system different. The arguments I have used would be compatible even with any law we can discover being only statistical. It has been suggested that the laws of physics do not apply to each single particle but are only statistics about the way in which most particles move, but there still must surely, it seems, be some reason in the nature of things why so many more particles move in one way than in another way.

Whether we are to maintain or reject the entailment theory depends largely on our attitude to the problem of induction. Modern logicians generally have tried to solve the problem of the validity of induction without assuming the entailment theory of causation and generally admit that they have failed. They have not, even according to themselves, shown why we are entitled to make inductive predictions in advance of experience. The main trouble is that there is no reason why we should think that A will be followed by B in the future merely because it has been so in the past. But if we suppose that the repeated experience in the past is an indication of something in the nature of A which entails B, that will be a good reason for expecting B to follow on future occasions also, even if we do not see why the assumed entailment should hold. No detailed theory of induction has been worked out on this basis, but it is significant that modern logicians who will not admit the entailment theory of causation have (usually according to their own admission) failed to produce any rational justification of induction. Nevertheless it has seemed so odd to many philosophers that there should be a relation of logical entailment between different events that they would rather admit all our induction to be irrational than save its rationality in such a fashion. Yet we cannot really suppose it irrational to believe that if we jump from a height we shall fall; and even if we say that all induction is in some sense irrational, it will still be incumbent on us to explain the distinction between scientific inductions and those inductions which would be accepted by no sensible person. What is the difference between the two kinds if they are both irrational?

It has been said that inductive arguments, though not rational in the same way as deductive arguments, are rational in some other way. It is easy enough to say this, but difficult to grasp what this sense of 'rational' could be. Inductive arguments are after all inferences, and for an inference to be valid the conclusion must follow from the premises. But for this to be so the premises must entail the conclusion, or at the very least be connected with it by a relation closely analogous to that of logical entailment. It is difficult to escape this argument. Nor have those who try to meet the difficulty by saying that induction is rational but rational in a different sense from deduction succeeded in defining the sense in which induction is rational. They have either left it undefined or defined it in terms of practical utility. In the latter case an inductive inference is rational if it is of a kind which is practically useful. But this seems hardly to solve the problem. It is clear that in order to act in a practically useful way it is not enough to do what has proved useful in the past unless this is an indication that it is likely to be useful also in the future, and it is just as much as induction to infer that something will have good practical results in the future from the results it has had in the past as it is to infer that something will be true of future events because it has been true of past.

It seems to me therefore that there is a strong case for the entailment theory of causation. But I must admit that this is not the opinion of the majority of contemporary philosophers. It is in any case a very important issue metaphysically. One of the most fundamental differences there are in philosophy is between those who think of the world as a rationally connected system and those who regard it as a mere collection of brute facts externally related, and which side we take in this controversy will depend chiefly on whether we, consciously or unconsciously, assume the entailment view of causation or not. One of the chief issues in philosophy through the ages has been that between monism and pluralism, between those who look on the unity of things as more important and those who give a more fundamental position to their plurality; and we shall certainly regard the world as much more of a unity if we adopt than if we do not adopt the entailment view of causation. If that view is true, everything in the world will be united in a logical system, since everything is causally connected with everything else either directly or indirectly. If that view is true, everything in the world will be a unity in a very important sense, for the very nature of a thing will also involve the other things with which it is causally connected.

Activity Theory

There is a third view of causation which is now generally known as the *activity view*. We are certainly apt to think of cause as a kind of depersonalized will, and some philosophers have thought that the key to the philosophical conception of causation lay in the notion of will. This view was taken by Berkeley. He argued that for a cause to produce something it must be 'active' and assumed that activity involved willing. He therefore contended that the only possible cause was a being possessed of will and used this as his chief argument for the existence of God, whom he, denying the material world in a realist sense, made the direct cause of everything which could not be attributed to the causation of human minds. Other philosophers, e.g. Locke, while admitting that material things could be proximate causes, insisted that, since causation ultimately involved will, the only ultimate cause must be mind or spirit. They could argue that, though a physical object once started in motion might move and otherwise affect other physical objects, it could not itself originate motion. We cannot think of a chair as getting up and moving about the room of its own accord, and if it apparently did we should feel forced to suppose either that it was moved in an unknown way by some mind external to it or that it was itself animated by some sort of rudimentary mind. In this fashion the activity view of cause has often been used as the basis for an argument to the existence of God in order to get the motion started originally. There are however forms of the activity view which would not involve such an argument. It might be held that the activity presupposed by causation was not conscious rational volition, but some kind of semi-conscious striving such as we commonly suppose to occur in the

lower animals and which we might then extend in a still more rudimentary form to what we call inanimate objects. The activity theory of causation would then involve panpsychism but not necessarily theism. Or we might go further still in the direction of attenuating the idea of activity, and say what is involved in causation is a quality which we experience consciously when we will but which can exist without being experienced in any way. It might in that case occur in objects which are in the full sense inanimate and might be supposed to constitute the essence also of their totally unconscious causality.

Again, the activity view has sometimes been combined with and sometimes given as an alternative to the entailment view. In modern times. Prof. Stout has first argued for the entailment view and then argued that the only instances in which we can conceive how the cause could entail the effect are instances where will or at least some sort of conation (striving or aiming at ends) is present, not necessarily in what we call the cause itself but in or behind the whole process. This then becomes an argument either for theism or panpsychism. The chief difficulty about this argument is to be sure whether it is really the case that the cause can entail the effect only if conation is supposed present. The cases I have mentioned in which we did seem to see causal connection directly and any other instances I could have given are cases in which conation is in some way present, but the fact that we can see causal connection only in such cases does not necessarily prove that it is only present in such cases. Others would oppose the activity view to the entailment view as providing an alternative account of the causal necessity which the regularity view errs in denying. They think of the effect as following necessarily in the sense of being forced by the cause but not in the sense of being logically entailed by it. This notion of forcing is certainly involved in the usual commonsense view of causation, but the commonsense view also involves the notion of explanation or reason, which can only be interpreted in terms of the entailment view as far as I can see. That the entailment view is, however, not a complete account of the common-sense view can easily be seen in the following way. Entailment, if it occurs, works both ways: it is just as true that the cause can be inferred from the effect as that the effect can be inferred from the cause, and so if inference presupposes entailment it will be just as true that the effect entails the cause as that the cause entails the effect. But there is certainly a sense in which we think of the cause as necessitating or determining the effect but do not think of the effect as necessitating or determining the cause. Causation is regarded as a one-sided or irreversible relation. If I hit somebody in the face and gave him a black eye, the black eye would be produced by my blow in a sense in which the black eye certainly did not produce the blow, and we think of the future as necessitated by the past in a sense in which we should never think of the past as necessitated by the future. But it is impossible to give arguments to show that this element in our ordinary conception of causation applies to the real world, so the activity view must remain inadequately grounded.

It may be further asked how we form the idea of causation at all. On the regularity view the answer is simple: all that causation means is regular sequence, and it is obvious that we can observe regular sequence. On the entailment view the situation is more complex. If it can be claimed that we even occasionally see some causal entailments, we might derive our idea from those we see and then could easily apply it also in cases where we do not ourselves see an entailment but suppose there must be some cause. Or it might be held that the entailment element in our common-sense view of causation was derived from the analogy of non-causal arguments, where we do admittedly see entailments. On the activity view of causation the idea of cause is usually held to be derived from the experience of volition. It is supposed that, when we voluntarily move a part of our body, we are, at least in some cases, immediately aware of our will causing our body to move.* The chief objection to this is constituted by the circumstance that an act of will never moves a part of the body by direct causation, but only by means of a number of intermediate links in the nervous system. Now it is difficult to hold that we can see directly C to cause E where C does not cause E directly, but only causes an intermediate term D (a set of vibrations in the nervous system), which then produces E without our being aware of D in the least, for we have only learnt of D not through the experience of willing in ourselves but through the reports of physiologists. It is less difficult, however, to hold that we can be immediately aware of our will as cause not of physical motion but of changes in our mental states, as when we will to attend to something. If we reject the regularity view but cannot explain how our idea of what there is in causation beyond regularity is derived, we can still fall back on the theory that it is an innate idea, but we should avoid this if possible.

STUDY QUESTIONS

1. How important is the concept of cause to empirical science? To practical life?
2. What is the regularity theory of causation? How is it different from the common-sense view of causation? What are its strengths as a theory? Its weaknesses?
3. What is the entailment theory of causation? Do you think it more or less plausible than the regularity theory? Explain.
4. Ewing believes that in certain situations we can have direct insight into the connection between a cause and its effect. What does he mean by this? What are his examples? Do you agree with him?

*The common objection that an act of will does not always produce motion, since we may be struck with paralysis, might be met by saying that we could still be aware in some cases of our will as at least *tending* to produce motion.

5. What is the activity theory of causation? How is it related to panpsychism? Do you find it plausible? Why or why not?
6. Under what conditions, if any, would you be willing to accept as an answer to the question "Why did this event occur?" "There is no explanation. The event was uncaused; it just happened"?

For Further Reading

Ayer, A. J. *The Foundations of Empirical Knowledge*. London: Macmillan, 1940 (Chapter 4).
Braithwaite, R. B. *Scientific Explanation*. New York: Cambridge University Press, 1953 (Chapters 9 and 10).
Burge, M. *Causality*. Cambridge, Mass.: Harvard University Press, 1959.
Ducasse, C. J. *Nature, Mind, and Death*. LaSalle, Ill.: Open Court, 1951 (Part II).
Hume, D. *An Enquiry Concerning Human Understanding* (esp. § 7).
Nagel, E. *The Structure of Science*. New York: Harcourt, 1961 (Chapter 4).
Russell, B. *Mysticism and Logic*. London: Allen and Unwin, 1917 (Chapter 9).

JAMES AND GRÜNBAUM: FREE WILL AND DETERMINISM

Most people believe in free will. They believe that when they make decisions they exercise a choice between genuine alternatives. They could have chosen otherwise than they in fact did. There are three main reasons for such a belief. First, when we choose, we are directly aware of the fact that our choice is free, that we are not bound to prefer the alternative we actually do but could have chosen something else instead. Second, we feel that freedom is necessary to our human dignity because, to be determined in what we do is to be constrained by forces ultimately outside ourselves, which is demeaning. Third, we believe that, if we are to be morally responsible for our actions, we must freely decide what we shall do. Yet many philosophers refuse to accept free will, mainly because of its implications. Free choices would constitute breaks in the cause-effect chain of events, thus introducing chance into the universe. It would be intrinsically impossible to predict the future on the basis of the past if doing so involved an appeal to human decisions. As a result, a scientific understanding of human events itself would become impossible. These issues are debated in the selections that follow, one defending free will and the other determinism.

William James (1842–1910) was one of the most eminent figures in the history of American philosophy and psychology. The son of a Swedenborgian theologian and brother of the famous novelist, Henry James, he received much of his early education abroad. On his return from Europe at the age of eighteen, he spent a year in Rhode Island studying painting, then entered Harvard University where he completed his studies in 1870 with an M.D. degree. Rather than practicing medicine, however, he became a teacher, serving on the faculty at Harvard for nearly thirty years, teaching mainly in philosophy and psychology. He was a founder of the philosophy of pragmatism (see page 00), which was to have profound effects on the life, both intellectual and practical, of American civilization in the twentieth century.

Adolf Grünbaum, who was born in Cologne, Germany, in 1923, came to America in 1938. He received his undergraduate education at Wesleyan University in Connecticut and his graduate education at Yale University. After teaching for ten years at Lehigh University, he moved to the University of Pittsburgh where he has since remained. His scholarly writing has been mainly in the area of philosophy of science.

✌ James: *The Dilemma of Determinism*

A common opinion prevails that the juice has ages ago been pressed out of the free-will controversy, and that no new champion can do more than warm up stale arguments which every one has heard. This is a radical mistake. I know of no subject less worn out, or in which inventive genius has a better chance of breaking open new ground—not, perhaps, of forcing a conclusion or of coercing assent, but of deepening our sense of what the issue between the two parties really is, of what the ideas of fate and of free will imply. At our very side almost, in the past few years, we have seen falling in rapid succession from the press works that present the alternative in entirely novel lights. Not to speak of the English disciples of Hegel, such as Green and Bradley; not to speak of Hinton and Hodgson, nor of Hazard here—we see in the writings of Renouvier, Fouillée, and Delboeuf how completely changed and refreshed is the form of all the old disputes. I cannot pretend to vie in originality with any of the masters I have named, and my ambition limits itself to just one little point. If I can make two of the necessarily implied corollaries of determinism clearer to you than they have been made before, I shall have made it possible for you to decide for or against that doctrine with a better understanding of what you are about. And if you prefer not to decide at all, but to remain doubters, you will at least see more plainly what the subject of your hesitation is. I thus disclaim openly on the threshold all pretension to prove to you that the freedom of the will is true. The most I hope is to induce some of you

First delivered as a lecture to Harvard divinity students and published in 1884.

to follow my own example in assuming it true, and acting as if it were true. If it be true, it seems to me that this is involved in the strict logic of the case. Its truth ought not to be forced willy-nilly down our indifferent throats. It ought to be freely espoused by men who can equally well turn their backs upon it. In other words, our first act of freedom, if we are free, ought in all inward propriety to be to affirm that we are free. This should exclude, it seems to me, from the free-will side of the question all hope of a coercive demonstration—a demonstration which I, for one, am perfectly contented to go without.

With this much understood at the outset, we can advance. But not without one more point understood as well. The arguments I am about to urge all proceed on two suppositions: first, when we make theories about the world and discuss them with one another, we do so in order to attain a conception of things which shall give us subjective satisfaction; and, second, if there be two conceptions and the one seems to us, on the whole, more rational than the other, we are entitled to suppose that the more rational one is the truer of the two. I hope that you are all willing to make these suppositions with me; for I am afraid that if there be any of you here who are not, they will find little edification in the rest of what I have to say. I cannot stop to argue the point; but I myself believe that all the magnificent achievements of mathematical and physical science—our doctrines of evolution, of uniformity of law, and the rest—proceed from our indomitable desire to cast the world into a more rational shape in our minds than the shape into which it is thrown there by the crude order of our experience. The world has shown itself, to a great extent, plastic to this demand of ours for rationality. How much farther it will show itself plastic, no one can say. Our only means of finding out is to try; and I, for one, feel as free to try conceptions of moral, as of mechanical or of logical, rationality. If a certain formula for expressing the nature of the world violates my moral demand, I shall feel as free to throw it overboard, or at least to doubt it, as if it disappointed my demand for uniformity of sequence, for example; the one demand being, so far as I can see, quite as subjective and emotional as the other is. The principle of causality, for example—what is it but a postulate, an empty name covering simply a demand that the sequence of events shall some day manifest a deeper kind of belonging of one thing with another than the mere arbitrary juxtaposition which now phenomenally appears? It is as much an altar to an unknown god as the one that Saint Paul found at Athens. All our scientific and philosophic ideals are altars to unknown gods. Uniformity is as much so as is free will. If this be admitted, we can debate on even terms. But if any one pretends that while freedom and variety are, in the first instance, subjective demands, necessity and uniformity are something altogether different, I do not see how we can debate at all.

To begin, then, I must suppose you are acquainted with all the usual arguments on the subject. I cannot stop to take up the old proofs from causation, from statistics, from the certainty with which we can foretell one another's conduct, from the fixity of character, and all the rest. But there are two *words* which usually encumber these classical arguments, and which we must immediately dispose of if we are to make any progress. One is the eulogistic word *freedom*, and the other is the opprobrious word *chance*. The word "chance" I wish to keep, but I wish to get rid of the word "freedom." Its eulogistic associations have so far overshadowed all the rest of its meaning that both parties claim the sole right to use it, and determinists today insist that they alone are freedom's champions. Old-fashioned determinism was what we may call *hard*-determinism. It did not shrink from such words as fatality, bondage of the will, necessitation, and the like. Nowadays, we have a *soft* determinism which abhors harsh words, and, repudiating fatality, necessity, and even predetermination, says that its real name is freedom; for freedom is only necessity understood, and bondage to the highest is identical with true freedom. Even a writer as little used to making capital out of soft words as Mr. Hodgson hesitates not to call himself a "free-will determinist."

Now, all this is a quagmire of evasion under which the real issue of fact has been entirely smothered. Freedom in all senses presents simply no problem at all. No matter what the soft determinist mean by it—whether he mean the acting without external constraint; whether he mean the acting rightly, or whether he mean the acquiescing in the law of the whole—who cannot answer him that sometimes we are free and sometimes we are not? But there *is* a problem, an issue of fact and not of words, an issue of the most momentous importance, which is often decided without discussion in one sentence—nay, in one clause of a sentence—by those very writers who spin out whole chapters in their efforts to show what "true" freedom is; and that is the question of determinism, about which we are to talk tonight.

Fortunately, no ambiguities hang about this word or about its opposite, indeterminism. Both designate an outward way in which things may happen, and their cold and mathematical sound has no sentimental associations that can bribe our partiality either way in advance. Now, evidence of an external kind to decide between determinism and indeterminism is, as I intimated a while back, strictly impossible to find. Let us look at the difference between them and see for ourselves. What does determinism profess?

It professes that those parts of the universe already laid down absolutely appoint and decree what the other parts shall be.

The future has no ambiguous possibilities hidden in its womb: the part we call the present is compatible with only one totality. Any other future complement than the one fixed from eternity is impossible. The whole is in each and every part, and welds it with the rest into an absolute unity, an iron block, in which there can be no equivocation or shadow of turning.

> "With earth's first clay they did the last man knead,
> And there of the last harvest sowed the seed.
> And the first morning of creation wrote
> What the last dawn of reckoning shall read."

Indeterminism, on the contrary, says that the parts have a certain amount of loose play on one another, so that the laying down of one of them does not necessarily determine what the others shall be. It admits that possibilities may be in excess of actualities, and that things not yet revealed to our knowledge may really in themselves be ambiguous. Of two alternative futures which we conceive, both may now be really possible; and the one becomes impossible only at the very moment when the other excludes it by becoming real itself. Indeterminism thus denies the world to be one unbending unit of fact. It says there is a certain ultimate pluralism in it; and, so saying, it corroborates our ordinary unsophisticated view of things. To that view, actualities seem to float in a wider sea of possibilities from out of which they are chosen; and *somewhere*, indeterminism says, such possibilities exist, and form a part of truth.

Determinism, on the contrary, says they exist *nowhere*, and that necessity, on the one hand, and impossibility, on the other, are the sole categories of the real. Possibilities that fail to get realized are, for determinism, pure illusions: they never were possibilities at all. There is nothing inchoate, it says, about this universe of ours, all that was or is or shall be actual in it having been from eternity virtually there. The cloud of alternatives our minds escort this mass of actuality withal is a cloud of sheer deceptions, to which "impossibilities" is the only name that rightfully belongs.

The issue, it will be seen, is a perfectly sharp one, which no eulogistic terminology can smear over or wipe out. The truth *must* lie with one side or the other, and its lying with one side makes the other false.

The question relates solely to the existence of possibilities, in the strict sense of the term, as things that may, but need not, be. Both sides admit that a volition, for instance, has occurred. The indeterminists say another volition might have occurred in its place: the determinists swear that nothing could possibly have occurrred in its place. Now, can science be called in to tell us which of these two point-blank contradicters of each other is right? Science professes to draw no conclusions but such as are based on matters of fact, things that have actually happened; but how can any amount of assurance that something actually happened give us the least grain of information as to whether another thing might or might not have happened in its place? Only facts can be proved by other facts. With things that are possibilities and not facts, facts have no concern. If we have no other evidence than the evidence of existing facts, the possibility-question must remain a mystery never to be cleared up.

And the truth is that facts practically have hardly anything to do with making us either determinists or indeterminists. Sure enough, we make a flourish of quoting facts this way or that; and if we are determinists, we talk about the infallibility with which we can predict one another's conduct; while if we are indeterminists, we lay great stress on the fact that it is just because we cannot foretell one another's conduct, either in war or statecraft or in any of the great and small intrigues and businesses of men, that life is so intensely anxious and hazardous a game. But who does not see the wretched insufficiency of this so-called objective testimony on both sides? What fills up the gaps in our minds is something not objective, not external. What divides us into possibility men and anti-possibility men is different faiths or postulates— postulates of rationality. To this man the world seems more rational with possibilities in it—to that man more rational with possibilities excluded; and talk as we will about having to yield to evidence, what makes us monists or pluralists, determinists or indeterminists, is at bottom always some sentiment like this.

The stronghold of the deterministic sentiment is the antipathy to the idea of chance. As soon as we begin to talk indeterminism to our friends, we find a number of them shaking their heads. This notion of alternative possibility, they say, this admission that any one of several things may come to pass, is, after all, only a roundabout name for chance; and chance is something the notion of which no sane mind can for an instant tolerate in the world. What is it, they ask, but barefaced crazy unreason, the negation of intelligibility and law? And if the slightest particle of it exist anywhere, what is to prevent the whole fabric from falling together, the stars from going out, and chaos from recommencing her topsy-turvy reign?

Remarks of this sort about chance will put an end to discussion as quickly as anything one can find. I have already told you that "chance" was a word I wished to keep and use. Let us then examine exactly what it means, and see whether it ought to be such a terrible bugbear to us. I fancy that squeezing the thistle boldly will rob it of its sting.

The sting of the word "chance" seems to lie in the assumption that it means something positive, and that if anything happens by chance, it must needs be something of an intrinsically irrational and preposterous sort. Now, chance means nothing of the kind. It is a purely negative and relative term, giving us no information about that of which it is predicated, except that it happens to be disconnected with something else—not controlled, secured, or necessitated by other things in advance of its own actual presence. As this point is the most subtle one of the whole lecture, and at the same time the point on which all the rest hinges, I beg you to pay particular attention to it. What I say is that it tells us nothing about what a thing may be in itself

to call it "chance." It may be a bad thing, it may be a good thing. It may be lucidity, transparency, fitness incarnate, matching the whole system of other things, when it has once befallen, in an unimaginably perfect way. All you mean by calling it "chance" is that this is not guaranteed, that it may also fall out otherwise. For the system of other things has no positive hold on the chance-thing. Its origin is, in a certain fashion, negative: it escapes, and says, "Hands off!" coming, when it comes, as a free gift, or not at all.

This negativeness, however, and this opacity of the chance-thing when thus considered *ab extra*, or from the point of view of previous things or distant things, do not preclude its having any amount of positiveness and luminosity from within, and at its own place and moment. All that its chance-character asserts about it is that there is something in it really of its own, something that is not the unconditional property of the whole. If the whole wants this property, the whole must wait till it can get it, if it be a matter of chance. That the universe may actually be a sort of joint-stock society of this sort, in which the sharers have both limited liabilities and limited powers, is of course a simple and conceivable notion.

Nevertheless, many persons talk as if the minutest dose of disconnectedness of one part with another, the smallest modicum of independence, the faintest tremor of ambiguity about the future, for example, would ruin everything, and turn this goodly universe into a sort of insane sand-heap or nulliverse, no universe at all. Since future human volitions are as a matter of fact the only ambiguous things we are tempted to believe in, let us stop for a moment to make ourselves sure whether their independent and accidental character need be fraught with such direful consequences to the universe as these.

What is meant by saying that my choice of which way to walk home after the lecture is ambiguous and matter of chance as far as the present moment is concerned? It means that both Divinity Avenue and Oxford Street are called; but that only one, and that one *either* one, shall be chosen. Now, I ask you seriously to suppose that this ambiguity of my choice is real; and then to make the impossible hypothesis that the choice is made twice over, and each time falls on a different street. In other words, imagine that I first walk through Divinity Avenue, and then imagine that the powers governing the universe annihilate ten minutes of time with all that it contained, and set me back at the door of this hall just as I was before the choice was made. Imagine then that, everything else being the same, I now make a different choice and traverse Oxford Street. You, as passive spectators, look on and see the two alternative universes—one of them with me walking through Divinity Avenue in it, the other with the same me walking through Oxford Street. Now, if you are determinists you believe one of these universes to have been from eternity impossible; you believe it to have been impossible because of the intrinsic irrationality or accidentality somewhere involved in it. But looking outwardly at these universes, can you say which is the impossible and accidental one, and which the rational and ncesssary one? I doubt if the most ironclad determinist among you could have the slightest glimmer of light on this point. In other words, either universe, *after the fact* and once there, would, to our means of observation and understanding, appear just as rational as the other. There would be absolutely no criterion by which we might judge one necessary and the other matter of chance. Suppose now we relieve the gods of their hypothetical task and assume my choice, once made, to be made forever. I go through Divinity Avenue for good and all. If as good determinists punctually do affirm, that in the nature of things I *couldn't* have gone through Oxford Street—had I done so it would have been chance, irrationality, insanity, a horrid gap in nature—I simply call your attention to this, that your affirmation is what the Germans call a *Machtspruch*, a mere conception fulminated as a dogma and based on no insight into details. Before my choice, either street seemed as natural to you as to

me. Had I happened to take Oxford Street, Divinity Avenue would have figured in your philosophy as the gap in nature; and you would have so proclaimed it with the best deterministic conscience in the world.

But what a hollow outcry, then, is this against a chance which, if it were present to us, we could by no character whatever distinguish from a rational necessity! I have taken the most trivial of examples, but no possible example could lead to any different result. For what are the alternatives which, in point of fact, offer themselves to human volition? What are those futures that now seem matters of chance? Are they not one and all like the Divinity Avenue and Oxford Street of our example? Are they not all of them *kinds* of things already here and based in the existing frame of nature? Is anyone ever tempted to produce an *absolute* accident, something utterly irrelevant to the rest of the world? Do not all the motives that assail us, all the futures that offer themselves to our choice, spring equally from the soil of the past; and would not either one of them, whether realized through chance or through necessity, the moment it was realized, seem to us to fit that past, and in the completest and most continuous manner to interdigitate with the phenomena already there?*

The more one thinks of the matter, the more one wonders that so empty and gratuitous a hubbub as this outcry against

---

*A favorite argument against free will is that if it be true, a man's murderer may as probably be his best friend as his worst enemy, a mother be as likely to strangle as to suckle her first-born, and all of us be as ready to jump from fourth-story windows as to go out of front doors, etc. Users of this argument should properly be excluded from debate till they learn what the real question is. "Free will" does not say that everything that is physically conceivable is also morally possible. It merely says that, of alternatives that really *tempt* our will, more than one is really possible. Of course, the alternatives that do thus tempt our will are vastly fewer than the physical possibilities we can coldly fancy. Persons really tempted often do murder their best friends, mothers do strangle their first-born, people do jump out of fourth-story windows, etc.

chance should have found so great an echo in the hearts of men. It is a word which tells us absolutely nothing about what chances, or about the *modus operandi* of the chancing; and the use of it as a war cry shows only a temper of intellectual absolutism, a demand that the world shall be a solid block, subject to one control—which temper, which demand, the world may not be bound to gratify at all. In every outwardly verifiable and practical respect, a world in which the alternatives that now actually distract *your* choice were decided by pure chance would be by *me* absolutely undistinguished from the world in which I now live. I am, therefore, entirely willing to call it, so far as your choices go, a world of chance for me. To *yourselves*, it is true, those very acts of choice, which to me are so blind, opaque, and external, are the opposites of this, for you are within them and effect them. To you they appear as decisions; and decisions, for him who makes them, are altogether peculiar psychic facts. Self-luminous and self-justifying at the living moment at which they occur, they appeal to no outside moment to put its stamp upon them or make them continuous with the rest of nature. Themselves, it is rather, who seem to make nature continuous; and in their strange and intense function of granting consent to one possibility and withholding it from another, to transform an equivocal and double future into an inalterable and simple past.

But with the psychology of the matter we have no concern this evening. The quarrel which determinism has with chance fortunately has nothing to do with this or that psychological detail. It is a quarrel altogether metaphysical. Determinism denies that ambiguity of future volitions, because it affirms that nothing can be ambiguous. But we have said enough to meet the issue. Indeterminate future volitions *do* mean chance. Let us not fear to shout it from the housetops if need be; for we know that the idea of chance is, at bottom, exactly the same thing as the idea of gift—the one simply being a disparaging, and the other a eulogistic, name for anything on which we have no effective *claim*. And whether the world be better or the worse for having either chances or gifts in it will depend altogether on *what* these uncertain and unclaimable things turn out to be.

And this at last brings us within sight of our subject. We have seen what determinism means: we have seen that indeterminism is rightly described as meaning chance; and we have seen that chance, the very name of which we are urged to shrink from as from metaphysical pestilence, means only the negative fact that no part of the world, however big, can claim to control absolutely the destinies of the whole. But although, in discussing the word "chance," I may at moments have seemed to be arguing for its real existence, I have not meant to do so yet. We have not yet ascertained whether this be a world of chance or no; at most, we have agreed that it seems so. And I now repeat what I said at the outset, that, from any strict theoretical point of view, the question is insoluble. To deepen our theoretic sense of the *difference* between a world with chances in it and a deterministic world is the most I can hope to do; and this I may now at last begin upon, after all our tedious clearing of the way.

I wish first of all to show you just what the notion that this is a deterministic world implies. The implications I call your attention to are all bound up with the fact that it is a world in which we constantly have to make what I shall, with your permission, call judgments of regret. Hardly an hour passes in which we do not wish that something might be otherwise; and happy indeed are those of us whose hearts have never echoed the wish of Omar Khayam—

"That we might clasp, ere closed, the book of fate,
And make the writer on a fairer leaf
Inscribe our names, or quite obliterate.

"Ah! Love, could you and I with fate conspire
To mend this sorry scheme of things entire,
Would we not shatter it to bits, and then
Remold it nearer to the heart's desire?"

Now, it is undeniable that most of these regrets are foolish, and quite on a par in point of philosophic value with the criticisms on the universe of that friend of our infancy, the hero of the fable "The Atheist and the Acorn,"—

"Fool! had that bough a pumpkin bore,
Thy whimsies would have worked no
more . . . ."

Even from the point of view of our own ends, we should probably make a botch of remodelling the universe. How much more then from the point of view of ends we cannot see! Wise men therefore regret as little as they can. But still some regrets are pretty obstinate and hard to stifle—regrets for acts of wanton cruelty or treachery, for example, whether performed by others or by ourselves. Hardly anyone can remain *entirely* optimistic after reading the confession of the murderer at Brockton the other day: to get rid of the wife whose continued existence bored him, he inveigled her into a desert spot, shot her four times, and then, as she lay on the ground and said to him, "You didn't do it on purpose, did you, dear?" replied, "No, I didn't do it on purpose," as he raised a rock and smashed her skull. Such an occurrence, with the mild sentence and self-satisfaction of the prisoner, is a field for a crop of regrets, which one need not take up in detail. We feel that, although a perfect mechanical fit to the rest of the universe, it is a bad moral fit, and that something else would really have been better in its place.

But, for the deterministic philosophy, the murder, the sentence, and the prisoner's optimism were all necessary from eternity; nothing else for a moment had a ghost of a chance of being put into their place. To admit such a chance, the determinists tell us, would be to make a suicide of reason; so we must steel our hearts against the thought. And here our plot thickens, for we see the first of those difficult implications of determinism and monism which it is my purpose to make you feel. If this Brockton murder was called for by the rest of the universe, if it

had come at its preappointed hour, and if nothing else would have been consistent with the sense of the whole, what are we to think of the universe? Are we stubbornly to stick to our judgment of regret, and say, though it *couldn't* be, yet it *would* have been a better universe with something different from this Brockton murder in it? That, of course, seems the natural and spontaneous thing for us to do; and yet it is nothing short of deliberately espousing a kind of pessimism. The judgment of regret calls the murder bad. Calling a thing bad means, if it means anything at all, that the thing ought not to be, that something else ought to be in its stead. Determinism, in denying that anything else can be in its stead, virtually defines the universe as a place in which what ought to be is impossible—in other words, as an organism whose constitution is afflicted with an incurable taint, an irremediable flaw. The pessimism of a Schopenhauer says no more than this—that the murder is a symptom; and that it is a vicious symptom because it belongs to a vicious whole, which can express its nature no otherwise than by bringing forth just such a symptom as that at this particular spot. Regret for the murder must transform itself, if we are determinists and wise, into a larger regret. It is absurd to regret the murder alone. Other things being what they are, *it* could not be different. What we should regret is that whole frame of things of which the murder is one member. I see no escape whatever from this pessimistic conclusion, if, being determinists, our judgment of regret is to be allowed to stand at all.

The only deterministic escape from pessimism is everywhere to abandon the judgment of regret. That this can be done, history shows to be not impossible. The devil, *quoad existentiam*, may be good. That is, although he be a *principle* of evil, yet the universe, with such a principle in it, may practically be a better universe than it could have been without. On every hand, in a small way, we find that a certain amount of evil is a condition by which a higher form of good is bought. There is nothing to prevent anybody from generalizing this view, and trusting that if we could but see things in the largest of all ways, even such matters as this Brockton murder would appear to be paid for by the uses that follow in their train. An optimism *quand même*, a systematic and infatuated optimism like that ridiculed by Voltaire in his *Candide*, is one of the possible ideal ways in which a man may train himself to look on life. Bereft of dogmatic hardness and lit up with the expression of a tender and pathetic hope, such an optimism has been the grace of some of the most religious characters that ever lived.

"Throb thine with Nature's throbbing breast,
And all is clear from east to west."

Even cruelty and treachery may be among the absolutely blessed fruits of time, and to quarrel with any of their detail may be blasphemy. The only real blasphemy, in short, may be that pessimistic temper of the soul which lets it give way to such things as regrets, remorse, and grief.

Thus, our deterministic pessimism may become a deterministic optimism at the price of extinguishing our judgments of regret.

But does not this immediately bring us into a curious logical predicament? Our determinism leads us to call our judgments of regret wrong, because they are pessimistic in implying that what is impossible yet ought to be. But how then about the judgments of regret themselves? If they are wrong, other judgments, judgments of approval presumably, ought to be in their place. But as they are necessitated, nothing else *can* be in their place; and the universe is just what it was before,—namely, a place in which what ought to be appears impossible. We have got one foot out of the pessimistic bog, but the other one sinks all the deeper. We have rescued our actions from the bonds of evil, but our judgments are now held fast. When murders and treacheries cease to be sins, regrets are theoretic absurdities and errors. The theoretic and the active life thus play a kind

of seesaw with each other on the ground of evil. The rise of either sends the other down. Murder and treachery cannot be good without regret being bad; regret cannot be good without treachery and murder being bad. Both, however, are supposed to have been foredoomed; so something must be fatally unreasonable, absurd, and wrong in the world. It must be a place of which either sin or error forms a necessary part. From this dilemma there seems at first sight no escape. Are we then so soon to fall back into the pessimism from which we thought we had emerged? And is there no possible way by which we may, with good intellectual consciences, call the cruelties and the treacheries, the reluctances and the regrets, *all* good together?

Certainly there is such a way, and you are probably most of you ready to formulate it yourselves. But, before doing so, remark how inevitably the question of determinism and indeterminism slides us into the question of optimism and pessimism, or, as our fathers called it, "the question of evil." The theological form of all these disputes is the simplest and the deepest, the form from which there is the least escape—not because, as some have sarcastically said, remorse and regret are clung to with a morbid fondness by the theologians as spiritual luxuries, but because they are existing facts of the world, and as such must be taken into account in the deterministic interpretation of all that is fated to be. If they are fated to be error, does not the bat's wing of irrationality still cast its shadow over the world?

The refuge from the quandary lies, as I said, not far off. The necessary acts we erroneously regret may be good, and yet our error in so regretting them may be also good, on one simple condition; and that condition is this: the world must not be regarded as a machine whose final purpose is the making real of any outward good, but rather as a contrivance for deepening the theoretic consciousness of what goodness and evil in their intrinsic natures are. Not the doing either of good or of evil is what nature cares for, but the knowing of them.

Life is one long eating of the fruit of the tree of *knowledge*. I am in the habit, in thinking to myself, of calling this point of view the *gnostical* point of view. According to it, the world is neither an optimism nor a pessimism, but a *gnosticism*. But as this term may perhaps lead to some misunderstandings, I will use it as little as possible here, and speak rather of *subjectivism*, and the *subjectivistic* point of view.

Subjectivism has three great branches—we may call them scientificism, sentimentalism, and sensualism, respectively. They all agree essentially about the universe, in deeming that what happens there is subsidiary to what we think or feel about it. Crime justifies its criminality by awakening our intelligence of that criminality, and eventually our remorses and regrets; and the error included in remorses and regrets, the error of supposing that the past could have been different, justifies itself by its use. Its use is to quicken our sense of *what* the irretrievably lost is. When we think of it as that which might have been: ("the saddest words of tongue or pen"), the quality of its worth speaks to us with a wilder sweetness; and, conversely, the dissatisfaction wherewith we think of what seems to have driven it from its natural place gives us the severer pang. Admirable artifice of nature! we might be tempted to exclaim—deceiving us in order the better to enlighten us, and leaving nothing undone to accentuate to our consciousness the yawning distance of those opposite poles of good and evil between which creation swings.

We have thus clearly revealed to our view what may be called the dilemma of determinism, so far as determinism pretends to think things out at all. A merely mechanical determinism, it is true, rather rejoices in not thinking them out. It is very sure that the universe must satisfy its postulate of a physical continuity and coherence, but it smiles at anyone who comes forward with a postulate of moral coherence as well. I may suppose, however, that the number of purely mechanical, or hard, determinists among you this evening is

small. The determinism to whose seductions you are most exposed is what I have called soft determinism—the determinism which allows considerations of good and bad to mingle with those of cause and effect in deciding what sort of universe this may rationally be held to be. The dilemma of this determinism is one whose left horn is pessimism and whose right horn is subjectivism. In other words, if determinism is to escape pessimism, it must leave off looking at the goods and ills of life in a simple objective way, and regard them as materials, indifferent in themselves, for the production of consciousness, scientific and ethical, in us.

To escape pessimism is, as we all know, no easy task. Your own studies have sufficiently shown you the almost desperate difficulty of making the notion that there is a single principle of things, and that principle absolute perfection, rhyme together with our daily vision of the facts of life. If perfection be the principle, how comes there any imperfection here? If God be good, how came he to create—or, if he did not create, how comes he to permit—the devil? The evil facts must be explained as seeming: the devil must be whitewashed, the universe must be disinfected, if neither God's goodness nor his unity and power are to remain impugned. And of all the various ways of operating the disinfection, and making bad seem less bad, the way of subjectivism appears by far the best.*

For, after all, is there not something rather absurd in our ordinary notion of external things being good or bad in them-

*To a reader who says he is satisfied with a pessimism, and has no objection to thinking the whole bad, I have no more to say: he makes fewer demands on the world than I, who, making them, wish to look a little further before I give up all hope of having them satisfied. If, however, all he means is that the badness of some parts does not prevent his acceptance of a universe whose *other* parts give him satisfaction, I welcome him as an ally. He has abandoned the notion of the *Whole*, which is the essence of deterministic monism, and views things as a pluralism, just as I do in this paper.

selves? Can murders and treacheries, considered as mere outward happenings, or motions of matter, be bad without anyone to feel their badness? And could paradise properly be good in the absence of a sentient principle by which the goodness was perceived? Outward goods and evils seem practically indistinguishable except insofar as they result in getting moral judgments made about them. But then the moral judgments seem the main thing, and the outward facts mere perishing instruments for their production. This is subjectivism. Everyone must at some time have wondered at that strange paradox of our moral nature, that, though the pursuit of outward good is the breath of its nostrils, the attainment of outward good would seem to be its suffocation and death. Why does the painting of any paradise or utopia, in heaven or on earth, awaken such yawnings for nirvana and escape? The white-robed, harp-playing heaven of our sabbath-schools, and the ladylike tea table elysium represented in Mr. Spencer's Data of Ethics, as the final consummation of progress, are exactly on a part in this respect—lubberlands, pure and simple, one and all. We look upon them from this delicious mess of insanities and realities, strivings and deadnesses, hopes and fears, agonies and exultations, which forms our present state, and *tedium vitae* is the only sentiment they awaken in our breasts. To our crepuscular natures, born for the conflict, the Rembrandtesque moral chiaroscuro, the shifting struggle of the sunbeam in the gloom, such pictures of light upon light are vacuous and expressionless, and neither to be enjoyed nor understood. If *this* be the whole fruit of the victory, we say; if the generations of mankind suffered and laid down their lives; if prophets confessed and martyrs sang in the fire, and all the sacred tears were shed for no other end than that a race of creatures of such unexampled insipidity should succeed, and protract in *saecula saeculorum* their contented and inoffensive lives—why, at such a rate better lose than win the battle, or at all events better ring down the curtain before the last act of the play so that a business that began so importantly may be saved from so singularly flat a winding-up.

All this is what I should instantly say, were I called on to plead for gnosticism; and its real friends of whom you will presently perceive I am not one, would say without difficulty a great deal more. Regarded as a stable finality, every outward good becomes a mere weariness to the flesh. It must be menaced, be occasionally lost, for its goodness to be fully felt as such. Nay, more than occasionally lost. No one knows the worth of innocence till he knows it is gone forever, and that money cannot buy it back. Not the saint, but the sinner that repenteth, is he to whom the full length and breadth, and height and depth, of life's meaning is revealed. Not the absence of vice, but vice there, and virtue holding her by the throat, seems the ideal human state. And there seems no reason to suppose it not a permanent human state. There is a deep truth in what the school of Schopenhauer insists on—the illusoriness of the notion of moral progress. The more brutal forms of evil that go are replaced by others more subtle and more poisonous. Our moral horizon moves with us as we move, and never do we draw nearer to the far-off line where the black waves and the azure meet. The final purpose of our creation seems most plausibly to be the greatest possible enrichment of our ethical consciousness, through the intensest play of contrasts and the widest diversity of characters. This of course obliges some of us to be vessels of wrath, while it calls others to be vessels of honor. But the subjectivist point of view reduces all these outward distinctions to a common denominator. The wretch languishing in the felon's cell may be drinking draughts of the wine of truth that will never pass the lips of the so-called favorite of fortune. And the peculiar consciousness of each of them is an indispensable note in the great ethical concert which the centuries as they roll are grinding out of the living heart of man.

So much for subjectivism! If the dilemma of determinism be to choose between it and pessimism, I see little room for hesitation from the strictly theoretical point of view. Subjectivism seems the more rational scheme. And the world may, possibly, for aught I know, be nothing else. When the healthy love of life is on one, and all its forms and its appetites seem so unutterably real; when the most brutal and the most spiritual things are lit by the same sun, and each is an integral part of the total richness—why, then it seems a grudging and sickly way of meeting so robust a universe to shrink from any of its facts and wish them not to be. Rather take the strictly dramatic point of view, and treat the whole thing as a great unending romance which the spirit of the universe, striving to realize its own content, is eternally thinking out and representing to itself.

No one, I hope, will accuse me, after I have said all this, of underrating the reasons in favor of subjectivism. And now that I proceed to say why those reasons, strong as they are, fail to convince my own mind, I trust the presumption may be that my objections are stronger still.

I frankly confess that they are of a practical order. If we practically take up subjectivism in a sincere and radical manner and follow its consequences, we meet with some that make us pause. Let a subjectivism begin in never so severe and intellectual a way, it is forced by the law of its nature to develop another side of itself and end with the corruptest curiosity. Once dismiss the notion that certain duties are good in themselves, and that we are here to do them, no matter how we feel about them; once consecrate the opposite notion that our performances and our violations of duty are for a common purpose, the attainment of subjective knowledge and feeling, and that the deepening of these is the chief end of our lives—and at what point on the downward slope are we to stop? In theology, subjectivism develops as its "left wing" antinomianism. In literature, its left wing is romanticism. And in practical life it is either a nerveless sentimentality or a sensualism without bounds.

Everywhere it fosters the fatalistic mood of mind. It makes those who are already too inert more passive still; it renders wholly reckless those whose energy is already in excess. All through history we find how subjectivism, as soon as it has a free career, exhausts itself in every sort of spiritual, moral, and practical license. Its optimism turns to an ethical indifference, which infallibly brings dissolution in its train. It is perfectly safe to say now that if the Hegelian gnosticism, which has begun to show itself here and in Great Britain, were to become a popular philosophy, as it once was in Germany, it would certainly develop its left wing here as there, and produce a reaction of disgust. Already I have heard a graduate of this very school express in the pulpit his willingness to sin like David, if only he might repent like David. You may tell me he was only sowing his wild, or rather his tame, oats; and perhaps he was. But the point is that in the subjectivistic or gnostical philosophy, oat-sowing, wild or tame, becomes a systematic necessity and the chief function of life. After the pure and classic truths, the exciting and rancid ones must be experienced; and if the stupid virtues of the Philistine herd do not then come and save society from the influence of the children of light, a sort of inward putrefaction becomes its inevitable doom.

• • •

And here I might legitimately stop, having expressed all I care to see admitted by others tonight. But I know that if I do stop here, misapprehensions will remain in the minds of some of you, and keep all I have said from having its effect; so I judge it best to add a few more words.

In the first place, in spite of all my explanations, the word "chance" will still be giving trouble. Though you may yourselves be adverse to the deterministic doctrine, you wish a pleasanter word than "chance" to name the opposite doctrine by; and you very likely consider my preference for such a word a perverse sort of a partiality on my part. It certainly *is* a bad word to make converts with; and you wish I had not thrust it so butt-foremost at you—you wish to use a milder term.

Well, I admit there may be just a dash of perversity in its choice. The spectacle of the mere word-grabbing game played by the soft determinists has perhaps driven me too violently the other way; and, rather than be found wrangling with them for the good words, I am willing to take the first bad one which comes along, provided it be unequivocal. The question is of things, not of eulogistic names for them; and the best word is the one that enables men to know the quickest whether they disagree or not about the things. But the word "chance," with its singular negativity, is just the word for this purpose. Whoever uses it instead of "freedom," squarely and resolutely gives up all pretense to control the things he says are free. For *him*, he confesses that they are no better than mere chance would be. It is a word of *impotence,* and is therefore the only sincere word we can use, if, in granting freedom to certain things, we grant it honestly, and really risk the game. "Who chooses me must give and forfeit all he hath." Any other word permits of quibbling, and lets us, after the fashion of the soft determinists, make a pretense of restoring the caged bird to liberty with one hand, while with the other we anxiously tie a string to its leg to make sure it does not get beyond our sight.

But now you will bring up your final doubt. Does not the admission of such an unguaranteed chance or freedom preclude utterly the notion of a Providence governing the world? Does it not leave the fate of the universe at the mercy of the chance-possibilities, and so far insecure? Does it not, in short, deny the craving of our nature for an ultimate peace behind all tempests, for a blue zenith above all clouds?

To this my answer must be very brief. The belief in free-will is not in the least incompatible with the belief in Providence, provided you do not restrict the Providence to fulminating nothing but *fatal* decrees. If you allow him to provide possibilities as well as actualities to the universe, and to carry on his own thinking in those two categories just as we do ours, chances may be there, uncontrolled even by him, and the course of the universe be really ambiguous; and yet the end of all things may be just what he intended it to be from all eternity.

An analogy will make the meaning of this clear. Suppose two men before a chessboard—the one a novice, the other an expert player of the game. The expert intends to beat. But he cannot foresee exactly what any one actual move of his adversary may be. He knows, however, all the *possible* moves of the latter; and he knows in advance how to meet each of them by a move of his own which leads in the direction of victory. And the victory infallibly arrives, after no matter how devious a course, in the one predestined form of checkmate to the novice's king.

Let now the novice stand for us finite free agents, and the expert for the infinite mind in which the universe lies. Suppose the latter to be thinking out his universe before he actually creates it. Suppose him to say, I will lead things to a certain end, but I will not *now* decide on all the steps thereto. At various points, ambiguous possibilities shall be left open, either of which, at a given instant, may become actual. But whichever branch of these bifurcations become real, I know what I shall do at the *next* bifurcation to keep things from drifting away from the final result I intend.

The Creator's plan of the universe would thus be left blank as to many of its actual details, but all possibilities would be marked down. The realization of some of these would be left absolutely to chance; that is, would only be determined when the moment of realization came. Other possibilities would be *contingently* determined; that is, their decision would have to wait till it was seen how the matters of absolute chance fell out. But the rest of the plan, including its final upshot, would be rigorously determined once for all. So the Creator himself would not need to know *all* the details of actuality until they came; and at any time his own view of the world would be a view partly of facts and partly of possibilities, exactly as ours is now. Of one thing, however, he might be certain; and that is that his world was safe, and that no matter how much it might zigzag he could surely bring it home at last.

Now, it is entirely immaterial, in this scheme, whether the Creator leave the absolute chance-possibilities to be decided by himself, each when its proper moment arrives, or whether, on the contrary, he alienate this power from himself, and leave the decision out-and-out to finite creatures such as we men are. The great point is that the possibilities are really *here*. Whether it be we who solve them or he working through us, at those soul-trying moments when fate's scales seem to quiver, and good snatches the victory from evil or shrinks nerveless from the fight, is of small account, so long as we admit that the issue is decided nowhere else than *here* and *now*. *That* is what gives the palpitating reality to our moral life and makes it tingle, as Mr. Mallock says, with so strange and elaborate an excitement. This reality, this excitement, are what the determinists, hard and soft alike, suppress by their denial that

anything is decided here and now, and their dogma that all things were foredoomed and settled long ago. If it be so, may you and I then have been foredoomed to the error of continuing to believe in liberty. It is fortunate for the winding up of controversy that in every discussion with determinism this *argumentum ad hominem* can be its adversary's last word.

STUDY QUESTIONS

1. What does James mean by "chance"? Why does he attach such importance to it?
2. How does James distinguish between determinism and indeterminism? Hard determinism and soft determinism?
3. What is the significance of James' "Divinity Avenue" and "Oxford Street" illustration?
4. Explain in your own words what James means by "the dilemma of determinism." Do you see any escape from this dilemma?
5. Do you agree with James that no objective resolution of the free will-determinism controversy is possible? Why then should anyone take a stand on either side?

For Further Reading appears on page 157.

✌ Grünbaum: *Causality and the Science of Human Behavior*

It is not uncommon to find that even those who have complete confidence in the continued success of the scientific method when applied to inanimate nature are highly skeptical of its applicability to the study of human behavior. Some go so far as to assert quite categorically that the methods of the natural sciences are in principle incompetent to yield predictions

From *American Scientist*, Vol. 40 (1952). Reprinted by permission of *American Scientist*, journal of Sigma Xi, The Scientific Research Society.

of man's individual or social behavior. Thus, for example, Dilthey and his followers in the *Geisteswissenschaften* movement*

---

*In the latter part of the nineteenth century, W. Dilthey spearheaded an influential movement whose representatives claimed that the theoretical task of the natural sciences is fundamentally different from that of the social sciences and humanities. The aim of the natural sciences was said to be generalization, whereas the social sciences were held to seek the articulation of individuality.

insist on the methodological autonomy of psychology and the social sciences, claiming that intelligent goal-seeking, which is so characteristic of man, calls for a method differing *toto genere* from that of the physical sciences.

Several important arguments have been offered against the hypothesis that cause-effect relationships exist in human behavior. These arguments are intended to deny the possibility of making the predictions which only the existence of such relationships would render feasible. In this article I shall attempt to show that the arguments in question are invalid and that there are good reasons for accepting the causal hypothesis against which they are directed. Many of the ideas to be discussed here have been previously outlined or developed by other authors in diverse contexts; wherever possible, references are given to these writings.

Before analyzing critically some of the reasons which have been given for supposing that human behavior is inherently unpredictable, I wish to point out several important consequences of this widely held belief, and also of its denial. It is essential to state explicitly what these consequences are, since few of the proponents of this doctrine realize all of its implications.

If human behavior, both individual and social, does not exhibit cause-effect sequences, then the scientific method is essentially irrelevant to the elucidation of the nature of man, and both scientific psychology and the social sciences are permanently barred from achieving the status of sciences. This conclusion follows, since it is the essence of a scientific explanation in any field outside of pure mathematics to "explain" a past phenomenon or predict a future event by showing that these are instances of a certain law (or laws) and that their occurrence is attributable to the fact that the conditions for the applicability of the relevant law(s) were satisfied. Therefore, scientific or rational learning from past experience consists in ascertaining causal regularities from which to anticipate the future. Accordingly, to deny the existence of uniformities in human behavior, both individual and social, is to assert that significant lessons cannot be drawn from the past and that man's future is capricious and elusive. Nevertheless, some historians and social scientists tell us that the absence of causal law is the distinguishing feature of their subject as contrasted with the natural sciences. In the same breath, they maintain that the only way in which individuals and nations will become manageable is by a drastic intensification in the cultivation of the social studies. It is plain that this position is untenable. For nothing can be learned from history regarding the wise conduct of international relations, if no such wisdom is to be found in history. The distinction between wisdom and foolishness in practical affairs first becomes meaningful through the existence of cause-effect relationships in human behavior, and by reference to the predictions which the existence of these relationships makes possible. Rules for managing individuals and nations can be based only on causal laws which tell us that *if* such and such is done, it is likely that the outcome will be thus and so, either in all cases or in an explicitly stated percentage of cases. It is useless to bemoan the great gap between our mastery of physical nature and our scientific understanding of man, if one denies the existence of the conditions which alone would make a scientific analysis of man possible. Only if human behavior does display some kind of causal law is it significant to emphasize the need for closing the dangerous gap between man's control over physical nature and his scientific knowledge of himself lest he destroy himself.

By contrast, the assumption that causal laws are discoverable in human behavior presents enormous possibilities. For in this case we can ask the social scientist to ascertain what means will bring about given ends. Thus it is possible to get a factually true rather than an emotional answer to some of the burning questions of our time. For example, we could hope for an authentic answer to the question, What system of organizing economic relationships will in fact lead to the maximum satisfaction of certain types of human needs? Whatever the answers to such questions, they would merit the assent of all rational men who share the same goals. To be sure, the history of physical science does record the defiance and acrimony evinced by men whose theories failed to be confirmed by the evidence. Nevertheless, we have learned to reject physical theories which fail to pass the test of observable fact, no matter how ingenious the theory or how dear it may be to our hearts when first propounded. For this reason the history of physical science is in a sense the history of discarded theories. What an advance toward sanity it would be, if it were equally generally accepted that theories of human nature, like physical theories, need careful, disciplined checking through observation. In our time, the ordinary person is very much aware of the need for scrupulous care in ascertaining the facts of nature but will hold forth dogmatically and evangelically about the alleged facts of "human nature." Despite the serious divisions among mankind today, most scientific knowledge concerning inanimate nature commands assent among thinking men everywhere. It would seem, therefore, that scientific knowledge of man, specifying the requirements for attaining given ends, would also merit such universal assent. In so far as this assent would actually be forthcoming, it would constitute a partial step toward human brotherhood.

So much for the implications of rival answers to the issue under discussion. Let us now deal directly with the merits of the answers themselves.

Arguments Against Causality in Human Behavior, and Their Refutation.
There are four arguments which I wish to consider against the hypothesis that causality is present in human behavior. These are:

1. Human behavior is not amenable to causal description and therefore not predictable, since each individual is unique and not exactly like anyone else.
2. Even if there is a causal order in the phenomena of human behavior, it is so complex as to elude discovery permanently.
3. In the physical sciences, a present fact is always determined by past facts, but in human behavior present behavior is oriented toward future goals and thus "determined" by these future goals.
4. If human behavior were part of the causal order of events and thereby in principle predictable, it would be futile to attempt to make a choice between good and evil, meaningless to hold men responsible for their deeds, unjust to inflict punishment, and naive to take seriously such remorse or guilt as is professed for past misdeeds. In short, the argument is that to assume the principle of causality in human behavior is incompatible with the known fact that people respond meaningfully to moral imperatives.

In the following pages I shall try to show that all four of these arguments are the result of superficial or specious analysis. The fourth has been by far the most influential and was invoked in the pages of this journal a few years ago.

Argument from the Uniqueness of Human Individuals.
This objection to the possibility of constructing a scientific psychology rests on several misunderstandings of the meaning of causality in science. To remove these misunderstandings it must be pointed out that *all* particulars in the world are unique, whether they are physical objects like trees, physical events like light flashes, or human beings. The mere assertion that a thing is a particular, means that it is in one way or another unique, different from all other objects of its own kind or of other kinds. Every insignificant tick of my watch is a unique event, for no two ticks can be simultaneous with a given third event. With respect to uniqueness, each tick is on a par with Lincoln's delivery of the Gettysburg address! It is clear, however, that the uniqueness of physical events does not pre-

vent them from being connected by causal laws, for present causal laws relate only *some* of the features of a given set of events with *some* of the features of another set of events. For example, frictional processes are accompanied by the development of heat in so far as they are frictional, whatever else they may be. A projectile fired under suitable conditions will describe a parabolic orbit regardless of the color of the projectile, its place of manufacture, and so on. Since the cause-effect relation is a relation between *kinds* of events, it is never necessary that all the features of a given cause be duplicated in order to produce the same kind of effect. It follows that when scientific psychologists assume the existence of causal laws for human behavior, this standpoint is not incompatible with the existence of great individual differences among men, nor does it infringe on the uniqueness and dignity of each particular person.

Every individual is unique by virtue of being a distinctive assemblage of characteristics not precisely duplicated in any other individual. Nevertheless, it is quite conceivable that the following psychological law *might* hold: If a male child having specifiable characteristics is subjected to maternal hostility and has a strong paternal attachment at a certain stage of his development, he will develop paranoia during adult life. If this law holds, then children who are subjected to the stipulated conditions would in fact become paranoiacs, however much they may have differed in other respects in childhood and whatever their other differences may be once they are already insane.

A variant of the argument against scientific psychology is that no psychologist can ever feel exactly like each of the diverse people whose feelings and behavior he is trying to understand. This form of the argument contains an additional misconception of the kind of understanding or explanation that is sought by science—the impression that in order to explain aspects of human experience or behavior scientifically, the psychologist must himself directly have the experience in question in all its complexity. One who objects to scientific psychology on these grounds virtually equates scientific understanding with genuinely empathic understanding. To understand a phenomenon scientifically, however, is, in the first place, to know the conditions necessary for its occurrence. A physician interested in understanding cancer (including the psychic consequences of that disease) is not interested in becoming a cancer victim himself but only in knowing the conditions associated with the occurrence and non-occurrence of cancer. Strictly empathic understanding may have great heuristic value and sometimes aesthetic value as well. However, from the standpoint of achieving scientific understanding and making the predictions which such mastery makes possible, the empathic method in psychology and in history (Dilthey) is quite insufficient.

The Argument from the Complexity of Human Behavior. This argument, it will be recalled, is to the effect that human behavior involves so complex a proliferation of factors that it is futile to attempt to unravel them. A glance at the history of science will deprive this point of view of such plausibility as it may possess. Consider what a person advancing such an argument about psychology today would have said about the physics of motion before the time of Galileo. Probably he would have said that it is hopeless to attempt to reduce the vast diversity of terrestrial and celestial motions to a few simple laws of motion. Before the rise of scientific chemistry, this kind of person would have dismissed the possibility of reducing the seemingly unsurveyable variety of substances in nature to some 96 elements. This argument rests its case on what is not known, and therefore, like all such arguments, it has no case.

The Argument from the "Determination" of the Present by the Future in Goal-seeking Human Behavior. If a person is now taking action toward the realization of a future goal, it is argued that the immediate action is the effect of a future cause—a kind of causation not encountered among physical phenomena. The answer to this contention is that, not the future goal-event, but rather the present expectation of its realization causally controls forward-looking behavior. Indeed, the goal sought may never be attained. Moreover, both the motives for achieving the given goal and the contemplation of action in its behalf function as antecedent conditions in the same way as the causal factors in physical phenomena. Thus in motivational situations causal determination is quite unaffected by the ideational reference of motives to the future.

The Argument from Moral Choice.   The name "determinism" is applied to the thesis that all phenomena, including those of human behavior, fall into causal patterns. This formulation of determinism is logically objectionable in some respects, but it will suffice for this discussion. It is clear that determinism is one of the key (regulative) principles of all scientific research. The denial of determinism is called "indeterminism," and the indeterminist argument from moral choice to be considered here has been summarized by a critic somewhat as follows: If determinism is true, then my will also is always determined by my character and my motives. Hence I do not make free choices and should not be held responsible for my acts, since I can do nothing about my decisions and cannot help doing what I do. If the determinist is right; I have not chosen either my motives or my character; my motives come to me from both external and internal causes and my character is the necessary product of the influences which have been effective during my lifetime. Thus determinism and moral responsibility are incompatible. Moral responsibility presupposes freedom, that is, exemption from causality.

The question before us is whether the argument of the indeterminist is valid. Before arguing that the answer to this question is emphatically in the negative, I wish to distinguish between two types of determinism and attempt to show that they must

each be objectionable to the indeterminist, once he has set forth his argument from moral choice.

The first type of determinism is the 100 per cent type, which maintains that under specifiable conditions a specifiable outcome will occur in all cases. For example, whenever a metal is heated (under ordinary conditions) it will expand. The second type of determinism is the statistical type, which maintains (roughly) that under specifiable conditions a certain result will occur but only in an explicitly stated percentage of cases. An instance of this is the statement that of all the people born in slums, 80 per cent will commit a crime at some time during their lifetime. The claim which I wish to make first is that if the moral argument of the indeterminist were valid against the 100 per cent type of determinism, it would also have relevance against the statistical type of determinism. This point is particularly important, since many indeterminists attempt to acknowledge the incontestable existence of an impressive measure of regularity in human behavior by emphasizing that they object on moral grounds only to the 100 per cent type of determinism and not to the statistical type.

To establish my case, let us suppose that, contrary to fact, we knew that all hunters are subject to the following 100 per cent deterministic law: All hunters commit homicide at some time after returning from jungle life. The indeterminist would say that if these hunters were really subject to such a causal law, they could not help becoming murderers and therefore we should have no right to punish them for their crimes. What would the position taken by the indeterminist have to be if we had a statistical type of law stating with near certainty that, of all the people born in slums, in the long run 80 per cent will commit a crime at some time during their lifetime? To be sure, this statistical law would not entitle us to say that any particular individual(s) born in the slums will become criminal; hence, it does not preclude the possibility that some particular person (or persons) be among the 20 per cent whose conduct is legal and that, to this extent, the person in question be regarded as having acted "freely" in the indeterminist sense. In so far as responsibility is an individual matter, it might even seem that our statistical law would permit the indeterminist to employ his own criteria for assigning individual responsibility to as many as 20 per cent of those persons originating in the slums. But if the 80 per cent who actually did commit a crime at some time during a long interval of time were simultaneously brought to trial before a judge holding the indeterminist point of view, the statistical law in question would deny him the logical right of making individual assignments of responsibility; this law would not enable the judge to designate among the culprits any one or any group of whom it could meaningfully be said that they "could" have avoided the crime by being among the 20 per cent who did, in fact, avoid it. For if a procedure for carrying out such a designation were possible—which it is not—the statistical law would remind us that not only all the remaining defendants arraigned before the judge but also some of those actually belonging to the 20 per cent *could then not have helped* violating the statutes. This means that if over a long period of time we select all those having originated in a slum and not guilty of any crime, the remainder having a similar origin will *always* as a matter of fact commit a crime and will constitute 80 per cent of those born in slums. Thus by the indeterminist's own criteria for assigning responsibility, the judge would not be able to carry out such an assignment individually as he must, because sufficient causality is assured by the statistical law to preclude his doing so consistently with indeterminist premises. If the indeterminist denies the justice of punishment, as he does in the case of 100 per cent determinism, he cannot assent to the punishment of individuals belonging to groups concerning which statistical laws make only a statistical prediction of conduct. Accordingly, the indeterminist must

have moral objections to 100 per cent determinism and statistical determinism alike. This means that he must be a foe of the belief that any kind of scientific study of man is possible!

To establish the invalidity of the moral argument offered by the indeterminist, I shall now try to show that there is no incompatibility between the deterministic assumptions of scientific psychology on the one hand and the meaningful assignment of responsibility, the infliction of punishment, and the existence of feelings of remorse or guilt on the other.

Causality and Moral Responsibility

The first point to be made clear is that determinism should never be identified with the prescientific and primitive doctrine of fatalism. The fatalist says that regardless of what we do, the outcome will be the same. By contrast, the determinist says that *if* we do such and such, *then* the effect will be thus and so. The fatalist thinks that if you go into combat, and if "some bullet has your name on it," you will be killed no matter what you do. Thus he would say that when a natural disaster occurs, it does not matter whether you are at the scene of the disaster or not; if you are not there but are "destined to die" that day, you will be destroyed some other way. The determinist maintains that a person will die on a certain day only if the conditions which lead to death materialize for that person on that day, as indeed they do at some time for each of us. Unlike fatalism, determinism allows causal efficacy to human actions.

The second point to keep in mind is that physical laws do not in any sense force bodies to behave in a certain way, but merely describe how, as a matter of fact, they do behave. Similarly, psychological laws do not force us to do or desire anything against our will. These laws merely state what, as a matter of fact, we do or desire under certain conditions. Thus if there were a psychological law enabling us to predict that under certain conditions a man will desire to commit a certain act, this law would not be making him act in a manner contrary to his own desires, for the desire would be his. It follows that neither the causes of our desires nor psychological laws, which state under what conditions our desires arise, compel us in any way to act in a manner contrary to our own will.

An illustration will show that district attorneys are determinists, since they assume in their work a definite casual connection between motives and acts. In a recent French film we find a district attorney married to a rather unsophisticated lady whom he had been suspecting of violating her marital vows. While speaking to her, he found a seemingly innocent way of mentioning the name of his rival. She promptly gulped, and then tried to maintain with studied innocence that she had had no motive at all for gulping. He insisted that she had had a very definite motive, and as it turned out he was right.

It should not be thought that the indeterminist is now prepared to surrender, for he has yet to use his strongest weapon. Says he: "We are all familiar with the fact that when we look back upon past conduct, we frequently feel very strongly that we could have done otherwise. If the determinist is right in saying that our behavior was unavoidably determined by earlier causes, this retrospective feeling of freedom either should not exist or else it is fraudulent. In either case, the burden of proof rests upon him." The determinist gladly accepts this challenge, and his reply is as follows: Let us carefully examine the content of the feeling that on a certain occasion we could have acted other than the way we did, in fact, act. What do we find? Does the feeling we have inform us that we could have acted otherwise *under exactly the same external and internal motivational conditions*? No, says the determinist, this feeling simply discloses that we were able to act in accord with our strongest desire at that time, and that we could indeed have acted otherwise if a different motive had prevailed at the time. Thus the determinist answer is that the content of this "consciousness of freedom" consists in our awareness that we were able to act in response to our strongest motive at

the time, and that we were not "under compulsion" in that sense. But the determinist reminds us that our feeling of "freedom" does not disclose that, given the motives which acted on us at the time and given their relative strength and distribution, we could have acted differently from the way in which we did, in fact, act. Neither do we feel that we could have responded to the weaker of two contending motives, or acted without a cause or motive, or chosen the motives which acted upon us. Since the retrospective feeling of freedom that we have does not report any of these results, its deliverances contain no facts incompatible with the claim of the determinist.

The analysis we have offered is applicable at once to the case of remorse, regret, or guilt. We sometimes experience remorse over past conduct when we reconsider that conduct in the light of *different* motives. Once we bring a different set of motives to bear on a given situation, we may feel that a different decision is called for. If our motives do not change, we do not regret a past deed no matter how reprehensible it would otherwise appear. Regret is an expression of our emotion toward the disvalue and injustice which issued from our past conduct, as seen in the light of the new motives. The regret we experience can then act as a deterrent against the repetition of past behavior which issued in disvalue. If the determinist expresses regret concerning past misconduct, he is applying motives of self-improvement to himself but not indulging in retroactive self-castigation or blame. Retroactive blame is futile, since the past will never return again. Thus, by responsibility the determinist does not mean retroactive blameworthiness, but rather liability to reformative or educative punishment. Punishment is educative in the sense that when properly administered it institutes counter-causes to the repetition of injurious conduct. The determinist rejects as barbarous the primitive vengeful idea of retaliatory punishment. He fails to see how the damage done by the wrongdoer is remedied by the mere infliction of pain or sorrow on the culprit, unless such infliction of pain promises to act as a *causal* deterrent against the repetition of evil conduct. We recall that the indeterminist accused the determinist of cruelly punishing people who, if determinism is true, cannot help acting as they do. The determinist now turns the tables on his anatagonist and accuses him of being gratuitously vengeful, on the grounds that the indeterminist is committed by his own theory to a retaliatory theory of punishment. The indeterminist cannot consistently expect to achieve anything better than retaliation by inflicting punishment; for were he to admit that punishment will causally influence all or some of the criminals, then he would be abandoning the basis of his entire argument against the determinist. We see that determinism does not entail the doctrine *tout comprendre, c'est tout pardonner.*

What does the determinist believe about the application of punishment? From his point of view, punishment should be administered to the person upon whom the decisive motive acted, for that person is the essential junction of causes, and it is he who is likely to cause harm again if unpunished. Thus the doctrine of the determinist does not commit him to punishing the parents or social environment of the culprit for the culprit's deeds, even though they are the basic cause of his misconduct. Such a procedure would be of no avail if the aim is to rehabilitate the wrongdoer. There are two types of cases, however, in which the determinist does not apply punishment. When a person is acting under compulsion, he is being prevented from implementing his own desires. In that event, his internal state irrelevant to what he does. Since his internal state needs no reforming, punishment would be completely misplaced in such a case. Again, in the case of insane behavior the determinist does not apply punishment, since insane people provide no unified point for the application of a counter-motive. More specifically, their internal state is not responsive to the external influences of punishment, and therefore the infliction of punishment

upon them cannot be counted on to change their future behavior in the desired direction. Once Ophelia had lost her mind, even Hamlet's words could have no effect on her, and similarly for Marguerite and Faust.

It is apparent that the entire problem of responsibility can be solved within the domain of deterministic assumptions. Thus the issue is not *whether* conduct is determined but rather *by what factors* it is determined, when responsibility is to be assigned. Far from facing insuperable difficulties with the problem of responsibility, the determinist and the scientific psychologist now challenge the indeterminist to provide a logical foundation for the penal system.

Other Arguments of the Indeterminist

It is sometimes said that, when applied to man, the deterministic doctrine becomes untenable by virtue of becoming self-contradictory. This contention is often stated as follows: "The determinist, by his own doctrine, must admit that his very acceptance of determinism was causally conditioned or determined. Since he could not help accepting it, he cannot argue that he has chosen a true doctrine." To justify this claim, it is first pointed out rightly that determinism implies a causal determination of its own acceptance by its defenders. Then it is further maintained, however, that since the determinist could not, by his own theory, help accepting determinism, he can have no confidence in its truth. Thus it is asserted that the determinist's acceptance of his own doctrine was forced upon him. I submit that this inference involves a radical fallacy. The proponent of this argument is gratuitously invoking the view that if our beliefs have causes, these causes *force* the beliefs in question upon us, against our better judgment, as it were. Nothing could be further from the truth. My belief that I am now looking at symbols on paper derives from the fact that their presence is causally inducing certain images on the retinas of my eyes, and that these images, in turn, cause me to infer that corresponding symbols are actually present before me. The reason why I do not suppose that I am now addressing a group of students in a classroom is that the images which the students would produce are not now in my visual field. The causal generation of a belief in no way detracts from its reliability. In fact, if a given belief were not produced in us by definite causes, we should have no reason to accept that belief as a correct description of the world, rather than some other belief arbitrarily selected. Far from making knowledge either adventitious or impossible, the deterministic theory about the origin of our beliefs alone provides the basis for thinking that our judgments of the world are or may be true. Knowing and judging are indeed causal processes in which the facts we judge are determining elements along with the cerebral mechanism employed in their interpretation. It follows that although the determinist's assent to his own doctrine is caused or determined, the truth of determinism is not jeopardized by this fact; if anything, it is made credible.

We have yet to consider the bearing of developments in atomic physics on this problem, since a number of writers have argued that these developments provide evidence for the indeterminist position.

It is known that for measurements in the domain of subatomic dimensions, the Heisenberg Uncertainty Relation comes into play. This relation states that for a given uncertainty or vagueness in the value of an observable quantity like position, there is a definite limit, imposed by the laws of nature, on the accuracy with which the simultaneous value of another empirical quantity like velocity can be known, and that this limit is independent of the paticular apparatus or method used in the determination. Since the apparatus used in measurement disturbs the system under observation, it would seem that the possibilities for refining measurements are not unlimited and that the dream of classical physics can therefore never come true. No refinement of experimental technique could ascertain the present values of the observables of a physical system accu-

rately enough to enable us to make a *precise* prediction of the future values. Consequently, the new quantum mechanics is content to specify the frequencies or probabilities with which different values will be found in a given set of measurements. These probability predictions are thus based on a statistico-determinism for the micro-processes of subatomic physics rather than upon the 100 per cent type of determinism which prevails in the physics of the macrocosm.

What are the implications of this situation for the controversy between the philosophical indeterminist and the scientific psychologist? In his *Atomic Theory and the Description of Nature*, Bohr gives several reasons for supposing that the most precise experimentally ascertainable knowledge of the momentary state of the constituent particles of the nervous system and of the external stimuli affecting it permits only a statistical prediction and not a completely detailed prediction of the fate of these stimuli in the nervous system. Nevertheless, there are important reasons why the philosophical indeterminist can derive no comfort from this situation. It has already been shown that if the moral argument for indeterminism is to be valid, statistico-determinism is objectionable along with 100 per cent determinism. For genuine free will would prevail only if the quantum theory were to conclude that all human acts (macrophenomena) can occur with the same frequency. But the theory does not make this assertion at all. The microscopic probabilities yielded by the theory are such that the acts which a macroscopic psychology would predict are overwhelmingly likely to occur. From the standpoint of the macrophenomena of human conduct, a 100 percent type of determinism holds, to all intents and purposes. As Cassirer has stated, the extent of the determination of human behavior is so great that the free will of the philosophical indeterminist can find no refuge in it. Schrödinger has aptly summarized these conclusions in the following words: "According to the evidence . . . the space-time events in the body of a living being which correspond to the activity of its mind, to its self-conscious or any other actions, are (considering also their complex structure and the accepted statistical explanation of physico-chemistry) if not strictly deterministic at any rate statistico-deterministic. To the physicist I wish to emphasize that in my opinion, and contrary to the opinion upheld in some quarters, *quantum indeterminacy* plays no biologically relevant role in them, except perhaps ... in such events as meiosis, natural and X-ray induced mutation and so on ... let me regard this as a fact, as I believe every unbiased biologist would, if there were not the well-known, unpleasant feeling about 'declaring oneself to be a pure mechanism'."

Conclusion

In this paper an attempt has been made to show that the arguments advanced against the possibility of a scientific study of man are without foundation. Of course, the truth of either strict determinism or statistico-determinism has not been established conclusively; for this cannot be done by logical analysis alone, but requires actual success in the scientific search for uniformities. Since the important arguments against determinism which we have considered are without foundation, the psychologist need not be deterred in his quest and can confidently use the causal hypothesis as a regulative principle, undaunted by the *caveat* of the philosophical indeterminist.

STUDY QUESTIONS

1. What, according to Grünbaum, are the results for the social sciences of the view that human actions are not governed by causal laws?
2. Who, in your opinion, has the better of the argument regarding the relationship between determinism, indeterminism and moral responsbiliity—Grünbaum or the indeterminists?
3. Do you agree with Grünbaum that our "consciousness of freedom" offers no support for the indeterminist cause?
4. How do you respond to Grünbaum's deterministic theory of punishment?
5. What relevance, if any, does the Heisenberg "uncertainty relation" have to the debate between determinism and indeterminism?

For Further Reading

Berofsky, B., ed. *Free Will and Determinism.* New York: 1966.
Dworkin, G., ed. *Determinism, Free Will, and Moral Responsibility.* Englewood Cliffs, N.J.: Prentice-Hall, 1970.
Enteman, W. F., ed. *The Problem of Free Will.* New York: Scribner's, 1967.
Hook, S., ed. *Determinism and Freedom.* New York: New York University Press, 1958.
Lehrer, K., ed. *Freedom and Determinism.* New York: Random House, 1966.
Morgenbesser, S., and Walsh, J., eds. *Free Will.* Englewood Cliffs, N.J.: 1962.
O'Connor, D. J. *Free Will.* Garden City, N.Y.: Doubleday, 1971.

DUCASSE AND HOLBACH: IMMORTALITY

Although both pre- and post-existence seem about equally related to the lives we now live, people have devoted little thought to the former but an immense amount to the latter. This difference in concern has an obviously practical basis; few of us much care whether we had an existence prior to our birth, but most of us care a great deal about the possibility of surviving our death. The intense and pervasive desire for immortality explains much of the perennial interest people have taken in religion. It also accounts for the vast amount of rubbish that is written and accepted about immortality. What they desperately want to believe, many people *will* believe, without regard to evidence, logic, or good sense. This does not mean that the subject cannot be approached objectively nor the issue it raises discussed on their merits. To do so is peculiarly the task of philosophers, whose concern is to come to intellectual grips with the fundamental issues of human existence. In the two selections that follow, the opposed sides of the issue are defended.

Curt John Ducasse (1881–1969) was born in France but received his higher education in America, first at the University of Washington and later at Harvard University. During a career that spanned a half-century, he taught first at the University of Washington and later for many years at Brown University. Besides philosophy, Ducasse had a deep interest in psychical research.

Born in southern Germany as Paul Heinrich Dietrich in 1723, Paul-Henri Thiry, Baron d'Holbach, changed his name as well as his nationality, after making a permanent move from his native land to Paris in 1749. On inheriting his title and munificent estates in 1753, Holbach turned his home into a *salon* that attracted the intellectual elite of the French world. For decades, major figures of the Enlightment, led by Denis Diderot and other famous contributors to the *Encyclopédie*, gathered regularly there to discuss philosophy, religion, politics and, in general, the state of the world. Because his own views were anti-clerical and anti-monarchist, Holbach was forced to publish most of his writings anonymously, in Holland. He died in 1789, on the eve of the French Revolution.

ℒ Ducasse: *Nature, Mind, and Death*

Chapter 19
The Case Against the Possibility of Survival

That a man's life continues in some form after the death of his body has always been believed by a large majority of mankind. Before we ask whether it is possible that this belief should be true, it will be well to ask first why it has so generally been held. But a word concerning two points of terminology is called for at the outset.

The first relates to the name by which we shall refer to the entity the possibility of whose survival is in question. It has been variously termed man's mind, personality, soul, or spirit—these words in most cases being defined either not at all or but

Reprinted from *Nature, Mind, and Death* by C. J. Ducasse by permission of The Open Court Publishing Company, La Salle, Illinois. Copyright by The Open Court Publishing Company, La Salle, Illinois, 1951.

loosely. For the present purpose there will be no need to take account of the more or less different meanings various writers have proposed for those terms; and since we have in preceding chapters reached a definite conception of the meaning implicit in the ordinary predicative usage of the term "mind," this term is the one we shall employ here. We shall assume that it includes such more special facts as the others may denote.

The other point of terminology concerns the common practice of describing as belief in "immortality" the belief that the human mind survives the death of its body. Strictly speaking immortality implies survival forever. But I believe few persons give much if any thought to the "forever" part of the hypothesis. It is survival of death that people are really interested in, and assurance of survival for some substantial period—say a thousand or even a hundred years—would probably have as much or nearly as much present psychological value as would assurance of survival strictly forever. Most men would be even less troubled by the idea of extinction at so distant a time than is a healthy and happy youth by the idea that he will die in fifty or sixty years. Therefore what I shall discuss will be the possibility that the human mind survives death of its body for some time whether finite or not, rather than that it survives it specifically forever.

1. Why Belief in Survival Is Easy and Widespread

This being understood, let us now consider what apparently are the chief psychological determinants of the belief in survival. One of them is what may be called psychological inertia—the natural tendency to assume that what we are accustomed to find present will continue to be so. Each of us having had conscious life at all times in the past which he can rememnber, he tacitly assumes that this will continue. As J. B. Pratt has pointed out, the child takes the continuity of life for granted. It is the fact of death that has to be taught him. But when he has learned it, and the idea of a future life is then put explicitly before his mind, it seems to him the most natural thing in the world.*

It is worth noting in this connection, that although we sometimes say that we were unconscious at certain times or that some person we observe is unconscious, nevertheless unconsciousness is nothing we ever really observe in ourselves or in anyone else. What we actually observe when we say that another person is unconscious is only the fact that his body does not then react to certain stimuli which at other times elicit perceptible responses. He is unconscious of those stimuli, but for all we know he may be vividly dreaming. And as regards ourselves, we of course are never conscious of being unconscious, for this is a contradiction. When we assert that we were

*Pratt, *The Religious Consciousness*, p. 225, Cf. C. D. Broad, *The Mind and Its Place in Nature*, p. 524.

unconscious during a certain period, what we really know is only that we have no memories relating to that period. This is no proof, and is even hardly evidence at all, that our consciousness was totally extinguished during that period; for if this followed, then the fact that we have no memories whatever of the first few years of our lives, nor of the vast majority of our days since, would equally require us to conclude that we were totally unconscious at all those times. But we have plenty of indirect evidence to the contrary.

Consciousness thus is something we have had at all times we can remember; and psychological inertia therefore makes natural and easy the idea that consciousness survives the death as it does the sleep, of the body.

Another psychological determinant of the belief in survival is the wish to survive. How subtle is this wish is shown by the fact that even persons who believe that death means complete extinction of the individual's consciousness often find comfort in various substitute conceptions of survival. They may, for instance, dwell on the continuity of the individual's germ plasm in his descendants. Or they find solace in the thought that, the past being indestructible, their individual life remains eternally an intrinsic part of the history of the world. Also—and more satisfying to one's craving for personal importance—there is the fact that since the acts of one's life have effects, and these in turn further effects, and so on, therefore what he has done goes on forever influencing remotely and sometimes greatly the course of future events. Gratifying to one's vanity, too, is the prospect that, if the achievements of one's life have been great or even conspicuous or his benefactions or evil deeds have been notable, his name may not only be remembered by acquaintances and relatives for a little while, but may live on in recorded history. But evidently survival in any of these senses is but a consolation prize—but a thin substitute for the continuation of conscious individual life, which may not be a fact, but which most men crave nonetheless.

The roots of this craving are certain desires which death appears to frustrate. For some, the chief of these is for union with persons dearly loved. For others whose lives have been wretched, it is the desire for another chance at the happiness they have missed. For others yet, it is desire for further opportunity to grow in ability, knowledge, or character. Often there is also the desire, already mentioned, to go on counting for something in the affairs of men. And again, a future life for oneself and others is often desired in order that the redressing of the many injustices of this life shall be possible. But it goes without saying that although belief in a future life is easy and desires such as these often suffice to induce it, they constitute no evidence at all that it is a fact.

. . .

3. The Case Against the Possibility of Survival

Although the belief in survival is easy, tempting, and widespread, critical reflection quickly brings forth a variety of *prima facie* strong reasons to regard that belief as illusory.*

There are first of all certain facts which definitely suggest that both the existence and the particular nature of consciousness at various times wholly depend on the presence of a functioning nervous system. Protagonists of the impossibility of survival remark, for example, that wherever consciousness is observed it is found associated with a living and functioning body. Further, when the body dies, or the head receives a heavy blow, or some anesthetic is

administered, all the familiar outward evidences of consciousness terminate, permanently or temporarily. Again, we know well that drugs of various kinds—alcohol, caffein, opium, heroin, and many others—cause specific changes at the time in the nature of a person's mental states. The secretions of the endocrine glands, or deficiency of them, also affect the mind in various ways. Also, by stimulating in appropriate ways the body's sense organs, corresponding states of consciousness—namely, the various kinds of sensations—can be caused at will. On the other hand, cutting a sensory nerve immediately eliminates a whole range of sensations. Again, the contents of consciousness, perceptual capacities, linguistic skills, and various mental powers and personality traits, are altered in characteristic ways when specific regions of the brain are destroyed by disease or injury or are disconnected from the rest surgically as in prefrontal lobotomy.

That the nervous system is the indispensable basis of mind is further suggested by the fact that, in the evolutionary scale, the degree of intelligence of various species of animals keeps pace closely with the degree of development of their brain; and that in an individual human being a similar correlation is to be observed between the growth and decay of his brain, and that of his mind, from infantility to maturity to senility.

That continued existence of mind after death is impossible has been argued also on the basis of theoretical considerations. It has been contended, for instance, that what we call states of consciousness—or more particularly, ideas, sensations, volitions, feelings, and the like—are really nothing but the minute physical or chemical events which take place in the tissues of the brain. For, it is urged, it would be absurd to suppose that an idea or a volition, if it is not itself a material thing or process, could cause material effects such as contractions of muscles. Moreover, it is maintained that the possibility of causation of a material event by an immaterial mental cause is ruled out *a priori* by the principle of the conservation of energy; for such

*An excellent statement of them is given by Gardner Murphy in the article, "Difficulties Confronting the Survival Hypothesis," *Jour. of the Amer. Soc. for Psych. Research*, Vol. XXXIX, No. 2 (April 1945), pp. 67–94. See also Corliss Lamont's *The Illusion of Immortality* (New York: Putnam, 1935); C. D. Broad's *The Mind and Its Place in Nature* (New York: Harcourt Brace, 1929), Chapters XI and XII *passim*, and especially pp. 526–33.

causation would mean that an additional quantity of energy suddenly pops into the nervous system out of nowhere.

Another conception of consciousness, which is more often met with today than the one just mentioned but which also implies that consciousness cannot survive death, is that "consciousness" is only the name we give to certain types of behavior which differentiate the higher animals from all other things in nature. According to this view, to say, for example, that an animal is conscious of a difference between two stimuli means nothing more than that it responds to each by different behavior. That is, the difference of behavior is what consciousness of difference between the stimuli consists in; and is not, as is commonly assumed, only the behavioral sign of something mental and not public, called "consciousness' that the stimuli are different.

Or again, consciousness of the typically human sort called thought is identified with the typically human form of behavior called speech; and this, again not in the sense that speech expresses or manifests something different from itself called "thought," but in the sense that speech—whether uttered or only whispered—is thought itself. And obviously, if thought, or any mental activity, is thus but some mode of behavior of the living body, the mind cannot possibly survive death.

A number of other difficulties of a different order also confront the survival hypothesis. Broad mentions two. One is "the apparently haphazard way in which men are born and die." Common sense rebels against the idea that, for instance, an unwanted child produced in a drunken orgy and dying of neglect or by infanticide six weeks after it is born is "a permanent and indestructible part of the universe, or indeed that it survives the death of its body at all." The other difficulty Broad mentions is "the continuity between men and animals." If the minds of men survive, why not also those of cats and dogs, and indeed those of lice and earwigs?

Still another difficulty becomes evident when one imagines in some detail what

survival would apparently have to include if it were to be survival in any sense important enough to warrant giving it any thought. It would, one feels, have to include persistence not alone of consciousness, but also of personality; that is, of personal character, acquired knowledge, cultural skills and interests, memories, and awareness of personal identity. But even this would not be enough, for "survival" means to live beyond the body's death; and to live means to meet new situations, and by exerting oneself to deal with them, to broaden and deepen one's experience and develop one's latent capacities. But it is hard to imagine this possible without a body and an environment for it, upon which to act and from which to receive impressions. And if a body and an environment were supposed, but not material and corruptible ones, then it is paradoxical to think that, under such radically different conditions, a given personality could persist. To take a crude but telling analogy, it is past belief that, if the body of any one of us were suddenly changed into that of a shark or an octopus, and placed in the ocean, his personality could, for more than a very short time if at all, survive intact so radical a change of environment and of bodily form.

Such, in brief, are the chief reasons commonly advanced for holding that survival is impossible. Scrutiny of them, however, will I think show that they are not as strong as they first seem, and far from strong enough to prove that there can be no life after death.

4. Critique of the Case Against the Possibility of Survival

Let us consider first the assertion that "thought," or "consciousness," is but another name for subvocal speech, or for some other form of behavior, or for molecular processes in the tissues of the brain. As Paulsen and others have pointed out* no evidence ever is or can be offered to support that assertion, because it is in

---

*F. Paulsen, *Introduction to Philosophy*, 2d ed. Translated by F. Thilly, pp. 82–83.

fact but a disguised proposal to make the words "thought," "feeling," "sensation," "desire," and so on, denote facts quite different from those which these words are commonly employed to denote. To say that those words are but other names for certain chemical or behavioral events is as grossly arbitrary as it would be to say that "wood" is but another name for glass, or "potato" but another name for cabbage. What thought, desire, sensation, and other mental states are like, each of us can observe directly by introspection; and what introspection reveals is that they do not in the least resemble muscular contraction, or glandular secretion, or any other known bodily events. No tampering with language can alter the observable fact that thinking is one thing and muttering quite another; that the feeling called anger has no resemblance to the bodily behavior which usually goes with it; or that an act of will is not in the least like anything we find when we open the skull and examine the brain. Certain mental events are doubtless connected in some way with certain bodily events, but they are not those bodily events themselves. The connection is not identity.

This being clear, let us next consider the arguments offered to show that mental processes, although not identical with bodily processes, nevertheless totally depend on them. We are told, for instance, that some head injuries, or anesthetics, totally extinguish consciousness for the time being. As already pointed out, however, the strict fact is only that the usual bodily signs of consciousness are then absent. But they are also absent when a person is asleep; and yet, at the same time, dreams, which are states of consciousness, may be occurring.

It is true that when the person concerned awakens, he often remembers his dreams, whereas the person that has been anesthetized or injured has usually no memories relating to the period of apparent blankness. But this could mean that his consciousness was, for the time, dissociated from its ordinary channels of manifestation, as was reported of the coconscious personalities of some of the patients of Dr.

Morton Prince.* Moreover, it sometimes occurs that a person who has been in an accident reports lack of memories not only for the period during which his body was unresponsive but also for a period of several hours before the accident, during which he had given to his associates all the ordinary external signs of being conscious as usual. As emphasized already in paragraph 1, if absence of memories relating to a given period proved unconsciousness for that period, this would force us to conclude that we were unconscious during the first few years of our lives, and indeed have been so most of the time since; for the fact is that we have no memories whatever of most of our days. That we were alive and conscious on any long past specific date is, with only a few exceptions, not something we actually remember, but only something which we infer must have been true.

We turn now to another of the arguments we mentioned against the possibility of survival. That states of consciousness somehow entirely depend on bodily processes and therefore cannot continue when the latter have ceased is proved, it is argued, by the fact that various states of consciousness—in particular, the several kinds of sensations—can, at will, be caused by appropriate stimulation of the body.

Now it is very true that sensations and some other mental states can be so caused; but we have just as good and abundant evidence that mental states can cause various bodily events. John Laird mentions, among others, the fact that merely willing to raise one's arm normally suffices to cause it to rise; that a hungry person's mouth is caused to water by the idea of food; that feelings of rage, fear, or excitement cause digestion to stop; that anxiety causes changes in the quantity and quality of the milk of a nursing mother; that certain thoughts cause tears, pallor, blushing, or fainting, and so on.* The evidence

*My Life as a Dissociated Personality, ed. by Morton Prince (Boston: Badger, 0000).

*John Laird, Our Minds and Their Bodies (London: Oxford University Press, 1925), pp. 16–19.

we have that the relation is one of cause and effect is exactly the same here as where bodily processes cause mental states.

It is said, of course, that to suppose something nonphysical, such as a thought, to be capable of causing motion of a physical object, such as the body, is absurd. But I submit that if the heterogeneity of mind and matter makes this absurd, then it makes equally absurd the causation of mental states by stimulation of the body. Yet no absurdity is commonly found in the assertion that cutting the skin causes a feeling of pain, or that alcohol, caffein, bromides, and other drugs, cause characteristic states of consciousness. Common sense here accords with Hume's demonstration, to which we have repeatedly referred, that no logical absurdity is ever involved in supposing an event of a given kind to cause any other particular kind of event, and therefore that only experience can tell us what in fact can cause what. And as we have also seen, the so-called principle of the conservation of energy precludes neither psycho-physical nor physico-psychical causation.

As regards the fact that certain mutilations of the body rob the mind of certain of its powers, this too is a fact, just as it is a fact that destruction of one's motor car, if one can get no other, destroys, not one's capacity to drive, but at least the possibility of exercising it. But it is equally true that certain mutilations of one's mind make it permanently or temporarily impossible for the body to exercise capacities which it still physiologically possesses. Impotence, deafness, or blindness caused by some psychological trauma are examples.

What it is essential to bear in mind in connection with the type of arguments we have just been considering is this: The fact that two substances, Mind and Brain, interact entails that some events in each can cause some events in the other, and indeed that the development of each is greatly affected by such events in the other. But this is quite compatible with a considerable range of autonomy in the body, and likewise in the mind. Hence no more con-

tradiction is involved in supposing that such activities of the mind as are autonomous, i.e., psycho-psychical, still go on when the connection between it and the body is temporarily severed—or, at death, permanently—than is involved in the fact that the autonomous activities of the body—breathing, circulation of the blood, metabolism, etc.—still go on during coma, deep sleep, or anesthesia, i.e., at times when psycho-physical and physico-psychical action is suspended.

A word, next, on the parallelism between the degree of development of the nervous systems of various animals and the degree of their intelligence. This is alleged to prove that the latter is the product of the former. But the facts lend themselves equally well to the supposition that, on the contrary, or at least in equal measure, an obscurely felt need for greater intelligence in the circumstances the animal faced brought about the variations which eventually resulted in a more adequate nervous organization. In the development of the individual, at all events, it seems clear, as we have pointed out, that the specific, highly complex nerve connections which become established in the brain and cerebellum of, for instance, a skilled pianist are the results of his will over many years to acquire the skill.

We must not forget in this context that there is a converse, equally consistent with the facts, for the theory, called epiphenomenalism, that mental states are related to the brain much as the halo is to the saint, that is, as effects but never themselves as causes. The converse theory, which might be called hypophenomenalism, and which is pretty well that of Schopenhauer, is that the instruments which the various mechanisms of the body constitute are the objective products of obscure cravings for corresponding powers; and, in particular, that the organization of the nervous system is the effect and material isomorph of the variety of mental functions exercised at a given level of animal or human existence. It is clear that epiphenomenalism, and likewise a hypophenomenalism that should assert psycho-physical but deny physico-psychical causation, would be not merely arbitrary, but would clash with facts which there are none but dogmatic reasons to refuse to take at their face value.

As regards the difficulty felt to arise from the haphazard way in which men are born and die, and from the continuity between men and animals, Broad, who in mentioning it says he is conscious that it affects him personally more than any others, nevertheless goes on to show with his usual admirable objectivity that these facts have no logical right to exert this influence. As to the first, he writes: "There is no logical transition from 'This [mind] is caused by the careless or criminal action of a human being' to: 'This [mind] is the kind of thing whose existence is transitory'." And as to the second, he concludes a detailed critique of it with the statement: "The alleged reasons for thinking it very unlikely that earwigs are immortal either are no reasons at all or they obviously depend on characteristics in which human beings and earwigs differ profoundly."

• • •

5. What Accounts for the Prima Facie Plausibility of the Arguments Against the Possibility of Survival

Our examination of the reasons commonly given for asserting the impossibility of survival has revealed that they are logically weak—far too much so even to show that survival is more unlikely than likely. The whole question will be placed in a useful perspective if we now ask why so many of the persons who advance those reasons nevertheless think them convincing.

This is, I believe, because they approach the question with a certain metaphysical bias. It derives from a particular initial assumption they tacitly make, namely, that to be real is to be material; and to be material, as we have seen, is to be some process or part of the perceptually public world.

Now the assumption that to be real is to be material is a useful and appropriate one for the purpose of discovering and employing the physico-physical properties of material things; and this purpose is a legitimate and very frequent one. But those persons, and most of us, do not ordinarily realize that the validity of that metaphysical assumption is strictly relative to that specific purpose; for what that assumption automatically does is to limit one's horizon to physical causes and physical effects, and thus to make the suggestion of any nonmaterial cause or effect of a material event seem incongruous—as indeed it is under, but only under, that assumption.

Because of one's ordinary failure to realize this state of affairs, he ordinarily continues making that assumption out of habit, and it continues to rule his judgments of relevance and plausibility in matters of causation even when, as now, the purpose in view is no longer that of discovering or employing such physico-physical properties as material things have, but is a different one, for which that assumption is no longer useful or even congruous.

The point is all important here and therefore worth stressing. Its essence is that the conception of the nature of reality that proposes to define the real as the material is not the expression of an observable fact to which everyone would have to bow, but is the expression only of a certain direction of interest on the part of the persons who so define reality—of interest, namely, which they have chosen to center wholly in the material, perceptually public world. This specialized interest is of course as legitimate as any other, but it automatically ignores all the facts, commonly called facts of mind, which only introspection directly reveals. And that specialized interest is what alone compels persons in its grip to employ the word "mind" to denote, instead of what it commonly does denote, something else altogether, namely, the public behavior of bodies that have minds; or makes it seem improbable or even absurd to them that any physical event could have any but a physical cause, or that anything but the material world and its processes should be self-sufficiently real. Only so long as one's judgment is swayed unawares by that special interest do the logically weak arguments against the possibility of survival which we have examined, seem strong.

It is possible, however, and just as legitimate, as well more conducive to fair judgment as to the possibility that a mind or some parts of it survives the death of its body, to center one's interest for a time on the facts of mind as introspectively observable—rank them for the time being as most real in the sense that they are facts the intrinsic nature of which we most directly experience; that they are the facts which we most certainly know to exist; and moreover, that they are the facts without the experiencing of which we should not know any other facts whatever—such, for instance, as those of the material world.

The sort of perspective one gets from this point of view equilibrates that which one gets from the materialistic point of view, and is what I propose now to sketch briefly. For one thing, the material world is then seen to be but one among other objects of our consciousness. Moreover, one becomes aware of the crucially important fact that it is an object known by interpretation rather than strictly given. Suppose that, perhaps in a restaurant we visit for the first time, an entire wall is occupied by a large mirror and we look into it without realizing it is a mirror. We then perceive in the part of space beyond it, various material objects, notwithstanding that in fact they have no existence there at all. A certain set of the vivid color images which we call visual sensations was all that was strictly given to us, and these we construed, automatically and instantaneously but nonetheless erroneously, as signs or appearances of the existence of certain material objects at a certain place.

Again, and similarly, we perceive in our dreams various objects which at the time we take as physical but which eventually we come to believe were not so. And this eventual conclusion, let it be noted, is

forced upon us not because we then detect that something called "physical substance" was lacking in those objects but only because we notice, as we did not at the time, that their behavior was erratic—incoherent with their ordinary one. That is, their appearance was a mere appearance, deceptive in the sense that it did not then predict truly, as ordinarily it does, their later appearances. This, it is important to notice, is the only way in which we ever discover that an object we perceive was not really physical, or was not the particular sort of physical object we judged it to be.

These two examples illustrate the fact that our perception of physical objects is sometimes erroneous. But the essential point is that, even when it is veridical instead of erroneous, all that is literally and directly given to our minds is still only some set of sensations. These, on a given occasion, may be only color sensations; but they often include also tactual sensations, sounds, odors, and so on. It is especially interesting, however, to remark here in passing that, with respect to almost all the many thousands of persons and other "physical" objects we have perceived in a lifetime, vivid color images were the only strict data our perceiving activity had to go by; so that, if the truth should happen to have been that those objects, like ghosts or images in a mirror, were actually intangible—that is, were only color images—we should never have discovered that this was the fact. For all we directly know, it may have been the fact!

To perceive a physical object, then, instead of merely experiencing passively certain sensations (something which perhaps hardly ever occurs), is always to interpret, that is, to construe, given sensations as signs of, and appearances to us of, a postulated something other than themselves, some event which is causing them in us; and other events which are capable of causing in us sensations of other specific kinds. This belief commonly is only tacit and instinctive; but when reflection considers it explicitly, it is vindicated by our belief—or our knowledge—that every event has some cause and therefore that our sensations too must have one, although we find none for them among our other mental states.

Such a postulated extramental something we call "a physical object." We say that we observe physical objects, and this is true. But it is important for the present purpose to be clear that we "observe" them never in any more direct or literal manner than is constituted by the process of interpretive postulation just described—never, for example, in the wholly direct and literal manner in which we are able to observe our sensations themselves and our other mental states.

That perception of a physical object is thus always the product of two factors—one, a set of sensations simply given to us, and the other an act of interpretation of these, performed by us—is something which easily escapes notice and has even been denied. This, however, is only because the interpretive act is almost always automatic, instantaneous and correct—like, for instance, that of thinking of the meaning of any familiar word we hear. But that an interpretive act does occur is forced on our attention when, in a particular case, we discover that the interpretation was incorrect—that is, we discover that we misconstrued the meaning of the sensations. Or again, the interpretive act is noticeable when, because the sensations are too scant and therefore ambiguous, we catch ourselves hesitating between two or more possible interpretations of them and say that we are not sure what object it is we see.

The remarks made in the present section have been intended to make evident that explanations in terms of material causes do not have the exclusive authoritativeness which they seem to many persons to possess, and that the tacit assumption of those persons that only material things, but not minds, can have independent existence, is quite gratuitous. We have supplemented those remarks by a sketch of the view of the universe obtained when one conceives oneself essentially as a mind rather than as a body. The enlarged perspective provided makes clear that no paradox at all is really involved in the supposition that some forms of consciousness may exist independently of connection with animal or human bodies.

STUDY QUESTIONS

1. Why do so many people believe in immortality? Do you think they can give persuasive reasons for this belief?
2. What are the main arguments against immortality? Which of these do you think is the strongest? Can any answer be given to it?
3. What is epiphenomenalism? Hypophenomenalism? Do you think either one is a plausible theory? Explain.
4. What, according to Ducasse, is the metaphysical assumption usually made by those who deny the possibility of immortality?
5. Can you imagine what a continued existence after death would be like? Do you think such an existence impossible? Barely possible? Probable? Certain?

For Further Reading **appears on page 173.**

✌ Holbach: *The System of Nature*

Chapter XIII

The reflections presented to the reader in this work, tend to show, what ought to be

First published in French in 1770. Translated by H. D. Robinson.

thought of the human soul, as well as of its operations and faculties: every thing proves, in the most convincing manner, that it acts and moves according to laws similar to those prescribed to the other beings of nature; that it cannot be distinguished from the body; that it is born with it; that it grows up with it; that it is modified in the same progression; in short, every thing ought to make man conclude that it perishes with it. This soul, as well as the body, passes through a state of weakness and infancy; it is in this stage of its existence that it is assailed by a multitude of modifications and of ideas which it receives from exterior objects through the medium of the organs; that it amasses facts; that it collects experience, whether true or false; that it forms to itself a system of conduct, according to which it thinks and acts, and from whence results either its happiness or its misery, its reason or its delirium, its virtues or its vices: arrived with the body at its full powers; having in conjunction with it reached maturity, it does not cease for a single instant to partake in common of its sensations, whether these are agreeable or disagreeable; in consequence it conjointly approves or disapproves its state; like it, it is either sound or diseased, active or languishing, awake or asleep. In old age, man extinguishes entirely, his fibres become rigid, his nerves lose their elasticity, his senses are obtunded, his sight grows dim, his ears lose their quickness, his ideas become unconnected, his memory fails, his imagination cools; what, then, becomes of his soul? Alas! it sinks down with the body; it gets benumbed as this loses its feeling, becomes sluggish as this decays in activity; like it, when enfeebled by years it fulfils its functions with pain; and this substance, which is deemed spiritual or *immaterial*, undergoes the same revolutions, and experiences the same vicissitudes as does the body itself.

In despite of this convincing proof of the materiality of the soul, and of its identity with the body, some thinkers have supposed that although the latter is perishable, the former does not perish; that this portion of man enjoys the especial privilege of *immortality*; that it is exempt from dissolution and free from those changes of form all the beings in nature undergo: in consequence of this, man has persuaded himself that this privileged soul does not die: its immortality above all appears indubitable

to those who suppose it spiritual: after having made it a simple being, without extent, devoid of parts, totally different from any thing of which he has a knowledge, he pretended that it was not subjected to the laws of decomposition common to all beings, of which experience shows him the continual operation.

•   •   •

Nothing is more popular than the doctrine of the *immortality of the soul*; nothing is more universally diffused than the expectation of another life. Nature having inspired man with the most ardent love for his existence, the desire of preserving himself for ever was a necessary consequence: this desire was presently coverted into certainty; from that desire of existing eternally, which nature has implanted in him, he made an argument to prove that man would never cease to exist. Abbadie says: "Our soul has no useless desires, it desires naturally an eternal life;" and by a very strange logic he concludes, that this desire could not fail to be fulfilled. However this may be, man, thus disposed, listened with avidity to those who announced to him systems so conformable with his wishes. Nevertheless, he ought not to regard as supernatural the desire of existing, which always was, and always will be, of the essence of man; it ought not to excite surprise if he received with eagerness an hypothesis that flattered his hopes, by promising that his desire would one day be gratified; but let him beware how he concludes, that this desire itself is an indubitable proof of the reality of this future life, with which, for his present happiness, he seems to be far too much occupied. The passion for existence, is in man only a natural consequence of the tendency of a sensible being, whose essence it is to be willing to conserve himself: in the human being, it follows the energy of his soul or keeps pace with the force of his imagination, always ready to realize that which he strongly desires. He desires the life of the body, nevertheless this desire is frustrated;

wherefore should not the desire for the life of the soul be frustrated like the other?

The most simple reflection upon the nature of his soul ought to convince man that the idea of its immortality is only an illusion of the brain. Indeed, what is his soul, save the principle of sensibility? What is it to think, to enjoy, to suffer; is it not to feel? What is life, except it be the assemblage of modifications, the congregation of motion, peculiar to an organized being? Thus, as soon as the body ceases to live, its sensibility can no longer exercise itself; therefore it can no longer have ideas, nor in consequence thoughts. Ideas, as we have proved, can only reach man through his senses; now, how will they have it, that once deprived of his senses, he is yet capable of receiving sensations, of having perceptions, of forming ideas? As they have made the soul of man a being separated from the animated body, wherefore have they not made life a being distinguished from the living body? Life in a body is the totality of its motion; feeling and thought make a part of this motion: thus, in the dead man, these motions will cease like all the others.

Indeed, by what reasoning will it be proved, that this soul, which cannot feel, think, will, or act, but by aid of man's organs, can suffer pain, be susceptible of pleasure, or even have a consciousness of its own existence, when the organs which should warn it of their presence, are decomposed or destroyed? Is it not evident that the soul depends on the arrangement of the various parts of the body, and on the order with which these parts conspire to perform their functions or motions? Thus the organic structure once destroyed, can it be doubted the soul will be destroyed also? Is it not seen, that during the whole course of human life, this soul is stimulated, changed, deranged, disturbed, by all the changes man's organs experience? And yet it will be insisted that this soul acts, thinks, subsists, when these same organs have entirely disappeared!

An organized being may be compared to a clock, which, once broken, is no longer suitable to the use for which it was designed. To say, that the soul shall feel, shall think, shall enjoy, shall suffer, after the death of the body, is to pretend, that a clock, shivered into a thousand pieces, will continue to strike the hour, and have the faculty of marking the progress of time. Those who say, that the soul of man is able to subsist notwithstanding the destruction of the body, evidently support the position, that the modification of a body will be enabled to conserve itself, after the subject is destroyed: but this is completely absurd.

It will be said, that the conservation of the soul after the death of the body, is an effect of the divine omnipotence: but this is supporting an absurdity by a gratuitous hypothesis. It surely is not meant by divine omnipotence, of whatever nature it may be supposed, that a thing shall exist and not exist at the same time: that a soul shall feel and think without the intermediates necessary to thought.

Let them, then, at least forbear asserting, that reason is not wounded by the doctrine of the immortality of the soul, or by the expectation of a future life. These notions, formed to flatter man, or to disturb the imagination of the uninformed who do not reason, cannot appear either convincing or probable to enlightened minds. Reason, exempted from the illusions of prejudice, is, without doubt, wounded by the supposition of a soul that feels, that thinks, that is afflicted, that rejoices, that has ideas, without having organs; that is to say, destitute of the only known and natural means by which it is possible for it to feel sensations, have perceptions, or form ideas. If it be replied, that other means are able to exist, which are *supernatural* or *unknown;* it may be answered, that these means of transmitting ideas to the soul separated from the body, are not better known to, or more within the reach of those who suppose it than they are of other men. It is at least very certain, that all those who reject the system of innate ideas, cannot, without contradicting their own principles, admit the groundless doctrine of the immortality of the soul.

In defiance of the consolation that so many persons pretend to find in the notion of an eternal existence; in despite of that firm persuasion, which such numbers of men assure us they have, that their souls will survive their bodies, they seem so very much alarmed at the dissolution of this body, that they do not contemplate their end, which they ought to desire as the period of so many miseries, but with the greatest inquietude: so true it is, that the real, the present, even accompanied with pain, has much more influence over mankind, than the most beautiful chimeras of the future, which he never views but through the clouds of uncertainty. Indeed the most religious men, notwithstanding the conviction they express of a blessed eternity, do not find these flattering hopes sufficiently consoling to repress their fears and trembling when they think on the necessary dissolution of their bodies. Death was always for mortals the most frightful point of view; they regard it as a strange phenomenon, contrary to the order of things, opposed to nature; in a word, as an effect of the celestial vengeance, as the *wages of sin*. Although every thing proves to man that death is inevitable, he is never able to familiarize himself with its idea; he never thinks on it without shuddering, and the assurance of possessing an immortal soul, but feebly indemnifies him for the grief he feels in the deprivation of his perishable body. Two causes contribute to strengthen and nourish his alarm; the one is, that this death, commonly accompanied with pain, wrests from him an existence that pleases him, with which he is acquainted, to which he is accustomed; the other is the uncertainty of the state that must succeed his actual existence.

The illustrious Bacon has said: that "Men fear death, for the same reason that children dread being alone in darkness." Man naturally challenges every thing with which he is unacquainted; he is desirous to see clearly, to the end that he may guaranty himself against those objects which may menace his safety, or that he may be enabled to procure for himself those which may be useful to him. The man who exists, cannot form to himself any idea of non-existence; as this circumstance disturbs him, for want of experience his imagination sets to work; this points out to him, either well or ill, this uncertain state: accustomed to think, to feel, to be stimulated into activity, to enjoy society, he contemplates as the greatest misfortune a dissolution that will strip him of these objects, and deprive him of those sensations which his present nature has rendered necessary to him; that will prevent his being warned of his own existence; that shall bereave him of his pleasures to plunge him into nothing. In supposing it even exempt from pain, he always looks upon this nothing as an afflicting solitude, as a heap of profound darkness; he sees himself in a state of general desolation, destitute of all assistance, and feeling the rigour of this frightful situation. But does not a profound sleep help to give him a true idea of this nothing? Does not that deprive him of every thing? Does it not appear to annihilate the universe to him, and him to the universe? Is death any thing more than a profound and permanent sleep? Is it for want of being able to form an idea of death, that man dreads it; if he could figure to himself a true image of this state of annihilation, he would from thence cease to fear it; but he is not able to conceive a state in which there is no feeling; he therefore believes, that when he shall no longer exist, he will have the same feelings and the same consciousness of things which during his existence appear to his mind in such gloomy colours: imagination pictures to him his funeral pomp; the grave they are digging for him; the lamentations that will accompany him to his last abode; he persuades himself that these melancholy objects will affect him as painfully, even after his decease, as they do in his present condition in which he is in full possession of his senses.

Mortal, led astray by fear! after thy death thine eyes will see no more; thine ears will hear no longer; in the depth of thy grave, thou wilt no more be witness to this scene which thine imagination at present represents to thee under such dismal colours; thou wilt no longer take part in what shall be done in the world; thou wilt no more be occupied with what may befall thine inanimate remains, than thou wast able to be the day previous to that which ranked thee among the beings of thy species. To die, is to cease to think, to feel, to enjoy, to suffer; thy sorrows will not follow thee to the silent tomb. Think of death, not to feed thy fears and to nourish thy melancholy, but to accustom thyself to look upon it with a peaceable eye, and to cheer thee up against those false terrours with which the enemies to thy repose labour to inspire thee!

The fears of death are vain illusions, that must disappear as soon as we learn to contemplate this necessary event under its true point of view. A great man has defined philosophy to be *a meditation on death*; he is not desirous by that to have it understood that man ought to occupy himself sorrowfully with his end, with a view to nourish his fears; on the contrary he wishes to invite him to familiarize himself with an object that nature has rendered necessary to him, and to accustom himself to expect it with a serene countenance. If life is a benefit, if it be necessary to love it, it is no less necessary to quit it, and reason ought to teach him a calm resignation to the decrees of fate: his welfare exacts that he should contract the habit of contemplating without alarm an event that his essence has rendered inevitable: his interest demands that he should not by continual dread imbitter his life, the charms of which he must inevitably destroy, if he can never view its termination but with trepidation. Reason and his interest concur to assure him against those vague terrors with which his imagination inspires him in this respect. If he was to call them to his assistance, they would reconcile him to an object that only startles him because he has no knowledge of it, or because it is only shown to him with those hideous accompaniments with which it is clothed by superstition. Let him, then, endeavour to despoil death of these vain illusions, and he will perceive that it is only the sleep of life; that this sleep will not be

disturbed with disagreeable dreams, and that an unpleasant awakening will never follow it. To die, is to sleep; it is to re-enter into the state of insensibility in which he was previous to his birth; before he had senses, before he was conscious of his actual existence. Laws, as necessary as those which gave him birth, will make him return into the bosom of nature from whence he was drawn, in order to reproduce him afterwards under some new form, which it would be useless for him to know: without consulting him, nature places him for a season in the order of organized beings; without his consent, she will oblige him to quit it to occupy some other order.

Let him not complain, then, that nature is callous; she only makes him undergo a law from which she does not exempt any one being she contains. If all are born and perish; if every thing is changed and destroyed; if the birth of a being is never more than the first step towards its end; how is it possible to expect that man, whose machine is so frail, of which the parts are so complicated, the whole of which possesses such extreme mobility, should be exempted from the common law which decrees that even the solid earth he inhabits shall experience change, shall undergo alteration—perhaps be destroyed! Feeble, frail mortal! thou pretendest to exist for ever; wilt thou, then, that for thee alone, eternal nature shall change her undeviating course? Dost thou not behold in those eccentric comets with which thine eyes are sometimes astonished, that the planets themselves are subject to death? Live then in peace, for the season that nature permits thee; and if thy mind be enlightened by reason, thou wilt die without terrour!

• • •

It will be asked, perhaps, by what road has man been conducted, to form to himself these strange and gratuitous ideas of another world? I reply, that it is a truth man has no idea of a future life, which does not exist for him; the ideas of the past and the present furnish his imagination with the materials of which he constructs the edifice of the regions of futurity; and Hobbes says, "We believe that that which is, will always be, and that the same causes will have the same effects." Man in his actual state, has two modes of feeling, one that he approves, another that he disapproves: thus, persuaded that these two modes of feeling must accompany him, even beyond his present existence, he placed in the regions of eternity two distinguished abodes; one destined to felicity, the other to misery: the one will contain the friends of his God; the other is a prison, destined to avenge Him on all those who shall not faithfully believe the doctrines promulgated by the ministers of a vast variety of superstitions.

Such is the origin of the ideas upon a future life, so diffused among mankind. Every where may be seen an *Elysium* and a *Tartarus*; a *Paradise* and a *Hell*; in a word, two distinguished abodes, constructed according to the imagination of the knaves or enthusiasts who have invented them, and who have accommodated them to the peculiar prejudices, to the hopes, to the fears, of the people who believe in them. The Indian figures the first of these abodes as one of inaction and of permanent repose, because, being the inhabitant of a hot climate, he has learned to contemplate rest as the extreme of felicity: the Mussulman promises himself corporeal pleasures, similar to those that actually constitute the object of his research in this life: the Christian hopes for ineffable and spiritual pleasures—in a word, for a happiness of which he has no idea.

Of whatever nature these pleasures may be, man perceived that a body was needful, in order that his soul might be enabled to enjoy the pleasures, or to experience the pains in reserve for him by the Divinity: from hence the doctrine of the *resurrection*; but as he beheld this body putrify, as he saw it dissolve, as he witnessed its decomposition after death, he therefore had recourse to the divine omnipotence, by whose interposition he now believes it will be formed anew. This opinion, so incom-

prehensible, is said to have originated in Persia, among the Magi, and finds a great number of adherents, who have never given it a serious examination. Others, incapable of elevating themselves to these sublime notions, believed, that under divers forms, man animated successively different animals, of various species, and that he never ceased to be an inhabitant of the earth; such was the opinion of those who adopted the doctrine of *Metempsychosis*.

As for the miserable abode of souls, the imagination of fanatics, who were desirous of governing the people, strove to assemble the most frightful images to render it still more terrible. Fire is of all beings that which produces in man the most pungent sensation; it was therefore supposed that God could not invent any thing more cruel to punish his enemies: then fire was the point at which their imagination was obliged to stop; and it was agreed pretty generally, that fire would one day avenge the offended divinity, thus they painted the victims to his anger as confined in fiery dungeons; as perpetually rolling a vortex of bituminous flames; as plunged in unfathomed gulfs of liquid sulphur; and making the infernal caverns resound with their useless groanings, and with their unavailing gnashing of teeth.

But it will perhaps be inquired, how could man reconcile himself to the belief of an existence accompanied with eternal torments; above all, as many according to their own religious systems had reason to fear it for themselves? Many causes have concurred to make him adopt so revolting an opinion. In the first place, very few thinking men have ever believed such an absurdity, when they have deigned to make use of their reason; or, when they have accredited it, this notion was always counterbalanced by the idea of the goodness, by a reliance on the mercy, which they attributed to their God. In the second place, those who were blinded by their fears, never rendered to themselves any account of these strange doctrines, which they either received with awe from their legislators, or which were transmitted to them by their fathers. In the third place each sees the object of his terrours only at a favourable distance; moreover superstition promises him the means of escaping the tortures he believes he has merited. At length, like those sick people whom we see cling with fondness even to the most painful life, man preferred the idea of an unhappy though unknown existence, to that of non-existence, which he looked upon as the most frightful evil that could befall him, either because he could form no idea of it, or, because his imagination painted to him this non-existence, this nothing, as the confused assemblage of all evils. A known evil, of whatever magnitude, alarmed him less, above all when there remained the hope of being able to avoid it, than an evil of which he knew nothing, upon which consequently his imagination was painfully employed, but to which he knew not how to oppose a remedy.

It will be seen, then, that superstition, far from consoling man upon the necessity of death, only redoubles his terrours, by the evils which it pretends his decease will be followed: these terrours are so strong, that the miserable wretches who believe strictly in these formidable doctrines, pass their days in affliction, bathed in the most bitter tears. What shall be said of an opinion, so destructive to society, yet adopted by so many nations, which announces to them, that a severe God, may at each instant, *like a thief*, take them unprovided; that at each moment they are liable to pass under the most rigorous judgment? What idea can be better suited to terrify man, what more likely to discourage him, what more calculated to damp the desire of ameliorating his condition, than the afflicting prospect of a world always on the brink of dissolution, and of a divinity seated upon the ruins of nature, ready to pass judgment on the human species? Such are, nevertheless, the fatal opinions with which the mind of nations has been fed for thousands of years; they are so dangerous, that if by a happy want of just inference, he did not derogate in his conduct from these afflicting ideas, he would fall into the most

abject stupidity. How could man occupy himself with a perishable world, ready every moment to crumble into atoms? How think of rendering himself happy on earth, when it is only the porch to an eternal kingdom? Is it, then, surprising that the superstitions to which such doctrines serve for a basis, have prescribed to their disciples a total detachment from things below: an entire renunciation of the most innocent pleasures; and have given birth to a sluggishness, to a pusillanimity, to an abjection of soul, to an insociability, that renders him useless to himself and dangerous to others? If necessity did not oblige man to depart in his practice from these irrational systems; if his wants did not bring him back to reason, in despite of his religious doctrines, the whole world would presently become a vast desert, inhabited by some few isolated savages, who would not even have courage to multiply themselves. What kind of notions are those which must necessarily be put aside, in order that human association may subsist?

Nevertheless, the doctrine of a future life, accompanied with rewards and punishments, has been regarded for a great number of ages as the most powerful, or even as the only motive capable of coercing the passions of man—as the sole means that can oblige him to be virtuous. By degrees, this doctrine has become the basis of almost all religious and political systems, so much so, that at this day it is said this prejudice cannot be attacked without absolutely rending asunder the bonds of society. The founders of religions have made use of it to attach their credulous disciples; legislators have looked at it as the curb best calculated to keep mankind under discipline. Many philosophers themselves have believed with sincerity, that this doctrine was requisite to terrify man, and thus divert him from crime.

It must indeed be allowed, that this doctrine has been of the greatest utility to those who have given religions to nations and made themselves its ministers: it was the foundation of their power; the source of their wealth; the permanent cause of that blindness, the solid basis of those terrors, which it was their interest to nourish in the human race. It was by this doctrine the priest became first the rival, then the master of kings: it is by this dogma that nations are filled with enthusiasts inebriated with religion, always more disposed to listen to its menaces than to the counsels of reason, to the orders of the sovereign, to the cries of nature, or to the laws of society. Politics itself, was enslaved to the caprice of the priest; the temporal monarch was obliged to bend under the yoke of the eternal monarch; the one only disposed of this perishable world; the other extended his power into the world to come, much more important for man than the earth, on which he is only a pilgrim, a mere passenger. Thus the doctrine of another life, placed the government itself in a state of dependence upon the priest; the monarch was nothing more than his first subject, and he was never obeyed, but when the two were in accord to oppress the human race. Nature in vain cried out to man, to be careful of his present happiness; the priest ordered him to be unhappy, in the expectation of future felicity. Reason in vain exhorted him to be peaceable, the priest breathed forth fanaticism and fury, and obliged him to disturb the public tranquillity, every time there was a question of the interests of the invisible monarch of another life, or the real interests of his ministers in this.

STUDY QUESTIONS

1. How, according to Holbach, is the soul related to the body?
2. Holbach asks: "Is death anything more than a profound and permanent sleep?" What is your response?
3. What, according to Holbach, are the moral effects of the traditional belief in immortality? Do you agree with him?
4. From your reading of the selection would you conclude that Holbach is an atheist?

For Further Reading

Augustine, St. *On the Immortality of the Soul.*

Brown, S. L., ed. *Reason and Religion.* Ithaca: Cornell University Press, 1977 (Part V).

Butler, J. *The Analogy of Religion.* (Part I, Chapter 1).

Dickinson, G. L. *Is Immortality Desirable?* Boston: Houghton, Mifflin, 1909.

Lamont, C. *The Illusion of Immortality.* New York: Putnam, 1935.

Montague, W. P. *The Chances of Surviving Death.* Cambridge, Mass.: Harvard University Press, 1934.

Plato. *Phaedo.*

Royce, J. *The Conception of Immortality.* Boston: Houghton Mifflin, 1900.

PART IV

---◁ ▷---

The Individual and Society

Although one may on occasion encounter a genuine misanthrope, such beings are relatively rare. Most of us enjoy the society of others and would find a life of solitude hard to bear. Not only do we take direct joy in the company of others but we find our lives enriched by the contributions our fellows make to them. But, as most of us learn before we grow very old, social life is a two-way street. If we are to receive, we must also give. For most of us, this is a hard lesson to learn, because giving, we discover, is much more difficult than receiving. At birth we are all total egoists. To transform such self-centered little animals into mature social beings is the work of many years, and it requires numerous sacrifices, usually on the part of one's parents and family.

Although philosophers, unlike educators and psychologists, are not involved in the practical process of making social beings out of us, they are concerned with understanding what the relationship between the individual and society should be. What benefits should each of us reasonably expect to receive from society as a whole and what duties do we owe to others? Before we can answer these questions, we must know what it is that others expect to receive from us as well as what we hope to gain from them. To respond to these issues in their most general terms, we can say that the aim of social cooperation is to realize the best possible life for all. But this answer, in turn, leads to further questions: What is the good life? What is good? The philosophical discipline that addresses itself to these and related issues is known as *ethics*.

To try to understand the problems raised in ethics, perhaps the best place to start is with ourselves. Almost everyone, at some time or other, asks himself, What should I seek in life? What is the greatest good that life can hold for me? Different people answer this question in different ways. Some say wealth, others fame, or power, or love, or security. But will such answers bear the test of time and life? Can anyone be sure that, if he succeeds in acquiring wealth, or gaining fame, or realizing some similar aim, he will attain the good life that he is seeking? How many millionaires have been bored, or lonely, or frightened? Although wealth may be very tempting, many of us would hesitate before trading the lives we live for theirs. Or consider power. Hitler could, and did, dictate life or death for millions of people, but he was feared and hated throughout the world and his name has become an epithet in history. If we stop to reflect, most of us will probably agree that the specific goals we set for ourselves cannot, in themselves, guarantee that our lives will fulfill our deepest desires. What more, then, is needed? Most philosophers have agreed with the response that Aristotle gave: "Happiness." Wealth without happiness is a curse, power without happiness hollow, and so with every other goal one may pursue. But, if we gain happiness, our life is complete; whatever our external condition may be, we need nothing more.

But, an oddity in philosophy, the conclusion we have just reached seems *too* general. If we agree, as almost everyone would, that happiness is the goal most worth seeking in life, we are still left with very little guidance about how we ought to live. Happiness is simply too abstract a concept to apply to the practical concerns of every day living. To make it more concrete so that we can use it to guide us in our choices and decisions, we must render it more specific, by answering the question: In what does the happy life consist?

Since the time of the Greeks, philosophers have addressed themselves to this question. The answers they have given can be divided into two main groups— those favoring hedonism, and those opposed to it. According to the hedonists, happiness is identical to pleasure. Thus our aim in life should always be to maximize the pleasures we can enjoy and minimize the pains we must endure. No other goal we seek, whether it be power, or wealth, or friendship, or anything else, has any value of its own. All are good only to the extent that they increase our pleasure. Here, however, an internal issue arises among hedonists. Are all pleasures on a par, or are some types of pleasure intrinsically higher or better than others? Are pleasures of the mind, for example, superior to pleasures of the body? The split among hedonists on this issue is exemplified by Jeremy Bentham and his pupil and follower, John Stuart Mill. According to Bentham, all pleasures are qualitatively on a par, so the only distinction that can be made between them is one of quantity. Mill, however, wrote, in a famous passage: "It is better to be a human being dissatisfied than a pig satisfied; better to be Socrates dissatisfied than a fool satisfied."

Although history has produced many defenders of hedonism, it has probably witnessed more who have been its critics. To such philosophers, the idea that the happiness one achieves in life must be equated with the pleasure he enjoys is demeaning to the human race. As Mill hints, such a view of the good life may be more appropriate to pigs than to people. Is there nothing higher to seek in human life than enjoyment? Many ethicists have believed that there is, but they have not agreed on what it is. A variety of different views regarding the happy life have been held. Aristotle, for example, equates happiness with a life in which the individual exercises his distinctive attributes as a human and, therefore, a rational being in an outstanding and meritorious manner. The German philosopher, Kant, takes quite a different view of ultimate value, writing, "Nothing can possibly be conceived in the world, or even out of it, which can be called good without qualification, except a good will." Still other philosophers have championed various candidates for the highest human good including such things as knowledge, friendship, the appreciation of beauty, and so on. Perhaps the best life possible would combine all of these things, and pleasure as well.

Our discussion of the good life arose out of questions we posed concerning the relationship between the individual and the rest of society. So let us return to that subject. Agreement on the following points would probably be general:

That every individual wants to be happy, that each one of us can promote (or hinder) the happiness of others, that if we help others we must often do so at the expense of our own happiness, and that most of us find it very hard to sacrifice our own happiness to that of someone else. On the basis of these facts we can ask: Why should any individual make such a sacrifice? According to those who defend ethical egoism, he should not. Stated in an extreme form, the egoistic view contends that every individual should seek his own good exclusively, without regard to that of anyone else. In a more moderate form, the theory holds that each individual should put his own good first, occupying himself with the good of others only when his doing so will not detract from his own good. Although the egoistic theory has considerable psychological appeal, and does, at least in its more moderate form, describe a way of living that undoubtedly has many followers, it is far from easy to see how it can be defended on rational grounds. One argument often offered in its support is that, if every individual pursued his own good exclusively, the result would be the greatest possible good for everyone. This would certainly be a strong argument, if it were true. But is it?

Critics of egoism point out that, if anything is good, it is equally good no matter who possesses it. My pleasure is no better than your equal pleasure, merely because it happens to be mine. It follows from this, that for me to pursue my own lesser pleasure at the expense of someone else's greater pleasure is to act irrationally. It is to prefer a lesser to a greater good. If we are rational, we must recognize that we ought not to promote *any* individual's good at the expense of that of anyone else; rather we ought to treat all equally. Because we often do not want to do this, the "ought" about which I have just spoken takes on a moral character; it lays down a duty that we owe to our fellows. But, as I said at the beginning, social life is a two-way street. Just as we have a duty to promote the good of others, they in turn have a like duty to promote ours.

Background Readings

Ewing, A. C. *Ethics.* New York: Macmillan, 1952.
Frankena, W. K. *Ethics.* Englewood Cliffs, N.J.: Prentice-Hall, 1963.
Harman, G. *The Nature of Morality.* London: Oxford University Press, 1977.
Hospers, J. *Human Conduct.* New York: Harcourt, 1961.
Johnson, O. A., ed. *Ethics.* 4th ed. New York: Holt, Rinehart and Winston, 1978.
Palmer, G. H. *The Field of Ethics.* Boston: Houghton Mifflin, 1901.

PLATO AND BROAD: EGOISM

Egoism, to be properly understood, needs to be discussed in two quite different contexts. The first is psychological. Here the basic question is: Are we all so constituted that we inevitably pursue our own welfare without regard to, or at the expense of, that of others? Those who answer this question affirmatively hold the theory of psychological egoism. The second context is moral, and the basic question is: *Ought* we always to pursue our own welfare without regard to, or at the expense of, that of others? Those who answer this question affirmatively hold the theory of moral egoism. Some philosophers have maintained that, if psychological egoism is true, moral egoism must be true as well. But this would seem to be a mistake. If the moral injunction "One ought always to pursue his own welfare regardless of that of others" is to have any weight, it would seem necessary that he should be able to do otherwise; that is, act in a way inconsistent with psychological egoism. Of course, none of this speaks to the question of the truth of either psychological or moral egoism; some philosophers, at least, claim both to be false. The issues of egoism are argued in the two selections that follow. It should, perhaps, be noted that Plato, in his story of Gyges, the Lydian, is not offering an account of human nature to which he himself subscribes.

For a biographical sketch of Plato see page 69 and of C. D. Broad see page 113.

℣ Plato: The Republic

Book II

The next point is that men practise it [justice] against the grain, for lack of power to do wrong. How true that is, we shall best see if we imagine two men, one just, the other unjust, given full licence to do whatever they like, and then follow them to observe where each will be led by his desires. We shall catch the just man taking the same road as the unjust; he will be moved by self-interest, the end which it is natural to every creature to pursue as good, until forcibly turned aside by law and custom to respect the principle of equality.

Now, the easiest way to give them that complete liberty of action would be to imagine them possessed of the talisman found by Gyges, the ancestor of the famous Lydian. The story tells how he was a shepherd in the King's service. One day there was a great storm, and the ground where his flock was feeding was rent by an earthquake. Astonished at the sight, he went down into the chasm and saw, among other wonders of which the story tells, a brazen horse, hollow, with windows in its sides. Peering in, he saw a dead body, which seemed to be of more than human size. It was naked save for a gold ring, which he took from the finger and made his way out. When the shepherds met, as they did every month, to send an account to the King of the state of his flocks, Gyges came wearing the ring. As he was sitting

From *The Republic of Plato* translated by F. M. Cornford and published by Oxford University Press (1941). Reprinted by permission of Oxford University Press.

with the others, he happened to turn the bezel of the ring inside his hand. At once he became invisible, and his companions, to his surprise, began to speak of him as if he had left them. Then, as he was fingering the ring, he turned the bezel outwards and became visible again. With that, he set about testing the ring to see if it really had this power, and always with the same result: according as he turned the bezel inside or out he vanished and reappeared. After this discovery he contrived to be one of the messengers sent to the court. There he seduced the Queen, and with her help murdered the King and seized the throne.

Now suppose there were two such magic rings, and one were given to the just man, the other to the unjust. No one, it is commonly believed, would have such iron strength of mind as to stand fast in doing right or keep his hands off other men's goods, when he could go to the market-place and fearlessly help himself to anything he wanted, enter houses and sleep with any woman he chose, set prisoners free and kill men at his pleasure, and in a word go about among men with the powers of a god. He would behave no better than the other; both would take the same course. Surely this would be strong proof that men do right only under compulsion; no individual thinks of it as good for him personally, since he does wrong whenever he finds he has the power. Every man believes that wrongdoing pays him personally much better, and, according to this theory, that is the truth. Granted full licence to do as he liked, people would think him a miserable fool if they found him refusing to wrong his neighbours or to touch their belongings, though in public they would keep up a pretence of praising his conduct, for fear of being wronged themselves. So much for that.

STUDY QUESTIONS

1. What does Plato mean by the statement that men practice justice against the grain?

2. Do you think this selection presents an accurate picture of human nature? Explain.

For Further Reading appears on page 187.

ℒ *Broad: Egoism as a Theory of Human Motives*

There seem *prima facie* to be a number of different kinds of ultimate desire which all or most men have. Plausible examples would be the desire to get pleasant experiences and to avoid unpleasant ones, the desire to get and exercise power over others, and the desire to do what is right and to avoid doing what is wrong. Very naturally philosophers have tried to reduce this plurality. They have tried to show that there is one and only one kind of ultimate desire, and that all other desires which seem at first sight to be ultimate are really subordinate to this. I shall call the view that there really are several different kinds of ultimate desire *Pluralism of ultimate desires*, and I shall call the view that there is really only one kind of ultimate desire *Monism of ultimate desires*. Even if a person were a Pluralist about ultimate desires, he might hold that there are certain important features common to all different kinds of ultimate desire.

Now much the most important theory on this subject is that all kinds of ultimate desire are *egoistic*. This is not in itself necessarily a monistic theory. For there might be several irreducibly different kinds of ultimate desire, even if they were all egoistic. Moreover, there might be several irreducibly different, though not necessarily unre-

C. D. Broad, "Egoism as a Theory of Human Motives," *Hibbert Journal*, vol. 48 (1950). Used with permission of The Hibbert Trustees.

lated, senses of the word 'egoistic'; and some desires might be egoistic in one sense and some in another, even if all were egoistic in some sense. But the theory often takes the special form that the only kind of ultimate desire is the desire to get or to prolong pleasant experiences, and to avoid or to cut short unpleasant experiences, for oneself. That *is* a monistic theory. I shall call the wider theory *Psychological Egoism*, and this special form of it *Psychological Hedonism*. Psychological Egoism might be true, even though Psychological Hedonism were false; but, if Psychological Egoism be false, Psychological Hedonism cannot be true.

I shall now discuss Psychological Egoism. I think it is best to begin by enumerating all the kinds of desire that I can think of which might reasonably be called 'egoistic' in one sense or another.

(1) Everyone has a special desire for the continued existence of himself in his present bodily life, and a special dread of his own death. This may be called *desire for self-preservation*. (2) Everyone desires to get and to prolong experiences of certain kinds, and to avoid and to cut short experiences of certain other kinds, because the former are pleasant to him and the latter unpleasant. This may be called *desire for one's own happiness*. (3) Everybody desires to acquire, keep, and develop certain mental and bodily powers and dispositions, and to avoid, get rid of or check certain others. In general he wants to be or to become a

person of a certain kind, and wants not to be or to become a person of certain other kinds. This may be called *desire to be a self of a certain kind*. (4) Everyone desires to feel certain kinds of emotion towards himself and his own powers and dispositions, and not to feel certain other kinds of reflexive emotion. This may be called *desire for self-respect*. (5) Everyone desires to get and to keep for himself the exclusive possession of certain material objects or the means of buying and keeping such objects. This may be called *desire to get and keep property*. (6) Everyone desires to get and to exercise power over certain other persons, so as to make them do what he wishes, regardless of whether they wish it or not. This may be called the *desire for self-assertion*. (7) Everyone desires that other persons shall believe certain things about him and feel certain kinds of emotion towards him. He wants to be noticed, to be respected by some, to be loved by some, to be feared by some, and so on. Under this head come the *desire for self-display*, for *affection*, and so on.

Lastly, it must be noted that some desires, which are concerned primarily with other things or persons, either would not exist at all or would be very much weaker or would take a different form if it were not for the fact that those things or persons already stand in certain relations to oneself. I shall call such relations *egoistic motive-stimulants*. The following are among the most important of these. (i) The relation of ownership. If a person owns a house or a wife, e.g., he feels a much stronger desire to improve the house or to make the woman happy than if the house belongs to another or the woman is married to someone else. (ii) Blood-relationship. A person desires, e.g., the well-being of his own children much more strongly than that of other children. (iii) Relations of love and friendship. A person desires strongly, e.g., to be loved and respected by those whom he loves. He may desire only to be feared by those whom he hates. And he may desire only very mildly, if at all, to be loved and respected by those to whom he feels indifferent. (iv) The relationship of being

fellow-members of an institution to which one feels loyalty and affection. Thus, e.g., an Englishman will be inclined to do services to another Englishman which he would not do for a foreigner, and an Old Etonian will be inclined to do services to another Old Etonian which he would not do for an Old Harrovian.

I think that I have now given a reasonably adequate list of motives and motive-stimulants which could fairly be called 'egoistic' in some sense or other. Our next business is to try to classify them and to consider their inter-relations.

(1) Let us begin by asking ourselves the following question. Which of these motives could act on a person if he had been the only person or thing that had ever existed? The answer is that he could still have had desires for *self-preservation*, for *his own happiness*, to be a *self of a certain kind*, and for *self-respect*. But he could not, unless he were under the delusion that there were other persons or other things, have desires for *property*, for *self-assertion*, or for *self-display*. Nor could he have any of those desires which are stimulated by family or other alio-relative relationships. I shall call those desires, and only those, which could be felt by a person who knew or believed himself to be the only existent in the universe, *self-confined*.

(2) Any desire which is not self-confined may be described as *extra-verted*; for the person who has such a desire is necessarily considering, not only himself and his own qualities, dispositions, and states, but also some other thing or person. If the desire is egoistic, it will also be *intro-verted*; for the person who has such a desire will also be considering himself and his relations to that other person or thing, and this will be an essential factor conditioning his experience. Thus a self-confined desire is purely intro-verted, whilst a desire which is egoistic but not self-confined is both intro-verted and extra-verted. Now we may subdivide desires of the latter kind into two classes, according as the primary emphasis is on the former or the latter aspect. Suppose that the person is concerned primarily

with himself and his own acts and experiences, and that he is concerned with the other thing or person only or mainly as an object of these acts or experiences or as the other term in a relationship to himself. Then I shall call the desire *self-centred*. I shall use the term *self-regarding* to include both desires which are self-centred and those which are self-confined. Under the head of self-centred desires come the desire for *property*, for *self-assertion*, for *self-display*, and for *affection*.

(3) Lastly, we come to desires which are both intro-verted and extra-verted, but where the primary emphasis is on the other person or thing and its states. Here the relationship of the other person or thing to oneself acts as a strong egoistic motive-stimulant, but one's primary desire is that the other person or thing shall be in a certain state. I will call such desires *other-regarding*. A desire which is other-regarding, but involves an egoistic motive-stimulant, may be described as *self-referential*. The desire of a mother to render services to her own children which she would not be willing to render to other children is an instance of a desire which is other-regarding but self-referential. So, too, is the desire of a man to inflict suffering on one who has injured him or whom he envies.

Having thus classified the various kinds of egoistic desire, I will now say something about their inter-relations.

(1) It is obvious that self-preservation may be desired as a necessary condition of one's own happiness; since one cannot acquire or prolong pleasant experiences unless one continues to exist. So the desire for self-preservation *may* be subordinate to the desire for one's own happiness. But it seems pretty clear that a person often desires to go on living even when there is no prospect that the remainder of his life will contain a balance of pleasant over unpleasant experiences.

(2) It is also obvious that property and power over others may be desired as a means to self-preservation or to happiness. So the desire to get and keep property, and the desire to get and exert power over others, *may* be subordinate to the desire for self-preservation or for one's own happiness. But it seems fairly certain that the former desires are sometimes independent of the latter. Even if a person begins by desiring property or power only as a means—and it is very doubtful whether we always do begin in that way—it seems plain that he often comes to desire them for themselves, and to sacrifice happiness, security, and even life for them. Any miser, and almost any keen politician, provides an instance of this.

It is no answer to this to say that a person who desires power or property enjoys the experiences of getting and exercising power or of amassing and owning property, and then to argue that therefore his ultimate desire is to give himself those pleasant experiences. The premise here is true, but the argument is self-stultifying. The experiences in question are pleasant to a person only in so far as he desires power or property. This kind of pleasant experience presupposes desires for something other than pleasant experiences, and therefore the latter desires cannot be derived from desire for that kind of pleasant experience.

Similar remarks apply to the desire for self-respect and the desire for self-display. If one already desires to feel certain emotions towards oneself, or to be the object of certain emotions in others, the experience of feeling those emotions or of knowing that others feel them towards you will be pleasant, because it will be the fulfilment of a pre-existing desire. But this kind of pleasure presupposes the existence of these desires, and therefore they cannot be derived from the desire for that kind of pleasure.

(3) Although the various kinds of egoistic desire cannot be reduced to a single ultimate egoistic desire, e.g., the desire for one's own happiness, they are often very much mixed up with each other. Take, e.g., the special desire which a mother feels for the health, happiness, and prosperity of her children. This is predominantly other-

regarding, though it is self-referential. The mother is directly attracted by the thought of her child as surviving, as having good dispositions and pleasant experiences, and as being the object of love and respect to other persons. She is directly repelled by the thought of his dying, or having bad dispositions or unpleasant experiences, or being the object of hatred or contempt to other persons. The desire is therefore other-regarding. It is self-referential, because the fact that it is *her* child and not another's acts as a powerful motive-stimulant. She would not be prepared to make the same sacrifices for the survival or the welfare of a child which was not her own. But this self-referential other-regarding motive is almost always mingled with other motives which are self-regarding. One motive which a woman has for wanting her child to be happy, healthy and popular is the desire that other women shall envy her as the mother of a happy, healthy and popular child. This motive is subordinate to the self-centred desire for self-display. Another motive, which may be present, is the desire not to be burdened with an ailing, unhappy, and unpopular child. This motive is subordinate to the self-contained desire for one's own happiness. But, although the self-referential other-regarding motive is nearly always mixed with the motives which are self-centred or self-confined, we cannot plausibly explain the behaviour of many mothers on many occasions towards their children without postulating the other-regarding motive.

We can now consider the various forms which Psychological Egoism might take. The most rigid form is that all human motives are ultimately egoistic, and that all egoistic motives are ultimately of one kind. That one kind has generally been supposed to be the desire for one's own happiness, and so this form of psychological Egoism may in practice be identified with Psychological Hedonism. This theory amounts to saying that the only ultimate motives are *self-confined*, and that the only ultimate self-confined motive is *desire for one's own happiness*.

I have already tried to show by examples that this is false. Among self-confined motives, e.g., is the desire for self-preservation, and this cannot be reduced to desire for one's own happiness. Then, again, there are self-regarding motives which are self-centred but not self-confined, such as the desire for affection, for gratitude, for power over others, and so on. And, finally, there are motives which are self-referential but predominantly other-regarding, such as a mother's desire for her children's welfare or a man's desire to injure one whom he hates.

It follows that the only form of Psychological Egoism that is worth discussing is the following. It might be alleged that all ultimate motives are *either* self-confined *or* self-centred *or* other-regarding but self-referential, some being of one kind and some of another. This is a much more modest theory than, e.g., Psychological Hedonism. I think that it covers satisfactorily an immensely wide field of human motivation, but I am not sure that it is true without exception. I shall now discuss it in the light of some examples.

Case A.

Take first the case of a man who does not expect to survive the death of his present body, and who makes a will, the contents of which will be known to no one during his lifetime.

(1) The motive of such a testator cannot possibly be the expectation of any experiences which he will enjoy after death through the provisions of his will being carried out; for he believes that he will have no more experiences after the death of his body. The only way in which this motive could be ascribed to such a man is by supposing that, although he is intellectually convinced of his future extinction, yet in practice he cannot help imagining himself as surviving and witnessing events which will happen after his death. I think that this kind of mental confusion is possible, and perhaps not uncommon; but I should doubt whether it is a plausible account of such a man's motives to say that they all involve this mistake.

(2) Can we say that his motive is the desire to enjoy during his life the pleasant experience of imagining the gratitude which the beneficiaries will feel towards him after his death? The answer is that this may well be *one* of his motives, but it cannot be primary, and therefore cannot be the only one. Unless he desired to be thought about in one way rather than another after his death, the present experience of imagining himself as becoming the object of certain retrospective thoughts and emotions on the part of the beneficiaries would be neither attractive nor repulsive to him.

(3) I think it is plain, then, that the ultimate motive of such a man cannot be desire for his own happiness. But it might be desire for power over others. For he may be said to be exercising this power when he makes his will, even though the effects will not begin until after his death.

(4) Can we say that his motive in making the will is simply to ensure that certain persons will think about him and feel towards him in certain ways after his death? In that case his motive would come under the head of self-display. (This must, of course, be distinguished from the question, already discussed, whether his motive might be to give himself the pleasant experience of imagining their future feelings of gratitude towards him). The answer is that self-display, in a wide sense, may be a motive, and a very strong one, in making a will; but it could hardly be the sole motive. A testator generally considers the relative needs of various possible beneficiaries, the question whether a certain person would appreciate and take care of a certain picture or house or book, the question whether a certain institution is doing work which he thinks important, and so on. In so far as he is influenced by these considerations, his motives are other-regarding. But they may be all self-referential. In making his will he may desire to benefit persons only in so far as they are *his* relatives or friends. He may desire to benefit institutions only in so far as *he* is or has been a member of them. And so on. I think that it would be quite plausible to hold that the motives of such a testator are all either self-regarding or self-referential, but that it would not be in the least plausible to say that they are all self-confined or that none of them are other-regarding.

Case B.

Let us next consider the case of a man who subscribes anonymously to a certain charity. His motive cannot possibly be that of self-display. Can we say that his motive is to enjoy the pleasant experience of self-approval and of seeing an institution in which he is interested flourishing? The answer is, again, that these motives may exist and may be strong, but they cannot be primary and therefore cannot be his only motives. Unless he wants the institution to flourish, there will be nothing to attract him in the experience of seeing it flourish. And, unless he subscribes from some other motive than the desire to enjoy a feeling of self-approval, he will not obtain a feeling of self-approval. So here, again, it seems to me that some of his motives must be other-regarding. But it is quite possible that his other-regarding motives may all be self-referential. An essential factor in making him want to benefit this institution may be that it is *his* old college or that a great friend of *his* is at the head of it.

The question, then, that remains is this. Are there any cases in which it is reasonable to think that a person's motive is not egoistic in any of the senses mentioned? In practice, as we now see, this comes down to the question whether there are any cases in which an other-regarding motive is not stimulated by an egoistic motive-stimulus, i.e., whether there is any other-regarding motive which is not also and essentially self-referential.

Case C.

Let us consider the case of a person who deliberately chooses to devote his life to working among lepers, in the full knowledge that he will almost certainly contract leprosy and die in a particularly loathsome way. This is not an imaginary case. To give the Psychological Egoist the longest possible run for his money I will suppose that a person is a Roman Catholic priest, who believes that his action may secure for him a place in heaven in the next world and a reputation for sanctity and heroism in this, that it may be rewarded posthumously with canonization, and that it will redound to the credit of the church of which he is an ordained member.

It is difficult to see what self-regarding or self-referential motives there could be *for* the action beside desire for happiness in heaven, desire to gain a reputation for sanctity and heroism and perhaps to be canonized after death, and desire to glorify the church of which one is a priest. Obviously there are extremely strong self-confined and self-centred motives *against* choosing this kind of life. And in many cases there must have been very strong self-referential other-regarding motives *against* it. For the person who made such a choice must sometimes have been a young man of good family and brilliant prospects, whose parents were heart-broken at his decision, and whose friends thought him an obstinate fool for making it.

Now there is no doubt at all that there was an other-regarding motive, viz. a direct desire to alleviate the sufferings of the lepers. No one who was not dying in the last ditch for an over-simple theory of human nature would deny this. The only questions that are worth raising about it are these: (1) Is this other-regarding motive stimulated by an egoistic motive–stimulus and thus rendered self-referential? (2) Suppose that this motive had not been supported by the various self-regarding and self-referential motives *for* deciding to go and work among the lepers, would it have sufficed, in presence of the motives *against* doing so, to ensure the choice that was actually made?

As regards the first question, I cannot see that there was any special pre-existing relationship between a young priest in Europe and a number of unknown lepers in Asia which might plausibly be held to act as an egoistic motive-stimulus. The lepers are neither his relatives nor his friends nor his benefactors nor members of any community or institution to which he belongs.

As regards the sufficiency of the other-regarding motive, whether stimulated egoistically or not, in the absence of all self-regarding motives tending in the same direction, no conclusive answer can be given. I cannot prove that a single person in the whole course of history *would* have decided to work among lepers, if all the motives against doing so had been present, whilst the hope of heaven, the desire to gain a reputation for sanctity and heroism, and the desire to glorify and extend one's church had been wholly absent. Nor can the Psychological Egoist prove that *no* single person would have so decided under these hypothetical conditions. Factors which cannot be eliminated cannot be shown to be necessary and cannot be shown to be superfluous; and there we must leave the matter.

I suspect that a Psychological Egoist might be tempted to say that the intending medical missionary found the experience of imagining the sufferings of the lepers intensely unpleasant, and that his primary motive for deciding to spend his life working among them was to get rid of this unpleasant experience. This, I think, is what Locke, e.g., would have had to say in accordance with his theory of motivation. About this suggestion there are two remarks to be made.

(1) This motive cannot have been primary, and therefore cannot have been the only motive. Unless this person desired that the lepers should have their sufferings alleviated, there is no reason why the thought of their sufferings should be an unpleasant experience to him. A malicious man, e.g., finds the thought of the sufferings of an enemy a very pleasant experience. This kind of pleasure presupposes a desire for the well-being or the ill-being of others.

(2) If his primary motive were to rid himself of the unpleasant experience of imagining the sufferings of the lepers, he could hardly choose a less effective means than to go and work among them. For the imagination would then be replaced by actual sense-perception; whilst, if he stayed

at home and devoted himself to other activities, he would have a reasonably good chance of diverting his attention from the sufferings of the lepers. In point of fact one knows that such a person would reproach himself in so far as he managed to forget about the lepers. He would *wish* to keep them and their sufferings constantly in mind, as an additional stimulus to doing what he believes he ought to do, viz. to take active steps to help and relieve them.

In this connection it is important to notice the following facts. For most people the best way to realize the sufferings of strangers is to imagine oneself or one's parents or children or some intimate and beloved friend in the situation in which the stranger is placed. This, as we say, 'brings home to one' his sufferings. A large proportion of the cruelty which decent people applaud or tolerate is applauded or tolerated by them only because they are either too stupid to put themselves imaginatively into the position of the victims or because they deliberately refrain from doing so. One important cause of their deliberately refraining is the notion of retributive justice, i.e., the belief that these persons, or a group taken as a collective whole to which they belong, have *deserved* suffering by wrongdoing, and the desire that they shall get their deserts. Another important cause of this deliberate refrainment is the knowledge that one is utterly powerless to help the victims. However this may be, the fact that imagining oneself in their position is often a necessary condition of desiring to relieve the sufferings of strangers does not make that desire self-referential. Imagining oneself in their place is merely a condition for becoming vividly *aware of* their sufferings. Whether one will then desire to relieve them or to prolong them or will remain indifferent to them, depends on motives which are not primarily self-regarding or self-referential.

I will now summarize the results of this discussion.

(1) If Psychological Egoism asserts that all ultimate motives are self-confined; or that they are all either self-confined or self-centred, some being of one kind and some of the other; or that all self-confined motives can be reduced to the desire for one's own happiness; it is certainly false. It is not even a close approximation of the truth.

(2) If it asserts that all ultimate motives are either self-regarding or self-referential, some being of one kind and some of the other; and that all other-regarding motives require a self-referential stimulus, it is a close approximation to the truth. It is true, I think, that in most people and at most times other-regarding motives are very weak unless stimulated by a self-referential stimulus. As England's wisest and wittiest statesman put it in his inimitable way: "Temporal things will have their weight in the world, and, though zeal may prevail for a time and get the better in a skirmish, yet the war endeth generally on the side of flesh and blood, and will do so until mankind is another thing than it is at present."*

(3) Nevertheless, Psychological Egoism, even in its most diluted form, is very doubtful if taken as a universal proposition. Some persons at some times are strongly influenced by other-regarding motives which cannot plausibly be held to be stimulated by a self-referential stimulus. It seems reasonable to hold that the presence of these other-regarding motives is *necessary* to account for their choice of alternatives which they do choose, and for their persistence in the course which they have adopted, though this can never be conclusively established in any particular case. Whether it is also *sufficient* cannot be decided with certainty, for self-regarding and self-referential components are always present in one's total motive for choosing such an action.

I think that the summary which I have just given fairly represents the results of introspection and reflection on one's own and other men's voluntary action. Yet Psychological Egoism in general and Psychological Hedonism in particular have seemed almost self-evident to many highly

*Halifax, *The Character of a Trimmer*.

intelligent thinkers, and they do still seem highly plausible to nearly everyone when he first begins to speculate on human motivation. I believe that this depends, not on empirical facts, but on certain verbal ambiguities and misunderstandings. As so often happens in philosophy, clever people accept a false general principle on *a priori* grounds and then devote endless labour and ingenuity to explaining away plain facts which obviously conflict with it. A full discussion of the subject would require an analysis of the confusions which have made these theories seem so plausible; but this must be omitted here.

I must content myself with the following remarks in conclusion. I have tried to show that Psychological Egoism, in the only form in which it could possibly fit the facts of human life, is not a monistic theory of motives. On this extended interpretation of the theory the only feature common to all motives is that every motive which can *act on* a person has one or another of a large number of different kinds of special *reference to* that person. I have tried to show that this certainly covers a very wide field, but that it is by no means certain that there is even this amount of unity among *all* human motives. I think that Psychological Egoism is much the most plausible attempt to reduce the *prima facie* plurality of ultimate kinds of desire to a unity. If it fails, I think it is most unlikely that any alternative attempt on a different basis will succeed.

For my part I am inclined to accept an irreducibly pluralistic view of human motives. This does not, of course, entail that the present irreducible plurality of ultimate motives may not have evolved, in some sense of that highly ambiguous word, out of fewer, either in the history of each individual or in that of the human race. About that I express no opinion here and now.

Now, if Psychological Hedonism had been true, all conflict of motives would have been between motives of the *same kind*. It would always be of the form "Shall I go to the dentist and certainly be hurt now but probably avoid thereby frequent and pro- longed toothache in future? Or shall I take the risk in order to avoid the certainty of being hurt by the dentist now?" On any pluralistic view there is also conflict between motives of irreducibly *different kinds*, e.g., between aversion to painful experience and desire to be thought manly, or between a desire to shine in conversation and aversion to hurting a sensitive person's feelings by a witty but wounding remark.

It seems to me plain that, in our ordinary moral judgments about ourselves and about others, we always unhesitatingly assume that there can be and often is conflict between motives of radically different kinds. Now I do not myself share that superstitious reverence for the beliefs of common sense which many contemporary philosophers profess. But I think that we must start from them, and that we ought to depart from them only when we find good reason to do so. If Psychological Hedonism, or any other monistic theory of motives had been true, we should have had to begin the study of ethics by recognizing that most moral judgments which we pass on ourselves or on others are made under a profound misapprehension of the psychological facts and are largely vitiated thereby. If Psychological Hedonism, e.g., had been true, the only ethical theory worth discussing would have been an egoistic form of ethical Hedonism. For one cannot be under an obligation to attempt to do what is psychologically impossible. And, on the hypothesis of Psychological Hedonism, it is psychologically impossible for anyone ultimately to desire anything except to prolong or acquire experiences which he knows or expects to be pleasant and to cut short or avoid experiences which he knows or expects to be unpleasant. If it were still possible to talk of having duties at all, each person's duties would be confined within the limits which that psychological impossibility marks out. And it would clearly be impossible to suppose that any part of anyone's ultimate motive for doing any act is his belief that it would be right in the circumstances together with his desire to do what is right as such. For, if Psychological Hedonism were true, a desire to do what is right could not be ultimate, it must be subordinate to the desire to get or prolong pleasant experiences and to avoid or cut short unpleasant ones.

Now it is plain that such consequences as these conflict sharply with common-sense notions of morality. If we had been obliged to accept Psychological Egoism, in any of its narrower forms, on its merits, we should have had to say: 'So much the worse for the common-sense notions of morality!' But, if I am right, the morality of common sense, with all its difficulties and incoherences, is immune at least to attacks from the basis of Psychological Egoism.

STUDY QUESTIONS

1. What does Broad mean by Psychological Egoism? Psychological Hedonism? How are they related? Do you think that either theory is true?

2. Do you think that Broad's analysis of the various kinds of desires and motives people have is accurate? Complete? Explain.

3. Do you accept the connection Broad draws between retributive punishment and cruelty?

4. Do you think the motives from which you act are always egoistic? Do you think they ought to be? Why or why not?

For Further Reading

Baier, K. *The Moral Point of View.* Ithaca: Cornell University Press, 1958 (Chapter 8).

Butler, J. *Fifteen Sermons Upon Human Nature.* (Sermon 11).

Ewing, A. C. *Ethics.* London: English Universities Press, 1953 (Chapter 2).

Gauthier, D. P., ed. *Morality and Rational Self-Interest.* Englewood Cliffs, N.J.: Prentice-Hall, 1970.

Mandeville, B. *Fable of the Bees.*

Nagel, T. *The Possibility of Altruism.* Oxford: Clarendon Press, 1970 (esp. Part Three).

Olson, R. G. *The Morality of Self-Interest.* New York: Harcourt, Brace & World, 1965 (esp. Chapter 1).

Rescher, N. *Unselfishness.* Pittsburgh: University of Pittsburgh Press, 1975.

BENTHAM: HEDONISM

If we agree, as most people do, that happiness is the most desirable thing in life, we are still left with the question: What does it mean to be happy? Among the oldest answers that have been given to this question is that of the hedonists. Happiness, they say, is the same thing as pleasure; unhappiness the same thing as pain. This does not mean, however, that one should spend his life in riotous living. As the ancient Greek hedonist, Epicurus, pointed out, a quiet, abstemious life produces more pleasure, and certainly less pain, in the long run than one of constant indulgence. Nor does it mean a self-centered pursuit of personal enjoyment. If pleasure is the only good, Jeremy Bentham argued, then any individual's pleasure is equally as good as that of any other. As we go about seeking our own pleasure, therefore, each of us has an obligation to promote a like pleasure for all those whose lives our actions affect. This obligation, Bentham adds, falls most heavily on those who hold positions of influence and power, for what they do has effects on the welfare of the entire society.

It is hard to say whether Jeremy Bentham (1748–1832) is more important as a philosopher or as a social reformer. Certainly he made great contributions as both. Nor were the two completely distinguishable, for most of his theoretical writings, besides being significant contributions to the history of thought, also served as foundations for campaigns of reform. During the course of Bentham's long active life, the central institutions of English political and social life underwent profound change, almost always for the better. A good portion of the credit for this change must be accorded to Jeremy Bentham.

✣ An Introduction to the Principles of Morals and Legislation

Chapter I
Of the Principle of Utility.

I

Nature has placed mankind under the governance of two sovereign masters, *pain* and *pleasure*. It is for them alone to point out what we ought to do, as well as to determine what we shall do. On the one hand, the standard of right and wrong, on the other, the chain of causes and effects, are fastened to their throne. They govern us in all we do, in all we say, in all we think: every effort we can make to throw off our subjection, will serve but to demonstrate and confirm it. In words, a man may pretend to abjure their empire: but, in reality, he will remain subject to it all the while. The *principle of utility* recognizes this subjection, and assumes it for the foundation of that system, the object of which is to tear the fabric of felicity by the hands of reason and of law. Systems which attempt to question it, deal in sounds instead of sense, in caprice instead of reason, in darkness instead of light.

But enough of metaphor and declamation: it is not by such means that moral science is to be improved.

II

The principle of utility is the foundation of the present work: it will be proper, therefore, at the outset to give an explicit and determinate account of what is meant by it. By the principle of utility is meant that principle which approves or disapproves of

every action whatsoever, according to the tendency which it appears to have to augment or diminish the happiness of the party whose interest is in question: or, what is the same thing in other words, to promote or to oppose that happiness. I say of every action whatsoever; and, therefore, not only of every action of a private individual, but of every measure of government.

III

By utility is meant that property in any object, whereby it tends to produce benefit, advantage, pleasure, good, or happiness (all this in the present case comes to the same thing), or (what comes again to the same thing) to prevent the happening of mischief, pain, evil, or unhappiness to the party whose interest is considered: if that party be the community in general, then the happiness of the community: if a particular individual, then the happiness of that individual.

IV

The interest of the community is one of the most general expressions that can occur in the phraseology of morals: no wonder that the meaning of it is often lost. When it has a meaning, it is this. The community is a fictitious *body*, composed of the individual persons who are considered as constituting, as it were, its *members*. The interest of the community then is, what?—the sum of the interests of the several members who compose it.

V

It is in vain to talk of the interest of the community, without understanding what is the interest of the individual. A thing is

First published in 1789. Bentham's footnotes and Chapter II, in which he criticizes other theories, are not included.

said to promote the interest, or to be *for* the interest, of an individual, when it tends to add to the sum total of his pleasures: or, what comes to the same thing, to diminish the sum total of his pains.

VI

An action, then, may be said to be conformable to the principle of utility, or, for shortness' sake, to utility (meaning with respect to the community at large), when the tendency it has to augment the happiness of the community is greater than any it has to diminish it.

VII

A measure of government (which is but a particular kind of action, performed by a particular person or persons) may be said to be conformable to or dictated by the principle of utility, when in like manner the tendency which it has to augment the happiness of the community is greater than any which it has to diminish it.

VIII

When an action, or in particular a measure of government, is supposed by a man to be conformable to the principle of utility, it may be convenient, for the purposes of discourse, to imagine a kind of law or dictate, called a law or dictate of utility: and to speak of the action in question, as being conformable to such law or dictate.

IX

A man may be said to be a partisan of the principle of utility, when the approbation or disapprobation he annexes to any action, or to any measure, is determined by and proportioned to the tendency which he conceives it to have to augment or to diminish the happiness of the community: or in other words, to its conformity or unconformity to the laws or dictates of utility.

X

Of an action that is conformable to the principle of utility, one may always say either that it is one that ought to be done, or at least that it is not one that ought not to be done. One may say also, that it is right it

should be done; at least that it is not wrong it should be done: that it is a right action; at least that it is not a wrong action. When thus interpreted, the words *ought*, and *right* and *wrong*, and others of that stamp, have a meaning: when otherwise, they have none.

XI

Has the rectitude of this principle been ever formally contested? It should seem that it had, by those who have not known what they have been meaning. Is it susceptible of any direct proof? It should seem not: for that which is used to prove everything else, cannot itself be proved: a chain of proofs must have their commencement somewhere. To give such proof is as impossible as it is needless.

XII

Not that there is or ever has been that human creature breathing, however stupid or perverse, who has not on many, perhaps on most occasions of his life, deferred to it. By the natural constitution of the human frame, on most occasions of their lives men in general embrace this principle, without thinking of it: if not for the ordering of their own actions, yet for the trying of their own actions, as well as of those of other men. There have been, at the same time, not many, perhaps, even of the most intelligent, who have been disposed to embrace it purely and without reserve. There are even few who have not taken some occasion or other to quarrel with it, either on account of their not understanding always how to apply it, or on account of some prejudice or other which they were afraid to examine into, or could not bear to part with. For such is the stuff that man is made of: in principle and in practice, in a right track and in a wrong one, the rarest of all human qualities is consistency.

XIII

When a man attempts to combat the principle of utility, it is with reasons drawn, without his being aware of it, from that very principle itself. His arguments, if they prove anything, prove not that the principle is *wrong*, but that, according to the applications he supposes to be made of it, it is *misapplied*. Is it possible for a man to move the earth? Yes, but he must first find out another earth to stand upon.

XIV

To disprove the propriety of it by arguments is impossible; but, from the causes that have been mentioned, or from some confused or partial view of it, a man may happen to be disposed not to relish it. Where this is the case, if he thinks the settling of his opinions on such a subject worth the trouble, let him take the following steps, and at length, perhaps, he may come to reconcile himself to it.

1. Let him settle with himself, whether he would wish to discard this principle altogether; if so, let him consider what it is that all his reasonings (in matters of politics especially) can amount to?

2. If he would, let him settle with himself, whether he would judge and act without any principle, or whether there is any other he would judge and act by?

3. If there be, let him examine and satisfy himself whether the principle he thinks he has found is really any separate intelligible principle; or whether it be not a mere principle in words, a kind of phrase, which at bottom expresses neither more nor less than the mere averment of his own unfounded sentiments; that is, what in another person he might be apt to call caprice?

4. If he is inclined to think that his own approbation or disapprobation, annexed to the idea of an act, without any regard to its consequences, is a sufficient foundation for him to judge and act upon, let him ask himself whether his sentiment is to be a standard of right and wrong, with respect to every other man, or whether every man's sentiment has the same privilege of being a standard to itself?

5. In the first case, let him ask himself whether his principle is not despotical, and hostile to all the rest of the human race?

6. In the second case, whether it is not anarchical, and whether at this rate there are not as many different standards of right and wrong as there are men? and

whether even to the same man, the same thing, which is right today, may not (without the least change in its nature) be wrong tomorrow? and whether the same thing is not right and wrong in the same place at the same time? and in either case, whether all argument is not at an end? and whether, when two men have said, "I like this," and "I don't like it," they can (upon such a principle) have anything more to say?

7. If he should have said to himself, No: for that the sentiment which he proposes as a standard must be grounded on reflection, let him say on what particulars the reflection is to turn? If on particulars having relation to the utility of the act, then let him say whether this is not deserting his own principle, and borrowing assistance from that very one in opposition to which he sets it up: or if not on those particulars, on what other particulars?

8. If he should be for compounding the matter, and adopting his own principle in part, and the principle of utility in part, let him say how far he will adopt it?

9. When he has settled with himself where he will stop, then let him ask himself how he justifies to himself the adopting it so far? and why he will not adopt it any farther?

10. Admitting any other principle than the principle of utility to be a right principle, a principle that it is right for a man to pursue; admitting (what is not true) that the word *right* can have a meaning without reference to utility, let him say whether there is any such thing as a *motive* that a man can have to pursue the dictates of it: if there is, let him say what that motive is, and how it is to be distinguished from those which enforce the dictates of utility: if not, then lastly let him say what it is this other principle can be good for?

Chapter III
Of the Four Sanctions or Sources of Pain and Pleasure.

I

It has been shown that the happiness of the individuals, of whom a community is composed, that is, their pleasures and their security, is the end and the sole end which the legislator ought to have in view: the sole standard in conformity to which each individual ought, as far as depends upon the legislator, to be *made* to fashion his behavior. But whether it be this or anything else that is to be *done*, there is nothing by which a man can ultimately be *made* to do it, but either pain or pleasure. Having taken a general view of these two grand objects (*viz.*, pleasure, and what comes to the same thing—immunity from pain) in the character of *final* causes; it will be necessary to take a view of pleasure and pain itself, in the character of *efficient* causes or means.

II

There are four distinguishable sources from which pleasure and pain are in use to flow: considered separately, they may be termed the *physical*, the *political*, the *moral*, and the *religious*; and inasmuch as the pleasures and pains belonging to each of them are capable of giving a binding force to any law or rule of conduct, they may all of them be termed *sanctions*.

III

If it be in the present life, and from the ordinary course of nature, not purposely modified by the interposition of the will of any human being, nor by any extraordinary interposition of any superior invisible being, that the pleasure or the pain takes place or is expected, it may be said to issue from, or to belong to, the *physical sanction*.

IV

If at the hands of a *particular* person or set of persons in the community, who under names correspondent to that of *judge*, are chosen for the particular purpose of dispensing it, according to the will of the sovereign or supreme ruling power in the state, it may be said to issue from the *political sanction*.

V

If at the hands of such *chance* persons in the community, as the party in question may happen in the course of his life to have concerns with, according to each man's spontaneous disposition, and not according to any settled or concerted rule, it may be said to issue from the *moral* or *popular sanction*.

VI

If from the immediate hand of a superior invisible being, either in the present life, or in a future, it may be said to issue from the *religious sanction*.

VII

Pleasures or pains which may be expected to issue from the *physical, political, or moral* sanctions, must all of them be expected to be experienced, if ever, in the *present* life: those which may be expected to issue from the *religious* sanction, may be expected to be experienced either in the *present* life or in a *future*.

VIII

Those which can be experienced in the present life, can of course be no others than such as human nature in the course of the present life is susceptible of: and from each of these sources may flow all the pleasures or pains of which, in the course of the present life, human nature is susceptible. With regard to these, then (with which alone we have in this place any concern), those of them which belong to any one of those sanctions, differ not ultimately in kind from those which belong to any one of the other three: the only difference there is among them lies in the circumstances that accompany their production. A suffering which befalls a man in the natural and spontaneous course of things, shall be styled, for instance, a *calamity*; in which case, if it be supposed to befall him through any imprudence of his, it may be styled a punishment issuing from the physical sanction. Now this same suffering, if inflicted by the law, will be what is commonly called a *punishment*; if incurred for want of friendly assistance, which the misconduct, or supposed misconduct, of the sufferer has occasioned to be withholden, a punishment issuing from the *moral* sanction; if through the immediate interposition of a particular providence, a punishment issuing from the religious sanction.

IX

A man's goods, or his person, are consumed by fire. If this happened to him by what is called an accident, it was a calamity: if by reason of his own imprudence (for instance, from his neglecting to put his candle out), it may be styled a punishment of the physical sanction: if it happened to him by the sentence of the political magistrate, a punishment belonging to the political sanction—that is, what is commonly called a punishment: if for want of any assistance which his *neighbor* withheld from him out of some dislike to his *moral* character, a punishment of the *moral* sanction: if by an immediate act of *God's* displeasure, manifested on account of some *sin* committed by him, or through any distraction of mind, occasioned by the dread of such displeasure, a punishment of the *religious* sanction.

X

As to such of the pleasures and pains belonging to the religious sanction, as regard a future life, of what kind these may be, we cannot know. These lie not open to our observation. During the present life they are matter only of expectation: and, whether that expectation be derived from natural or revealed religion, the particular kind of pleasure or pain, if it be different from all those which lie open to our observation, is what we can have no idea of. The best ideas we can obtain of such pains and pleasures are altogether unliquidated [i.e., unclear —ed.] in point of quality. In what other respects our ideas of them *may* be liquidated, will be considered in another place.

XI

Of these four sanctions, the physical is altogether, we may observe, the groundwork of the political and the moral: so is it also of the religious, in as far as the latter bears relation to the present life. It is included in each of those other three. This may operate in any case (that is, any of the pains or pleasures belonging to it may operate) independently of *them*: none of *them* can operate but by means of this. In a word, the powers of nature may operate of themselves; but neither the magistrate, nor men at large, *can* operate, nor is God in the case in question *supposed* to operate, but through the powers of nature.

XII

For these four objects, which in their nature have so much in common, it seemed of use to find a common name. It seemed of use, in the first place, for the convenience of giving a name to certain pleasures and pains, for which a name equally characteristic could hardly otherwise have been found: in the second place, for the sake of holding up the efficacy of certain moral forces, the influence of which is apt not to be sufficiently attended to. Does the political sanction exert an influence over the conduct of mankind? The moral, the religious sanctions, do so too. In every inch of his career are the operations of the political magistrate liable to be aided or impeded by these two foreign powers: who, one or other of them, or both, are sure to be either his rivals or his allies. Does it happen to him to leave them out in his calculations? He will be sure almost to find himself mistaken in the result. Of all this we shall find abundant proofs in the sequel of this work. It behooves him, therefore, to have them continually before his eyes; and that under such a name as exhibits the relation they bear to his own purposes and designs.

Chapter IV
Value of a Lot of Pleasure or Pain, How to be Measured.

I

Pleasures, then, and the avoidance of pains are the *ends* which the legislator has in view: it behooves him therefore to understand their *value*. Pleasures and pains are the *instruments* he has to work with: it behooves him therefore to understand their force, which is again, in another point of view, their value.

II

To a person considered *by himself*, the value of a pleasure or pain considered *by itself*, will be greater or less, according to the four following circumstances:

1. Its *intensity*.
2. Its *duration*.
3. Its *certainty* or *uncertainty*.
4. Its *propinquity* or *remoteness*.

III

These are the circumstances which are to be considered in estimating a pleasure or a pain considered each of them by itself. But when the value of any pleasure or pain is considered for the purpose of estimating the tendency of any *act* by which it is produced, there are two other circumstances to be taken into the account; these are:

5. Its *fecundity*, or the chance it has of being followed by sensations of the *same* kind: that is, pains, if it be a pleasure: pains, if it be a pain.

6. Its *purity*, or the chance it has of *not* being followed by sensations of the *opposite* kind: that is, pains if it be a pleasure: pleasures, if it be a pain.

These two last, however, are in strictness scarcely to be deemed properties of the pleasure or the pain itself; they are not, therefore, in strictness to be taken into the account of the value of that pleasure or that pain. They are in strictness to be deemed properties only of the act, or other event, by which such pleasure or pain has been produced; and accordingly are only to be taken into the account of the tendency of such act or such event.

IV

To a *number* of persons, with reference to each of whom the value of a pleasure or a pain is considered, it will be greater or less, according to seven circumstances: to wit, the six preceding ones; *viz.*,

1. Its *intensity*.
2. Its *duration*.

3. Its *certainty* or *uncertainty*.
4. Its *propinquity* or *remoteness*.
5. Its *fecundity*.
6. Its *purity*.

And one other; to wit:

7. Its *extent*; that is, the number of persons to whom it *extends*; or (in other words) who are affected by it.

V

To take an exact account, then, of the general tendency of any act, by which the interests of a community are affected, proceed as follows. Begin with any one person of those whose interests seem most immediately to be affected by it; and take an account:

1. Of the value of each distinguishable *pleasure* which appears to be produced by it in the *first* instance.

2. Of the value of each *pain* which appears to be produced by it in the *first* instance.

3. Of the value of each pleasure which appears to be produced by it *after* the first. This constitutes the *fecundity* of the first *pleasure* and the *impurity* of the first *pain*.

4. Of the value of each *pain* which appears to be produced by it after the first. This constitutes the *fecundity* of the first *pain*, and the *impurity* of the first pleasure.

5. Sum up all the values of all the *pleasures* on the one side, and those of all the pains on the other. The balance, if it be on the side of pleasure, will give the *good* tendency of the act upon the whole, with respect to the interests of that *individual* person; if on the side of pain, the *bad* tendency of it upon the whole.

6. Take an account of the *number* of persons whose interests appear to be concerned; and repeat the above process with respect to each. *Sum up* the numbers expressive of the degrees of *good* tendency, which the act has, with respect to each individual, in regard to whom the tendency of it is *good* upon the whole: do this again with respect to each individual, in regard to whom the tendency of it is *bad* upon the whole. Take the *balance*; which, if on the side of *pleasure*, will give the general *good* tendency of the act, with respect to the total

number or community of individuals concerned; if on the side of pain, the general *evil tendency*, with respect to the same community.

VI

It is not to be expected that the process should be strictly pursued previously to every moral judgment, or to every legislative or judicial operation. It may, however, be always kept in view: and as near as the process actually pursued on these occasions approaches to it, so near will such process approach to the character of an exact one.

STUDY QUESTIONS

1. Bentham begins the selection with an affirmation of a theory known as "psychological hedonism." What is this theory? How is it related to ethical hedonism? Do you think it is true? Explain.

2. What does Bentham mean by the "principle of utility"? How is it related to hedonism?

3. What does Bentham mean by a sanction? What does his theory of sanctions imply concerning human nature? Do you agree with him on this point?

4. Bentham's "hedonistic calculus," or measurement of pleasures and pains, is meant to be a guide for us to follow in deciding how we should act. Do you think it is an adequate practical guide?

5. "Quantity of pleasure being equal, pushpin is as good as poetry" (Bentham). Do you agree? If not, why not? Do your answers help you to decide whether or not you are a hedonist?

For Further Reading

Baumgardt, D. *Bentham and the Ethics of Today*. Princeton, N.J.: Princeton University Press, 1952 (pp. 165–320).

Bayles, M. D., ed. *Contemporary Utilitarianism*. Garden City, N.Y.: Doubleday, 1968.

Lyons, D. *Forms and Limits of Utilitarianism*. Oxford: Clarendon Press, 1965.

Mill, J. S. *Utilitarianism*.

Moore, G. E. *Ethics*. London: Oxford University Press, 1912 (Chapters 1 and 2).

———. *Principia Ethica*. Cambridge, England: At the University Press, 1903 (Chapter 3).

Rashdall, H. *The Theory of Good and Evil*. Oxford: Clarendon Press, 1907 (Vol. I. Chapter 2).

Stephen, L. *The English Utilitarians*. London: Duckworth, 1900 (Vol. I, Chapters 5 and 6).

EPICTETUS: STOICISM

Although Stoicism had its origins among the Greeks during the Hellenistic period, it reached its full fruition in Rome, particularly during the Empire, counting among its adherents the emperor Marcus Aurelius and the statesman Seneca. There is a deep ambivalence in the Stoic view of life. In theory the Stoics held the universe to be good, because ruled by reason. Since nature is good, the individual should always try to conform to it, accepting whatever life brings. In fact, however, the practical admonitions of Stoic writers like Epictetus portray life as a burden that must be "stoically" endured. Despite this curious vacillation between theoretical optimism and practical pessimism, the Stoics advocated a way of life for the individual in society that seems generally as viable in the twentieth century as it must have been in the first.

Epictetus was a slave. A native of Asia Minor, he was sold into slavery while still a child and transported to Rome where he became a member of the household of an officer of Nero's imperial guard. Fortunately, his unusual talents were recognized and he was given an education. Later, he was freed from slavery and became a teacher of philosophy and one of the leading exponents of the doctrines of Stoicism. Epictetus, the date of whose birth is not known, died in A.D. 120, one of the most respected figures of his time.

🦋 *The Enchiridion*

I

Of things some are in our power, and others are not. In our power are opinion, movement towards a thing, desire, aversion; and in a word, whatever are our own acts: not in our power are the body, property, reputation, offices, and in a word, whatever are not our own acts. And the things in our power are by nature free, not subject to restraint nor hindrance: but the things not in our power are weak, slavish, subject to restraint, in the power of others. Remember then that if you think the things which are by nature slavish to be free, and the things which are in the power of others to be your own, you will be hindered, you will lament, you will be disturbed, you will blame both gods and men: but if you think that only which is your own to be your own, and if you think that what is another's, as it really is, belongs to another, no man will ever compel you, no man will hinder you, you will never blame any man, you will accuse no man, you will do nothing involuntarily, no man will harm you, you will have no enemy, for you will not suffer any harm.

If then you desire such great things, remember that you must not lay hold of them with a small effort; but you must leave alone some things entirely, and postpone others for the present. But if you wish for these things also, and power and wealth, perhaps you will not gain even these very things because you aim also at those former things: certainly you will fail in those things through which alone happiness and freedom are secured. Straight-

Translated by George Long.

way then practise saying to every harsh appearance, You are an appearance, and in no manner what you appear to be. Then examine it by the rules which you possess, and by this first and chiefly, whether it relates to the things which are in our power or to things which are not in our power: and if it relates to any thing which is not in our power, be ready to say, that it does not concern you.

II

Remember that desire contains in it the profession of obtaining that which you desire; and the profession in aversion is that you will not fall into that which you attempt to avoid: and he who fails in his desire is unfortunate; and he who falls into that which he would avoid, is unhappy. If then you attempt to avoid only the things contrary to nature which are within your power, you will not be involved in any of the things which you would avoid. But if you attempt to avoid disease or death or poverty, you will be unhappy. Take away then aversion from all things which are not in our power, and transfer it to the things contrary to nature which are in our power. But destroy desire completely for the present. For if you desire anything which is not in our power, you must be unfortunate: but of the things in our power, and which it would be good to desire, nothing yet is before you. But employ only the power of moving towards an object and retiring from it; and these powers indeed only slightly and with exceptions and with remission.

III

In every thing which pleases the soul, or supplies a want, or is loved, remember to add this to the description; what is the nature of each thing, beginning from the smallest? If you love an earthen vessel, say it is an earthen vessel which you love; for when it has been broken, you will not be disturbed. If you are kissing your child or wife, say that it is a human being whom you are kissing, for when the wife or child dies, you will not be disturbed.

IV

When you are going to take in hand any act, remind yourself what kind of an act it is. If you are going to bathe, place before yourself what happens in the bath: some splashing the water, others pushing against one another, others abusing one another, and some stealing: and thus with more safety you will undertake the matter, if you say to yourself, I now intend to bathe, and to maintain my will in a manner comformable to nature. And so you will do in every act: for thus if any hindrance to bathing shall happen, let this thought be ready: it was not this only that I intended, but I intended also to maintain my will in a way conformable to nature; but I shall not maintain it so, if I am vexed at what happens.

V

Men are disturbed not by the things which happen, but by the opinions about the things: for example, death is nothing terrible, for if it were, it would have seemed so to Socrates; for the opinion about death, that it is terrible, is the terrible thing. When then we are impeded or disturbed or grieved, let us never blame others but ourselves, that is, our opinions. It is the act of an ill-instructed man to blame others for his own bad condition; it is the act of one who has begun to be instructed, to lay the blame on himself; and of one whose instruction is completed, neither to blame another, nor himself.

VI

Be not elated at any advantage which belongs to another. If a horse when he is elated should say, I am beautiful, one might endure it. But when you are elated, and say, I have a beautiful horse, you must know that you are elated at having a good horse. What then is your own? The use of appearances. Consequently when in the use of appearances you are conformable to nature, then you will be elated, for then you will be elated at something good which is your own.

VII

As on a voyage when the vessel has reached a port, if you go out to get water, it is an amusement by the way to pick up a shell fish or some bulb, but your thoughts ought to be directed to the ship, and you ought to be constantly watching if the captain should call, and then you must throw away all those things, that you may not be bound and pitched into the ship like sheep: so in life also, if there be given to you instead of a little bulb and a shell a wife and child, there will be nothing to prevent you from taking them. But if the captain should call, run to the ship, and leave all those things without regard to them. But if you are old, do not even go far from the ship, lest when you are called you make default.

VIII

Seek not that the things which happen should happen as you wish: but wish the things which happen to be as they are, and you will have a tranquil flow of life.

IX

Disease is an impediment to the body, but not to the will, unless the will itself chooses. Lameness is an impediment to the leg, but not to the will. And add this reflection on the occasion of every thing that happens; for you will find it an impediment to something else, but not to yourself.

X

On the occasion of every accident that befalls you, remember to turn to yourself and inquire what power you have for turning it to use. If you see a fair man or a fair woman, you will find that the power to resist is temperance. If labour be presented to you, you will find that it is endurance. If it be abusive words, you will find it to be patience. And if you have been thus formed to the proper habit, the appearances will not carry you along with them.

XI

Never say about any thing, I have lost it, but say I have restored it. Is your child dead? It has been restored. Is your wife dead? She has been restored. Has your estate been taken from you? Has not then this also been restored? But he who has taken it from me is a bad man. But what is it to you, by whose hands the giver demanded it back? So long as he may allow you, take care of it as a thing which belongs to another, as travellers do with their inn.

XII

If you intend to improve, throw away such thoughts as these: if I neglect my affairs, I shall not have the means of living: unless I chastise my slave, he will be bad. For it is better to die of hunger and so to be released from grief and fear than to live in abundance with perturbation; and it is better for your slave to be bad than for you to be unhappy. Begin then from little things. Is the oil spilled? Is a little wine stolen? Say on the occasion, at such price is sold freedom from perturbation; at such price is sold tranquillity, but nothing is got for nothing. And when you call your slave, consider that it is possible that he does not hear; and if he does hear, that he will do nothing which you wish. But matters are not so well with him, but altogether well with you, that it should be in his power for you to be not disturbed.

XIII

If you would improve, submit to be considered without sense and foolish with respect to externals. Wish to be considered to know nothing: and if you shall seem to some to be a person of importance, distrust yourself. For you should know that it is not easy both to keep your will in a condition conformable to nature and to secure external things: but if a man is careful about the one, it is an absolute necessity that he will neglect the other.

XIV

If you would have your children and your wife and your friends to live for ever, you are silly; for you would have the things which are not in your power to be in your power, and the things which belong to others to be yours. So if you would have your slave to be free from faults, you are a fool; for you would have badness not to be badness, but something else. But if you wish not to fail in your desires, you are able to do that. Practise then this which you are able to do. He is the master of every man who has the power over the things, which another person wishes or does not wish, the power to confer them on him or to take them away. Whoever then wishes to be free, let him neither wish for any thing nor avoid anything which depends on others: if he does not observe this rule, he must be a slave.

XV

Remember that in life you ought to behave as at a banquet. Suppose that something is carried round and is opposite to you. Stretch out your hand and take a portion with decency. Suppose that it passes by you. Do not detain it. Suppose that it is not yet come to you. Do not send your desire forward to it, but wait till it is opposite to you. Do so with respect to children, so with respect to a wife, so with respect to magisterial offices, so with respect to wealth, and you will be some time a worthy partner of the banquets of the gods. But if you take none of the things which are set before you, and even despise them, then you will be not only a fellow banqueter with the gods, but also a partner with them in power. For by acting thus Diogenes and Heracleitus and those like them were deservedly divine, and were so called.

XVI

When you see a person weeping in sorrow either when a child goes abroad or when he is dead, or when the man has lost his property, take care that the appearance do not hurry you away with it, as if he were suffering in external things. But straightway make a distinction in your own mind, and be in readiness to say, it is not that which has happened that afflicts this man, for it does not afflict another, but it is the opinion about this thing which afflicts the man. So far as words then do not be unwilling to show him sympathy, and even if it happens so, to lament with him. But take care that you do not lament internally also.

XVII

Remember that thou art an actor in a play, of such a kind as the author may choose; if short, of a short one; if long, of a long one: if he wishes you to act the part of a poor man, see that you act the part naturally; if the part of a lame man, of a magistrate, of a private person, do the same. For this is your duty, to act well the part that is given to you; but to select the part, belongs to another.

XVIII

When a raven has croaked inauspiciously, let not the appearance hurry you away with it; but straightway make a distinction in your mind and say, None of these things is signified to me, but either to my poor body, or to my small property, or to my reputation, or to my children, or to my wife: but to me all significations are auspicious if I choose. For whatever of these things results, it is in my power to derive benefit from it.

XIX

You can be invincible, if you enter into no contest in which it is not in your power to conquer. Take care then when you observe a man honoured before others or possessed of great power or highly esteemed for any reason, not to suppose him happy, and be not carried away by the appearance. For if the nature of the good is in our power, neither envy nor jealousy will have a place in us. But you yourself will not wish to be a general or senator or consul, but a free man: and there is only one way to this,

to despise the things which are not in our power.

XX

Remember that is not he who reviles you or strikes you, who insults you, but it is your opinion about these things as being insulting. When then a man irritates you, you must know that it is your own opinion which has irritated you. Therefore especially try not to be carried away by the appearance. For if you once gain time and delay, you will more easily master yourself.

XXI

Let death and exile and every other thing which appears dreadful be daily before your eyes; but most of all death: and you will never think of any thing mean nor will you desire any thing extravagantly.

XXII

If you desire philosophy, prepare yourself from the beginning to be ridiculed, to expect that many will sneer at you, and say, He has all at once returned to us as a philosopher; and whence does he get this supercilious look for us? Do you not show a supercilious look; but hold on to the things which seem to you best as one appointed by God to this station. And remember that if you abide in the same principles, these men who first ridiculed will afterwards admire you: but if you shall have been overpowered by them, you will bring on yourself double ridicule.

XXIII

If it should ever happen to you to be turned to externals in order to please some person, you must know that you have lost your purpose in life. Be satisfied then in every thing with being a philosopher; and if you wish to seem also to any person to be a philosopher, appear so to yourself, and you will be able to do this.

XXIV

Let not these thoughts afflict you, I shall live unhonoured and be nobody nowhere.

For if want of honour is an evil, you cannot be in evil through the means of another any more than you can be involved in any thing base. Is it then your business to obtain the rank of a magistrate, or to be received at a banquet? By no means. How then can this be want of honour? And how will you be nobody nowhere, when you ought to be somebody in those things only which are in your power, in which indeed it is permitted to you to be a man of the greatest worth? But your friends will be without assistance! What do you mean by being without assistance? They will not receive money from you, nor will you make them Roman citizens. Who then told you that these are among the things which are in our power, and not in the power of others? And who can give to another what he has not himself? Acquire money then, your friends say, that we also may have something. If I can acquire money and also keep myself modest, and faithful and magnanimous, point out the way, and I will acquire it. But if you ask me to lose the things which are good and my own, in order that you may gain the things which are not good, see how unfair and silly you are. Besides, which would you rather have, money or a faithful and modest friend? For this end then rather help me to be such a man, and do not ask me to do this by which I shall lose that character. But my country, you say, as far as it depends on me, will be without my help. I ask again, what help do you mean? It will not have porticoes or baths through you. And what does this mean? For it is not furnished with shoes by means of a smith, nor with arms by means of a shoemaker. But it is enough if every man fully discharges the work that is his own: and if you provided it with another citizen faithful and modest, would you not be useful to it? Yes. Then you also cannot be useless to it. What place then, you say, shall I hold in the city? Whatever you can, if you maintain at the same time your fidelity and modesty. But if when you wish to be useful to the state, you shall lose these qualities, what profit could you be to it, if you were made shameless and faithless?

XXV

Has any man been preferred before you at a banquet, or in being saluted, or in being invited to a consultation? If these things are good, you ought to rejoice that he has obtained them: but if bad, be not grieved because you have not obtained them; and remember that you cannot, if you do not the same things in order to obtain what is not in our own power, be considered worthy of the same things. For how can a man obtain an equal share with another when he does not visit a man's doors as that other man does, when he does not attend him when he goes abroad, as the other man does; when he does not praise him as another does? You will be unjust then and insatiable, if you do not part with the price, in return for which those things are sold, and if you wish to obtain them for nothing. Well, what is the price of lettuces? An obolus perhaps. If then a man gives up the obolus, and receives the lettuces, and if you do not give up the obolus and do not obtain the lettuces, do not suppose that you receive less than he who has got the lettuces; for as he has the lettuces, so you have the obolus which you did not give. In the same way then in the other matter also you have not been invited to a man's feast, for you did not give to the host the price at which the supper is sold; but he sells it for praise, he sells it for personal attention. Give then the price, if it is for your interest, for which it is sold. But if you wish both not to give the price and to obtain the things, you are insatiable and silly. Have you nothing then in place of the supper? You have indeed, you have the not flattering of him, whom you did not choose to flatter; you have the not enduring of the man when he enters the room.

XXVI

We may learn the will of nature from the things in which we do not differ from one another: for instance, when your neighbour's slave has broken his cup, or any thing else, we are ready to say forthwith, that it is one of the things which happen. You must know then that when your cup also is broken, you ought to think as you did when your neighbour's cup was broken. Transfer this reflection to greater things also. Is another man's child or wife dead? There is no one who would not say, this is an event incident to man. But when a man's own child or wife is dead, forthwith he calls out, Wo to me, how wretched I am. But we ought to remember how we feel when we hear that it has happened to others.

XXVII

As a mark is not set up for the purpose of missing the aim, so neither does the nature of evil exist in the world.

XXVIII

If any person was intending to put your body in the power of any man whom you fell in with on the way, you would be vexed: but that you put your understanding in the power of any man whom you meet, so that if he should revile you, it is disturbed and troubled, are you not ashamed at this?

XXIX

In every act observe the things which come first, and those which follow it; and so proceed to the act. If you do not, at first you will approach it with alacrity, without having thought of the things which will follow; but afterwards, when certain base things have shown themselves, you will be ashamed. A man wishes to conquer at the Olympic games. I also wish indeed, for it is a fine thing. But observe both the things which come first, and the things which follow; and then begin the act. You must do every thing according to rule, eat according to strict orders, abstain from delicacies, exercise yourself as you are bid at appointed times, in heat, in cold, you must not drink cold water, nor wine as you choose; in a word, you must deliver yourself up to the exercise master as you do to the physician, and then proceed to the contest. And sometimes you will strain the hand, put the ankle out of joint, swallow much dust, sometimes be flogged, and after all this be defeated. When you have considered all this, if you still choose, go to the contest: if you do not, you will behave like children, who at one time play at wrestlers, another time as flute players, again as gladiators, then as trumpeters, then as tragic actors: so you also will be at one time an athlete, at another a gladiator, then a rhetorician, then a philosopher, but with your whole soul you will be nothing at all; but like an ape you imitate every thing that you see, and one thing after another pleases you. For you have not undertaken any thing with consideration, nor have you surveyed it well; but carelessly and with cold desire. Thus some who have seen a philosopher and having heard one speak, as Euphrates speaks,—and who can speak as he does?—they wish to be philosophers themselves also. My man, first of all consider what kind of thing it is: and then examine your own nature, if you are able to sustain the character. Do you wish to be a pentathlete or a wrestler? Look at your arms, your thighs, examine your loins. For different men are formed by nature for different things. Do you think that if you do these things, you can eat in the same manner, drink in the same manner, and in the same manner loathe certain things? You must pass sleepless nights, endure toil, go away from your kinsmen, be despised by a slave, in every thing have the inferior part, in honour, in office, in the courts of justice, in every little matter. Consider these things, if you would exchange for them, freedom from passions, liberty, tranquillity. If not, take care that, like little children, you be not now a philosopher, then a servant of the publicani, then a rhetorician, then a procurator for Caesar. These things are not consistent. You must be one man, either good or bad. You must either cultivate your own ruling faculty, or external things; you must either exercise your skill on internal things or on external things; that is you must either maintain the position of a philosopher or that of a common person.

XXX

Duties are universally measured by relations. Is a man a father? The precept is to take care of him, to yield to him in all things, to submit when he is reproachful, when he inflicts blows. But suppose that he is a bad father. Were you then by nature made akin to a good father? No; but to a father. Does a brother wrong you? Maintain then your own position towards him, and do not examine what he is doing, but what you must do that your will shall be conformable to nature. For another will not damage you, unless you choose: but you will be damaged then when you shall think that you are damaged. In this way then you will discover your duty from the relation of a neighbour, from that of a citizen, from that of a general, if you are accustomed to contemplate the relations.

XXXI

As to piety towards the Gods you must know that this is the chief thing, to have right opinions about them, to think that they exist, and that they administer the All well and justly; and you must fix yourself in this principle, to obey them, and to yield to them in every thing which happens, and voluntarily to follow it as being accomplished by the wisest intelligence. For if you do so, you will never either blame the Gods, nor will you accuse them of neglecting you. And it is not possible for this to be done in any other way than by withdrawing from the things which are not in our power, and by placing the good and the evil only in those things which are in our power. For if you think that any of the things which are not in our power is good or bad, it is absolutely necessary that, when you do not obtain what you wish, and when you fall into those things which you do not wish, you will find fault and hate those who are the cause of them; for every animal is formed by nature to this, to fly from and to turn from the things which appear harmful and the things which are the cause of the harm, but to follow and admire the things which are useful and the causes of the useful. It is impossible then for a person

who thinks that he is harmed to be delighted with that which he thinks to be the cause of the harm, as it is also impossible to be pleased with the harm itself. For this reason also a father is reviled by his son, when he gives no part to his son of the things which are considered to be good: and it was this which made Polynices and Eteocles enemies, the opinion that royal power was a good. It is for this reason that the cultivator of the earth reviles the Gods, for this reason the sailor does, and the merchant, and for this reason those who lose their wives and their children. For where the useful is, there also piety is. Consequently he who takes care to desire as he ought and to avoid as he ought, at the same time also cares after piety. But to make libations and to sacrifice and to offer first fruits according to the custom of our fathers, purely and not meanly nor carelessly nor scantily nor above our ability, is a thing which belongs to all to do.

XXXII

When you have recourse to divination, remember that you do not know how it will turn out, but that you are come to inquire from the diviner. But of what kind it is, you know when you come, if indeed you are a philosopher. For if it is any of the things which are not in our power, it is absolutely necessary that it must be neither good nor bad. Do not then bring to the diviner desire or aversion: if you do, you will approach him with fear. But having determined in your mind that every thing which shall turn out is indifferent, and does not concern you, and whatever it may be, for it will be in your power to use it well, and no man will hinder this, come then with confidence to the Gods as your advisers. And then when any advice shall have been given, remember whom you have taken as advisers, and whom you will have neglected, if you do not obey them. And go to divination, as Socrates said that you ought, about those matters in which all the inquiry has reference to the result, and in which means are not given either by reason nor by any other art for knowing the thing which is the subject of the inquiry. Wherefore when we ought to share a friend's danger or that of our country, you must not consult the diviner whether you ought to share it. For even if the diviner shall tell you that the signs of the victims are unlucky, it is plain that this is a token of death or mutilation of part of the body or of exile. But reason prevails that even with these risks we should share the dangers of our friend and of our country. Therefore attend to the greater diviner, the Pythian God, who ejected from the temple him who did not assist his friend when he was being murdered.

XXXIII

Immediately prescribe some character and some form to yourself, which you shall observe both when you are alone and when you meet with men.

And let silence be the general rule, or let only what is necessary be said, and in few words. And rarely and when the occasion calls we shall say something; but about none of the common subjects, not about gladiators, nor horse races, nor about athletes, nor about eating or drinking, which are the usual subjects; and especially not about men, as blaming them or praising them, or comparing them. If then you are able, bring over by your conversation the conversation of your associates to that which is proper; but if you should happen to be confined to the company of strangers, be silent.

Let not your laughter be much, nor on many occasions, nor excessive. Refuse altogether to take an oath, if it is possible: if it is not, refuse as far as you are able.

Avoid banquets which are given by strangers and by ignorant persons. But if ever there is occasion to join in them, let your attention be carefully fixed, that you slip not into the manners of the vulgar. For you must know, that if your companion be impure, he also who keeps company with him must become impure, though he should happen to be pure.

Take the things which relate to the body as far as the bare use, as food, drink, clothing, house, and slaves: but exclude every thing which is for show or luxury.

As to pleasure with women, abstain as far as you can before marriage: but if you do indulge in it, do it in the way which is conformable to custom. Do not however be disagreeable to those who indulge in these pleasures, or reprove them; and do not often boast that you do not indulge in them yourself.

If a man has reported to you, that a certain person speaks ill of you, do not make any answer to what has been told you: but reply, The man did not know the rest of my faults, for he would not have mentioned these only.

It is not necessary to go to the theatres often: but if there is ever a proper occasion for going, do not show yourself as being a partisan of any man except yourself, that is, desire only that to be done which is done, and for him only to gain the prize who gains the prize; for in this way you will meet with no hindrance. But abstain entirely from shouts and laughter at any thing or person, or violent emotions. And when you are come away, do not talk much about what has passed on the stage, except about that which may lead to your own improvement. For it is plain, if you do talk much that you admired the spectacle.

Do not go to the hearing of certain persons' recitations nor visit them readily. But if you do attend, observe gravity and sedateness, and also avoid making yourself disagreeable.

When you are going to meet with any person, and particularly one of those who are considered to be in a superior condition, place before yourself what Socrates or Zeno would have done in such circumstances, and you will have no difficulty in making a proper use of the occasion.

When you are going to any of those who are in great power, place before yourself that you will not find the man at home, that you will be excluded, that the door will not be opened to you, that the man will not care about you. And if with all this it is your duty to visit him, bear what happens, and never say to yourself that it was not worth the trouble. For this is silly, and marks the character of a man who is offended by externals.

In company take care not to speak much and excessively about your own acts or dangers: for as it is pleasant to you to make mention of your own dangers, it is not so pleasant to others to hear what has happened to you. Take care also not to provoke laughter; for this is a slippery way towards vulgar habits, and is also adapted to diminish the respect of your neighbours. It is a dangerous habit also to approach obscene talk. When then any thing of this kind happens, if there is a good opportunity, rebuke the man who has proceeded to this talk: but if there is not an opportunity, by your silence at least, and blushing and expression of dissatisfaction by your countenance, show plainly that you are displeased at such talk.

XXXIV

If you have received the impression of any pleasure, guard yourself against being carried away by it: but let the thing wait for you, and allow yourself a certain delay on your own part. Then think of both times, of the time when you will enjoy the pleasure, and of the time after the enjoyment of the pleasure when you will repent and will reproach yourself. And set against these things how you will rejoice if you have abstained from the pleasure, and how you will commend yourself. But if it seem to you reasonable to undertake the thing, take care that the charm of it, and the pleasure, and the attraction of it shall not conquer you: but set on the other side the consideration how much better it is to be conscious that you have gained this victory.

XXXV

When you have decided that a thing ought to be done and are doing it, never avoid being seen doing it, though the many shall form an unfavourable opinion about it. For if it is not right to do it, avoid doing the thing; but if it is right, why are you afraid of those who shall find fault wrongly?

XXXVI

As the proposition it is either day or it is night is of great importance for the disjunctive argument, but for the conjunctive is of no value, so in a symposium to select the larger share is of great value for the body, but for the maintenance of the social feeling is worth nothing. When then you are eating with another, remember to look not only to the value for the body of the things set before you, but also to the value of the behaviour towards the host which ought to be observed.

XXXVII

If you have assumed a character above your strength, you have both acted in this matter in an unbecoming way, and you have neglected that which you might have fulfilled.

XXXVIII

In walking about as you take care not to step on a nail or to sprain your foot, so take care not to damage your own ruling faculty: and if we observe this rule in every act, we shall undertake the act with more security.

XXXIX

The measure of possession is to every man the body, as the foot is of the shoe. If then you stand on this rule, you will maintain the measure: but if you pass beyond it, you must then of necessity be hurried as it were down a precipice. As also in the matter of the shoe, if you go beyond the necessities of the foot, the shoe is gilded, then of a purple colour, then embroidered: for there is no limit to that which has once passed the true measure.

XL

Women forthwith from the age of fourteen are called by the men mistresses. Therefore since they see that there is nothing else that they can obtain, but only the power of lying with men, they begin to decorate themselves, and to place all their hopes in this. It is worth our while then to take care that they may know that they are valued by men for nothing else than appearing decent and modest and discreet.

XLI

It is a mark of a mean capacity to spend much time on the things which concern the body, such as much exercise, much eating, much drinking, much easing of the body, much copulation. But these things should be done as subordinate things: and let all your care be directed to the mind.

XLII

When any person treats you ill or speaks ill of you, remember that he does this or says this because he thinks that it is his duty. It is not possible then for him to follow that which seems right to you, but that which seems right to himself. Accordingly if he is wrong in his opinion, he is the person who is hurt, for he is the person who has been deceived; for if a man shall suppose the true conjunction to be false, it is not the conjunction which is hindered, but the man who has been deceived about it. If you proceed then from these opinions, you will be mild in temper to him who reviles you: for say on each occasion, It seemed so to him.

XLIII

Every thing has two handles, the one by which it may be borne, the other by which it may not. If your brother acts unjustly, do not lay hold of the act by that handle wherein he acts unjustly, for this is the handle which cannot be borne: but lay hold of the other, that he is your brother, that he was nurtured with you, and you will lay hold of the thing by that handle by which it can be borne.

XLIV

These reasonings do not cohere: I am richer than you, therefore I am better than you; I am more eloquent than you, therefore I am better than you. On the contrary these rather cohere, I am richer than you, therefore my possessions are greater than yours: I am more eloquent than you, there-fore my speech is superior to yours. But you are neither possession nor speech.

XLV

Does a man bathe quickly? do not say that he bathes badly, but that he bathes quickly. Does a man drink much wine? do not say that he does this badly, but say that he drinks much. For before you shall have determined the opinion, how do you know whether he is acting wrong? Thus it will not happen to you to comprehend some appearances which are capable of being comprehended, but to assent to others.

XLVI

On no occasion call yourself a philosopher, and do not speak much among the uninstructed about theorems: but do that which follows from them. For example at a banquet do not say how a man ought to eat, but eat as you ought to eat. For remember that in this way Socrates also altogether avoided ostentation: persons used to come to him and ask to be recommended by him to philosophers, and he used to take them to philosophers: so easily did he submit to being overlooked. Accordingly if any conversation should arise among uninstructed persons about any theorem, generally be silent; for there is great danger that you will immediately vomit up what you have not digested. And when a man shall say to you, that you know nothing, and you are not vexed, then be sure that you have begun the work of philosophy. For even sheep do not vomit up their grass and show to the shepherds how much they have eaten; but when they have internally digested the pasture, they produce externally wool and milk. Do you also show not your theorems to the uninstructed, but show the acts which come from their digestion.

XLVII

When at a small cost you are supplied with every thing for the body, do not be proud of this; nor, if you drink water, say on every occasion, I drink water. But consider first how much more frugal the poor are than we, and how much more enduring of labour. And if you ever wish to exercise yourself in labour and endurance, do it for yourself, and not for others: do not embrace statues. But if you are ever very thirsty, take a draught of cold water, and spit it out, and tell no man.

XLVIII

The condition and characteristic of an uninstructed person is this: he never expects from himself profit nor harm, but from externals. The condition and characteristic of a philosopher is this: he expects all advantage and all harm from himself. The signs of one who is making progress are these: he censures no man, he praises no man, he blames no man, he accuses no man, he says nothing about himself as if he were somebody or knew something; when he is impeded at all or hindered, he blames himself: if a man praises him, he ridicules the praiser to himself: if a man censures him, he makes no defence: he goes about like weak persons, being careful not to move any of the things which are placed, before they are firmly fixed: he removes all desire from himself, and he transfers aversion to those things only of the things within our power which are contrary to nature: he employs a moderate movement towards every thing: whether he is considered foolish or ignorant, he cares not: and in a word he watches himself as if he were an enemy and lying in ambush.

XLIX

When a man is proud because he can understand and explain the writings of Chrysippus, say to yourself, If Chrysippus had not written obscurely, this man would have had nothing to be proud of. But what is it that I wish? To understand Nature and to follow it. I inquire therefore who is the interpreter: and when I have heard that it is Chrysippus, I come to him. But I do not understand what is written, and therefore I seek the interpreter. And so far there is yet nothing to be proud of. But when I shall have found the interpreter, the thing that

remains is to use the precepts. This itself is the only thing to be proud of. But if I shall admire the exposition, what else have I been made unless a grammarian instead of a philosopher? except in one thing, that I am explaining Chrysippus instead of Homer. When then any man says to me, Read Chrysippus to me, I rather blush, when I cannot show my acts like to and consistent with his words.

L

Whatever things are proposed to you for the conduct of life abide by them, as if they were laws, as if you would be guilty of impiety if you transgressed any of them. And whatever any man shall say about you, do not attend to it: for this is no affair of yours. How long will you then still defer thinking yourself worthy of the best things, and in no matter transgressing the distinctive reason? Have you accepted the theorems, which it was your duty to agree to, and have you agreed to them? what teacher then do you still expect that you defer to him the correction of yourself? You are no longer a youth, but already a full-grown man. If then you are negligent and slothful, and are continually making procrastination after procrastination, and proposal after proposal, and fixing day after day, after which you will attend to yourself, you will not know that you are not making improvement, but you will continue ignorant both while you live and till you die. Immediately then think it right to live as a full-grown man, and one who is making proficiency, and let every thing which appears to you to be the best be to you a law which must not be transgressed. And if any thing laborious, or pleasant or glorious or inglorious be presented to you, remember that now is the contest, now are the Olympic games, and they cannot be deferred; and that it depends on one defeat and one giving way that progress is either lost or maintained. Socrates in this way became perfect, in all things improving himself, attending to nothing except to reason. But you, though you are not yet a

Socrates, ought to live as one who wishes to be a Socrates.

LI

The first and most necessary part in philosophy is the use of theorems, for instance, that we must not lie: the second part is that of demonstrations, for instance, How is it proved that we ought not to lie: the third is that which is confirmatory of these two and explanatory, for example, How is this a demonstration? For what is demonstration, what is consequence, what is contradiction, what is truth, what is falsehood? The third part is necessary on account of the second, and the second on account of the first; but the most necessary and that on which we ought to rest is the first. But we do the contrary. For we spend our time on the third topic, and all our earnestness is about it: but we entirely neglect the first. Therefore we lie; but the demonstration that we ought not to lie we have ready to hand.

LII

In every thing we should hold these maxims ready to hand:

Lead me, O Zeus, and thou O Destiny,
The way that I am bid by you to go:
To follow I am ready. If I choose not,

I make myself a wretch, and still must follow.

But whoso nobly yields unto necessity,
We hold him wise, and skill'd in things divine.

And the third also: O Crito, if so it pleases the Gods, so let it be; Anytus and Melitus are able indeed to kill me, but they cannot harm me.

STUDY QUESTIONS

1. What does Epictetus mean by the admonition, "Keep your will conformable to nature"? Why should one do so?
2. Do you agree with what Epictetus says in §VII? Explain.
3. What does Epictetus mean by freedom? How does one achieve it?
4. In §XXVII Epictetus makes an important statement about God and the universe. State his point in your own words.
5. Epictetus was a Stoic. What does this mean, as far as his teachings are concerned? Would you call him an optimist or a pessimist? Explain.
6. Do you think that the kind of life Epictetus recommends is one you could follow? Should follow?

For Further Reading
Blanshard, B. *Reason and Goodness.* London: Allen and Unwin, 1961 (Chapter 2).
Edelstein, L. *The Meaning of Stoicism.* Cambridge, Mass.: Harvard University Press, 1966 (esp. Chapter 4).
Hicks, R.D. *Stoic and Epicurean.* New York: Russell and Russell, 1962 (Chapter 3).
Marcus Aurelius. *The Meditations.*
Zeller, E. *The Stoics, Epicureans and Sceptics.* London: Longman's, 1880 (Chapters 10 through 12).

ARISTOTLE: THE LIFE OF MODERATION

Aristotle's "Golden Mean" is one of the most famous ideas in the history of thought about how we should best live our lives. With its emphasis on balance and moderation, it reflects one of the main ideals of Greek civilization, which manifests itself most clearly in the arts and is most strikingly exemplified in the

Parthenon. To what extent the Greeks followed the mean in their social relationships is difficult now even to speculate about but, whatever they actually did, we can still consider the mean as an ideal to which they aspired and which we might ourselves pursue. In the latter case, we need to ask ourselves: Would adherence to the mean provide an individual with a guide that he should be willing conscientiously to follow in all his encounters with those around him?

A native of Macedonia, Aristotle (384–322 B.C.) journeyed to Athens at the age of eighteen to enroll in Plato's Academy. There he remained for twenty years, until the death of the master. A little later he was recalled to his native land to serve as tutor to the young heir to the throne, Alexander (later the Great). Before long, the two parted—Alexander to conquer Asia Minor and Aristotle to establish a school in Athens, the Lyceum, where he spent the remainder of his life. In 323 the young Alexander died suddenly. Aristotle, fearing mob violence against himself because of his former association with Alexander, and recalling the fate of Socrates, fled the city, saying he did not wish "to give the Athenians a second chance of sinning against philosophy." He died in exile the following year.

ℒ The Nicomachean Ethics

Book I
The End

Every art and every kind of inquiry, and likewise every act and purpose, seems to aim at some good: and so it has been well said that the good is that at which everything aims.

But a difference is observable among these aims or ends. What is aimed at is sometimes the exercise of a faculty, sometimes a certain result beyond that exercise. And where there is an end beyond the act, there the result is better than the exercise of the faculty.

Now since there are many kinds of actions and many arts and sciences, it follows that there are many ends also; e.g. health is the end of medicine, ships of shipbuilding, victory of the art of war, and wealth of economy.

But when several of these are subordinated to some one art or science,—as the making of bridles and other trappings to the art of horsemanship, and this in turn, along with all else that the soldier does, to the art of war, and so on,—then the end of the master-art is always more desired than

Translated by F. H. Peters.

the ends of the subordinate arts, since these are pursued for its sake. And this is equally true whether the end in view be the mere exercise of a faculty or something beyond that, as in the above instances.

If then in what we do there be some end which we wish for on its own account, choosing all the others as means to this, but not every end without exception, as a means to something else (for so we should go on *ad infinitum*, and desire would be left void and objectless),—this evidently will be the good or the best of all things.

And surely from a practical point of view it much concerns us to know this good; for then, like archers shooting at a definite mark, we shall be more likely to attain what we want.

If this be so, we must try to indicate roughly what it is, and first of all to which of the arts or sciences it belongs.

It would seem to belong to the supreme art or science, that one which most of all deserves the name of master-art or master-science.

Now Politics seems to answer to this description. For it prescribes which of the sciences a state needs, and which each man shall study, and up to what point; and to it we see subordinated even the highest arts, such as economy, rhetoric, and the art of war.

Since then it makes use of the other practical sciences, and since it further ordains what men are to do and from what to refrain, its end must include the ends of the others, and must be the proper good of man.

For though this good is the same for the individual and the state, yet the good of the state seems a grander and more perfect thing both to attain and to secure; and glad as one would be to do this service for a single individual, to do it for a people and for a number of states is nobler and more divine.

This then is the aim of the present inquiry, which is a sort of political inquiry.

We must be content if we can attain to so much precision in our statement as the subject before us admits of; for the same degree of accuracy is no more to be expected in all kinds of reasoning than in all kinds of manufacture.

Now what is noble and just (with which Politics deals) is so various and so uncertain, that some think these are merely conventional and not natural distinctions.

There is a similar uncertainty also about what is good, because good things often do people harm: men have before now been ruined by wealth, and have lost their lives through courage.

Our subject, then, and our data being of this nature, we must be content if we can indicate the truth roughly and in outline, and if, in dealing with matters that are not amenable to immutable laws, and reasoning from premises that are but probable, we can arrive at probable conclusions.

The reader, on his part, should take each of my statements in the same spirit; for it is the mark of an educated man to require, in each kind of inquiry, just so much exactness as the subject admits of: it is equally absurd to accept probable reasoning from a mathematician, and to demand scientific proof from an orator.

But each man can form a judgment about what he knows, and is called "a good judge" of that—of any special matter when he has received a special education therein, "a good judge" (without any qualifying epithet) when he has received a universal education. And hence a young man is not qualified to be a student of Politics; for he lacks experience of the affairs of life, which form the data and the subject-matter of Politics.

Further, since he is apt of be swayed by his feelings, he will derive no benefit from a study whose aim is not speculative but practical.

But in this respect young in character counts the same as young in years; for the young man's disqualification is not a matter of time, but is due to the fact that feeling rules his life and directs all his desires. Men of this character turn the knowledge they get to no account in practice, as we see with those we call incontinent; but those who direct their desires and actions by reason will gain much profit from the knowledge of these matters.

So much then by way of preface as to the student, and the spirit in which he must accept what we say, and the object which we propose to ourselves.

Since—to resume—all knowledge and all purpose aims at some good, what is this which we say is the aim of Politics; or, in other words, what is the highest of all realizable goods?

As to its name, I suppose nearly all men are agreed; for the masses and the men of culture alike declare that it is happiness, and hold that "to live well" or to "do well" is the same as to be "happy."

But they differ as to what this happiness is, and the masses do not give the same account of it as the philosophers.

The former take it to be something palpable and plain, as pleasure or wealth or fame; one man holds it to be this, and another that, and often the same man is of different minds at different times,—after sickness it is health, and in poverty it is wealth; while when they are impressed with the consciousness of their ignorance, they admire most those who say grand things that are above their comprehension.

Some philosophers, on the other hand, have thought that, beside these several good things, there is an "absolute" good which is the cause of their goodness.

As it would hardly be worth while to review all the opinions that have been held, we will confine ourselves to those which are most popular, or which seem to have some foundation in reason.

But we must not omit to notice the distinction that is drawn between the method of proceeding from your starting-points or principles, and the method of working up to them. Plato used with fitness to raise this question, and to ask whether the right way is from or to your starting-points, as in the racecourse you may run from the judges to the boundary, or *vice versa*.

Well, we must start from what is known.

But "what is known" may mean two things: "what is known to us," which is one thing, or "what is known" simply, which is another.

I think it is safe to say that *we* must start from what is known to *us*.

And on this account nothing but a good moral training can qualify a man to study what is noble and just—in a word, to study questions of Politics. For the undemonstrated fact is here the starting-point, and if this undemonstrated fact be sufficiently evident to a man, he will not require a "reason why." Now the man who has had a good moral training either has already arrived at starting-points or principles of action, or will easily accept them when pointed out. But he who neither has them nor will accept them may hear what Hesiod says—

The best is he who of himself doth know;
Good too is he who listens to the wise;
But he who neither knows himself nor heeds
The words of others, is a useless man.

Let us now take up the discussion at the point from which we digressed.

As to men's notions of the good or happiness, it seems (to judge, as we reasonably may, from their lives) that the masses, who are the least refined, hold it to be pleasure, and so accept the life of enjoyment as their ideal.

For the most conspicuous kinds of life are three: this life of enjoyment, the life of the statesman, and, thirdly, the contemplative life.

The mass of men show themselves utterly slavish in their preference for the life of brute beasts, but their views receive consideration because many of those in high places have the tastes of Sardanapalus.

Men of refinement with a practical turn prefer honour; for I suppose we may say that honour is the aim of the statesman's life.

But this seems too superficial to be the good we are seeking: for it appears to depend upon those who give rather than upon those who receive it; while we have a presentiment that the good is something that is peculiarly a man's own and can scarce be taken away from him.

Moreover, these men seem to pursue honour, in order that they may be assured of their own excellence,—at least, they wish to be honoured by men of sense, and by those who know them, and on the ground of their virtue or excellence. It is plain, then, that in their view, at any rate, virtue or excellence is better than honour; and perhaps we should take this to be the end of the statesman's life, rather than honour.

But virtue or excellence also appears too incomplete to be what we want; for it seems that a man might have virtue and yet be asleep or be inactive all his life, and, moreover, might meet with the greatest disasters and misfortunes; and no one would maintain that such a man is happy, except for argument's sake. But we will not dwell on these matters now, for they are sufficiently discussed in the popular treatises.

The third kind of life is the life of contemplation: we will treat of it further on.

As for the money-making life, it is something quite contrary to nature; and wealth evidently is not the good of which we are in search, for it is merely useful as a means to something else. So we might rather take pleasure and virtue or excellence to be ends than wealth; for they are chosen on their own account. But it seems that not even they are the end, though much breath has been wasted in attempts to show that they are . . . .

Leaving these matters, then, let us return once more to the question, what this good can be of which we are in search.

It seems to be different in different kinds of action and in different arts,—one thing in medicine and another in war, and so on. What then is the good in each of these cases? Surely that for the sake of which all else is done. And that in medicine is health, in war is victory, in building is a house,—a different thing in each different case, but always, in whatever we do and in whatever we choose, the end. For it is always for the sake of the end that all else is done.

If then there be one end of all that man does, this end will be the realizable good,—or these ends, if there be more than one. Our argument has thus come round by a different path to the same point as before. This point we must try to explain more clearly.

We see that there are many ends. But some of these are chosen only as means, as wealth, flutes, and the whole class of instruments. And so it is plain that not all ends are final.

But the best of all things must, we conceive, be something final.

If then there be only one final end, this will be what we are seeking,—or if there be more than one, then the most final of them.

Now that which is pursued as an end in itself is more final than that which is pursued as means to something else, and that which is never chosen as means than that which is chosen both as an end in itself and as means, and that is strictly final which is always chosen as an end in itself and never as means.

Happiness seems more than anything else to answer to this description: for we always choose it for itself, and never for the sake of something else; while honour and pleasure and reason, and all virtue or excellence, we choose partly indeed for themselves (for, apart from any result, we should choose each of them), but partly also for the sake of happiness, supposing that they will help to make us happy. But no one chooses happiness for the sake of these things, or as a means to anything else at all.

We seem to be led to the same conclusion when we start from the notion of self-sufficiency.

The final good is thought to be self-sufficing. In applying this term we do not regard a man as an individual leading a solitary life, but we also take account of parents, children, wife, and, in short, friends and fellow-citizens generally, since man is naturally a social being. Some limits must indeed be set to this; for if you go on to parents and descendants and friends of friends, you will never come to a stop. But this we will consider further on: for the present we will take self-sufficing to mean what by itself makes life desirable and in want of nothing. And happiness is believed to answer to this description.

And further, happiness is believed to be the most desirable thing in the world, and that not merely as one among other good things: if it were merely one among other good things, it is plain that the addition of the least of other goods must make it more desirable; for the addition becomes a surplus of good, and of two goods the greater is always more desirable.

Thus it seems that happiness is something final and self-sufficing, and is the end of all that man does.

But perhaps the reader thinks that though no one will dispute the statement that happiness is the best thing in the world, yet a still more precise definition of it is needed.

This will best be gained, I think, by asking, What is the function of man? For as the goodness and the excellence of a piper or a sculptor, or the practiser of any art, and generally of those who have any function or business to do, lies in that function, so man's good would seem to lie in his function, if he has one.

But can we suppose that, while a carpenter and a cobbler has a function and a business of his own, man has no business and no function assigned him by nature? Nay, surely as his several members, eye and hand and foot, plainly have each his own functions so we must suppose that man also has some function over and above all these.

What then is it?

Life evidently he has in common even with the plants, but we want that which is peculiar to him. We must exclude, therefore, the life of mere nutrition and growth.

Next to this comes the life of sense; but this too he plainly shares with horses and cattle and all kinds of animals.

There remains then the life whereby he acts—the life of his rational nature, with its two sides or divisions, one rational as obeying reason, the other rational as having and exercising reason.

But as this expression is ambiguous, we must be understood to mean thereby the life that consists in the exercise of the faculties; for this seems to be more properly entitled to the name.

The function of man, then, is exercise of his vital faculties on one side in obedience to reason, and on the other side with reason.

But what is called the function of a man of any profession and the function of a man who is good in that profession are generically the same, e.g. of a harper and of a good harper; and this holds in all cases without exception, only that in the case of the latter his superior excellence at his work is added; for we say a harper's function is to harp, and a good harper's to harp well.

Man's function being, as we say, a kind of life—that is to say, exercise of his faculties and action of various kinds with reason—the good man's function is to do this well and beautifully.

But the function of anything is done well when it is done in accordance with the proper excellence of that thing.

Putting all this together, then, we find that the good of man is exercise of his faculties in accordance with excellence or virtue, or, if there be more than one, in accordance with the best and most complete virtue.

But there must also be a full term of years for this exercise; for one swallow or one fine day does not make a spring, nor does one day or any small space of time make a blessed or happy man.

• • •

Since happiness is an exercise of the vital faculties in accordance with perfect virtue or excellence, we will now inquire about virtue or excellence; for this will probably help us in our inquiry about happiness.

And indeed the true statesman seems to be especially concerned with virtue, for he wishes to make the citizens good and obedient to the laws. Of this we have an example in the Cretan and the Lacedaemonian lawgivers, and any others who have resembled them. But if the inquiry belongs to Politics or the science of the state, it is plain that it will be in accordance with our original purpose to pursue it.

The virtue or excellence that we are to consider is, of course, the excellence of man; for it is the good of man and the happiness of man that we started to seek. And by the excellence of man I mean excellence not of body, but of soul, just as the man who is to heal the eye or the whole body must have some knowledge of them, and that the more in proportion as the science of the state is higher and better than medicine. But all educated physicians take much pains to know about the body.

As statesmen, then, we must inquire into the nature of the soul, but in so doing we must keep our special purpose in view and go only so far as that requires; for to go into minuter detail would be too laborious for the present undertaking.

Now, there are certain points which are stated with sufficient precision even in the popular accounts of the soul, and these we will adopt.

For instance, they distinguish an irrational and a rational part.

Whether these are separated as are the parts of the body or any divisible thing, or whether they are only distinguishable in thought but in fact inseparable, like concave and convex in the circumference of a circle, makes no difference for our present purpose.

Of the irrational part, again, one division seems to be common to all things that live, and to be possessed by plants—I mean that which causes nutrition and growth; for we must assume that all things that take nourishment have a faculty of this kind, even when they are embryos, and have the same faculty when they are full grown; at least, this is more reasonable than to suppose that they then have a different one.

The excellence of this faculty, then, is plainly one that man shares with other beings, and not specifically human.

And this is confirmed by the fact that this part of the soul, or this faculty, is thought to be most active in sleep, while the distinction between the good and the bad man shows itself least in sleep—whence the saying that for half their lives there is no difference between the happy and the miserable. This indeed is what we should expect; for sleep is the cessation of the soul from those functions in respect of which it is called good or bad, except in so far as the motions of the body may sometimes make their way in, and give occasion to dreams which are better in the good man than in ordinary people.

However, we need not pursue this further, and may dismiss the nutritive principle, since it has no place in the excellence of man.

But there seems to be another vital principle that is irrational, and yet in some way partakes of reason. In the case of the continent and of the incontinent man alike we praise the reason or the rational part, for it exhorts them rightly and urges them to do what is best; but there is plainly present in them another principle besides the rational one, which fights and struggles against the reason. For just as a paralyzed limb, when you will to move it to the right, moves on the contrary to the left, so it is with the soul; the incontinent man's impulses run counter to his reason. Only whereas we see the refractory member in the case of the body, we do not see it in the case of the soul. But we must nevertheless, I think, hold that in the soul too there is something beside the reason, which opposes and runs counter to it (though in what sense it is distinct from the reason does not matter here).

It seems, however, to partake of reason also, as we said: at least, in the continent man it submits to the reason; while in the temperate and courageous man we may say it is still more obedient; for in him it is altogether in harmony with the reason.

The irrational part, then, it appears, is twofold. There is the vegetative faculty, which has no share of reason; and the faculty of appetite or of desire in general, which partakes of reason in a manner—that is, in so far as it listens to reason and submits to its sway. But when we say "partakes of reason" or "listens to reason," we mean this in the sense in which we talk of "listening to reason" from parents or friends, not in the sense in which we talk of listening to the reasonings of mathematicians.

Further, all advice and all rebuke and exhortation testifies that the irrational part is in some way amenable to reason.

If then we like to say that this part, too, has a share of reason, the rational part also will have two divisions: one rational in the strict sense as possessing reason in itself, the other rational as listening to reason as a man listens to his father.

Now, on this division of the faculties is based the division of excellence; for we speak of intellectual excellences and of moral excellences; wisdom and understanding and prudence we call intellectual, liberality and temperance we call moral virtues or excellences. When we are speaking of a man's moral character we do not say that he is wise or intelligent, but that he is gentle or temperate. But we praise the wise man, too, for his habit of mind or trained faculty; and a habit or trained faculty that is praiseworthy is what we call an excellence or virtue.

Book II
Moral Virtue

Excellence, then, being of these two kinds, intellectual and moral, intellectual excellence owes its birth and growth mainly to instruction, and so requires time and experience, while moral excellence is the result of habit or custom, and has accordingly in our language received a name formed by a slight change from *ethos*.

From this it is plain that none of the moral excellences or virtues is implanted in us by nature; for that which is by nature cannot be altered by training. For instance, a stone naturally tends to fall downwards, and you could not train it to rise upwards, though you tried to do so by throwing it up ten thousand times, nor could you train fire to move downwards, nor accustom anything which naturally behaves in one way to behave in any other way.

The virtues, then, come neither by nature nor against nature, but nature gives the capacity for acquiring them, and this is developed by training.

Again, where we do things by nature we get the power first, and put this power forth in act afterwards: as we plainly see in the case of the senses; for it is not by constantly seeing and hearing that we acquire those faculties, but, on the contrary, we had the power first and then used it, instead of acquiring the power by the use. But the virtues we acquire by doing the acts, as is the case with the arts too. We learn an art by doing that which we wish to do when we have learned it; we become builders by building, and harpers by harping. And so by doing just acts we become just, and by doing acts of temperance and courage we become temperate and courageous. This is attested, too, by what occurs in states; for the legislators make their citizens good by training, i.e. this is the wish of all legislators, and those who do not succeed in this miss their aim, and it is

this that distinguishes a good from a bad constitution.

Again, both the moral virtues and the corresponding vices result from and are formed by the same acts; and this is the case with the arts also. It is by harping that good harpers and bad harpers alike are produced: and so with builders and the rest; by building well they will become good builders, and bad builders by building badly. Indeed, if it were not so, they would not want anybody to teach them, but would all be born either good or bad at their trades. And it is just the same with the virtues also. It is by our conduct in our intercourse with other men that we become just or unjust, and by acting in circumstances of danger, and training ourselves to feel fear or confidence, that we become courageous or cowardly. So, too, with our animal appetites and the passion of anger; for by behaving in this way or in that on the occasions with which these passions are concerned, some become temperate and gentle, and others profligate and ill-tempered. In a word, acts of any kind produce habits or characters of the same kind.

Hence we ought to make sure that our acts be of a certain kind; for the resulting character varies as they vary. It makes no small difference, therefore, whether a man be trained from his youth up in this way or in that, but a great difference, or rather all the difference.

But our present inquiry has not, like the rest, a merely speculative aim; we are not inquiring merely in order to know what excellence or virtue is, but in order to become good; for otherwise it would profit us nothing. We must ask therefore about these acts, and see of what kind they are to be; for, as we said, it is they that determine our habits or character.

First of all, then, that they must be in accordance with right reason is a common characteristic of them which we shall here take for granted, reserving for future discussion the question what this right reason is, and how it is related to the other excellences.

But let it be understood, before we go on, that all reasoning on matters of practice must be in outline merely, and not scientifically exact: for, as we said at starting, the kind of reasoning to be demanded varies with the subject in hand; and in practical matters and questions of expedience there are no invariable laws, any more than in questions of health.

And if our general conclusions are thus inexact, still more inexact is all reasoning about particular cases; for these fall under no system of scientifically established rules or traditional maxims, but the agent must always consider for himself what the special occasion requires, just as in medicine or navigation.

But though this is the case we must try to render what help we can.

First of all, then, we must observe that, in matters of this sort, to fall short and to exceed are alike fatal. This is plain (to illustrate what we cannot see by what we can see) in the case of strength and health. Too much and too little exercise alike destroy strength, and to take too much meat and drink, or to take too little, is equally ruinous to health, but the fitting amount produces and increases and preserves them. Just so, then, is it with temperance also, and courage, and the other virtues. The man who shuns and fears everything and never makes a stand, becomes a coward; while the man who fears nothing at all, but will face anything, becomes foolhardy. So, too, the man who takes his fill of any kind of pleasure, and abstains from none, is a profligate, but the man who shuns all (like him whom we call a "boor") is devoid of sensibility. For temperance and courage are destroyed both by excess and defect, but preserved by moderation.

But habits or types of character are not only produced and preserved and destroyed by the same occasions and the same means, but they will also manifest themselves in the same circumstances. This is the case with palpable things like strength. Strength is produced by taking plenty of nourishment and doing plenty of hard work, and the strong man, in turn has the greatest capacity for these. And the case is

the same with the virtues: by abstaining from pleasure we become temperate, and when we have become temperate we are best able to abstain. And so with courage: by habituating ourselves to despise danger, and to face it, we become courageous; and when we have become courageous, we are best able to face danger.

The pleasure or pain that accompanies the acts must be taken as a test of the formed habit or character. He who abstains from the pleasures of the body and rejoices in the abstinence is temperate, while he who is vexed at having to abstain is profligate; and again, he who faces danger with pleasure, or, at any rate, without pain, is courageous, but he to whom this is painful is a coward.

For moral virtue or excellence is closely concerned with pleasure and pain. It is pleasure that moves us to do what is base, and pain that moves us to refrain from what is noble. And therefore, as Plato says, man needs to be so trained from his youth up as to find pleasure and pain in the right objects. This is what sound education means.

Another reason why virtue has to do with pleasure and pain, is that it has to do with actions and passions or affections; but every affection and every act is accompanied by pleasure or pain.

The fact is further attested by the employment of pleasure and pain in correction; they have a kind of curative property, and a cure is effected by administering the opposite of the disease.

Again, as we said before, every type of character is essentially relative to, and concerned with, those things that form it for good or for ill; but it is through pleasure and pain that bad characters are formed— that is to say, through pursuing and avoiding the wrong pleasures and pains, or pursuing and avoiding them at the wrong time, or in the wrong manner, or in any other of the various ways of going wrong that may be distinguished.

And hence some people go so far as to define the virtues as a kind of impassive or neutral state of mind. But they err in stating this absolutely, instead of qualifying it by the addition of the right and wrong manner, time, etc.

We may lay down, therefore, that this kind of excellence makes us do what is best in matters of pleasure and pain, while vice or badness has the contrary effect.

The following considerations will throw additional light on the point.

There are three kinds of things that move us to choose, and three that move us to avoid them: on the one hand, the beautiful or noble, the advantageous, the pleasant; on the other hand, the ugly or base, the hurtful, the painful. Now, the good man is apt to go right, and the bad man to go wrong, about them all, but especially about pleasure: for pleasure is not only common to man with animals, but also accompanies all pursuit or choice; since the noble, and the advantageous also, are pleasant in idea.

Again, the feeling of pleasure has been fostered in us all from our infancy by our training, and has thus become so engrained in our life that it can scarce be washed out. And, indeed, we all more or less make pleasure our test in judging of actions. For this reason too, then, our whole inquiry must be concerned with these matters; since to be pleased and pained in the right or the wrong way has great influence on our actions.

Again, to fight with pleasure is harder than to fight with wrath (which Heraclitus says is hard), and virtue, like art, is always more concerned with what is harder; for the harder the task the better is success. For this reason also, then, both virtue or excellence and the science of the state must always be concerned with pleasures and pains; for he that behaves rightly with regard to them will be good, and he that behaves badly will be bad.

We will take it as established, then, that excellence or virtue has to do with pleasures and pains; and that the acts which produce it develop it, and also, when differently done, destroy it; and that it manifests itself in the same acts which produced it.

But here we may be asked what we mean by saying that men can become just

and temperate only by doing what is just and temperate: surely, it may be said, if their acts are just and temperate, they themselves are already just and temperate, as they are grammarians and musicians if they do what is grammatical and musical.

We may answer, I think, firstly, that this is not quite the case even with the arts. A man may do something grammatical by chance, or at the prompting of another person: he will not be grammatical till he not only does something grammatical, but also does it grammatically, i.e. in virtue of his own knowledge of grammar.

But, secondly, the virtues are not in this point analogous to the arts. The products of art have their excellence in themselves, and so it is enough if when produced they are of a certain quality; but in the case of the virtues, a man is not said to act justly or temperately if what he does merely be of a certain sort—he must also be in a certain state of mind when he does it; i.e. first of all, he must know what he is doing; secondly, he must choose it, and choose it for itself; and, thirdly, his act must be the expression of a formed and stable character. Now, of these conditions, only one, the knowledge, is necessary for the possession of any art; but for the possession of the virtues knowledge is of little or no avail, while the other conditions that result from repeatedly doing what is just and temperate are not a little important, but all-important.

The thing that is done, therefore, is called just or temperate when it is such as the just or temperate man would do; but the man who does it is not just or temperate, unless he also does it in the spirit of the just or temperate man.

It is right, then, to say that by doing what is just a man becomes just, and temperate by doing what is temperate, while without doing thus he has no chance of ever becoming good.

But most men, instead of doing thus, fly to theories, and fancy that they are philosophizing and that this will make them good, like a sick man who listens attentively to what the doctor says and then disobeys all his orders. This sort of philosophizing will no more produce a healthy habit of mind than this sort of treatment will produce a healthy habit of body.

We have next to inquire what excellence or virtue is.

A quality of the soul is either (1) a passion or emotion, or (2) a power or faculty, or (3) a habit or trained faculty; and so virtue must be one of these three. By (1) a passion or emotion we mean appetite, anger, fear, confidence, envy, joy, love, hate, longing, emulation, pity, or generally that which is accompanied by pleasure or pain; (2) a power or faculty is that in respect of which we are said to be capable of being affected in any of these ways, as, for instance, that in respect of which we are able to be angered or pained or to pity; and (3) a habit or trained faculty is that in respect of which we are well or ill regulated or disposed in the matter of our affections; as, for instance, in the matter of being angered, we are ill regulated if we are too violent or too slack, but if we are moderate in our anger we are well regulated. And so with the rest.

Now, the virtues are not emotions, nor are the vices—(1) because we are not called good or bad in respect of our emotions, but are called so in respect of our virtues or vices; (2) because we are neither praised nor blamed in respect of our emotions (a man is not praised for being afraid or angry, nor blamed for being angry, simply, but for being angry in a particular way), but we are praised or blamed in respect of our virtues or vices; (3) because we may be angered or frightened without deliberate choice, but the virtues are a kind of deliberate choice, or at least are impossible without it; and (4) because in respect of our emotions we are said to be moved, but in respect of our virtues and vices we are not said to be moved, but to be regulated or disposed in this way or in that.

For these same reasons also they are not powers or faculties; for we are not called either good or bad for being merely capable of emotion, nor are we either praised or blamed for this. And further, while nature gives us our powers or faculties, she does not make us either good or bad.

If, then, the virtues be neither emotions nor faculties, it only remains for them to be habits or trained faculties.

We have thus found the genus to which virtue belongs; but we want to know, not only that it is a trained faculty, but also what species of trained faculty it is.

We may safely assert that the virtue or excellence of a thing causes that thing both to be itself in good condition and to perform its function well. The excellence of the eye, for instance, makes both the eye and its work good; for it is by the excellence of the eye that we see well. So the proper excellence of the horse makes a horse what he should be, and makes him good at running, and carrying his rider, and standing a charge.

If, then, this holds good in all cases, the proper excellence or virtue of man will be a habit or trained faculty that makes a man good and makes him perform his function well.

How this is to be done we have already said, but we may exhibit the same conclusion in another way, by inquiring what the nature of this virtue is.

Now, if we have any quantity, whether continuous or discrete, it is possible to take either a larger, or a smaller, or an equal amount, and that either absolutely or relatively to our own needs.

By an equal or fair amount I understand a mean amount, or one that lies between excess and deficiency.

By the absolute mean, or mean relatively to the thing itself, I understand that which is equidistant from both extremes, and this is one and the same for all.

By the mean relatively to us I understand that which is neither too much nor too little for us; and this is not one and the same for all.

For instance, if ten be larger and two be smaller, if we take six we take the mean relatively to the thing itself; for it exceeds one extreme by the same amount by which it is exceeded by the other extreme: and this is the mean in arithmetical proportion.

But the mean relatively to us cannot be found in this way. If ten pounds of food is too much for a given man to eat, and two pounds too little, it does not follow that the trainer will order him six pounds: for that also may perhaps be too much for the man in question, or too little; too little for Milo [a famous wrestler —ed.], too much for the beginner. The same holds true in running and wrestling.

And so we may say generally that a master in any art avoids what is too much and what is too little, and seeks for the mean and chooses it—not the absolute but the relative mean.

Every art or science, then, perfects its work in this way, looking to the mean and bringing its work up to this standard; so that people are wont to say of a good work that nothing could be taken from it or added to it, implying that excellence is destroyed by excess or deficiency, but secured by observing the mean. And good artists, as we say, do in fact keep their eyes fixed on this in all that they do.

Virtue therefore, since like nature it is more exact and better than any art, must also aim at the mean—virtue of course meaning moral virtue or excellence; for it has to do with passions and actions, and it is these that admit of excess and deficiency and the mean. For instance, it is possible to feel fear, confidence, desire, anger, pity, and generally to be affected pleasantly and painfully, either too much or too little, in either case wrongly; but to be thus affected at the right times, and on the right occasions, and towards the right persons, and with the right object, and in the right fashion, is the mean course and the best course, and these are characteristics of virtue. And in the same way our outward acts also admit of excess and deficiency, and the mean or due amount.

Virtue, then, has to deal with feelings or passions and with outward acts, in which excess is wrong and deficiency also is blamed, but the mean amount is praised and is right—both of which are characteristics of virtue.

Virtue, then, is a kind of moderation, inasmuch as it aims at the mean or moderate amount.

Again, there are many ways of going wrong (for evil is infinite in nature, to use a Pythagorean figure, while good is finite), but only one way of going right; so that the one is easy and the other hard—easy to miss the mark and hard to hit. On this account also, then, excess and deficiency are characteristic of vice, hitting the mean is characteristic of virtue.

Goodness is simple, ill takes any shape.

Virtue, then, is a habit or trained faculty of choice, the characteristic of which lies in moderation or observance of the mean relatively to the persons concerned, as determined by reason, i.e. as the prudent man would determine it.

And it is a moderation, firstly, inasmuch as it comes in the middle or mean between two vices, one on the side of excess, the other on the side of defect; and, secondly, inasmuch as, while these vices fall short of or exceed the due measure in feeling and in action, it finds and chooses the mean, middling, or moderate amount.

Regarded in its essence, therefore, or according to the definition of its nature, virtue is a moderation or middle state, but viewed in its relation to what is best and right it is the extreme of perfection.

But it is not all actions nor all passions that admit of moderation; there are some whose very names imply badness, as malevolence, shamelessness, envy, and, among acts, adultery, theft, murder. These and all other like things are blamed as being bad in themselves and not merely in their excess or deficiency. It is impossible therefore to go right in them; they are always wrong; rightness and wrongness in such things (e.g. in adultery) does not depend upon whether it is the right person and occasion and manner, but the mere doing of any one of them is wrong.

It would be equally absurd to look for moderation or excess or deficiency in unjust, cowardly or profligate conduct; for then there would be moderation in excess or deficiency, and excess in excess, and deficiency in deficiency.

The fact is that just as there can be no excess or deficiency in temperance or courage because the mean or moderate amount is, in a sense, an extreme, so in these kinds of conduct also there can be no moderation or excess or deficiency, but the acts are wrong however they be done. For, to put it generally, there cannot be moderation in excess or deficiency, nor excess or deficiency in moderation.

But it is not enough to make these general statements: we must go on and apply them to particulars. For in reasoning about matters of conduct general statements are too vague, and do not convey so much truth as particular propositions. It is with particulars that conduct is concerned: our statements, therefore, when applied to these particulars, should be found to hold good.

These particulars then, we will take from the following table.

Moderation in the feelings of fear and confidence is courage: of those that exceed, he that exceeds in fearlessness has no name (as often happens), but he that exceeds in confidence is foolhardy, while he that exceeds in fear, but is deficient in confidence, is cowardly.

Moderation in respect of certain pleasures and also (though to a less extent) certain pains is temperance, while excess is profligacy. But defectiveness in the matter of these pleasures is hardly ever found, and so this sort of people also have as yet received no name: let us put them down as "void of sensibility."

In the matter of giving and taking money, moderation is liberality, excess and deficiency are prodigality and illiberality. But these two vices exceed and fall short in contrary ways: the prodigal exceeds in spending, but falls short in taking; while the illiberal man exceeds in taking, but falls short in spending.

But, besides these, there are other dispositions in the matter of money: there is a moderation which is called magnificence (for the magnificent is not the same as the liberal man: the former deals with large sums, the latter with small), and an excess which is called bad taste or vulgarity, and a deficiency which is called meanness; and these vices differ from those which are opposed to liberality: how they differ will be explained later.

With respect to honour and disgrace, there is a moderation which is high-mindedness, an excess which may be called vanity, and a deficiency which is little-mindedness.

But just as we said that liberality is related to magnificence, differing only in that it deals with small sums, so here is a virtue related to high-mindedness; and differing only in that it is concerned with small instead of great honours. A man may have a due desire for honour, and also more or less than a due desire: he that carries this desire to excess is called ambitious, he that has not enough of it is called unambitious, but he that has the due amount has no name. There are also no abstract names for the characters, except "ambition," corresponding to ambitious. And on this account those who occupy the extremes lay claim to the middle place. And in common parlance, too, the moderate man is sometimes called ambitious and sometimes unambitious, and sometimes the ambitious man is praised and sometimes the unambitious. Why this is we will explain afterwards; for the present we will follow out our plan and enumerate the other types of character.

In the matter of anger we also find excess and deficiency and moderation. The characters themselves hardly have recognized names, but as the moderate man is here called gentle, we will call his character gentleness; of those who go into extremes, we may take the term wrathful for him who exceeds, with wrathfulness for the vice, and wrathless for him who is deficient, with wrathlessness for his character.

Besides these, there are three kinds of moderation, bearing some resemblance to one another, and yet different. They all have to do with intercourse in speech and action, but they differ in that one has to do with the truthfulness of this intercourse, while the other two have to do with its pleasantness—one of the two with pleasantness in matters of amusement, the other with pleasantness in all the relations of life. We must therefore speak of these qualities also in order that we may the more plainly see how, in all cases, moderation is praiseworthy, while the extreme courses are neither right nor praiseworthy, but blamable.

In these cases also names are for the most part wanting, but we must try, here as elsewhere, to coin names ourselves, in order to make our argument clear and easy to follow.

In the matter of truth, then, let us call him who observes the mean a true person, and observance of the mean truth: pretence, when it exaggerates, may be called boasting, and the person a boaster; when it understates, let the names be irony and ironical.

With regard to pleasantness in amusement, he who observes the mean may be called witty, and his character wittiness; excess may be called buffoonery, and the man a buffoon; while boorish may stand for the person who is deficient, and boorishness for his character.

With regard to pleasantness in the other affairs of life, he who makes himself properly pleasant may be called friendly, and his moderation friendliness; he that exceeds may be called obsequious if he have no ulterior motive, but a flatterer if he has an eye to his own advantage; he that is deficient in this respect, and always makes himself disagreeable, may be called a quarrelsome or peevish fellow.

STUDY QUESTIONS

1. Do you agree with Aristotle that everything aims at the good?
2. What does Aristotle mean by the term "virtue"? How does his meaning differ from our meaning of this word?
3. Describe in your own words what Aristotle means by happiness.
4. In what way does Aristotle base his theory of moral excellence on his analysis of human nature?
5. Would you consider following Aristotle's "golden mean" as a guide in your everyday life? Can you foresee situations in which you feel you would find it necessary to depart from it?

For Further Reading

Allan, D. J. *The Philosophy of Aristotle*. London: Oxford University Press, 1952 (Chapter 13).

Huby, P. *Greek Ethics*. London: Macmillan, 1967 (Chapter 5).

Joachim, H. H. *Aristotle: The Nicomachean Ethics*. Oxford: Clarendon Press, 1951 (esp. Books I, II, and VIII).

Ross, W. D. *Aristotle*. London: Methuen, 1923 (Chapter 7).

Taylor, A. E. *Aristotle*. rev. ed. New York: Dover, 1955 (Chapter 5).

Walsh, J. J., and Shapiro, H. L., eds. *Aristotle's Ethics*. Belmont, Calif.: Wadsworth, 1967.

NIETZSCHE: THE ARISTOCRATIC IDEAL

Nietzsche is an extremely provocative writer; he meant to be. His conception of the ideal society, divided into "masters" and "slaves," is particularly repugnant to most Americans, who have been nurtured in democracy and accept as a basic article of faith the notion of human equality. Why, then, should we read him seriously? In the first place, he does us a service by questioning our deepest ideals, forcing us to reexamine the grounds on which our society rests. Second, we must, if we are candid, concede that many of his remarks about human nature and social relationships are extremely perceptive. Nietzsche is a writer with an almost uncanny eye for the foibles of humanity. Finally, we should be aware that his purpose is not destructive. Although he wishes to destroy the civilization of nineteenth-century Europe, he does so with the further aim of replacing it with a society he conceives to be better. We may disagree violently with his ideal but that is not to deny that, beneath his caustic surface, Nietzsche was an idealist.

Friedrich Nietzsche, one of the most controversial philosophers of modern times, was born in Prussia in 1844, the son of a Lutheran minister. While he was a student at the University of Leipzig, a professorship in classical philology became vacant at the University of Basel in Switzerland. Nietzsche was recommended for the position and was appointed at the age of twenty-four. He remained at Basel for ten years but his health, delicate at best, finally broke down and he was forced into a premature retirement. He spent the next decade seeking to regain his health and writing many of his greatest works. In 1889 he suffered a mental breakdown from which he never recovered, and died in 1900. One of the main episodes of his life was his friendship with the German composer, Richard Wagner, which finally came to a bitter end when Nietzsche concluded that Wagner was compromising his artistic integrity to gain fame and fortune.

✌ *Beyond Good and Evil*

What Is Noble?

Every elevation of the type "man," has hitherto been the work of an aristocratic society—and so will it always be—a society believing in a long scale of gradations of rank and differences of worth among human beings, and requiring slavery in some form or other. Without the *pathos of distance*, such as grows out of the incarnated difference of classes, out of the constant outlooking and down-looking of the ruling caste on subordinates and instruments, and out of their equally constant practice of obeying and commanding, of keeping down and keeping at a distance—that other more mysterious pathos could never have arisen, the longing for an ever new widening of distance within the soul itself, the formation of ever higher, rarer, further,

Reprinted from F. Nietzsche, *Beyond Good and Evil*, translated by H. Zimmern, with permission of the publisher, George Allen & Unwin.

more extended, more comprehensive states, in short, just the elevation of the type "man," the continued "self-surmounting of man," to use a moral formula in a supermoral sense. To be sure, one must not resign oneself to any humanitarian illusions about the history of the origin of an aristocratic society (that is to say, of the preliminary condition for the elevation of the type "man"); the truth is hard. Let us acknowledge unprejudicedly how every higher civilization hitherto has *originated!* Men with a still natural nature, barbarians in every terrible sense of the word, men of prey, still in possession of unbroken strength of will and desire for power, threw themselves upon weaker, more moral, more peaceful races (perhaps trading or cattle-rearing communities), or upon old mellow civilizations in which the final vital force was flickering out in brilliant fireworks of wit and depravity. At the commencement, the noble caste was always the barbarian caste: their superiority did not consist first of all in their physical, but in their psychical power—they were more *complete* men (which at every point also implies the same as "more complete beasts").

Corruption—as the indication that anarchy threatens to break out among the instincts, and that the foundation of the emotions, called "life," is convulsed—is something radically different according to the organization in which it manifests itself. When, for instance, an aristocracy like that of France at the beginning of the Revolution, flung away its privileges with sublime disgust and sacrificed itself to an excess of its moral sentiments, it was corruption—it was really only the closing act of the corruption which had existed for centuries, by virtue of which that aristocracy had abdicated step by step its lordly prerogatives and lowered itself to a *function* of royalty (in the end even to its decoration and parade-dress). The essential thing, however, in a good and healthy aristocracy is that it should *not* regard itself as a function either of the kingship or the commonwealth, but as the *significance* and highest justification thereof—that it should therefore accept with a good conscience the sacrifice of a legion of individuals, who, *for its sake,* must be suppressed and reduced to imperfect men, to slaves and instruments. Its fundamental belief must be precisely that society is *not* allowed to exist for its own sake, but only as a foundation and scaffolding, by means of which a select class of beings may be able to elevate themselves to their higher duties, and in general to a higher *existence:* like those sun-seeking climbing plants in Java—they are called *Sipo Matador*—which encircle an oak so long and so often with their arms, until at last, high above it, but supported by it, they can unfold their tops in the open light, and exhibit their happiness.

To refrain mutually from injury, from violence, from exploitation, and put one's will on a par with that of others: this may result in a certain rough sense in good conduct among individuals when the necessary conditions are given (namely, the actual similarity of the individuals in amount of force and degree of worth, and their co-relation within one organization). As soon, however, as one wished to take this principle more generally, and if possible even as *the fundamental principle of society,* it would immediately disclose what it really is—namely, a Will to the *denial* of life, a principle of dissolution and decay. Here one must think profoundly to the very basis and resist all sentimental weakness: life itself is *essentially* appropriation, injury, conquest of the strange and weak, suppression, severity, obtrusion of peculiar forms, incorporation, and at the least, putting it mildest, exploitation;—but why should one forever use precisely these words on which for ages a disparaging purpose has been stamped? Even the organization within which, as was previously supposed, the individuals treat each other as equal—it takes place in every healthy aristocracy—must itself, if it be a living and not a dying organization, do all that towards other bodies, which the individuals within it refrain from doing to each other: it will have to be the incarnated Will to Power, it will endeavor to grow, to gain ground, attract to itself and acquire ascendency—not owing to any morality or immorality, but because it *lives,* and because life *is* precisely Will to Power. On no point, however, is the ordinary consciousness of Europeans more unwilling to be corrected than on this matter; people now rave everywhere, even under the guise of science, about coming conditions of society in which "the exploiting character" is to be absent:—that sounds to my ears as if they promised to invent a mode of life which should refrain from all organic functions. "Exploitation" does not belong to a depraved, or imperfect and primitive society: it belongs to the *nature* of the living being as a primary organic function; it is a consequence of the intrinsic Will to Power, which is precisely the Will to Life.—Granting that as a theory this is a novelty—as a reality it is the *fundamental fact* of all history: let us be so far honest towards ourselves!

In a tour through the many finer and coarser moralities which have hitherto prevailed or still prevail on the earth, I found certain traits recurring regularly together, and connected with one another, until finally two primary types revealed themselves to me, and a radical distinction was brought to light. There is *master-morality* and *slave-morality*;—I would at once add, however, that in all higher and mixed civilizations, there are also attempts at the reconciliation of the two moralities; but one finds still oftener the confusion and mutual misunderstanding of them, indeed, sometimes their close juxtaposition—even in the same man, within one soul. The distinctions of moral values have either originated in a ruling caste, pleasantly conscious of being different from the ruled—or among the ruled class, the slaves and dependents of all sorts. In the first case, when it is the rulers who determine the conception "good," it is the exalted, proud disposition which is regarded as the distinguishing feature, and that which determines the order of rank. The noble type of man separates from himself the beings in whom the opposite of this exalted, proud disposition displays itself: he despises them. Let it at once be noted that in this first kind of morality the antithesis "good" and "bad" means practically the same as "noble" and "despicable";—the antithesis "good" and "*evil*" is of a different origin. The cowardly, the timid, the insignificant, and those thinking merely of narrow utility are despised; moreover, also, the distrustful, with their constrained glances, the self-abasing, the dog-like kind of men who let themselves be abused, the mendicant flatterers, and above all the liars:—it is a fundamental belief of all aristocrats that the common people are untruthful. "We truthful ones"—the nobility in ancient Greece called themselves. It is obvious that everywhere the designations of moral value were at first applied to *men*, and were only derivatively and at a later period applied to *actions;* it is a gross mistake, therefore, when historians of morals start with questions like, "Why have sympathetic actions been praised?" The noble type of man regards *himself* as a determiner of values;

he does not require to be approved of; he passes the judgment: "What is injurious to me is injurious in itself"; he knows that it is he himself only who confers honor on things; he is a *creator of values.* He honors whatever he recognizes in himself: such morality is self-glorification. In the foreground, there is the feeling of plenitude, of power, which seeks to overflow, the happiness of high tension, the consciousness of a wealth which would fain give and bestow:—the noble man also helps the unfortunate, but not—or scarcely—out of pity, but rather from an impulse generated by the super-abundance of power. The noble man honors in himself the powerful one, him also who has power over himself, who knows how to speak and how to keep silence, who takes pleasure in subjecting himself to severity and hardness, and has reverence for all that is severe and hard. "Wotan placed a hard heart in my breast," says an old Scandinavian saga: it is thus rightly expressed from the soul of a proud Viking. Such a type of man is even proud of *not* being made for sympathy; the hero of the saga therefore adds warningly: "He who has not a hard heart when young, will never have one." The noble and brave who think thus are the furthest removed from the morality which sees precisely in sympathy, or in acting for the good of others, or in *désintéressement,* the characteristic of the moral; faith in oneself, pride in oneself, a radical enmity and irony towards "selflessness," belong as definitely to noble morality, as do a careless scorn and precaution in presence of sympathy and the "warm heart."—It is the powerful who *know* how to honor, it is their art, their domain for invention. The profound reverence for age and for tradition—all law rests on this double reverence—the belief and prejudice in favor of ancestors and unfavorable to newcomers, is typical in the morality of the powerful; and if, reversely, men of "modern ideas" believe almost instinctively in "progress" and the "future," and are more and more lacking in respect for old age, the ignoble origin of these "ideas" has complacently betrayed itself thereby. A morality of the ruling class, however, is more especially foreign and irritating to present-day taste in the sternness of its principle that one has duties only to one's equals; that one may act towards beings of a lower rank, towards all that is foreign, just as seems good to one, or "as the heart desires," and in any case "beyond good and evil": it is here that sympathy and similar sentiments can have a place. The ability and obligation to exercise prolonged gratitude and prolonged revenge—both only within the circle of equals—artfulness in retaliation, *raffinement* of the idea in friendship, a certain necessity to have enemies (as outlets for the emotions of envy, quarrelsomeness, arrogance—in fact, in order to be a good *friend*): all these are typical characteristics of the noble morality, which, as has been pointed out, is not the morality of "modern ideas," and is therefore at present difficult to realize, and also to unearth and disclose.—It is otherwise with the second type of morality, *slave-morality*. Supposing that the abused, the oppressed, the suffering, the unemancipated, the weary, and those uncertain of themselves, should moralize, what will be the common element in their moral estimates? Probably a pessimistic suspicion with regard to the entire situation of man will find expression, perhaps a condemnation of man, together with his situation. The slave has an unfavorable eye for the virtues of the powerful; he has a skepticism and distrust, a *refinement* of distrust of everything "good" that is there honored—he would fain persuade himself that the very happiness there is not genuine. On the other hand, *those* qualities which serve to alleviate the existence of sufferers are brought into prominence and flooded with light; it is here that sympathy, the kind, helping hand, the warm heart, patience, diligence, humility, and friendliness attain to honor; for here these are the most useful qualities, and almost the only means of supporting the burden of existence. Slave-morality is essentially the morality of utility. Here is the seat of the origin of the famous antithesis "good" and "*evil*":—power and dangerousness are as-

sumed to reside in the evil, a certain dreadfulness, subtlety, and strength, which do not admit of being despised. According to slave-morality, therefore, the "evil" man arouses fear; according to master-morality, it is precisely the "good" man who arouses fear and seeks to arouse it, while the bad man is regarded as the despicable being. The contrast attains its maximum when, in accordance with the logical consequences of slave-morality, a shade of depreciation—it may be slight and well-intentioned—at last attaches itself even to the "good" man of this morality; because, according to the servile mode of thought, the good man must in any case be the *safe* man: he is good-natured, easily deceived, perhaps a little stupid, *un bonhomme*. Everywhere that slave-morality gains the ascendency, language shows a tendency to approximate the significance of the words "good" and "stupid."—A last fundamental difference: the desire for *freedom*, the instinct for happiness and the refinements of the feeling of liberty belong as necessarily to slave-morals and morality, as artifice and enthusiasm in reverence and devotion are the regular symptoms of an aristocratic mode of thinking and estimating.—Hence we can understand without further detail why love *as a passion*—it is our European specialty—must absolutely be of noble origin; as is well known, its invention is due to the Provencal poet-cavaliers, those brilliant ingenious men of the "*gai Saber*," to whom Europe owes so much, and almost owes itself.

Vanity is one of the things which are perhaps most difficult for a noble man to understand: he will be tempted to deny it, where another kind of man thinks he sees it self-evidently. The problem for him is to represent to his mind beings who seek to arouse a good opinion of themselves which they themselves do not possess—and consequently also do not "deserve"—and who yet *believe* in this good opinion afterwards. This seems to him on the one hand such bad taste and so self-disrespectful, and on the other hand so grotesquely unreasonable, that he would like to consider vanity an exception, and is doubtful about it in most cases when it is spoken of. He will say, for instance: "I may be mistaken about my value, and on the other hand may nevertheless demand that my value should be acknowledged by others precisely as I rate it:—that, however, is not vanity (but self-conceit, or, in most cases, that which is called 'humility,' and also 'modesty')." Or he will even say: "For many reasons I can delight in the good opinion of others, perhaps because I love and honor them, and rejoice in all their joys, perhaps also because their good opinion endorses and strengthens my belief in my own good opinion, perhaps because the good opinion of others, even in cases where I do not share it, is useful to me, or gives promise of usefulness:—all this, however, is not vanity." The man of noble character must first bring it home forcibly to his mind, especially with the aid of history, that, from time immemorial, in all social strata in any way dependent, the ordinary man *was* only that which he *passed for*:—not being at all accustomed to fix values, he did not assign even to himself any other value than that which his master assigned to him (it is the peculiar *right of masters* to create values). It may be looked upon as the result of an extraordinary atavism, that the ordinary man, even at present, is still always *waiting* for an opinion about himself, and then instinctively submitting himself to it; yet by no means only to a "good" opinion, but also to a bad and unjust one (think, for instance, of the greater part of the self-appreciations and self-depreciations which believing women learn from their confessors, and which in general the believing Christian learns from his Church). In fact, comformably to the slow rise of the democratic social order (and its cause, the blending of the blood of masters and slaves), the originally noble and rare impulse of the masters to assign a value to themselves and to "think well" of themselves, will now be more and more encouraged and extended; but it has at all times an older, ampler, and more radically ingrained propensity opposed to it—and in the phenomenon of "vanity" this

older propensity overmasters the younger. The vain person rejoices over *every* good opinion which he hears about himself (quite apart from the point of view of its usefulness, and equally regardless of its truth or falsehood), just as he suffers from every bad opinion: for he subjects himself to both, he *feels* himself subjected to both, by that oldest instinct of subjection which breaks forth in him.—It is "the slave" in the vain man's blood, the remains of the slave's craftiness—and how much of the "slave" is still left in woman, for instance!—which seeks to *seduce* to good opinions of itself; it is the slave, too, who immediately afterwards falls prostrate himself before these opinions, as though he had not called them forth.—And to repeat it again: vanity is an atavism.

A *species* originates, and a type becomes established and strong in the long struggle with essentially constant *unfavorable* conditions. On the other hand, it is known by the experience of breeders that species which receive superabundant nourishment, and in general a surplus of protection and care, immediately tend in the most marked way to develop variations, and are fertile in prodigies and monstrosities (also in monstrous vices). Now look at an aristocratic commonwealth, say an ancient Greek *polis,* or Venice, as a voluntary or involuntary contrivance for the purpose of *rearing* human beings; there are men beside one another, thrown upon their own resources, who want to make their species prevail, chiefly because they *must* prevail, or else run the terrible danger of being exterminated. The favor, the superabundance, the protection are there lacking under which variations are fostered; the species needs itself as species, as something which, precisely by virtue of its hardness, its uniformity, and simplicity of structure, can in general prevail and make itself permanent in constant struggle with its neighbors, or with rebellious or rebellion-threatening vassals. The most varied experience teaches it what are the qualities to which it principally owes the fact that it still exists, in spite of all Gods and men, and has hitherto been victorious; these qualities it calls virtues, and these virtues alone it develops to maturity. It does so with severity, indeed it desires severity; every aristocratic morality is intolerant in the education of youth, in the control of women, in the marriage customs, in the relations of old and young, in the penal laws (which have an eye only for the degenerating): it counts intolerance itself among the virtues, under the name of "justice." A type with few, but very marked features, a species of severe, war-like, wisely silent, reserved and reticent men (and as such, with the most delicate sensibility for the charm and *nuances* of society) is thus established, unaffected by the vicissitudes of generations; the constant struggle with uniform *unfavorable* conditions is, as already remarked, the cause of a type becoming stable and hard. Finally, however, a happy state of things results, the enormous tension is relaxed; there are perhaps no more enemies among the neighboring peoples, and the means of life, even of the enjoyment of life, are present in superabundance. With one stroke the bond and constraint of the old discipline severs: it is no longer regarded as necessary, as a condition of existence—if it would continue, it can only do so as a form of *luxury,* as an archaizing *taste.* Variations, whether they be deviations (into the higher, finer, and rarer), or deteriorations and monstrosities, appear suddenly on the scene in the greatest exuberance and splendor; the individual dares to be individual and detach himself. At this turning-point of history there manifest themselves, side by side, and often mixed and entangled together, a magnificent, manifold, virgin-forest-like up-growth and up-striving, a kind of *tropical tempo* in the rivalry of growth, and an extraordinary decay and self-destruction, owing to the savagely opposing and seemingly exploding egoisms, which strive with one another "for sun and light," and can no longer assign any limit, restraint, or forbearance for themselves by means of the hitherto existing morality. It was this morality itself which piled up the strength so enormously, which bent the bow in so threatening a manner:—it is now "out of date," it is getting "out of date." The dangerous and disquieting point has been reached when the greater, more manifold, more compehensive life *is lived beyond* the old morality; the "individual" stands out, and is obliged to have recourse to his own lawgiving, his own arts and artifices for self-preservation, self-elevation, and self-deliverance. Nothing but new "Whys," nothing but new "Hows," no common formulas any longer, misunderstanding and disregard in league with each other, decay, deterioration, and the loftiest desires frightfully entangled, the genius of the race overflowing from all the cornucopias of good and bad, a portentous simultaneousness of spring and autumn, full of new charms and mysteries peculiar to the fresh, still inexhausted, still unwearied corruption. Danger is again present, the mother of morality, great danger; this time shifted into the individual, into the neighbor and friend, into the street, into their own child, into their own heart, into all the most personal and secret recesses of their desires and volitions. What will the moral philosophers who appear at this time have to preach? They discover, these sharp onlookers and loafers, that the end is quickly approaching, that everything around them decays and produces decay, that nothing will endure until the day after tomorrow, except one species of man, the incurably *mediocre.* The mediocre alone have a prospect of continuing and propagating themselves—they will be the men of the future, the sole survivors; "be like them! become mediocre!" is now the only morality which has still a significance, which still obtains a hearing.—But it is difficult to preach this morality of mediocrity! it can never avow what it is, and what it desires! it has to talk of moderation and dignity and duty and brotherly love—it will have difficulty *in concealing its irony!*

There is an *instinct for rank,* which more than anything else is already the sign of a *high* rank; there is a *delight* in the *nuances* of reverence which leads one to infer noble origin and habits. The refinement, goodness, and loftiness of a soul are put to a perilous test when something passes by that is of the highest rank, but is not yet protected by the awe of authority from obtrusive touches and incivilities: something that goes its way like a living touchstone, undistinguished, undiscovered, and tentative, perhaps voluntarily veiled and disguised. He whose task and practice it is to investigate souls, will avail himself of many varieties of this very art to determine the ultimate value of a soul, the unalterable, innate order of rank to which it belongs: he will test it by its *instinct for reverence. Différence engendre haine:* The vulgarity of many a nature spurts up suddenly like dirty water, when any holy vessel, any jewel from closed shrines, any book bearing the marks of great destiny, is brought before it; while on the other hand, there is an involuntary silence, a hesitation of the eye, a cessation of all gestures, by which it is indicated that a soul *feels* the nearness of what is worthiest of respect. The way in which, on the whole, the reverence for the Bible has hitherto been maintained in Europe, is perhaps the best example of discipline and refinement of manners which Europe owes to Christianity: books of such profoundness and supreme significance require for their protection an external tyranny of authority, in order to acquire the *period* of thousands of years which is necessary to exhaust and unriddle them. Much has been achieved when the sentiment has been at last instilled into the masses (the shallow-pates and the boobies of every kind) that they are not allowed to touch everything, that there are holy experiences before which they must take off their shoes and keep away the unclean hand—it is almost their highest advance towards humanity. On the contrary in the so-called cultured classes, the believers in "modern ideas," nothing is perhaps so repulsive as their lack of shame, the easy insolence of eye and hand with which they touch, taste, and finger everything; and it is possible that even yet there is more *relative* nobility of taste, and more tact for reverence among the people, among the lower

classes of the people, especially among peasants, than among the newspaper-reading demimonde of intellect, the cultured class.

It cannot be effaced from a man's soul what his ancestors have preferably and most constantly done: whether they were perhaps diligent economizers attached to a desk and a cash-box, modest and citizen-like in their desires, modest also in their virtues; or whether they were accustomed to commanding from morning till night, fond of rude pleasures and probably of still ruder duties and responsibilities; or whether, finally, at one time or another, they have sacrificed old privileges of birth and possession, in order to live wholly for their faith—for their "God"—as men of an inexorable and sensitive conscience, which blushes at every compromise. It is quite impossible for a man *not* to have the qualities and predilections of his parents and ancestors in his constitution, whatever appearances may suggest to the contrary. This is the problem of race. Granted that one knows something of the parents, it is admissible to draw a conclusion about the child: any kind of offensive incontinence, any kind of sordid envy, or of clumsy self-vaunting—the three things which together have constituted the genuine plebeian type in all times—such must pass over to the child, as surely as bad blood; and with the help of the best education and culture one will only succeed in *deceiving* with regard to such heredity.—And what else does education and culture try to do nowadays! In our very democratic, or rather, very plebeian age, "education" and "culture" *must* be essentially the art of deceiving—deceiving with regard to origin, with regard to the inherited plebeianism in body and soul. An educator who nowadays preached truthfulness above everything else, and called out constantly to his pupils: "Be true! Be natural! Show yourselves as you are!"—even such a virtuous and sincere ass would learn in a short time to have recourse to the *furca* of Horace, *naturam expellere:* with what results? "Plebeianism" *usque recurret.*

At the risk of displeasing innocent ears,

I submit that egoism belongs to the essence of a noble soul; I mean the unalterable belief that to a being such as "we," other beings must naturally be in subjection, and have to sacrifice themselves. The noble soul accepts the fact of his egoism without question, and also without consciousness of harshness, constraint, or arbitrariness therein, but rather as something that may have its basis in the primary law of things:—if he sought a designation for it he would say: "It is justice itself." He acknowledges under certain circumstances, which made him hesitate at first, that there are other equally privileged ones; as soon as he has settled this question of rank, he moves among those equals and equally privileged ones with the same assurance, as regards modesty and delicate respect, which he enjoys in intercourse with himself—in accordance with an innate heavenly mechanism which all the stars understand. It is an *additional* instance of his egoism, this artfulness and self-limitation in intercourse with his equals—every star is a similar egoist; he honors *himself* in them, and in the rights which he concedes to them, he has no doubt that the exchange of honors and rights, as the *essence* of all intercourse, belongs also to the natural condition of things. The noble soul gives as he takes, prompted by the passionate and sensitive instinct of requital, which is at the root of his nature. The notion of "favor" has, *inter pares*, neither significance nor good repute; there may be a sublime way of letting gifts, as it were, light upon one from above, and of drinking them thirstily like dewdrops; but for those arts and displays the noble soul has no aptitude. His egoism hinders him here: in general, he looks "aloft" unwillingly—he looks either *forward*, horizontally and deliberately, or downwards— *he knows that he is on a height.*

STUDY QUESTIONS

1. On what grounds does Nietzsche justify slavery?
2. What does Nietzsche mean when he says that life is Will to Power? What conclusions does he draw from this view?
3. What is Nietzsche's opinion of democracy? Of modern European civilization?
4. Nietzsche divides humans into two classes—masters and slaves. After reading his descriptions of these two classes, into which would you place yourself? Are you content to be there?
5. Nietzsche has a vision of an ideal civilization. Can anything good be said about this vision? If so, what?

For Further Reading

Copleston, F. *Friedrich Nietzsche*. London: Burns Oates and Washburne, 1942 (Chapter 5).
Danto, A. C. *Nietzche. as Philosopher*. New York: Macmillan, 1965 (esp. Chapter 5).
Hollingdale, R. J. *Nietzsche*. London: Routledge & Kegan Paul, 1973 (Chapter 5, §V).
Kaufmann, W. A. *Nietzsche*. 4th ed. Princeton, N.J.: Princeton University Press, 1974 (Chapters 7 through 10).
Solomon, R. C., ed. *Nietzsche*. Garden City, N.Y.: Doubleday, 1973 (Chapters 8 through 11).

KANT: THE CATEGORICAL IMPERATIVE

Students sometimes find Kant's theory of the moral life hard to understand. Part of the reason for the difficulty undoubtedly lies in the complexity of Kant's thought, but probably more results from the language he used to express that thought. Two clues may be helpful in unraveling Kant's views. For him, to live morally is to act rationally and honestly. If we examine our relationships with our fellows, our reason is capable of discerning a rule of action that we ought to follow. The only obstacle to our acting morally then becomes our self-interest; we know what we ought to do but we don't want to do it. Hence we begin searching for excuses to avoid doing our duty. Honesty then becomes essential; we must possess the will to do what we have recognized to be our duty simply because of our recognition that it is our duty.

Immanuel Kant (1724–1804) is generally regarded to be the greatest of the modern philosophers. Born in the small university city of Königsberg on the shores of the Baltic Sea, he spent his entire life there, hardly ever traveling out of town. After working several years as a private tutor, he joined the faculty of the University of Königsberg where he gained fame for his witty and eloquent lectures. A life-time bachelor, he organized his day on a rigorous schedule, which began each morning at four forty-five. His afternoon walk was a ritual. Rain or shine he set forth, followed by his servant carrying an umbrella. It is said that the people of Königsberg set their clocks by his appearance on the street.

Fundamental Principles of the Metaphysic of Morals

First Section Transition From the Common Rational Knowledge of Morality to the Philosophical

Nothing can possibly be conceived in the world, or even out of it, which can be called good, without qualification, except a Good Will. Intelligence, wit, judgment, and the other *talents* of the mind, however they may be named, or courage, resolution, perseverance, as qualities of temperament, are undoubtedly good and desirable in many respects; but these gifts of nature may also become extremely bad and mischievous if the will which is to make use of them, and which, therefore, constitutes what is called *character,* is not good. It is the same with the *gifts of fortune.* Power, riches, honor, even health, and the general well-being and contentment with one's condition which is called *happiness,* inspire pride, and often presumption, if there is not a good will to correct the influence of these on the mind, and with this also to rectify the whole principle of acting, and adapt it to its end. The sight of a being who is not adorned with a single feature of a pure and good will, enjoying unbroken prosperity, can never give pleasure to an impartial rational spectator. Thus a good will appears to constitute the indispensable condition even of being worthy of happiness.

First published in German in 1785. Translated by T. K. Abbott. Kant's footnotes have not been included.

There are even some qualities which are of service to this good will itself, and may facilitate its action, yet which have no intrinsic unconditional value, but always presuppose a good will, and this qualifies the esteem that we justly have for them, and does not permit us to regard them as absolutely good. Moderation in the affections and passions, self-control, and calm deliberation are not only good in many respects, but even seem to constitute part of the intrinsic worth of the person; but they are far from deserving to be called good without qualification, although they have been so unconditionally praised by the ancients. For without the principles of a good will, they may become extremely bad; and the coolness of a villain not only makes him far more dangerous, but also directly makes him more abominable in our eyes than he would have been without it.

A good will is good not because of what it performs or effects, not by its aptness for the attainment of some proposed end, but simply by virtue of the volition, that is, it is good in itself, and considered by itself is to be esteemed much higher than all that can be brought about by it in favour of any inclination, nay, even of the sum-total of all inclinations. Even if it should happen that, owing to special disfavour of fortune, or the niggardly provision of a step-motherly nature, this will should wholly lack power to accomplish its purpose, if with its greatest efforts it should yet achieve nothing, and there should remain only the good will (not, to be sure, a mere wish, but the summoning of all means in our power), then, like a jewel, it would still shine by its own light, as a thing which has its whole value in itself. Its usefulness or fruitlessness can neither add to nor take away anything from this value. It would be, as it were, only the setting to enable us to handle it the more conveniently in common commerce, or to attract to it the attention of those who are not yet connoisseurs, but not to recommend it to true connoisseurs, or to determine its value.

There is, however, something so strange in this idea of the absolute value of the mere will, in which no account is taken of its utility, that notwithstanding the thorough assent of even common reason to the idea, yet a suspicion must arise that it may perhaps really be the product of mere high-flown fancy, and that we may have misunderstood the purpose of nature in assigning reason as the governor of our will. Therefore we will examine this idea from this point of view.

In the physical constitution of an organized being, that is, a being adapted suitably to the purposes of life, we assume it as a fundamental principle that no organ for any purpose will be found but what is also the fittest and best adapted for that purpose. Now in a being which has reason and a will, if the proper object of nature were its *conservation,* its *welfare,* in a word, its *happiness,* then nature would have hit upon a very bad arrangement in selecting the reason of the creature to carry out this purpose. For all the actions which the creature has to perform with a view to this purpose, and the whole rule of its conduct, would be far more surely prescribed to it by instinct, and that end would have been attained thereby much more certainly than

it ever can be by reason. Should reason have been communicated to this favored creature over and above, it must only have served it to contemplate the happy constitution of its nature, to admire it, to congratulate itself thereon, and to feel thankful for it to the beneficent cause, but not that it should subject its desires to that weak and delusive guidance, and meddle bunglingly with the purpose of nature. In a word, nature would have taken care that reason should not break forth into *practical exercise,* nor have the presumption, with its weak insight, to think out for itself the plan of happiness, and of the means of attaining it. Nature would not only have taken on herself the choice of the ends, but also of the means, and with wise foresight would have entrusted both to instinct.

. . .

For as reason is not competent to guide the will with certainty in regard to its objects and the satisfaction of all our wants (which it to some extent even multiplies), this being an end to which an implanted instinct would have led with much greater certainty; and since, nevertheless, reason is imparted to us as a practical faculty, *i.e.,* as one which is to have influence on the *will,* therefore, admitting that nature generally in the distribution of her capacities has adapted the means to the end, its true destination must be to produce a *will,* not merely good as a *means* to something else, but *good in itself,* for which reason was absolutely necessary. This will then, though not indeed the sole and complete good, must be the supreme good and the condition of every other, even of the desire of happiness. Under these circumstances, there is nothing inconsistent with the wisdom of nature in the fact that the cultivation of the reason, which is requisite for the first and unconditional purpose, does in many ways interfere, at least in this life, with the attainment of the second, which is always conditional, namely, happiness. Nay, it may even reduce it to nothing, without nature thereby failing of her purpose. For reason recognizes the establishment of a good will as its highest practical destination, and in attaining this purpose is capable only of a satisfaction of its own proper kind, namely, that from the attainment of an end, which end again is determined by reason only, notwithstanding that this may involve many a disappointment to the ends of inclination.

We have then to develop the notion of a will which deserves to be highly esteemed for itself, and is good without a view to anything further, a notion which exists already in the sound natural understanding, requiring rather to be cleared up than to be taught, and which in estimating the value of our actions always takes the first place, and constitutes the condition of all the rest. In order to do this, we will take the notion of duty, which includes that of a good will, although implying certain subjective restrictions and hindrances. These, however, far from concealing it, or rendering it unrecognizable, rather bring it out by contrast, and make it shine forth so much the brighter.

I omit here all actions which are already recognized as inconsistent with duty, although they may be useful for this or that purpose, for with these the question whether they are done *from duty* cannot arise at all, since they even conflict with it. I also set aside those actions which really conform to duty, but to which men have no direct *inclination*, performing them because they are impelled thereto by some other inclination. For in this case we can readily distinguish whether the action which agrees with duty is done *from duty*, or from a selfish view. It is much harder to make this distinction when the action accords with duty, and the subject has besides a *direct* inclination to it. For example, it is always a matter of duty that a dealer should not overcharge an inexperienced purchaser; and wherever there is much commerce the prudent tradesman does not overcharge, but keeps a fixed price for everyone, so that a child buys of him as well as any other. Men are thus *honestly* served; but this is not enough to make us believe

that the tradesman has so acted from duty and from principles of honesty: his own advantage required it; it is out of the question in this case to suppose that he might besides have a direct inclination in favour of the buyers, so that, as it were, from love he should give no advantage to one over another. Accordingly the action was done neither from duty nor from direct inclination, but merely with a selfish view.

On the other hand, it is a duty to maintain one's life; and, in addition, everyone has also a direct inclination to do so. But on this account the often anxious care which most men take for it has no intrinsic worth, and their maxim has no moral import. They preserve their life *as duty requires,* no doubt, but not *because duty requires.* On the other hand, if adversity and hopeless sorrow have completely taken away the relish for life; if the unfortunate one, strong in mind, indignant at his fate rather than desponding or dejected, wishes for death, and yet preserves his life without loving it—not from inclination or fear, but from duty—then his maxim has a moral worth.

To be beneficent when we can is a duty; and besides this, there are many minds so sympathetically constituted that, without any other motive of vanity or self-interest, they find a pleasure in spreading joy around them, and can take delight in the satisfaction of others so far as it is their own work. But I maintain that in such a case an action of this kind, however proper, however amiable it may be, has nevertheless no true moral worth, but is on a level with other inclinations, *e.g.* the inclination to honor, which, if it is happily directed to that which is in fact of public utility and accordant with duty, and consequently honorable, deserves praise and encouragement, but not esteem. For the maxim lacks the moral import, namely, that such actions be done *from duty,* not from inclination. Put the case that the mind of that philanthropist was clouded by sorrow of his own, extinguishing all sympathy with the lot of others, and that while he still has the power to benefit others in distress, he is not touched by their trouble because he is absorbed with his own; and now suppose that he tears himself out of this dead insensibility, and performs the action without any inclination to it, but simply from duty, then first has his action its genuine moral worth. Further still; if nature has put little sympathy in the heart of this or that man; if he, supposed to be an upright man, is by temperament cold and indifferent to the sufferings of others, perhaps because in respect of his own he is provided with the special gift of patience and fortitude, and supposes, or even requires, that others should have the same—and such a man would certainly not be the meanest product of nature—but if nature had not specially framed him for a philanthropist, would he not still find in himself a source from whence to give himself a far higher worth than that of a good-natured temperament could be? Unquestionably. It is just in this that the moral worth of the character is brought out which is incomparably the highest of all, namely, that he is beneficent, not from inclination, but from duty.

To secure one's own happiness is a duty, at least indirectly; for discontent with one's condition, under a pressure of many anxieties and amidst unsatisfied wants, might easily become a great *temptation to transgression of duty*. But here again, without looking to duty, all men have already the strongest and most intimate inclination to happiness, because it is just in this idea that all inclinations are combined in one total. But the precept of happiness is often of such a sort that it greatly interferes with some inclinations, and yet a man cannot form any definite and certain conception of the sum of satisfaction of all of them which is called happiness. It is not then to be wondered at that a single inclination, definite both as to what it promises and as to the time within which it can be gratified, is often able to overcome such a fluctuating idea, and that a gouty patient, for instance, can choose to enjoy what he likes, and to suffer what he may, since, according to his calculation, on this occasion at least, he has not sacrificed the enjoyment of the present

moment to a possibly mistaken expectation of a happiness which is supposed to be found in health. But even in this case, if the general desire for happiness did not influence his will, and supposing that in his particular case health was not a necessary element in this calculation, there yet remains in this, as in all other cases, this law, namely, that he should promote his happiness not from inclination but from duty, and by this would his conduct first acquire true moral worth.

It is in this manner, undoubtedly, that we are to understand those passages of Scripture also in which we are commanded to love our neighbor, even our enemy. For love, as an affection, cannot be commanded, but beneficence for duty's sake may; even though we are not impelled to it by any inclination—nay, are even repelled by a natural and unconquerable aversion. This is *practical* love, and not *pathological*—a love which is seated in the will, and not in the propensions of sense—in principles of action and not of tender sympathy; and it is this love alone which can be commanded.

The second* proposition is: That an action done from duty derives its moral worth, *not from the purpose* which is to be attained by it, but from the maxim by which it is determined, and therefore does not depend on the realization of the object of the action, but merely on the *principle of volition* by which the action has taken place, without regard to any object of desire. It is clear from what precedes that the purposes which we may have in view in our actions, or their effects regarded as ends and springs of the will, cannot give to actions any unconditional or moral worth. In what, then can their worth lie, if it is not to consist in the will and in reference to its expected effect? It cannot lie anywhere but in the principle of the will without regard to the ends which can be attained by the action. For the will stands between its *à priori* principle, which is formal, and its *à posteriori* spring, which is material, as between two

---

*The first proposition was that to have moral worth an action must be done from duty.

roads, and as it must be determined by something, it follows that it must be determined by the formal principle of volition when an action is done from duty, in which case every material principle has been withdrawn from it.

The third proposition, which is a consequence of the two preceding, I would express thus: *Duty is the necessity of action from respect for the law.* I may have *inclination* for an object as the effect of my proposed action, but I cannot have *respect* for it, just for this reason, that it is an effect and not an energy of will. Similarly, I cannot have respect for inclination, whether my own or another's; I can at most, if my own, approve it; if another's, sometimes even love it; *i.e.* look on it as favourable to my own interest. It is only what is connected with my will as a principle, by no means as an effect—what does not subserve my inclination, but overpowers it, or at least in case of choice excludes it from its calculation—in other words, simply the law of itself, which can be an object of respect, and hence a command. Now an action done from duty must wholly exclude the influence of inclination, and with it every object of the will, so that nothing remains which can determine the will except objectively the *law,* and subjectively *pure respect* for this practical law, and consequently the maxim that I should follow this law even to the thwarting of all my inclinations.

Thus the moral worth of an action does not lie in the effect expected from it, nor in any principle of action which requires to borrow its motive from this expected effect. For all these effects—agreeableness of one's condition, and even the promotion of the happiness of others—could have been also brought about by other causes, so that for this there would have been no need of the will of a rational being; whereas it is in this alone that the supreme and unconditional good can be found. The preeminent good which we call moral can therefore consist in nothing else than *the conception of law* in itself, which certainly is only *possible in a rational being,* in so far as this conception, and not the expected ef-

fect, determines the will. This is a good which is already present in the person who acts accordingly, and we have not to wait for it to appear first in the result.

But what sort of law can that be, the conception of which must determine the will, even without paying any regard to the effect expected from it, in order that this will may be called good absolutely and without qualification? As I have deprived the will of every impulse which could arise to it from obedience to any law, there remains nothing but the universal conformity of its actions to law in general, which alone is to serve the will as a principle, *i.e.* I am never to act otherwise than so *that I could also will that my maxim should become a universal law.* Here, now, it is the simple conformity to law in general, without assuming any particular law applicable to certain actions, that serves the will as its principle, and must so serve it, if duty is not to be a vain delusion and a chimerical notion. The common reason of men in its practical judgments perfectly coincides with this, and always has in view the principle here suggested. Let the question be, for example: May I when in distress make a promise with the intention not to keep it? I readily distinguish here between the two significations which the question may have: Whether it is prudent, or whether it is right, to make a false promise? The former may undoubtedly often be the case. I see clearly indeed that it is not enough to extricate myself from a present difficulty by means of this subterfuge, but it must be well considered whether there may not hereafter spring from this lie much greater inconvenience than that from which I now free myself, and as, with all my supposed *cunning,* the consequences cannot be so easily foreseen but that credit once lost may be much more injurious to me than any mischief which I seek to avoid at present, it should be considered whether it would not be more *prudent* to act herein according to a universal maxim, and to make it a habit to promise nothing except with the intention of keeping it. But it is soon clear to me that such a maxim will still only be based on the fear of consequences. Now it is a wholly different thing to be truthful from duty, and to be so from apprehension of injurious consequences. In the first case, the very notion of the action already implies a law for me; in the second case, I must first look about elsewhere to see what results may be combined with it which would affect myself. For to deviate from the principle of duty is beyond all doubt wicked; but to be unfaithful to my maxim of prudence may often be very advantageous to me, although to abide by it is certainly safer. The shortest way, however, and an unerring one, to discover the answer to this question whether a lying promise is consistent with duty, is to ask myself, Should I be content that my maxim (to extricate myself from difficulty by a false promise) should hold good as a universal law, for myself as well as for others? and should I be able to say to myself, "Every one may make a deceitful promise when he finds himself in a difficulty from which he cannot otherwise extricate himself"? Then I presently become aware that while I can will the lie, I can by no means will that lying should be a universal law.

• • •

Second Section
TRANSITION FROM POPULAR MORAL PHILOSOPHY TO THE METAPHYSIC OF MORALS

• • •

Everything in nature works according to laws. Rational beings alone have the faculty of acting according *to the conception* of laws, that is according to principles, *i.e.* have a *will.* Since the deduction of actions from principles requires *reason,* the will is nothing but practical reason. If reason infallibly determines the will, then the actions of such a being which are recognized as objectively necessary are subjectively necessary also, *i.e.* the will is a faculty to choose *that only* which reason independent on inclina-

tion recognizes as practically necessary, *i.e.* as good. But if reason of itself does not sufficiently determine the will, if the latter is subject also to subjective conditions (particular impulses) which do not always coincide with the objective conditions; in a word, if the will does not *in itself* completely accord with reason (which is actually the case with men), then the actions which objectively are recognized as necessary are subjectively contingent, and the determination of such a will according to objective laws is *obligation,* that is to say, the relation of the objective laws to a will that is not thoroughly good is conceived as the determination of the will of a rational being by principles of reason, but which the will from its nature does not of necessity follow.

The conception of an objective principle, in so far as it is obligatory for a will, is called a command (of reason), and the formula of the command is called an Imperative.

All imperatives are expressed by the word *ought,* and thereby indicate the relation of an objective law of reason to a will, which from its subjective constitution is not necessarily determined by it (an obligation). They say that something would be good to do or to forbear, but they say it to a will which does not always do a thing because it is conceived to be good to do it. That is practically *good,* however, which determines the will by means of the conception of reason, and consequently not from subjective causes, but objectively, that is on principles which are valid for every rational being as such. It is distinguished from the *pleasant,* as that which influences the will only by means of sensation from merely subjective causes, valid only for the sense of this or that one, and not as a principle of reason, which holds for every one.

A perfectly good will would therefore be equally subject to objective laws (viz. laws of good), but could not be conceived as *obliged* thereby to act lawfully, because of itself from its subjective constitution it can only be determined by the conception of good. Therefore no imperatives hold for the Divine will, or in general for a *holy* will; *ought* is here out of place, because the volition is already of itself necessarily in unison with the law. Therefore imperatives are only formulae to express the relation of objective laws of all volition to the subjective imperfection of the will of this or that rational being, *e.g.* the human will.

Now all *imperatives* command either *hypothetically* or *categorically.* The former represent the practical necessity of a possible action as means to something else that is willed (or at least which one might possibly will). The categorical imperative would be that which represented an action as necessary of itself without reference to another end, *i.e.,* as objectively necessary.

Since every practical law represents a possible action as good, and on this account, for a subject who is practically determinable by reason, necessary, all imperatives are formulae determining an action which is necessary according to the principle of a will good in some respects. If now the action is good only as a means *to something else*, then the imperative is hypothetical; if it is conceived as good *in itself* and consequently as being necessarily the principle of a will which of itself conforms to reason, then it is *categorical.*

Thus the imperative declares what action possible by me would be good, and presents the practical rule in relation to a will which does not forthwith perform an action simply because it is good, whether because the subject does not always know that it is good, or because even if it knows this, yet its maxims might be opposed to the objective principles of practical reason.

Accordingly the hypothetical imperative only says that the action is good for some purpose, *possible* or *actual.* In the first case it is a Problematical, in the second an Assertorial practical principle. The categorical imperative which declares an action to be objectively necessary in itself without reference to any purpose, *i.e.* without any other end, is valid as an Apodictic (practical) principle.

Whatever is possible only by the power of some rational being may also be conceived as a possible purpose of some will; and therefore the principles of action as regards the means necessary to attain some possible purpose are in fact infinitely numerous. All sciences have a practical part, consisting of problems expressing that some end is possible for us, and of imperatives directing how it may be attained. These may, therefore, be called in general imperatives of Skill. Here there is no question whether the end is rational and good, but only what one must do in order to attain it. The precepts for the physician to make his patient thoroughly healthy, and for a poisoner to ensure certain death, are of equal value in this respect, that each serves to effect its purpose perfectly. Since in early youth it cannot be known what ends are likely to occur to us in the course of life, parents seek to have their children taught a *great many things,* and provide for their *skill* in the use of means for all sorts of arbitrary ends, of none of which can they determine whether it may not perhaps hereafter be an object to their pupil, but which it is at all events *possible* that he might aim at; and this anxiety is so great that they commonly neglect to form and correct their judgment on the value of the things which may be chosen as ends.

There is *one* end, however, which may be assumed to be actually such to all rational beings (so far as imperatives apply to them, viz. as dependent beings), and, therefore, one purpose which they not merely *may* have, but which we may with certainty assume that they all actually *have* by natural necessity, and this is *happiness.* The hypothetical imperative which expresses the practical necessity of an action as means to the advancement of happiness is Assertorial. We are not to present it as necessary for an uncertain and merely possible purpose, but for a purpose which we may presuppose with certainty and *à priori* in every man, because it belongs to his being. Now skill in the choice of means to his own greatest well-being may be called *prudence,* in the narrowest sense. And thus the imperative which refers to the choice of means to one's own happiness, *i.e.* the precept of prudence, is still always *hypothetical;* the action is not commanded absolutely, but only as means to another purpose.

Finally, there is an imperative which commands a certain conduct immediately, without having as its condition any other purpose to be attained by it. This imperative is Categorical. It concerns not the matter of the action, or its intended result, but its form and the principle of which it is itself a result; and what is essentially good in it consists in the mental disposition, let the consequence be what it may. This imperative may be called that of Mortality.

There is a marked distinction also between the volitions on these three sorts of principles in the *dissimilarity* of the obligation of the will. In order to mark this difference more clearly, I think they would be most suitably named in their order if we said they are either *rules* of skill, or *counsels* of prudence, or *commands (laws)* of morality. For it is *law* only that involves the conception of an *unconditional* and objective necessity, which is consequently universally valid; and commands are laws which must be obeyed, that is, must be followed, even in opposition to inclination. *Counsels,* indeed, involve necessity, but one which can only hold under a contingent subjective condition, viz. they depend on whether this or that man reckons this or that as part of his happiness; the categorical imperative, on the contrary, is not limited by any condition, and as being absolutely, although practically, necessary may be quite properly called a command. We might also call the first kind of imperatives *technical* (belonging to art), the second *pragmatic* (to welfare), the third *moral* (belonging to free conduct generally, that is, to morals).

• • •

When I conceive a hypothetical imperative, in general I do not know beforehand what it will contain until I am given the condition. But when I conceive a categorical imperative, I know at once what it contains. For as the imperative contains besides the law only the necessity that the maxims shall conform to this law, while the law contains no conditions restricting it, there remains nothing but the general statement that the maxim of the action should conform to a universal law, and it is this conformity also that the imperative properly represents as necessary.

There is therefore but one categorical imperative, namely, this: *Act only on that maxim whereby thou canst at the same time will that it should become a universal law.*

• • •

Now I say: man and generally any rational being *exists* as an end in himself, *not merely as a means* to be arbitrarily used by this or that will, but in all his actions, whether they concern himself or other rational beings, must be always regarded at the same time as an end. All objects of the inclinations have only a conditional worth; for if the inclinations and the wants founded on them did not exist, then their object would be without value. But the inclinations themselves being sources of want are so far from having an absolute worth for which they should be desired, that, on the contrary, it must be the universal wish of every rational being to be wholly free from them. Thus the worth of any object which is *to be acquired* by our action is always conditional. Beings whose existence depends not on our will but on nature's, have nevertheless, if they are rational beings, only a relative value as means, and are therefore called *things;* rational beings, on the contrary, are called *persons,* because their very nature points them out as ends in themselves, that is as something which must not be used merely as means, and so far therefore restricts freedom of action (and is an object of respect). These, therefore, are not merely subjective ends whose existence has a worth *for us* as an effect of our action, but *objective ends,* that is things whose existence is an end in itself: an end moreover for which no other can be substituted, which they should subserve merely as means, for otherwise nothing whatever would possess *absolute worth;* but if all worth were conditioned and therefore contingent, then there would be no supreme practical principle of reason whatever.

If then there is a supreme practical principle or, in respect of the human will, a categorical imperative, it must be one which, being drawn from the conception of that which is necessarily an end for everyone because it is *an end in itself,* constitutes an *objective* principle of will, and can therefore serve as a universal practical law. The foundation of this principle is: *rational nature exists at as end in itself.* Man necessarily conceives his own existence as being so: so far then this is a *subjective* principle of human actions. But every other rational being regards its existence similarly, just on the same rational principle that holds for me: so that it is at the same time an objective principle, from which as a supreme practical law all laws of the will must be capable of being deduced. Accordingly the practical imperative will be as follows: *So act as to treat humanity, whether in thine own person or in that of any other, in every case as an end withal, never as means only.*

• • •

This principle, that humanity and generally every rational nature is *an end in itself,* (which is the supreme limiting condition of every man's freedom of action), is not borrowed from experience, *firstly,* because it is universal, applying as it does to all rational beings whatever, and experience is not capable of determining anything about them; *secondly,* because it does not present humanity as an end to men (subjectively), that is as an object which men do of themselves actually adopt as an end; but as an objective end, which must as a law constitute the supreme limiting condition of all our subjective ends, let them be what we will; it must therefore spring from pure reason. In fact the objective principle of all practical legislation lies (according to the first principle) in *the rule* and its form of universality which makes it capable of being a law (say, *e.g.* a law of nature); but the *subjective* principle is in the *end;* now by

the second principle the subject of all ends is each rational being inasmuch as it is an end in itself. Hence follows the third practical principle of the will, which is the ultimate condition of its harmony with the universal practical reason, viz.: The idea of *the will of every rational being as a universally legislative will.*

On this principle all maxims are rejected which are inconsistent with the will being itself universal legislator. Thus the will is not subject simply to the law, but so subject that it must be regarded *as itself giving the law,* and on this ground only, subject to the law (of which it can regard itself as the author).

In the previous imperatives, namely, that based on the conception of the conformity of actions to general laws, as in a *physical system of nature,* and that based on the universal *prerogative* of rational beings as *ends* in themselves—these imperatives just because they were conceived as categorical excluded from any share in their authority all admixture of any interest as a spring of action; they were, however, only *assumed* to be categorical, because such an assumption was necessary to explain the conception of duty. But we could not prove independently that there are practical propositions which command categorically, nor can it be proved in this section; one thing, however, could be done, namely, to indicate in the imperative itself by some determinate expression, that in the case of volition from duty all interest is renounced, which is the specific criterion of categorical as distinguished from hypothetical imperatives. This is done in the present (third) formula of the principle, namely, in the idea of the will of every rational being as a universally legislating will.

For although a will *which is subject to laws* may be attached to this law by means of an interest, yet a will which is itself a supreme lawgiver so far as it is such cannot possibly depend on any interest, since a will so dependent would itself still need another law restricting the interest of its self-love by the condition that it should be valid as universal law.

Thus the *principle* that every human will

is *a will which in all its maxims gives universal laws,* provided it be otherwise justified, would be very *well adapted* to be the categorical imperative, in this respect, namely, that just because of the idea of universal legislation it is *not based on any interest,* and therefore it alone among all possible imperatives can be *unconditional.* Or still better, converting the proposition, if there is a categorical imperative (*i.e.* a law for the will of every rational being), it can only command that everything be done from maxims of one's will regarded as a will which could at the same time will that it should itself give universal laws, for in that case only the practical principle and the imperative which it obeys are unconditional, since they cannot be based on any interest.

Looking back now on all previous attempts to discover the principle of morality, we need not wonder why they all failed. It was seen that man was bound to laws by duty, but it was not observed that the laws to which he is subject are *only those of his own giving,* though at the same time they are *universal,* and that he is only bound to act in conformity with his own will; a will, however, which is designed by nature to give universal laws. For when one has conceived man only as subject to a law (no matter what), then this law required some interest, either by way of attraction or constraint, since it did not originate as a law from *his own* will, but this will was according to a law obliged by *something else* to act in a certain manner. Now by this necessary consequence all the labour spent in finding a supreme principle of *duty* was irrevocably lost. For man never elicited duty, but only a necessity of acting from a certain interest. Whether this interest was private or otherwise, in any case the imperative must be conditional, and could not by any means be capable of being a moral command. I will therefore call this the principle of *Autonomy* of the will, in contrast with every other which I accordingly reckon as *Heteronomy.*

The conception of every rational being as one which must consider itself as giving in all the maxims of its will universal laws, so as to judge itself and its actions from this point of view—this conception leads to another which depends on it and is very fruitful, namely, that of a *kingdom of ends.*

By a *kingdom* I understand the union of different rational beings in a system by common laws. Now since it is by laws that ends are determined as regards their universal validity, hence, if we abstract from the personal differences of rational beings, and likewise from all the content of their private ends, we shall be able to conceive all ends combined in a systematic whole (including both rational beings as ends in themselves, and also the special ends which each may propose to himself), that is to say, we can conceive a kingdom of ends, which on the preceding principles is possible.

For all rational beings come under the *law* that each of them must treat itself and all others *never merely as means,* but in every case *at the same time as ends in themselves.* Hence results a systematic union of rational beings by common objective laws, *i.e.,* a kingdom which may be called a kingdom of ends, since what these laws have in view is just the relation of these beings to one another as ends and means. It is certainly only an ideal.

A rational being belongs as a *member* to the kingdom of ends when, although giving universal laws in it, he is also himself subject to these laws. He belongs to it *as sovereign* when, while giving laws, he is not subject to the will of any other.

A rational being must always regard himself as giving laws either as member or as sovereign in a kingdom of ends which is rendered possible by the freedom of will. He cannot, however, maintain the latter position merely by the maxims of his will, but only in case he is a completely independent being without wants and with unrestricted power adequate to his will.

Morality consists then in the reference of all action to the legislation which alone can render a kingdom of ends possible. This legislation must be capable of existing in every rational being, and of emanating from his will, so that the principle of this will is, never to act on any maxim which could not without contradiction be also a universal law, and accordingly always so to act *that the will could at the same time regard itself as giving in its maxims universal laws.* If now the maxims of rational beings are not by their own nature coincident with this objective principle, then the necessity of acting on it is called practical necessitation, i.e. *duty*. Duty does not apply to the sovereign in the kingdom of ends, but it does to every member of it and to all in the same degree.

The practical necessity of acting on this principle, *i.e.*, duty, does not rest at all on feelings, impulses, or inclinations, but solely on the relation of rational beings to one another, a relation in which the will of a rational being must always be regarded as *legislative*, since otherwise it could not be conceived as *an end in itself*. Reason then refers every maxim of the will, regarding it as legislating universally, to every other will and also to every action towards oneself; and this not on account of any other practical motive or any future advantage, but from the idea of the *dignity* of a rational being, obeying no law but that which he himself also gives.

In the kingdom of ends everything has either Value or Dignity. Whatever has a value can be replaced by something else which is *equivalent;* whatever, on the other hand, is above all value, and therefore admits of no equivalent, has a dignity.

Whatever has reference to the general inclinations and wants of mankind has a *market value*; whatever, without presupposing a want, corresponds to a certain taste, that is to a satisfaction in the mere purpose-less play of our faculties, has a *fancy value;* but that which constitutes the condition under which alone anything can be an end in itself, this has not merely a relative worth, *i.e.*, value, but an intrinsic worth, that is *dignity*.

Now morality is the condition under which alone a rational being can be an end in himself, since by this alone it is possible that he should be a legislating member in the kingdom of ends. Thus morality, and humanity as capable of it, is that which alone has dignity. Skill and diligence in labour have a market value; wit, lively imagination, and humour, have fancy value; on the other hand, fidelity to promises, benevolence from principle (not from instinct), have an intrinsic worth.

STUDY QUESTIONS

1. Do you agree with the first sentence in the selection? Why or why not?
2. What does Kant mean by the moral law? Respect for the law? How is the moral law related to the categorical imperative?
3. If you always followed the categorical imperative in all your actions, would what you did always be morally right? Explain.
4. Why does Kant conclude that we ought never to treat human beings as means only? Do you agree with him?
5. Suppose Kant's "kingdom of ends" to be realized. What kind of a society would it be? Would there be any crime in it? Injustice?

For Further Reading

Acton, H. B. *Kant's Moral Philosophy*. London: Macmillan, 1970.

Broad, C. D. *Five Types of Ethical Theory*. London: Kegan & Paul, 1930 (Chapter 5).

Korner, S. *Kant*. Baltimore: Penguin, 1955 (Chapters 6 and 7).

Murphy, J. G. *Kant: The Philosophy of Right*. London: Macmillan, 1970 (Chapters 2 and 3).

Nell, O. *Acting on Principle*. New York: Columbia University Press, 1975.

Paton, H. J. *The Categorical Imperative*. Chicago: University of Chicago Press, 1948.

Teale, A. E. *Kantian Ethics*. London: Oxford University Press, 1951.

Williams, T. C. *The Concept of the Categorical Imperative*. Oxford: Clarendon Press, 1968.

Wolff, R. P. *The Autonomy of Reason*. New York: Harper & Row, 1973.

RAWLS: JUSTICE AS FAIRNESS

We all believe in justice—but we by no means all agree what justice is. One of the earliest definitions of justice can be found at the beginning of Plato's *Republic,* where it is described as "giving to everyone what is his due." The difficulty with this conception is that it offers little guidance to one who is prepared to act justly but doesn't know what he ought to do in order to be just. Before he can give anyone his due, he must know what that individual's due is. Much of the writing on justice since Plato's time has been devoted to attempts to explain what each person's due is and why it is his due, thus giving those who wish to be just some practical guidance in the way in which they ought to act. One of the latest and most interesting of these attempts is that of John Rawls, who maintains that to act justly is to act fairly. This answer, of course, leaves us with the question: What is fairness? The selection that follows addresses itself to that question, as well as several others.

John Rawls was born in Baltimore in 1921. He studied at Princeton and Cornell Universities receiving his doctorate from the former in 1950. He has for many years been a professor of philosophy at Harvard University. After writing the selection that appears below, Rawls continued to develop the ideas contained in it, publishing these finally in 1971 in his important and influential book, *A Theory of Justice.*

ℒ *Justice as Fairness*

The fundamental idea in the concept of justice is that of fairness.* It is this aspect of justice for which utilitarianism, in its classical form, is unable to account, but which is represented, even if misleadingly so, in the idea of the social contract. To establish these propositions I shall develop, but of necessity only very briefly, a particular conception of justice by stating two principles which specify it and by considering how they may be thought to arise. The parts of this conception are familiar; but perhaps it is possible by using the notion of fairness as a framework to assemble and to look at them in a new way.

1. Throughout I discuss justice as a virtue of institutions constituting restrictions as to how they may define offices and powers, and assign rights and duties; and not as a virtue of particular actions, or persons. Justice is but one of many virtues of institutions, for these may be inefficient, or degrading, or any of a number of things, without being unjust. Essentially justice is the elimination of arbitrary distinctions and the establishment, within the structure of a practice, of a proper balance between competing claims. I do not argue that the principles given below are *the* principles of justice. It is sufficient for my purposes that they be typical of the family of principles which might reasonably be called principles of justice as shown by the background against which they may be thought to arise.

The first principle is that each person participating in a practice, or affected by it, has an equal right to the most extensive

Reprinted from *The Journal of Philosophy,* Vol. 54 (1957), with permission of the author and *The Journal of Philosophy.*

*Considerations of space have made it impossible to give appropriate references. I must, however, mention that, in the second paragraph of section 3, I am indebted to H. L. A. Hart. See his paper "Are There Any Natural Rights?," *Philosophical Review,* LXIV (1955), pp. 185 f.

liberty compatible with a like liberty for all; and the second is that inequalities are arbitrary unless it is reasonable to expect that they will work out for everyone's advantage and unless the offices to which they attach, or from which they may be gained, are open to all. These principles express justice as a complex of three ideas: liberty, equality, and reward for contributions to the common advantage.

The first principle holds, of course, only *ceteris paribus:* while there must always be a justification for departing from the initial position of equal liberty (which is defined by the pattern of rights and duties), and the burden of proof is placed upon him who would depart from it, nevertheless, there can be, and often there is, a justification for doing so. One can view this principle as containing the principle that similar cases be judged similarly, or if distinctions are made in the handling of cases, there must be some relevant difference between them (a principle which follows from the concept of a judgment of any kind). It could be argued that justice requires only an equal liberty; but if a greater liberty were possible for all without loss or conflict, then it would be irrational to settle on a lesser liberty. There is no reason for circumscribing rights until they mutually interfere with one another. Therefore no serious distortion of the concept of justice is likely to follow from including within it the concept of the greatest equal liberty instead of simply equal liberty.

The second principle specifies what sorts of inequalities are permissible, where by inequalities it seems best to understand not any difference between offices and positions, since structural differences are not usually an issue (people do not object to there being different offices as such, and so to there being the offices of president, senator, governor, judge, and so on), but differences in the benefits and burdens attached to them either directly or indirectly, such as prestige and wealth, or liability to taxation and compulsory service. An inequality is allowed only if there is reason to believe that the practice with the inequal-ity will work to the advantage of *every* party. This is interpreted to require, first, that there must normally be evidence acceptable to common sense and based on a common fund of knowledge and belief which shows that this is in fact likely to be the case. The principle does not rule out, however, arguments of a theological or metaphysical kind to justify inequalities (e.g., a religious basis for a caste system) provided they belong to common belief and are freely acknowledged by people who may be presumed to know what they are doing.

Second, an inequality must work for the common advantage; and since the principle applies to practices, this implies that the representative man in *every* office or position of the practice, when he views it as a going institution, must find it reasonable to prefer his condition and prospects with the inequality to what they would be without it. And finally, the various offices to which special benefits and burdens attach are required to be open to all; and so if, for example, it is to the common advantage to attach benefits to offices (because by doing so not only is the requisite talent attracted to them, but encouraged to give its best efforts once there), they must be won in a fair competition in which contestants are judged on their merits. If some offices were not open, those excluded would normally be justified in feeling wronged, even if they benefited from the greater efforts of those who were allowed to compete for them. Assuming that offices are open, it is necessary only to consider the design of the practices themselves and how they jointly, as a system, work together. It is a mistake to fix attention on the varying relative positions of particular persons and to think that each such change, as a once-for-all transaction, must be in itself just. The system must be judged from a general point of view: unless one is prepared to criticize it from the standpoint of a representative man holding some particular office, one has no complaint against it.

2. Given these principles, one might try to derive them from *a priori* principles of

reason, or offer them as known by intuition. These are familiar steps, and, at least in the case of the first principle, might be made with some success. I wish, however, to look at the principles in a different way.

Consider a society where certain practices are already established, and whose members are mutually self-interested: their allegiance to the established practices is founded on the prospect of self-advantage. It need not be supposed that they are incapable of acting from any other motive: if one thinks of the members of this society as families, the individuals thereof may be bound by ties of sentiment and affection. Nor must they be mutually self-interested under all circumstances, but only under those circumstances in which they ordinarily participate in their common practices. Imagine also that the persons in this society are rational: they know their own interests more or less accurately; they are capable of tracing out the likely consequences of adopting one practice rather than another and of adhering to a decision once made; they can resist present temptations and attractions of immediate gain; and the knowledge, or the perception, of the difference between their condition and that of others is not, in itself, a source of great dissatisfaction. Finally, they have roughly similar needs and interests and are sufficiently equal in power and ability to assure that in normal circumstances none is able to dominate the others.

Now suppose that on some particular occasion several members of this society come together to discuss whether any of them has a legitimate complaint against their established institutions. They try first to arrive at the principles by which complaints, and so practices themselves, are to be judged. Their procedure for this is the following: each is to propose the principles upon which he wishes his complaints to be tried with the understanding that, if acknowledged, the complaints of others will be similarly tried, and that no complaints will be heard at all until everyone is roughly of one mind as to how complaints are to be judged. They understand further that the

principles proposed and acknowledged on this occasion are to be binding on future occasions. Thus each will be wary of proposing principles which give him a peculiar advantage, supposing them to be accepted, in his present circumstances, since he will be bound by it in future cases the circumstances of which are unknown and in which the principle might well be to his detriment. Everyone is, then, forced to make in advance a firm commitment, which others also may reasonably be expected to make, and no one is able to tailor the canons of a legitimate complaint to fit his own special condition. Therefore each person will propose principles of a general kind which will, to a large degree, gain their sense from the various applications to be made of them. These principles will express the conditions in accordance with which each is least unwilling to have his interests limited in the design of practices on the supposition that the interests of others will be limited likewise. The restrictions which would so arise might be thought of as those a person would keep in mind if he were designing a practice in which his enemy were to assign him his place.

In this account of a hypothetical society the character and respective situations of the parties reflect the circumstances in which questions of justice may be said to arise, and the procedure whereby principles are proposed and acknowledged represents constraints, analogous to those of having a morality, whereby rational and mutually self-interested parties are brought to act reasonably. Given all conditions are described, it would be natural to accept the two principles of justice. Since there is no way for anyone to win special advantage for himself, each might consider it reasonable to acknowledge equality as an initial principle. There is, however, no reason why they should regard this position as final; for if there are inequalities which satisfy the second principle, the immediate gain which equality would allow can be considered as intelligently invested in view of its future return. If, as is quite likely, these inequalities work as incentives to draw out better efforts, the members of this society may look upon them as concessions to human nature: they, like us, may think that people ideally should want to serve one another. But as they are mutually self-interested, their acceptance of these inequalities is merely the acceptance of the relations in which they actually stand. They have no title to complain of one another. And so, provided the conditions of the principle are met, there is no reason why they should reject such inequalities in the design of their social practices. Indeed, it would be short-sighted of them to do so, and could result, it seems, only from their being dejected by the bare knowledge, or perception, that others are better situated. Each person will, however, insist on a common advantage, for none is willing to sacrifice anything for the others.

These remarks are not, of course, offered as a proof that persons so circumstanced would settle upon the two principles, but only to show that the principles of justice could have such a background; and so can be viewed as those principles which mutually self-interested and rational persons, when similarly situated and required to make in advance a firm commitment, could acknowledge as restrictions governing the assignment of rights and duties in their common practices, and thereby accept as limiting their rights against one another.

3. That the principles of justice can be regarded in this way is an important fact about them. It brings out the idea that fundamental to justice is the concept of fairness which relates to right dealing between persons who are cooperating with or competing against one another, as when one speaks of fair games, fair competition, and fair bargains. The question of fairness arises when free persons, who have no authority over one another, are engaging in a joint activity and amongst themselves settling or acknowledging the rules which define it and which determine the respective shares in its benefits and burdens. A practice will strike the parties as fair if none

feels that, by participating in it, he, or any of the others, is taken advantage of, or forced to give in to claims which he does not regard as legitimate. This implies that each has a conception of legitimate claims which he thinks it reasonable that others as well as himself should acknowledge. If one thinks of the principles of justice as arising in the way described, then they do define this sort of conception. A practice is just, then, when it satisfies the principles which those who participate in it could propose to one another for mutual acceptance under the aforementioned circumstances. Persons engaged in a just, or fair, practice can face one another honestly, and support their respective positions, should they appear questionable, by reference to principles which it is reasonable to expect each to accept. It is this notion of the possibility of mutual acknowledgment which makes the concept of fairness fundamental to justice. Only if such acknowledgment is possible, can there be true community between persons in their common practices; otherwise their relations will appear to them as founded to some extent on force and violence. If, in ordinary speech, fairness applies more particularly to practices in which there is a choice whether to engage or not, and justice to practices in which there is no choice and one must play, the element of necessity does not alter the basic conception of the possibility of mutual acceptance, although it may make it much more urgent to change unjust than unfair institutions.

Now if the participants in a practice accept its rules as fair, and so have no complaint to lodge against it, there arises a *prima facie* duty (and a corresponding *prima facie* right) of the parties to each other to act in accordance with the practice when it falls upon them to comply. When any number of persons engage in a practice, or conduct a joint undertaking, according to rules, and thus restrict their liberty, those who have submitted to these restrictions when required have a right to a similar acquiescence on the part of those who have benefited by their submission.

These conditions will, of course, obtain if a practice is correctly acknowledged to be fair, for in this case, all who participate in it will benefit from it. The rights and duties so arising are special rights and duties in that they depend on previous voluntary actions—in this case, on the parties' having engaged in a common practice and accepted its benefits. It is not, however, an obligation which presupposes a deliberate performative act in the sense of a promise, or contract, and the like. It is sufficient that one has knowingly participated in a practice acknowledged to be fair and accepted the resulting benefits. This *prima facie* obligation may, of course, be overridden: it may happen, when it comes one's turn to follow a rule, that other considerations will justify not doing so. But one cannot, in general, be released from this obligation by denying the justice of the practice only when it falls on one to obey. If a person rejects a practice, he should, as far as possible, declare his intention in advance, and avoid participating in it or accepting its benefits.

This duty may be called that of fair play, which is, perhaps, to extend the ordinary notion; for acting unfairly is usually not so much the breaking of any particular rule, even if the infraction is difficult to detect (cheating), but taking advantage of loopholes or ambiguities in rules, availing oneself of unexpected or special circumstances which make it impossible to enforce them, insisting that rules be enforced when they should be suspended, and, more generally, acting contrary to the intention of a practice. (Thus one speaks of the sense of fair play: acting fairly is not simply following rules; what is fair must be felt or perceived.) Nevertheless, it is not an unnatural extension of the duty of fair play to have it include the obligation which participants in a common practice owe to each other to act in accordance with it when their performance falls due. Consider the tax dodger, or the free rider.

The duty of fair play stands beside those of fidelity and gratitude as a fundamental moral notion; and like them it im-plies a constraint on self-interest in particular cases. I make this point to avoid a misunderstanding: the conception of the mutual acknowledgment of principles under special circumstances is used to analyze the concept of justice. I do not wish to imply that the acceptance of justice in actual conduct depends solely on an existing equality of conditions. My own view, which is perhaps but one of several compatible with the preceding analysis, and which I can only suggest here, is that the acknowledgement of the duty of fair play, as shown in acting on it, and wishing to make amends and the like when one has been at fault, is one of the forms of conduct in which participants in a common practice show their recognition of one another as persons. In the same way that, failing a special explanation, the criterion for the recognition of suffering is helping him who suffers, acknowledging the duty of fair play is the criterion for recognizing another as a person with similar capacities, interests, and feelings as oneself. The acceptance by participants in a common practice of this duty is a reflection in each of the recognition of the aspirations of the others to be realized by their joint activity. Without this acceptance they would recognize one another as but complicated objects in a complicated routine. To recognize another as a person one must respond to him and act towards him as one: and these forms of action and response include, among other things, acknowledging the duty of fair play. These remarks are unhappily obscure; their purpose here is to forestall the misunderstanding mentioned above.

The conception at which we have arrived, then, is that the principles of justice may be thought of as arising once the constraints of having a morality are imposed upon rational and mutually self-interested parties who are related and situated in a special way. A practice is just if it is in accordance with the principles which all who participate in it might reasonably be expected to propose or to acknowledge before one another when they are similarly circumstanced and required to make a firm commitment in advance; and thus when it meets standards which the parties could accept as fair should occasion arise for them to debate its merits. Once persons knowingly engage in a practice which they acknowledge to be fair and accept the benefits of doing so, they are bound by the duty of fair play which implies a limitation on self-interest in particular cases.

Now if a claim fails to meet this conception of justice there is no moral value in granting it, since it violates the conditions of reciprocity and community amongst persons: he who presses it, not being willing to acknowledge it when pressed by another, has no grounds for complaint when it is denied; whereas him against whom it is pressed can complain. As it cannot be mutually acknowledged, it is a resort to coercion: granting the claim is only possible if one party can compel what the other will not admit. Thus in deciding on the justice of a practice it is not enough to ascertain that it answers to wants and interest in the fullest and most effective manner. For if any of these be such that they conflict with justice, they should not be counted; their satisfaction is no reason for having a practice. It makes no sense to concede claims the denial of which gives rise to no complaint in preference to claims the denial of which can be objected to. It would be irrelevant to say, even if true, that it resulted in the greatest satisfaction of desire.

4. This conception of justice differs from that of the stricter form of utilitarianism (Bentham and Sidgwick), and its counterpart in welfare economics, which assimilates justice to benevolence and the latter in turn to the most efficient design of institutions to promote the general welfare. Now it is said occasionally that this form of utilitarianism puts no restrictions on what might be a just assignment of rights and duties. But this is not so. Beginning with the notion that the general happiness can be represented by a social utility function consisting of the sum of individual utility functions with identical weights (this being the meaning of the maxim that each counts for one and no more than one), it is commonly assumed that the utility functions of individuals are similar in all essential respects. Differences are laid to accidents of education and upbringing, and should not be taken into account; and this assumption, coupled with that of diminishing marginal utility, results in a *prima facie* case for equality. But even if such restrictions are built into the utility function, and have, in practice, much the same result as the application of the principles of justice (and appear, perhaps, to be ways of expressing these principles in the language of mathematics and psychology), the fundamental idea is very different from the conception of justice as reciprocity. Justice is interpreted as the contingent result of a higher order administrative decision whose form is similar to that of an entrepreneur deciding how much to produce of this or that commodity in view of its marginal revenue, or to that of someone distributing goods to needy persons according to the relative urgency of their wants. The choice between practices is thought of as being made on the basis of the allocation of benefits and burdens to individuals (measured by the present capitalized value of the utility of these benefits over the full period of the practice's existence) which results from the distribution of rights and duties established by a practice. The individuals receiving the benefits are not thought of as related in any way: they represent so many different directions in which limited resources may be allocated. Preferences and interest are taken as given; and their satisfaction has value irrespective of the relations between persons which they represent and the claims which the parties are prepared to make on one another. This value is properly taken into account by the (ideal) legislator who is conceived as adjusting the rules of the system from the center so as to maximize the present capitalized value of the social utility function. The principles of justice will not be violated by a legal system so conceived provided these executive decisions are correctly made; and in this fact the principles of justice are said to find their derivation and explanation.

Some social decisions are, of course, of an administrative sort; namely, when the decision turns on social utility in the ordinary sense: on the efficient use of common means for common ends whose benefits are impartially distributed, or in connection with which the question of distribution is misplaced, as in the case of maintaining public order, or national defense. But as an interpretation of the basis of the principles of justice the utilitarian conception is mistaken. It can lead one to argue against slavery on the grounds that the advantages to the slaveholder do not counter-balance the disadvantages to the slave and to society at large burdened by a comparatively inefficient system of labor. The conception of justice as fairness, when applied to the offices of slaveholder and slave, would forbid counting the advantages of the slaveholder at all. These offices could not be founded on principles which could be mutually acknowledged, so the question whether the slaveholder's gains are great enough to counter-balance the losses to the slave and society cannot arise in the first place.

The difference between the two conceptions is whether justice is a fundamental moral concept arising directly from the reciprocal relations of persons engaging in common practices, and its principles those which persons similarly circumstanced could mutually acknowledge; or whether justice is derivative from a kind of higher order executive decision as to the most efficient design of institutions conceived as general devices for distributing benefits to individuals the worth of whose interests is defined independently of their relations to each other. Now even if the social utility function is constructed so that the practices chosen by it would be just, at least under normal circumstances, there is still the further argument against the utilitarian conception that the various restrictions on the utility function needed to get this result are borrowed from the conception of justice as fairness. The notion that individuals have similar utility functions, for example, is really the first principle of justice under the guise of a psychological law. It is assumed not in the manner of an empirical hypothesis concerning actual desires and interests, but from sensing what must be laid down if justice is not to be violated. There is, indeed, irony in this conclusion; for utilitarians attacked the notion of the original contract not only as a historical fiction but as a superfluous hypothesis: they thought that utility alone provides sufficient grounds for all social obligation, and is in any case the real basis of contractual obligations. But this is not so unless one's conception of social utility embodies within it restrictions whose basis can be understood only if one makes reference to one of the ideas of contractarian thought: that persons must be regarded as possessing an original and equal liberty, and their common practices are unjust unless they accord with principles which persons so circumstanced and related could freely accept.

STUDY QUESTIONS

1. What does Rawls mean by saying that justice is a virtue of institutions?
2. State Rawls' two principles of justice in your own words. On what grounds does he claim that individuals interested in their own welfare should accept these principles?
3. What does Rawls mean when he speaks of justice as fairness? What is the relationship between fairness and our recognizing each other as persons?
4. What does Rawls mean by the utilitarian theory of justice? Do you agree with him that his own theory is preferable to it?

For Further Reading

Barry, B. M. *The Liberal Theory of Justice*. Oxford: Clarendon Press, 1973.
Daniels, N., ed. *Reading Rawls*. New York: Basic Books, 1975.
Ethics, 85, No. 1 (October 1974).

Hall, E. W. "Justice as Fairness: A Modernized Version of the Social Contract." *The Journal of Philosophy* 54 (1957) pp. 662–70.

Rawls, J. *A Theory of Justice.* Cambridge, Mass.: Harvard University Press, 1971.

Social Theory and Practice, Vol. III. No. 1 (Spring 1974).

Wolff, R. P. *Understanding Rawls.* Princeton, N.J.: Princeton University Press, 1977.

SUMNER: CULTURAL RELATIVISM

As we gain knowledge of societies separated from our own, whether by space, time or level of cultural development, we are forced to recognize that the moral and social relationships between individuals in these groups often differ markedly from our own. Actions we condemn as wrong, they praise as right, and the reverse. When we encounter such divergencies our natural inclination (if we do not simply condemn the foreign beliefs and practices outright) is to ask: Who is correct, we or they? To this question the cultural relativist responds: Neither. Such a question is based on the false assumption that there *is* a right or wrong way of conducting ourselves in society. But no such absolute right or wrong exists; rather all we find are the various beliefs and practices about right and wrong that different cultures accept. They differ from each other but none is any better, or any worse, than any other. As ordinary human beings living in a specific social group our task is to follow as best we can, but not question, the moral practices of that society.

William Graham Sumner (1840–1910) was one of America's first and most important cultural anthropologists. A graduate of Yale University, he studied further abroad before returning to Yale briefly as an instructor and then becoming an Episcopalian minister. After three years, Sumner left the clerical profession to return to Yale and teaching. There he remained for the rest of a long career, gaining fame as a brilliant and influential teacher. His book *Folkways,* from which our selection is taken, is a classic in its field.

✒ *Folkways*

1. DEFINITION AND MODE OF ORIGIN OF THE FOLKWAYS. If we put together all that we have learned from anthropology and ethnography about primitive men and primitive society, we perceive that the first task of life is to live. Men begin with acts, not with thoughts. Every moment brings necessities which must be satisfied at once. Need was the first experience, and it was followed at once by a blundering effort to satisfy it. It is generally

First published in 1907. Sumner's footnoes are not included.

taken for granted that men inherited some guiding instincts from their beast ancestry, and it may be true, although it has never been proved. If there were such inheritances, they controlled and aided the first efforts to satisfy needs. Analogy makes it easy to assume that the ways of beasts had produced channels of habit and predisposition along which dexterities and other psychophysical activities would run easily. Experiments with newborn animals show that in the absence of any experience of the relation of means to ends, efforts to satisfy needs are clumsy and blundering. The method is that of trial and failure, which produces repeated pain, loss, and disappointments. Nevertheless, it is a method of rude experiment and selection. The earliest efforts of men were of this kind. Need was the impelling force. Pleasure and pain, on the one side and the other, were the rude constraints which defined the line on which efforts must proceed. The ability to distinguish between pleasure and pain is the only psychical power which is to be assumed. Thus ways of doing things were selected, which were expedient. They answered the purpose better than other ways, or with less toil and pain. Along the course on which efforts were compelled to go, habit, routine, and skill were developed. The struggle to maintain existence was not carried on individually but in groups. Each profited by the other's experience; hence there was concurrence towards that which proved to be most expedient. All at last adopted the same way for the same purpose; hence the ways turned into customs and became mass phenomena. Instincts were developed in connection with them. In this way folkways arise. The young learn them by tradition, imitation, and authority. The folkways, at a time, provide for all the needs of life then and there. They are uniform, universal in the group, imperative, and invariable. As time goes on, the folkways become more and more arbitrary, positive, and imperative. If asked why they act in a certain way in certain cases, primitive people always answer that it is because they and their ancestors always have done so. A sanction also arises from ghost fear. The ghosts of ancestors would be angry if the living should change the ancient folkways.

2. THE FOLKWAYS ARE A SOCIETAL FORCE. The operation by which folkways are produced consists in the frequent repetition of petty acts, often by great numbers acting in concert, or, at least, acting in the same way when face to face with the same need. The immediate motive is interest. It produces habit in the individual and custom in the group. It is, therefore, in the highest degree original

and primitive. By habit and custom it exerts a strain on every individual within its range; therefore it rises to a societal force to which great classes of societal phenomena are due. Its earliest stages, its course, and laws may be studied; also its influence on individuals and their reaction to it. It is our present purpose so to study it. We have to recognize it as one of the chief forces by which a society is made to be what it is. Out of the unconscious experiment which every repetition of the ways includes, there issues pleasure or pain, and then, so far as the men are capable of reflection, convictions that the ways are conducive to societal welfare. These two experiences are not the same. The most uncivilized men, both in the food quest and in war, do things which are painful, but which have been found to be expedient. Perhaps these cases teach the sense of social welfare better than those which are pleasurable and favorable to welfare. The former cases call for some intelligent reflection on experience. When this conviction as to the relation to welfare is added to the folkways they are converted into mores, and, by virtue of the philosophical and ethical element added to them, they win utility and importance and become the source of the science and the art of living.

3. FOLKWAYS ARE MADE UNCONSCIOUSLY. It is of the first importance to notice that, from the first acts by which men try to satisfy needs, each act stands by itself, and looks no further than the immediate satisfaction. From recurrent needs arise habits for the individual and customs for the group, but these results are consequences which were never conscious, and never foreseen or intended. They are not noticed until they have long existed, and it is still longer before they are appreciated. Another long time must pass, and a higher stage of mental development must be reached, before they can be used as a basis from which to deduce rules for meeting, in the future, problems whose pressure can be foreseen. The folkways, therefore, are not creations of human purpose and wit.

They are like products of natural forces which men unconsciously set in operation, or they are like the instinctive ways of animals, which are developed out of experience, which reach a final form of maximum adaption to an interest, which are handed down by tradition and admit of no exception or variation, yet change to meet new conditions, still within the same limited methods, and without rational reflection or purpose. From this it results that all the life of human beings, in all ages and stages of culture, is primarily controlled by a vast mass of folkways handed down from the earliest existence of the race, having the nature of the ways of other animals, only the topmost layers of which are subject to change and control, and have been somewhat modified by human philosophy, ethics, and religion, or by other acts of intelligent reflection. We are told of savages that: "It is difficult to exhaust the customs and small ceremonial usages of a savage people. Custom regulates the whole of a man's actions,—his bathing, washing, cutting his hair, eating, drinking, and fasting. From his cradle to his grave he is the slave of ancient usage. In his life there is nothing free, nothing original, nothing spontaneous, no progress towards a higher and better life, and no attempt to improve his condition, mentally, morally, or spiritually." All men act in this way with only a little wider margin of voluntary variation.

28. FOLKWAYS DUE TO FALSE INFERENCE. Furthermore, folkways have been formed by accident, that is, by irrational and incongruous action, based on pseudo-knowledge. In Molembo a pestilence broke out soon after a Portuguese had died there. After that the natives took all possible measures not to allow any white man to die in their country. On the Nicobar islands some natives who had just begun to make pottery died. The art was given up and never again attempted. White men gave to one Bushman in a kraal a stick ornamented with buttons as a symbol of authority. The recipient died leaving the stick to his son. The son soon died. Then the Bushmen brought back the stick lest all should die. Until recently no building of incombustible materials could be built in any big town of the central province of Madagascar, on account of some ancient prejudice. A party of Eskimos met with no game. One of them returned to their sledges and got the ham of a dog to eat. As he returned with the ham bone in his hand he met and killed a seal. Ever afterwards he carried a ham bone in his hand when hunting. The Belenda women (peninsula of Malacca) stay as near to the house as possible during the period. Many keep the door closed. They know no reason for this custom. "It must be due to some now forgotten superstition." Soon after the Yakuts saw a camel for the first time smallpox broke out amongst them. They thought the camel to be the agent of the disease. A woman amongst the same people contracted an endogamous marriage. She soon afterwards became blind. This was thought to be on account of the violation of ancient customs. A very great number of such cases could be collected. In fact they represent the current mode of reasoning of nature people. It is their custom to reason that, if one thing follows another, it is due to it. A great number of customs are traceable to the notions of the evil eye, many more to ritual notions of uncleanness. No scientific investigation could discover the origin of the folkways mentioned, if the origin had not chanced to become known to civilized men. We must believe that the known cases illustrate the irrational and incongruous origin of many folkways. In civilized history also we know that customs have owed their origin to "historical accident,"—the vanity of a princess, the deformity of a king, the whim of a democracy, the love intrigue of a statesman or prelate. By the institutions of another age it may be provided that no one of these things can affect decisions, acts, or interests, but then the power to decide the ways may have passed to clubs, trades unions, trusts, commercial rivals, wire-pullers, politicians, and political fanatics. In these cases also the causes and origins may escape investigation.

31. THE FOLKWAYS ARE "RIGHT." RIGHTS. MORALS.

The folkways are the "right" ways to satisfy all interests, because they are traditional, and exist in fact. They extend over the whole of life. There is a right way to catch game, to win a wife, to make one's self appear, to cure disease, to honor ghosts, to treat comrades or strangers, to behave when a child is born, on the warpath, in council, and so on in all cases which can arise. The ways are defined on the negative side, that is, by taboos. The "right" way is the way which the ancestors used and which has been handed down. The tradition is its own warrant. It is not held subject to verification by experience. The notion of right is in the folkways. It is not outside of them, of independent origin, and brought to them to test them. In the folkways, whatever is, is right. This is because they are traditional, and therefore contain in themselves the authority of the ancestral ghosts. When we come to the folkways we are at the end of our analysis. The notion of right and ought is the same in regard to all the folkways, but the degree of it varies with the importance of the interest at stake. The obligation of conformable and cooperative action is far greater under ghost fear and war than in other matters, and the social sanctions are severer, because group interests are supposed to be at stake. Some usages contain only a slight element of right and ought. It may well be believed that notions of right and duty, and of social welfare, were first developed in connection with ghost fear and other-worldliness, and therefore that, in that field also, folkways were first raised to mores. "Rights" are the rules of mutual give and take in the competition of life which are imposed on comrades in the in-group, in order that the peace may prevail there which is essential to the group strength. Therefore rights can never be "natural" or "God-given," or absolute in any sense. The morality of a group at a time is the sum of the taboos and prescriptions in the folkways by which right conduct is defined. Therefore morals can never be intuitive. They are historical, institutional, and empirical.

World philosophy, life policy, right, rights, and morality are all products of the folkways. They are reflections on, and generalizations from, the experience of pleasure and pain which is won in efforts to carry on the struggle for existence under actual life conditions. The generalizations are very crude and vague in their germinal forms. They are all embodied in folklore, and all our philosophy and science have been developed out of them.

41. INTEGRATION OF THE MORES OF A GROUP OR AGE.

In further development of the same interpretation of the phenomena we find that changes in history are primarily due to changes in life conditions. Then the folkways change. The new philosophies and ethical rules are invented to try to justify the new ways. The whole vast body of modern mores has thus been developed out of the philosophy and ethics of the Middle Ages. So the mores which have been developed to suit the system of great secular states, world commerce, credit institutions, contract wages and rent, emigration to outlying continents, etc., have become the norm for the whole body of usages, manners, ideas, faiths, customs, and institutions which embrace the whole life of a society and characterize an historical epoch. Thus India, Chaldea, Assyria, Egypt, Greece, Rome, the Middle Ages, Modern Times, are cases in which the integration of the mores upon different life conditions produced societal states of complete and distinct individuality (ethos). Within any such societal status the great reason for any phenomenon is that it conforms to the mores of the time and place. Historians have always recognized incidentally the operation of such a determining force. What is now maintained is that it is not incidental or subordinate. It is supreme and controlling. Therefore the scientific discussion of a usage, custom, or institution consists in tracing its relation to the mores, and the discussion of societal crises and changes consists in showing their connection with changes in the life conditions, or with the readjustment of the mores to changes in those conditions.

42. PURPOSE OF THE PRESENT WORK. "Ethology" would be a convenient term for the study of manners, customs, usages, and mores, including the study of the way in which they are formed, how they grow or decay, and how they affect the interests which it is their purpose to serve. The Greeks applied the term "ethos" to the sum of the characteristic usages, ideas, standards, and codes by which a group was differentiated and individualized in character from other groups. "Ethics" were things which pertained to the ethos and therefore the things which were the standard of right. The Romans used "mores" for customs in the broadest and richest sense of the word, including the notion that customs served welfare, and had traditional and mystic sanction, so that they were properly authoritative and sacred. It is a very surprising fact that modern nations should have lost these words and the significant suggestions which inhere in them. The English language has no derivative noun from "mores," and no equivalent for it. The French *moeurs* is trivial compared with "mores." The German *Sitte* renders "mores" but very imperfectly. The modern peoples have made morals and morality a separate domain, by the side of religion, philosophy, and politics. In that sense, morals is an impossible and unreal category. It has no existence, and can have none. The word "moral" means what belongs or appertains to the mores. Therefore the category of morals can never be defined without reference to something outside of itself. Ethics, having lost connection with the ethos of a people, is an attempt to systematize the current notions of right and wrong upon some basic principle, generally with the purpose of establishing morals on an absolute doctrine, so that it shall be universal, absolute, and everlasting. In a general way also, whenever a thing can be called moral, or connected with some ethical generality, it is thought to be "raised," and disputants whose method is to employ ethical generalities assume especial authority for themselves and their views. These methods of discussion are most employed in treating of social topics, and they are disastrous to sound study of facts. They help to hold the social sciences under the dominion of metaphysics. The abuse has been most developed in connection with political economy, which has been almost robbed of the character of a serious discipline by converting the discussions into ethical disquisitions.

43. WHY USE THE WORD MORES. "Ethica," in the Greek sense, or "ethology," as above defined, would be good names for our present work. We aim to study the ethos of groups, in order to see how it arises, its power and influence, the modes of its operation on members of the group, and the various attributes of it (ethica). "Ethology" is a very unfamiliar word. It has been used for the mode of setting forth manners, customs, and mores in satirical comedy. The Latin word "mores" seems to be, on the whole, more practically convenient and available than any other for our purpose, as a name for the folkways with the connotations of right and truth in respect to welfare, embodied in them. The analysis and definition above given show that in the mores we must recognize a dominating force in history, constituting a condition as to what can be done, and as to the methods which can be employed.

44. MORES ARE A DIRECTIVE FORCE. Of course the view which has been stated is antagonistic to the view that philosophy and ethics furnish creative and determining forces in society and history. That view comes down to us from the Greek philosophy and it has now prevailed so long that all current discussion conforms to it. Philosophy and ethics are pursued as independent disciplines, and the results are brought to the science of society and to statesmanship and legislation as authoritative dicta. We also have *Volkerpsychologie, Sozialpolitik,* and other intermediate forms which show the struggle of metaphysics to retain control of the science of society. The "historic sense," the *Zeitgeist,* and other terms of similar import are partial recognitions of the mores and their importance in the science of society. We shall see below that philosophy and ethics are products of the folkways. They are taken out of the mores, but are never original and creative; they are secondary and derived. They often interfere in the second stage of the sequence,—act, thought, act. Then they produce harm, but some ground is furnished for the claim that they are creative or at least regulative. In fact, the real process in great bodies of men is not one of deduction from any great principle of philosophy or ethics. It is one of minute efforts to live well under existing conditions, which efforts are repeated indefinitely by great numbers, getting strength from habit and from the fellowship of united action. The resultant folkways become coercive. All are forced to conform, and the folkways dominate the societal life. Then they seem true and right, and arise into mores as the norm of welfare. Thence are produced faiths, ideas, doctrines, religions, and philosophies, according to the stage of civilization and the fashions of reflection and generalization.

65. WHAT IS GOODNESS OR BADNESS OF THE MORES. It is most important to notice that, for the people of a time and place, their own mores are always good, or rather that for them there can be no question of the goodness or badness of their mores. The reason is because the standards of good and right are in the mores. If the life conditions change, the traditional folkways may produce pain and loss, or fail to produce the same good as formerly. Then the loss of comfort and ease brings doubt into the judgment of welfare (causing doubt of the pleasure of the gods, or of war power, or of health), and thus disturbs the unconscious philosophy of the morse. Then a later time will pass judgment on the mores. Another society may also pass judgment on the mores. In our literary and historical study of the mores we want to get from them their educational value, which consists in the stimulus or warning as to what is, in its effects, societally good or bad. This may lead us to reject or neglect a phenomenon like infanticide, slavery, or witchcraft, as an old "abuse" and "evil," or to pass by the crusades as a folly which cannot recur. Such a course would be a great error. Everything in the mores of a time and place must be regarded as justified with regard to that time and place. "Good" mores are those which are well adapted to the situation. "Bad" mores are those which are not so adapted. The mores are not so stereotyped and changeless as might appear, because they are forever moving towards more complete adaptation to conditions and interests, and also towards more complete adjustment to each other. People in mass have never made or kept up a custom in order to hurt their own interests. They have made innumerable errors as to what their interests were and how to satisfy them, but they have always aimed to serve their interests as well as they could. This gives the standpoint for the student of the mores. All things in them come before him on the same plane. They all bring instruction and warning. They all have the same relation to power and welfare. The mistakes in them are component parts of them. We do not study them in order to approve some of them and condemn others. They are all equally worthy of attention from the fact that they existed and were used. The chief object of study in them is their adjustment to interests, their relation to welfare, and their coordination in a harmonious system of life policy. For the men of the time there are no "bad" mores. What is traditional and current is the standard of what ought to be. The masses never raise any question about such things.

If a few raise doubts and questions, this proves that the folkways have already begun to lose firmness and the regulative element in the mores has begun to lose authority. This indicates that the folkways are on their way to a new adjustment. The extreme of folly, wickedness, and absurdity in the mores is witch persecutions, but the best men of the seventeenth century had no doubt that witches existed, and that they ought to be burned. The religion, statecraft, jurisprudence, philosophy, and social system of that age all contributed to maintain that belief. It was rather a culmination than a contradiction of the current faiths and convictions, just as the dogma that all men are equal and that one ought to have as much political power in the state as another was the culmination of the political dogmatism and social philosophy of the nineteenth century. Hence our judgments of the good or evil consequences of folkways are to be kept separate from our study of the historical phenomena of them, and of their strength and the reasons for it. The judgments have their place in plans and doctrines for the future, not in a retrospect.

80. THE MORES HAVE THE AU-THORITY OF FACTS. The mores come down to us from the past. Each individual is born into them as he is born into the atmosphere, and he does not reflect on them, or criticize them any more than a baby analyzes the atmosphere before he begins to breathe it. Each one is subjected to the influence of the mores, and formed by them, before he is capable of reasoning about them. It may be objected that nowadays, at least, we criticize all traditions, and accept none just because they are handed down to us. If we take up cases of things which are still entirely or almost entirely in the mores, we shall see that this is not so. There are sects of free-lovers amongst us who want to discuss pair marriage. They are not simply people of evil life. They invite us to discuss rationally our inherited customs and ideas as to marriage, which, they say, are by no means so excellent and

elevated as we believe. They have never won any serious attention. Some others want to argue in favor of polygamy on grounds of expediency. They fail to obtain a hearing. Others want to discuss property. In spite of some literary activity on their part, no discussion of property, bequest, and inheritance has ever been opened. Property and marriage are in the mores. Nothing can ever change them but the unconscious and imperceptible movement of the mores. Religion was originally a matter of the mores. It became a societal institution and a function of the state. It has now to a great extent been put back into the mores. Since laws with penalties to enforce religious creeds or practices have gone out of use any one may think and act as he pleases about religion. Therefore, it is not now "good form" to attack religion. Infidel publications are now tabooed by the mores, and are more effectually repressed than ever before. They produce no controversy. Democracy is in our American mores. It is a product of our physical and economic conditions. It is impossible to discuss or criticize it. It is glorified for popularity, and is a subject of dithyrambic rhetoric. No one treats it with complete candor and sincerity. No one dares to analyze it as he would aristocracy or autocracy. He would get no hearing and would only incur abuse. The thing to be noticed in all these cases is that the masses oppose a deaf ear to every argument against the mores. It is only in so far as things have been transferred from the mores into laws and positive institutions that there is discussion about them or rationalizing upon them. The mores contain the norm by which, if we should discuss the mores, we should have to judge the mores. We learn the mores as unconsciously as we learn to walk and eat and breathe. The masses never learn how to walk, and eat, and breathe, and they never know any reason why the mores are what they are. The justification of them is that when we wake to consciousness of life we find them facts which already hold us in the bonds of tradition, custom, and habit. The mores contain embodied in them notions, doctrines, and maxims, but they are facts. They are in the present tense. They have nothing to do with what ought to be, will be, may be, or once was, if it is not now.

81. BLACKS AND WHITES IN SOUTHERN SOCIETY.

In our southern states, before the civil war, whites and blacks had formed habits of action and feeling towards each other. They lived in peace and concord, and each one grew up in the ways which were traditional and customary. The civil war abolished legal rights and left the two races to learn how to live together under other relations than before. The whites have never been converted from the old mores. Those who still survive look back with regret and affection to the old social usages and customary sentiments and feelings. The two races have not yet made new mores. Vain attempts have been made to control the new order by legislation. The only result is the proof that legislation cannot make mores. We see also that mores do not form under social convulsion and discord. It is only just now that the new society seems to be taking shape. There is a trend in the mores now as they begin to form under the new state of things. It is not at all what the humanitarians hoped and expected. The two races are separating more than ever before. The strongest point in the new code seems to be that any white man is boycotted and despised if he "associates with negroes." Some are anxious to interfere and try to control. They take their stand on ethical views of what is going on. It is evidently impossible for any one to interefere. We are like spectators at a great natural convulsion. The results will be such as the facts and forces call for. We cannot foresee them. They do not depend on ethical views any more than the volcanic eruption on Martinique contained an ethical element. All the faiths, hopes, energies, and sacrifices of both whites and blacks are components in the new construction of folkways by which the two races will learn how to live together. As we go along with the construc-

tive process it is very plain that what once was, or what any one thinks ought to be, but slightly affects what, at any moment, is. The mores which once were are a memory. Those which any one thinks ought to be are a dream. The only thing with which we can deal are those which are.

232. MORES AND MORALS: SOCIAL CODE.

For every one the mores give the notion of what ought to be. This includes the notion of what ought to be done, for all should cooperate to bring to pass, in the order of life, what ought to be. All notions of propriety, decency, chastity, politeness, order, duty, right, rights, discipline, respect, reverence, cooperation, and fellowship, especially all things in regard to which good and ill depend entirely on the point at which the line is drawn, are in the mores. The mores can make things seem right and good to one group or one age which to another seem antagonistic to every instinct of human nature. The thirteenth century bred in every heart such a sentiment in regard to heretics that inquisitors had no more misgivings in their proceedings than men would have now if they should attempt to exterminate rattlesnakes. The sixteenth century gave to all such notions about witches that witch persecutors thought they were waging war on enemies of God and man. Of course the inquisitors and witch persecutors constantly developed the notions of heretics and witches. They exaggerated the notions and then gave them back again to the mores, in their expanded form, to inflame the hearts of men with terror and hate and to become, in the next stage, so much more fantastic and ferocious motives. Such is the reaction between the mores and the acts of the living generation. The world philosophy of the age is never anything but the reflection on the mental horizon, which is formed out of the mores, of the ruling ideas which are in the mores themselves. It is from a failure to recognize the to and fro in this reaction that the current notion arises that mores are produced by doctrines. The "morals" of an age are never anything but the consonance between what is done and what the mores of the age require. The whole revolves on itself, in the relation of the specific to the general, within the horizon formed by the mores. Every attempt to win an outside standpoint from which to reduce the whole to an absolute philosophy of truth and right, based on an unalterable principle, is a delusion. New elements are brought in only by new conquests of nature through science and art. The new conquests change the conditions of life and the interests of the members of the society. Then the mores change by adaptation to new conditions and interests. The philosophy and ethics then follow to account for and justify the changes in the mores; often, also, to claim that they have caused the changes. They never do anything but draw new lines of bearing between the parts of the mores and the horizon of thought within which they are inclosed, and which is a deduction from the mores. The horizon is widened by more knowledge, but for one age it is just as much a generalization from the mores as for another. It is always unreal. It is only a product of thought. The ethical philosophers select points on this horizon from which to take their bearings, and they think that they have won some authority for their systems when they travel back again from the generalization to the specific custom out of which it was deduced. The cases of the inquisitors and witch persecutors who toiled arduously and continually for their chosen ends, for little or no reward, show us the relation between mores on the one side and philosophy, ethics, and religion on the other.

STUDY QUESTIONS

1. What does Sumner mean by folkways? Mores? Do you agree with him that "the notion of right is in the folkways"? Explain.
2. Why is Sumner called a cultural relativist? What implications does cultural relativism have for ethics?
3. What can a study of anthropology teach us about ethics? Can a study of ethics teach us anything about anthropology?
4. Has history borne out Sumner's predictions about social relationships in the South?
5. Some critics have charged that Sumner commits the "genetic fallacy." What does this mean? Do you think the charge is justified?

For Further Reading

Ginsberg, M. *Essays in Sociology and Social Philosophy.* Vol. 1. New York: Macmillan, 1957 (esp. Chapter 7).

"Is Ethical Relativity Necessary?" A Symposium. *Aristotelian Society.* Supp. Vol. 17 (1938), pp. 152–94.

Ladd, J., ed. *Ethical Relativism.* Belmont, Calif.: Wadsworth, 1973.

Stace, W. T. *The Concept of Morals.* New York: Macmillan, 1937 (Chapters 1 and 2).

Westermarck, E. *Ethical Relativity.* New York: Harcourt, 1932 (Chapters 1 and 2).

PART V

——— ⊂━┥ ┝━ ———

The Individual and the State

Unlike nature or the human beings who make up society, the state is an entity whose existence requires justification. We do not ask, Why must we live in nature and among other people? We recognize that no life outside of a natural and human context is possible. But many of us, at least occasionally, ask, Why must we live in a state? Such a question naturally arises when some act of government affects us adversely; we are called before the internal revenue inspectors to explain our income tax return, or we are drafted to perform military service, and so on.

One of the main aims of political philosophy is to justify the existence of the state. Part V includes some of the most famous attempts made by theorists in the Western tradition to accomplish this goal. Since the primary means by which we justify the existence of anything is through showing that it makes possible the realization of some value that could not have been gained without it, we shall find political philosophers concentrating their attention on the goods that we can enjoy only if we live in an organized state. Since different writers have differing views about the relative values of the various goods of human existence, they frequently reach quite different conclusions about the nature of the best possible state.

One of the earliest and historically most influential justifications of the state appears in Aristotle's book *The Politics*. In Aristotle's view, the good to be gained through living in a state is literally coextensive with human life itself. We may exist outside of a state but such an existence is barely human, being more akin to that of animals. To live a truly human life, in which we realize the kind of values that sets us apart from all other living creatures, it is necessary for us to live in an organized society governed by law. Thus Aristotle is led to one of his most widely quoted characterizations of human nature: "Man is a political animal," or, expanded somewhat, "Man is an animal whose distinctive human nature can be realized only through life in a state."

Few of the modern political philosophers tie the state so closely as Aristotle does to human nature, though most agree with him in believing it to be necessary to the good life. The seventeenth-century English philosopher John Locke, for example, sees the state as a human creation, the result of a deliberate social act. Viewed in such a way the existence of the state is not necessary to human life, and Locke makes a point of emphasizing that human, social life is quite possible even without a state. What the state contributes to human welfare is stability in the securing and maintaining of basic rights to its members. The Lockian conception and justification of the state received its greatest practical fulfillment in the American *Declaration of Independence*, in the justly famous passage: "We hold these truths to be self-evident, that all men are created equal, that they are endowed by their Creator with certain unalienable rights, that among these are life, liberty and the pursuit of happiness. That to secure these rights, governments are instituted among men, deriving their just powers from the consent of the governed."

Although he agreed with his younger contemporary, Locke, in thinking the state to be a human creation, Thomas Hobbes was much closer to Aristotle in his view of its necessity to human life. Yet his reasons for believing this were considerably different from those of Aristotle. Hobbes recognized the possibility that humans can live without government, but he judged that such a life would be so miserable as to be hardly worth living. The reason lies in human nature itself. We are all by nature egoists, interested only in our own welfare. Left to our own devices, without any laws to govern our behavior, we would be constantly at each other's throats. In such a situation no one has much chance for survival. Recognizing the self-destructive character of life in such a "state of nature," individuals have got together to form governments to protect their lives and vital interests. Because their motivation in forming the state is self-protection, Hobbes concluded, the best state is one that keeps the peace. Thus he argued in favor of a single central authority with the power both to make and to enforce laws. Carried to its logical conclusion, his conception of government becomes a police state.

The dominant tradition in Western thought has been to find a justification for the state in the contribution it makes to the realization of values, whether these be simple survival, the protection of basic human rights, or the higher achievements of mankind in such pursuits as science, literature, religion, technology, art, and philosophy. But, we might ask, is the state really necessary for all that? Could humanity not have achieved everything it has and avoided the inconvenience and repressions that have plagued every historical society, if the state, with its machinery, had never been brought into existence? A minor note has been struck throughout the history of political thought by those who have claimed that no satisfactory justification can be given for the state. These are the anarchists. Historically, little attention has been given to them, largely because their views have usually been "utopian," in the derogatory sense that their conceptions of a society without a state are too simple to be practicable in a civilization of the size and complexity of the modern world. But within the last century or so, a new form of anarchism—perhaps "anarchism as an ideal for the future" would be a more accurate description—has arisen, one that overcomes the main deficiencies of the traditional forms of anarchistic view. This is Marxism, named after its founder, the nineteenth-century economist and philosopher, Karl Marx.

In order to understand the Marxist conception and evaluation of the state, it is necessary to begin with economics, for, according to Marx, economic conditions are the determining causes of which political institutions and practices are the effects. In the Marxian view, the manner in which goods are produced and distributed determines the nature of society. To understand any social institution, therefore, we must examine the economic system that produced it and determined the form it would take. Applying this general theory to the state, the Marxists developed the view that, if we examine societies historically, we find a recurring situation in which a small minority of the populace have gained control of the economic forces of their society at the expense of the vast majority. Thus, past societies have always been made up of a minority of exploiters and a majority of exploited. One of the main devices that the exploiters have developed to maintain their control over the people at large is the state. In every historical epoch the state has been an instrument wielded by the economically privileged to suppress the rest. Rather than being a natural condition of human life, it is completely artificial, the deliberate creation of a small segment of society without the consent and against the interests of everyone else. As a result, instead of releasing human nature to pursue higher goals, it stultifies our intellectual and creative capacities.

Because the state is an instrument of repression, it should be opposed by everyone concerned with human welfare. But the Marxists hold a stronger, more optimistic view (and herein lies their anarchism). Although the state, as a repressive force, has existed throughout history, it is doomed. Economic changes are even now taking place that will lead to the elimination of the exploiting class. Once the exploiters have gone and economic power is transferred to the people, the state will no longer have any function to perform, for no one will remain to be repressed. The state will then disappear or, to use the more descriptive phrase of the literature, the state will simply "wither away." The difficulty with this view, which is practical but apparent, lies in the refusal of Marxian states in the contemporary world to heed the prediction of Marx and disappear from the social scene.

Background Reading

Burns, C. D. *Political Ideals: Their Nature and Development.* London: Oxford University Press, 1917.

Feinberg, J. *Social Philosophy.* Englewood Cliffs, N.J.: Prentice-Hall, 1973

Jenkin, T. P. *The Study of Political Theory.* New York: Random House, 1955.

Murphy, J. S. *Political Theory: A Conceptual Analysis.* Homewood, Ill: The Dorsey Press, 1968.

Quinton, A., ed. *Political Philosophy.* London: Oxford University Press, 1967.

Thomson, D., ed. *Political Ideas.* New York: Basic Books, 1966.

Zollinger, P. *The Political Creature: An Evolutionary Reorientation.* New York: George Braziller, 1967 (esp. Part III).

ARISTOTLE: THE STATE AND THE CITIZEN

Most modern political philosophers have thought it necessary to offer arguments to *justify* the existence of the state. The reason for this is largely historical. As it slowly emerged from the feudal society of the middle ages, the modern state developed as powerful individuals gradually gathered political power into their own hands. Such a concentration of power reached its culmination in seventeenth-century France, enabling Louis XIV to proclaim *"L'etat, c'est moi."* The following century witnessed a progression of revolutions. Writing under quite different circumstances, and with a breadth of vision rarely equalled, Aristotle recognized no need to justify the state, arguing, instead, that life in a state is advantageous for human beings because only under such conditions can we realize the highest values we are capable of pursuing. The individual and the state, therefore, are not in opposition to, but rather in harmony with, each other.

For a biographical sketch of Aristotle see page 207.

❦ *The Politics*

Book I

Every state is a community of some kind, and every community is established with a view to some good; for mankind always act in order to obtain that which they think good. But, if all communities aim at some good, the state or political community, which is the highest of all, and which embraces all the rest, aims, and in a greater degree than any other, at the highest good.

Now there is an erroneous opinion that a statesman, king, householder, and master are the same, and that they differ, not in kind, but only in the number of their subjects. For example, the ruler over a few called a master; over more, the manager of a household; over a still larger number, a statesman or king, as if there were no difference between a great household and a small state. The distinction which is made between the king and the statesman is as follows: When the government is personal, the ruler is a king; when, according to the principles of the political science, the citizens rule and are ruled in turn, then he is called a statesman.

But all this is a mistake; for governments differ in kind, as will be evident to any one who considers the matter according to the method which has hitherto guided us. As in other departments of science, so in politics, the compound should always be resolved into the simple elements or least parts of the whole. We must therefore look at the elements of which the state is composed, in order that we may see in what they differ from one

Translated by B. Jowett.

another, and whether any scientific distinction can be drawn between the different kinds of rule.

He who thus considers things in their first growth and origin, whether a state or anything else, will obtain the clearest view of them. In the first place (1) there must be a union of those who cannot exist without each other; for example, of male and female, that the race may continue; and this is a union which is formed, not of deliberate purpose, but because, in common with other animals and with plants, mankind have a natural desire to leave behind them an image of themselves. And (2) there must be a union of natural ruler and subject, that both may be preserved. For he who can foresee with his mind is by nature intended to be lord and master, and he who can work with his body is a subject, and by nature a slave; hence master and slave have the same interest. Nature, however, has distinguished between the female and the slave. For she is not niggardly, like the smith who fashions the Delphian knife for many uses; she makes each thing for a single use, and every instrument is best made when intended for one and not for many uses. But among barbarians no distinction is made between women and slaves, because there is no natural ruler among them: they are a community of slaves, male and female. Wherefore the poets say—

"It is meet that Hellenes should rule
over barbarians;"
as if they thought that the barbarian and the slave were by nature one.

Out of these two relationships between man and woman, master and slave, the family first arises, and Hesiod is right when he says—

"First house and wife and an ox for the plough,"

for the ox is the poor man's slave. The family is the association established by nature for the supply of men's every day wants, and the members of it are called by Charondas "companions of the cupboard," and by Epimenides the Cretan, "companions of the manger." But when several families are united, and the association aims at something more than the supply of daily needs, then comes into existence the village. And the most natural form of the village appears to be that of a colony from the family, composed of the children and grandchildren, who are said to be "suckled with the same milk." And this is the reason why Hellenic states were originally governed by kings; because the Hellenes were under royal rule before they came together, as the barbarians still are. Every family is ruled by the eldest, and therefore in the colonies of the family the kingly form of government prevailed because they were of the same blood. As Homer says:—

"Each one gives law to his children and to his wives."

For they lived dispersedly, as was the manner in ancient times. Wherefore men say that the Gods have a king, because they themselves either are or were in ancient times under the rule of a king. For they imagine, not only the forms of the Gods, but their ways of life to be like their own.

When several villages are united in a single community, perfect and large enough to be nearly or quite self-sufficing, the state comes into existence, originating in the bare needs of life, and continuing in existence for the sake of a good life. And therefore, if the earlier forms of society are natural, so is the state, for it is the end of them, and the completed nature is the end. For what each thing is when fully developed, we call its nature, whether we are speaking of a man, a horse, or a family. Besides, the final cause and end of a thing is the best, and to be self-sufficing is the end and the best.

Hence it is evident that the state is a creation of nature, and that man is by nature a political animal. And he who by nature and not by mere accident is without a state, is either above humanity, or below it; he is the

"Tribeless, lawless, heartless one,"

whom Homer denounces—the outcast who is a lover of war; he may be compared to a bird which flies alone.

Now the reason why man is more of a political animal than bees or any other gregarious animals is evident. Nature, as we often say, makes nothing in vain, and man is the only animal whom she has endowed with the gift of speech. And whereas mere sound is but an indication of pleasure or pain, and is therefore found in other animals (for their nature attains to the perception of pleasure and pain and the intimation of them to one another, and no further), the power of speech is intended to set forth the expedient and inexpedient, and likewise the just and the unjust. And it is a characteristic of man that he alone has any sense of good and evil, of just and unjust; and the association of living beings who have this sense makes a family and a state.

Thus the state is by nature clearly prior to the family and to the individual, since the whole is of necessity prior to the part; for example, if the whole body be destroyed, there will be no foot or hand, except in an equivocal sense, as we might speak of a stone hand; for when destroyed the hand will be no better. But things are defined by their working and power; and we ought not to say that they are the same when they are no longer the same, but only that they have the same name. The proof that the state is a creation of nature and prior to the individual is that the individual, when isolated, is not self-sufficing; and therefore he is like a part in relation to the whole. But he who is unable to live in society, or who has no need because he is sufficient for himself, must be either a beast or a god: he is no part of a state. A social instinct is implanted in all men by nature, and yet he who first founded the state was the greatest of benefactors. For man, when perfected, is the best of animals, but, when separated from law and justice, he is the worst of all; since armed injustice is the more dangerous, and he is equipped at birth with the arms of intelligence and with moral qualities which he may use for the worst ends. Wherefore, if he have not virtue, he is the most unholy and the most savage of animals, and the most full of lust and gluttony. But justice is the bond of men in states, and the administration of justice, which is the determination of what is just, is the principle of order in political society.

. . .

Book III

. . .

We have next to consider whether there is only one form of government or many, and if many, what they are, and how many, and what are the differences between them.

A constitution is the arrangement of magistracies in a State, especially of the highest of all. The government is everywhere sovereign in the State, and the constitution is in fact the government. For example, in democracies the people are supreme, but in oligarchies, the few; and, therefore, we say that these two forms of government are different: and so in other cases.

First, let us consider what is the purpose of a State, and how many forms of government there are by which human society is regulated. We have already said, in the former part of this treatise, when drawing a distinction between household management and the rule of a master, that man is by nature a political animal. And therefore, men, even when they do not require one another's help, desire to live together all

the same, and are in fact brought together by their common interests in proportion as they severally attain to any measure of well-being. This is certainly the chief end, both of individuals and of States. And also for the sake of mere life (in which there is possibly some noble element) mankind meet together and maintain the political community, so long as the evils of existence do not greatly overbalance the good. And we all see that men cling to life even in the midst of misfortune, seeming to find in it a natural sweetness and happiness.

There is no difficulty in distinguishing the various kinds of authority; they have been often defined already in popular works. The rule of a master, although the slave by nature and the master by nature have in reality the same interests, is nevertheless exercised primarily with a view to the interest of the master, but accidentally considers the slave, since, if the slave perish, the rule of the master perishes with him. On the other hand, the government of a wife and children and of a household, which we have called household management, is exercised in the first instance for the good of the governed or for the common good of both parties, but essentially for the good of the governed, as we see to be the case in medicine, gymnastic, and the arts in general, which are only accidentally concerned with the good of the artists themselves. (For there is no reason why the trainer may not sometimes practise gymnastics, and the pilot is always one of the crew.) The trainer or the pilot considers the good of those committed to his care. But, when he is one of the persons taken care of, he accidentally participates in the advantage, for the pilot is also a sailor, and the trainer becomes one of those in training. And so in politics: when the State is framed upon the principle of equality and likeness, the citizens think that they ought to hold office by turns. In the order of nature everyone would take his turn of service; and then again, somebody else would look after his interest, just as he, while in office, had looked after theirs. But nowadays, for the sake of the advantage which is to be gained from the public revenues and from office, men want to be always in office. One might imagine that the rulers, being sickly, were only kept in health while they continued in office; in that case we may be sure that they would be hunting after places. The conclusion is evident: that governments, which have a regard to the common interest, are constituted in accordance with strict principles of justice, and are therefore true forms; but those which regard only the interest of the rulers are all defective and perverted forms, for they are despotic, whereas a State is a community of freemen.

Having determined these points, we have next to consider how many forms of government there are, and what they are; and in the first place what are the true forms, for when they are determined the perversions of them will at once be apparent. The words "constitution" and "government" have the same meaning, and the government, which is the supreme authority in States, must be in the hands of one, or of a few, or of many. The true forms of government, therefore, are those in which the one, or the few, or the many, govern with a view to the common interest; but governments which rule with a view to the private interest, whether of the one, or of the few, or of the many, are perversions. For citizens, if they are truly citizens, ought to participate in the advantages of a State. Of forms of government in which one rules, we call that which regards the common interests, kingship or royalty; that in which more than one, but not many, rule, aristocracy (the rule of the best); and it is so called, either because the rulers are the best men, or because they have at heart the best interests of the State and of the citizens. But when the citizens at large administer the State for the common interest, the government is called by the generic name—a constitution. And there is a reason for this use of language. One man or a few may excel in virtue; but of virtue there are many kinds: and as the number increases it becomes more difficult for them to attain perfection in very kind, though

they may in military virtue, for this is found in the masses. Hence, in a constitutional government the fighting-men have the supreme power, and those who possess arms are the citizens.

Of the above-mentioned forms, the perversions are as follows:—of royalty, tyranny; of aristocracy, oligarchy; of constitutional government, democracy. For tyranny is a kind of monarchy which has in view the interest of the monarch only; oligarchy has in view the interest of the wealthy; democracy, of the needy: none of them the common good of all.

But there are difficulties about these forms of government, and it will therefore be necessary to state a little more at length the nature of each of them. For he who would make a philosophical study of the various sciences, and does not regard practice only, ought not to overlook or omit anything, but to set forth the truth in every particular. Tyranny, as I was saying, is monarchy exercising the rule of a master over political society; oligarchy is when men of property have the government in their hands; democracy, the opposite, when the indigent, and not the men of property, are the rulers. And here arises the first of our difficulties, and it relates to the definition just given. For democracy is said to be the government of the many. But what if the many are men of property and have the power in their hands? In like manner oligarchy is said to be the government of the few; but what if the poor are fewer than the rich, and have the power in their hands because they are stronger? In these cases the distinction which we have drawn between these different forms of government would no longer hold good.

Suppose, once more, that we add wealth to the few and poverty to the many, and name the governments accordingly—an oligarchy is said to be that in which the few and the wealthy, and a democracy that in which the many and the poor are the rulers—there will still be a difficulty. For, if the only forms of government are the ones already mentioned, how shall we describe those other governments also just mentioned by us, in which the rich are the more numerous and the poor are the fewer, and both govern in their respective States?

The argument seems to show that, whether in oligarchies or in democracies, the number of the governing body, whether the greatest number, as in a democracy, or the smaller number, as in an oligarchy, is an accident due to the fact that the rich everywhere are few, and the poor numerous. But if so, there is a misapprehension of the causes of the difference between them. For the real difference between democracy and oligarchy is poverty and wealth. Wherever men rule by reason of their wealth, whether they be few or many, that is an oligarchy, and where the poor rule, that is a democracy. But as a fact the rich are few and the poor many: for few are well-to-do, whereas freedom is enjoyed by all, and wealth and freedom are the grounds on which the oligarchical and democratical parties respectively claim power in the State.

Let us begin by considering the common definitions of oligarchy and democracy, and what is justice oligarchical and democratical. For all men cling to justice of some kind, but their conceptions are imperfect and they do not express the whole idea. For example, justice is thought by them to be, and is, equality, not, however, for all, but only for equals. And inequality is thought to be, and is, justice; neither is this for all, but only for unequals. When the persons are omitted, then men judge erroneously. The reason is that they are passing judgment on themselves, and most people are bad judges in their own case. And whereas justice implies a relation to persons as well as to things, and a just distribution, as I have already said in the "Ethics," embraces alike persons and things, they acknowledge the equality of the things, but dispute about the merit of the persons, chiefly for the reason which I have just given—because they are bad judges in their own affairs; and secondly, because both the parties to the argument are speaking of a limited and partial justice, but imagine themselves to be speaking of

absolute justice. For those who are unequal in one respect, for example wealth, consider themselves to be unequal in all; and any who are equal in one respect, for example freedom, consider themselves to be equal in all. But they leave out the capital point. For if men met and associated out of regard to wealth only, their share in the State would be proportioned to their property, and the oligarchical doctrine would then seem to carry the day. It would not be just that he who paid one mina should have the same share of a hundred minae, whether of the principal or of the profits, as he who paid the remaining ninety-nine. But a state exists for the sake of a good life, and not for the sake of life only: if life only were the object, slaves and brute animals might form a State, but they cannot, for they have no share in happiness or in a life of free choice. Nor does a State exist for the sake of alliance and security from injustice, nor yet for the sake of exchange and mutual intercourse; for then the Tyrrhenians and the Carthaginians, and all who have commercial treaties with one another, would be the citizens of one State. True, they have agreements about imports, and engagements that they will do no wrong to one another, and written articles of alliance. But there are no magistracies common to the contracting parties who will enforce their engagements; different States have each their own magistracies. Nor does one State take care that the citizens of the other are such as they ought to be, nor see that those who come under the terms of the treaty do no wrong or wickedness at all, but only that they do no injustice to one another. Whereas, those who care for good government take into consideration [the larger question of] virtue and vice in States. Whence it may be further inferred that virtue must be the serious care of a State which truly deserves the name: for [without this ethical end] the community becomes a mere alliance which differs only in place from alliances of which the members live apart; and law is only a convention, "a surety to one another of justice," as the sophist Lycophron says, and has no real power to make the citizens good and just.

This is obvious; for suppose distinct places, such as Corinth and Megara, to be united by a wall, still they would not be one city, not even if the citizens had the right to intermarry, which is one of the rights peculiarly characteristic of States. Again, if men dwelt at a distance from one another, but not so far off as to have no intercourse, and there were laws among them that they should not wrong each other in their exchanges, neither would this be a State. Let us suppose that one man is a carpenter, another a husbandman, another a shoemaker, and so on, and that their number is ten thousand: nevertheless, if they have nothing in common but exchange, alliance, and the like, that would not constitute a State. Why is this? Surely not because they are at a distance from one another: for even supposing that such a community were to meet in one place, and that each man had a house of his own, which was in a manner his State, and that they made alliance with one another, but only against evil-doers; still an accurate thinker would not deem this to be a State, if their intercourse with one another was of the same character after as before their union. It is clear then that a state is not a mere society, having a common place, established for the prevention of crime and for the sake of exchange. These are conditions without which a State cannot exist; but all of them together do not constitute a State, which is a community of well-being in families and aggregations of families, for the sake of a perfect and self-sufficing life. Such a community can only be established among those who live in the same place and intermarry. Hence arise in cities family connections, brotherhoods, common sacrifices, amusements which draw men together. They are created by friendship, for friendship is the motive of society. The end is the good life, and these are the means towards it. And the State is the union of families and villages having for an end a perfect and self-sufficing life, by which we mean a happy and honorable life.

Our conclusion, then, is that political society exists for the sake of noble actions, and not of mere companionship. And they who contribute most to such a society have a greater share in it than those who have the same or a greater freedom or nobility of birth but are inferior to them in political virtue; or than those who exceed them in wealth but are surpassed by them in virtue.

From what has been said it will be clearly seen that all the partisans of different forms of government speak of a part of justice only.

There is also a doubt as to what is to be the supreme power in the State:—Is it the multitude? Or the wealthy? Or the good? Or the one best man? Or a tyrant? Any of these alternatives seems to involve disagreeable consequences. If the poor, for example, because they are more in number, divide among themselves the property of the rich—is not this unjust? No, by heaven (will be the reply), for the lawful authority (*i.e.* the people) willed it. But if this is not injustice, pray what is? Again, when (in the first division) all has been taken, and the majority divide anew the property of the minority, is it not evident, if this goes on, that they will ruin the State? Yet surely, virtue is not the ruin of those who possess her, nor is justice destructive of a State; and therefore this law of confiscation clearly cannot be just. If it were, all the acts of a tyrant must of necessity be just; for he only coerces other men by superior power, just as the multitude coerce the rich. But is it just then that the few and the wealthy should be the rulers? And what if they, in like manner, rob and plunder the people—is this just? If so, the other case [*i.e.* the case of the majority plundering the minority] will likewise be just. But there can be no doubt that all these things are wrong and unjust.

Then ought the good to rule and have supreme power? But in that case everybody else, being excluded from power, will be dishonored. For the offices of a State are posts of honor; and if one set of men always hold them, the rest must be deprived of them. Then will it be well that the one best man should rule? Nay, that is still more oligarchical, for the number of those who are dishonored is thereby increased. Some one may say that it is bad for a man, subject as he is to all the accidents of human passion, to have the supreme power, rather than the law. But what if the law itself be democratical or oligarchical, how will that help us out of our difficulties? Not at all; the same consequences will follow.

Most of these questions may be reserved for another occasion. The principle that the multitude ought to be supreme rather than the few best is capable of a satisfactory explanation, and though not free from difficulty, yet seems to contain an element of truth. For the many, of whom each individual is but an ordinary person, when they meet together may very likely be better than the few good, if regarded not individually but collectively, just as a feast to which many contribute is better than a dinner provided out of a single purse. For each individual among the many has a share of virtue and prudence, and when they meet together they become in a manner one man, who has many feet, and hands, and senses; that is a figure of their mind and disposition. Hence the many are better judges than a single man of music and poetry; for some understand one part, and some another, and among them, they understand the whole. There is a similar combination of qualities in good men, who differ from any individual of the many, as the beautiful are said to differ from those who are not beautiful, and works of art from realities, because in them the scattered elements are combined, although, if taken separately, the eye of one person or some other feature in another person would be fairer than in the picture. Whether this principle can apply to every democracy, and to all bodies of men, is not clear. Or rather, by heaven, in some cases it is impossible of application; for the argument would equally hold about brutes; and wherein, it will be asked, do some men differ from brutes? But there may be bodies of men about whom our statement is nevertheless true.

Book IV

• • •

We have now to inquire what is the best constitution for most States, and the best life for most men, neither assuming a standard of virtue which is above ordinary persons, nor an education which is exceptionally favored by nature and circumstances, nor yet an ideal State which is an aspiration only, but having regard to the life in which the majority are able to share, and to the form of government which States in general can attain. As to those aristocracies, as they are called, of which we were just now speaking, they either lie beyond the possibilities of the greater number of States, or they approximate to the so-called constitutional government, and therefore need no separate discussion. And in fact the conclusion at which we arrive respecting all these forms rests upon the same grounds. For if it has been truly said in the "Ethics" that the happy life is the life according to unimpeded virtue, and that virtue is a mean, then the life which is in a mean, and in a mean attainable by everyone, must be the best. And the same principles of virtue and vice are characteristic of cities and of constitutions; for the constitution is in a figure the life of a city.

Now in all States there are three elements; one class is very rich, another very poor, and a third in a mean. It is admitted that moderation and the mean are best, and therefore it will clearly be best to possess the gifts of fortune in moderation; for in that condition of life men are most ready to listen to reason. But he who greatly excels in beauty, strength, birth or wealth, or on the other hand who is very poor, or very weak, or very much disgraced, finds it difficult to follow reason. Of these two the one sort grow into violent and great criminals, the others into rogues and petty rascals. And two sorts of offences correspond to them, the one committed from violence, the other from roguery. The petty rogues are disinclined to hold office, whether military or civil, and their aversion to these two duties is as great an injury to the State as their tendency to crime. Again, those who have too much of the goods of fortune, strength, wealth, friends, and the like, are neither willing nor able to submit to authority. The evil begins at home: for when they are boys, by reason of the luxury in which they are brought up, they never learn, even at school, the habit of obedience. On the other hand, the very poor, who are in the opposite extreme, are too degraded. So that the one class cannot obey, and can only rule despotically; the other knows not how to command and must be ruled like slaves. Thus arises a city, not of freemen, but of masters and slaves, the one despising, the other envying; and nothing can be more fatal to friendship and good-fellowship in States than this: for good fellowship tends to friendship; when men are at enmity with one another, they would rather not even share the same path. But a city ought to be composed, as far as possible, of equals and similars; and these are generally the middle classes. Wherefore the city which is composed of middle-class citizens is necessarily best governed; they are, as we say, the natural elements of a State. And this is the class of citizens which is most secure in a State, for they do not, like the poor, covet their neighbors' goods; nor do others covet theirs, as the poor covet the goods of the rich; and as they neither plot against others, nor are themselves plotted against, they pass through life safely. Wisely then did Phocylides pray, "Many things are best in the mean; I desire to be of a middle condition in my city."

Thus it is manifest that the best political community is formed by citizens of the middle class, and that those States are likely to be well administered, in which the middle class is large, and larger if possible than both the other classes, or at any rate than either singly; for the addition of the middle class turns the scale, and prevents either of the extremes from being dominant. Great then is the good fortune of a State in which the citizens have a moderate and sufficient property; for where some possess much, and the others nothing, there may arise an extreme democracy, or a pure oligarchy; or a tyranny may grow out of either extreme—either out of the most rampant democracy, or out of an oligarchy; but it is not so likely to arise out of a middle and nearly equal condition.

STUDY QUESTIONS

1. Do you think Aristotle is right in his belief that the state aims at the highest good?
2. What does Aristotle mean by saying "man is by nature a political animal"? Do you agree?
3. How does Aristotle distinguish between good and bad forms of government?
4. What is the relationship, in Aristotle's terminology, between the form of government he calls a constitution and a democracy?
5. What, according to Aristotle, are the requirements for the existence of a state?
6. What are Aristotle's arguments in support of middle-class government?

For Further Reading

Barker, E. *The Political Thought of Plato and Aristotle.* New York: Putnam's, 1906 (Chapters 5 through 8 and 10 through 11).

Barnes, J.; Schofield, M; and Sorabji, R. *Articles on Aristotle: Ethics and Politics.* New York: St. Martin's, 1978 (Vol. II, Chapters 11 through 17).

Morrall, J. B. *Aristotle.* London: Allen and Unwin, 1977.

Mulgan, R. G. *Aristotle's Political Theory.* New York: Oxford University Press, 1977.

Sabine, G. H. *A History of Political Theory.* 2d ed. New York: Holt, Rinehart and Winston, 1973 (Chapters 5 and 6).

HOBBES: ABSOLUTISM

History has witnessed many leaders who have ruled their states with an absolute, or nearly absolute, hand. On the other hand, it has produced few philosophers who have undertaken to justify such absolutism. The most important exception is Thomas Hobbes, who believed that, if society is to survive, someone must be entrusted with absolute power to keep the human mob under control. Hobbes based his defense of absolutism on his analysis of human nature, which he held in low esteem. Motivated only by self-interest and haunted by a constant fear of death, each individual, if left to his own devices, will do everything he can to gain an advantage over his fellows. The result of this struggle for supremacy, according to Hobbes, is a constant war in which human life becomes "solitary, poor, nasty, brutish, and short." To rescue humanity from such destructive anarchy, it is necessary to establish a civil society with laws to govern our conduct and with someone in control, not only with authority to enforce the laws but power to punish whoever breaks them.

Thomas Hobbes was born in 1588—prematurely, it is said—because of his mother's fright at the approach of the Spanish Armada to the shores of England. As he remarked about the event later, "Fear and I, like twins, were born together." Because of his absolutistic political views, he found it expedient to leave England for France in 1640 before the onset of the Puritan Revolution, which drove the Stuarts from the English throne and King Charles I to the scaffold. While in France, he acted as tutor to the future King Charles II, who was also in exile. He returned to England in 1651, where he lived a long life, punctuated by intellectual controversies, until his death in 1679 at the age of ninety-one.

❧ Leviathan

Part I: Of Man
Chapter XIII
Of the natural condition of mankind as concerning their felicity, and misery

Nature hath made men so equal, in the faculties of the body, and mind; as that though there be found one man sometimes manifestly stronger in body, or of quicker mind than another; yet when all is reckoned together, the difference between man, and man, is not so considerable, as that one man can thereupon claim to himself any benefit, to which another may not pretend, as well as he. For as to the strength of body, the weakest has strength enough to kill the strongest, either by se-

First published in 1651.

cret machination, or by confederacy with others, that are in the same danger with himself.

And as to the faculties of the mind, setting aside the arts grounded upon words, and especially that skill of proceeding upon general, and infallible rules, called science; which very few have, and but in few things; as being not a native faculty, born with us; nor attained, as prudence, while we look after somewhat else, I find yet a greater equality amongst men, than that of strength. For prudence, is but experience; which equal time, equally bestows on all men, in those things they equally apply themselves unto. That which may perhaps make such equality incredible, is but a vain conceit of one's own wisdom, which almost all men think they have in a greater degree, than the vulgar; that is, than all men but themselves, and a few others, whom by fame, or for concurring with themselves, they approve. For such is the nature of men, that howsoever they may acknowledge many others to be more witty, or more eloquent, or more learned; yet they will hardly believe there be many so wise as themselves; for they see their own wit at hand, and other men's at a distance. But this proveth rather that men are in that point equal, than unequal. For there is not ordinarily a greater sign of the equal distribution of any thing, than that every man is contented with his share.

From this equality of ability, ariseth equality of hope in the attaining of our ends. And therefore if any two men desire the same thing, which nevertheless they cannot both enjoy, they become enemies; and in the way to their end, which is principally their own conservation, and sometimes their delectation only, endeavour to destroy, or subdue one another. And from hence it comes to pass, that where an invader hath no more to fear, than another man's single power; if one plant, sow, build, and possess a convenient seat, others may probably be expected to come prepared with forces united, to dispossess, and deprive him, not only of the fruit of his labour, but also of his life, or liberty. And the invader again is in the like danger of another.

And from this diffidence of one another, there is no way for any man to secure himself, so reasonable, as anticipation; that is, by force, or wiles, to master the persons of all men he can, so long, till he see no other power great enough to endanger him: and this is no more than his own conservation requireth, and is generally allowed. Also because there be some, that taking pleasure in contemplating their own power in the acts of conquest, which they pursue farther than their security requires; if others, that otherwise would be glad to be at ease within modest bounds, should not by invasion increase their power, they would not be able, long time, by standing only on their defence, to subsist. And by consequence, such augmentation of dominion over men being necessary to a man's conservation, it ought to be allowed him.

Again, men have no pleasure, but on the contrary a great deal of grief, in keeping company, where there is no power able to over-awe them all. For every man looketh that his companion should value him, at the same rate he sets upon himself: and upon all signs of contempt, or undervaluing, naturally endeavours, as far as he dares, (which amongst them that have no common power to keep them in quiet, is far enough to make them destroy each other), to extort a greater value from his contemners, by damage; and from others, by the example.

So that in the nature of man, we find three principal causes of quarrel. First, competition; secondly, diffidence; thirdly, glory.

The first, maketh men invade for gain; the second, for safety; and the third, for reputation. The first use violence, to make themselves masters of other men's persons, wives, children, and cattle; the second, to defend them; the third, for trifles, as a word, a smile, a different opinion, and any other sign of undervalue, either direct in their persons, or by reflection in their kindred, their friends, their nation, their profession, or their name.

Hereby it is manifest, that during the time men live without a common power to keep them all in awe, they are in that condition which is called war; and such a war, as is of every man, against every man. For WAR, consisteth not in battle only, or the act of fighting; but in a tract of time, wherein the will to contend by battle is sufficiently known: and therefore the notion of *time*, is to be considered in the nature of war; as it is in the nature of weather. For as the nature of foul weather, lieth not in a shower or two of rain; but in an inclination thereto of many days together: so the nature of war, consisteth not in actual fighting; but in the known disposition thereto, during all the time there is no assurance to the contrary. All other time is PEACE.

Whatsoever therefore is consequent to a time of war, where every man is enemy to every man; the same is consequent to the time, wherein men live without other security, than what their own strength, and their own invention shall furnish them withal. In such condition, there is no place for industry; because the fruit thereof is uncertain: and consequently no culture of the earth; no navigation, nor use of the commodities that may be imported by sea; no commodious building; no instruments of moving, and removing, such things as require much force; no knowledge of the face of the earth; no account of time; no arts; no letters; no society; and which is worst of all, continual fear, and danger of violent death; and the life of man, solitary, poor, nasty, brutish, and short.

It may seem strange to some man, that has not well weighed these things; that nature should thus dissociate, and render men apt to invade, and destroy one another: and he may therefore, not trusting to this inference, made from the passions, desire perhaps to have the same confirmed by experience. Let him therefore consider with himself, when taking a journey, he arms himself, and seeks to go well accompanied; when going to sleep, he locks his doors; when even in his house he locks his chests; and this when he knows there be laws, and public officers, armed, to revenge all injuries shall be done him; what opinion he has of his fellow-subjects, when he rides armed; of his fellow citizens, when he locks his doors, and of his children, and servants, when he locks his chests. Does he not there as much accuse mankind by his actions, as I do by my words? But neither of us accuse man's nature in it. The desires, and other passions of man, are in themselves no sin. No more are the actions, that proceed from those passions, till they know a law that forbids them: which till laws be made they cannot know: nor can any law be made, till they have agreed upon the person that shall make it.

It may peradventure be thought, there was never such a time, nor condition of war as this; and I believe it was never generally so, over all the world: but there are many places, where they live so now. For the savage people in many places of America, except the government of small families, the concord whereof dependeth on natural lust, have no government at all; and live at this day in that brutish manner, as I said before. Howsoever, it may be perceived what manner of life there would be, where there were no common power to fear, by the manner of life, which men that have formerly lived under a peaceful government, use to degenerate into, in a civil war.

But though there had never been any time, wherein particular men were in a condition of war one against another; yet in all times, kings, and persons of sovereign authority, because of their independency, are in continual jealousies, and in the state and posture of gladiators; having their weapons pointing, and their eyes fixed on one another; that is, their forts, garrisons, and guns upon the frontiers of their kingdoms; and continual spies upon their neighbours; which is a posture of war. But because they uphold thereby, the industry of their subjects; there does not follow from it, that misery, which accompanies the liberty of particular men.

To this war of every man, against every man, this also is consequent; that nothing can be unjust. The notions of right and wrong, justice and injustice have there no place. Where there is no common power, there is no law: where no law, no injustice. Force, and fraud, are in war the two cardinal virtues. Justice, and injustice are none of the faculties neither of the body, or mind. If they were, they might be in a man that were alone in the world, as well as his senses, and passions. They are qualities, that relate to men in society, not in solitude. It is consequent also to the same condition, that there be no propriety, no dominion, no *mine* and *thine* distinct; but only that to be every man's, that he can get; and for so long, as he can keep it. And thus much for the ill condition, which man by mere nature is actually placed in; though with a possibility to come out of it, consisting partly in the passions, partly in his reason.

The passions that incline men to peace, are fear of death; desire of such things as are necessary to commodious living; and a hope by their industry to obtain them. And reason suggesteth convenient articles of peace, upon which men may be drawn to agreement. These articles, are they, which otherwise are called the Laws of Nature, whereof I shall speak more particularly, in the two following chapters.

Chapter XIV
Of the first and second natural laws, and of contracts

The RIGHT OF NATURE, which writers commonly call *jus naturale*, is the liberty each man hath, to use his own power, as he will himself, for the preservation of his own nature; that is to say, of his own life; and consequently, of doing any thing, which in his own judgment, and reason, he shall conceive to be the aptest means thereunto.

By LIBERTY, is understood, according to the proper signification of the word, the absence of external impediments: which impediments, may oft take away part of a man's power to do what he would; but cannot hinder him from using the power left him, according as his judgment, and reason shall dictate to him.

A LAW OF NATURE, *lex naturalis*, is a precept or general rule, found out by reason, by which a man is forbidden to do that, which is destructive of his life, or taketh away the means of preserving the same; and to omit that, by which he thinketh it may be best preserved. For though they that speak of this subject, use to confound *jus*, and *lex*, *right* and *law:* yet they ought to be distinguished; because RIGHT, consisteth in liberty to do, or to forbear; whereas LAW, determineth, and bindeth to one of them: so that law, and right, differ as much, as obligation, and liberty; which in one and the same matter are inconsistent.

And because the condition of man, as hath been declared in the precedent chapter, is a condition of war of every one against every one: in which case every one is governed by his own reason; and there is nothing he can make use of, that may not be a help unto him, in preserving his life against his enemies; it followeth, that in such a condition, every man has a right to every thing; even to one another's body. And therefore, as long as this natural right of every man to every thing endureth, there can be no security to any man, how strong or wise soever he be, of living out the time, which nature ordinarily alloweth men to live. And consequently it is a precept, or general rule of reason, *that every man, ought to endeavor peace, as far as he has hope of obtaining it; and when he cannot obtain it, that he may seek, and use, all helps, and advantages of war.* The first branch of which rule, containeth the first and fundamental law of nature; which is, *to seek peace, and follow it.* The second, the sum of the right of nature; which is, *by all means we can, to defend ourselves.*

From this fundamental law of nature, by which men are commanded to endeavour peace, is derived this second law; *that a man be willing, when others are so too, as far-forth, as for peace, and defence of himself he shall think it necessary, to lay down this right to all things; and be contented with so much liberty against other men as he would allow other men against himself.* For as long as every man holdeth this right, of doing any thing he liketh; so long are all men in the condition of war. But if other men will not lay down their right, as well as he; then there is no reason for any one, to divest himself of his: for that were to expose himself to prey, which no man is bound to, rather than to dispose himself to peace. This is that law of the Gospel; *whatsoever you require that others should do to you, that do ye to them.* And that law of all men, *quod tibi fieri non vis, alteri ne feceris.*

To *lay down* a man's *right* to any thing, is to *divest* himself of the *liberty*, of hindering another of the benefit of his own right to the same. For he that renounceth, or passeth away his right, giveth not to any other man a right which he had not before; because there is nothing to which every man had not right by nature: but only standeth out of his way, that he may enjoy his own original right, without hindrance from him; not without hindrance from another. So that the effect which redoundeth to one man, by another man's defect of right, is but so much diminution of impediments to the use of his own right original.

Right is laid aside, either by simply renouncing it; or by transferring it to another. By *simply* RENOUNCING; when he cares not to whom the benefit thereof redoundeth. By TRANSFERRING; when he intendeth the benefit thereof to some certain person, or persons. And when a man hath in either manner abandoned, or granted away his right, then is he said to be OBLIGED, or BOUND, not to hinder those, to whom such right is granted, or abandoned, from the benefit of it: and that he *ought,* and it is his DUTY, not to make void that voluntary act of his own: and that such hindrance is INJUSTICE, and IN-JURY, and being *sine jure;* the right being before renounced, or transferred. So that *injury,* or *injustice,* in the controversies of the world, is somewhat like to that, which in the disputations of scholars is called *absurdity.* For as it is there called an absurdity, to contradict what one maintained in the beginning: so in the world, it is called injustice, and injury, voluntarily to undo that, which from the beginning he had voluntarily done. The way by which a man either simply renounceth, or transferreth his right, is a declaration, or signification, by some voluntary and sufficient sign, or signs, that he doth so renounce, or transfer; or hath so renounced, or transferred the same, to him that accepteth it. And these signs are either words only, or actions only; or, as it happeneth most often, both words, and actions. And the same are the BONDS, by which men are bound, and obliged: bonds, that have their strength, not from their own nature, for nothing is more easily broken than a man's word, but from fear of some evil consequences upon the rupture.

Whensoever a man transferreth his right, or renounceth it; it is either in con-sideration of some right reciprocally trans-ferred to himself; or for some other good he hopeth for thereby. For it is a voluntary act: and of the voluntary acts of every man the object is some *good to himself.* And therefore there be some rights, which no man can be understood by any words, or other signs, to have abandoned, or trans-ferred. As first a man cannot lay down the right of resisting them, that assault him by force, to take away his life; because he cannot be understood to aim thereby, at any good to himself. The same may be said of wounds, and chains, and imprisonment; both because there is no benefit consequent to such patience; as there is to the patience of suffering another to be wounded, or imprisoned: as also because a man cannot tell, when he seeth men proceed against him by violence, whether they intend his death or not. And lastly the motive, and end for which this renouncing, and trans-ferring of rights is introduced, is nothing else but the security of a man's person, in his life, and in the means of so preserving life, as not to be weary of it. And therefore if a man by words, or other signs, seem to despoil himself of the end, for which those signs were intended; he is not to be un-derstood as if he meant it, or that it was his will; but that he was ignorant of how such words and actions were to be interpreted.

The mutual transferring of right, is that which men call CONTRACT.

• • •

If a covenant be made, wherein neither of the parties perform presently, but trust one another; in the condition of mere nature, which is a condition of war of every man against every man, upon any reason-able suspicion, it is void: but if there be a common power set over them both, with right and force sufficient to compel per-formance, it is not void. For he that per-formeth first, has no assurance the other will perform after; because the bonds of words are too weak to bridle men's ambi-tion, avarice, anger, and other passions, without the fear of some coercive power;

which in the condition of mere nature, where all men are equal, and judges of the justness of their own fears, cannot possibly be supposed. And therefore he which performeth first, does but betray himself to his enemy; contrary to the right, he can never abandon, of defending his life, and means of living.

But in a civil estate, where there is a power set up to constrain those that would otherwise violate their faith, that fear is no more reasonable; and for that cause, he which by the covenant is to perform first, is obliged so to do.

• • •

The force of words, being, as I have formerly noted, too weak to hold men to the performance of their covenants; there are in man's nature, but two imaginable helps to strengthen it. And those are either a fear of the consequence of breaking their word; or a glory, or pride in appearing not to need to break it. This latter is a generosity too rarely found to be presumed on, especially in the pursuers of wealth, command, or sensual pleasure; which are the greatest part of mankind. The passion to be reckoned upon, is fear.

• • •

Chapter XV
Of other laws of nature

From that law of nature, by which we are obliged to transfer to another, such rights, as being retained, hinder the peace of mankind, there followeth a third; which is this, *that men perform their covenants made*: without which, covenants are in vain, and but empty words; and the right of all men to all things remaining, we are still in the condition of war.

And in this law of nature, consisteth the fountain and original of JUSTICE. For where no covenant hath preceded, there hath no right been transferred, and every man has right to every thing; and consequently, no action can be unjust. But when a covenant is made, then to break it is *unjust*: and the definition of INJUSTICE,

is no other than *the not performance of covenant*. And whosoever is not unjust, is *just*.

But because covenants of mutual trust, where there is a fear of not performance on either part, as hath been said in the former chapter, are invalid; though the original of justice be the making of covenants; yet injustice actually there can be none, till the cause of such fear be taken away; which while men are in the natural condition of war, cannot be done. Therefore before the names of just, and unjust can have place, there must be some coercive power, to compel men equally to the performance of their covenants, by the terror of some punishment, greater than the benefit they expect by the breach of their covenant; and to make good that propriety, which by mutual contract men acquire, in recompense of the universal right they abandon: and such power there is none before the erection of a commonwealth. And this is also to be gathered out of the ordinary definition of justice in the Schools: for they say, that *justice is the constant will of giving to every man his own*. And therefore where there is no *own*, that is no propriety, there is no injustice; and where there is no coercive power erected, that is, where there is no commonwealth, there is no propriety; all men having right to all things: therefore where there is no commonwealth, there nothing is unjust. So that the nature of justice, consisteth in keeping of valid covenants: but the validity of covenants begins not but with the constitution of a civil power, sufficient to compel men to keep them: and then it is also that propriety begins.

• • •

Part II: Of Commonwealth
Chapter XVII
Of the causes, generation, and definition of a commonwealth

The final cause, end, or design of men, who naturally love liberty, and dominion over others, in the introduction of that restraint upon themselves, in which we see them live in commonwealths, is the foresight of their own preservation, and of a more contented life thereby; that is to say, of getting themselves out from that miserable condition of war, which is necessarily consequent, as hath been shown in Chapter XIII, to the natural passions of men, when there is no visible power to keep them in awe, and tie them by fear of punishment to the performance of their covenants, and observation of those laws of nature set down in the fourteenth and fifteenth chapters.

For the laws of nature, as *justice, equity, modesty, mercy,* and in sum, *doing to others, as we would be done to,* of themselves, without the terror of some power, to cause them to be observed, are contrary to our natural passions, that carry us to partiality, pride, revenge, and the like. And covenants, without the sword, are but words, and of no strength to secure a man at all. Therefore notwithstanding the laws of nature, which every one hath then kept, when he has the will to keep them, when he can do it safely, if there be no power erected, or not great enough for our security; every man will, and may lawfully rely on his own strength and art, for caution against all other men. And in all places, where men have lived by small families, to rob and spoil one another, has been a trade, and so far from being reputed against the law of nature, that the greater spoils they gained, the greater was their honour; and men observed no other laws therein, but the laws of honour; that is, to abstain from cruelty, leaving to men their lives, and instruments of husbandry. And as small families did then; so now do cities and kingdoms which are but greater families, for their own security, enlarge their dominions, upon all pretences of danger, and fear of invasion, or assistance that may be given to invaders, and endeavour as much as they can, to subdue, or weaken their neighbours, by open force, and secret arts, for want of other caution, justly; and are remembered for it in after ages with honour.

Nor is it the joining together of a small number of men, that gives them this security; because in small numbers, small actions on the one side or the other, make the advantage of strength so great, as is sufficient to carry the victory; and therefore gives encouragement to an invasion. The multitude sufficient to confide in for our security, is not determined by any certain number, but by comparison with the enemy we fear; and is then sufficient, when the odds of the enemy is not of so visible and conspicuous moment, to determine the event of war, as to move him to attempt.

And be there never so great a multitude; yet if their actions be directed according to their particular judgments, and particular appetites, they can expect thereby no defence, nor protection, neither against a common enemy, nor against the injuries of one another. For being distracted in opinions concerning the best use and application of their strength, they do not help but hinder one another; and reduce their strength by mutual opposition to nothing: whereby they are easily, not only subdued by a very few that agree together; but also when there is no common enemy, they make war upon each other, for their particular interests. For if we could suppose a great multitude of men to consent in the observation of justice, and other laws of nature, without a common power to keep them all in awe; we might as well suppose all mankind to do the same; and then there neither would be, nor need to be any civil government, or commonwealth at all; because there would be peace without subjection.

Nor is it enough for the security, which men desire should last all the time of their life, that they be governed, and directed by one judgment, for a limited time; as in one battle, or one war. For though they obtain a victory by their unanimous endeavour against a foreign enemy; yet afterwards, when either they have no common enemy, or he that by one part is held for an enemy, is by another part held for a friend, they must needs by the difference of their interest dissolve, and fall again into a war amongst themselves.

It is true, that certain living creatures, as bees, and ants, live sociably one with another, which are therefore by Aristotle numbered amongst political creatures; and yet have no other direction, than their particular judgments and appetites; nor speech, whereby one of them can signify to another, what he thinks expedient for the common benefit: and therefore some man may perhaps desire to know, why mankind cannot do the same. To which I answer.

First, that men are continually in competition for honour and dignity, which these creatures are not; and consequently amongst men there ariseth on that ground, envy and hatred, and finally war; but amongst these not so.

Secondly, that amongst these creatures, the common good differeth not from the private; and being by nature inclined to their private, they procure thereby the common benefit. But man, whose joy consisteth in comparing himself with other men, can relish nothing but what is eminent.

Thirdly, that these creatures, having not, as man, the use of reason, do not see, nor think they see any fault, in the administration of their common business; whereas amongst men, there are very many, that think themselves wiser, and abler to govern the public, better than the rest; and these strive to reform and innovate, one this way, another that way; and thereby bring it into distraction and civil war.

Fourthly, that these creatures, though they have some use of voice, in making known to one another their desires, and other affections; yet they want that art of words, by which some men can represent to others, that which is good, in the likeness of evil; and evil, in the likeness of good; and augment, or diminish the apparent greatness of good and evil; discontenting men, and troubling their peace at their pleasure.

Fifthly, irrational creatures cannot distinguish between *injury,* and *damage*; and therefore as long as they be at ease, they are not offended with their fellows: whereas man is then most troublesome, when he is most at ease: for then it is that he loves to shew his wisdom, and control the actions of them that govern the commonwealth.

Lastly, the agreement of these creatures is natural; that of men, is by covenant only, which is artificial: and therefore it is no wonder if there be somewhat else required, besides covenant, to make their agreement constant and lasting; which is a common power, to keep them in awe, and to direct their actions to the common benefit.

The only way to erect such a common power, as may be able to defend them from the invasion of foreigners, and the injuries of one another, and thereby to secure them in such sort, as that by their own industry, and by the fruits of the earth, they may nourish themselves and live contentedly; is, to confer all their power and strength upon one man, or upon one assembly of men, that may reduce all their wills, by plurality of voices, unto one will: which is as much as to say, to appoint one man, or assembly of men, to bear their person; and every one to own, and acknowledge himself to be author of whatsoever he that so beareth their person, shall act, or cause to be acted, in those things which concern the common peace and safety; and therein to submit their wills, every one to his will, and their judgments, to his judgment. This is more than consent, or concord; it is a real unity of them all, in one and the same person, made by covenant of every man with every man, in such a manner, as if every man should say to every man, *I authorise and give up my right of governing myself, to this man, or to this assembly of men, on this condition, that thou give up thy right to him, and authorise all his actions in like manner.* This done, the multitude so united in one person, is called a COMMONWEALTH, in Latin CIVITAS. This is the generation of that great LEVIATHAN, or rather, to speak more reverently, of that *mortal god,* to which we owe under the *immortal God,* our peace and defence. For by this authority, given him by every particular man in the commonwealth, he hath the use of so much power and strength conferred on him, that by terror thereof, he is enabled to perform the wills of them all, to peace at home, and mutual aid against their enemies abroad. And in him consisteth the essence of the commonwealth; which, to define it, is *one person, of whose acts a great multitude, by mutual covenants one with another, have made themselves every one the author, to the end he may use the strength and means of them all, as he shall think expedient, for their peace and common defence.*

And he that carrieth this person, is called SOVEREIGN, and said to have *sovereign power*; and every one besides, his SUBJECT.

STUDY QUESTIONS

1. What do you think of Hobbes' view of human nature? If people are as he describes, do you believe they could ever join forces to form a stable society?

2. Do you agree with Hobbes that where there is no law, nothing is right or wrong, just or unjust? Would Robinson Crusoe have been morally blameless if he had murdered Friday?

3. What does Hobbes mean by the right of nature? A law of nature?

4. For what reason do individuals accept the social contract and join societies under government? What does their reason for doing so tell you about human nature, as Hobbes views it?

5. Why does Hobbes believe that government must have absolute power over the populace? Who will there be to control the actions of the sovereign?

For Further Reading

Gauthier, D. P. *The Logic of Leviathan.* Oxford: Clarendon Press, 1969 (Chapters 1 through 4).

Goldsmith, M. M. *Hobbes' Science of Politics.* New York: Columbia University Press, 1966 (Chapters 3 through 6).

Lemos, R. P. *Hobbes and Locke.* Athens, Ga.: University of Georgia Press, 1978 (Part I).

McNeilly, F. S. *The Anatomy of Leviathan.* London: Macmillan. 1968 (Parts II and III).

Sabine, G. H. *A History of Political Theory.* 2d ed. New York: Holt, Rinehart and Winston, 1973 (Chapter 23).

Warrender, H. *The Political Philosophy of Hobbes.* Oxford: Clarendon Press, 1957.

LOCKE: THE SOCIAL CONTRACT

Unless it is considered to be arbitrary, the power that the state exercises over its citizens requires justification. The question, Why should we obey the laws? needs an answer. Socrates discussed this issue with Crito as he awaited execution in his Athenian prison, concluding that he should not follow Crito's plan to escape because he had, by living his entire life in Athens, agreed to abide by its laws. This Socratic notion of government by consent, or the social contract theory, has had a long history in Western thought. It became particularly important in the early modern world, as the various countries of Western Europe strove to throw off the yoke of absolute monarchy. One of its most important spokesmen was John Locke, who wrote at the time of the Glorious Revolution in late seventeenth-century England. His ideas about government by consent of the governed were to bear particularly significant fruit a century later when a group of men in a colony in North America gathered together to produce a revolutionary document known as the Declaration of Independence.

By profession John Locke (1632–1704) was a doctor. A few years after completing his studies at Oxford University, he accepted the position of physician to Lord Ashley, who later became Earl of Shaftesbury. His association with Shaftesbury profoundly affected the course of his life. During the troubled times of the seventeenth century, Shaftesbury's political fortunes, and hence those of Locke, fluctuated wildly. In 1672 Shaftesbury became Lord Chancellor, and Locke was appointed to an important position in the government. A few years later, however, Shaftesbury supported a losing cause, so had to flee to Holland where he died in 1683. Locke followed his patron into exile, remaining in Holland until 1689, when he was able to return to England in triumph, a supporter of the Glorious Revolution and friend of the newly crowned monarchs, William and Mary.

❦ The Second Treatise of Civil Government

I

I think it may not be amiss to set down what I take to be political power; that the power of a magistrate over a subject may be distinguished from that of a father over his children, a master over his servants, a husband over his wife, and a lord over his slave. All which distinct powers happening sometimes together in the same man, if he be considered under these different relations, it may help us to distinguish these powers one from another, and show the difference betwixt a ruler of a commonwealth, a father of a family, and a captain of a galley.

Political power, then, I take to be a right of making laws with penalties of death, and consequently all less penalties, for the regulating and preserving of property, and of employing the force of the community, in the execution of such laws, and in the defence of the commonwealth from foreign injury; and all this only for the public good.

II

Of the state of nature

To understand political power right, and derive it from its original, we must consider what state all men are naturally in, and that

First published in 1690.

is, a state of perfect freedom to order their actions and dispose of their possessions and persons, as they think fit, within the bounds of the law of nature; without asking leave, or depending upon the will of any other man.

A state also of equality, wherein all the power and jurisdiction is reciprocal, no one having more than another; there being nothing more evident, than that creatures of the same species and rank, promiscuously born to all the same advantages of nature, and the use of the same faculties, should also be equal one amongst another without subordination or subjection; unless the lord and master of them all should, by any manifest declaration of his will, set one above another, and confer on him, by an evident and clear appointment, an undoubted right to dominion and sovereignty . . . .

But though this be a state of liberty, yet it is not a state of licence: though man in that state have an uncontrollable liberty to dispose of his person or possessions, yet he has not liberty to destroy himself, or so much as any creature in his possession, but where some nobler use than its bare preservation calls for it. The state of nature has a law of nature to govern it, which obliges every one: and reason, which is that law, teaches all mankind, who will but consult it, that being all equal and independent, no one ought to harm another in his life, health, liberty, or possessions: for men being all the workmanship of one omnipotent and infinitely wise Maker; all the servants of one sovereign master, sent into the world by his order, and about his business; they are his property, whose workmanship they are, made to last during his, not another's pleasure: and being furnished with like faculties, sharing all in one community of nature, there cannot be supposed any such subordination among us, that may authorize us to destroy another, as if we were made for one another's uses, as the inferior ranks of creatures are for ours. Every one, as he is bound to preserve himself, and not to quit his station wilfully, so by the like reason, when his own preservation comes not in competition, ought he, as much as he can, to preserve the rest of mankind, and may not, unless it be to do justice to an offender, take away or impair the life, or what tends to the preservation of life, the liberty, health, limb, or goods of another.

And that all men may be restrained from invading others' rights, and from doing hurt to one another, and the law of nature be observed, which willeth the peace and preservation of all mankind, the execution of the law of nature is, in that state, put into every man's hands, whereby every one has a right to punish the transgressors of that law to such a degree as may hinder its violation: for the law of nature would, as all other laws that concern men in this world, be in vain, if there were nobody that in the state of nature had a power to execute that law, and thereby preserve the innocent and restrain offenders. And if any one in the state of nature may punish another for any evil he has done, every one may do so: for in that state of perfect equality, where naturally there is no superiority or jurisdiction of one over another, what any may do in prosecution of that law, every one must needs have a right to do.

And thus, in the state of nature, "one man comes by a power over another"; but yet no absolute or arbitrary power, to use a criminal, when he has got him in his hands, according to the passionate heats, or boundless extravagancy of his own will; but only to retribute to him, so far as calm reason and conscience dictate, what is proportionate to his transgression; which is so much as may serve for reparation and restraint: for these two are the only reasons, why one man may lawfully do harm to another, which is that we call punishment. In transgressing the law of nature, the offender declares himself to live by another rule than that of reason and common equity, which is that measure God has set to the actions of men, for their mutual security; and so he becomes dangerous to mankind, the tie, which is to secure them from injury and violence, being slighted and broken by him. Which being a trespass against the whole species, and the peace and safety of it, provided for by the law of nature; every man upon this score, by the right he hath to preserve mankind in general, may restrain, or, where it is necessary, destroy things noxious to them, and so may bring such evil on any one, who hath transgressed that law, as may make him repent the doing of it, and thereby deter him, and by his example others, from doing the like mischief. And in this case, and upon this ground, "every man hath a right to punish the offender, and be executioner of the law of nature."

III

Of the state of war

The state of war is a state of enmity and destruction: and therefore declaring by word or action, not a passionate and hasty, but a sedate settled design upon another man's life, puts him in a state of war with him against whom he has declared such an intention, and so has exposed his life to the other's power to be taken away by him, or any one that joins with him in his defence, and espouses his quarrel; it being reasonable and just, I should have a right to destroy that which threatens me with destruction; for, by the fundamental law of nature, man being to be preserved as much as possible, when all cannot be preserved, the safety of the innocent is to be preferred: and one may destroy a man who makes war upon him, or has discovered an enmity to his being, for the same reason that he may kill a wolf or a lion; because such men are not under the ties of the common law of reason, have no other rule, than that of force and violence, and so may be treated as beasts of prey, those dangerous and noxious creatures, that will be sure to destroy him whenever he falls into their power.

And hence it is, that he who attempts to get another man into his absolute power, does thereby put himself into a state of war with him; it being to be understood as a declaration of a design upon his life: for I have reason to conclude, that he who would get me into his power without my consent, would use me as he pleased when he got me there, and destroy me too when he had a fancy to it; for nobody can desire to have me in his absolute power, unless it be to compel me by force to that which is against the right of my freedom, *i.e.*, make me a slave. To be free from such force is the only security of my preservation; and reason bids me look on him, as an enemy to my preservation, who would take away that freedom which is the fence to it; so that he who makes an attempt to enslave me, thereby puts himself into a state of war with me. He that, in the state of nature, would take away the freedom that belongs to any one in that state, must necessarily be supposed to have a design to take away every thing else, that freedom being the foundation of all the rest; as he that, in the state of society, would take away the freedom belonging to those of that society or commonwealth, must be supposed to design to take away from them every thing else, and so be looked on as in a state of war.

This makes it lawful for a man to kill a thief, who has not in the least hurt him, nor declared any design upon his life, any farther than, by the use of force, so to get him in his power, as to take away his money, or what he pleases, from him; because using force, where he has no right,

to get me into his power, let his pretence be what it will, I have no reason to suppose, that he, who would take away my liberty, would not, when he had me in his power, take away every thing else. And therefore it is lawful for me to treat him as one who has put himself into a state of war with me, *i.e.*, kill him if I can; for to that hazard does he justly expose himself, whoever introduces a state of war, and is aggressor in it.

And here we have the plain "difference between the state of nature and the state of war," which however some men have confounded, are as far distant, as a state of peace, good-will, mutual assistance and preservation, and a state of enmity, malice, violence and mutual destruction, are one from another. Men living together according to reason, without a common superior on earth, with authority to judge between them, is properly the state of nature. But force, or a declared design of force, upon the person of another, where there is no common superior on earth to appeal to for relief, is the state of war: and it is the want of such an appeal gives a man the right of war even against an aggressor, though he be in society and a fellow-subject.

IV

Of slavery

The natural liberty of man is to be free from any superior power on earth, and not to be under the will or legislative authority of man, but to have only the law of nature for his rule. The liberty of man, in society, is to be under no other legislative power, but that established, by consent, in the commonwealth; nor under the dominion of any will, or restraint of any law, but what that legislative shall enact, according to the trust put in it. Freedom then is not what Sir Robert Filmer tells us, "a liberty for every one to do what he lists, to live as he pleases, and not to be tied by any laws": but freedom of men under government is, to have a standing rule to live by, common to every one of that society, and made by the legislative power erected in it; a liberty to follow my own will in all things, where the rule prescribes not; and not to be subject to the inconstant, uncertain, unknown, arbitrary will of another man: as freedom of nature is, to be under no other restraint but the law of nature.

This freedom from absolute, arbitrary power, is so necessary to, and closely joined with a man's preservation, that he cannot part with it, but by what forfeits his preservation and life together.

V

Of property

God, who hath given the world to men in common, hath also given them reason to make use of it to the best advantage of life, and convenience. The earth, and all that is therein, is given to men for the support and comfort of their being. And though all the fruits it naturally produces, and beasts it feeds, belong to mankind in common, as they are produced by the spontaneous hand of nature; and nobody has originally a private dominion, exclusive of the rest of mankind, in any of them, as they are thus in their natural state; yet being given for the use of men, there must of necessity be a means to appropriate them some way or other, before they can be of any use, or at all beneficial to any particular man. The fruit, or venison, which nourishes the wild Indian, who knows no enclosure, and is still a tenant in common, must be his, and so his, *i.e.,* a part of him, that another can no longer have any right to it, before it can do him any good for the support of his life.

Though the earth, and all inferior creatures, be common to all men, yet every man has a property in his own person: this nobody has any right to but himself. The labour of his body, and the work of his hands, we may say, are properly his. Whatsoever then he removes out of the state that nature hath provided, and left it in, he hath mixed his labour with, and joined to it something that is his own, and thereby makes it his property. It being by him removed from the common state nature hath placed it in, it hath by this labour something annexed to it, that excludes the common right of other men. For this labour being the unquestionable property of the labourer, no man but he can have a right to what that is once joined to, at least where there is enough, and as good, left in common for others.

He that is nourished by the acorns he picked up under an oak, or the apples he gathered from the trees in the wood, has certainly appropriated them to himself. Nobody can deny but the nourishment is his. I ask then, when did they begin to be his? when he digested? or when he eat? or when he boiled? or when he brought them home? or when he picked them up? and it is plain, if the first gathering made them not his, nothing else could. That labour put a distinction between them and common: that added something to them more than nature, the common mother of all, had done and so they became his private right. And will any one say he had no right to those acorns or apples he thus appropriated, because he had not the consent of all mankind to make them his? was it a robbery thus to assume to himself what belonged to all in common? If such a consent as that was necessary, man had starved, notwithstanding the plenty God had given him. We see in commons, which remain so by compact, that it is the taking any part of what is common, and removing it out of the state nature leaves it in, which begins the property; without which the common is of no use. And the taking of this or that part does not depend on the express consent of all the commoners. Thus the grass my horse has bit; the turfs my servant has cut; and the ore I have digged in any place, where I have a right to them in common with others, become my property, without the assignation or consent of any body. The labour that was mine, removing them out of that common state they were in, hath fixed my property in them.

• • •

It will perhaps be objected to this, that "if gathering the acorns, or other fruits of the earth, &c. makes a right to them, then any one may engross as much as he will." To which I answer, Not so. The same law of nature, that does by this means give us property, does also bound that property too. "God has given us all things richly," I Tim. vi. 17, is the voice of reason confirmed by inspiration. But how far has he given it us? To enjoy. As much as any one can make use of to any advantage of life before it spoils, so much he may by his labour fix a property in: whatever is beyond this, is more than his share, and belongs to others. Nothing was made by God for man to spoil or destroy. And thus, considering the plenty of natural provisions there was a long time in the world, and the few spenders; and to how small a part of that provision the industry of one man could extend itself, and engross it to the prejudice of others; especially keeping within the bounds, set by reason, of what might serve for his use; there could be then little room for quarrels or contentions about property so established.

But the chief matter of property being now not the fruits of the earth, and the beasts that subsist on it, but the earth itself; as that which takes in, and carries with it all the rest; I think it is plain, that property in that too is acquired as the former. As much land as a man tills, plants, improves, cultivates, and can use the product of, so much is his property. He by his labour does, as it were, enclose it from the common. Nor will it invalidate his right, to say every body else has an equal title to it, and therefore he cannot appropriate, he cannot enclose, without the consent of all his fellow commoners, all mankind. God, when he gave the world in common to all mankind, commanded man also to labour, and the penury of his condition required it of him. God and his reason commanded him to subdue the earth, i.e., improve it for the benefit of life, and therein lay out something upon it that was his own, his labour. He that, in obedience to this command of God, subdued, tilled, and sowed any part of it, thereby annexed to it something that was his property, which another had no

title to, nor could without injury take from him.

• • •

Nor is it so strange, as perhaps before consideration it may appear, that the property of labour should be able to overbalance the community of land: for it is labour indeed that puts the difference of value on every thing; and let any one consider what the difference is between an acre of land planted with tobacco or sugar, sown with wheat or barley, and an acre of the same land lying in common, without any husbandry upon it, and he will find, that the improvement of labour makes the far greater part of the value. I think it will be but a very modest computation to say, that of the products of the earth useful to the life of man, nine-tenths are the effects of labour: nay, if we will rightly estimate things as they come to our use, and cast up the several expenses about them, what in them is purely owing to nature, and what to labour, we shall find, that in most of them ninety-nine hundredths are wholly to be put on the account of labour.

VII
Of political or civil society
Whenever . . . any number of men are so united into one society, as to quit everyone his executive power of the law of nature, and to resign it to the public, there and there only is a political, or civil society. And this is done, wherever any number of men, in the state of nature, enter into society to make one people, one body politic, under one supreme government; or else when any one joins himself to, and incorporates with any government already made: for hereby he authorizes the society, or, which is all one, the legislative thereof, to make laws for him, as the public good of the society shall require; to the execution whereof, his own assistance (as to his own decrees) is due. And this puts men out of a state of nature into that of a common-

wealth, by setting up a judge on earth, with authority to determine all the controversies, and redress the injuries that may happen to any member of the commonwealth: which judge is the legislative, or magistrate appointed by it. And wherever there are any number of men, however associated, that have no such decisive power to appeal to, there they are still in the state of nature.

Hence it is evident, that absolute monarchy, which by some men is counted the only government in the world, is indeed inconsistent with civil society, and so can be no form of civil government at all; for the end of civil society being to avoid and remedy those inconveniences of the state of nature, which necessarily follow from every man being judge in his own case, by setting up a known authority, to which every one of that society may appeal upon any injury received, or controversy that may arise, and which every one of the society ought to obey; wherever any persons are, who have not such an authority to appeal to for the decision of any difference between them, there those persons are still in the state of nature and so is every absolute prince, in respect of those who are under his dominion.

For he being supposed to have all, both legislative and executive power in himself alone, there is no judge to be found, no appeal lies open to any one, who may fairly and indifferently, and with authority decide, and from whose decision relief and redress may be expected of any injury or inconveniency that may be suffered from the prince, or by his order: so that such a man, however intitled, czar, or grand seignior, or how you please, is as much in the state of nature, with all under his dominion, as he is with the rest of mankind: for wherever any two men are, who have no standing rule, and common judge to appeal to on earth, for the determination of controversies of right betwixt them, there they are still in the state of nature, and under all the inconveniences of it with only this woeful difference to the subject, or rather slave of an absolute prince; that

whereas in the ordinary state of nature he has a liberty to judge of his right, and, according to the best of his power, to maintain it; now whenever his property is invaded by the will and order of his monarch, he has not only no appeal, as those in society ought to have, but, as if he were degraded from the common state of rational creatures, is denied a liberty to judge of, or to defend his right; and so is exposed to all the misery and inconveniences, that a man can fear from one, who being in the unrestrained state of nature, is yet corrupted with flattery, and armed with power.

For he that thinks absolute power purifies men's blood, and corrects the baseness of human nature, need read but the history of this or any other age, to be convinced of the contrary.

VIII
Of the beginning of political societies

Men being, as has been said, by nature, all free, equal, and independent, no one can be put out of this estate, and subjected to the political power of another, without his own consent. The only way, whereby any one divests himself of his natural liberty, and puts on the bonds of civil society, is by agreeing with other men to join and unite into a community, for their comfortable, safe, and peaceable living one amongst another, in a secure enjoyment of their properties, and a greater security against any, that are not of it. This any number of men may do, because it injures not the freedom of the rest; they are left as they were in the liberty of the state of nature. When any number of men have so consented to make one community or government, they are thereby presently incorporated, and make one body politic, wherein the majority have a right to act and conclude the rest.

For when any number of men have, by the consent of every individual, made a community, they have thereby made that community one body, with a power to act as one body, which is only by the will and determination of the majority: for that which acts any community, being only the consent of the individuals of it, and it being necessary to that which is one body to move one way; it is necessary the body should move that way whither the greater force carries it, which is the consent of the majority: or else it is impossible it should act or continue one body, one community, which the consent of every individual that united into it, agreed that it should; and so every one is bound by that consent to be concluded by the majority. And therefore we see, that in assemblies, impowered to act by positive laws, where no number is set by that positive law which impowers them, the act of the majority passes for the act of the whole, and of course determines; as having, by the law of nature and reason, the power of the whole.

And thus every man, by consenting with others to make one body politic under one government, puts himself under an obligation, to every one of that society, to submit to the determination of the majority, and to be concluded by it; or else this original compact, whereby he with others incorporate into one society, would signify nothing, and be no compact, if he be left free, and under no other ties than he was in before in the state of nature.

IX

Of the ends of political society and government

If man in the state of nature be so free, as has been said; if he be absolute lord of his own person and possessions, equal to the greatest, and subject to nobody, why will he part with his freedom? why will he give up his empire, and subject himself to the dominion and control of any other power? To which it is obvious to answer, that though in the state of nature he hath such a right, yet the enjoyment of it is very uncertain, and constantly exposed to the invasion of others; for all being kings as much as he, every man his equal, and the greater part

no strict observers of equity and justice, the enjoyment of the property he has in this state is very unsafe, very unsecure. This makes him willing to quit a condition, which, however free, is full of fears and continual dangers: and it is not without reason, that he seeks out, and is willing to join in society with others, who are already united, or have a mind to unite, for the mutual preservation of their lives, liberties, and estates, which I call by the general name, property.

The great and chief end, therefore, of men's uniting into commonwealths, and putting themselves under government, is the preservation of their property. To which in the state of nature there are many things wanting.

First, There wants an established, settled, known law, received and allowed by common consent to be the standard of right and wrong, and the common measure to decide all controversies between them: for though the law of nature be plain and intelligible to all rational creatures; yet men being biased by their interest, as well as ignorant for want of studying it, are not apt to allow of it as a law binding to them in the application of it to their particular cases.

Secondly, In the state of nature there wants a known and indifferent judge, with authority to determine all differences according to the established law: for every one in that state being both judge and executioner of the law of nature, men being partial to themselves, passion and revenge is very apt to carry them too far, and with too much heat, in their own cases; as well as negligence, and unconcernedness, to make them too remiss in other men's.

Thirdly, In the state of nature, there often wants power to back and support the sentence when right, and to give it due execution. They who by any injustice offend, will seldom fail, where they are able, by force to make good their injustice; such resistance many times makes the punishment dangerous, and frequently destructive, to those who attempt it.

Thus mankind, notwithstanding all the privileges of the state of nature, being but in an ill condition, while they remain in it, are quickly driven into society. Hence it comes to pass that we seldom find any number of men live any time together in this state. The inconveniences that they are therein exposed to, by the irregular and uncertain exercise of the power every man has of punishing the transgressions of others, make them take sanctuary under the established laws of government, and therein seek the preservation of their property. It is this makes them so willingly give up every one his single power of punishing, to be exercised by such alone, as shall be appointed to it amongst them; and by such rules as the community, or those authorized by them to that purpose, shall agree on. And in this we have the original right of both the legislative and executive power, as well as of the governments and societies themselves.

. . .

But though men, when they enter into society, give up the equality, liberty, and executive power they had in the state of nature, into the hands of the society, to be so far disposed of by the legislative, as the good of the society shall require; yet it being only with an intention in every one the better to preserve himself, his liberty and property; (for no rational creature can be supposed to change his condition with an intention to be worse) the power of the society, or legislative constituted by them, can never be supposed to extend farther, than the common good; but is obliged to secure every one's property, by providing against those three defects above mentioned, that made the state of nature so unsafe and uneasy. And so whoever has the legislative or supreme power of any commonwealth, is bound to govern by established standing laws, promulgated and known to the people, and not by extemporary decrees; by indifferent and upright judges, who are to decide controversies by those laws; and to employ the force of the community at home, only in the execution of such laws; or abroad to prevent or redress foreign injuries, and secure the community from inroads and invasion. And all this to be directed to no other end, but the peace, safety, and public good of the people.

XIII

Of the subordination of the powers of the commonwealth

Though in a constituted commonwealth, standing upon its own basis, and acting according to its own nature, that is, acting for the preservation of the community, there can be but one supreme power, which is the legislative, to which all the rest are and must be subordinate; yet the legislative being only a fiduciary power to act for certain ends, there remains still "in the people a supreme power to remove or alter the legislative," when they find the legislative act contrary to the trust reposed in them: for all power given with trust for the attaining an end, being limited by that end; whenever that end is manifestly neglected or opposed, the trust must necessarily be forfeited, and the power devolve into the hands of those that gave it, who may place it anew where they shall think best for their safety and security. And thus the community perpetually retains a supreme power of saving themselves from the attempts and designs of any body, even of their legislators, whenever they shall be so foolish, or so wicked, as to try and carry on designs against the liberties and properties of the subject: for no man, or society of men, having a power to deliver up their preservation, or consequently the means of it, to the absolute will and arbitrary dominion of another; whenever any one shall go about to bring them into such a slavish condition, they will always have a right to preserve what they have not a power to part with; and to rid themselves of those who invade this fundamental, sacred, and unalterable law of self-preservation, for which they entered into society. And thus the community may be said in this respect to be always the supreme power.

XIX
Of the dissolution of government
The reason why men enter into society, is the preservation of their property; and the end why they choose and authorize a legislative, is, that there may be laws made, and rules set, as guards and fences to the properties of all the members of the society: to limit the power, and moderate the dominion, of every part and member of the society: for since it can never be supposed to be the will of the society, that the legislative should have a power to destroy that which every one designs to secure by entering into society, and for which the people submitted themselves to legislators of their own making; whenever the legislators endeavour to take away and destroy the property of the people, or to reduce them to slavery under arbitrary power, they put themselves into a state of war with the people, who are thereupon absolved from any farther obedience, and are left to the common refuge, which God hath provided for all men, against force and violence. Whensoever therefore the legislative shall transgress this fundamental rule of society; and either by ambition, fear, folly or corruption, endeavour to grasp themselves, or put into the hands of any other, an absolute power over the lives, liberties, and estates of the people; by this breach of trust they forfeit the power the people had put into their hands for quite contrary ends, and it devolves to the people, who have a right to resume their original liberty, and, by the establishment of a new legislative, (such as they shall think fit) provide for their own safety and security, which is the end for which they are in society. What I have said here, concerning the legislative in general, holds true also concerning the supreme executor, who having a double trust put in him, both to have a part in the legislative, and the supreme execution of the law, acts against both, when he goes about to set up his own arbitrary will as the law of the society. He acts also contrary to his trust, when he either employs the force, treasure, and offices of the society to corrupt the representatives, and gain them to his purposes; or openly pre-engages the electors, and prescribes to their choice, such, whom he has, by solicitations, threats, promises, or otherwise, won to his designs: and employs them to bring in such, who have promised beforehand what to vote, and what to enact. Thus to regulate candidates and electors, and new-model the ways of election, what is it but to cut up the government by the roots, and poison the very fountain of public security?

• • •

But it will be said, this hypothesis lays a ferment for frequent rebellion. To which I answer,

First, no more than any other hypothesis: for when the people are made miserable, and find themselves exposed to the ill-usage of arbitrary power, cry up their governors as much as you will, for sons of Jupiter; let them be sacred or divine, descended, or authorized from heaven; give them out for whom or what you please, the same will happen. The people generally ill-treated, and contrary to right, will be ready upon any occasion to ease themselves of a burden that sits heavy upon them. They will wish, and seek for the opportunity, which in the change, weakness, and accidents of human affairs, seldom delays long to offer itself. He must have lived but a little while in the world, who has not seen examples of this in his time; and he must have read very little, who cannot produce examples of it in all sorts of governments in the world.

Secondly, I answer, such revolutions happen not upon every little mismanagement in public affairs. Great mistakes in the ruling part, many wrong and inconvenient laws, and all the slips of human frailty, will be borne by the people without mutiny or murmur. But if a long train of abuses, prevarications and artifices, all tending the same way, make the design visible to the people, and they cannot but feel what they lie under, and see whither they are going; it is not to be wondered, that they should then rouse themselves, and endeavour to put the rule into such hands which may secure to them the ends for which government was at first erected; and without which, ancient names, and specious forms, are so far from being better, that they are much worse, than the state of nature, or pure anarchy; the inconveniencies being all as great and as near, but the remedy farther off and more difficult.

Thirdly, I answer, that this doctrine of a power in the people of providing for their safety anew, by a new legislative, when their legislators have acted contrary to their trust, by invading their property, is the best fence against rebellion, and the probablest means to hinder it: for rebellion being an opposition, not to persons, but authority, which is founded only in the constitutions and laws of the government; those, whoever they be, who by force break through, and by force justify their violation of them, are truly and properly rebels: for when men, by entering into society and civil government, have excluded force, and introduced laws for the preservation of property, peace, and unity amongst themselves; those who set up force again in opposition to the laws, do *rebellare*, that is, bring back again the state of war, and are properly rebels; which they who are in power, (by the pretence they have to authority, the temptation of force they have in their hands, and the flattery of those about them) being likeliest to do; the properest way to prevent the evil, is to show them the danger and injustice of it, who are under the greatest temptation to run into it.

In both the forementioned cases, when either the legislative is changed, or the legislators act contrary to the end for which they were constituted, those who are guilty are guilty of rebellion; for if any one by force takes away the established legislative of any society, and the laws by them made

pursuant to their trust, he thereby takes away the umpirage, which every one had consented to, for a peaceable decision of all their controversies, and a bar to the state of war amongst them. They who remove, or change the legislative, take away this decisive power, which nobody can have but by the appointment and consent of the people; and so destroying the authority which the people did, and nobody else can set up, and introducing a power which the people hath not authorized, they actually introduce a state of war, which is that of force without authority; and thus by removing the legislative established by the society, (in whose decisions the people acquiesced and united, as to that of their own will) they untie the knot, and expose the people anew to the state of war. And if those, who by force take away the legislative, are rebels, the legislators themselves, as has been shown, can be no less esteemed so; when they, who were set up for the protection and preservation of the people, their liberties and properties, shall by force invade and endeavour to take them away; and so by putting themselves into a state of war with those who made them the protectors and guardians of their peace, are properly, and with the greatest aggravation, *rebellantes*, rebels.

But if they, who say, "it lays a foundation for rebellion," mean that it may occasion civil wars, or intestine broils, to tell the people they are absolved from obedience when illegal attempts are made upon their liberties or properties, and may oppose the unlawful violence of those who were their magistrates, when they invade their properties contrary to the trust put in them; and that therefore this doctrine is not to be allowed, being so destructive to the peace of the world: they may as well say, upon the same ground, that honest men may not oppose robbers or pirates, because this may occasion disorder or bloodshed. If any mischief come in such cases, it is not to be charged upon him who defends his own right, but on him that invades his neighbour's. If the innocent honest man must quietly quit all he has, for peace sake, to him who will lay violent hands upon it, I desire it may be considered, what a kind of peace there will be in the world, which consists only in violence and rapine; and which is to be maintained only for the benefit of robbers and oppressors.

• • •

Whosoever uses force without right, as every one does in society, who does it without law, puts himself into a state of war with those against whom he so used it; and in that state all former ties are cancelled, all other rights cease, and every one has a right to defend himself, and to resist the aggressor.

STUDY QUESTIONS

1. Locke describes political power as a right. Does it follow from this that he would deny that a tyrannical despot has any political power? Explain.
2. How does Locke describe the state of nature? What is the law of nature?
3. How does Locke justify private property? Does he place any limits on the amount of property any individual may own?
4. Do you agree with Locke's labor theory of value? Explain.
5. What is Locke's objection to absolutism?
6. Under what conditions is revolution justified, according to Locke? Do you agree with him?

For Further Reading

Gough, J. W. *John Locke's Political Philosophy.* 2d ed. Oxford: Clarendon Press, 1973 (Chapters 1 through 5).

Lamprecht, S. *The Moral and Political Philosophy of John Locke.* New York: Russell and Russell, 1962 (Book III).

Lemos, R. M. *Hobbes and Locke.* Athens, Ga.: University of Georgia Press, 1978 (Part II).

Mabbott, J. D. *John Locke.* London: Macmillan, 1973 (Part IV).

Rousseau, J. J. *The Social Contract.*

Sabine, G. H. *A History of Political Theory.* 2d ed. New York: Holt, Rinehart and Winston, 1973 (Chaper 26).

MILL: LIBERALISM

The geographical expansion of the state in modern times, combined with the increasing complexity of society, has led to the diminution of the individual. As writers have often pointed out, we are being reduced to cogs in a machine or to marks on a tape in some governmental vault. Increasingly, people find themselves powerless to exert influence in the direction of political affairs or even in the control of their own careers. The liberal tradition in political thought has resisted such subjugation of the individual to the state, pointing out that it reverses the proper order of our values. The individual does not exist for the sake of the state; rather the state exists for the sake of the individual. Translated into practice the liberal ideal demands the greatest possible liberty for each individual person compatible with a like liberty for everyone else.

John Stuart Mill (1806–1873) was an unusually precocious child. Educated at home by his father, an eminent intellectual, and Jeremy Bentham (see page 187), he progressed rapidly, beginning the study of Greek at the age of three, Latin at eight, and philosophy at twelve. While still in his teens, he took a position as a clerk in the London headquarters of the East India Company where he remained for thirty-five years and rose to an executive position, occupying his spare time with writing, mostly on philosophical and political issues. In 1865 he won a seat in Parliament, where he served for two years. Throughout his life he was very active in the political affairs of England, always on the side of reform.

𝕏 *On Liberty*

Chapter I
Introductory . . .

The object of this Essay is to assert one very simple principle, as entitled to govern absolutely the dealings of society with the individual in the way of compulsion and control, whether the means used be physical force in the form of legal penalties, or the moral coercion of public opinion. That principle is, that the sole end for which mankind are warranted, individually or collectively, in interfering with the liberty of action of any of their number, is self-protection. That the only purpose for which power can be rightfully exercised over any member of a civilized community, against his will, is to prevent harm to others. His own good, either physical or moral, is not a sufficient warrant. He cannot rightfully be compelled to do or forbear because it will be better for him to do so, because it will make him happier, because, in the opinions of others, to do so would be wise, or even right. These are good reasons for remonstrating with him, or reasoning with him, or persuading him, or entreating him, but not for compelling him, or visiting him with any evil in case he do otherwise. To justify that, the conduct from which it is desired to deter him must be calculated to produce evil to some one else. The only part of the conduct of any one, for which he is amenable to society, is that which concerns others. In the part which merely concerns himself, his independence is, of right, absolute. Over himself, over his own body and mind, the individual is sovereign.

It is, perhaps, hardly necessary to say that this doctrine is meant to apply to

First published in 1859.

human beings in the maturity of their faculties. We are not speaking of children, or of young persons below the age which the law may fix as that of manhood or womanhood. Those who are still in a state to require being taken care of by others, must be protected against their actions as well as against external injury. For the same reason, we may leave out of consideration those backward states of society in which the race itself may be considered as in its nonage. The early difficulties in the way of spontaneous progress are so great, that there is seldom any choice of means for overcoming them; and a ruler full of the spirit of improvement is warranted in the use of any expedients that will attain an end, perhaps otherwise unattainable. Despotism is a legitimate mode of government in dealing with barbarians, provided the end be their improvement, and the means justified by actually effecting that end. Liberty, as a principle, has no application to any state of things anterior to the time when mankind have become capable of being improved by free and equal discussion. Until then, there is nothing for them but implicit obedience to an Akbar or a Charlemagne, if they are so fortunate as to find one. But as soon as mankind have attained the capacity of being guided to their own improvement by conviction or persuasion (a period long since reached in all nations with whom we need here concern ourselves), compulsion, either in the direct form or in that of pains and penalties for non-compliance, is no longer admissible as a means to their own good, and justifiable only for the security of others.

It is proper to state that I forego any advantage which could be derived to my argument from the idea of abstract right, as a thing independent of utility. I regard utility as the ultimate appeal on all ethical questions; but it must be utility in the largest sense, grounded on the permanent interests of a man as a progressive being. Those interests, I contend, authorise the subjection of individual spontaneity to external control, only in respect to those actions of each, which concern the interest of other people. If any one does an act hurtful to others, there is a *prima facie* case for punishing him, by law, or, where legal penalties are not safely applicable, by general disapprobation. There are also many positive acts for the benefit of others, which he may rightfully be compelled to perform; such as to give evidence in a court of justice; to bear his fair share in the common defence, or in any other joint work necessary to the interest of the society of which he enjoys the protection; and to perform certain acts of individual beneficence, such as saving a fellow-creature's life, or interposing to protect the defenceless against ill-usage, things which whenever it is obviously a man's duty to do, he may rightfully be made responsible to society for not doing. A person may cause evil to others not only by his actions but by his inaction, and in either case he is justly accountable to them for the injury. The latter case, it is true, requires a much more cautious exercise of compulsion than the former. To make any one answerable for doing evil to others is the rule; to make him answerable for not preventing evil is, comparatively speaking, the exception. Yet there are many cases clear enough and grave enough to justify that exception. In all things which regard the external relations of the individual, he is *de jure* amenable to those whose interests are concerned, and, if need be, to society as their protector. There are often good reasons for not holding him to the responsibility; but these reasons must arise from the special expediencies of the case: either because it is a kind of case in which he is on the whole likely to act better, when left to his own discretion, than when controlled in any way in which society have it in their power to control him; or because

the attempt to exercise control would produce other evils, greater than those which it would prevent. When such reasons as these preclude the enforcement of responsibility, the conscience of the agent himself should step into the vacant judgment seat, and protect those interests of others which have no external protection; judging himself all the more rigidly, because the case does not admit of his being made accountable to the judgment of his fellow-creatures.

But there is a sphere of action in which society, as distinguished from the individual, has, if any, only an indirect interest; comprehending all that portion of a person's life and conduct which affects only himself, or if it also affects others, only with their free, voluntary, and undeceived consent and participation. When I say only himself, I mean directly, and in the first instance; for whatever affects himself, may affect others through himself; and the objection which may be grounded on this contingency, will receive consideration in the sequel. This, then, is the appropriate region of human liberty. It comprises, first, the inward domain of consciousness; demanding liberty of conscience in the most comprehensive sense; liberty of thought and feeling; absolute freedom of opinion and sentiment on all subjects, practical or speculative, scientific, moral, or theological. The liberty of expressing and publishing opinions may seem to fall under a different principle, since it belongs to that part of the conduct of an individual which concerns other people; but, being almost of as much importance as the liberty of thought itself, and resting in great part on the same reasons, is practically inseparable from it. Secondly, the principle requires liberty of tastes and pursuits; of framing the plan of our life to suit our own character; of doing as we like, subject to such consequences as may follow: without impediment from our fellow-creatures, so long as what we do does not harm them, even though they should think our conduct foolish, perverse, or wrong. Thirdly, from this liberty of each individual, follows the liberty, within the same limits, of combination among individuals; freedom to unite, for any purpose not involving harm to others; the persons combining being supposed to be of full age, and not forced or deceived.

No society in which these liberties are not, on the whole, respected, is free, whatever may be its form of government; and none is completely free in which they do not exist absolute and unqualified. The only freedom which deserves the name, is that of pursuing our own good in our own way, so long as we do not attempt to deprive others of theirs, or impede their efforts to obtain it. Each is the proper guardian of his own health, whether bodily, *or* mental and spiritual. Mankind are greater gainers by suffering each other to live as seems good to themselves, than by compelling each to live as seems good to the rest.

Chapter II
Of The Liberty of Thought and Discussion

The time, it is to be hoped, is gone by, when any defence would be necessary of the 'liberty of the press' as one of the securities against corrupt or tyrannical government. No argument, we may suppose, can now be needed, against permitting a legislature or an executive, not identified in interest with the people, to prescribe opinions to them, and determine what doctrines or what arguments they shall be allowed to hear. This aspect of the question, besides, has been so often and so triumphantly enforced by preceding writers, that it needs not be specially insisted on in this place. Though the law of England, on the subject of the press, is as servile to this day as it was in the time of the Tudors, there is little danger of its being actually put in force against political discussion, except during some temporary panic, when fear of insurrection drives ministers and judges from their propriety, and, speaking generally, it is not, in constitutional countries, to be apprehended, that the government, whether completely responsible to the people or not, will often attempt to control the expression of opinion, except when in doing

so it makes itself the organ of the general intolerance of the public. Let us suppose, therefore, that the government is entirely at one with the people, and never thinks of exerting any power of coercion unless in agreement with what it conceives to be their voice. But I deny the right of the people to exercise such coercion, either by themselves or by their government. The power itself is illegitimate. The best government has no more title to it than the worst. It is as noxious, or more noxious, when exerted in accordance with public opinion, than when in opposition to it. If all mankind minus one were of one opinion, and only one person were of the contrary opinion, mankind would be no more justified in silencing that one person, than he, if he had the power, would be justified in silencing mankind. Were an opinion a personal possession of no value except to the owner; if to be obstructed in the enjoyment of it were simply a private injury, it would make some difference whether the injury was inflicted only on a few persons or on many. But the peculiar evil of silencing the expression of opinion is, that it is robbing the human race; posterity as well as the existing generation; those who dissent from the opinion, still more than those who hold it. If the opinion is right, they are deprived of the opportunity of exchanging error for truth; if wrong, they lose, what is almost as great a benefit, the clearer perception and livelier impression of truth, produced by its collision with error.

• • •

Mankind can hardly be too often reminded, that there was once a man named Socrates, between whom and the legal authorities and public opinion of his time there took place a memorable collision. Born in an age and country abounding in individual greatness, this man has been handed down to us by those who best knew both him and the age, as the most virtuous man in it; while *we* know him as the head and prototype of all subsequent teachers of virtue, the source equally of the lofty inspiration of Plato and the judicious utilitarianism of Aristotle, 'i maëstri di color che sanno' ["the masters of whose who know"], the two headsprings of ethical as of all other philosophy. This acknowledged master of all the eminent thinkers who have since lived—whose fame still growing after more than two thousand years, all but outweighs the whole remainder of the names which make his native city illustrious—was put to death by his countrymen, after a judicial conviction, for impiety and immorality. Impiety, in denying the gods recognized by the State; indeed his accuser asserted (see the 'Apologia') that he believed in no gods at all. Immorality, in being, by his doctrines and instructions, a 'corrupter of youth.' Of these charges the tribunal, there is every ground for believing, honestly found him guilty, and condemned the man who probably of all then born had deserved best of mankind to be put to death as a criminal.

To pass from this to the only other instance of judicial iniquity, the mention of which, after the condemnation of Socrates, would not be an anti-climax: the event which took place on Calvary rather more than eighteen hundred years ago. The man who left on the memory of those who witnessed his life and conversation such an impression of his moral grandeur that eighteen subsequent centuries have done homage to him as the Almighty in person, was ignominiously put to death, as what? As a blasphemer. Men did not merely mistake their benefactor; they mistook him for the exact contrary of what he was, and treated him as that prodigy of impiety which they themselves are now held to be for their treatment of him. The feelings with which mankind now regard these lamentable transactions, especially the later of the two, render them extremely unjust in their judgment of the unhappy actors. These were, to all appearance, not bad men—not worse than men commonly are, but rather the contrary; men who possessed in a full, or somewhat more than a full measure, the religious, moral, and patriotic feelings of their time and people: the

very kind of men, who, in all times, our own included, have every chance of passing through life blameless and respected. The high-priest who rent his garments when the words were pronounced, which, according to all the ideas of his country, constituted the blackest guilt, was in all probability quite as sincere in his horror and indignation as the generality of respectable and pious men now are in the religious and moral sentiments they profess; and most of those who now shudder at his conduct, if they had lived in his time, and been born Jews, would have acted precisely as he did. Orthodox Christians who are tempted to think that those who stoned to death the first martyrs must have been worse men than they themselves are, ought to remember that one of those persecutors was Saint Paul.

• • •

Before quitting the subject of freedom of opinion, it is fit to take some notice of those who say that the free expression of all opinions should be permitted, on condition that the manner be temperate, and do not pass the bounds of fair discussion. Much might be said on the impossibility of fixing where these supposed bounds are to be placed; for if the test be offence to those whose opinions are attacked, I think experience testifies that this offence is given whenever the attack is telling and powerful, and that every opponent who pushes them hard, and whom they find it difficult to answer, appears to them, if he shows any strong feeling on the subject, an intemperate opponent. But this, though an important consideration on a practical point of view, merges in a more fundamental objection. Undoubtedly the manner of asserting an opinion, even though it be a true one, may be very objectionable, and may justly incur severe censure. But the principal offences of the kind are such as it is mostly impossible, unless by accidental self-betrayal, to bring home to conviction. The gravest of them is, to argue sophistically, to suppress facts or arguments, to misstate the elements of the case, or misrepresent the opposite opinion. But all this, even to the most aggravated degree, is so continually done in perfect good faith, by persons who are not considered, and in many other respects may not deserve to be considered, ignorant or incompetent, that it is rarely possible, on adequate grounds, conscientiously to stamp the misrep. esentation as morally culpable; and still less could law presume to interfere with this kind of controversial misconduct. With regard to what is commonly meant by intemperate discussion, namely invective, sarcasm, personality, and the like, the denunciation of these weapons would deserve more sympathy if it were ever proposed to interdict them equally to both sides; but it is only desired to restrain the employment of them against the prevailing opinion; against the unprevailing they may not only be used without general disapproval, but will be likely to obtain for him who uses them the praise of honest zeal and righteous indignation. Yet whatever mischief arises from their use is greatest when they are employed against the comparatively defenceless; and whatever unfair advantage can be derived by any opinion from this mode of asserting it, accrues almost exclusively to received opinions. The worst offence of this kind which can be committed by a polemic is to stigmatise those who hold the contrary opinion as bad and immoral men. To calumny of this sort, those who hold any unpopular opinion are peculiarly exposed, because they are in general few and uninfluential, and nobody but themselves feels much interested in seeing justice done them; but this weapon is, from the nature of the case, denied to those who attack a prevailing opinion: they can neither use it with safety to themselves, nor, if they could, would it do anything but recoil on their own cause. In general, opinions contrary to those commonly received can only obtain a hearing by studied moderation of language, and the most cautious avoidance of unnecessary offence, from which they hardly ever deviate even in a slight degree without

losing ground: while unmeasured vituperation employed on the side of the prevailing opinion really does deter people from professing contrary opinions, and from listening to those who profess them. For the interest, therefore, of truth and justice, it is far more important to restrain this employment of vituperative language than the other; and, for example, if it were necessary to choose, there would be much more need to discourage offensive attacks on infidelity than on religion. It is, however, obvious that law and authority have no business with restraining either, while opinion ought, in every instance, to determine its verdict by the circumstances of the individual case; condemning every one, on whichever side of the argument he places himself, in whose mode of advocacy either want of candour, or malignity, bigotry, or intolerance of feeling manifest themselves; but not inferring these vices from the side which a person takes, though it be the contrary side of the question to our own; and giving merited honour to every one, whatever opinion he may hold, who has calmness to see and honesty to state what his opponents and their opinions really are, exaggerating nothing to their discredit, keeping nothing back which tells, or can be supposed to tell, in their favour. This is the real morality of public discussion: and if often violated, I am happy to think that there are many controversialists who to a great extent observe it, and a still greater number who conscientiously strive towards it.

Chapter III
Of Individuality, as One of the Elements of Well-Being

Such being the reasons which make it imperative that human beings should be free to form opinions, and to express their opinions without reserve; and such the baneful consequences to the intellectual, and through that to the moral nature of man, unless this liberty is either conceded, or asserted in spite of prohibition; let us next examine whether the same reasons do not require that men should be free to act upon their opinions—to carry these out in their lives, without hindrance, either physical or moral, from their fellow-men, so long as it is at their own risk and peril. This last proviso is of course indispensable. No one pretends that actions should be as free as opinions. On the contrary, even opinions lose their immunity when the circumstances in which they are expressed are such as to constitute their expression a positive instigation to some mischievous act. An opinion that corn-dealers are starvers of the poor, or that private property is robbery, ought to be unmolested when simply circulated through the press, but may justly incur punishment when delivered orally to an excited mob assembled before the house of a corn-dealer, or when handed about among the same mob in the form of a placard. Acts, of whatever kind, which, without justifiable cause, do harm to others, may be, and in the more important cases absolutely require to be, controlled by the unfavourable sentiments, and, when needful, by the active interference of mankind. The liberty of the individual must be thus far limited; he must not make himself a nuisance to other people. But if he refrains from molesting others in what concerns them, and merely acts according to his own inclination and judgment in things which concern himself, the same reasons which show that opinion would be free, prove also that he should be allowed, without molestation, to carry his opinions into practice at his own cost. That mankind are not infallible; that their truths, for the most part, are only half-truths; that unity of opinion, unless resulting from the fullest and freest comparison of opposite opinions, is not desirable, and diversity not an evil, but a good, until mankind are much more capable than at present of recognising all sides of the truth, are principles applicable to men's modes of action, not less than to their opinions. As it is useful that while mankind are imperfect there should be different opinions, so it is that there should be different experiments of living; that free scope should be given to varieties of character, short of injury to others; and

that the worth of different modes of life should be proved practically, when any one thinks fit to try them. It is desirable, in short, that in things which do not primarily concern others, individuality should assert itself. Where, not the person's own character, but the traditions or customs of other people are the rule of conduct, there is wanting one of the principal ingredients of human happiness, and quite the chief ingredient of individual and social progress.

In maintaining this principle, the greatest difficulty to be encountered does not lie in the appreciation of means towards an acknowledged end, but in the indifference of persons in general to the end itself. If it were felt that the free development of individuality is one of the leading essentials of well-being; that it is not only a co-ordinate element with all that is designated by the terms civilization, instruction, education, culture, but is itself a necessary part and condition of all those things; there would be no danger that liberty should be under-valued, and the adjustment of the boundaries between it and social control would present no extraordinary difficulty. But the evil is, that individual spontaneity is hardly recognized by the common modes of thinking as having any intrinsic worth, or deserving any regard on its own account. The majority, being satisfied with the ways of mankind as they now are (for it is they who make them what they are), cannot comprehend why those ways should not be good enough for everybody; and what is more, spontaneity forms no part of the ideal of the majority of moral and social reformers, but is rather looked on with jealousy, as a troublesome and perhaps rebellious obstruction to the general acceptance of what these reformers, in their own judgment, think would be best for mankind. Few persons, out of Germany, even comprehend the meaning of the doctrine which Wilhelm von Humboldt, so eminent both as a *savant* and as a politician, made the text of a treatise—that 'the end of man, or that which is prescribed by the eternal or immutable dictates of reason, and not suggested by vague and transient desires, is the highest and most harmonious development of his powers to a complete and consistent whole;' that, therefore, the object 'towards which every human being must ceaselessly direct his efforts, and on which especially those who design to influence their fellow-men must ever keep their eyes, is the individuality of power and development;' that for this there are two requisites, 'freedom and variety of situations;' and that from the union of these arise 'individual vigour and manifold diversity,' which combine themselves in 'originality.'*

Little, however, as people are accustomed to a doctrine like that of Von Humboldt, and surprising as it may be to them to find so high a value attached to individuality, the question, one must nevertheless think, can only be one of degree. No one's idea of excellence in conduct is that people should do absolutely nothing but copy one another. No one would assert that people ought not to put into their mode of life, and into the conduct of their concerns, any impress whatever of their own judgment, or of their own individual character. On the other hand, it would be absurd to pretend that people ought to live as if nothing whatever had been known in the world before they came into it; as if experience had as yet done nothing towards showing that one mode of existence, or of conduct, is preferable to another. Nobody denies that people should be so taught and trained in youth as to know and benefit by the ascertained results of human experience. But it is the privilege and proper condition of a human being, arrived at the maturity of his faculties, to use and interpret experience in his own way. It is for him to find out what part of recorded experience is properly applicable to his own circumstances and character. The traditions and customs of other people are, to a certain extent, evidence of what their experience has taught *them;* presumptive evidence, and as such, have a claim to his

*The Sphere and Duties of Government, from the German of Baron Wilhelm von Humboldt, pp. 11–13.

deference; but, in the first place, their experience may be too narrow; or they may not have interpreted it rightly. Secondly, their interpretation of experience may be correct, but unsuitable to him. Customs are made for customary circumstances and customary characters; and his circumstances or his character may be uncustomary. Thirdly, though the customs be both good as customs, and suitable to him, yet to conform to custom, merely *as* custom, does not educate or develop in him any of the qualities which are the distinctive endowment of a human being. The human faculties of perception, judgment, discriminative feeling, mental activity, and even moral preference, are exercised only in making a choice. He who does anything because it is the custom makes no choice. He gains no practice either in discerning or in desiring what is best. The mental and moral, like the muscular powers, are improved only by being used. The faculties are called into no exercise by doing a thing merely because others do it, no more than by believing a thing only because others believe it. If the grounds of an opinion are not conclusive to the person's own reason, his reason cannot be strengthened, but is likely to be weakened, by his adopting it: and if the inducements to an act are not such as are consentaneous to his own feelings and character (where affection, or the rights of others, are not concerned) it is so much done towards rendering his feelings and character inert and torpid, instead of active and energetic.

He who lets the world, or his own portion of it, choose his plan of life for him, has no need of any other faculty than the ape-like one of imitation. He who chooses his plan for himself, employs all his faculties. He must use observation to see, reasoning and judgment to foresee, activity to gather materials for decision, discrimination to decide, and when he has decided, firmness and self-control to hold to his deliberate decision. And these qualities he requires and exercises exactly in proportion as the part of his conduct which he determines according to his own judgment and feelings is a large one. It is possible that he might be guided in some good path, and kept out of harm's way, without any of these things. But what will be his comparative worth as a human being? It really is of importance, not only what men do, but also what manner of men they are that do it. Among the works of man, which human life is rightly employed in perfecting and beautifying, the first in importance surely is man himself. Supposing it were possible to get houses built, corn grown, battles fought, causes tried, and even churches erected and prayers said, by machinery—by automatons in human form—it would be a considerable loss to exchange for these automatons even the men and women who at present inhabit the more civilised parts of the world, and who assuredly are but starved specimens of what nature can and will produce. Human nature is not a machine to be built after a model, and set to do exactly the work prescribed for it, but a tree, which requires to grow and develop itself on all sides, according to the tendency of the inward forces which make it a living thing.

It will probably be conceded that it is desirable people should exercise their understandings, and that an intelligent following of custom, or even occasionally an intelligent deviation from custom, is better than a blind and simply mechanical adhesion to it. To a certain extent it is admitted that our understanding should be our own: but there is not the same willingness to admit that our desires and impulses should be our own likewise; or that to possess impulses of our own, and of any strength, is anything but a peril and a snare. Yet desires and impulses are as much a part of a perfect human being as beliefs and restraints: and strong impulses are only perilous when not properly balanced; when one set of aims and inclinations is developed into strength, while others, which ought to co-exist with them, remain weak and inactive. It is not because men's desires are strong that they act ill; it is because their consciences are weak. There is no natural connection between strong impulses and a weak conscience. The natural connection is the other way. To say that

one person's desires and feelings are stronger and more various than those of another, is merely to say that he has more of the raw material of human nature, and is therefore capable, perhaps, of more evil, but certainly of more good. Strong impulses are but another name for energy. Energy may be turned to bad uses; but more good may always be made of an energetic nature, than of an indolent and impassive one. Those who have most natural feeling are always those whose cultivated feelings may be made the strongest. The same strong susceptibilities which make the personal impulses vivid and powerful, are also the source from whence are generated the most passionate love of virtue, and the sternest self-control. It is through the cultivation of these that society both does its duty and protects its interests: not by rejecting the stuff of which heroes are made, because it knows not how to make them. A person whose desires and impulses are his own—are the expression of his own nature, as it has been developed and modified by his own culture—is said to have a character. One whose desires and impulses are not his own, has no character, no more than a steam-engine has a character. If, in addition to being his own, his impulses are strong, and are under the government of a strong will, he has an energetic character. Whoever thinks that individuality of desires and impulses should not be encouraged to unfold itself, must maintain that society has no need of strong natures—is not the better for containing many persons who have much character—and that a high general average of energy is not desirable.

In some early states of society, these forces might be, and were, too much ahead of the power which society then possessed of disciplining and controlling them. There has been a time when the element of spontaneity and individuality was in excess, and the social principle had a hard struggle with it. The difficulty then was to induce men of strong bodies or minds to pay obedience to any roles which required them to control their impulses. To overcome this difficulty, law and discipline, like the Popes struggling against the Emperors, asserted a power over the whole man, claiming to control all his life in order to control his character—which society had not found any other sufficient means of binding. But society has now fairly got the better of individuality; and the danger which threatens human nature is not the excess, but the deficiency, of personal impulses and preferences. Things are vastly changed since the passions of those who were strong by station or by personal endowment were in a state of habitual rebellion against laws and ordinances, and required to be rigorously chained up to enable the persons within their reach to enjoy any particle of security. In our times, from the highest class of society down to the lowest, every one lives as under the eye of a hostile and dreaded censorship. Not only in what concerns others, but in what concerns only themselves, the individual or the family do not ask themselves—what do I prefer? or, what would suit my character and disposition? or, what would allow the best and highest in me to have fair play, and enable it to grow and thrive? They ask themselves, what is suitable to my position? what is usually done by persons of my station and pecuniary circumstances? or (worse still) what is usually done by persons of a station and circumstances superior to mine? I do not mean that they choose what is customary in preference to what suits their own inclination. It does not occur to them to have any inclination, except for what is customary. Thus the mind itself is bowed to the yoke: even in what people do for pleasure, conformity is the first thing thought of; they live in crowds; they exercise choice only among things commonly done; peculiarity of taste, eccentricity of conduct, are shunned equally with crimes: until by dint of not following their own nature they have no nature to follow: their human capacities are withered and starved: they become incapable of any strong wishes or native pleasures, and are generally without either opinions or feelings of home growth, or properly their own. Now is this, or is it not, the desirable condition of human nature?

It is so, on the Calvinistic theory. According to that, the one great offence of man is self-will. All the good of which humanity is capable is comprised in obedience. You have no choice; thus you must do, and no otherwise: 'whatever is not a duty, is a sin.' Human nature being radically corrupt, there is no redemption for any one until human nature is killed within him. To one holding this theory of life, crushing out any of the human faculties, capacities, and susceptibilities, is no evil: man needs no capacity, but that of surrendering himself to the will of God: and if he uses any of his faculties for any other purpose but to do that supposed will more effectually, he is better without them. This is the theory of Calvinism; and it is held, in a mitigated form, by many who do not consider themselves Calvinists; the mitigation consisting in giving a less ascetic interpretation to the alleged will of God; asserting it to be his will that mankind should gratify some of their inclinations; of course not in the manner they themselves prefer, but in the way of obedience, that is, in a way prescribed to them by authority; and, therefore, by the necessary condition of the case, the same for all.

In some such insidious form there is at present a strong tendency to this narrow theory of life, and to the pinched and hidebound type of human character which it patronises. Many persons, no doubt, sincerely think that human beings thus cramped and dwarfed are as their Maker designed them to be; just as many have thought that trees are a much finer thing when clipped into pollards, or cut out into figures of animals, than as nature made them. But if it be any part of religion to believe that man was made by a good Being, it is more consistent with that faith to believe that this Being gave all human faculties that they might be cultivated and unfolded, not rooted out and consumed, and that he takes delight in every nearer approach made by his creatures to the ideal conception embodied in them, every increase in any of their capabilities of comprehension, of action, or of enjoyment. There is a different type of human excellence from the Calvinistic: a conception of humanity as having its nature bestowed on it for other purposes than merely to be abnegated. 'Pagan self-assertion' is one of the elements of human worth, as well as 'Christian self-denial.' There is a Greek ideal of self-development, which the Platonic and Christian ideal of self-government blends with, but does not supersede. It made be better to be a John Knox than an Alcibiades, but it is better to be a Pericles than either; nor would a Pericles, if we had one in these days, be without anything good which belonged to John Knox.

It is not by wearing down into uniformity all that is individual in themselves, but by cultivating it, and calling it forth, within the limits imposed by the rights and interests of others, that human beings become a noble and beautiful object of contemplation; and as the works partake the character of those who do them, by the same process human life also becomes rich, diversified, and animating, furnishing more abundant aliment to high thoughts and elevating feelings, and strengthening the tie which binds every individual to the race, by making the race infinitely better worth belonging to. In proportion to the development of his individuality, each person becomes more valuable to himself, and is therefore capable of being more valuable to others. There is a greater fulness of life about his own existence, and when there is more life in the units there is more in the mass which is composed of them. As much compression as is necessary to prevent the stronger specimens of human nature from encroaching on the rights of others cannot be dispensed with; but for this there is ample compensation even in the point of view of human development. The means of development which the individual loses by being prevented from gratifying his inclinations to the injury of others, are chiefly obtained at the expense of the development of other people. And even to himself there is a full equivalent in the better development of the social part of his nature, rendered possible by the restraint put upon the selfish part. To be held to rigid rules of justice for the sake of others, develops the feelings and capacities which have the good of others for their object. But to be restrained in things not affecting their good, by their mere displeasure, develops nothing valuable, except such force of character as may unfold itself in resisting the restraint. If acquiesced in, it dulls and blunts the whole nature. To give any fair play to the nature of each, it is essential that different persons should be allowed to lead different lives. In proportion as this latitude has been exercised in any age, has that age been noteworthy to posterity. Even despotism does not produce its worst effects, so long as individuality exists under it; and whatever crushes individuality is despotism, by whatever name it may be called, and whether it professes to be enforcing the will of God or the injunctions of men.

STUDY QUESTIONS

1. What, according to Mill, is the appropriate region of human liberty?

2. Do you agree with Mill that society ought not to exercise coercion over an individual, for his own good? Can you think of any exceptions to this rule?

3. "If all mankind minus one were of one opinion, and only one person were of the contrary opinion, mankind would be no more justified in silencing that one person, than he, if he had the power, would be justified in silencing mankind." Do you agree?

4. Why, according to Mill, should the actions of an individual be more subject to constraint by society than his opinions?

5. Mill defends the view that everyone should do his own thing. What are his reasons for defending this view? Do you find his argument persuasive?

For Further Reading

Anschutz, R. P. *The Philosophy of J. S. Mill.* Oxford: Clarendon Press, 1953 (Chapters 2 through 4).

Britton, K. *John Stuart Mill*. Baltimore: Penguin, 1953 (Chapter 3).

Cowling, M. *Mill and Liberalism*. Cambridge: Cambridge University Press, 1963.

Mill, J. S. *Representative Government*.

Radcliffe, P., ed. *Limits of Liberty: Studies of Mill's On Liberty*. Belmont, Calif.: Wadsworth, 1966.

Sabine, G. H. *A History of Political Theory*. 2d ed. New York: Holt, Rinehart and Winston, 1973 (Chapter 32).

MARX AND ENGELS: SOCIALISM

The American and French revolutions of the late-eighteenth century spawned a flood of political thought and agitation in the century that followed. Taking their cue from several French writers, many of the nineteenth-century political theorists espoused socialism, in some form. Among these, one of the most prominent, and ultimately by far the most important, was Karl Marx. The chief difference between the Marxian version of socialism and that of its rivals is revealed in the title of the essay from which our selection is taken. In describing Marx's socialistic theory as "scientific" as opposed to "utopian" (an obvious term of derision), Engels is emphasizing the fact that Marx based his politics on a general theory of philosophy and history. The philosophical foundation for Marxian socialism lies in a modified version of the idealism of the German philospher, Hegel, called dialectical materialism; the historical basis is found in a novel and penetrating theory known as the economic interpretation of history. That the "scientific" character of his socialism has been a major reason for its practical success, as Marx himself would surely have believed, is a point on which many historians, at least, would demur.

The author of the selection that follows is Friedrich Engels (1820–1895), the life-long friend, collaborator, and benefactor of Karl Marx (1818–1883). Born in the German Rhineland, the son of a wealthy textile manufacturer, Engels spent many years in England operating a family cotton mill in Manchester. Although Engels wrote the essay *Socialism: Utopian and Scientific*, the ideas it contains were generated by Karl Marx, with the possible exception of Charles Darwin, the most influential thinker of the nineteenth century. Marx, also, was born in the Rhineland, of a Jewish family that had converted to Protestantism. When the newspaper he was editing in Cologne was suppressed because of its liberal stance, Marx went into exile from Germany, first to Paris, then to Brussels, back to Paris, then briefly to Cologne again, and finally to London, where he lived for the rest of his life, supporting himself and his family by writing and through the generosity of his friend, Engels.

❧ Engels: Socialism: Utopian and Scientific

I

Modern socialism is, in its essence, the direct product of the recognition, on the one

First published in German in 1883 and translated into Engish by E. Aveling.

hand, of the class antagonisms, existing in the society of today, between proprietors and non-proprietors, between capitalists and wage workers; on the other hand, of the anarchy existing in production. But, in its theoretical form, modern socialism originally appears ostensibly as a more logical extension of the principles laid down by the great French philosophers of the eighteenth century. Like every new theory, modern socialism had, at first, to connect itself with the intellectual stock-in-trade ready to its hand, however deeply its roots lay in material economic facts.

The great men, who in France prepared men's minds for the coming revolution, were themselves extreme revolutionists. They recognized no external authority of any kind whatever. Religion, natural science, society, political institutions, everything, was subjected to the most unsparing criticism: everything must justify its existence before the judgment seat of reason, or give up existence. Reason became the sole measure of everything. It was the time when, as Hegel says, the world stood upon its head; first, in the sense that the human head, and the principles arrived at by its thought, claimed to be the basis of all human action and association; but by and by, also, in the wider sense that the reality which was in contradiction to these principles had, in fact, to be turned upside down. Every form of society and government then existing, every old traditional notion was flung into the lumber room as irrational; the world had hitherto allowed itself to be led solely by prejudices; everything in the past deserved only pity and contempt. Now, for the first time, appeared the light of day, the kingdom of reason; henceforth superstition, injustice, privilege, oppression, were to be superseded by eternal truth, eternal right, equality based on nature and the inalienable rights of man.

We know today that this kingdom of reason was nothing more than the idealized kingdom of the bourgeoisie; that this eternal right found its realization in bourgeois justice; that this equality reduced itself to bourgeois equality before the law; that bourgeois property was proclaimed as one of the essential rights of man; and that the government of reason, the *Contrat Social* of Rousseau, came into being, and only could come into being, as a democratic bourgeois republic. The great thinkers of the eighteenth century could, no more than their predecessors, go beyond the limits imposed upon them by their epoch.

But, side by side with the antagonism of the feudal nobility and the burghers, who claimed to represent all the rest of society, was the general antagonism of exploiters and exploited, of rich idlers and poor workers. It was this very circumstance that made it possible for the representatives of the bourgeoisie to put themselves forward as representing not one special class, but the whole of suffering humanity. Still further. From its origin, the bourgeoisie was saddled with its antithesis: capitalists cannot exist without wage workers, and, in the same proportion as the medieval burgher of the guild developed into the modern bourgeois, the guild journeyman and the day laborer, outside the guilds, developed into the proletarian. And although, upon the whole, the bourgeoisie, in their struggle with the nobility, could claim to represent at the same time the interests of the different working classes of that period, yet in every great bourgeois movement there were independent outbursts of that class which was the forerunner, more or less developed, of the modern proletariat.

II

In 1831, the first working class rising took place in Lyons; between 1838 and 1842, the first national working class movement, that of the English Chartists, reached its height. The class struggle between proletariat and bourgeoisie came to the front in the history of the most advanced countries in Europe, in proportion to the development, upon the one hand, of modern industry, upon the other, of the newly-acquired political supremacy of the bourgeoisie. Facts more and more strenuously gave the lie to the teachings of bourgeois economy as to the identity of the interests of capital and labor, as to the universal harmony and universal prosperity that would be the consequence of unbridled competition. All these things could no longer be ignored, any more than the French and English socialism, which was their theoretical, though very imperfect expression. But the old idealist conception of history, which was not yet dislodged, knew nothing of class struggles based upon economic interests, knew nothing of economic interests; production and all economic relations appeared in it only as incidental, subordinate elements in the "history of civilization."

The new facts made imperative a new examination of all past history. Then it was seen that *all* past history, with the exception of its primitive stages, was the history of class struggles; that these warring classes of society are always the products of the modes of production and of exchange—in a word, of the *economic* conditions of their time; that the economic structure of society always furnishes the real basis, starting from which we can alone work out the ultimate explanation of the whole superstructure of juridical and political institutions as well as of the religious, philosophical and other ideas of a given historical period. Hegel had freed history from metaphysics—he had made it dialectic; but his conception of history was essentially idealistic. But now idealism was driven from its last refuge, the philosophy of history; now a materialistic treatment of history was propounded, and a method found of explaining man's "knowing" by his "being," instead of, as heretofore, his "being" by his "knowing."

From that time forward socialism was no longer an accidental discovery of this or that ingenious brain, but the necessary outcome of the struggle between two historically developed classes—the proletariat and the bourgeoisie. Its task was no longer to manufacture a system of society as perfect as possible, but to examine the historico-economic succession of events from which these classes and their antagonism had of necessity sprung, and to discover in the economic conditions thus created the means of ending the conflict. But the socialism of earlier days was as incompatible with this materialistic conception as the conception of nature of the French materialists was with dialectics and modern natural science.

The socialism of earlier days certainly criticized the existing capitalistic mode of production and its consequences. But it could not explain them, and, therefore, could not get the mastery of them. It could only simply reject them as bad. The more strongly this earlier socialism denounced the exploitation of the working class, inevitable under capitalism, the less able was it clearly to show in what this exploitation consisted and how it arose. But for this it was necessary—(1) to present the capitalistic method of production in its historical connection and its inevitableness during a particular historical period, and therefore, also, to present its inevitable downfall; and (2) to lay bare its essential character, which was still a secret. This was done by the discovery of *surplus value*. It was shown that the appropriation of unpaid labor is the basis of the capitalist mode of production and of the exploitation of the worker that occurs under it; that even if the capitalist buys the labor power of his laborer at its full value as a commodity on the market, he yet extracts more value from it than he paid for; and that in the ultimate analysis this surplus value forms those sums of value from which are heaped up the constantly increasing masses of capital in the hands of the possessing classes. The genesis of capitalist production and the production of capital were both explained.

III

These two great discoveries, the materialistic conception of history and the revolution of the secret of capitalistic production through surplus value, we owe to Marx. With these discoveries, socialism became a science. The next thing was to work out all its details and relations.

The materialist conception of history starts from the proposition that the production of the means to support human life and, next to production, the exchange of things produced, is the basis of all social structure; that in every society that has appeared in history, the manner in which wealth is distributed and society divided into classes or orders is dependent upon what is produced, how it is produced, and how the products are exchanged. From this point of view the final causes of all social changes and political revolutions are to be sought, not in men's brains, not in man's better insight into external truth and justice, but in changes in the modes of production and exchange. They are to be sought, not in the *philosophy*, but in the *economics* of each particular epoch. The growing perception that existing social institutions are unreasonable and unjust, that reason has become unreason, and right wrong, is only proof that in the modes of production and exchange changes have silently taken place, with which the social order, adapted to earlier economic conditions, is no longer in keeping. From this it also follows that the means of getting rid of the incongruities that have been brought to light must also be present, in a more or less developed condition, within the changed modes of production themselves. These means are not to be invented by deduction from fundamental principles, but are to be discovered in the stubborn facts of the existing system of production.

What is, then, the position of modern socialism in this connection?

The present structure of society—this is now pretty generally conceded—is the creation of the ruling class of today, of the bourgeoisie. The mode of production peculiar to the bourgeoisie, known, since Marx, as the capitalist mode of production, was incompatible with the feudal system, with the privileges it conferred upon individuals, entire social ranks and local corporations, as well as with the hereditary ties of subordination which constituted the framework of its social organization. The bourgeoisie broke up the feudal system and built upon its ruins the capitalist order of society, the kingdom of free competition, of personal liberty, of equality before the law of all commodity owners, and of all the rest of the capitalist blessings. Thenceforward, the capitalist mode of production could develop in freedom. Since steam, machinery and the making of machines by machinery transformed the older man-

ufacture into modern industry, the productive forces evolved under the guidance of the bourgeoisie developed with a rapidity and in a degree unheard of before. But just as the older manufacture, in its time, and handicraft, becoming more developed under its influence, had come into collision with the feudal trammels of the guilds, so now modern industry, in its more complete development, comes into collision with the bounds within which the capitalistic mode of production holds it confined. The new productive forces have already outgrown the capitalistic mode of using them. And this conflict between productive forces and modes of production is not a conflict engendered in the mind of man, like that between original sin and divine justice. It exists, in fact, objectively, outside us, independently of the will and actions even of the men that have brought it on. Modern socialism is nothing but the reflex, in thought, of this conflict in fact; its ideal reflection in the minds, first, of the class directly suffering under it, the working class.

Now, in what does this conflict consist?

Before capitalistic production, *i.e.*, in the Middle Ages, the system of petty industry obtained generally, based upon the private property of the laborers in their means of production; in the country, the agriculture of the small peasant, freeman or serf; in the towns, the handicrafts organized in guilds. The instruments of labor—land, agricultural implements, the workshop, the tool—were the instruments of labor of single individuals, adapted for the use of one worker, and, therefore, of necessity, small, dwarfish, circumscribed. But for this very reason they belonged, as a rule, to the producer himself. To concentrate these scattered, limited means of production, to enlarge them, to turn them into the powerful levers of production of the present day—this was precisely the historic role of capitalist production and of its upholder, the bourgeoisie. In Part IV of *Capital*, Marx has explained in detail how since the fifteenth century this has been historically worked out through the three phases of simple cooperation, manufacture, and modern industry. But the bourgeoisie, as is also shown there, could not transform these puny means of production into mighty productive forces, without transforming them, at the same time, from means of production of the individual into *social* means of production only workable by a collectivity of men. The spinning-wheel, the hand-loom, the blacksmith's hammer were replaced by the spinning machine, the power-loom, the steam-hammer; the individual workshop, by the factory, implying the cooperation of hundreds and thousands of workmen. In like manner, production itself changed from a series of individual into a series of social acts, and the products from individual to social products. The yarn, the cloth, the metal articles that now came out of the factory were the joint product of many workers, through whose hands they had successively to pass before they were ready. No one person could say of them: "I made that; this is *my* product."

But where, in a given society, the fundamental form of production is that spontaneous division of labor which creeps in gradually and not upon any preconceived plan, there the products take on the form of *commodities*, whose mutual exchange, buying and selling, enable the individual producers to satisfy their manifold wants. And this was the case in the Middle Ages. The peasant, *e.g.*, sold to the artisan agricultural products and bought from him the products of handicraft. Into this society of individual producers, of commodity producers, the new mode of production thrust itself. In the midst of the old division of labor, grown up spontaneously and upon *no definite plan*, which had governed the whole society, now arose division of labor upon *a definite plan*, as organized in the factory; side by side with *individual* production appeared *social* production. The products of both were sold in the same market, and, therefore, at prices at least approximately equal. But organization upon a definite plan was stronger than spontaneous division of labor. The factories working with the combined social forces of a collectivity of individuals produced their commodities far more cheaply than the individual small producers. Individual production succumbed in one department after another. Socialized production revolutionized all the old methods of production. But its revolutionary character was, at the same time, so little recognized, that it was, on the contrary, introduced as a means of increasing and developing the production of commodities. When it arose, it found ready-made, and made liberal use of, certain machinery for the production and exchange of commodities; merchants' capital, handicraft, wage labor. Socialized production thus introducing itself as a new form of the production of commodities, it was a matter of course that under it the old forms of appropriation remained in full swing, and were applied to its products as well.

In the medieval stage of evolution of the production of commodities, the question as to the owner of the product of labor could not arise. The individual producer, as a rule, had, from raw material belonging to himself, and generally his own handiwork, produced it with his own tools, by the labor of his own hands or of his family. There was no need for him to appropriate the new product. It belonged wholly to him, as a matter of course. His property in the product was, therefore, based *upon his own labor*. Even where external help was used, this was, as a rule, of little importance, and very generally was compensated by something other than wages. The apprentices and journeymen of the guilds worked less for board and wages than for education, in order that they might become master craftsmen themselves.

Then came the concentration of the means of production and of the producers in large workshops and manufactories, their transformation into actual socialized means of production and socialized producers. But the socialized producers and means of production and their products were still treated, after this change, just as they had been before, *i.e.*, as the means of production and the products of individuals. Hitherto, the owner of the instruments of labor had himself appropriated the product, because as a rule it was his own product and the assistance of others was the exception. Now the owner of the instruments of labor always appropriated to himself the product, although it was no longer *his* product, but exclusively the product of the *labor of others*. Thus, the products now produced socially were not appropriated by those who had actually set in motion the means of production and actually produced the commodities, but by the *capitalists*. The means of production, and production itself, had become in essence socialized. But they were subjected to a form of appropriation which presupposes the private production of individuals, under which, therefore, everyone owns his own product and brings it to market. The mode of production is subjected to this form of appropriation, although it abolishes the conditions upon which the latter rests.

This contradiction, which gives to the new mode of production its capitalistic character, *contains the germ of the whole of the social antagonisms of today*. The greater the mastery obtained by the new mode of production over all important fields of production and in all manufacturing countries, the more it reduced individual production to an insignificant residuum, *the more clearly was brought out the incompatibility of socialized production with capitalistic appropriation.*

The first capitalists found, as we have said, alongside of other forms of labor, wage labor ready-made for them on the market. But it was exceptional, complementary, accessory, transitory wage labor. The agricultural laborer, though, upon occasion, he hired himself out by the day, had a few acres of his own land on which he could at all events live at a pinch. The guilds were so organized that the journeyman of today became the master of tomorrow. But all this changed, as soon as the means of production became socialized and concentrated in the hands of capitalism. The means of production, as well as the product of the individual pro-

ducer became more and more worthless; there was nothing left for him but to turn wage worker under the capitalist. Wage labor, aforetime the exception and accessory, now became the rule and basis of all production; aforetime complementary, it now became the sole remaining function of the worker. The wage worker for a time became a wage worker for life. The number of these permanent wage workers was further enormously increased by the breaking up of the feudal system that occurred at the same time, by the disbanding of the retainers of the feudal lords, the eviction of the peasants from their homesteads, etc. The separation was made complete between the means of production concentrated in the hands of the capitalists on the one side, and the producers, possessing nothing but their labor power, on the other. *The contradiction between socialized production and capitalistic appropriation manifested itself as the antagonism of proletariat and bourgeoisie.*

We have seen that the capitalistic mode of production thrust its way into a society of commodity producers, of individual producers, whose social bond was the exchange of their products. But every society, based upon the production of commodities, has this peculiarity: that the producers have lost control over their own social interrelations. Each man produces for himself with such means of production as he may happen to have, and for such exchange as he may require to satisfy his remaining wants. No one knows how much of his particular article is coming on the market, nor how much of it will be wanted. No one knows whether his individual product will meet an actual demand, whether he will be able to make good his cost of production or even to sell his commodity at all. Anarchy reigns in socialized production.

But the production of commodities, like every other form of production, has its peculiar inherent laws inseparable from it; and these laws work, despite anarchy, in and through anarchy. They reveal themselves in the only persistent form of social inter-relations, *i.e.*, in exchange, and here they affect the individual producers as compulsory laws of competition. They are, at first, unknown to these producers themselves, and have to be discovered by them gradually and as the result of experience. They work themselves out, therefore, independently of the producers, and in antagonism to them, as inexorable natural laws of their particular form of production. The product governs the producers.

In medieval society, especially in the earlier centuries, production was essentially directed towards satisfying the wants of the individual. It satisfied, in the main, only the wants of the producer and his family. Where relations of personal dependence existed, as in the country, it also helped to satisfy the wants of the feudal lord. In all this there was, therefore, no exchange; the products, consequently, did not assume the character of commodities. The family of the peasant produced almost everything they wanted: clothes and furniture, as well as means of subsistence. Only when it began to produce more than was sufficient to supply its own wants and the payments in kind to the feudal lord, only then did it also produce commodities. This surplus, thrown into socialized exchange and offered for sale, became commodities.

The artisans of the towns, it is true, had from the first to produce for exchange. But they, also, themselves supplied the greatest part of their own individual wants. They had gardens and plots of land. They turned their cattle out into the communal forest, which, also, yielded them timber and firing. The women spun flax, wool, and so forth. Production for the purpose of exchange, production of commodities was only in its infancy. Hence, exchange was restricted, the market narrow, the methods of production stable; there was local exclusiveness without, local unity within; the mark,* in the country, in the town, the guild.

But with the extension of the production of commodities, and especially with

*A form of medieval social and political organization, based on the land. —Ed.

the introduction of the capitalist mode of production, the laws of commodity production, hitherto latent, came into action more openly and with greater force. The old bonds were loosened, the old exclusive limits broken through, the producers were more and more turned into independent, isolated producers of commodities. It became apparent that the production of society at large was ruled by absence of plan, by accident, by anarchy; and this anarchy grew to greater and greater height. But the chief means by aid of which the capitalist mode of production intensified this anarchy of socialized production was the exact opposite of anarchy. It was the increasing organization of production, upon a social basis, in every individual productive establishment. By this, the old, peaceful, stable condition of things was ended. Wherever this organization of production was introduced into a branch of industry, it brooked no other method of production by its side. The field of labor became a battleground. The great geographical discoveries, and the colonization following upon them, multiplied markets and quickened the transformation of handicraft into manufacture. The war did not simply break out between the individual producers of particular localities. The local struggles begat in their turn national conflicts, the commercial wars of the seventeenth and the eighteenth centuries.

Finally, modern industry and the opening of the world market made the struggle universal, and at the same time gave it an unheard-of virulence. Advantages in natural or artificial conditions of production now decide the existence or nonexistence of individual capitalists, as well as of whole industries and countries. He that falls is remorselessly cast aside. It is the Darwinian struggle of the individual for existence transferred from nature to society with intensified violence. The conditions of existence natural to the animal appear as the final term of human development. The contradiction between socialized production and capitalistic appropriation now presents itself as *an antagonism between the organization of production in the individual workshop and the anarchy of production in society generally.*

The capitalistic mode of production moves in these two forms of the antagonism immanent to it from its very origin. It is never able to get out of that "vicious circle," which Fourier had already discovered. What Fourier could not, indeed, see in his time is: that this circle is gradually narrowing; that the movement becomes more and more a spiral, and must come to an end, like the movement of the planets, by collision with the center. It is the compelling force of anarchy in the production of society at large that more and more completely turns the great majority of men into proletarians; and it is the masses of the proletariat again who will finally put an end to anarchy in production. It is the compelling force of anarchy in social production that turns the limitless perfectibility of machinery under modern industry into a compulsory law by which every individual industrial capitalist must perfect his machinery more and more, under penalty of ruin.

But the perfecting of machinery is making human labor superfluous. If the introduction and increase of machinery means the displacement of millions of manual, by a few machine workers, improvement in machinery means the displacement of more and more of the machine workers themselves. It means, in the last instance, the production of a number of available wage workers in excess of the average needs of capital, the formation of a complete industrial reserve army, as I called it in 1845, available at the times when industry is working at high pressure, to be cast out upon the street when the inevitable crash comes, a constant dead weight upon the limbs of the working class in its struggle for existence with capital, a regulator for the keeping of wages down to the low level that suits the interests of capital. Thus it comes about, to quote Marx, that machinery becomes the most powerful weapon in the war of capital against the working class; that the instruments of labor

constantly tear the means of subsistence out of the hands of the laborer; that the very product of the worker is turned into an instrument for his subjugation. Thus it comes about that the economizing of the instruments of labor becomes at the same time, from the outset, the most reckless waste of labor power, and robbery based upon the normal conditions under which labor functions; that machinery, "the most powerful instrument for shortening labor time, becomes the most unfailing means for placing every moment of the laborer's time and that of his family at the disposal of the capitalist for the purpose of expanding the value of his capital." (Marx, *Capital*). Thus it comes about that overwork of some becomes the preliminary condition for the idleness of others, and that modern industry, which hunts after new consumers over the whole world, forces the consumption of the masses at home down to a starvation minimum, and in doing thus destroys its own home market. "The law that always equilibrates the relative surplus population, or industrial reserve army, to the extent and energy of accumulation, this law rivets the laborer to capital more firmly than the wedges of Vulcan did Prometheus to the rock. It establishes an accumulation of misery, corresponding with accumulation of capital. Accumulation of wealth at one pole is, therefore, at the same time, accumulation of misery, agony of toil, slavery, ignorance, brutality, mental degradation, at the opposite pole, *i.e.,* on the side of the class that produces *its own product in the form of capital.*" (Marx, *Capital*). And to expect any other division of the products from the capitalistic mode of production is the same as expecting the electrodes of a battery not to decompose acidulated water, not to liberate oxygen at the positive, hydrogen at the negative pole, so long as they are connected with the battery.

We have seen that the ever-increasing perfectibility of modern machinery is, by the anarchy of social production, turned into a compulsory law that forces the individual industrial capitalist always to improve his machinery, always to increase its productive force. The bare possibility of extending the field of production is transformed for him into a similar compulsory law. The enormous expansive force of modern industry, compared with which that of gases is mere child's play, appears to us now as a *necessity* for expansion, both qualitative and quantitative, that laughs at all resistance. Such resistance is offered by consumption, by sales, by the markets for the products of modern industry. But the capacity for extension, extensive and intensive, of the markets is primarily governed by quite different laws, that work much less energetically. The extension of the markets cannot keep pace with the extension of production. The collision becomes inevitable, and as this cannot produce any real solution so long as it does not break in pieces the capitalist mode of production, the collisions become periodic. Capitalist production has begotten another "vicious circle."

As a matter of fact, since 1825, when the first general crisis broke out, the whole industrial and commercial world, production and exchange among all civilized peoples and their more or less barbaric hangers-on, are thrown out of joint about once every ten years. Commerce is at a standstill, the markets are glutted, products accumulate, as multitudinous as they are unsaleable, hard cash disappears, credit vanishes, factories are closed, the mass of the workers are in want of the means of subsistence, because they have produced too much of the means of subsistence; bankruptcy follows upon bankruptcy, execution upon execution. The stagnation lasts for years, productive forces and products are wasted and destroyed wholesale, until the accumulated mass of commodities finally filter off, more or less depreciated in value, until production and exchange gradually begin to move again. Little by little the pace quickens. It becomes a trot. The industrial trot breaks into a canter, the canter in turn grows into the headlong gallop of a perfect steeple-chase of industry, commercial credit and speculation, which finally, after breakneck leaps, ends where it began—in the ditch of a crisis. And so over and over again.

• • •

If the crises demonstrate the incapacity of the bourgeoisie for managing any longer modern productive forces, the transformation of the great establishments for production and distribution into joint-stock companies, trusts and state property, show how unnecessary the bourgeoisie are for that purpose. All the social functions of the capitalist are now performed by salaried employees. The capitalist has no further social function than that of pocketing dividends, tearing off coupons, and gambling on the Stock Exchange, where the different capitalists despoil one another of their capital. At first the capitalistic mode of production forces out the workers. Now it forces out the capitalists, and reduces them, just as it reduced the workers, to the ranks of the surplus population, although not immediately into those of the industrial reserve army.

But the transformation, either into joint-stock companies and trusts, or into state ownership, does not do away with the capitalistic nature of the productive forces. In the joint-stock companies and trusts this is obvious. And the modern state, again, is only the organization that bourgeois society takes on in order to support the external conditions of the capitalist mode of production against the encroachments, as well of the workers as of individual capitalists. The modern state, no matter what its form, is essentially a capitalist machine, the state of the capitalists, the ideal personification of the total national capital. The more it proceeds to the taking over of productive forces, the more does it actually become the national capitalist, the more citizens does it exploit. The workers remain wage workers—proletarians. The capitalist relation is not done away with. It is rather brought to a head. But, brought to a head, it topples over. State ownership of the productive forces is not the solution of the conflict, but concealed within it are the technical conditions that form the elements of that solution.

This solution can only consist in the practical recognition of the social nature of the modern forces of production, and therefore in the harmonizing of the modes of production, appropriation and exchange with the socialized character of the means of production. And this can only come about by society openly and directly taking possession of the productive forces which have outgrown all control except that of society as a whole. The social character of the means of production and of the products today reacts against the producers, periodically disrupts all production and exchange, acts only like a law of nature working blindly, forcibly, destructively. But with the taking over by society of the productive forces, the social character of the means of production and of the products will be utilized by the producers with a perfect understanding of its nature, and instead of being a source of disturbance and periodical collapse, will become the most powerful lever of production itself.

Active social forces work exactly like natural forces; blindly, forcibly, destructively, so long as we do not understand and reckon with them. But when once we understand them, when once we grasp their action, their direction, their effects, it depends only upon ourselves to subject them more and more to our own will, and by means of them to reach our own ends. And this holds quite especially of the mighty productive forces of today. As long as we obstinately refuse to understand the nature and the character of these social means of action—and this understanding goes against the grain of the capitalist mode of production and its defenders—so long these forces are at work in spite of us, in opposition to us, so long they master us, as we have shown above in detail.

But when once their nature is understood, they can, in the hands of the producers working together, be transformed from master demons into willing servants. The difference is as that between the destructive force of electricity in the lightning of the storm, and electricity under command in the telegraph and the voltaic arc; the difference between a conflagration, and fire working in the service of man. With this recognition at last of the real nature of the productive forces of today, the social anarchy of production gives place to a social regulation of production upon a definite plan, according to the needs of the community and of each individual. Then the capitalist mode of appropriation, in which the product enslaves first the producer and then the appropriator, is replaced by the mode of appropriation of the products that is based upon the nature of the modern means of production; upon the one hand, direct social appropriation, as means to the maintenance and extension of production—on the other, direct individual appropriation, as means of subsistence and of enjoyment.

Whilst the capitalist mode of production more and more completely transforms the great majority of the population into proletarians, it creates the power which, under penalty of its own destruction, is forced to accomplish this revolution. Whilst it forces on more and more the transformation of the vast means of production, already socialized, into state property, it shows itself the way to accomplishing this revolution. *The proletariat seizes political power and turns the means of production into state property.*

But, in doing this, it abolishes itself as proletariat, abolishes all class distinctions and class antagonisms, abolishes also the state as state. Society thus far, based upon class antagonisms, had need of the state. That is, of an organization of the particular class which was *pro tempore* the exploiting class, an organization for the purpose of preventing any interference from without with existing conditions of production, and therefore, especially, for the purpose of forcibly keeping the exploited classes in the condition of oppression corresponding with the given mode of production (slavery, serfdom, wage labor). The state was the official representative of society as a whole; the gathering of it together into a visible embodiment. But it was this only in so far as it was the state of that class which itself represented, for the time being, society as a whole; in ancient times, the state of slave-owning citizens; in the Middle Ages, the feudal lords; in our own time, the bourgeoisie. When at last it becomes the real representative of the whole of society, it renders itself unnecessary. As soon as there is no longer any social class to be held in subjection; as soon as class rule and the individual struggle for existence based upon our present anarchy in production, with the collisions and excesses arising from these, are removed, nothing more remains to be repressed, and a special repressive force, a state, is no longer necessary. The first act by virtue of which the state really constitutes itself the representative of the whole of society—the taking possession of the means of production in the name of society—this is, at the same time, its last independent act as a state. State interference in social relations becomes, in one domain after another, superfluous, and then dies out of itself; the government of persons is replaced by the administration of things, and by the conduct of processes of production. The state is not "abolished." *It dies out.*

STUDY QUESTIONS

1. What does Engels mean by the words "bourgeoisie," "proletariat"?
2. The philosophical theory underlying Marxism is known as "dialectical materialism." Can you explain what this means?
3. According to Engels, all past history is the history of class struggles. What does he mean by this and why does he think it to be true?
4. What is the labor theory of value? The theory of surplus value?
5. What is the economic interpretation of history? How important do you consider this theory to be? Explain.
6. What role has the state played historically, according to Engels? Under what conditions, and for what reasons, will it "die out" in the future?

For Further Reading

Avineri, S. *The Social and Political Thought of Karl Marx.* London: Cambridge University Press, 1968.

Cole, G. D. H. *What Marx Really Meant.* New York: Knopf, 1934 (esp. Chapters 2 through 6).

Marx, K., and Engels, F. *The Communist Manifesto.*

Mayo, H. B. *Introduction to Marxist Theory.* New York: Oxford University Press, 1960 (esp. Chapters 3 through 5).

Popper, K. R. *The Open Society and Its Enemies.* Princetown, N.J.: Princeton University Press, 1950 (Chapters 13 and 14).

Sabine, G. H. *A History of Political Theory.* 2d ed. New York: Holt, Rinehart and Winston, 1973 (Chapter 33).

DEWEY: DEMOCRACY

For Americans, "democracy" is a "good" word. As a result, democracy is perennially lauded but seldom analyzed dispassionately. What does democracy mean and how does it differ from other forms of government and society? The crucial factor that distinguishes forms of government from each other—no matter what labels they may give to themselves—is the ultimate repository of political power. In a democracy that repository is the people themselves. They may exercise this power directly, as they did in Athens twenty-five centuries ago and still do in New England town meetings, or they may exercise it indirectly through representatives whom they elect and hold responsible to themselves, as they must do in all large political groups. Since democracy, in contrast to other forms of political organization, is uniquely government by the people, if it is to function successfully, those who hold the ultimate power must participate in an active and enlightened way in the political process.

John Dewey (1859–1952) is often called the philosopher of American democracy. A native of Vermont, he studied philosophy at Johns Hopkins University where he received his doctorate in 1884. In the following years, while teaching at the Universities of Michigan and Chicago, he became a follower of William James and his philosophy of pragmatism or, as Dewey chose to call it, instrumentalism. Applying his ideas to education, Dewey through the years wrought a transformation in both the theory and practice of American education. He completed his academic career at Columbia University, where he taught for twenty-five years.

✍ *Democracy and Educational Administration*

Democracy is much broader than a special political form, a method of conducting government, of making laws and carrying on governmental administration by means of popular suffrage and elected officers. It is that, of course. But it is something broader and deeper than that. The political and governmental phase of democracy is a means, the best means so far found, for realizing ends that lie in the wide domain of human relationships and the development of human personality. It is, as we often say, though perhaps without appreciating all that is involved in the saying, a way of life, social and individual. The key-note of democracy as a way of life may be expressed, it seems to me, as the necessity for the participation of every mature human being in formation of the values that regulate the living of men together: which is necessary from the standpoint of both the general social welfare and the full development of human beings as individuals.

Universal suffrage, recurring elections, responsibility of those who are in political power to the voters, and the other factors of democratic government are means that have been found expedient for realizing democracy as the truly human way of living. They are not a final end and a final

Reprinted from *School & Society*. Copyright, 1937 by Society for the Advancement of Education.

value. They are to be judged on the basis of their contribution to the end. It is a form of idolatry to erect means into the end which they serve. Democratic political forms are simply the best means that human wit has devised up to a special time in history. But they rest back upon the idea that no man or limited set of men is wise enough or good enough to rule others without their consent; the positive meaning of this statement is that all those who are affected by social institutions must have a share in producing and managing them. The two facts that each one is influenced in what he does and enjoys and in what he becomes by the institutions under which he lives, and that therefore he shall have, in a democracy, a voice in shaping them, are the passive and active sides of the same fact.

The development of political democracy came about through substitution of the method of mutual consultation and voluntary agreement for the method of subordination of the many to the few enforced from above. Social arrangements which involve fixed subordination are maintained by coercion. The coercion need not be physical. There have existed, for short periods, benevolent despotisms. But coercion of some sort there has been; perhaps economic, certainly psychological and moral. The very fact of exclusion from participation is a subtle form of suppression. It gives individuals no opportunity to reflect and decide upon what is good for them. Others who are supposed to be wiser and who in any case have more power decide the question for them and also decide the methods and means by which subjects may arrive at the enjoyment of what is good for them. This form of coercion and suppression is more subtle and more effective than is overt intimidation and restraint. When it is habitual and embodied in social institutions, it seems the normal and natural state of affairs. The mass usually become unaware that they have a claim to a development of their own powers. Their experience is so restricted that they are not conscious of restriction. It is part of the democratic conception that they as individuals are not the only sufferers, but that the whole social body is deprived of the potential resources that should be at its service. The individuals of the submerged mass may not be very wise. But there is one thing they are wiser about than anybody else can be, and that is where the shoe pinches, the troubles they suffer from.

The foundation of democracy is faith in the capacities of human nature; faith in human intelligence and in the power of pooled and cooperative experience. It is not belief that these things are complete but that if given a show they will grow and be able to generate progressively the knowledge and wisdom needed to guide collective action. Every autocratic and authoritarian scheme of social action rests on a belief that the needed intelligence is confined to a superior few, who because of inherent natural gifts are endowed with the ability and the right to control the conduct of others; laying down principles and rules and directing the ways in which they are carried out. It would be foolish to deny that much can be said for this point of view. It is that which controlled human relations in social groups for much the greater part of human history. The democratic faith has emerged very, very recently in the history of mankind. Even where democracies now exist, men's minds and feelings are still permeated with ideas about leadership imposed from above, ideas that developed in the long early history of mankind. After

democratic political institutions were nominally established, beliefs and ways of looking at life and of acting that originated when men and women were externally controlled and subjected to arbitrary power, persisted in the family, the church, business and the school, and experience shows that as long as they persist there, political democracy is not secure.

Belief in equality is an element of the democratic credo. It is not, however, belief in equality of natural endowments. Those who proclaimed the idea of equality did not suppose they were enunciating a psychological doctrine, but a legal and political one. All individuals are entitled to equality of treatment by law and in its administration. Each one is affected equally in quality if not in quantity by the institutions under which he lives and has an equal right to express his judgment, although the weight of his judgment may not be equal in amount when it enters into the pooled result to that of others. In short, each one is equally an individual and entitled to equal opportunity of development of his own capacities, be they large or small in range. Moreover, each has needs of his own, as significant to him as those of others are to them. The very fact of natural and psychological inequality is all the more reason for establishment by law of equality of opportunity, since otherwise the former becomes a means of oppression of the less gifted.

While what we call intelligence be distributed in unequal amounts, it is the democratic faith that it is sufficiently general so that each individual has something to contribute, whose value can be assessed only as it enters into the final pooled intelligence constituted by the contributions of all. Every authoritarian scheme, on the contrary, assumes that its value may be assessed by some *prior* principle, if not of family and birth or race and color or possession of material wealth, then by the position and rank a person occupies in the existing social scheme. The democratic faith in equality is the faith that each individual shall have the chance and opportunity to contribute whatever he is capable of contributing and that the value of his contribution be decided by its place and function in the organized total of similar contributions, not on the basis of prior status of any kind whatever.

I have emphasized in what precedes the importance of the effective release of intelligence in connection with personal experience in the democratic way of living. I have done so purposely because democracy is so often and so naturally associated in our minds with freedom of *action,* forgetting the importance of freed intelligence which is necessary to direct and to warrant freedom of action. Unless freedom of individual action has intelligence and informed conviction back of it, its manifestation is almost sure to result in confusion and disorder. The democratic idea of freedom is not the right of each individual to *do* as he pleases, even if it be qualified by adding "provided he does not interfere with the same freedom on the part of others." While the idea is not always, not often enough, expressed in words, the basic freedom is that of freedom of *mind* and of whatever degree of freedom of action and experience is necessary to produce freedom of intelligence. The modes of freedom guaranteed in the Bill of Rights are all of this nature: Freedom of belief and conscience, of expression of opinion, of assembly for discussion and conference, of the press as an organ of communication. They are guaranteed because without them individuals are not free to develop and society is deprived of what they might contribute.

There is some kind of government, of control, wherever affairs that concern a number of persons who act together are engaged in. It is a superficial view that holds government is located in Washington and Albany. There is government in the family, in business, in the church, in every social group. There are regulations, due to custom if not to enactment, that settle how individuals in a group act in connection with one another.

It is a disputed question of theory and practice just how far a democratic political government should go in control of the conditions of action within special groups. At the present time, for example, there are those who think the federal and state governments leave too much freedom of independent action to industrial and financial groups, and there are others who think the government is going altogether too far at the present time. I do not need to discuss this phase of the problem, much less to try to settle it. But it must be pointed out that if the methods of regulation and administration in vogue in the conduct of secondary social groups are non-democratic, whether directly or indirectly or both, there is bound to be an unfavorable reaction back into the habits of feeling, thought and action of citizenship in the broadest sense of that word. The way in which any organized social interest is controlled necessarily plays an important part in forming the dispositions and tastes, the attitudes, interests, purposes and desires, of those engaged in carrying on the activities of the group. For illustration, I do not need to do more than point to the moral, emotional and intellectual effect upon both employers and laborers of the existing industrial system. Just what the effects specifically are is a matter about which we know very little. But I suppose that everyone who reflects upon the subject admits that it is impossible that the ways in which activities are carried on for the greater part of the waking hours of the day; and the way in which the share of individuals are involved in the management of affairs in such a matter as gaining a livelihood and attaining material and social security, can not but be a highly important factor in shaping personal dispositions; in short, forming character and intelligence.

In the broad and final sense all institutions are educational in the sense that they operate to form the attitudes, dispositions, abilities and disabilities that constitute a concrete personality. The principle applies with special force to the school. For it is the main business of the family and the school to influence directly the formation and growth of attitudes and dispositions, emotional, intellectual and moral. Whether this educative process is carried on in a predominantly democratic or non-democratic way becomes, therefore, a question of transcendent importance not only for education itself but for its final effect upon all the interests and activities of a society that is committed to the democratic way of life.

• • •

I conclude by saying that the present subject is one of peculiar importance at the present time.* The fundamental beliefs and practices of democracy are now challenged as they never have been before. In some nations they are more than challenged. They are ruthlessly and systematically destroyed. Everywhere there are waves of criticism and doubt as to whether democracy can meet pressing problems of order and security. The causes for the de-

struction of political democracy in countries where it was nominally established are complex. But of one thing I think we may be sure. Wherever it has fallen it was too exclusively political in nature. It had not become part of the bone and blood of the people in daily conduct of its life. Democratic forms were limited to Parliament, elections and combats between parties. What is happening proves conclusively, I think, that unless democratic habits of thought and action are part of the fiber of a people, political democracy is insecure. It can not stand in isolation. It must be buttressed by the presence of democratic methods in all social relationships.

*This was written about two years before the outbreak of World War II. —ed.

STUDY QUESTIONS

1. What is Dewey's ethical interpretation of democracy?
2. For what kind of equality does democracy stand?
3. What relationship does Dewey draw between freedom of action and intelligence? Do you think he is right?

For Further Reading

Bishop, H. M. and Hendel, S., eds. *Basic Issues of American Democracy*. 3d ed. New York: Appleton-Century-Crofts, 1956.

Cohen, C. *Democracy*. Athens, Ga.: University of Georgia Press, 1971.

Dewey, J. *Freedom and Culture*. New York: Putnam's, 1939.

———. *Liberalism and Social Action*. New York: G. P. Putnam's Sons, 1935 (esp. Chapter 3).

Edman, I. *John Dewey*. Indianapolis: Bobbs-Merrill, 1955 (Chapter 8).

Frankel, C. "John Dewey's Social Philosophy." In *New Studies in the Philosophy of John Dewey*. ed. S. M. Cahn. Hanover: The University Press of New England, 1977 (Chapter 1).

Hallowell, J.H. *The Moral Foundation of Democracy*. Chicago: University of Chicago Press, 1954.

Lindsay, A. D. *The Essentials of Democracy*. 2d ed. London: Oxford University Press, 1935.

PART VI

---⊰⊱---

The Individual
and God

Jesus said, "Come unto me, all ye that labor and are heavy laden, and I will give you rest." Karl Marx said, "Religion is the opium of the masses." Diametrically opposed in tone and spirit though these two statements may be, they still have something in common; both speak to the common people of this earth and both are concerned with the question of the value of religion to their lives. Jesus delivers a message of comfort and hope, but Marx implies that the consolations that religion offers to the downtrodden are as spurious as the dreams of a drug addict.

Is it possible to find any rational grounds for choosing between such radically different assessments of the worth of religion, or is the matter one about which feeling must be the final arbiter? Although spokesmen can be found for both sides of this question, philosophers and theologians have, as should be expected, sought rational grounds either to support, or to undercut, religious belief. In the Western tradition, the focus of the religious issue has always been concentrated on the being of God. Does there exist a being eternal, omnipotent, and perfect who created the universe out of nothing? On the answer one gives to this question turn the most significant issues of which the human mind can conceive. Does the universe have any meaning? Does history have a goal or is the universe doomed to destruction? Is human life meaningful? Is death its final end or can we look forward to a further life beyond the grave? Will good ultimately triumph over evil or is this itself a meaningless question?

Because of their belief that the answers we must give to such questions depend on the conclusion we reach about the existence of God, theologians have usually made this issue their primary concern. The first four selections of Part VI include some of the most famous arguments that have been offered in support of the proposition that God exists, along with criticisms of those arguments. Those who believe that it is possible to prove that God exists have attempted to do so by arguments of two different types. The first of these are *a posteriori* arguments. Here the believer begins with an account of certain features of the world in which we live; for example, the fact that events are linked

311

together through a chain of causes and effects or the fact that individual parts of the human body, like the eye, are designed to serve a specific purpose, and then goes on to argue that these experienced natural facts cannot be accounted for satisfactorily unless we assume the existence of a God who has created the universe in the particular way in which we find it to be. The other type of argument is *a priori*. Instead of seeking evidence on which to base his conclusion about God's existence, the believer argues that all one need to do to be assured that God exists is to understand his nature. A being with the attributes possessed by God *must* exist because it is logically impossible that anything with such a nature not exist. The main *a priori* proof of God's existence is the celebrated ontological argument of St. Anselm of Canterbury, which appears, along with a criticism, in the second selection of this Part.

The very idea of offering an argument to prove the existence of God suggests the possibility, at least, that his existence may be doubted. Else why the need of providing a proof? This entire perspective regarding the relationship between the believer and God is rejected by the mystic. To know that God exists, Evelyn Underhill believes, no proof is needed, because no doubts on this subject can arise. Knowledge of God is the surest of any knowledge we can ever have because it is gained through a direct "face-to-face" meeting between the individual and God. This meeting, or communion, is more intimate than anything that can take place between separate human individuals because, in it, the person is literally dissolved into the infinite being of God, so that, while the mystical experience lasts, she possesses no separate individuality of her own at all.

For mystics, the existence of God is not an issue. They "know," because they have directly experienced the divine reality. But what are the rest of us to say? Unfortunately, most of us have been denied the privilege of a mystical experience. If God exists, why, we are tempted to ask, does he reveal himself to so few? The suspicion occurs that the mystic may be misled; what she accepts as a meeting with God may well have another, less exalted explanation. Recent discoveries in psychology, furthermore, offer us a wide range of alternative interpretations of an alleged mystical experience, which to many outside observers appear more plausible than the account offered by the mystic. Yet, such negative evidence is not conclusive; the mystic *may* be right in interpreting her experience as a meeting with God. The problem for those on the outside, however, remains: Since we have no independent means of corroborating the mystic's testimony, we must, it would appear, simply either accept, or reject, the truth of what she reports.

The doubts just expressed about the mystical route to God can be broadened. Some philosophers have come to the conclusion that neither the mystics, nor the theologians, have been successful in their attempts to establish the existence of God. On the contrary, the weight of the evidence and argument supports the conclusion that the universe contains no such being as God. This view is called atheism, in contrast to theism, or the belief that God exists. Yet another group of philosophers are dubious of the claims of both theists and atheists, holding both to be equally presumptuous, on the grounds that the question of God's existence is an issue beyond the capacity of humans to answer. For this position the English biologist and philosopher, T. H. Huxley, coined the name "agnosticism."

Although the question of God's existence is the central problem of theology, it is by no means the sole matter of the theologians' concern. One's entire view of the world and of humanity's fate will vary markedly, depending on whether he is a theist or an atheist. As Bertrand Russell makes abundantly clear in his essay, *A*

Free Man's Worship, atheism leads to pessimism. In a universe ruled not by God but by blind matter all values are doomed to ultimate destruction as is the universe itself. The only comfort for the individual, likewise doomed by death, is to create something of worth that he and others can appreciate and enjoy, even if but for a short while. Through his actions in the creation of things of value the individual realizes his freedom and demonstrates his moral superiority over the forces of destruction that will finally overpower him.

The theist, although he need not succumb to the deep pessimism of the atheist, has formidable problems of his own. He offers us a conception of reality in which the universe, and everything it contains, has been created by and is under the control of an omnipotent, perfect being. To the impartial, but sceptical, observer an obvious question arises: If God created the universe, and he is the kind of being he is described to be, how are we to explain the obvious mess he made of things? Even without any pretensions to the infinite abilities of God, some of us may be inclined to think that, given the opportunities to create that he had, we might have done a better job than he did.

One of the main tasks that theistic theologians have undertaken is to show that the existence of the world as we actually find it to be, including what we call the human condition, is compatible with the existence of a creative God, possessing the qualities traditionally attributed to him. Arguments to achieve this end or, to use Milton's powerful phrase, to "justify the ways of God to men" make up a sub-discipline of theology known as *theodicy*. The main issues raised by theodicy, which are discussed in the final two selections of this Part, are summed up in the problem of evil. Evil presents us with an ethical problem by being what it is but it presents us with a theological problem by existing at all. Why, in a universe created and controlled by God, should there be any evil? Since evil exists, it must be permitted by God and since God is perfect, this evil cannot be gratuitous. Rather, God must have a reason for allowing evil to exist and his reason must be a good one. Most of the issues of theodicy arise from attempts theologians have made to find reasons capable of explaining why God permits the existence of all the evils that experience reveals to us. A number of different solutions, some quite ingenious, have been offered to this problem but all seem to have some implications that are hard to accept. Perhaps the most reasonable response we can make to the problem of evil is to recognize it as an issue that remains unresolved.

Background Readings

The Bible.

Ducasse, C. J. *A Philosophical Scrutiny of Religion.* New York: Ronald, 1953.

James, W. *The Varieties of Religious Experience.*

Kaufmann, W. *Critique of Religion and Philosophy.* New York: Harper, 1958.

Matson, W. I. *The Existence of God.* Ithaca: Cornell University Press, 1965.

Mill, J. S. *Three Essays on Religion.*

Wilson, J. *Philosophy and Religion.* London: Oxford University Press, 1961.

ST. THOMAS: THE FIVE WAYS

The history of theological literature contains a multitude of different "proofs" of the existence of God. Although all of the various arguments probably have a certain amount of merit, some are considerably more persuasive than others. The crucial question, of course, is: Do any of these arguments, or all together, succeed in establishing that God exists? Here no unanimity can be found. Those who offered the arguments undoubtedly found them conclusive, and they have succeeded in convincing many others of their cogency. But critics of the arguments have also been many. To the uncommitted, perhaps the best advice would be to point out that the issue of God's existence remains an open question, subject to investigation and debate. To aid in coming to grips with the problem perhaps no better starting place can be found than St. Thomas' five brief arguments on the affirmative side of the question.

St. Thomas Aquinas (1225–1274) was the most important intellectual figure of the high middle ages. Born in Italy of a noble family, he entered the Dominican order, much to the displeasure of his family who had higher aspirations for him than the life of a monk. When he refused to abandon his monkish vows, they imprisoned him in the family castle, where he remained incarcerated for two years, finally escaping with his mother's help. After studying in Cologne, he became a professor at the University of Paris, where his teaching was so popular that it was difficult to find a classroom large enough to accommodate the students who flocked to hear him. A prolific writer, Thomas completed seventeen volumes on philosophy and theology in the short span of twenty years.

❦ *Summa Theologica*

First Part
Question 2
Third Article

The existence of God can be proved in five ways.

The first and more manifest way is the argument from motion. It is certain, and evident to our senses, that in the world some things are in motion. Now whatever is in motion is put in motion by another, for nothing can be in motion except it is in potentiality to that towards which it is in motion; whereas a thing moves inasmuch as it is in act. For motion is nothing else than the reduction of something from potentiality to actuality. But nothing can be

Translated by the Fathers of the English Dominican Province.

reduced from potentiality to actuality, except by something in a state of actuality. Thus that which is actually hot, as fire, makes wood, which is potentially hot, to be actually hot, and thereby moves and changes it. Now it is not possible that the same thing should be at once in actuality and potentiality in the same respect, but only in different respects. For what is actually hot cannot simultaneously be potentially hot; but it is simultaneously potentially cold. It is therefore impossible that in the same respect and in the same way a thing should be both mover and moved, *i.e.,* that it should move itself. Therefore, whatever is in motion must be put in motion by another. If that by which it is put in motion be itself put in motion, then this also must need be put in motion by another, and that by another again. But this cannot go on to infinity, because then there would be no first mover, and, consequently, no other mover; seeing that subsequent movers move only inasmuch as they are put in motion by the first mover; as the staff moves only because it is put in motion by the hand. Therefore it is necessary to arrive at a first mover, put in motion by no other; and this everyone understands to be God.

The second way is from the nature of the efficient cause. In the world of sense we find there is an order of efficient causes. There is no case known (neither is it, indeed, possible) in which a thing is found to be the efficient cause of itself; for so it would be prior to itself, which is impossible. Now in efficient causes it is not possible to go on to infinity, because in all efficient causes following in order, the first is the cause of the intermediate cause, and the intermediate is the cause of the ultimate cause, whether the intermediate cause be several, or one only. Now to take away the cause is to take away the effect. Therefore, if there be no first cause among efficient causes, there will be no ultimate, nor any intermediate cause. But if in efficient causes it is possible to go on to infinity, there will be no first efficient cause, neither will there be an ultimate effect, nor any intermediate efficient causes; all of which is plainly false. Therefore it is necessary to admit a first efficient cause, to which everyone gives the name of God.

The third way is taken from possibility and necessity, and runs thus. We find in nature things that are possible to be and not to be, since they are found to be generated, and to corrupt, and consequently, they are possible to be and not to be. But it is impossible for these always to exist, for that which is possible not to be at some time is not. Therefore, if everything is possible not to be, then at one time there could have been nothing in existence. Now if this were true, even now there would be nothing in existence, because that which does not exist only begins to exist by something already existing. Therefore, if at one time nothing was in existence, it would have been impossible for anything to have begun to exist; and thus even now nothing would be in existence—which is absurd. Therefore, not all beings are merely possible, but there must exist something the existence of which is necessary. But every necessary thing either has its necessity caused by another, or not. Now it is impossible to go on to infinity in necessary things which have their necessity caused by another, as has been already proved in regard to efficient causes. Therefore we cannot but postulate the existence of some being having of itself its own necessity, and not receiving it from another, but rather causing in others their necessity. This all men speak of as God.

The fourth way is taken from the gradation to be found in things. Among beings there are some more and some less good, true, noble, and the like. But "more" and "less" are predicated of different things, according as they resemble in their different ways something which is the maximum, as a thing is said to be hotter according as it more nearly resembles that which is hottest; so that there is something which is uttermost being; for those things noblest, and, consequently, something which is uttermost being; for thos things that are greatest in truth are greatest in being, as it is written in *Metaph.* ii. Now the maximum in any genus is the cause of all in that genus; as fire, which is the maximum of heat, is the cause of all hot things. Therefore there must also be something which is to all beings the cause of their being, goodness, and every other perfection; and this we call God.

The fifth way is taken from the governance of the world. We see that things which lack intelligence, such as natural bodies, act for an end, and this is evident from their acting always, or nearly always, in the same way, so as to obtain the best result. Hence it is plain that not fortuitously, but designedly, do they achieve their end. Now whatever lacks intelligence cannot move towards an end, unless it be directed by some being endowed with knowledge and intelligence; as the arrow is shot to its mark by the archer. Therefore some intelligent being exists by whom all natural things are directed to their end; and this being we call God.

STUDY QUESTIONS

1. Do you see any difficulty in Thomas' conception of God as a first mover that is moved by nothing else? A first, hence uncaused, cause?

2. On what grounds does Thomas argue that God is a necessary being? Do you find his argument convincing? Explain.

3. Could Thomas use a variation of his fourth argument to prove the existence of Satan?

4. Do you agree with the facts, as Thomas describes them in his fifth argument? Do you think he gives the correct explanation of these facts? Why or why not?

For Further Reading

Bonnette, D. *Aquinas' Proofs for God's Existence.* The Hague: Martinus Nijhoff, 1972 (esp. Part II).

Kant, I. *Critique of Pure Reason.* Translated by N. K. Smith. London: Macmillan, 1929 (pp. 507–14).

Kenny, A. *The Five Ways.* New York: Schocken Books, 1969.

Reichenbach, B. R. *The Cosmological Argument.* Springfield, Ill.: Charles C. Thomas, 1972.

Rowe, W. L. *The Cosmological Argument.* Princeton, N.J.: Princeton University Press, 1975.

ST. ANSELM AND GAUNILON: THE ONTOLOGICAL ARGUMENT

Things that exist can be divided into contingent beings and necessary beings. Contingent beings are those things that may or may not exist, necessary beings those things that must exist. Almost all objects we know—trees, houses, people, our planet, the solar system—are contingent beings; none of these things exists necessarily. Is there anything, then, that does so exist? According to St. Anselm there is, and it is God. His ontological argument is an attempt to demonstrate that a being with the characteristics possessed by God must exist. The argument is short but so powerful that philosophers and theologians have debated its merits for nearly a thousand years. Among those who were not convinced that the argument proves its conclusion was a monk named Gaunilon, a contemporary of Anselm. His criticism of the ontological argument is included in the selection that follows.

St. Anselm of Canterbury (1033–1109), a major theologian and religious leader of the early middle ages, was born of a noble family in Aosta, in northern Italy. He entered the Benedictine order and was for much of his life associated with the monastery of Bec, in France, becoming abbot in 1078. Under his leadership Bec became a major center of medieval learning. In 1093 Anselm was appointed Archbishop of Canterbury. Gaunilon, who criticizes Anselm's ontological argument in the selection that follows, was also a Benedictine monk, from the monastery of Marmoutier.

℣ St. Anselm: Proslogium

Chapter II

Truly there is a God, although the fool hath said in his heart, There is no God.

And so, Lord, do thou, who dost give understanding to faith, give me, so far as thou knowest it to be profitable, to understand that thou art as we believe; and that thou art that which we believe. And, indeed, we believe that thou art a being than which nothing greater can be conceived. Or is there no such nature, since the fool hath said in his heart, there is no God? (Psalms xiv. 1). But, at any rate, this very fool, when he hears of this being of which I speak—a being than which nothing greater can be conceived—understands what he hears, and what he understands is in his understanding; although he does not understand it to exist.

For, it is one thing for an object to be in the understanding, and another to understand that the object exists. When a painter first conceives of what he will afterwards peform, he has it in his understanding, but he does not yet understand it to be, because he has not yet performed it. But after he has made the painting, he both has it in his understanding, and he understands that it exists, because he has made it.

Hence, even the fool is convinced that something exists in the understanding, at least, than which nothing greater can be conceived. For, when he hears of this, he understands it. And whatever is understood, exists in the understanding. And assuredly that, than which nothing greater can be conceived, cannot exist in the understanding alone. For, suppose it exists in the understanding alone: then it can be conceived to exist in reality; which is greater.

Therefore, if that, than which nothing greater can be conceived, exists in the understanding alone, the very being, than which nothing greater can be conceived, is one, than which a greater can be conceived. But obviously this is impossible. Hence, there is no doubt that there exists a being, than which nothing greater can be conceived, and it exists both in the understanding and in reality.

Chapter III

. . .

God cannot be conceived not to exist.—God is that, than which nothing greater can be conceived.—That which can be conceived not to exist is not God.

And it assuredly exists so truly, that it cannot be conceived not to exist. For, it is possible to conceive of a being which cannot be conceived not to exist; and this is greater than one which can be conceived not to exist. Hence, if that, than which nothing greater can be conceived, can be conceived not to exist, it is not that, than which nothing greater can be conceived. But this is an irreconcilable contradiction. There is, then, so truly a being than which nothing greater can be conceived to exist, that it cannot even be conceived not to exist; and this being thou art, O Lord, our God.

So truly, therefore, dost thou exist, O Lord, my God, that thou canst not be conceived not to exist; and rightly. For, if a mind could conceive of a being better than thee, the creature would rise above the Creator; and this is most absurd. And, indeed, whatever else there is, except thee alone, can be conceived not to exist. To thee alone, therefore, it belongs to exist more truly than all other beings, and hence in a higher degree than all others. For, whatever else exists does not exist so truly,

Reprinted from *Proslogium, Monologium, An Appendix in Behalf of the Fool by Gaunilon; and Cur Deus Homo,* by St. Anselm, translated by S. N. Deane. By permission of The Open Court Publishing Company, La Salle, Illinois. Copyrighted by The Open Court Publishing Co., 1903.

and hence in a less degree it belongs to it to exist. Why, then, has the fool said in his heart, there is no God (Psalms xiv. I), since it is so evident, to a rational mind, that thou dost exist in the highest degree of all? Why, except that he is dull and a fool?

• • •

An Answer to the Argument of Anselm in the Proslogium.
By Gaunilon, a Monk of Marmoutier.

1. If one doubts or denies the existence of a being of such a nature that nothing greater than it can be conceived, he receives this answer:

The existence of this being is proved, in the first place, by the fact that he himself, in his doubt or denial regarding this being, already has it in his understanding; for in hearing it spoken of he understands what is spoken of. It is proved, therefore, by the fact that what he understands must exist not only in his understanding, but in reality also.

And the proof of this is as follows.—It is a greater thing to exist both in the understanding and in reality than to be in the understanding alone. And if this being is in the understanding alone, whatever has even in the past existed in reality will be greater than this being. And so that which was greater than all beings will be less than some being, and will not be greater than all: which is a manifest contradiction.

And hence, that which is greater than all, already proved to be in the understanding, must exist not only in the understanding, but also in reality: for otherwise it will not be greater than all other beings.

2. The fool might make this reply:

This being is said to be in my understanding already, only because I understand what is said. Now could it not with equal justice be said that I have in my understanding all manner of unreal objects, having absolutely no existence in themselves, because I understand these things if one speaks of them, whatever they may be?

Unless indeed it is shown that this being is of such a character that it cannot be held in concept like all unreal objects, or objects whose existence is uncertain: and hence I am not able to conceive of it when I hear of it, or to hold it in concept; but I must understand it and have it in my understanding; because, it seems, I cannot conceive of it in any other way than by understanding it, that is, by comprehending in my knowledge its existence in reality.

But if this is the case, in the first place there will be no distinction between what has precedence in time—namely, the having of an object in the understanding—and what is subsequent in time—namely, the understanding that an object exists; as in the example of the picture, which exists first in the mind of the painter, and afterwards in his work.

Moreover, the following assertion can hardly be accepted: that this being, when it is spoken of and heard of, cannot be conceived not to exist in the way in which even God can be conceived not to exist. For if this is impossible, what was the object of this argument against one who doubts or denies the existence of such a being?

Finally, that this being so exists that it cannot be perceived by an understanding convinced of its own indubitable existence, unless this being is afterwards conceived of—this should be proved to me by an indisputable argument, but not by that which you have advanced: namely, that what I understand, when I hear it, already is in my understanding. For thus in my understanding, as I still think, could be all sorts of things whose existence is uncertain, or which do not exist at all, if some one whose words I should understand mentioned them. And so much the more if I should be deceived, as often happens, and believe in them: though I do not yet believe in the being whose existence you would prove.

3. Hence, your example of the painter who already has in his understanding what he is to paint cannot agree with this argument. For the picture, before it is made, is contained in the aritificer's art itself; and

any such thing, existing in the art of an aritficer, is nothing but a part of his understanding itself. A joiner, St. Augustine says, when he is about to make a box in fact, first has it in his art. The box which is made in fact is not life; but the box which exists in his art is life. For the artificer's soul lives, in which all these things are, before they are produced. Why, then, are these things life in the living soul of the artificer, unless because they are nothing else than the knowledge or understanding of the soul itself?

With the exception, however, of those facts which are known to pertain to the mental nature, whatever, on being heard and thought out by the understanding, is perceived to be real, undoubtedly that real object is one thing and the understanding itself, by which the object is grasped, is another. Hence, even if it were true that there is a being than which a greater is inconceivable: yet to this being, when heard of and understood, the not yet created picture in the mind of the painter is not analogous.

4. Let us notice also the point touched on above, with regard to this being which is greater than all which can be conceived, and which, it is said, can be none other than God himself. I, so far as actual knowledge of the object, either from its specific or general character, is concerned, am as little able to conceive of this being when I hear of it, or to have it in my understanding, as I am to conceive of or understand God himself: whom, indeed, for this very reason I can conceive not to exist. For I do not know that reality itself which God is, nor can I form a conjecture of that reality from some other like reality. For you yourself assert that that reality is such that there can be nothing else like it.

For, suppose that I should hear something said of a man absolutely unknown to me, of whose very existence I was unaware. Through that special or general knowledge by which I know what man is, or what men are, I could conceive of him also, according to the reality itself, which man is. And yet it would be possible, if the person who told

me of him deceived me, that the man himself, of whom I conceived, did not exist; since that reality according to which I conceived of him, though a no less indisputable fact, was not that man, but any man.

Hence, I am not able, in the way in which I should have this unreal being in concept or in understanding, to have that being of which you speak in concept or in understanding, when I hear the word *God* or the words, *a being greater than all other beings.* For I can conceive of the man according to a fact that is real and familiar to me: but of God, or a being greater than all others, I could not conceive at all, except merely according to the word. And an object can hardly or never be conceived according to the word alone.

For when it is so conceived, it is not so much the word itself (which is, indeed, a real thing—that is, the sound of the letters and syllables) as the signification of the word, when heard, that is conceived. But it is not conceived as by one who knows what is generally signified by the word; by whom, that is, it is conceived according to a reality and in true conception alone. It is conceived as by a man who does not know the object, and conceives of it only in accordance with the movement of his mind produced by hearing the word, the mind attempting to image for itself the signification of the word that is heard. And it would be surprising if in the reality of fact it could ever attain to this.

Thus, it appears, and in no other way, this being is also in my understanding, when I hear and understand a person who says that there is a being greater than all conceivable beings. So much for the assertion that this supreme nature already is in my understanding.

5. But that this being must exist, not only in the understanding but also in reality, is thus proved to me:

If it did not so exist, whatever exists in reality would be greater than it. And so the being which has been already proved to exist in my understanding, will not be greater than all other beings.

I still answer: if it should be said that a being which cannot be even conceived in terms of any fact, is in the understanding, I do not deny that this being is, accordingly, in my understanding. But since through this fact it can in no wise attain to real existence also, I do not yet concede to it that existence at all, until some certain proof of it shall be given.

For he who says that this being exists, because otherwise the being which is greater than all will not be greater than all, does not attend strictly enough to what he is saying. For I do not yet say, no, I even deny or doubt that this being is greater than any real object. Nor do I concede to it any other existence than this (if it should be called existence) which it has when the mind, according to a word merely heard, tries to form the image of an object absolutely unknown to it.

How, then, is the veritable existence of that being proved to me from the assumption, by hypothesis, that it is greater than all other beings? For I should still deny this, or doubt your demonstration of it, to this extent, that I should not admit that this being is in my understanding and concept even in the way in which many objects whose real existence is uncertain and doubtful, are in my understanding and concept. For it should be proved first that this being itself really exists somewhere; and then, from the fact that it is greater than all, we shall not hesitate to infer that it also subsists in itself.

6. For example: it is said that somewhere in the ocean is an island, which because of the difficulty, or rather the impossibility, of discovering what does not exist, is called the lost island. And they say that this island has an inestimable wealth of all manner of riches and delicacies in greater abundance than is told of the Islands of the Blest; and that having no owner or inhabitant, it is more excellent than all other countries, which are inhabited by mankind, in the abundance with which it is stored.

Now is some one should tell me that there is such an island, I should easily understand his words, in which there is no difficulty. But suppose that he went on to say, as if by a logical inference: "You can no longer doubt that this island which is more excellent than all lands exists somewhere, since you have no doubt that it is in your understanding. And since it is more excellent not to be in the understanding alone, but to exist both in the understanding and in reality, for this reason it must exist. For if it does not exist, any land which really exists will be more excellent than it; and so the island already understood by you to be more excellent will not be more excellent."

If a man should try to prove to me by such reasoning that this island truly exists, and that its existence should no longer be doubted, either I should believe that he was jesting, or I know not which I ought to regard as the greater fool: myself, supposing that I should allow this proof; or him, if he should suppose that he had established with any certainty the existence of this island. For he ought to show first that the hypothetical excellence of this island exists as a real and indubitable fact, and in no wise as any unreal object, or one whose existence is uncertain, in my understanding.

7. This, in the mean time, is the answer the fool could make to the arguments urged against him. When he is assured in the first place that this being is so great that its non-existence is not even conceivable, and that this in turn is proved on no other ground than the fact that otherwise it will not be greater than all things, the fool may make the same answer, and say:

When did I say that any such being exists in reality, that is, a being greater than all others?—that on this ground it should be proved to me that it also exists in reality to such a degree that it cannot even be conceived not to exist? Whereas in the first place it should be in some way proved that a nature which is higher, that is, greater and better, than all other natures, exists; in order that from this we may then be able to to prove all attributes which necessarily the being that is greater and better than all possesses.

STUDY QUESTIONS

1. What does Anselm mean by the phrase "that than which nothing greater can be conceived?" Can you conceive of a being than which nothing greater can be conceived?

2. On what grounds does Anselm argue that that than which nothing greater can be conceived cannot exist in the understanding alone, but must exist in reality?

3. How does Anselm try to prove that God alone necessarily exists?

4. How does Gaunilon use the illustration of a perfect lost island as an objection to Anselm? Do you find any weakness in this argument?

For Further Reading

Barnes, J. *The Ontological Argument*. London: Macmillan, 1972.

Descartes, R. *Meditation* III.

Hick, J. and McGill, A. C., eds. *The Many-Faced Argument*. New York: Macmillan, 1967.

Kant. I. *Critique of Pure Reason*. Translated by N. K. Smith. London: Macmillan, 1929 (pp. 500–507).

Plantinga, A., ed. *The Ontological Argument*. Garden City, N.Y.: Doubleday, 1965.

PALEY AND HUME: THE TELEOLOGICAL ARGUMENT

The teleological argument for the existence of God is based on an analogy. We are surrounded by manufactured products, some of which are extraordinarily complex and sophisticated, like computers and space vehicles. We know that these machines have been designed by human minds and produced by human artificers. But we are surrounded, as well, by countless natural objects. Some of these, like the heavenly constellations, are unimaginably vast; others, like a human brain, are many times more complex than any object ever produced by human ingenuity. We must conclude, by analogy with manufactured products that require a designer, that these natural objects, too, must have been designed and produced by some intelligent being and that this being must be possessed of powers commensurate with the scope and complexity of the natural world that he has created. In the two selections that follow, this argument is defended by William Paley and criticized by David Hume.

William Paley (1743–1805) was educated at Cambridge University. Although he studied mathematics there, his real interests lay in theology and moral philosophy. After teaching at Cambridge for several years, he became a clergyman and subsequently held a number of important posts in the Church of England. He failed to become a bishop, presumably because a satire he had written on private property was ill-received by the ecclesiastical hierarchy of his time. For many decades, Paley's book, *A View of the Evidences of Christianity,* was required reading for undergraduates at Cambridge.

For a biographical sketch of David Hume see page 258.

❧ *Paley: Natural Theology*

Chapter I

In crossing a heath, suppose I pitched my foot against a *stone,* and were asked how the stone came to be there; I might possibly answer, that, for anything I knew to the contrary, it had lain there forever: nor would it perhaps be very easy to show the absurdity of this answer. But suppose I had found a *watch* upon the ground, and it should be inquired how the watch happened to be in that place; I should hardly think of the answer which I had before given, that, for anything I knew, the watch might have always been there. Yet why should not this answer serve for the watch as well as for the stone? Why is it not as admissible in the second case, as in the first? For this reason, and for no other, viz. that, when we come to inspect the watch, we perceive (what we could not discover in the stone) that its several parts are framed and put together for a purpose, *e.g.* that they are so formed and adjusted as to produce motion, and that motion so regulated as to point out the hour of the day; that if the different parts had been differently shaped from what they are, of a different size from what they are, or placed after any other manner, or in any other order, than that in which they are placed, either no motion at all would have been carried on in the machine, or none which would have answered the use that is now served by it. To reckon up a few of the plainest of these parts, and of their offices, all tending to one result:—We see a cylindrical box containing a coiled elastic spring, which, by its endeavor to relax itself, turns round the box. We next observe a flexible chain (artificially wrought for the sake of flexure) communicating the action of the spring from the box to the fusee. We then find a series of wheels, the teeth of which catch in, and apply to each other, conducting the motion from the fusee to the balance, and from the balance to the pointer; and at the

same time, by the size and shape of those wheels, so regulating that motion, as to terminate in causing an index, by an equable and measured progression, to pass over a given space in a given time. We take notice that the wheels are made of brass in order to keep them from rust; the springs of steel, no other metal being so elastic; that over the face of the watch there is placed a glass, a material employed in no other part of the work; but in the room of which, if there had been any other than a transparent substance, the hour could not be seen without opening the case. This mechanism being observed (it requires indeed an examination of the instrument, and perhaps some previous knowledge of the subject, to perceive and understand it; but being once, as we have said, observed and understood), the inference, we think, is inevitable; that the watch must have had a maker; that there must have existed, at sometime, and at some place or other, an artificer or artificers, who formed it for the purpose which we find it actually to answer; who comprehended its construction, and designed its use.

I. Nor would it, I apprehend, weaken the conclusion, that we had never seen a watch made: that we had never known an artist capable of making one; that we were altogether incapable of executing such a piece of workmanship ourselves, or of understanding in what manner it was performed; all this being no more than what is true of some exquisite remains of ancient art, of some lost arts, and, to the generality of mankind, of the more curious productions of modern manufacture. Does one man in a million know how oval frames are turned? Ignorance of this kind exalts our opinion of the unseen and unknown artist's skill, if he be unseen and unknown, but raises no doubt in our minds of the existence and agency of such an artist, at some former time, and in some place or other. Nor can I perceive that it varies at all the inference, whether the question arise concerning a human agent, or concerning an agent of a different species, or an agent possessing, in some respects, a different nature.

II. Neither, secondly, would it invalidate our conclusion, that the watch sometimes went wrong, or that it seldom went exactly right. The purpose of the machinery, the design and the designer, might be evident, and in the case supposed would be evident, in whatever way we accounted for the irregularity of the movement, or whether we could account for it or not. It is not necessary that a machine be perfect, in order to show with what design it was made: still less necessary, where the only question is, whether it were made with any design at all.

III. Nor, thirdly, would it bring any uncertainty into the argument, if there were a few parts of the watch, concerning which we could not discover, or had not yet discovered, in what manner they conduced to the general effect; or even some parts, concerning which we could not ascertain whether they conduced to that effect in any manner whatever. For, as to the first branch of the case; if by the loss, or disorder, or decay of the parts in question, the movement of the watch were found in fact to be stopped, or disturbed, or retarded, no doubt would remain in our minds as to the utility or intention of these parts, although we should be unable to investigate the manner according to which, or the connexion by which, the ultimate effect depended upon their action or assistance; and the more complex is the machine, the more likely is this obscurity to arise. Then, as to the second thing supposed, namely, that there were parts which might be spared, without prejudice to the movement of the watch, and that we had proved this by experiment—these superfluous parts, even if we were completely assured that they were such, would not vacate the reasoning which we had instituted concerning other parts. The indication of contrivance remained, with respect to them, nearly as it was before.

IV. Nor, fourthly, would any man in his senses think the existence of the watch, with its various machinery, accounted for, by being told that it was one out of possible combinations of material forms; that whatever he had found in the place where he found the watch, must have contained some internal configuration or other; and that this configuration might be the structure now exhibited, viz. of the works of a watch, as well as a different structure.

V. Nor, fifthly, would it yield his inquiry more satisfaction to be answered, that there existed in things a principle of order, which had disposed the parts of the watch into their present form and situation. He never knew a watch made by the principle of order; nor can he even form to himself an idea of what is meant by a principle of order distinct from the intelligence of the watchmaker.

VI. Sixthly, he would be surprised to hear that the mechanism of the watch was no proof of contrivance, only a motive to induce the mind to think so.

VII. And not less surprised to be informed, that the watch in his hand was nothing more than the result of the laws of *metallic* nature. It is a perversion of language to assign any law as the efficient, operative cause of anything. A law presupposes an agent; for it is only the mode according to which an agent proceeds: it implies a power; for it is the order, according to which that power acts. Without this agent, without this power, which are both distinct from itself, the *law* does nothing; is nothing. The expression, "the law of metallic nature," may sound strange and harsh to a philosophic ear; but it seems quite as justifiable as some others which are more familiar to him, such as "the law of vegetable nature," "the law of animal nature," or indeed as "the law of nature" in general, when assigned as the cause of phenomena, in exclusion of agency and power; or when it is substituted into the place of these.

VIII. Neither, lastly, would our observer be driven out of his conclusion, or from his confidence in its truth, by being told that he knew nothing at all about the matter. He knows enough for his argument. He knows the utility of the end: he knows the subserviency and adaptation of the means to the end. These points being known, his ignorance of other points, his doubts concerning other points, affect not the certainty of his reasoning. The consciousness of knowing little need not beget a distrust of that which he does know.

Chapter II

Suppose, in the next place, that the person who found the watch, should, after sometime, discover, that, in addition to all the properties which he had hitherto observed in it, it possessed the unexpected property of producing, in the course of its movement, another watch like itself, (the thing is conceivable;) that it contained within it a mechanism, a system of parts, a mould for instance, or a complex adjustment of lathes, files, and other tools, evidently and separately calculated for this purpose; let us inquire, what effect ought such a discovery to have upon his former conclusion.

I. The first effect would be to increase his admiration of the contrivance, and his conviction of the consummate skill of the contriver. Whether he regarded the object of the contrivance, the distinct apparatus, the intricate, yet in many parts intelligible mechanism, by which it was carried on, he would perceive, in this new observation, nothing but an additional reason for doing what he had already done,—for referring the construction of the watch to design, and to supreme art. If that construction *without* this property, or, which is the same thing, before this property had been noticed, proved intention and art to have been employed about it, still more strong would the proof appear, when he came to the knowledge of this farther property, the crown and perfection of all the rest.

II. He would reflect, that though the watch before him were, *in some sense*, the maker of the watch which was fabricated in the course of its movements, yet it was in a very different sense from that in which a carpenter, for instance, is the maker of a chair; the author of its contrivance, the cause of the relation of its parts to their use.

With respect to these, the first watch was no cause at all to the second: in no such sense as this was it the author of the constitution and order, either of the parts which the new watch contained, or of the parts by the aid and instrumentality of which it was produced. We might possibly say, but with great latitude of expression, that a stream of water ground corn; but no latitude of expression would allow us to say, no stretch of conjecture could lead us to think, that the stream of water built the mill, though it were too ancient for us to know who the builder was. What the stream of water does in the affair, is neither more nor less than this; by the application of an unintelligent impulse to a mechanism previously arranged, arranged independently of it, and arranged by intelligence, an effect is produced, viz. the corn is ground. But the effect results from the arrangement. The force of the stream cannot be said to be the cause or author of the effect, still less of the arrangement. Understanding and plan in the formation of the mill were not the less necessary, for any share which the water has in grinding the corn; yet is this share the same as that which the watch would have contributed to the production of the new watch, upon the supposition assumed in the last section. Therefore,

III. Though it be now no longer probable, that the individual watch which our observer had found was made immediately by the hand of an artificer, yet doth not this alteration in any-wise affect the inference, that an artificer had been originally employed and concerned in the production. The argument from design remains as it was. Marks of design and contrivance are no more accounted for now than they were before. In the same thing, we may ask for the cause of different properties. We may ask for the cause of the color of a body, of its hardness, of its heat; and these causes may be all different. We are now asking for the cause of that subserviency to a use, that relation to an end, which we have remarked in the watch before us. No answer is given to this question by telling us that a preceding watch produced it. There cannot be design without a designer; contrivance without a contriver; order, without choice; arrangement, without anything capable of arranging; subserviency and relation to a purpose, without that which could intend a purpose; means suitable to an end, and executing their office in accomplishing that end, without the end ever having been contemplated, or the means accommodated to it. Arrangement, disposition of parts, subserviency of means to an end, relation of instruments to a use, imply the presence of intelligence and mind. No one, therefore, can rationally believe, that the insensible, inanimate watch, from which the watch before us issued, was the proper cause of the mechanism we so much admire in it;—could be truly said to have constructed the instrument, disposed its parts, assigned their office, determined their order, action, and mutual dependency, combined their several motions into one result, and that also a result connected with the utilities of other beings. All these properties, therefore, are as much unaccounted for as they were before.

IV. Nor is anything gained by running the difficulty farther back, *i.e.* by supposing the watch before us to have been produced from another watch, that from a former, and so on indefinitely. Our going back ever so far brings us no nearer to the least degree of satisfaction upon the subject. Contrivance is still unaccounted for. We still want a contriver. A designing mind is neither supplied by this supposition, nor dispensed with. If the difficulty were diminished the farther we went back, by going back indefinitely we might exhaust it. And this is the only case to which this sort of reasoning applies. Where there is a tendency, or, as we increase the number of terms, a continual approach towards a limit, *there*, by supposing the number of terms to be what is called infinite, we may conceive the limit to be attained: but where there is no such tendency, or approach, nothing is effected by lengthening the series. There is no difference, as to the point in question, (whatever there may be as to many points,) between one series and

another; between a series which is finite, and a series which is infinite. A chain, composed of an infinite number of links, can no more support itself, than a chain composed of a finite number of links. And of this we are assured, (though we never *can* have tried the experiment,) because, by increasing the number of links, from ten, for instance, to a hundred, from a hundred to a thousand, &c. we make not the smallest approach, we observe not the smallest tendency, towards self-support. There is no difference in this respect (yet there may be a great difference in several respects) between a chain of a greater or less length, between one chain and another, between one that is finite and one that is infinite. This very much resembles the case before us. The machine which we are inspecting demonstrates, by its construction, contrivance and design. Contrivance must have had a contriver; design, a designer; whether the machine immediately proceeded from another machine or not. That circumstance alters not the case. That other machine may, in like manner, have proceeded from a former machine: nor does that alter the case; contrivance must have had a contriver. That former one from one preceding it: no alteration still; a contriver is still necessary. No tendency is perceived, no approach towards a diminution of this necessity. It is the same with any and every succession of these machines; a succession of ten, of a hundred, of a thousand; with one series as with another; a series which is finite, as with a series which is infinite. In whatever other respects they may differ, in this they do not. In all, equally, contrivance and design are unaccounted for.

The question is not simply, How came the first watch into existence? which question, it may be pretended, is done away by supposing the series of watches thus produced from one another to have been infinite, and consequently to have had no such *first*, for which it was necessary to provide a cause. This, perhaps, would have been nearly the state of the question, if nothing had been before us but an unorganized, unmechanized substance, without mark or indication of contrivance. It might be difficult to show that such substance could not have existed from eternity, either in succession (if it were possible, which I think it is not, for unorganized bodies to spring from one another) or by individual perpetuity. But that is not the question now. To suppose it to be so, is to suppose that it made no difference whether we had found a watch or a stone. As it is, the metaphysics of that question have no place; for, in the watch which we are examining, are seen contrivance, design; an end, a purpose; means for the end, adaptation to the purpose. And the question which irresistibly presses upon our thoughts, is, whence this contrivance and design? The thing required is the intending mind, the adapting hand, the intelligence by which that hand was directed. This question, this demand, is not shaken off, by increasing a number or succession of substances, destitute of these properties; nor the more, by increasing that number to infinity. If it be said, that, upon the supposition of one watch being produced from another in the course of that other's movements, and by means of the mechanism within it, we have a cause for the watch in my hand, viz. the watch from which it proceeded: I deny, that for the design, the contrivance, the suitableness of means to an end, the adaptation of instruments to a use, (all which we discover in a watch,) we have any cause whatever. It is in vain, therefore, to assign a series of such causes, or to allege that a series may be carried back to infinity; for I do not admit that we have yet any cause at all of the phenomena, still less any series of causes either finite or infinite. Here is contrivance, but no contriver; proofs of design, but no designer.

V. Our observer would farther also reflect, that the maker of the watch before him, was, in truth and reality, the maker of every watch produced from it; there being no difference (except that the latter manifests a more exquisite skill) between the making of another watch with his own hands, by the mediation of files, lathes, chisels, &c. and the disposing, fixing, and inserting of these instruments, or of others equivalent to them, in the body of the watch already made, in such a manner as to form a new watch in the course of the movements which he had given to the old one. It is only working by one set of tools instead of another.

The conclusion which the *first* examination of the watch, of its works, construction, and movement, suggested, was, that it must have had, for the cause and author of that construction, an artificer, who understood its mechanism, and designed its use. This conclusion is invincible. A *second* examination presents us with a new discovery. The watch is found, in the course of its movement, to produce another watch, similar to itself: and not only so, but we perceive in it a system or organization, separately calculated for that purpose. What effect would this discovery have or ought it to have, upon our former inference? What, as hath already been said, but to increase, beyond measure, our admiration of the skill which had been employed in the formation of such a machine! Or shall it, instead of this, all at once turn us round to an opposite conclusion, viz. that no art or skill whatever has been concerned in the business, although all other evidences of art and skill remain as they were, and this last and supreme piece of art be now added to the rest? Can this be maintained without absurdity? Yet this is atheism.

Chapter III

This is atheism: for every indication of contrivance, every manifestation of design, which existed in the watch, exists in the works of nature; with the difference, on the side of nature, of being greater and more, and that in a degree which exceeds all computation. I mean, that the contrivances of nature surpass the contrivances of art, in the complexity, subtilty, and curiosity of the mechanism; and still more, if possible, do they go beyond them in number and variety: yet, in a multitude of cases, are not less evidently mechanical, not less evidently contrivances, not less evidently accommodated to their end, or suited to their office, than are the most perfect productions of human ingenuity.

I know no better method of introducing so large a subject, than that of comparing a single thing with a single thing; an eye, for example, with a telescope. As far as the examination of the instrument goes, there is precisely the same proof that the eye was made for vision, as there is that the telescope was made for assisting it. They are made upon the same principles; both being adjusted to the laws by which the transmission and refraction of rays of light are regulated. I speak not of the origin of the laws themselves; but such laws being fixed, the construction, in both cases, is adapted to them. For instance; these laws require, in order to produce the same effect, that the rays of light, in passing from water into the eye, should be refracted by a more convex surface than when it passes out of air into the eye. Accordingly we find, that the eye of a fish, in that part of it called the crystalline lens, is much rounder than the eye of terrestrial animals. What plainer manifestation of design can there be than this difference? What could a mathematical instrument-maker have done more, to show his knowledge of his principle, his application of that knowledge, his suiting of his means to his end; I will not say to display the compass or excellence of his skill and art, for in these all comparison is indecorous, but to testify counsel, choice, consideration, purpose?

Chapter VI

Were there no example in the world of contrivance except that of the *eye,* it would be alone sufficient to support the conclusion which we draw from it, as to the necessity of an intelligent Creator. It could never be got rid of; because it could not be accounted for by any other supposition, which did not contradict all the principles we possess of knowledge: the principles, according to which things do, as often as they can be brought to the test of experience, turn out to be true or false. Its coats and humours constructed as the lenses of a telescope are constructed for the refraction of rays of light to a point, which forms the proper office of the organ: the provision in its muscles for turning its pupil to the object, similar to that which is given to the telescope by screws, and upon which power of direction in the eye, the exercise of its office as an optical instrument depends; the farther provision for its defence, its constant lubricity and moisture, which we see in its socket and its lids, in its gland for the secretion of the matter of tears, its outlet or communication with the nose for carrying off the liquid after the eye is washed with it; these provisions compose altogether an apparatus, a system of parts, a preparation of means, so manifest in their design, so exquisite in their contrivance, so successful in their issue, so precious, and so infinitely beneficial in their use, as, in my opinion, to bear down all doubt that can be raised upon the subject. And what I wish, under the title of the present chapter, to observe is, that if other parts of nature were inaccessible to our inquiries, or even if other parts of nature presented nothing to our examination but disorder and confusion, the validity of this example would remain the same. If there were but one watch in the world, it would not be less certain that it had a maker. If we had never in our lives seen any but one single kind of hydraulic machine, yet, if of that one kind we understood the mechanism and use, we should be as perfectly assured that it proceeded from the hand, and thought, and skill of a workman, as if we visited a museum of the arts, and saw collected there twenty different kinds of machines for drawing water, or a thousand different kinds for other purposes. Of this point, each machine is a proof, independently of all the rest. So it is with the evidences of a divine agency. The proof is not a conclusion which lies at the end of a chain of reasoning, of which chain each instance of contrivance is only a link, and of which, if one link fail, the whole falls; but it is an argument separately supplied by every separate example. An error in stating an example affects only that example. The argument is cumulative, in the fullest sense of that term. The eye proves it without the ear; the ear without the eye. The proof in each example is complete; for when the design of the part, and the conduciveness of its structure to that design is shown, the mind may set itself at rest; no future consideration can detract anything from the force of the example.

STUDY QUESTIONS
1. What is the point of Paley's detailed description of a watch?

2. What is the point of Paley's discussion of the watch that makes new watches?
3. What does Paley mean by atheism? What connection does it have with watches?
4. Construct in your own words the analogy that Paley presents in the selection to prove the existence of God.

For Further Reading appears on page 337.

🌿 *Hume: Dialogues Concerning Natural Religion*

Part II

"Not to lose any time in circumlocutions," said Cleanthes, addressing himself to Demea, "much less in replying to the pious declamations of Philo, I shall briefly explain how I conceive this matter. Look round the world: contemplate the whole and every part of it: You will find it to be nothing but one great machine, subdivided into an infinite number of lesser machines, which again admit of subdivisions, to a degree beyond what human senses and faculties can trace and explain. All these various machines, and even their most minute parts, are adjusted to each other with an accuracy, which ravishes into admiration all men, who have ever contemplated them. The curious adapting of means to ends, throughout all nature, resembles exactly, though it much exceeds, the productions of human contrivance; of human design, thought, wisdom, and intelligence. Since therefore the effects resemble each other, we are led to infer, by all the rules of analogy, that the causes also resemble; and that the Author of Nature is somewhat similar to the mind of man; though possessed of much larger faculties, proportioned to the grandeur of the work, which he has executed. By this argument *a posteriori*, and by this argument alone, do we prove at once

First published posthumously in 1779.

the existence of a Deity, and his similarity to human mind and intelligence."

"I shall be so free, Cleanthes," said Demea, "as to tell you, that from the beginning, I could not approve of your conclusion concerning the similarity of the Deity to men; still less can I approve of the mediums, by which you endeavour to establish it. What! No demonstration of the Being of a God! No abstract arguments! No proofs *a priori!* Are these, which have hitherto been so much insisted on by philosophers, all fallacy, all sophism? Can we reach no farther in this subject than experience and probability? I will not say, that this is betraying the cause of a deity: But surely, by this affected candor, you give advantage to atheists, which they never could obtain, by the mere dint of argument and reasoning."

"What I chiefly scruple in this subject," said Philo, "is not so much, that all religious arguments are by Cleanthes reduced to experience, as that they appear not to be even the most certain and irrefragable of that inferior kind. That a stone will fall, that fire will burn, that the earth has solidity, we have observed a thousand and a thousand times; and when any new instance of this nature is presented, we draw without hesitation the accustomed inference. The exact similarity of the cases gives us a perfect assurance of a similar event; and a stronger evidence is never desired nor sought after. But wherever you depart, in the least, from the similarity of the cases, you diminish proportionably the evidence; and may at last bring it to a very weak *analogy*, which is confessedly liable to error and uncertainty. After having experienced the circulation of the blood in human creatures, we make no doubt that it takes place in Titius and Maevius: but from its circulation in frogs and fishes, it is only a presumption, though a strong one, from analogy, that it takes place in men and other animals. The analogical reasoning is much weaker, when we infer the circulation of the sap in vegetables from our experience, that the blood circulates in animals; and those, who hastily followed that imperfect analogy, are found, by more accurate experiments, to have been mistaken.

"If we see a house, Cleanthes, we conclude, with the greatest certainty, that it had an architect or builder; because this is precisely that species of effect, which we have experienced to proceed from that species of cause. But surely you will not affirm, that the universe bears such a resemblance to a house, that we can with the same certainty infer a similar cause, or that the analogy is here entire and perfect. The dissimilitude is so striking, that the utmost you can here pretend to is a guess, a conjecture, a presumption concerning a similar cause; and how that pretension will be received in the world, I leave you to consider."

"It would surely be very ill received," replied Cleanthes; "and I should be deservedly blamed and detested, did I allow, that the proofs of a Deity amounted to no more than a guess or conjecture. But is the whole adjustment of means to ends in a house and in the universe so slight a resemblance? The economy of final causes? The order, proportion, and arrangement of every part? Steps of a stair are plainly contrived, that human legs may use them in mounting; and this inference is certain and infallible. Human legs are also contrived for walking and mounting; and this inference, I allow, is not altogether so cer-

tain, because of the dissimilarity which you remark; but does it, therefore, deserve the name only of presumption or conjecture?"

"Good God!" cried Demea, interrupting him, "where are we? Zealous defenders of religion allow, that the proofs of a Deity fall short of perfect evidence! And you, Philo, on whose assistance I depended, in proving the adorable mysteriousness of the Divine Nature, do you assent to all these extravagant opinions of Cleanthes? For what other name can I give them? Or why spare my censure, when such principles are advanced, supported by such an authority, before so young a man as Pamphilus?"

"You seem not to apprehend," replied Philo, "that I argue with Cleanthes in his own way; and by showing him the dangerous consequences of his tenets, hope at last to reduce him to our opinion. But what sticks most with you, I observe, is the representation which Cleanthes has made of the argument *a posteriori;* and finding that that argument is likely to escape your hold and vanish into air, you think it so disguised, that you can scarcely believe it to be set in its true light. Now, however much I may dissent, in other respects, from the dangerous principles of Cleanthes, I must allow, that he has fairly represented that argument; and I shall endeavor so to state the matter to you, that you will entertain no farther scruples with regard to it.

"Were a man to abstract from everything which he knows or has seen, he would be altogether incapable, merely from his own ideas, to determine what kind of scene the universe must be, or to give the preference to one state or situation of things above another. For as nothing which he clearly conceives, could be esteemed impossible or implying a contradiction, every chimera of his fancy would be upon an equal footing; nor could he assign any just reason, why he adheres to one idea or system, and rejects the others, which are equally possible.

"Again; after he opens his eyes, and contemplates the world, as it really is, it would be impossible for him, at first, to assign the cause of any one event; much less, of the whole of things or of the universe. He might set his fancy a rambling; and she might bring him in an infinite variety of reports and representations. These would all be possible; but being all equally possible, he would never, of himself, give a satisfactory account for his preferring one of them to the rest. Experience alone can point out to him the true cause of any phenomenon.

"Now, according to this method of reasoning, Demea, it follows (and is, indeed, tacitly allowed by Cleanthes himself) that order, arrangement, or the adjustment of final causes is not, of itself, any proof of design; but only so far as it has been experienced to proceed from that principle. For aught we can know *a priori*, matter may contain the source or spring of order originally, within itself, as well as mind does; and there is no more difficulty in conceiving, that the several elements, from an internal unknown cause, may fall into the most exquisite arrangement, than to conceive that their ideas, in the great, universal mind, from a like internal, unknown cause, fall into that arrangement. The equal possibility of both these suppositions is allowed. But by experience we find (according to Cleanthes), that there is a difference between them. Throw several pieces of steel together, without shape or form; they will never arrange themselves so as to compose a watch: stone, and mortar, and wood, without an architect, never erect a house. But the ideas in a human mind, we see, by an unknown, inexplicable economy, arrange themselves so as to form the plan of a watch or house. Experience, therefore, proves, that there is an original principle of order in mind, not in matter. From similar effects we infer similar causes. The adjustment of means to ends is alike in the universe, as in a machine of human contrivance. The causes, therefore, must be resembling.

"I was from the beginning scandalized, I must own, with this resemblance, which is asserted, between the Deity and human creatures; and must conceive it to imply such a degradation of the Supreme Being

as no sound Theist could endure. With your assistance, therefore, Demea, I shall endeavor to defend what you justly called the adorable mysteriousness of the Divine Nature, and shall refute this reasoning of Cleanthes, provided he allows, that I have made a fair representation of it."

When Cleanthes had assented, Philo, after a short pause, proceeded in the following manner.

"That all inferences, Cleanthes, concerning fact, are founded on experience, and that all experimental reasonings are founded on the supposition, that similar causes prove similar effects, and similar effects similar causes, I shall not, at present, much dispute with you. But observe, I entreat you, with what extreme caution all just reasoners proceed in the transferring of experiments to similar cases. Unless the cases be exactly similar, they repose no perfect confidence in applying their past observation to any particular phenomenon. Every alteration of circumstance occasions a doubt concerning the event; and it requires new experiments to prove certainly, that the new circumstances are of no moment or importance. A change in bulk, situation, arrangement, age, disposition of the air, or surrounding bodies; any of these particulars may be attended with the most unexpected consequences: and unless the objects be quite familiar to us, it is the highest temerity to expect with assurance, after any of these changes, an event similar to that which before fell under our observation. The slow and deliberate steps of philosophers, here, if any where, are distinguished from the precipitate march of the vulgar, who, hurried on by the smallest similitudes, are incapable of all discernment or consideration.

"But can you think, Cleanthes, that your usual phlegm and philosophy have been preserved in so wide a step as you have taken, when you compared to the universe, houses, ships, furniture, machines; and from their similarity in some circumstances inferred a similarity in their causes? Thought, design, intelligence, such as we discover in men and other animals, is no more than one of the springs and principles of the universe, as well as heat or cold, attraction or repulsion, and a hundred others, which fall under daily observation. It is an active cause, by which some particular parts of nature, we find, produce alterations on other parts. But can a conclusion, with any propriety, be transferred from parts to the whole? Does not the great disproportion bar all comparison and inference? From observing the growth of a hair, can we learn any thing concerning the generation of a man? Would the manner of a leaf's blowing, even though perfectly known, afford us any instruction concerning the vegetation of a tree?

"But allowing that we were to take the *operations* of one part of nature upon another for the foundation of our judgment concerning the *origin* of the whole (which never can be admitted), yet why select so minute, so weak, so bounded a principle as the reason and design of animals is found to be upon this planet? What particular privilege has this little agitation of the brain which we call *thought,* that we must thus make it the model of the whole universe? Our partiality in our own favor does indeed present it on all occasions; but sound philosophy ought carefully to guard against so natural an illusion.

"So far from admitting," continued Philo, "that the operations of a part can afford us any just conclusion concerning the origin of the whole, I will not allow any one part to form a rule for another part, if the latter be very remote from the former. Is there any reasonable ground to conclude, that the inhabitants of other planets possess thought, intelligence, reason, or anything similar to these faculties in men? When Nature has so extremely diversified her manner of operation in this small globe; can we imagine, that she incessantly copies herself throughout so immense a universe? And if thought, as we may well suppose, be confined merely to this narrow corner, and has even there so limited a sphere of action; with what propriety can we assign it for the original cause of all things? The narrow views of a peasant, who

makes his domestic economy the rule for the government of kingdoms, is in comparison a pardonable sophism.

"But were we ever so much assured, that a thought and reason, resembling the human, were to be found throughout the whole universe, and were its activity elsewhere vastly greater and more commanding than it appears in this globe; yet I cannot see, why the operations of a world, constituted, arranged, adjusted, can with any propriety be extended to a world, which is in its embryo-state, and is advancing towards that constitution and arrangement. By observation, we know somewhat of the economy, action, and nourishment of a finished animal; but we must transfer with great caution that observation to the growth of a fetus in the womb, and still more, to the formation of an animalcule in the loins of its male parent. Nature, we find, even from our limited experience, possesses an infinite number of springs and principles, which incessantly discover themselves on every change of her position and situation. And what new and unknown principles would actuate her in so new and unknown a situation as that of the formation of a universe, we cannot, without the utmost temerity, pretend to determine.

"A very small part of this great system, during a very short time, is very imperfectly discovered to us: and do we thence pronounce decisively concerning the origin of the whole?

"Admirable conclusion! Stone, wood, brick, iron, brass, have not, at this time, in this minute globe of earth, an order of arrangement without human art and contrivance: therefore the universe could not originally attain its order and arrangement, without something similar to human art. But is a part of nature a rule for another part very wide of the former? Is it a rule for the whole? Is a very small part a rule for the universe? Is nature in one situation a certain rule for nature in another situation, vastly different from the former?

"And can you blame me, Cleanthes, if I here imitate the prudent reserve of Simonides, who according to the noted story, being asked by Hiero *What God was?* desired a day to think of it, and then two days more; and after that manner continually prolonged the term, without ever bringing in his definition or description? Could you even blame me, if I had answered at first *that I did not know,* and was sensible that this subject lay vastly beyond the reach of my faculties? You might cry out sceptic and railer as much as you pleased: but having found, in so many other subjects, much more familiar, the imperfections and even contradictions of human reason, I never should expect any success from its feeble conjectures, in a subject, so sublime, and so remote from the sphere of our observation. When two *species* of objects have always been observed to be conjoined together, I can *infer,* by custom, the existence of one wherever I *see* the existence of the other: and this I call an argument from experience. But how this argument can have place, where the objects, as in the present case, are single, individual, without parallel or specific resemblance, may be difficult to explain. And will any man tell me with a serious countenance, that an orderly universe must arise from some thought and art, like the human; because we have experience of it? To ascertain this reasoning, it were requisite, that we had experience of the origin of worlds; and it is not sufficient surely, that we have seen ships and cities arise from human art and contrivance . . . ."

Philo was proceeding in this vehement manner, somewhat between jest and earnest, as it appeared to me; when he observed some signs of impatience in Cleanthes, and then immediately stopped short. "What I had to suggest," said Cleanthes, "is only that you would not abuse terms, or make use of popular expressions to subvert philosophical reasonings. You know, that the vulgar often distinguish reason from experience, even where the question relates only to matter of fact and existence; even though it is found, where that *reason* is properly analyzed, that it is nothing but a species of experience. To prove by experience the origin of the universe from mind is not more contrary to common speech than to prove the motion of the earth from the same principle. And a caviller might raise all the same objections to the Copernican system, which you have urged against my reasonings. Have you other earths, might he say, which you have seen to move? Have. . . ."

"Yes!" cried Philo, interrupting him, "we have other earths. Is not the moon another earth, which we see to turn round its center? Is not Venus another earth, where we observe the same phenomenon? Are not the revolutions of the sun also a confirmation, from analogy, of the same theory? All the planets, are they not earths, which revolve about the sun? Are not the satellites moons, which move round Jupiter and Saturn, and along with these primary planets, round the sun? These analogies and resemblances, with others, which I have not mentioned, are the sole proofs of the Copernican system: and to you it belongs to consider, whether you have any analogies of the same kind to support your theory.

"In reality, Cleanthes," continued he, "the modern system of astronomy is now so much received by all inquirers, and has become so essential a part even of our earliest education, that we are not commonly very scrupulous in examining the reasons upon which it is founded. It is now become a matter of mere curiosity to study the first writers on that subject, who had the full force of prejudice to encounter, and were obliged to turn their arguments on every side, in order to render them popular and convincing. But if we peruse Galileo's famous *Dialogues* concerning the system of the world, we shall find, that the great genius, one of the sublimest that ever existed, first bent all his endeavors to prove, that there was no foundation for the distinction commonly made between elementary and celestial substances. The schools, proceeding from the illusions of sense, had carried this distinction very far; and had established the latter substances to be ingenerable, incorruptible, unalterable, impassable; and had assigned all the opposite qualities to the former. But Galileo, beginning with the moon, proved its similarity in every particular to the earth; its convex figure, its natural darkness when not illuminated, its density, its distinction into solid and liquid, the variations of its phases, the mutual illuminations of the earth and moon, their mutual eclipses, the inequalities of the lunar surface, etc. After many instances of this kind, with regard to all the planets, men plainly saw, that these bodies became proper objects of experience; and that the similarity of their nature enabled us to extend the same arguments and phenomena from one to the other.

"In this cautious proceeding of the astronomers, you may read your own condemnation, Cleanthes; or rather you may see, that the subject in which you are engaged exceeds all human reason and inquiry. Can you pretend to show any such similarity between the fabric of a house, and the generation of a universe? Have you ever seen nature in any such situation as resembles the first arrangement of the elements? Have worlds ever been formed under your eye? and have you had leisure to observe the whole progress of the phenomenon, from the first appearance of order to its final consummation? If you have, then cite your experience, and deliver your theory."

Part III

"How the most absurd argument," replied Cleanthes, "in the hands of a man of ingenuity and invention, may acquire an air of probability! Are you not aware, Philo, that it became necessary for Copernicus and his first disciples to prove the similarity of the terrestrial and celestial matter; because several philosophers, blinded by old systems, and supported by some sensible appearances, had denied this similarity? But that it is by no means necessary, that Theists should prove the similarity of the works of Nature to those of Art; because this similarity is self-evident and undeniable? The same matter, a like form: what more is requisite to show an analogy between their causes, and to ascertain the ori-

gin of all things from a divine purpose and intention? Your objections, I must freely tell you, are no better than the abstruse cavils of those philosophers who denied motion; and ought to be refuted in the same manner, by illustrations, examples, and instances, rather than by serious argument and philosophy.

"Suppose, therefore, that an articulate voice were heard in the clouds, much louder and more melodious than any which human art could ever reach: suppose, that this voice were extended in the same instant over all nations, and spoke to each nation in its own language and dialect: suppose, that the words delivered not only contain a just sense and meaning, but convey some instruction altogether worthy of a benevolent being, superior to mankind: could you possibly hesitate a moment concerning the cause of this voice? and must you not instantly ascribe it to some design or purpose? Yet I cannot see but all the same objections (if they merit that appellation) which lie against the system of Theism, may also be produced against this inference.

"Might you not say, that all conclusions concerning fact were founded on experience: that when we hear an articulate voice in the dark, and thence infer a man, it is only the resemblance of the effects, which leads us to conclude that there is a like resemblance in the cause: but that this extraordinary voice, by its loudness, extent, and flexibility to all languages, bears so little analogy to any human voice, that we have no reason to suppose any analogy in their causes: and consequently, that a rational, wise, coherent speech proceeded, you knew not whence, from some accidental whistling of the winds, not from any divine reason or intelligence? You see clearly your own objections in these cavils and I hope too, you see clearly, that they cannot possibly have more force in the one case than in the other.

"But to bring the case still nearer the present one of the universe, I shall make two suppositions, which imply not any absurdity or impossibility. Suppose, that there is a natural, universal, invariable language, common to every individual of the human race, and that books are natural productions, which perpetuate themselves in the same manner with animals and vegetables, by descent and propagation. Several expressions of our passions contain a universal language: all brute animals have a natural speech, which, however limited, is very intelligible to their own species. And as there are infinitely fewer parts and less contrivance in the finest composition of eloquence, than in the coarsest organized body, the propagation of an *Iliad* or *Aeneid* is an easier supposition than that of any plant or animal.

"Suppose, therefore, that you enter into your library, thus peopled by natural volumes, containing the most refined reason and most exquisite beauty: could you possibly open one of them, and doubt, that its original cause bore the strongest analogy to mind and intelligence? When it reasons and discourses; when it expostulates, argues, and enforces its views and topics; when it applies sometimes to the pure intellect, sometimes to the affections; when it collects, disposes, and adorns every consideration suited to the subject: could you persist in asserting, that all this, at the bottom, had really no meaning, and that the first formation of this volume in the loins of its original parent proceeded not from thought and design? Your obstinacy, I know, reaches not that degree of firmness: even your skeptical play and wantonness would be abashed at so glaring an absurdity.

"But if there be any difference, Philo, between this supposed case and the real one of the universe, it is all to the advantage of the latter. The anatomy of an animal affords many stronger instances of design than the perusal of Livy or Tacitus: and any objection which you start in the former case, by carrying me back to so unusual and extraordinary a scene as the first formation of worlds, the same objection has place on the supposition of our vegetating library. Choose, then, your party, Philo, without ambiguity or evasion; assert either that a rational volume is no proof of a rational cause, or admit of a similar cause to all the works of nature. ·

"Let me here observe too," continued Cleanthes, "that this religious argument, instead of being weakened by that skepticism, so much affected by you, rather acquires force from it, and becomes more firm and undisputed. To exclude all arguments or reasoning of every kind is either affectation or madness. The declared profession of every reasonable skeptic is only to reject abstruse, remote, and refined arguments; to adhere to common sense and the plain instincts of nature; and to assent, wherever any reasons strike him with so full a force, that he cannot, without the greatest violence, prevent it. Now the arguments for Natural Religion are plainly of this kind; and nothing but the most perverse, obstinate metaphysics can reject them. Consider, anatomize the eye; survey its structure and contrivance; and tell me, from your own feeling, if the idea of a contriver does not immediately flow in upon you with a force like that of sensation. The most obvious conclusion surely is in favor of design; and it requires time, reflection and study, to summon up those frivolous, though abstruse objections, which can support infidelity. Who can behold the male and female of each species, the correspondence of their parts and instincts, their passions and whole course of life before and after generation, but must be sensible, that the propagation of the species is intended by Nature? Millions and millions of such instances present themselves through every part of the universe; and no language can convey a more intelligible, irresistible meaning, than the curious adjustment of final causes. To what degree, therefore, of blind dogmatism must one have attained, to reject such natural and such convincing arguments?

"Some beauties in writing we may meet with, which seem contrary to rules, and which gain the affections, and animate the imagination, in opposition to all the precepts of criticism, and to the authority of the established masters of art. And if the argument for Theism be, as you pretend, contradictory to the principles of logic; its universal, its irresistible influence proves clearly, that there may be arguments of a like irregular nature. Whatever cavils may be urged; an orderly world, as well as a coherent, articulate speech, will still be received as an incontestable proof of design and intention.

"It sometimes happens, I own, that the religious arguments have not their due influence on an ignorant savage and barbarian; not because they are obscure and difficult, but because he never asks himself any question with regard to them. Whence arises the curious structure of an animal? From the copulation of its parents. And these whence? From *their* parents? A few removes set the objects at such a distance, that to him they are lost in darkness and confusion; nor is he actuated by any curiosity to trace them farther. But this is neither dogmatism nor skepticism, but stupidity; a state of mind very different from your sifting, inquisitive disposition, my ingenious friend. You can trace causes from effects: you can compare the most distant and remote objects: and your greatest errors proceed not from barrenness of thought and invention, but from too luxuriant a fertility, which suppresses your natural good sense, by a profusion of unnecessary scruples and objections."

• • •

Part V

• • •

"Now, Cleanthes," said Philo, with an air of alacrity and triumph, "mark the consequences. *First,* by this method of reasoning, you renounce all claim to infinity in any of the attributes of the Deity. For as the cause ought only to be proportioned to the effect, and the effect, so far as it falls under our cognizance, is not infinite; what pretensions have we, upon your suppositions, to ascribe that attribute to the divine Being? You will still insist, that, by removing him so much from all similarity to human creatures, we give in to the most arbitrary hypothesis, and at the same time weaken all proofs of his existence.

"*Secondly,* you have no reason, on your theory, for ascribing perfection to the Deity, even in his finite capacity; or for supposing him free from every error, mistake, or incoherence in his undertakings. There are many inexplicable difficulties in the works of Nature, which, if we allow a perfect author to be proved *a priori,* are easily solved, and become only seeming difficulties, from the narrow capacity of man, who cannot trace infinite relations. But according to your method of reasoning, these difficulties become all real; and perhaps will be insisted on, as new instances of likeness to human art and contrivance. At least, you must acknowledge, that it is impossible for us to tell, from our limited views, whether this system contains any great faults, or deserves any considerable praise, if compared to other possible, and even real systems. Could a peasant, if the *Aeneid* were read to him, pronounce that poem to be absolutely faultless, or even assign to it its proper rank among the productions of human wit; he, who had never seen any other production?

"But were this world ever so perfect a production, it must still remain uncertain, whether all the excellences of the work can justly be ascribed to the workman. If we survey a ship, what an exalted idea must we form of the ingenuity of the carpenter, who framed so complicated, useful, and beautiful a machine? And what surprise must we feel, when we find him a stupid mechanic, who imitated others, and copied an art, which, through a long succession of ages, after multiplied trials, mistakes, corrections, deliberations, and controversies, had been gradually improving? Many worlds might have been botched and bungled, throughout an eternity, ere this system was struck out: much labor lost: many fruitless trials made: and a slow, but continued improvement carried on during infinite ages in the art of world-making. In such subjects, who can determine, where the truth; nay, who can conjecture where the probability lies; amidst a great number of hypotheses which may be proposed, and a still greater number which may be imagined?

"And what shadow of an argument," continued Philo, "can you produce, from your hypothesis, to prove the unity of the Deity? A great number of men join in building a house or ship, in rearing a city, in framing a commonwealth: why may not several deities combine in contriving and framing a world? This is only so much greater similarity to human affairs. By sharing the work among several, we may so much further limit the attributes of each, and get rid of that extensive power and knowledge, which must be supposed in one deity, and which, according to you, can only serve to weaken the proof of his existence. And if such foolish, such vicious creatures as man can yet often unite in framing and executing one plan; how much more those deities or demons, whom we may suppose several degrees more perfect?

"To multiply causes, without necessity, is indeed contrary to true philosophy: but this principle applies not to the present case. Were one deity antecedently proved by your theory, who were possessed of every attribute, requisite to the production of the universe; it would be needless, I own (though not absurd) to suppose any other deity existent. But while it is still a question, whether all these attributes are united in one subject, or dispersed among several independent beings: by what phenomena in nature can we pretend to decide the controversy? Where we see a body raised in a scale, we are sure that there is in the opposite scale, however concealed from sight, some counterpoising weight equal to it: but it is still allowed to doubt, whether that weight be an aggregate of several distinct bodies, or one uniform united mass. And if the weight requisite very much exceeds anything which we have ever seen conjoined in any single body, the former supposition becomes still more probable and natural. An intelligent being of such vast power and capacity, as is necessary to produce the universe, or, to speak in the language of ancient philosophy, so prodigious an animal, exceeds all analogy, and even comprehension.

"But farther, Cleanthes; men are mortal, and renew their species by generation; and this is common to all living creatures.

The two great sexes of male and female, says Milton, animate the world. Why must this circumstance, so universal, so essential, be excluded from those numerous and limited deities? Behold then the theogony of ancient times brought back upon us.

"And why not become a perfect Anthropomorphite? Why not assert the deity or deities to be corporeal, and to have eyes, a nose, mouth, ears, &c.? Epicurus maintained, that no man had ever seen reason but in a human figure; therefore the gods must have a human figure. And this argument, which is deservedly so much ridiculed by Cicero, becomes, according to you, solid and philosophical.

"In a word, Cleanthes, a man who follows your hypothesis is able, perhaps, to assert, or conjecture, that the universe, sometime, arose from something like design: but beyond that position he cannot ascertain one single circumstance, and is left afterwards to fix every point of his theology, by the utmost license of fancy and hypothesis. This world, for aught he knows, is very faulty and imperfect, compared to a superior standard; and was only the first rude essay of some infant deity, who afterwards abandoned it, ashamed of his lame performance; it is the work only of some dependent, inferior deity; and is the object of derision to his superiors: it is the production of old age and dotage in some superannuated deity; and ever since his death, has run on at adventures, from the first impulse and active force, which it received from him.

STUDY QUESTIONS

1. In what ways does Philo attempt to weaken the analogy on which the teleological argument rests? How does Cleanthes answer him?

2. What does Hume mean when he calls the teleological argument an *a posteriori* argument? Contrast this with an *a priori* argument.

3. Describe the views defended in the discussion by Cleanthes, Demea, and Philo. Which of the three seems the most persuasive to you?

4. Since Hume's time a scientific theory about the nature of the world and, particularly, of living creatures has been developed that has a profound effect on the credibility of the teleological argument. What is it?

For Further Reading

Darrow, C. *The Story of My Life.* London: Watts, 1932 (Chapter 44).

Drake, D. *Problems of Religion.* Boston: Houghton Mifflin, 1916 (Chapter 19).

Hick, J. *Arguments for the Existence of God.* New York: Seabury Press, 1971 (Chapters 1 and 2).

Hurlbutt, R. H. *Hume, Newton, and the Design Argument.* Lincoln, Neb.: University of Nebraska Press, 1965 (esp. Part III).

Jeffner, A. *Butler and Hume on Religion.* Stockholm, 1966 (esp. Chapter 6).

Kant, I. *Critique of Pure Reason.* Translated by N. K. Smith. London: Macmillan, 1929 (pp. 518–24).

McPherson, T. *The Argument from Design.* London: Macmillan, 1972.

Taylor, A. E. *Does God Exist?* London: Macmillan, 1948.

Tennant, F. R. *Philosophical Theology.* Cambridge: Cambridge University Press, 1928, (Vol. II, Chapter 4).

RUSSELL: ATHEISM

Strictly speaking, atheism is a purely negative position. The atheist simply claims that the universe contains no being who answers to the description of God. In the hands of imaginative thinkers like Bertrand Russell, however, atheism gains a positive content. In the selection that follows, Russell addresses himself to the question, "How should the individual respond to the realization that the universe is the product, not of a wise and benevolent deity, but of blind and unconscious force?" That we are doomed to final defeat and death must be acknowledged; yet, Russell believes, we can create things of value that, while they last, successfully defy the insensate forces that will ultimately destroy both them and us.

Bertrand Russell (1872–1970), one of the leading intellectual figures of the twentieth century, had a lonely childhood. After his parents died in his infancy, he went to live in the home of his grandfather, a former British prime minister. He was educated at home by private tutors and hardly ever saw anyone his own age until he enrolled in Cambridge University when he was eighteen. During his long career he published dozens of influential books. Most important was the monumental, three-volume *Principia Mathematica,* written in collaboration with A. N. Whitehead. During the first world war, Russell was imprisoned because of his anti-war activities. He was awarded the Nobel prize for literature in 1950.

✣ *A Free Man's Worship*

To Dr. Faustus in his study Mephistopheles told the history of the Creation saying:

First published in 1903. Reprinted from B. Russell, *Mysticism and Logic,* with permission of the publisher, George Allen & Unwin., London.

"The endless praises of the choirs of angels had begun to grow wearisome; for, after all, did he not deserve their praise? Had he not given them endless joy? Would it not be more amusing to obtain undeserved praise, to be worshipped by beings whom he tortured? He smiled inwardly, and resolved that the great drama should be performed.

"For countless ages the hot nebula whirled aimlessly through space. At length it began to take shape, the central mass threw off planets, the planets cooled, boiling seas and burning mountains heaved and tossed, from black masses of cloud hot sheets of rain deluged the barely solid crust. And now the first germ of life grew in the depths of the ocean, and developed rapidly in the fructifying warmth into vast forest trees, huge ferns springing from the damp mold, sea monsters breeding, fighting, devouring, and passing away. And from the monsters, as the play unfolded itself, Man was born, with the power of thought, the knowledge of good and evil, and the cruel thirst for worship. And Man saw that all is passing in this mad, monstrous world, that all is struggling to snatch, at any cost, a few brief moments of life before Death's inexorable decree. And Man said: 'There is a hidden purpose, could we but fathom it, and the purpose is good; for we must reverence something, and in the visible world there is nothing worthy of reverence.' And Man stood aside from the struggle, resolving that God intended harmony to come out of chaos by human efforts. And when he followed the instincts which God had transmitted to him from his ancestry of beasts of prey, he called it Sin, and asked God to forgive him. But he doubted whether he could be justly forgiven, until he invented a divine Plan by which God's wrath was to have been appeased. And seeing the present was bad, he made it yet worse, that thereby the future might be better. And he gave God thanks for the strength that enabled him to forego even the joys that were possible. And God smiled; and when he saw that Man had become perfect in renunciation and worship, he sent another sun through the sky, which crashed into Man's sun; and all returned again to nebula.

" 'Yes,' he murmured, 'it was a good play; I will have it performed again.' "

Such, in outline, but even more pur-poseless, more void of meaning, is the world which science presents for our belief. Amid such a world, if anywhere, our ideals henceforward must find a home. That Man is the product of causes which had no prevision of the end they were achieving; that his origin, his growth, his hopes and fears, his loves and his beliefs, are but the outcome of accidental collocations of atoms; that no fire, no heroism, no intensity of thought and feeling, can preserve an individual life beyond the grave; that all the labors of the ages, all the devotion, all the inspiration, all the noonday brightness of human genius, are destined to extinction in the vast death of the solar system, and that the whole temple of Man's achievement must inevitably be buried beneath the debris of a universe in ruins—all these things, if not quite beyond dispute, are yet so nearly certain, that no philosophy which rejects them can hope to stand. Only within the scaffolding of these truths, only on the firm foundation of unyielding despair, can the soul's habitation henceforth be safely built.

How, in such an alien and inhuman world, can so powerless a creature as Man preserve his aspirations untarnished? A strange mystery it is that Nature, omnipotent but blind, in the revolutions of her secular hurryings through the abysses of space, has brought forth at last a child, subject still to her power, but gifted with sight, with knowledge of good and evil, with the capacity of judging all the works of his unthinking Mother. In spite of Death, the mark and seal of the parental control, Man is yet free, during his brief years, to examine, to criticize, to know, and in imagination to create. To him alone, in the world with which he is acquainted, this freedom belongs; and in this lies his superiority to the resistless forces that control his outward life.

The savage, like ourselves, feels the oppression of his impotence before the powers of Nature; but having in himself nothing that he respects more than Power, he is willing to prostrate himself before his gods, without inquiring whether they are worthy of his worship. Pathetic and very terrible is the long history of cruelty and torture, of degradation and human sacrifice, endured in the hope of placating the jealous gods: surely, the trembling believer thinks, when what is most precious has been freely given, their lust for blood must be appeased, and more will not be required. The religion of Moloch—as such creeds may be generically called—is in essence the cringing submission of the slave, who dare not, even in his heart, allow the thought that his master deserves no adulation. Since the independence of ideals is not yet acknowledged, Power may be freely worshipped, and receive an unlimited respect, despite its wanton infliction of pain.

But gradually, as morality grows bolder, the claim of the ideal world begins to be felt; and worship, if it is not to cease, must be given to gods of another kind than those created by the savage. Some, though they feel the demands of the ideal, will still consciously reject them, still urging that naked Power is worthy of worship. Such is the attitude inculcated in God's answer to Job out of the whirlwind: the divine power and knowledge are paraded, but of the divine goodness there is no hint. Such also is the attitude of those who, in our own day, base their morality upon the struggle for survival, maintaining that the survivors are necessarily the fittest. But others, not content with an answer so repugnant to the moral sense, will adopt the position which we have become accustomed to regard as specially religious, maintaining that, in some hidden manner, the world of fact is really harmonious with the world of ideals. Thus Man creates God, all-powerful and all-good, the mystic unity of what is and what should be.

But the world of fact, after all, is not good; and, in submitting our judgment to it, there is an element of slavishness from which our thoughts must be purged. For in all things it is well to exalt the dignity of Man, by freeing him as far as possible from the tyranny of nonhuman Power. When we have realised that Power is largely bad, that man, with his knowledge of good and evil, is but a helpless atom in a world which has no such knowledge, the choice is again presented to us: Shall we worship Force, or shall we worship Goodness? Shall our God exist and be evil, or shall he be recognized as the creation of our own conscience?

The answer to this question is very momentous, and affects profoundly our whole morality. The worship of Force, to which Carlyle and Nietzsche and the creed of militarism have accustomed us, is the result of failure to maintain our own ideals against a hostile universe: it is itself a prostrate submission to evil, a sacrifice of our best to Moloch. If strength indeed is to be respected, let us respect rather the strength of those who refuse that false "recognition of facts" which fails to recognize that facts are often bad. Let us admit that, in the world we know, there are many things that would be better otherwise, and that the ideals to which we do and must adhere are not realized in the realm of matter. Let us preserve our respect for truth, for beauty, for the ideal of perfection which life does not permit us to attain, though none of these things meet with the approval of the unconscious universe. If Power is bad, as it seems to be, let us reject it from our hearts. In this lies Man's true freedom: in determination to worship only the God created by our own love of the good, to respect only the heaven which inspires the insight of our best moments. In action, in desire, we must submit perpetually to the tyranny of outside forces; but in thought, in aspiration, we are free, free from our fellowmen, free from the petty planet on which our bodies impotently crawl, free even, while we live, from the tyranny of death. Let us learn, then, that energy of faith which enables us to live constantly in the vision of the good; and let us descend, in action, into the world of fact, with that vision always before us.

When first the opposition of fact and ideal grows fully visible, a spirit of fiery revolt, of fierce hatred of the gods, seems necessary to the assertion of freedom. To defy with Promethean constancy a hostile universe, to keep its evil always in view, always actively hated, to refuse no pain that the malice of Power can invent, appears to be the duty of all who will not bow before the inevitable. But indignation is still a bondage, for it compels our thoughts to be occupied with an evil world; and in the fierceness of desire from which rebellion springs there is a kind of self-assertion which it is necessary for the wise to overcome. Indignation is a submission of our thoughts but not of our desires; the Stoic freedom in which wisdom consists is found in the submission of our desires, but not of our thoughts. From the submission of our desires springs the virtue of resignation; from the freedom of our thoughts springs the whole world of art and philosophy, and the vision of beauty by which, at last, we half reconquer the reluctant world. But the vision of beauty is possible only to unfettered contemplation, to thoughts not weighted by the load of eager wishes; and thus Freedom comes only to those who no longer ask of life that it shall yield them any of those personal goods that are subject to the mutations of Time.

Although the necessity of renunciation is evidence of the existence of evil, yet Christianity, in preaching it, has shown a wisdom exceeding that of the Promethean philosophy of rebellion. It must be admitted that, of the things we desire, some, though they prove impossible, are yet real goods; others, however, as ardently longed for, do not form part of a fully purified ideal. The belief that what must be renounced is bad, though sometimes false, is far less often false than untamed passion supposes; and the creed of religion, by providing a reason for proving that it is never false, has been the means of purifying our hopes by the discovery of many austere truths.

But there is in resignation a further good element: even real goods, when they are unattainable, ought not to be fretfully desired. To every man comes, sooner or later, the great renunciation. For the young, there is nothing unattainable; a good thing desired with the whole force of a passionate will, and yet impossible, is to them not credible. Yet, by death, by illness, by poverty, or by the voice of duty, we must learn, each one of us, that the world was not made for us, and that, however beautiful may be the things we crave, Fate may nevertheless forbid them. It is the part of courage, when misfortune comes, to bear without repining the ruin of our hopes, to turn away our thoughts from vain regrets. This degree of submission to Power is not only just and right: it is the very gate of wisdom.

But passive renunciation is not the whole of wisdom; for not by renunciation alone can we build a temple for the worship of our own ideals. Haunting foreshadowings of the temple appear in the realm of imagination, in music, in architecture, in the untroubled kingdom of reason, and in the golden sunset magic of lyrics, where beauty shines and glows, remote from the fear of change, remote from the failures and disenchantments of the world of fact. In the contemplation of these things the vision of heaven will shape itself in our hearts, giving at once a touchstone to judge the world about us, and an inspiration by which to fashion to our needs whatever is not incapable of serving as a stone in the sacred temple.

Except for those rare spirits that are born without sin, there is a cavern of darkness to be traversed before that temple can be entered. The gate of the cavern is despair, and its floor is paved with the gravestones of abandoned hopes. There Self must die; there the eagerness, the greed of untamed desire must be slain, for only so can the soul be freed from the empire of Fate. But out of the cavern the Gate of Renunciation leads again to the daylight of wisdom, by whose radiance a new insight, a new joy, a new tenderness, shine forth to gladden the pilgrim's heart.

When, without the bitterness of impotent rebellion, we have learnt both to resign ourselves to the outward rule of Fate and to recognize that the non-human world is unworthy of our worship, it becomes possible at last so to transform and refashion the unconscious universe, so to transmute it in the crucible of imagination, that a new image of shining gold replaces the old idol of clay. In all the multiform facts of the world—in the visual shapes of trees and mountains and clouds, in the events of the life of man, even in the very omnipotence of Death—the insight of creative idealism can find the reflection of a beauty which its own thoughts first made. In this way mind asserts its subtle mastery over the thoughtless forces of Nature. The more evil the material with which it deals, the more thwarting to untrained desire, the greater is its achievement in inducing the reluctant rock to yield up its hidden treasures, the prouder its victory in compelling the opposing forces to swell the pageant of its triumph. Of all the arts, Tragedy is the proudest, the most triumphant; for it builds its shining citadel in the very centre of the enemy's country, on the very summit of his highest mountain; from its impregnable watchtowers, his camps and arsenals, his columns and forts, are all revealed; within its walls the free life continues, while the legions of Death and Pain and Despair, and all the servile captains of tyrant Fate, afford the burghers of that dauntless city new spectacles of beauty. Happy those sacred ramparts, thrice happy the dwellers on that all-seeing eminence. Honor to those brave warriors who, through countless ages of warfare, have preserved for us the priceless heritage of liberty, and have kept undefiled by sacrilegious invaders the home of the unsubdued.

But the beauty of Tragedy does but make visible a quality which, in more or less obvious shapes, is present always and everywhere in life. In the spectacle of Death, in the endurance of intolerable pain, and in the irrevocableness of a vanished past, there is a sacredness, an overpowering awe, a feeling of the vastness, the depth, the inexhaustible mystery of existence, in which, as by some strange marriage of pain, the sufferer is bound to the world by bonds of sorrow. In these moments of insight, we lose all eagerness of temporary desire, all struggling and striving for petty ends, all care for the little trivial things that, to a superficial view, make up the common life of day by day; we see, surrounding the narrow raft illumined by the flickering light of human comradeship, the dark ocean on whose rolling waves we toss for a brief hour; from the great night without, a chill blast breaks in upon our refuge; all the loneliness of humanity and hostile forces is concentrated upon the individual soul, which must struggle alone, with what of courage it can command, against the whole weight of a universe that cares nothing for its hopes and fears. Victory, in this struggle with the powers of darkness, is the true baptism into the glorious company of heroes, the true initiation into the overmastering beauty of human existence. From that awful encounter of the soul with the outer world, renunciation, wisdom, and charity are born; and with their birth a new life begins. To take into the inmost shrine of the soul the irresistible forces whose puppets we seem to be—Death and change, the irrevocableness of the past, and the powerlessness of man before the blind hurry of the universe from vanity to vanity—to feel these things and know them is to conquer them.

This is the reason why the Past has such magical power. The beauty of its motionless and silent pictures is like the enchanted purity of late autumn, when the leaves, though one breath would make them fall, still glow against the sky in golden glory. The Past does not change or strive; like Duncan, after life's fitful fever it sleeps well; what was eager and grasping, what was petty and transitory, has faded away, the things that were beautiful and eternal shine out of it like stars in the night. Its beauty, to a soul not worthy of it, is unendurable; but, to a soul which has conquered Fate it is the key of religion.

The life of Man, viewed outwardly, is but a small thing in comparison with the forces of Nature. The slave is doomed to worship Time and Fate and Death, because they are greater than anything he finds in himself, and because all his thoughts are of things which they devour. But, great as they are, to think of them greatly, to feel their passionless splendor, is greater still. And such thought makes us free men; we no longer bow before the inevitable in Oriental subjection, but we absorb it, and make it a part of ourselves. To abandon the struggle for private happiness, to expel all eagerness of temporary desire, to burn with passion for eternal things—this is emancipation, and this is the free man's worship. And this liberation is effected by a contemplation of Fate; for Fate itself is subdued by the mind which leaves nothing to be purged by the purifying fire of Time.

United with his fellowmen by the strongest of all ties, the tie of a common doom, the free man finds that a new vision is with him always, shedding over every daily task the light of love. The life of Man is a long march through the night, surrounded by invisible foes, tortured by weariness and pain, towards a goal that few can hope to reach, and where none may tarry long. One by one, as they march, our comrades vanish from our sight, seized by the silent orders of omnipotent Death. Very brief is the time in which we can help them, in which their happiness or misery is decided. Be it ours to shed sunshine on their path, to lighten their sorrows by the balm of sympathy, to give them the pure joy of a never-tiring affection, to strengthen failing courage, to instill faith in hours of despair. Let us not weigh in grudging scales their merits and demerits, but let us think only of their need—of the sorrows, the difficulties, perhaps the blindnesses, that make the misery of their lives; let us remember that they are fellow-sufferers in the same darkness, actors in the same tragedy with ourselves. And so, when their day is over, when their good and their evil have become eternal by the immortality of the past, be it ours to feel that, where they suffered, where they failed, no deed of ours was the cause; but wherever a spark of the divine fire kindled in their hearts, we were ready with encour-agement, with sympathy, with brave words in which high courage glowed.

Brief and powerless is Man's life; on him and all his race the slow, sure doom falls pitiless and dark. Blind to good and evil, reckless of destruction, omnipotent matter rolls on its relentless way; for Man, condemned today to lose his dearest, to-morrow himself to pass through the gate of darkness, it remains only to cherish, ere yet the blow falls, the lofty thoughts that enno-ble his little day; disdaining the coward ter-rors of the slave of Fate, to worship at the shrine that his own hands have built; un-dismayed by the empire of chance, to pre-serve a mind free from the wanton tyranny that rules his outward life; proudly defiant of the irresistible forces that tolerate, for a moment, his knowledge and his condemna-tion, to sustain alone, a weary but unyield-ing Atlas, the world that his own ideals have fashioned despite the trampling march of unconscious power.

STUDY QUESTIONS

1. Do you agree with Russell that the world science presents to us is purposeless? Explain.

2. Russell is generally considered to be an atheist. Do you agree with this view? How then can he also be described, as he sometimes is, as a religious man?

3. What does Russell mean by "a free man's worship"? In what ways does such worship differ from orthodox worship?

4. Overall, Russell is a pessimist. Is there anything that is optimistic in his essay?

5. Do you find yourself sympathetic with, or antagonistic to the view of the world and our place in it that Russell de-scribes? Explain.

For Further Reading

Ayer, A. J. *Language, Truth and Logic.* 2d ed. London: Victor Gollancz, 1948 (pp. 114–20).

Flew, A. *The Presumption of Atheism.* London: Elek/Pemberton, 1976 (Chapter 1).

Nielsen, K. *Scepticism.* London: Macmillan, 1973.

Nietzsche, F. "What Our Cheerfulness Signifies." In *Joyful Wisdom.* (Book V, §343).

Robinson, R. *An Atheist's Values.* Oxford: Clarendon Press, 1964.

Strunk, O. *The Choice Called Atheism.* Nashville: Abingdon Press, 1968.

Thrower, J. *A Short History of Western Atheism.* London: Pemberton Books, 1971.

HUXLEY: AGNOSTICISM

The agnostic is a theological conservative. Unlike the theist, who affirms that God exists, and the atheist, who denies this, he refuses to commit himself either way but instead reserves judgment. The question of God's existence, he maintains, is a matter on which the evidence we have and the arguments we can marshall are insufficient to justify us in reaching any conclusion, whether positive or negative. To join the camp either of the theist or the atheist under these circumstances, therefore, is to commit ourselves to a belief that we cannot support. On the question, "Is the issue of God's existence intrinsically irresolvable or may we look forward to a time when we shall have sufficient evidence to warrant a decision?" agnostics are not in full agreement. Some argue that the problem is of a type that is beyond human capacities ever to resolve; others contend that we simply have insufficient evidence at this time to answer it.

Thomas Henry Huxley (1825–1895) was born in the environs of London. With almost no previous formal education he entered Charing Cross hospital in London at the age of seventeen to study medicine. At twenty he graduated and qualified as a surgeon. Almost immediately after he published the first of the many papers that were to establish his reputation as a biologist and paleontologist. A champion of scientific method as the only reliable way of gaining knowledge, Huxley accepted the theory of evolution when Darwin's *Origin of Species* was published in 1859, becoming its chief public defender against its opponents, most of whom criticized it on religious grounds. Despite his doubts about orthodox religion, he remained an agnostic (a term he originated) rather than an atheist.

✢ *Agnosticism and Agnosticism and Christianity*

When I reached intellectual maturity and began to ask myself whether I was an atheist, a theist, or a pantheist; a materialist or an idealist; a Christian or a freethinker; I found that the more I learned and reflected, the less ready was the answer; until, at last, I came to the conclusion that I had neither art nor part with any of these denominations, except the last. The one thing in which most of these good people were agreed was the one thing in which I differed from them. They were quite sure they had attained a certain "gnosis,"—had, more or less successfully, solved the problem of existence; while I was quite sure I had not, and had a pretty strong conviction that the problem was insoluble. . . .

This was my situation when I had the

Both essays from which the selection was taken were published in 1889.

good fortune to find a place among the members of that remarkable confraternity of antagonists, long since deceased, but of green and pious memory, the Metaphysical Society. Every variety of philosophical and theological opinion was represented there, and expressed itself with entire openness; most of my colleagues were -*ists* of one sort or another; and, however kind and friendly they might be, I, the man without a rag of a label to cover himself with, could not fail to have some of the uneasy feelings which must have beset the historical fox when, after leaving the trap in which his tail remained, he presented himself to his normally elongated companions. So I took thought, and invented what I conceived to be the appropriate title of "agnostic." It came into my head as suggestively antithetic to the "gnostic" of Church history, who professed to know so much about the very things of which I was ignorant; and I took the earliest opportunity of parading it at our Society, to show that I, too, had a tail, like the other foxes. To my great satisfaction, the term took; and when the *Spectator* had stood godfather to it, any suspicion in the minds of respectable people, that a knowledge of its parentage might have awakened was, of course, completely lulled.

That is the history of the origin of the terms "agnostic" and "agnosticism. . . ."

Agnosticism, in fact, is not a creed, but a method, the essence of which lies in the rigorous application of a single principle. That principle is of great antiquity; it is as old as Socrates; as old as the writer who said, "Try all things, hold fast by that which is good;" it is the foundation of the Reformation, which simply illustrated the axiom that every man should be able to give a reason for the faith that is in him; it is the great principle of Descartes; it is the fundamental axiom of modern science. Positively the principle may be expressed: In matters of the intellect, follow your reason as far as it will take you, without regard to any other consideration. And negatively: In matters of the intellect do not pretend that conclusions are certain which are not demonstrated or demonstrable. That I take to be the agnostic faith, which if a man keep whole and undefiled, he shall not be ashamed to look the universe in the face, whatever the future may have in store for him.

The results of the working out of the agnostic principle will vary according to individual knowledge and capacity, and according to the general condition of science. That which is unproven today may be proven by the help of new discoveries tomorrow. The only negative fixed points will be those negations which flow from the demonstrable limitation of our faculties. And the only obligation accepted is to have the mind always open to conviction. Agnostics who never fail in carrying out their principles are, I am afraid, as rare as other people of whom the same consistency can be truthfully predicated. But, if you were to meet with such a phoenix and to tell him that you had discovered that two and two

make five, he would patiently ask you to state your reasons for that conviction, and express his readiness to agree with you if he found them satisfactory. The apostolic injunction to "suffer fools gladly" should be the rule of life of a true agnostic. I am deeply conscious how far I myself fall short of this ideal, but it is my personal conception of what agnostics ought to be.

• • •

Agnosticism is not properly described as a "negative" creed, nor indeed as a creed of any kind, except in so far as it expresses absolute faith in the validity of a principle, which is as much ethical as intellectual. This principle may be stated in various ways, but they all amount to this: that it is wrong for a man to say that he is certain of the objective truth of any proposition unless he can produce evidence which logically justifies that certainty. This is what Agnosticism asserts; and, in my opinion, it is all that is essential to Agnosticism. That which Agnostics deny and repudiate, as immoral, is the contrary doctrine, that there are propositions which men ought to believe, without logically satisfactory evidence; and that reprobation ought to attach to the profession of disbelief in such inadequately supported propositions. The justification of the Agnostic principle lies in the success which follows upon its application, whether in the field of natural, or in that of civil, history; and in the fact that, so far as these topics are concerned, no sane man thinks of denying its validity.

Still speaking for myself, I add, that though Agnosticism is not, and cannot be, a creed, except in so far as its general principle is concerned; yet that the application of that principle results in the denial of, or the suspension of judgment concerning, a number of propositions respecting which our contemporary ecclesiastical "gnostics" profess entire certainty. And, in so far as these ecclesiastical persons can be justified in their old-established custom (which many nowadays think more honoured in the breach than the observance) of using approbrious names to those who differ from them, I fully admit their right to call me and those who think with me "Infidels"; all I have ventured to urge is that they must not expect us to speak of ourselves by that title.

The extent of the region of the uncertain, the number of the problems the investigation of which ends in a verdict of not proven, will vary according to the knowledge and the intellectual habits of the individual Agnostic. I do not very much care to speak of anything as "unknowable." What I am sure about is that there are many topics about which I know nothing; and which, so far as I can see, are out of reach of my faculties. But whether these things are knowable by any one else is exactly one of those matters which is beyond my knowledge, though I may have a tolerably strong opinion as to the probabilities of the case. Relatively to myself, I am quite sure that the region of uncertainty—the nebulous country in which words play the part of realities—is far more extensive than I could wish. Materialism and Idealism; Theism and Atheism; the doctrine of the soul and its mortality or immortality—appear in the history of philosophy like the shades of Scandinavian heroes, eternally slaying one another and eternally coming to life again in a metaphysical "Nifelheim." It is getting on for twenty-five centuries, at least, since mankind began seriously to give their minds to these topics. Generation after generation, philosophy has been doomed to roll the stone uphill; and, just as all the world swore it was at the top, down it has rolled to the bottom again. All this is written in innumerable books; and he who will toil through them will discover that the stone is just where it was when the work began. Hume saw this; Kant saw it; since their time, more and more eyes have been cleansed of the films which prevented them from seeing it; until now the weight and number of those who refuse to be the prey of verbal mystifications has begun to tell in practical life.

It was inevitable that a conflict should arise between Agnosticism and Theology; or rather, I ought to say, between Agnosticism and Ecclesiasticism. For Theology, the science, is one thing; and Ecclesiasticism, the championship of a foregone conclusion as to the truth of a particular form of Theology, is another. With scientific Theology, Agnosticism has no quarrel. On the contrary, the Agnostic, knowing too well the influence of prejudice and idiosyncrasy, even on those who desire most earnestly to be impartial, can wish for nothing more urgently than that the scientific theologian should not only be at perfect liberty to thresh out the matter in his own fashion; but that he should, if he can, find flaws in the Agnostic position; and, even if demonstration is not to be had, that he should put, in their full force, the grounds of the conclusions he thinks probable. The scientific theologian admits the Agnostic principle, however widely his results may differ from those reached by the majority of Agnostics.

But, as between Agnosticism and Ecclesiasticism, or, as our neighbours across the Channel call it, Clericalism, there can be neither peace nor truce. The Cleric asserts that it is morally wrong not to believe certain propositions, whatever the results of a strict scientific investigation of the evidence of these propositions. He tells us "that religious error is, in itself, of an immoral nature." He declares that he has prejudged certain conclusions, and looks upon those who show cause for arrest of judgment as emissaries of Satan. It necessarily follows that, for him, the attainment of faith, not the ascertainment of truth, is the highest aim of mental life. And, on careful analysis of the nature of this faith, it will too often be found to be, not the mystic process of unity with the Divine, understood by the religious enthusiast; but that which the candid simplicity of a Sunday scholar once defined it to be. "Faith," said this unconscious plagiarist of Tertullian, "is the power of saying you believe things which are incredible."

STUDY QUESTIONS

1. What does Huxley mean by the term "agnostic"?
2. Huxley defends agnosticism on moral grounds. How does he do this? Do you think he is correct in doing so?

3. How is agnosticism related to theism? Atheism? Do you find it more or less plausible than either of these other positions? Explain.

For Further Reading

Burtt, E. A. *Types of Religious Philosophy*. 2d ed. New York: Harper & Row, 1951 (Chapter 8).

Flint, R. *Agnosticism*. Edinburgh: Blackwood and Sons, 1903 (Chapters 1, 9, and 10).

Paradis, J. G. *T. H. Huxley: Man's Place in Nature*. Lincoln, Neb.: University of Nebraska Press, 1978 (Chapter 3).

Spalding, J. L. *Religion, Agnosticism and Education*. Chicago: McClurg, 1902 (Chapters 2 and 3).

Stephen, L. *An Agnostic's Apology*. London: Smith, Elder, 1893 (Chapter 1).

UNDERHILL: MYSTICISM

Outsiders are prone to dismiss the mystic, with his claim to "out-of-the-world" experiences, as being somewhat abnormal and hence not to be taken seriously. The mystics would agree with this judgment, at least in part. Their experiences *are* abnormal and out-of-this-world. But they are profoundly serious. The mystic is granted the rare privilege of direct "face-to-face" communion with God. Because such an experience has nothing in common with ordinary life, it is totally inexplicable to an outsider. There is only one way in which an individual can understand what mysticism is—by having a mystical experience himself. Nevertheless, as Evelyn Underhill emphasizes in the selection that follows, mysticism is much more than just communing with God; it is an entire way of life in which one's self and one's relation to others are transformed by that act of communion.

Evelyn Underhill (1875–1941) was born in Wolverhampton, England, but lived most of her life in London. She began to write at an early age, first short stories, then poetry and novels. She showed little interest in religion until she became an adult but then devoted the remainder of her life to it. Unlike the great mystics, about whom she wrote so much, she did not herself have any extraordinary "mystical experiences."

✿ *What is Mysticism*

What is Mysticism? is a very difficult question to answer, unless we first deal with the things which mysticism is not, but with which it is too commonly confused. In spite of the great Christian mystical tradition which we have inherited, and because of

By permission of A. A. Mowbray & Co. Ltd., London. First published in 1936.

the bad company the word often keeps, many people assume that it is merely another name for religious queerness or religious vagueness: for visions, voices, ecstasies and other symptoms of psychic instability, and even far less reputable forms of abnormality. Thus it has gradually become one of the most ambiguous and unsatisfactory words in the English language, arousing violent prejudice in those who hear it; and those who care most deeply for that which it really means often find themselves respecting the critics of mysticism far more than they respect many of its friends.

It is true that certain abnormal states of mind and even of body, which as yet we hardly understand, do sometimes appear in connection with mysticism, attracting an attention out of all proportion to their importance. But they can never be more than its by-products; and the tendency to exaggerate them has, more than any other cause, brought misunderstanding and discredit on the great souls of the mystics. A mystic is not a person who has queer experiences; but a person for whom God is the one reality of life, the supreme Object of love. He is a religious realist. Mysticism, then, far from being abnormal, is an essential part of all religion which is fully and deeply alive; it is the light which the mystics cast on the normal spiritual life, their disclosure of the landscape in which we really live, not their occasional excursions into an abnormal spiritual life, which gives them their great importance.

Francis Thompson, in that beautiful poem, "Any Saint," describes man as a

> Swinging-wicket, set
> Between
> The Unseen and Seen.

Man, that is, is the child both of the natural and the spiritual worlds. He is placed on the borderland; through him, there is a certain communication between them. In one way or another that is an idea which is quite familiar to us. We accept it, as we accept familiar food, without too much examination. But if we put that idea alongside one of our average acquaintances—or even alongside ourselves—we feel a certain contrast between the poet's view of humanity and our ordinary experience of humanity. We do not notice a general tendency in average men and women to swing out vigorously towards the Unseen, or even a marked desire to do so. The hinges of the wicket-gate seem to be differently adjusted in people of different types.

In many, it swings so widely and persistently open towards the visible side that nothing from the Unseen squeezes through. It is not noticed, and it is not missed. Those are the people who are commonly regarded as practical and sensible men. Their philosophy, unless it is a mere intellectual hobby unrelated to life, is always utilitarian. Their religion, when they have one, is practical, ethical, mainly expressed in fellowship and good works. They value it because it helps them to do their duty here and now; to live good lives. In some people, the wicket seems beautifully balanced. They take up and use together both sides of our wonderful human inheritance, moving to and fro between the temporal world and the eternal world, between communion with God and communion with their fellow-men; as Christ did during His life on earth. In a few, however, the hinges are so adjusted that, left to themselves, they always tend to swing out towards the Unseen. There they find, though they may not be able to describe it, the object of their love, and the whole meaning of their life. Those are the mystics.

So the beginning of an answer to the question, "What is mysticism?" must be this: Mysticism is the passionate longing of the soul for God, the Unseen Reality, loved, sought and adored in Himself for Himself alone. It is, to use a favourite phrase of Baron von Hügel, a "metaphysical thirst." A mystic is not a person who practises unusual forms of prayer, but a person whose life is ruled by this thirst. He feels and responds to the overwhelming attraction of God, is sensitive to that attraction; perhaps a little in the same way as the artist is sensitive to the mysterious attraction of visible beauty, and the musician to the mysterious attraction of harmonized sound. And as the painter comes to know a visible reality, a secret wonder revealed in form and colour, which wholly escapes the casual eye, and the musician to know a reality revealed in music of which the ordinary listener can only receive a fraction, and both are lifted by this experience to fresh levels of life; so the mystic, because of that loving and devoted attention which we call contemplation—"gazing into heaven with his ghostly eye," as one of them said—comes to know a spiritual reality to which we are deaf and blind. He knows it, but he cannot describe it; as we know but cannot describe the atmosphere of our own country, our own home. Its awful beauty and its living peace lie beyond the resources of our limited thought and clumsy tongues, which are adjusted to other levels of existence.

We begin, therefore, to see why mysticism has been called the science of the love of God; and why St. Augustine's great saying, "Thou hast made us for Thyself, and our hearts shall find no rest save in Thee," remains the best explanation of its undying appeal. For on the one hand, human beings do many hard and strange things when they are trying to express, or respond to, great love; and the real mystic always feels called to great sacrifices, much self-discipline, and the willing endurance of long periods of obscurity. The emphasis for him does not lie on his own wonderful experiences, his ardent and delightful feelings, his lovely visions, or anything like that. Very often his feelings are not ardent and delightful; and, even when they are, they carry with them a sense of obligation which kills all self-seeking, and compels him to consecrate the whole of his life to the purposes of God. He has seen Perfection, and wants to serve it, however much it costs. The life of the artist or musician, serving beauty and revealing beauty, is not easy. The life of the mystic, serving God, and by that very act revealing God, is harder still. For him, suffering and love are much the same thing—two forms of self-offering to God; and it is on God that the emphasis lies.

And, on the other hand, the knowledge that comes through love is the only knowledge that is really worth having; and this is specially true of the knowledge of Reality, of God. "He may well be loved but not thought. . . . By love He may be gotten and holden, by thought never," said the greatest of our English mystics. This is not an invitation to religious emotionalism. It states a profound philosophical truth, which is a central truth of Christian theology too. The typical mystic, then, is the person who has a certain first-hand experience and knowledge of God through love; and the literature of mysticism tell us, or tries to tell us, what the finite human spirit has come to know through love of the relation between the little half-made spirit of man and the Infinite Spirit—God.

This experience of God may come in many ways and under many symbolic disguises. It may be steady or fleeting, dim or intense. But in so far as it is direct and intuitive it is always a mystical experience. Various things may result from it; a total change and reorientation of life, a long, hard discipline and inward growth, an immense transformation of personality, great creative power. Those whom we speak of as the great mystics are seldom dreamy contemplatives, but are people whose whole lives have been re-made in harmony with this overwhelming experience of God; and who have at last achieved that union with His spirit in which, as one of them said, they "are to the Eternal Goodness what his own hand is to a man," and act within the temporal order with a strange originality and power. St. Augustine and St. Francis, St. Catherine of Siena and St. Teresa, George Fox and Elizabeth Fry, are each in their different ways and degrees examples of this.

So a first-hand experience of God, the Absolute reality, and a life controlled by the overwhelming love which that experience awakens—this is what unites all mystics, Christian and non-Christian alike. As one of them said, they "mean only God, and none of His works," going straight beyond all symbols, definitions and images to the unspeakable fact of God, exceeding all that we can think or feel. They are the great experimental theists; so numerous and so distinctive that no theory of human knowledge, still less of human religion, which aims at completeness can possibly neglect their reports. The reports will vary, because the mystic, like the artist, is always showing us reality through his own temperament: a temperament which is immersed in history, and coloured by its social and religious surroundings. Only a few are able, like Ruysbroeck, to discriminate "between God and the light in which we see Him." But what matters to us and gives their great religious importance to the mystics is the massive agreement which underlies all their various experiences—the way these experiences, taken together, witness to the living fact of God and His relation to the created spirit of man.

St. Augustine's saying, "God is the only reality and we are only real in so far as we are in His order and He in us," gives us in a phrase the central conviction of every mystic; and we notice at once its intensely objective character. Their concern is with God. He is. That is what matters; not the ecstatic feelings which I may happen to have about him. For mystics, God is the fact of facts. They long for self-loss in Him, even while they know themselves eternally distinct from Him. For, intensely conscious of the contrast between His perfect and eternal Being and our imperfect changeful life, they know that only an effort and growth to ever closer union with that God, and at last a life so re-made in His order that He is all in all, can ever satisfy the soul's thirst.

So mysticism is man's conscious Godward trend; the response of his small dependent spirit to the pressure and invitation of the real God, the magnet of the universe. Such a definition as that relieves us from narrow and exclusive conceptions; since God's demand on the soul and call to the soul is a universal truth experienced by different men in many different ways and degrees. This definition, of course, begs the central question of theology—the very existence of God. But here we can hardly avoid that; for unless we accept the reality of God, mysticism ceases to have any meaning at all. When we speak of a mystic, we speak of a person who knows that his relation to this real God takes precedence of everything else; although this Godward longing and this Godward life may be expressed in many different ways.

I think this statement covers all the mystics; from the impersonal ecstasy of the pagan Plotinus with his longing to attain the One, to the Christocentric passion of St. Bernard or Richard Rolle and many others, who find in the Person of Christ the Divine Object of contemplation and love; from the Eucharistic mysticism of St. Thomas Aquinas or St. Catherine of Genoa, to the Inner Light of the Quaker saints. It shows us mysticism as the flaming heart of personal religion; and the mystic as a person whose function in the Church is to produce and keep burning this vivid sense of God. "Thou are great and dost wondrous things! Thou art God alone!" That is the substance of the mystic's affirmation. And over against that we have the deep longing of the soul for union with that transcendent God. "O knit my soul unto Thee!" says the Psalmist. That is the substance of the mystic's prayer. Where we find anyone whose life is ruled by this realistic passion for God, this inability to be satisfied with anything less than God, we are in the presence of a mystic; whether that life is lived inside or outside the cloister, inside or outside the Christian Church; and whatever the symbols he may use to describe or suggest the unseen Object of his love, whatever the work that love drives him to do.

This passion for God, this eager response of the soul to the living touch of God, appears within all the great religions. It must appear, I think, in any creed which has as its first term God, and which wakes human souls up to a realization of God; and as a matter of fact the Hindu, Moslem, and Jewish religions all have their mystics, their God-intoxicated men. When these speak of their desires and their experiences, they all, up to a point, seem to speak in the same tongue: for each is reaching out in his own way to the Eternal, and is speaking of that Object of love to which religion directs the soul of man.

"I should not exist, wert not Thou already with me!" says St. Augustine.

"I exist in God and am altogether His," says Rabi'a, the Mahommedan contemplative who has been called "the Moslem St. Teresa."

"My Me is God nor do I know my selfhood save in Him," says St. Catherine of Genoa, the lady of the Renaissance, who was the creator of modern hospital work.

"To be absorbed in God filled me with joy and delight," says the Franciscan Angela of Foligno.

"My hope is for union with Thee—that is the goal of my desire!" says Rabi'a again.

"Who dwelleth in love dwelleth in God," says St. John.

"From the beginning until the end of time there is love between me and Thee and how shall such love be extinguished?" says the Hindu Kabir.

"Thou art the love wherewith the heart loves Thee," says St. Augustine again.

"Thou dost fashion thy lovers to beauty and make them also worthy of love," says the pagan Plotinus.

There we have the typical declarations of the mystics; and it would be hard to pick out with a sure hand Christian from non-Christian in that list. There are ungenerous spirits who actually think that is a suspicious circumstance, and tends to discredit mysticism. But fortunately God is greater than their hearts, and the rewarder of all who diligently seek Him; whether or not they are on the Church roll.

All this surely means that the longing for God, the diligent search for Him, and the adoring delight in Him, are genuine characteristics of the human soul: and indeed that the human soul in which they seem to be absent has not yet developed its full powers. There is something in man which longs for the Perfect and the Unchanging, and is sure, in spite of the confusions, the evils, the rough and tumble of life, that the Perfect and the Unchanging is the Real. I believe this longing and this cer-

tainty are latent in everyone, in a more or less rudimentary condition, and that they are the best clue we possess to the mysterious nature of man and the true meaning of prayer. It is part of the business of organized worship to arouse and feed this Godward thirst, and so to make us more completely human, more alive. In many people it is dormant throughout life; in others, more or less awake even though dimly understood. In a few the longing for Reality blazes up into a great passion, which triumphs over every obstacle and every other interest. The eternal Me, the indwelling spirit, emerges and recognizes that its home, its satisfaction, is not here. Its real home, its real satisfaction, is God.

If we leave these general ideas, and consider what mysticism is and means within Christianity we see that the great Christian mystical tradition, having its roots in the New Testament and including as it does some of the greatest of the saints, has a special quality which distinguishes it from those who have responded to the attraction of God from within other faiths. We should, of course, expect this, if the claim of Christianity to be a unique revelation of God, and the claim of the Church to be a supernatural society fostering the supernatural life of the soul, are true. Christianity is the religion of the Word Incarnate, and in the great Christian mystic something which has a certain relation to the mystery of the Incarnation takes place. He becomes at his full development a creative personality, a tool of God. The promise made in the first chapter of Acts is literally fulfilled in him; his loving contemplation of the Eternal, his prayer in the Spirit, produces power.

A non-Christian mystic, such as the great Plotinus, may describe his ecstatic experience of God as a solitary flight from this world with its demands, imperfections, and confusions, and a self-loss in the peace and blessedness of eternity. The Christian mystic knows these wonderful moments too; but for him they are only wonderful moments. His experience of eternal life includes the Incarnation, with its voluntary acceptance of all the circumstances of our common situation, its ministry of healing and enlightenment, its redemptive suffering. He cannot, therefore, contract out of existence with its tensions and demands. For him union with God means self-giving to the purposes of the divine energy and love.

Here is the secret of the strange power of St. Paul, St. Bernard, St. Francis, John Wesley, Elizabeth Fry, the Curé d'Ars, and thousands more. "Our works," says St. Teresa, speaking for all of them, "are the best proof that the favours we have received come from God." Thus she and her companion, St. John of the Cross, the prince of transcendentalists, labour and suffer for the reform of the religious life; Wesley takes the world for his parish; the Curé d'Ars becomes the conscience of France. "All Friends everywhere," said George Fox, "keep all your meetings waiting on the Light." That is a demand for a corporate act of mystical devotion; and we know what the lives of Friends in the world were required to be. All these endorse the saying of Ruysbroeck that the final state of the mystic is not ecstatic self-loss in the Godhead but something at once more difficult and more divine—"a widespreading love towards all in common." Indeed this must be so, because the God with whom he is united is the Absolute Love.

That which makes Christian mysticism so rich, deep, life-giving, and beautiful is, therefore, the Christian doctrine of the nature and action of God. It is different because it is based on the Incarnation, the redemptive self-giving of the Eternal Charity. The Christian mystic tries to continue in his own life Christ's balanced life of ceaseless communion with the Father and homely service to the crowd. His love of God and thirst for God have been cleansed by long discipline from all self-interest; and the more profound his contemplation of God, the more he loves the world and tries to serve it as a tool of the divine creative love. And indeed, a spiritual life which cuts the world into two mutually exclusive halves, and tries to achieve the Infinite by

ignoring the finite and its obligations, could never be satisfactory for men; who need, in proportion to their spiritual enthusiasm, a constant remembrance of Plato's warning that it is not well to exercise the soul without the body or the body without the soul.

Though mysticism be indeed the living heart of all religion, this does not mean that religion does, or can, consist of nothing but heart. The Church is a Body with head, hands, feet, flesh, and hard bones: none of them any use, it is true, if the heart does not function, but all needed for the full expression of the Christian spiritual life. This acceptance of our whole life of thought, feeling, and action, as material to be transformed and used in our life towards God, is what Baron von Hügel meant by "inclusive mysticism." It alone is truly Christian; because its philosophic basis is the doctrine of the Incarnation, with its continuance in the Church and Sacraments. Its opposite, exclusive mysticism, the attempt to ascend to the vision of God by turning away from His creatures by an unmitigated otherworldliness, is not Christian at all. It ends, says that same great theologian, in something which cannot be distinguished from mere Pantheism; or, on more popular levels, in sloppy claims to be in tune with the Infinite.

Finally, the thoroughly organic, deeply human character of real mysticism is surely brought home to us when we see how gradually a mystic grows, what hard work he is called upon to do, and how many things he often has to suffer in getting rid of all that prevents him from swinging easily and peacefully between the Unseen and the Seen; how marked are the moral and psychological changes which must take place in him, and the different kinds of prayer which express his increasing communion with God.

Most people have heard of the "Mystic Way" with its three stages of Purgation, Illumination and Union. Though this ancient formula, borrowed by Christian writers from the Neo-Platonists, cannot be applied rigidly to all cases, it does in a general sense describe the great phases of growth which gradually make our ordinary, faulty, earthbound human nature capable of communion with the Eternal God. All indeed have to pass through a process much like this on their way to the full living-out of any kind of life. The artist, explorer, scientist, philanthropist, must root out everything that conflicts with his vocation and impedes his progress—all forms of self-occupation, pride, ambition, love of comfort; all competing interests, pleasures and affections—and such self-conquest is the very essence of the mystic's purgation. But the purity of heart demanded of him is much greater and more searching, because his objective is God, who asks his undivided devotedness and love. And because his special art, the medium of his communion with God, is prayer, this too must be developed, spiritualized, cleansed from self-will and self-interest and all unworthy images of God.

The reward of this courage and single-mindedness, this stern training in detachment, is always a great increase in knowledge and understanding. The power of the artist grows with his concentration; he is able to perceive and convey beauty in a way that he did not do before. So too the purified soul of the mystic, in proportion to his self-abandonment, sees all the truths of religion glowing with new beauty, reality and life. But the fullness and creative quality of the life to which he is called is only developed in him when he passes, and usually by way of great suffering, beyond this to a further stage: a state in which he is so penetrated, so sunk in and united to that divine life and divine beauty, that he seems to live in and with its very life, with the freedom, ease and simplicity of a fish at home in the sea. The mystics are fond of this metaphor—"I live in the ocean of God as a fish in the sea." That is the life of union, of conscious abiding in God; the full expansion of man's spiritual possibilities, and full satisfaction of his deepest desires. It brings with it great creative power. Once more we come back for our best definition to St. Paul's "I live, yet not I."

It is hardly strange that such a transformation of existence, such an ascent to the very summits of human nature, is seldom achieved; and costs those who do achieve it a good deal. We like to look on the spiritual life as something very noble, very holy; but also very peaceful and consoling. The word "contemplation" easily tempts those who have not tried it to think that the mystical life consists in looking at the Everlasting Hills, and having nice feelings about God. But the world of contemplation is really continuous with the world of prayer, in the same way as the high Alps are continuous with the lower pastures. To enter it means exchanging the lovely view for the austere reality: penetrating the strange hill-country, slogging up stony tracks in heavy boots, bearing fatigue and risking fog and storm, helping fellow-climbers at one's own cost. It means renouncing the hotel-life level of religion with its comforts and conveniences, and setting our face towards the snows; not for any personal ambition or enjoyment, but driven by the strange mountain love. "Thou hast made us for Thyself and our hearts shall have no rest save in Thee." Narrow rough paths, slippery shale, the glimpse of awful crevasses, terrible storms, cold, bewildering fog and darkness—all these wait for the genuine mountaineer. The great mystics experience all of them, and are well content so to do.

One of the best of all guides to these summits, St. John of the Cross, drew for his disciples a picturesque map of the route. It starts straight up a very narrow path. There are two much wider and better paths going left and right; one of them is marked "the advantages of this world" and the other "the advantages of the next world." Both must be avoided; for both end in the foot-hills, with no road further on. The real path goes very steeply up the mountain, to a place where St. John has written, "After this there is no path at all"; and the climber says with St. Paul, "Having nothing, I possess all things."

Here we are already a long way from the valley; and have reached the stage which is familiar to all climbers, when we feel exhilarated because we think we see the top, but are really about to begin the true climb. This is the Illuminative Life; and here, says St. John, on these levels, the majority of souls come to a halt. For the next thing he shows us is an immense precipice; towering above us, and separating the lovely Alpine pastures of the spiritual life from the awful silence of the Godhead, the mysterious region of the everlasting snows. No one can tell the climber how to tackle the precipice. Here he must be led by the Spirit of God; and his success must depend on his self-abandonment and his courage—his willingness to risk, to trust, and to endure to the very end. Every one suffers on the precipice. Here all landmarks and all guides seem to fail, and the naked soul must cling as best it can to the naked rock of reality. This is the experience which St. John calls in another place the Dark Night of the Spirit. It is a rare experience, but the only way to the real summit; the supernatural life of perfect union with the self-giving and outpouring love of God. There His reality, His honour and His glory alone remain; the very substance of the soul's perpetual joy. And that, and only that, is the mystic goal.

STUDY QUESTIONS

1. What does Underhill mean by mysticism? What part do abnormal states of body and mind play in it?
2. What is a mystical experience? What are its main practical results?
3. How does the mystic know God? Does she require an argument that proves God's existence? Do you think it possible that the mystic is simply deluded? Probable? Why or why not?
4. Suppose you had a "mystical experience." How do you think you would react?

For Further Reading

Inge, W. R. *Mysticism in Religion.* Chicago: University of Chicago Press, 1948.
Leuba, J. H. *The Psychology of Religious Mysticism.* New York: Harcourt Brace, 1926.
Pratt, J. B. *The Religious Consciousness.* New York: Macmillan, 1920 (Chapters 17 to 20).
Russell, B. *Religion and Science.* London: Oxford University Press, 1935 (Chapter 7).
Stace, W. T. *Mysticism and Philosophy.* Philadelphia: Lippincott, 1960.
Zaehner, R. C. *Mysticism: Sacred and Profane.* New York: Oxford University Press, 1957.

LEIBNIZ and McTAGGART: THE PROBLEM OF EVIL

It is difficult to deny the existence of evil. When we look around us we find people suffering from disease, malnutrition, injustice, and a host of other calamities. When we contemplate history, we find it too often a record of war, bloodshed, and disaster. If we adopt a naturalistic explanation of the universe, we have little trouble in accounting for these evils. But, if we accept the view that the universe was created by an omnipotent, perfect God, we discover it to be extremely difficult to provide a satisfactory explanation of evil. If God could have prevented evil, why didn't he? and if he could not, why not? Theologians have wrestled with these problems for centuries but have not reached agreement about their correct resolution. In the two selections that follow, Leibniz attempts to show that the existence of God is compatible with the reality of evil, but McTaggart raises issues that cast doubt on this traditional view.

Gottfried Wilhelm Leibniz (1646–1716) was born in Leipzig, the son of a professor. Soon after finishing his education he moved to Paris, where he lived for four years and became acquainted with many leading French philosophers and scientists. From Paris he moved to Hanover, where he held a position in the ducal court for the remainder of his life. In addition to being an eminent philosopher, Leibniz was a brilliant mathematician. Concurrently with but independently of Isaac Newton, he discovered the calculus. A Protestant, Leibniz was concerned about the doctrinal splits in Christianity and spent many years trying to effect a union between Protestants and Catholics, a task in which he gained scant success.

John McTaggart Ellis McTaggart (1866–1925) owes his odd-sounding name to a will. To inherit a bequest, his father, Francis Ellis, added the family name (McTaggart) of a distant relation to his own. Having given his son that same name as his middle name, he was thus obliged to add it to his name a second time, at the end. Born in London, McTaggart completed his education at Cambridge University, where he remained as a member of the faculty for the rest of his career, until his retirement in 1923.

ℒ Leibniz: Theodicy

Summary of the Controversy Reduced to Formal Arguments

Some persons of discernment have wished me to make this addition. I have the more readily deferred to their opinion, because of the opportunity thereby gained for meeting certain difficulties, and for making observations on certain matters which were not treated in sufficient detail in the work itself.

Objection I

Whoever does not choose the best course is lacking either in power, or knowledge, or goodness.

God did not choose the best course in creating this world.

Therefore God was lacking in power, or knowledge, or goodness.

Answer

I deny the minor, that is to say, the second premise of this syllogism, and the opponent proves it by this.

First published in 1710. Reprinted from G. W. Leibniz, *Theodicy*. Translated by E. M. Huggard, London, 1951, with the permission of the publishers, Routledge & Kegan Paul Ltd.

Prosyllogism

Whoever makes things in which there is evil, and which could have been made without any evil, or need not have been made at all, does not choose the best course.

God made a world wherein there is evil; a world, I say, which could have been made without any evil or which need not have been made at all.

Therefore God did not choose the best course.

Answer

I admit the minor of this prosyllogism: for one must confess that there is evil in this world which God has made, and that it would have been possible to make a world without evil or even not to create any world, since its creation depended upon the free will of God. But I deny the major, that is, the first of the two premises of the prosyllogism, and I might content myself with asking for its proof. In order, however, to give a clearer exposition of the matter, I would justify this denial by pointing out that the best course is not always that one which tends towards avoiding evil, since it is possible that the evil may be accompanied by a greater good. For example, the general of an army will prefer a great victory with a slight wound to a state of affairs without wound and without victory. I have proved this in further detail in this work by pointing out, through instances taken from mathematics and elsewhere, that an imperfection in the part may be required for a greater perfection in the whole. I have followed therein the opinion of St. Augustine, who said a hundred times that God permitted evil in order to derive from it a good, that is to say, a greater good; and Thomas Aquinas says that the permission of evil tends towards the good of the universe. I have shown that among older writers the fall of Adam was termed *felix culpa*, a fortunate sin, because it had been expiated with immense benefit by the incarnation of the Son of God: for he gave to the universe something more noble than anything there would otherwise have been amongst created beings. For the better understanding of the matter I added, following the example of many good authors, that it was consistent with order and the general good for God to grant to certain of his creatures the opportunity to exercise their freedom, even when he foresaw that they would turn to evil: for God could easily correct the evil, and it was not fitting that in order to prevent sin he should always act in an extraordinary way. It will therefore sufficiently refute the objection to show that a world with evil may be better than a world without evil. But I have gone still further in the work, and have even shown that this universe must be indeed better than every other possible universe.

Objection II

If there is more evil than good in intelligent creatures, there is more evil than good in all God's work.

Now there is more evil than good in intelligent creatures.

Therefore there is more evil than good in all God's work.

Answer

I deny the major and the minor of this conditional syllogism. As for the major, I do not admit it because this supposed inference from the part to the whole, from intelligent creatures to all creatures, assumes tacitly and without proof that creatures devoid of reason cannot be compared or taken into account with those that have reason. But why might not the surplus of good in the non-intelligent creatures that fill the world compensate for and even exceed incomparably the surplus of evil in rational creatures? It is true that the value of the latter is greater; but by way of compensation the others are incomparably greater in number; and it may be that the proportion of number and quantity surpasses that of value and quality.

The minor also I cannot admit, namely, that there is more evil than good in intelligent creatures. One need not even agree that there is more evil than good in the human kind. For it is possible, and even a very reasonable thing, that the glory and the perfection of the blessed may be incomparably greater than the misery and imperfection of the damned, and that here the excellence of the total good in the smaller number may exceed the total evil which is in the greater number. The blessed draw near to divinity through a divine Mediator, so far as can belong to these created beings, and make such progress in good as is impossible for the damned to make in evil, even though they should approach as nearly as may be the nature of demons. God is infinite, and the Devil is finite; good can and does go on *ad infinitum*, whereas evil has its bounds. It may be therefore, and it is probable, that there happens in the comparison between the blessed and the damned the opposite of what I said could happen in the comparison between the happy and the unhappy, namely that in the latter the proportion of degrees surpasses that of numbers, while in the comparison between intelligent and non-intelligent the proportion of numbers is greater than that of values. One is justified in assuming that a thing may be so as long as one does not prove that it is impossible, and indeed what is here put forward goes beyond assumption.

But secondly, even should one admit

that there is more evil than good in the human kind, one still has every reason for not admitting that there is more evil than good in all intelligent creatures. For there is an inconceivable number of Spirits, and perhaps of other rational creatures besides: and an opponent cannot prove that in the whole City of God, composed as much of Spirits as of rational animals without number and of endless different kinds, the evil exceeds the good. Although one need not, in order to answer an objection, prove that a thing is, when its mere possibility suffices, I have nevertheless shown in this present work that it is a result of the supreme perfection of the Sovereign of the Universe that the kingdom of God should be the most perfect of all states or governments possible, and that in consequence what little evil there is should be required to provide the full measure of the vast good existing there.

. . .

Objection IV

Whoever can prevent the sin of others and does not so, but rather contributes to it, although he be fully apprised of it, is accessary thereto.

God can prevent the sin of intelligent creatures; but he does not so, and he rather contributes to it by his co-operation and by the opportunities he causes, although he is fully cognizant of it.

Therefore, etc.

Answer

I deny the major of this syllogism. It may be that one can prevent the sin, but that one ought not to do so, because one could not do so without committing a sin oneself, or (when God is concerned) without acting unreasonably. I have given instances of that, and have applied them to God himself. It may be also that one contributes to the evil, and that one even opens the way to it sometimes, in doing things one is bound to do. And when one does one's duty, or (speaking of God) when, after full consideration, one does that which reason de-

mands, one is not responsible for events, even when one foresees them. One does not will these evils; but one is willing to permit them for a greater good, which one cannot in reason help preferring to other considerations. This is a *consequent* will, resulting from acts of *antecedent* will, in which one wills the good. I know that some persons, in speaking of the antecedent and consequent will of God, have meant by the antecedent that which wills that all men be saved, and by the consequent that which wills, in consequence of persistent sin, that there be some damned, damnation being a result of sin. But these are only examples of a more general notion, and one may say with the same reason, that God wills by his antecedent will that men sin not, and that by his consequent or final and decretory will (which is always followed by its effect) he wills to permit that they sin, this permission being a result of superior reasons. One had indeed justification for saying, in general, that the antecedent will of God tends towards the production of good and the prevention of evil, each taken in itself, and as it were detached according to the measure of the degree of each good or of each evil. Likewise one may say that the consequent, or final and total, divine will tends towards the production of as many goods as can be put together, whose combination thereby becomes determined, and involves also the permission of some evils and the exclusion of some goods, as the best possible plan of the universe demands.

. . .

Objection VIII

Whoever cannot fail to choose the best is not free.

God cannot fail to choose the best.

Therefore God is not free.

Answer

I deny the major of this argument. Rather is it true freedom, and the most perfect, to be able to make the best use of one's free will, and always to exercise this power, without being turned aside either by outward force or by inward passions, whereof the one enslaves our bodies and the other our souls. There is nothing less servile and more befitting the highest degree of freedom than to be always led towards the good, and always by one's own inclination, without any constraint and without any displeasure. And to object that God therefore had need of external things is only a sophism. He creates them freely: but when he had set before him an end, that of exercising his goodness, his wisdom determined him to choose the means most appropriate for obtaining this end. To call that a *need* is to take the term in a sense not usual, which clears it of all imperfection, somewhat as one does when speaking of the wrath of God.

Seneca says somewhere, that God commanded only once, but that he obeys always, because he obeys the laws that he willed to ordain for himself: *semel jussit, semper paret.* But he had better have said, that God always commands and that he is always obeyed: for in willing he always follows the tendency of his own nature, and all other things always follow his will. And as this will is always the same one cannot say that he obeys that will only which he formerly had. Nevertheless, although his will is always indefectible and always tends towards the best, the evil or the lesser good which he rejects will still be possible in itself. Otherwise the necessity of good would be geometrical (so to speak) or metaphysical, and altogether absolute; the contingency of things would be destroyed, and there would be no choice. But necessity of this kind, which does not destroy the possibility of the contrary, has the name by analogy only: it becomes effective not through the mere essence of things, but through that which is outside them and above them, that is, through the will of God. This necessity is called moral, because for the wise what is necessary and what is owing are equivalent things; and when it is always followed by its effect, as it indeed is in the perfectly wise, that is, in God, one can say that it is a happy necessity. The more nearly creatures approach this, the closer do they come to perfect felicity. Moreover, necessity of this

kind is not the necessity one endeavours to avoid, and which destroys morality, reward and commendation. For that which it brings to pass does not happen whatever one may do and whatever one may will, but because one desires it. A will to which it is natural to choose well deserves most to be commended; and it carries with in its own reward, which is supreme happiness. And as this constitution of the divine nature gives an entire satisfaction to him who possesses it, it is also the best and the most desirable from the point of view of the creatures who are all dependent upon God. If the will of God had not as its rule the principle of the best, it would tend towards evil, which would be worst of all; or else it would be indifferent somehow to good and to evil, and guided by chance. But a will that would always drift along at random would scarcely be any better for the government of the universe than the fortuitous concourse of corpuscles, without the existence of divinity. And even though God should abandon himself to chance only in some cases, and in a certain way (as he would if he did not always tend entirely towards the best, and if he were capable of preferring a lesser good to a greater good, that is, an evil to a good, since that which prevents a greater good is an evil) he would be no less imperfect than the object of his choice. Then he would not deserve absolute trust; he would act without reason in such a case, and the government of the universe would be like certain games equally divided between reason and luck. This all proves that this objection which is made against the choice of the best perverts the notions of free and necessary, and represents the best to us actually as evil: but that is either malicious or absurd.

STUDY QUESTIONS

1. How does Leibniz support his view that a world containing evil can be better than one without evil? Do you agree with him?

2. Leibniz claimed that we live in "the best of all possible worlds." What do you think of this claim?

3. In what sense does God act freely, even if he must always choose what is best?
4. Do you agree with Leibniz that (assuming the existence of God) God always chooses for the best, considering the nature of the world we find ourselves in?

For Further Reading appears on page 363.

❧ McTaggart: Some Dogmas of Religion

Chapter VI
God as Omnipotent

We now come to the relation of omnipotence to goodness. There is evil in the universe. It is not necessary to inquire how great or how small the amount of evil may be. All that is important for the present discussion is that there is some evil, and this is beyond doubt. A single pang of toothache, a single ungenerous thought, in the midst of a universe otherwise perfectly good, would prove the existence of evil.

The existence of evil is beyond doubt in the sense that no one denies the existence of pain and sin in experience, and that no one denies that pain and sin are, from the point of view of ordinary life, to be considered evil. But it has been asserted that the universe, when looked at rightly, may be completely good. Sometimes the standard is challenged, and it is suggested that pain and sin are really good, though we think them evil. Sometimes our comprehension of the facts is challenged; it is admitted that pain and sin, if they existed, would be bad, but it is maintained that they do not really exist.

The first of these alternatives means complete ethical scepticism. There is no judgement about the good of whose truth we are more certain than the judgement that what is painful or sinful cannot be perfectly good. If we distrust this judgement, we have no reason to put any trust in any judgement of good or evil. In that case we should have no right to call anything or anybody good, and therefore it would be

First published in 1906.

impossible to justify any belief in God, whose definition includes goodness. This objection, therefore, cannot consistently be used, by the believers in an omnipotent God, against the existence of evil.

The second alternative is one which can only be supported by metaphysical arguments of a somewhat abstruse and elaborate nature. To expound and examine these arguments in detail would take us too far from our subject. I will only say briefly that the theory of the unreality of evil now seems to me untenable. Supposing that it could be proved that all that we think evil was in reality good, the fact would still remain that we think it evil. This may be called a delusion or a mistake. But a delusion or mistake is as *real* as anything else. A savage's erroneous belief that the earth is stationary is just as real a fact as an astronomer's correct belief that it moves. The delusion that evil exists, then, is real. But then, to me at least, it seems certain that a delusion or an error which hid from us the goodness of the universe would itself be evil. And so there would be real evil after all. If, again, the existence of the delusion is pronounced to be a delusion, then this second delusion, which would be admitted to be real, must be pronounced evil, since it is now this delusion which decives us about the true nature of reality, and hides its goodness from us. And so on indefinitely. However many times we pronounce evil unreal, we always leave a reality behind, which in its turn is to be pronounced evil.

An omnipotent God is conceived as creating the universe. In that case it seems a natural inference that he is the cause of all the evil in the universe. But some people, who maintain the existence of a creative omnipotent God, maintain also that the choice of the human will between motives has no cause, and, therefore, is not ultimately caused by the creator. They admit, however, that God could have dispensed with the freedom of the human will, if he had chosen to do so.*

We may therefore say that an omnipotent God could have prevented all the evil in the universe if he had willed to do so. It is impossible to deny this, if omnipotence is to have any meaning, for to deny it would be to assert that there was something that God could not do if he willed to do it.

What bearing has this on the question of God's goodness? It is clear that man may act rightly in permitting evil, and even in directly causing it. It is evil that a child should lose his leg, for the loss deprives him of much happiness, and causes him much pain. But the surgeon who performs the operation, and the parent who allows it to be performed, may be perfectly justified. For amputation may be the only alternative to evils much greater than those it produces.

And, again, the production of sin may under certain circumstances be justified. Supposing that it were true—fortunately there is no reason to believe that it is true—that employment as an executioner tended to degrade morally a large proportion of those who were employed, it would by no means follow that men ought not to be induced to act as executioners. The evil results which might follow from having no hangman might far outweigh the evil done to morality by having one.

But the justification in these cases depends entirely on the limited powers of the agents. The father and the surgeon are justified because it is only through the evils of

*It seems curious that believers in human free will should often accept the argument for God's existence from the necessity of a first cause. If human volition is not completely determined, the law of causality is not universally valid. And, in that case, what force remains in the argument for a first cause?

amputation that worse evils can be avoided. If they could have avoided those worse evils by some other course that would not have been evil at all, they would not have been justified in deciding on the amputation.

Now the power of an omnipotent God is not limited. He can effect whatever he wills. If he wills to have A without B, he can have A without B, however closely A and B may be connected in the present scheme of the universe. For that scheme also is dependent on his will. It thus appears that his action cannot be justified as the amputation was. It rather resembles that of a father who should first gratuitously break his son's leg, or permit it to be broken, and should then decide for amputation, although a complete cure was possible.

If a man did this we should call him wicked. We do not wait to call a man wicked till he does more evil than good. If a man should, at the risk of his life, save all the crew of a sinking ship but one, and should then, from mere caprice, leave that man to sink, whom he could easily have saved, we should say that he had acted wickedly. Nor is it necessary that a man should do evil for the sake of evil. To desire to attend a concert is not a desire for evil as such, but if I killed a man in order to acquire his ticket, I should have acted wickedly.

Now in what way would the conduct of an omnipotent God, who permitted the existence of evil, differ from the conduct of such men, except for the worse? There are palliations of men's guilt, but what palliations could there be for such a God? A man may have lived a long life of virtue before he fell into sin, or, again, we may have reason to hope that he will repent and amend. But could we have any reason for hoping that the omnipotent God would repent and amend? It seems difficult to imagine such a reason. Again, a man may be excused to some extent for his sin, if ignorance or folly prevents him from realizing the full meaning of his action. But if an omnipotent God is not omniscient (and it seems most natural to suppose that he is), at any rate he could be so if he chose. Or again, a man may have a genuine repugnance for his sin, and only commit it under extreme temptation. A man who betrays his country under torture is less wicked than if he had betrayed it for money. But an omnipotent God can be forced to nothing, and can therefore not be forced to choose between wickedness and suffering.

Such conduct, then, as we must attribute to an omnipotent God, would be called wicked in men, although the amount of evil for which any man is responsible is insignificant as compared with the sum of all evil, and although men have in most cases excuses which would not apply to an omnipotent God. Yet this being is still called God, by people who admit that goodness is part of the definition of God. Why is God called good, when his action is asserted to be such as would prove a man to be a monster of wickedness? Two lines of defence have been tried. The first is, in substance, that the omnipotent and good God is not really good, the second that he is not really omnipotent.

The form in which the first is put by its supporters is that goodness in God is of a different nature from what it is in man. Thus Mansel says that 'the infliction of physical suffering, the permission of moral evil' and various other things 'are facts which no doubt are reconcilable, we know not how, with the infinite Goodness of God, but which certainly are not to be explained on the supposition that its sole and sufficient type is to be found in the finite goodness of man.' And he goes on to say that the difference is not one of degree only, but of kind. Pascal is still more plain-spoken: 'What can be more opposed to our wretched rules of justice than the eternal damnation of a child without any will of its own for a sin in which it seems to have had so little share that it was committed six thousand years before the said child came into existence.' Nevertheless Pascal continued to call good, and to worship, a God whom he believed to have done this.

But why should the word good be used in two senses absolutely opposed to one another? The senses are not merely dif-

ferent, as they would be if, for example, it was proposed to use the word good to indicate what is generally meant by the word scarlet. For what is called good in God would be called wicked in men, and good and wicked are predicates directly contrary to one another.

Is the alteration to be considered as one of mere caprice? Are the people who say that God is good, while Nero was wicked, in the same position as a man who should call Everest a valley, while he called Snowdon a mountain? It seems to me that there is more than this involved, and that the real ground of the alteration is that good is a word of praise, and that wicked is a word of blame, and that it is felt to be desirable to praise God rather than to blame him.

But why is it desirable to praise him? Certainly not for the reasons which make us praise Socrates and blame Nero. For the conduct which in God we call good is conduct for some faint and imperfect approximation to which we blame Nero. What other reason is left? I can only see one—that an omnipotent God is, and will remain, infinitely more powerful than Nero ever was.

On this subject Mill has spoken, and it is unnecessary to quote words which form one of the great turning-points in the religious development of the world. Yet when Mill says that rather than worship such a God he would go to hell, it is possible to raise a doubt. To call such a being good, and to worship him, is to lie and to be degraded. But it is not certain that nothing could be a greater evil than to lie and to be degraded. It is not impossible that God's goodness, as explained by Pascal and Mansel, should include the infliction of such tortures, physical and mental, on one who refused to worship him that they would be a greater evil than lying and degradation. Unless it is said that moral degradation is absolutely incommensurable with suffering—and I doubt if this can be maintained—the case does not seem impossible. Nor need the motive of the worshipper be selfish. The goodness of God, like the wickedness of some men, might include the torture of the culprit's friends as well as of himself.

We may doubt, then, whether we should be bound, or justified, in refusing to misapply the predicate good to such an omnipotent being, if the use of the word would diminish our chances of unending torture. But it seems just as likely to increase them. There are, no doubt, men who are prepared to inflict suffering on all who do not flatter them, even when they know that the flattery is empty and undeserved. But, granted that God has some qualities which would be called wicked in men, it does not follow that he has all qualities which would be called wicked in men, and there is no reason to suppose that he has this particular quality. Many men, bad as well as good, are not appeased by such flattery, but rather irritated by it, especially if they know it to be insincere, or to have been insincere when it began. God may resemble these men rather than the others. Indeed, the probability seems to be that he would do so, since pleasure in such flattery is generally a mark of a weak intellect, and even if God's goodness is like our wickedness, it can scarcely be suggested that his wisdom is like our folly. Or, again, God's goodness may induce him to damn us whatever we do, in which case we shall gain nothing by lying.

When everything is so doubtful there does not seem to be the least prudence in flattery. Nor can we rest our actions on any statement made by God as to the conduct which he will pursue. For, if goodness in God is different from goodness in us, we should have no reason to believe a statement to be true rather than false, even if it were certain that it came from God. Divine goodness may not exclude the desire to destroy our happiness by false statements.

There remains the attempt to save the goodness of an omnipotent God by giving up the reality of his omnipotence, while retaining the name. Various elements in the universe have been taken either as good or as inevitable, and the evil in the universe explained as the necessary consequence of the reality of these elements.

Thus, for example, the sin of the universe has been accounted for by the free will of the sinners, and the suffering explained as the necessary consequence, in some way, of the sin. Thus all the evil in the universe, it is asserted, is a necessary consequence of free will, and it is said that free will is so good that God was justified in choosing a universe with all the present evil in it, rather than surrender free will.

Or, again, it is said that it is impossible that there should not be some evil in a universe which was governed according to general laws, and that to be governed according to general laws is so great a perfection in the universe that God did well to choose it with all the evil that it involves.

It seems to me rather difficult to see such supreme value in free will that it would be worth more than the absence of all the present evil of the universe. It might be doubted, even, whether the advantage of unbroken general laws is so great that the evil of the universe would not be cheaply removed at the cost of frequent miracles.* But we need not discuss this. For it is quite evident that a God who cannot create a universe in which all men have free will, and which is at the same time free from all evil, is not an omnipotent God, since there is one thing which he cannot do. In the same way, a God who cannot ordain a series of general laws, the uniform working of which would exclude all evil from the universe, is not an omnipotent God.

Or, once more, it is said that a universe without evil would involve in some way the violation of such laws as the law of Contradiction or of Excluded Middle, and that these laws are so fundamental that the existence of evil in the universe is inevitable.

Even if there were any ground for believing that the absence of evil from the universe would violate such laws as these, it is clear that a God who is bound by any laws

*The supporters of this view of the supreme value of unbroken general laws, have often, it may be noted, been men who believed that God did well in permitting the human will to be undetermined, and in working occasional miracles.

is not omnipotent, since he cannot alter them. If it is said—as it may very reasonably be said—that these laws are so fundamental that it is unmeaning to speak of a being who is not bound by them, the proper conclusion is not that an omnipotent God is bound by them, but that, if there is a God, he is not omnipotent.

It is necessary to emphasize this point because, remarkable as it may appear, it is not an unusual position to maintain that God is absolutely omnipotent, and, at the same time, to believe that there are certain things he cannot do, and even to be quite certain what those things are. As against such a view as this it seems necessary to emphasize the tolerably obvious fact that, if there is anything which God could not do if he wished, he is not omnipotent.

It may be said that we are attaching too much importance to a slight inaccuracy of language. If people say that there are certain things which God could not do, then they do not believe him to be omnipotent, and they are simply using the wrong word when they say that they do believe him to be omnipotent.

But then why do they use the word? It seems to me that the confusion of language covers a confusion of thought. Many people are unwilling to accept the idea that God is not omnipotent. It is held to detract from his perfection, and to render it difficult to regard him as the creator of the universe.

And there is another point of grave importance. If God is not omnipotent, the fact that God exists and is good gives us no guarantee that the universe is more good than bad, or even that it is not very bad. If God exists and is good, the universe will of course be as good as he can make it. But, if there are some things that he cannot do, how can we tell that among these impossibilities may not be the impossibility of preventing the world from being more bad than good, or of preventing it from being very bad? If it could be shown that God's power, though limited, was strong enough to prevent this, it could only be by a deter-

mination of the precise limits of his power, and, if this could be done at all, it could only be done by an elaborate metaphysical investigation. Such investigations are open to few, and their results are frequently highly controversial. It is not strange that popular theology is unwilling to accept the position that the goodness of the universe can only be proved in such a way.

And thus popular theology has two conflicting impulses. It desires, among other things, to show that the universe is more good than bad—at any rate in the long run. The only means of its disposal for showing this—if it is to remain popular—is its belief in the existence of a God to whose will all evil is repugnant, and who is powerful enough to effect the predominance of good. But if God is to be taken as omnipotent, it is certain that all evil is not repugnant to his will, and if he is to be taken as not omnipotent, it is not certain that he is powerful enough to effect the predominance of good.

The inaccurate use of the word omnipotence hides this dilemma. When popular theology is pressed to reconcile the present existence of evil with the goodness of God, then it pleads that omnipotent does not mean omnipotent, but only very powerful. But when the sceptic has been crushed, and what is wanted is a belief in the future extinction of evil, then omnipotence slides back into its strict meaning, and it is triumphantly asserted that the cause which has an omnipotent God on its side must certainly win. The confusion is unintentional, no doubt, but it is dangerous.

It seems to me that when believers in God save his goodness by saying that he is not really omnipotent, they are taking the best course open to them, since both the personality and the goodness of God present much fewer difficulties if he is not conceived as omnipotent. But then they must accept the consequences of their choice, and realize that the efforts of a non-omnipotent God in favor of good may, for anything they have yet shown, be doomed to almost total defeat. It is not a very cheerful creed, unless it can be supplemented by some other dogmas which can assure us of God's eventual victory. But it is less depressing and less revolting than the belief that the destinies of the universe are at the mercy of a being who, with the resources of omnipotence at his disposal, decided to make a universe no better than this.

STUDY QUESTIONS

1. State in your own words McTaggart's objection to the view that all evil is illusory. Do you find his argument convincing? Explain.

2. Do you think that a God could have created a universe in which there is no evil at all? Why or why not?

3. What do you think of McTaggart's "hangman" argument?

4. What is the problem that must be faced by anyone who believes that the universe contains evil but was created by a perfect, omnipotent God? What, in your opinion, is the best solution to this problem?

For Further Reading

Ahern, M. B. *The Problem of Evil.* London: Routledge & Kegan Paul, 1971.
The Book of Job.
Laird, J. *Mind and Deity.* London: Allen and Unwin, 1941 (Chapter 6).
McCloskey, H. J. *God and Evil.* The Hague: Martinus Nijhoff, 1974.
Mill, J. S. "Nature." In *Three Essays on Religion.*
Pike, N., ed. *God and Evil.* Englewood Cliffs, N.J.: Prentice-Hall, 1964.
Voltaire. *Candide.*

PART VII

———◁▷———

The Individual as Knower

Aristotle begins his great work *Metaphysics* with the pronouncement, "All men by nature desire to know." In one sense this statement is obviously false; yet in another sense it expresses an important truth. If we take Aristotle's view to be a generalization about human attitudes, it seems only too evident that he is mistaken. Rather than desiring to know, many people probably prefer to remain in ignorance, particularly if the truth about an issue conflicts with their personal preconceptions or prejudices. The aphorism "Ignorance is bliss" may seem trite; yet it describes a gospel to which many of us, to a greater or lesser degree, do in fact subscribe.

Aristotle's thesis about human nature may, however, be interpreted in quite a different way. So understood, it differentiates humans from all other beings by emphasizing that they alone have the capacity for knowledge. Furthermore, the ability to know not only distinguishes us from other beings, it is the mark of distinction that uniquely constitutes our humanity. To be a human is to be able to think and thus to know. So Aristotle is led to his most famous definition, "Man is a rational animal," that is, man is the only animal that has the capacity for reason. Aristotle goes one step further and argues that humans not only are able to think but that they gain satisfaction from doing so. Having the capacity to understand the world, they alone are truly curious. And in this he certainly seems to be right. So we can agree with Aristotle that man *by nature* does desire to know.

If our goal is to understand the world, we need some guideposts to point us along the way and keep us from going astray. One of the main purposes of the philosophical discipline of epistemology (or theory of knowledge) is to provide such guideposts. Before that can be done, however, we must specify our objective so that we have a clear conception of what we are seeking. What, precisely, do we mean by the quest for knowledge? What is knowledge? Perhaps the best way to set about answering these questions is to recognize that all of us, as thinking beings, believe a great number of things—about ourselves, about other people, about the world we live in, and so on. To believe something is to accept it as true. If I believe that all physical bodies are governed by the law of gravitation,

I shall accept it as true that, if I fall from a height, I shall plummet to the ground. Furthermore, I shall govern my actions by this belief by refraining, for example, from making a quick exit from a tall building by leaping from a tenth-floor window. If we wish to understand, we shall try to believe, or accept as true, only those things that *are* true, recognizing that, unless what we believe is true, we have no right to claim it as something we know. At this point we might be tempted to conclude that, just as we can't know unless what we believe is true, if something we believe *is* true, then it constitutes something we know. But that would be a mistake for a very obvious reason. Suppose someone were to ask me "What is the population of Chad?" and I were to reply, "I believe the population of Chad is X" (giving some number). Suppose, further, that the number I give is correct, the population of Chad *is* X. My belief, thus, is true; does it follow that I know the population of Chad? In fact, the number I would give if asked such a question would be little more than a guess. I certainly would not be able to offer any reasons for selecting it because I know nothing about Chad except that it is located in Africa. This illustration indicates the addition that needs to be made to complete our definition of knowledge. For someone to know, it is not enough that what he believes is true; he must also be able to offer reasons in support of his belief capable of establishing its truth. These considerations have led most epistemologists to agree in defining knowledge as "justified, true belief."

With a clear conception of what knowledge is in hand, it would seem a relatively simple task to determine what things we know. All we need to do is to decide which of our beliefs we can justify as true. Unfortunately, at this point, we run into opposition, for some philosophers claim that no one can ever succeed in justifying the truth of *anything* he believes. Thus the goal that we seek—knowledge, or an understanding of the world—is unattainable. Such philosophers are called epistemological sceptics. Two of the most famous sceptics in the history of philosophy were the Roman philosopher of the second century A.D., Sextus Empiricus, and the eighteenth-century Scottish philosopher, David Hume. Through the ages, the sceptics have attacked the possibility of our gaining any knowledge by a wide variety of arguments. Among the most telling of the sceptical arguments is that given by the French philosopher, René Descartes, who was anything but a sceptic himself. His purpose in offering the argument was to make plain the nature and magnitude of the difficulties confronting any philosopher who attempts to defend the view that we can know things. Descartes' case for scepticism, with which he begins his *Meditations*, appears in the first of the selections that follow.

In their attempts to combat scepticism by showing that we can indeed know things, epistemologists have usually avoided adopting the obvious device; namely, of pointing out various individual things that we know. Instead they have taken a more general and hence theoretically more powerful line. They have argued that, by appealing to a certain methodology, or type of justification procedure, we can succeed in justifying the truth of many of our beliefs, hence can count all of them as things we know. But about the correct methodology to adopt, they have been in disagreement. Some say we can justify our beliefs by an appeal to reason; these are the rationalists. Others say we must appeal to experience; these are the empiricists. Each of these two opposed positions has been defended by a major tradition in epistemology. They are represented in the selections that follow by their leading exponents—René Descartes and John Locke.

In my discussion of knowledge and scepticism, I have devoted my attention mainly to the notion of justification, the means by which we attempt to transform what we merely believe into something we know. To justify any belief, I have said, is to establish that it is true. But what does this mean? What is truth? Although this may seem an easy question to answer, philosophers have not found it so. On the contrary, they have developed a number of quite different definitions of truth. Three of the most important appear in the last three selections of the book—correspondence, coherence, and pragmatism. These three theories are defended, respectively, by Bertrand Russell, Brand Blanshard, and William James.

Background Reading
Chisholm, R. M. *Theory of Knowledge.* 2d ed. Englewood Cliffs, N.J.: Prentice-Hall, 1977.
Hamlyn, D. W. *The Theory of Knowledge.* Garden City, N.Y.: Doubleday, 1970 (Part I).
Hill, T. E. *Contemporary Theories of Knowledge.* New York: Ronald, 1961.
Pears, D. *What Is Knowledge?* New York: Harper & Row, 1971.
White, A. R. *Truth.* London: Macmillan, 1970.
Woozley, A. D. *Theory of Knowledge.* London: Hutchinson University Library, 1949.

DESCARTES: RATIONALISM

The term rationalism is used in two different ways by philosophers. In its broader sense, it describes the view that we should base our beliefs about the nature of things on reason rather than on superstition, hearsay, authority, or some other nonrational source. When it is used in this way, rationalism is a view to which practically all philosophers obviously would subscribe. But rationalism has a narrower sense as well, to describe the epistemological theory that reason, as a faculty of the mind to be distinguished particularly from sense experience, is the sole source of human knowledge. According to the epistemological rationalists, only those things whose truth we can demonstrate constitute something we can legitimately claim to know. One of the results of rationalism is to constrict quite sharply the scope of human knowledge. Excluded, for example, are almost all the beliefs of ordinary life, beliefs most of us take for granted as things we know. René Descartes begins the selection that follows by offering some compelling reasons for doubting particularly our senses as sources of knowledge.

For a biographical sketch of René Descartes see page 101.

℣ *Rules for the Direction of the Mind*

Rule I.

The end of study should be to direct the mind towards the enunciation of sound and correct judgments on all matters that come before it.

Written probably in 1628 but not published until 1701. Reprinted from *The Philosophical Works of Descartes.* Translated by E. S. Haldane and G. R. T. Ross. Vol. I. With permission of the publisher, Cambridge University Press, London.

Whenever men notice some similarity between two things, they are wont to ascribe to each, even in those respects in which the two differ, what they have found to be true of the other. Thus they erroneously compare the sciences, which entirely consist in the cognitive exercise of the mind, with the arts, which depend upon an exercise and disposition of the body. They see that not all the arts can be acquired by the same man, but that he who restricts himself to one, most readily becomes the best executant, since it is not so easy for the same hand to adapt itself both to agricultural operations and to harp-playing, or to the performance of several such tasks as to one alone. Hence they have held the same to be true of the sciences also, and distinguishing them from one another according to their subject matter, they have imagined that they ought to be studied separately, each in isolation from all the rest. But this is certainly wrong. For since the sciences taken all together are identical with human wisdom, which always remains one and the same, however applied to different subjects—and suffers no more differentiation proceeding from them than the light of the sun experiences from the variety of the things which it illumines—there is no need for minds to be confined at all within limits, for neither does the knowing of one truth have an effect like that of the acquisition of one art and prevent us from finding out another—it rather aids us to do so. Certainly it appears to me strange that so many people should investigate human customs with such care, the virtues of plants, the motions of the stars, the transmutations of metals, and the objects of similar sciences, while at the same time practically none bethink themselves about good understanding, or universal Wisdom, though nevertheless all other studies are to be esteemed not so much for their own value as because they contribute something to this. Consequently, we are justified in bringing forward this as the first rule of all, since there is nothing more prone to turn us aside from the correct way of seeking out truth than this directing of our inquiries, not towards their general end, but towards certain special investigations. I do not here refer to perverse and censurable pursuits like empty glory or base gain; obviously counterfeit reasonings and quibbles suited to vulgar understanding open up a much more direct route to such a goal than does a sound apprehension of the truth. But I have in view even honorable and laudable pursuits, because these mislead us in a more subtle fashion. For example, take our investigations of those sciences conducive to the conveniences of life or which yield that pleasure which is found in the contemplation of truth, practically the only joy in life that is complete and untroubled with any pain. There we may indeed expect to receive the legitimate fruits of scientific inquiry; but if, in the course of our study, we think of them, they frequently cause us to omit many facts which are necessary to the understanding of other matters, because they seem to be either of slight value or of little interest. Hence we must believe that all the sciences are so interconnected, that it is much easier to study them all together than to isolate one from all the others. If, therefore, anyone wishes to search out the truth of things in serious earnest, he ought not to select one special science; for all the sciences are conjoined with each other and interdependent: he ought rather to think how to increase the natural light of reason, not for the purpose of resolving this or that difficulty of scholastic type, but in order that his understanding may light his will to its proper choice in all the contingencies of life. In a short time he will see with amazement that he has made much more progress than those who are eager about particular ends, and that he has not only obtained all that they desire, but even higher results than fall within his expectation.

Rule II.

Only those objects should engage our attention, to the sure and indubitable knowledge of which our mental powers seem to be adequate.

Science in its entirety is true and evident cognition. He is no more learned who has doubts on many matters than the man who has never thought of them; nay he appears to be less learned if he has formed wrong opinions on any particulars. Hence it were better not to study at all than to occupy one's self with objects of such difficulty, that, owing to our inability to distinguish true from false, we are forced to regard the doubtful as certain; for in those matters any hope of augmenting our knowledge is exceeded by the risk of diminishing it. Thus in accordance with the above maxim we reject all such merely probable knowledge and make it a rule to trust only what is completely known and incapable of being doubted. No doubt men of education may persuade themselves that there is but little of such certain knowledge, because, forsooth, a common failing of human nature has made them deem it too easy and open to everyone, and so led them to neglect to think upon such truths; but I nevertheless announce that there are more of these than they think—truths which suffice to give a rigorous demonstration of innumerable propositions, the discussion of which they have hitherto been unable to free from the element of probability. Further because they have believed that it was unbecoming for a man of education to confess ignorance on any point, they have so accustomed themselves to trick out their fabricated explanations, that they have ended by gradually imposing on themselves, and thus have issued them to the public as genuine.

But if we adhere closely to this rule we shall find left but few objects of legitimate study. For there is scarce any question occurring in the sciences about which talented men have not disagreed. But whenever two men come to opposite decisions about the same matter one of them at least must certainly be in the wrong, and apparently there is not even one of them who knows; for if the reasoning of the second was sound and clear he would be able so to lay it before the other as finally to succeed in convincing *his* understanding also. Hence apparently we cannot attain to a perfect knowledge in any such case of probable opinion, for it would be rashness to hope for more than others have attained to. Consequently, if we reckon correctly, of the sciences already discovered, Arithmetic and Geometry alone are left, to which the observance of this rule reduces us.

Yet we do not therefore condemn that method of philosophizing which others have already discovered and those weapons of the schoolmen, probable syllogisms, which are so well suited for polemics. They indeed give practice to the wits of youths and, producing emulation among them, act as a stimulus; and it is much better for their minds to be molded by opinions of this sort, uncertain though they appear, as being objects of controversy among the learned, than to be left entirely to their own devices. For thus, through lack of guidance, they might stray into some abyss; but as long as they follow in their masters' footsteps, though they may diverge at times from the truth, they will yet certainly find a path which is at least in this respect safer, that it has been approved of by more prudent people. We ourselves rejoice that we in earlier years experienced this scholastic training; but now, being released from that oath of allegiance which bound us to our old masters, and since, as becomes our riper years, we are no longer subject to the ferule, if we wish in earnest to establish for ourselves those rules which shall aid us in scaling the heights of human knowledge, we must admit assuredly among the primary members of our catalogue that maxim which forbids us to abuse our leisure as many do, who neglect all easy quests and take up their time only with difficult matters; for they, though certainly making all sorts of subtle conjectures and elaborating most plausible arguments with great ingenuity, frequently find too late that after all their labors they have only increased the multitude of their doubts, without acquiring any knowledge whatsoever.

But now let us proceed to explain more carefully our reasons for saying, as we did a little while ago, that of all the sciences known as yet, Arithmetic and Geometry alone are free from any taint of falsity or uncertainty. We must note then that there are two ways by which we arrive at the knowledge of facts, viz., by experience and by deduction. We must further observe that while our inferences from experience are frequently fallacious, deduction, or the pure illation of one thing from another, though it may be passed over, if it is not seen through, cannot be erroneous when performed by an understanding that is in the least degree rational. And it seems to me that the operation is profited but little by those constraining bonds by means of which the Dialecticians claim to control human reason, though I do not deny that that discipline may be serviceable for other purposes. My reason for saying so is that none of the mistakes which men can make (men, I say, not beasts) are due to faulty inference; they are caused merely by the fact that we found upon a basis of poorly comprehended experiences, or that propositions are posited which are hasty and groundless.

This furnishes us with an evident explanation of the great superiority in certitude of Arithmetic and Geometry to other sciences. The former alone deal with an object so pure and uncomplicated, that they need make no assumptions at all which experience renders uncertain, but wholly consist in the rational deduction of consequences. They are on that account much the easiest and clearest of all, and possess an object such as we require, for in them it is scarce humanly possible for anyone to err except by inadvertence. And yet we should not be surprised to find that plenty of people of their own accord prefer to apply their intelligence to other studies, or to Philosophy. The reason for this is that every person permits himself the liberty of making guesses in the matter of an obscure subject with more confidence than in one which is clear, and that it is much easier to have some vague notion about any subject, no matter what, than to arrive at the real truth about a single question, however simple that may be.

But one conclusion now emerges out of these considerations, viz., not, indeed, that Arithmetic and Geometry are the sole sciences to be studied, but only that in our search for the direct road towards truth we should busy ourselves with no object about which we cannot attain a certitude equal to that of the demonstrations of Arithmetic and Geometry.

Rule III

In the subjects we propose to investigate, our inquiries should be directed, not to what others have thought, nor to what we ourselves conjecture, but to what we can clearly and perspicuously behold and with certainty deduce; for knowledge is not won in any other way.

• • •

We shall here take note of all those mental operations by which we are able, wholly without fear of illusion, to arrive at the knowledge of things. Now I admit only two, viz., intuition and deduction.

By *intuition* I understand, not the fluctuating testimony of the senses, nor the misleading judgment that proceeds from the blundering constructions of imagination, but the conception which an unclouded and attentive mind gives us so readily and distinctly that we are wholly freed from doubt about that which we understand. Or, what comes to the same thing, *intuition* is the undoubting conception of an unclouded and attentive mind, and springs from the light of reason alone; it is more certain than deduction itself, in that it is simpler, though deduction, as we have noted above, cannot by us be erroneously conducted. Thus each individual can mentally have intuition of the fact that he exists, and that he thinks; that the triangle is bounded by three lines only, the sphere by a single superficies, and so on. Facts of such a kind are far more numerous than many people think, disdaining as they do to direct their attention upon such simple matters.

But in case anyone may be put out by this new use of the term intuition and of other terms which in the following pages I am similarly compelled to dissever from their current meaning, I here make the general announcement that I pay no attention to the way in which particular terms have of late been employed in the schools, because it would have been difficult to employ the same terminology while my theory was wholly different. All that I take note of is the meaning of the Latin of each word, when, in cases where an appropriate term is lacking, I wish to transfer to the vocabulary that expresses my own meaning those that I deem most suitable.

This evidence and certitude, however, which belongs to intuition, is required not only in the enunciation of propositions, but also in discursive reasoning of whatever sort. For example consider this consequence: 2 and 2 amount to the same as 3 and 1. Now we need to see intuitively not only that 2 and 2 make 4, and that likewise 3 and 1 make 4, but further that the third of the above statements is a necessary conclusion from these two.

Hence now we are in a position to raise the question as to why we have, besides intuition, given this supplementary method of knowing, viz., knowing by *deduction,* by which we understand all necessary inference from other facts that are known with certainty. This, however, we could not avoid, because many things are known with certainty, though not by themselves evident, but only deduced from true and known principles by the continuous and uninterrupted action of a mind that has a clear vision of each step in the process. It is in a similar way that we know that the last link in a long chain is connected with the first, even though we do not take in by means of one and the same act of vision all the intermediate links on which that connection depends, but only remember that we have taken them successively under review and that each single one is united to its neighbor, from the first even to the last. Hence we distinguish this mental intuition from deduction by the fact that into the conception of the latter there enters a certain movement or succession, into that of the former there does not. Further, deduction does not require an immediately presented evidence such as intuition possesses; its certitude is rather conferred upon it in some way by memory. The upshot of the matter is that it is possible to say that those propositions indeed which are immediately deduced from first principles are known now by intuition, now by deduction, *i.e.,* in a way that differs according to our point of view. But the first principles themselves are given by intuition alone, while, on the contrary, the remote conclusions are furnished only by deduction.

These two methods are the most certain routes to knowledge, and the mind should admit no others. All the rest should be rejected as suspect of error and dangerous.

🍃 *Meditations on the First Philosophy*

Meditation I.
Of the things which may be brought within the sphere of the doubtful.

It is now some years since I detected how many were the false beliefs that I had from my earliest youth admitted as true, and how doubtful was everything I had since constructed on this basis; and from that time I was convinced that I must once for all seriously undertake to rid myself of all the opinions which I had formerly accepted; and commence to build anew from the foundation, if I wanted to establish any firm and permanent structure in the sciences. But as this enterprise appeared to be a very great one, I waited until I had attained an age so mature that I could not hope that at any later date I should be better fitted to execute my design. This reason caused me to delay so long that I should feel that I was doing wrong were I to occupy in deliberation the time that yet remains to me for action. Today, then, since very opportunely for the plan I have in view I have delivered my mind from every care and am happily agitated by no passions and since I have procured for myself an assured leisure in a peaceable retirement, I shall at last seriously and freely address myself to the general upheaval of all my former opinions.

Now for this object it is not necessary that I should show that all of these are false—I shall perhaps never arrive at this end. But inasmuch as reason already persuades me that I ought no less carefully to withhold my assent from matters which are not entirely certain and indubitable than from those which appear to me manifestly to be false, if I am able to find in each one some reason to doubt, this will suffice to justify my rejecting the whole. And for that end it will not be requisite that I should examine each in particular, which would be an endless undertaking; for owing to the fact that the destruction of the foundations of necessity brings with it the downfall of the rest of the edifice, I shall only in the first place attack those principles upon which all my former opinions rested.

All that up to the present time I have accepted as most true and certain I have learned either from the senses or through the senses; but it is sometimes proved to me that these senses are deceptive, and it is wiser not to trust entirely to any thing by which we have once been deceived.

But it may be that although the senses sometimes deceive us concerning things which are hardly perceptible, or very far away, there are yet many others to be met with as to which we cannot reasonably have any doubt, although we recognize them by their means. For example, there is the fact that I am here, seated by the fire, attired in a dressing gown, having this paper in my hands and other similar matters. And how could I deny that these hands and this body are mine, were it not perhaps that I compare myself to certain persons, devoid of sense, whose cerebella are so troubled and clouded by the violent vapours of black bile, that they constantly assure us that they think they are kings when they are really quite poor, or that they are clothed in purple when they are really without covering, or who imagine that they have an earthenware head or are nothing but pumpkins or are made of glass. But they are mad, and I should not be any the less insane were I to follow examples so extravagant.

At the same time I must remember that I am a man, and that consequently I am in the habit of sleeping, and in my dreams representing to myself the same things or sometimes even less probable things, than do those who are insane in their waking moments. How often has it happened to me that in the night I dreamt that I found myself in this particular place, that I was dressed and seated near the fire, whilst in reality I was lying undressed in bed! At this moment it does indeed seem to me that it is with eyes awake that I am looking at this paper; that this head which I move is not asleep, that it is deliberately and of set purpose that I extend my hand and perceive it; what happens in sleep does not appear so clear nor so distinct as does all this. But in thinking over this, I remind myself that on many occasions I have in sleep been deceived by similar illusions, and in dwelling carefully on this reflection I see so manifestly that there are no certain indications by which we may clearly distinguish wakefulness from sleep that I am lost in astonishment. And my astonishment is such that it is almost capable of persuading me that I now dream.

Now let us assume that we are asleep and that all these particulars, e.g., that we open our eyes, shake our head, extend our hands, and so on, are but false delusions; and let us reflect that possibly neither our hands nor our whole body are such as they appear to us to be. At the same time we must at least confess that the things which are represented to us in sleep are like painted representations which can only have been formed as the counterparts of something real and true, and that in this way those general things at least, i.e., eyes, a head, hands, and a whole body, are not imaginary things, but things really existent. For, as a matter of fact, painters, even when they study with the greatest skill to represent sirens and satyrs by forms the most strange and extraordinary, cannot give them natures which are entirely new, but merely make a certain medley of the members of different animals; or if their imagination is extravagant enough to invent something so novel that nothing similar has ever before been seen, and that then their work represents a thing purely fictitious and absolutely false, it is certain all the same that the colors of which this is composed are necessarily real. And for the same reason, although these general things, to wit, a body, eyes, a head, hands, and such like, may be imaginary, we are bound at the same time to confess that there are at least some other objects yet more simple and more universal, which are real and true; and of these just in the same way as with certain real colors, all these images of things which dwell in our thoughts, whether true and real or false and fantastic, are formed.

To such a class of things pertains corporeal nature in general, and its extension, the figure of extended things, their quantity or magnitude and number, as also the place in which they are, the time which measures their duration, and so on.

That is possibly why our reasoning is not unjust when we conclude from this that Physics, Astronomy, Medicine and all other sciences which have as their end the consideration of composite things, are very dubious and uncertain; but that Arithmetic, Geometry and other sciences of that kind which only treat of things that are very simple and very general, without taking great trouble to ascertain whether they are actually existent or not, contain some measure of certainty and an element of the indubitable. For whether I am awake or alseep, two and three together always form five, and the square can never have more than four sides, and it does not seem possible that truths so clear and apparent can be suspected of any falsity or uncertainty.

Nevertheless I have long had fixed in my mind the belief that an all-powerful God existed by whom I have been created such as I am. But how do I know that He has not brought it to pass that there is no earth, no heaven, no extended body, no magnitude, no place, and that nevertheless I possess the perceptions of all these things and that they seem to me to exist just exactly as I now see them? And, besides, as I sometimes imagine that others deceive themselves in the things which they think they know best, how do I know that I am not deceived every time that I add two and

three, or count the sides of a square, or judge of things yet simpler, if anything simpler can be imagined? But possibly God has not desired that I should be thus deceived, for He is said to be supremely good. If, however, it is contrary to His goodness to have made me such that I constantly deceive myself, it would also appear to be contrary to His goodness to permit me to be sometimes deceived, and nevertheless I cannot doubt that He does permit this.

There may indeed be those who would prefer to deny the existence of a God so powerful, rather than believe that all other things are uncertain. But let us not suppose them for the present, and grant that all that is here said of a God is a fable; nevertheless, in whatever way they suppose that I have arrived at the state of being that I have reached—whether they attribute it to fate or to accident, or make out that it is by a continual succession of antecedents, or by some other method—since to err and deceive oneself is a defect, it is clear that the greater will be the probability of my being so imperfect as to deceive myself ever, as is the Author to whom they assign my origin the less powerful. To these reasons I have certainly nothing to reply, but at the end I feel constrained to confess that there is nothing in all that I formerly believed to be true, of which I cannot in some measure doubt, and that not merely through want of thought or through levity, but for reasons which are very powerful and maturely considered; so that henceforth I ought not the less carefully to refrain from giving credence to these opinions than to that which is manifestly false, if I desire to arrive at any certainty.

But it is not sufficient to have made these remarks; we must also be careful to keep them in mind. For these ancient and commonly held opinions still revert frequently to my mind, long and familiar custom having given them the right to occupy my mind against my inclination and rendered them almost masters of my belief; nor will I ever lose the habit of deferring to them or of placing my confidence in them, so long as I consider them as they really are, *i.e.,* opinions in some measure doubtful, as I have just shown, and at the same time highly probable, so that there is much more reason to believe in than to deny them. That is why I consider that I shall not be acting amiss, if, taking of set purpose a contrary belief, I allow myself to be deceived, and for a certain time pretend that all these opinions are entirely false and imaginary, until at last, having thus balanced my former prejudices with my latter so that they cannot divert my opinions more to one side than to the other, my judgment will no longer be dominated by bad usage or turned away from the right knowledge of the truth. For I am assured that there can be neither peril nor error in this course, and that I cannot at present yield too much to distrust, since I am not considering the question of action, but only of knowledge.

I shall then suppose, not that God who is supremely good and the fountain of truth, but some evil genius not less powerful than deceitful, has employed his whole energies in deceiving me; I shall consider that the heavens, the earth, colors, figures, sound, and all other external things are nought but the illusions and dreams of which this genius has availed himself in order to lay traps for my credulity; I shall consider myself as having no hands, no eyes, no flesh, no blood, nor any senses, yet falsely believing myself to possess all these things; I shall remain obstinately attached to this idea, and if by this means it is not in my power to arrive at the knowledge of any truth, I may at least do what is in my power (i.e., suspend my judgment), and with firm purpose avoid giving credence to any false thing, or being imposed upon by this arch deceiver, however powerful and deceptive he may be. But this task is a laborious one, and insensibly a certain lassitude leads me into the course of my ordinary life. And just as a captive who in sleep enjoys an imaginary liberty, when he begins to suspect that the liberty is but a dream, fears to awaken, and conspires with these agreeable illusions that the deception may be prolonged, so insensibly of my own accord I

fall back into my former opinions, and I dread awakening from this slumber, lest the laborious wakefulness which would follow the tranquility of this repose should have to be spent not in daylight, but in the excessive darkness of the difficulties which have just been discussed.

Meditation II.
Of the Nature of the Human Mind; and that it is more easily known than the Body.

The Meditation of yesterday filled my mind with so many doubts that it is no longer in my power to forget them. And yet I do not see in what manner I can resolve them; and, just as if I had all of a sudden fallen into very deep water, I am so disconcerted that I can neither make certain of setting my feet on the bottom, nor can I swim and so support myself on the surface. I shall nevertheless make an effort and follow anew the same path as that on which I yesterday entered, *i.e.,* I shall proceed by setting aside all that in which the least doubt could be supposed to exist, just as if I had discovered that it was absolutely false; and I shall ever follow in this road until I have met with something which is certain, or at least, if I can do nothing else, until I have learned for certain that there is nothing in the world that is certain. Archimedes, in order that he might draw the terrestrial globe out of its place, and transport it elsewhere, demanded only that one point should be fixed and immovable; in the same way I shall have the right to conceive high hopes if I am happy enough to discover one thing only which is certain and indubitable.

I suppose, then, that all the things that I see are false; I persuade myself that nothing has ever existed of all that my fallacious memory represents to me. I consider that I possess no senses; I imagine that body, figure, extension, movement, and place are but the fictions of my mind. What, then can be esteemed as true? Perhaps nothing at all, unless that there is nothing in the world that is certain.

But how can I know there is not something different from those things that I have just considered, of which one cannot have the slightest doubt? Is there not some God, or some other being by whatever name we call it, who puts these reflections into my mind? That is not necessary, for is it not possible that I am capable of producing them myself? I myself, am I not at least something? But I have already denied that I had senses and body. Yet I hesitate, for what follows from that? Am I so dependent on body and senses that I cannot exist without these? But I was persuaded that there was nothing in all the world, that there was no heaven, no earth, that there were no minds, nor any bodies: was I not then likewise persuaded that I did not exist? Not at all; of a surety I myself did exist since I persuaded myself of something or merely because I thought of something. But there is some deceiver or other, very powerful and very cunning, who ever employs his ingenuity in deceiving me. Then without doubt I exist also if he deceives me, and let him deceive me as much as he will, he can never cause me to be nothing so long as I think that I am something. So that after having reflected well and carefully examined all things, we must come to the definite conclusion that this proposition: *I am, I exist,* is necessarily true each time I pronounce it, or that I mentally conceive it.

STUDY QUESTIONS

1. What does Descartes mean by knowledge? What kinds of things can we know?
2. What does Descartes mean by intuition? How does it differ from experience? From deduction? What role does it play in the acquisition of knowledge?
3. What are Descartes' objections to the appeal to sense experience as a source of knowledge?
4. What is the "evil genius" argument? What is its point? How does Descartes go about answering it? Do you think he is successful?
5. Do you agree that Descartes should be labelled as a rationalist? Explain.

For Further Reading

Aune, B. *Rationalism, Empiricism, and Pragmatism.* New York: Random House, 1970 (Chapter 1).

Descartes, R. *Discourse on Method.*

Doney, W., ed. *Descartes.* Garden City, N.Y.: Doubleday, 1967.

Frankfurt, H. G. *Demons, Dreamers, and Madmen: The Defense of Reason in Descartes' Meditations.* Indianapolis: Bobbs-Merrill, 1970.

Kenny, A. *Descartes.* New York: Random House, 1968 (esp. Chapters 2 through 5).

Spinoza, B. *On the Improvement of the Understanding.*

LOCKE: EMPIRICISM

In contrast to rationalism, which attempts to explain human knowledge by an appeal to reason, empiricism turns to experience as the ultimate source of what we know. All the information that comes to us to provide the content of our knowledge, or our ideas, arrives through our senses (sight, hearing, etc.). The human mind, although completely passive at birth, becomes increasingly active as its stock of ideas enlarges, arranging and combining these ideas in a great variety of ways and thus expanding the range of our knowledge. How far knowledge gained in this way can reach and what its limits are is a point of serious dispute among epistemologists. One of the greatest of the historical empiricists,

David Hume, found himself forced to the conclusion that, if experience is the source of our knowledge, there is little of importance that we can really know. With this pessimistic conclusion, however, John Locke, the author of the selection that follows, does not agree.

For a biographical sketch of John Locke see page 275.

❧ *An Essay Concerning Human Understanding*

Book II
Chapter I
Of Ideas in General, and Their Original

Every man being conscious to himself, that he thinks, and that which his mind is applied about, whilst thinking, being the ideas that are there, it is past doubt, that men have in their minds several ideas, such as are those expressed by the words, whiteness, hardness, sweetness, thinking, motion, man, elephant, army, drunkenness, and others. It is in the first place then to be inquired, how he comes by them. I know it is a received doctrine, that men have native ideas, and original characters, stamped upon their minds, in their very first being. This opinion I have, at large, examined already; and, I suppose, what I have said, in the foregoing book, will be much more easily admitted, when I have shown, whence the understanding may get all the ideas it has, and by what ways and degrees they may come into the mind; for which I shall appeal to everyone's own observation and experience.

Let us then suppose the mind to be, as we say, white paper, void of all characters, without any ideas; how comes it to be furnished? Whence comes it by that vast store which the busy and boundless fancy of man has painted on it, with an almost endless variety? Whence has it all the materials of reason and knowledge? To this I answer in one word, from experience; in that all our knowledge is founded, and from that it ultimately derives itself. Our observation, employed either about external sensible objects, or about the internal operations of our minds, perceived and reflected on by ourselves, is that which supplies our understandings with all the materials of thinking. These two are the fountains of knowledge, from whence all the ideas we have, or can naturally have, do spring.

First, our senses, conversant about particular sensible objects, do convey into the mind several distinct perceptions of things, according to those various ways wherein those objects do affect them: and thus we come by those ideas we have, of yellow, white, heat, cold, soft, hard, bitter, sweet, and all those which we call sensible qualities; which when I say the senses convey into the mind, I mean, they from external objects convey into the mind what produces there those perceptions. This great source of most of the ideas we have, depending wholly upon our senses, and derived by them to the understanding, I call *sensation.*

Secondly, the other fountain, from which experience furnisheth the understanding with ideas, is the perception of the operations of our own mind within us, as it is employed about the ideas it has got; which operations when the soul comes to reflect on and consider, do furnish the understanding with another set of ideas, which could not be had from things without; and such are perception, thinking, doubting, believing, reasoning, knowing, willing, and all the different actings of our own minds; which we being conscious of and observing in ourselves, do from these receive into our understandings as distinct ideas, as we do from bodies affecting our senses. This source of ideas every man has wholly in himself: and though it be not

First published in 1690.

sense, as having nothing to do with external objects, yet it is very like it, and might properly enough be called internal sense. But as I call the other *sensation*, so I call this *reflection*, the ideas it affords being such only as the mind gets by reflecting on its own operations within itself. By *reflection* then, in the following part of this discourse, I would be understood to mean that notice which the mind takes of its own operations, and the manner of them; by reason whereof there come to be ideas of these operations in the understanding. These two, I say, viz., external material things, as the objects of sensation; and the operations of our own minds within, as the objects of reflection, are to me the only originals from whence all our ideas take their beginnings. The term *operations* here I use in a large sense, as comprehending not barely the actions of the mind about its ideas, but some sort of passions arising sometimes from them, such as is the satisfaction or uneasiness arising from any thought.

The understanding seems to me not to have the least glimmering of any ideas, which it doth not receive from one of these two. External objects furnish the mind with the ideas of sensible qualities, which are all of those different perceptions they produce in us: and the mind furnishes the understanding with ideas of its own operations.

These, when we have taken a full survey of them and their several modes, combinations, and relations, we shall find to contain all our whole stock of ideas; and that we have nothing in our minds which did not come in one of these two ways. Let any one examine his own thoughts, and thoroughly search into his understanding; and then let him tell me, whether all the original ideas he has there, are any other than of the objects of his senses, or of the operations of his mind, considered as objects of his reflection: and how great a mass of knowledge soever he imagines to be lodged there, he will, upon taking a strict view, see that he has not any idea in his mind, but what one of these two have imprinted; though perhaps, with infinite variety compounded and enlarged by the understanding, as we shall see hereafter.

• • •

Chapter VIII
Some Further Considerations Concerning Our Simple Ideas of Sensation

• • •

To discover the nature of our ideas the better, and to discourse of them intelligibly, it will be convenient to distinguish them as they are ideas or perceptions in our minds, and as they are modifications of matter in the bodies that cause such perception in us: that so we may not think (as perhaps usually is done) that they are exactly the images and resemblances of something inherent in the subject; most of those of sensation being in the mind no more the likeness of something existing without us, than the names that stand for them are the likeness of our ideas, which yet upon hearing they are apt to excite in us.

Whatsoever the mind perceives in itself, or is the immediate object of perception, thought, or understanding, that I call idea; and the power to produce any idea in our mind I call quality of the subject wherein that power is. Thus a snowball having the power to produce in us the ideas of white, cold, and round, the powers to produce those ideas in us, as they are in the snowball, I call *qualities;* and as they are sensations or perceptions in our understandings, I call them *ideas;* which ideas, if I speak of sometimes, as in the things themselves, I would be understood to mean those qualities in the objects which produce them in us.

Qualities thus considered in bodies are, first, such as are utterly inseparable from the body, in what estate soever it be; such as in all the alterations and changes it suffers, all the force can be used upon it, it constantly keeps; and such as sense constantly finds in every particle of matter which has bulk enough to be perceived, and the mind finds inseparable from every particle of matter, though less than to make itself singly be perceived by our senses. For example, take a grain of wheat, divide it into two parts—each part has still solidity, extension, figure, and mobility; divide it again, and it retains still the same qualities; and so divide it on till the parts become insensible, they must retain still each of them all those qualities. For division (which is all that a mill, or pestle, or any other body does upon another, in reducing it to insensible parts) can never take away either solidity, extension, figure, or mobility from any body, but only makes two or more distinct separate masses of matter, of that which was but one before; all which distinct masses, reckoned as so many distinct bodies, after division make a certain number. These I call original, or primary, qualities of body, which I think we may observe to produce simple ideas in us, viz., solidity, extension, figure, motion or rest, and number.

Secondly, such qualities which in truth are nothing in the objects themselves, but powers to produce various sensations in us by their primary qualities, *i.e.,* by the bulk, figure, texture, and motion of their insensible parts, as colors, sounds, tastes, etc. These I call secondary qualities. To these might be added a third sort, which are allowed to be barely powers, though they are as much real qualities in the subject, as those which I, to comply with the common way of speaking, call qualities, but for distinction, secondary qualities. For the power in fire to produce a new color, or consistency, in wax or clay, by its primary qualities, is as much a quality in fire, as the power it has to produce in me a new idea or sensation of warmth or burning, which I felt not before, by the same primary qualities, viz., the bulk, texture, and motion of its insensible parts.

The next thing to be considered is, how bodies produce ideas in us; and that is manifestly by impulse, the only way which we can conceive bodies to operate in.

If then external objects be not united to our minds, when they produce ideas therein, and yet we perceive these original qualities in such of them as singly fall under our senses, it is evident that some motion must be thence continued by our nerves or animal spirits, by some parts of our bodies, to the brain, or the seat of sensation, there to produce in our minds the particular ideas we have of them. And since the extension, figure, number, and motion of bodies, of an observable bigness, may be perceived at a distance by the sight, it is evident some singly imperceptible bodies must come from them to the eyes, and thereby convey to the brain some motion, which produces these ideas which we have of them in us.

After the same manner that the ideas of these original qualities are produced in us, we may conceive that the ideas of secondary qualities are also produced, viz., by the operations of insensible particles on our senses. For it being manifest that there are bodies, and good store of bodies, each whereof are so small, that we cannot, by any of our senses, discover either their bulk, figure, or motion, as is evident in the particles of the air and water, and others extremely smaller than those, perhaps as much smaller than the particles of air and water are smaller than peas or hailstones: let us suppose at present, that the different motions and figures, bulk and number of such particles, affecting the several organs of our senses, produce in us those different sensations, which we have from the colors and smells of bodies; for example, that of violet, by the impulse of such insensible particles of matter of peculiar figures and bulks, and in different degrees and modifications of their motions, causes the ideas of the blue color and sweet scent of that flower, to be produced in our minds; it being no more impossible to conceive that God should annex such ideas to such motions, with which they have no similitude, than that he should annex the idea of pain to the motion of a piece of steel dividing our flesh, with which that idea hath no resemblance.

What I have said concerning colors and

smells may be understood also of tastes and sounds, and other the like sensible qualities; which, whatever reality we by mistake attribute to them, are in truth nothing in the objects themselves, but powers to produce various sensations in us, and depend on those primary qualities, viz., bulk, figure, texture, and motion of parts; as I have said.

From whence I think it easy to draw this observation, that the ideas of primary qualities of bodies are resemblances of them, and their patterns do really exist in the bodies themselves; but the ideas, produced in us by these secondary qualities, have no resemblance of them at all. There is nothing like our ideas existing in the bodies themselves. They are in the bodies, we denominate from them, only a power to produce those sensations in us: and what is sweet, blue, or warm in idea, is but the certain bulk, figure, and motion of the insensible parts in the bodies themselves, which we call so.

. . .

Chapter XXIII
Of Our Complex Ideas of Substances

The mind being, as I have declared, furnished with a great number of the simple ideas, conveyed in by the senses, as they are found in exterior things, or by reflection on its own operations, takes notice also, that a certain number of these simple ideas go constantly together; which being presumed to belong to one thing, and words being suited to common apprehensions, and made use of for quick dispatch, are called, so united in one subject, by one name; which, by inadvertency, we are apt afterward to talk of, and consider as one simple idea, which indeed is a complication of many ideas together: because, as I have said, not imagining how these simple ideas can subsist by themselves, we accustom ourselves to suppose some substratum wherein they do subsist, and from which they do result: which therefore we call substance.

So that if anyone will examine himself concerning his notion of pure substance in general, he will find he has no other idea of it at all, but only a supposition of he knows not what support of such qualities, which are capable of producing simple ideas in us; which qualities are commonly called accidents. If anyone should be asked, what is the subject wherein color or weight inheres, he would have nothing to say, but the solid extended parts: and if he were demanded, what is it that that solidity and extension adhere in, he would not be in a much better case than the Indian beforementioned, who, saying that the world was supported by a great elephant, was asked what the elephant rested on; to which his answer was, a great tortoise. But being again pressed to know what gave support to the broad-backed tortoise, replied, something, he knew not what. And thus here, as in all other cases where we use words without having clear and distinct ideas, we talk like children; who being questioned what such a thing is, which they know not, readily give this satisfactory answer, that it is something: which in truth signifies no more, when so used either by children or men, but that they know not what; and that the thing they pretend to know and talk of, is what they have no distinct idea of at all, and so are perfectly ignorant of it, and in the dark. The idea then we have, to which we give the general name substance, being nothing but the supposed, but unknown support of those qualities we find existing, which we imagine cannot subsist, *sine re substante*, without something to support them, we call that support *substantia;* which, according to the true import of the word, is, in plain English, standing under or upholding.

An obscure and relative idea of substance in general being thus made, we come to have the ideas of particular sorts of substances, by collecting such combinations of simple ideas, as are by experience and observation of men's senses taken notice of to exist together, and are therefore supposed to flow from the particular internal constitution, or unkown essence of that substance. Thus we come to have the ideas of a man, horse, gold, water, etc., of which substances, whether anyone has any other clear idea, further than of certain simple ideas coexistent together, I appeal to everyone's own experience. It is the ordinary qualities observable in iron, or a diamond, put together, that make the true complex idea of those substances, which a smith or a jeweller commonly knows better than a philosopher; who, whatever substantial forms he may talk of, has no other idea of those substances, than what is framed by a collection of those simple ideas which are to be found in them: only we must take notice, that our complex ideas of substances, besides all those simple ideas they are made up of, have always the confused idea of something to which they belong, and in which they subsist. And therefore when we speak of any sort of substance, we say it is a thing having such or such qualities; as body is a thing that is extended, figured, and capable of motion; spirit, a thing capable of thinking; and so hardness, friability, and power to draw iron, we say, are qualities to be found in a loadstone. These, and the like fashions of speaking, intimate, that the substance is supposed always something besides the extension, figure, solidity, motion, thinking, or other observable ideas, though we know not what it is.

Hence, when we talk or think of any particular sort of corporeal substances, as horse, stone, etc., though the idea we have of either of them be but the complication or collection of those several simple ideas of sensible qualities, which we used to find united in the thing called horse or stone; yet because we cannot conceive how they should subsist alone, nor one in another, we suppose them existing in and supported by some common subject; which support we denote by the name substance, though it be certain we have no clear or distinct idea of that thing we suppose a support.

The same thing happens concerning the operations of the mind, viz., thinking, reasoning, fearing, etc., which we concluding not to subsist of themselves, nor apprehending how they can belong to body,

or be produced by it, we are apt to think these the actions of some other substance, which we call spirit: whereby yet it is evident, that having no other idea or notion of matter, but something wherein those many sensible qualities which affect our senses do subsist; by supposing a substance, wherein thinking, knowing, doubting, and a power of moving, etc., do subsist, we have as clear a notion of the substance of spirit, as we have of body; the one being supposed to be (without knowing what it is) the substratum to those simple ideas we have from without; and the other supposed (with a like ignorance of what it is) to be the substratum to those operations we experiment in ourselves within. It is plain then, that the idea of corporeal substance in matter is as remote from our conceptions and apprehensions, as that of spiritual substance or spirit: and therefore from our not having any notion of the substance of spirit, we can no more conclude its non-existence, than we can for the same reason deny the existence of body; it being as rational to affirm there is no body, because we have no clear and distinct idea of the substance of matter, as to say there is no spirit, because we have no clear and distinct idea of the substance of a spirit.

STUDY QUESTIONS

1. What does Locke mean by an idea? What does he believe the original sources of our ideas to be? Do you think all of our ideas can be accounted for as he does?

2. If the mind is conceived of originally as blank, white paper, how does it become active and produce what Locke calls ideas of reflection?

3. What does Locke mean by qualities? How are they related to ideas? What is the distinction between primary and secondary qualities?

4. What does Locke mean by substance? What are the two kinds of substances? How do we gain an idea of substance?

5. Why is Locke called an empiricist? Do you think the term appropriate?

For Further Reading

Aaron, R. I. *John Locke.* 3d ed. Oxford: Clarendon Press, 1971 (Part II, Chapter 3).

Blanshard, B. *The Nature of Thought.* London: Allen and Unwin, 1939 (Vol. II, Chapter 28).

Gibson, J. *Locke's Theory of Knowledge and Its Historical Relations.* Cambridge: At the University Press, 1938 (Chapters 3 through 7).

Mackie, J. L. *Problems from Locke.* Oxford: Clarendon Press, 1976 (Chapter 7).

Vesey, G. N. A., ed. *Impressions of Empiricism.* New York: St. Martin's, 1976.

RUSSELL: TRUTH AS CORRESPONDENCE

To most of us, before we reflect on the matter, the correspondence theory of truth seems obviously true. Suppose someone says "President Kennedy was assassinated in Dallas." We should all agree that this statement is true only if Kennedy was in fact assassinated in Dallas, that is to say, only if what is asserted corresponds with what actually took place. If it does not so correspond, we should conclude that the statement is false. Nevertheless, there are problems with the correspondence theory. These are mainly concerned with its ability to provide a comprehensive account of the meaning of truth. In the first sentence of this paragraph I wrote that, to most of us, the correspondence theory seems obviously *true*. What did I mean by my use of the word "true" there? To what fact does the correspondence theory, if it is true, correspond? Questions such as these have forced epistemologists to the conclusion that the notion of truth is more elusive than it might at first glance appear to be, even leading some of them to offer alternative theories of truth to replace, or at least to supplement, the correspondence theory.

For a biographical sketch of Bertrand Russell see page 337.

ℒ *The Problems of Philosophy*

Truth and Falsehood

Our knowledge of truths, unlike our knowledge of things, has an opposite, namely *error*. So far as things are concerned, we may know them or not know them, but there is no positive state of mind which can be described as erroneous knowledge of things, so long, at any rate, as we confine ourselves to knowledge by acquaintance. Whatever we are acquainted

From *The Problems of Philosophy* by Bertrand Russell, published by Oxford University Press, London, 1912. Reprinted by permission of Oxford University Press.

with must be something; we may draw wrong inferences from our acquaintance, but the acquaintance itself cannot be deceptive. Thus there is no dualism as regards acquaintance. But as regards knowledge of truths, there is a dualism. We may believe what is false as well as what is true. We know that on very many subjects different people hold different and incompatible opinions: hence some beliefs must be erroneous. Since erroneous beliefs are often held just as strongly as true beliefs, it becomes a difficult question how they are to be distinguished from true beliefs. How are we to know, in a given case, that our belief is not erroneous? This is a question of the very greatest difficulty, to which no completely satisfactory answer is possible. There is, however, a preliminary question which is rather less difficult, and that is: What do we *mean* by truth and falsehood? It is this preliminary question which is to be considered in this chapter.

In this chapter we are not asking how we can know whether a belief is true or false: we are asking what is meant by the question whether a belief is true or false. It is to be hoped that a clear answer to this question may help us to obtain an answer to the question what beliefs are true, but for the present we ask only "What is truth?" and "What is falsehood?"—not "What beliefs are true?" and "What beliefs are false?" It is very important to keep these different questions entirely separate, since any confusion between them is sure to produce an answer which is not really applicable to either.

There are three points to observe in the attempt to discover the nature of truth, three requisites which any theory must fulfil.

(1) Our theory of truth must be such as to admit of its opposite, falsehood. A good many philosophers have failed adequately to satisfy this condition: they have constructed theories according to which all our thinking ought to have been true, and have then had the greatest difficulty in finding a place for falsehood. In this respect our theory of belief must differ from our theory of acquaintance, since in the case of acquaintance it was not necessary to take account of any opposite.

(2) It seems fairly evident that if there were no beliefs there could be no falsehood, and no truth either, in the sense in which truth is correlative to falsehood. If we imagine a world of mere matter, there would be no room for falsehood in such a world, and although it would contain what may be called "facts," it would not contain any truths, in the sense in which truths are things of the same kind as falsehoods. In fact, truth and falsehood are properties of beliefs and statements: hence a world of

mere matter, since it would contain no beliefs or statements, would also contain no truth or falsehood.

(3) But, as against what we have just said, it is to be observed that the truth or falsehood of a belief always depends upon something which lies outside the belief itself. If I believe that Charles I died on the scaffold, I believe truly, not because of any intrinsic quality of my belief, which could be discovered by merely examining the belief but because of an historical event which happened two and a half centuries ago. If I believe that Charles I died in his bed, I believe falsely: no degree of vividness in my belief, or of care in arriving at it, prevents it from being false, again because of what happened long ago, and not because of any intrinsic property of my belief. Hence, although truth and falsehood are properties of beliefs, they are properties dependent upon the relations of the beliefs to other things, not upon any internal quality of the beliefs.

The third of the above requisites leads us to adopt the view—which has on the whole been commonest among philosophers—that truth consists in some form of correspondence between belief and fact. It is, however, by no means an easy matter to discover a form of correspondence to which there are no irrefutable objections. By this partly—and partly by the feeling that, if truth consists in a correspondence of thought with something outside thought, thought can never know when truth has been attained—many philosophers have been led to try to find some definition of truth which shall not consist in relation to something wholly outside belief. The most important attempt at a definition of this sort is the theory that truth consists in *coherence*. It is said that the mark of falsehood is failure to cohere in the body of our beliefs, and that it is the essence of a truth to form part of the completely rounded system which is "The Truth."

There is, however, a great difficulty in this view, or rather two great difficulties. The first is that there is no reason to suppose that only *one* coherent body of beliefs is possible. It may be that, with sufficient imagination, a novelist might invent a past for the world that would perfectly fit on to what we know, and yet be quite different from the real past. In more scientific matters, it is certain that there are often two or more hypotheses which account for all the known facts on some subject, and although, in such cases, men of science endeavor to find facts which will rule out all the hypotheses except one, there is no reason why they should always succeed.

In philosophy, again, it seems not uncommon for two rival hypotheses to be both able to account for all the facts. Thus, for example, it is possible that life is one long dream, and that the outer world has only that degree of reality that the objects of dreams have; but although such a view does not seem inconsistent with known facts, there is no reason to prefer it to the common-sense view, according to which other people and things do really exist. Thus coherence as the definition of truth fails because there is no proof that there can be only one coherent system.

The other objection to this defintion of truth is that it assumes the meaning of "coherence" known, whereas, in fact, "coherence" presupposes the truth of the laws of logic. Two propositions are coherent when both may be true, and are incoherent when one at least must be false. Now in order to know whether two propositions can both be true, we must know such truths as the law of contradiction. For example, the two propositions, "this tree is a beech" and "this tree is not a beech," are not coherent, because of the law of contradiction. But if the law of contradiction itself were subjected to the test of coherence, we should find that, if we choose to suppose it false, nothing will any longer be incoherent with anything else. Thus the laws of logic supply the skeleton or framework within which the test of coherence applies, and they themselves cannot be established by this test.

For the above two reasons, coherence cannot be accepted as giving the *meaning* of truth, though it is often a most important *test* of truth after a certain amount of truth has become known.

Hence we are driven back to *correspondence with fact* as constituting the nature of truth. It remains to define precisely what we mean by "fact," and what is the nature of the correspondence which must subsist between belief and fact, in order that belief may be true.

In accordance with our three requisites, we have to seek a theory of truth which (1) allows truth to have an opposite, namely falsehood, (2) makes truth a property of beliefs, but (3) makes it a property wholly dependent upon the relation of the beliefs to outside things.

The necessity of allowing for falsehood makes it impossible to regard belief as a relation of the mind to a single object, which could be said to be what is believed. If belief were so regarded, we should find that, like acquaintance, it would not admit of the opposition of truth and falsehood, but would have to be always true. This may be made clear by examples. Othello believes falsely that Desdemona loves Cassio. We cannot say that this belief consists in a relation to a single object, "Desdemona's love for Cassio" for if there were such an object, the belief would be true. There is in fact no such object, and therefore Othello cannot have any relation to such an object. Hence his belief cannot possibly consist in a relation to this object.

It might be said that his belief is a relation to a different object, namely, "that Desdemona loves Cassio"; but it is almost as difficult to suppose that there is such an object as this, when Desdemona does not love Cassio, as it was to suppose that there is "Desdemona's love for Cassio." Hence it will be better to seek for a theory of belief which does not make it consist in a relation of the mind to a single object.

It is common to think of relations as though they always held between *two* terms, but in fact this is not always the case. Some relations demand three terms, some four, and so on. Take, for instance, the relation "between." So long as only two terms come in, the relation "between" is impossible: three terms are the smallest number that render it possible. York is between London and Edinburgh; but if London and Edinburgh were the only places in the world, there could be nothing which was between one place and another. Similarly, *jealousy* requires three people: there can be no such relation that does not involve three at least. Such a proposition as "*A* wishes *B* to promote *C*'s marriage with *D*" involves a relation of four terms; that is to say, *A* and *B* and *C* and *D* all come in, and the relation involved cannot be expressed otherwise than in a form involving all four. Instances might be multiplied indefinitely, but enough has been said to show that there are relations which require more than two terms before they can occur.

The relation involved in *judging* or *believing* must, if falsehood is to be duly allowed for, be taken to be a relation between several terms, not between two. When Othello believes that Desdemona loves Cassio, he must not have before his mind a single object, "Desdemona's love for Cassio," or "that Desdemona loves Cassio," for that would require that there should be objective falsehoods, which subsist independently of any minds; and this, though not logically refutable, is a theory to be avoided if possible. Thus it is easier to account for falsehood if we take judgment to be a relation to which the mind and the various objects concerned all occur severally; that is to say, Desdemona and loving and Cassio must all be terms in the relation which subsists when Othello believes that Desdemona loves Cassio. This relation, therefore, is a relation of four terms, since Othello also is one of the terms of the relation. When we say that it is a relation of four terms, we do not mean that Othello has a certain relation to Desdemona, and has the same relation to loving and also to Cassio. This may be true of some other relation than believing; but believing, plainly, is not a relation which Othello has to *each* of the three terms concerned, but to *all* of them together: there is only one example of the relation of believing involved, but this one example knits together four terms. Thus the actual occur-

rence, at the moment when Othello is entertaining his belief, is that the relation called "believing" is knitting together into one complex whole the four terms Othello, Desdemona, loving, and Cassio. What is called belief or judgment is nothing but this relation of believing or judging, which relates a mind to several things other than itself. An *act* of belief or of judgment is the occurrence between certain terms at some particular time, of the relation of believing or judging.

We are now in a position to understand what it is that distinguishes a true judgment from a false one. For this purpose we will adopt certain definitions. In every act of judgment there is a mind which judges, and there are terms concerning which it judges. We will call the mind the *subject* in the judgment, and the remaining terms the *objects*. Thus, when Othello judges that Desdemona loves Cassio, Othello is the subject, while the objects are Desdemona and loving and Cassio. The subject and the objects together are called the constituents of the judgment. It will be observed that the relation of judging has what is called a "sense" or "direction." We may say, metaphorically, that it puts its objects in a certain *order*, which we may indicate by means of the order of the words in the sentence. (In an inflected language, the same thing will be indicated by inflections, *e.g.*, by the difference between nominative and accusative.) Othello's judgment that Cassio loves Desdemona differs from his judgment that Desdemona loves Cassio, in spite of the fact that it consists of the same constituents, because the relation of judging places the constituents in a different order in the two cases. Similarly, if Cassio judges that Desdemona loves Othello, the constituents of the judgment are still the same, but their order is different. This property of having a "sense" or "direction" is one which the relation of judging shares with all other relations. The "sense" of relations is the ultimate source of order and series and a host of mathematical concepts; but we need not concern ourselves further with this aspect.

We spoke of the relation called "judging" or "believing" as knitting together into one complex whole the subject and the objects. In this respect, judging is exactly like every other relation. Whenever a relation holds between two or more terms, it unites the terms into a complex whole. If Othello loves Desdemona, there is such a complex whole as "Othello's love for Desdemona." The terms united by the relation may be themselves complex, or may be simple, but the whole which results from their being united must be complex. Wherever there is a relation which relates certain terms, there is a complex object formed of the union of those terms; and conversely, wherever there is a complex object, there is a relation which relates its constituents. When an act of believing occurs, there is a complex, in which "believing" is the uniting relation, and subject and objects are arranged in a certain order by the "sense" of the relation of believing. Among the objects, as we saw in considering "Othello believes that Desdemona loves Cassio" one must be a relation—in this instance, the relation "loving." But this relation, as it occurs in the act of believing, is not the relation which creates the unity of the complex whole consisting of the subject and the objects. The relation "loving," as it occurs in the act of believing, is one of the objects—it is a brick in the structure, not the cement. The cement is the relation "believing." When the belief is *true*, there is another complex unity, in which the relation which was one of the objects of the belief relates the other objects. Thus, *e.g.,* if Othello believes *truly* that Desdemona loves Cassio, then there is a complex unity, "Desdemona's love for Cassio" which is composed exclusively of the *objects* of the belief, in the same order as they had in the belief, with the relation which was one of the objects occurring now as the cement that binds together the other objects of the belief. On the other hand, when a belief is *false*, there is no such complex unity composed only of the objects of the belief. If Othello believes *falsely* that Desdemona loves Cassio, then there is no such complex unity as "Desdemona's love for Cassio."

Thus a belief is *true* when it *corresponds* to a certain associated complex, and *false* when it does not. Assuming, for the sake of definiteness, that the objects of the belief are two terms and a relation, the terms being put in a certain order by the "sense" of the believing, then if the two terms in that order are united by the relation into a complex, the belief is true; if not, it is false. This constitutes the definition of truth and falsehood that we were in search of. Judging or believing is a certain complex unity of which a mind is a constituent; if the remaining constituents, taken in the order which they have in the belief, form a complex unity, then the belief is true; if not, it is false.

Thus although truth and falsehood are properties of beliefs, yet they are in a sense extrinsic properties, for the condition of the truth of a belief is something not involving beliefs, or (in general) any mind at all, but only the *objects* of the belief. A mind, which believes, believes truly when there is a *corresponding* complex not involving the mind, but only its objects. This correspondence ensures truth, and its absence entails falsehood. Hence we account simultaneously for the two facts that beliefs (a) depend on minds for their *existence,* (b) do not depend on minds for their *truth*.

We may restate our theory as follows: If we take such a belief as "Othello believes that Desdemona loves Cassio" we will call Desdemona and Cassio the *object-terms,* and loving the *object-relation.* If there is a complex unity "Desdemona's love for Cassio," consisting of the object-terms related by the object-relation in the same order as they have in the belief, then this complex unity is called the *fact corresponding to the belief.* Thus, a belief is true when there is a corresponding fact, and is false when there is no corresponding fact.

It will be seen that minds do not *create* truth or falsehood. They create beliefs, but when once the beliefs are created, the mind cannot make them true or false, except in the special case where they concern future things which are within the power of the person believing, such as catching trains. What makes a belief true is a *fact,* and this fact does not (except in exceptional cases) in any way involve the mind of the person who has the belief.

STUDY QUESTIONS

1. What three requirements must an acceptable theory of truth satisfy?
2. What is meant by the correspondence theory of truth? How does it differ from the coherence theory? What are Russell's objections to the coherence theory?
3. State in your own terms Russell's analysis of the nature of belief or judgment?
4. What does Russell mean by a fact? What kind of existence do you think facts have?

For Further Reading

Acton, H. B. "The Correspondence Theory of Truth." *Proceedings of the Aristotelian Society* 35 (1935), 177–94.

Blanshard, B. *The Nature of Thought.* London: Allen and Unwin, 1939 (Vol. II, pp. 225–37).

Joachim, H. H. *The Nature of Truth.* Oxford: Clarendon Press, 1906 (Chapter 1).

O'Connor, D. J. *The Correspondence Theory of Truth.* London: Hutchinson University Library, 1975 (Part I).

Williams, C. J. F. *What Is Truth?* Cambridge: Cambridge University Press, 1976 (Chapter 5).

BLANSHARD: TRUTH AS COHERENCE

According to defenders of the coherence theory of truth, their analysis most accurately describes the way in which we actually make judgments of truth and falsity. To support this claim, they usually appeal to the procedures of the empirical sciences. To use an example offered by Brand Blanshard, in his book *The Nature of Thought* (II, 235–37) he describes some experiments conducted by an English scientist in which a medium in a trance was able to materialize disembodied spirits. The evidence that she had done so was beyond question, yet no reputable member of the scientific community would accept it. Why not? According to Blanshard, it was rejected because it failed to cohere or fit in with the established body of scientific theory. In this situation, although the statement: "There are materialized disembodied spirits in this laboratory" would be true, according to the correspondence theory, because it corresponds with the facts, or the observed evidence, it would be false, according to the coherence theory—and the entire scientific community were in agreement in calling it false.

Brand Blanshard, one of the most eminent of contemporary American philosophers, was born in 1892 in Ohio. As an undergraduate he studied at the University of Michigan; his graduate education was completed at Columbia and Harvard Universities. He also studied at Oxford University as a Rhodes scholar. During his long career, he taught at several schools, including the University of Michigan, Swarthmore College, and finally Yale University. In 1952 he was invited to deliver the Gifford lectures in Scotland, the highest recognition that can be granted a philosopher in the English-speaking world.

❧ The Nature of Thought

Chapter XXVI
Coherence as the Nature of Truth

• • •

To think is to seek understanding. And to seek understanding is an activity of mind that is marked off from all other activities by a highly distinctive aim. This aim, as we saw in our chapter on the general nature of understanding, is to achieve systematic vision, so to apprehend what is now unknown to us as to relate it, and relate it necessarily, to what we know already. We think to solve problems; and our method of solving problems is to build a bridge of intelligible relation from the continent of our knowledge to the island we wish to include in it. Sometimes this bridge is causal, as when we try to explain a disease; sometimes teleological, as when we try to fathom the move of an opponent over the chess board; sometimes geometrical, as in Euclid. But it is always systematic; thought in its very nature is the attempt to bring something unknown or imperfectly known into a subsystem of knowledge, and thus also into that larger system that forms the world of accepted beliefs. That is what explanation is. *Why* is it that thought desires this ordered vision? Why should such a vision give satisfaction when it comes? To these questions there is no answer, and if there were, it would be an answer only because it had succeeded in supplying the characteristic satisfaction to this unique desire.

But may it not be that what satisfies thought fails to conform to the real world? Where is the guarantee that when I have brought my ideas into the form my ideal requires, they should be *true*? Here we come round again to the tortured problem of Book II. In our long struggle with the relation of thought to reality, we saw that if

B. Blanshard, *The Nature of Thought.* Reprinted with the permission of the publishers, George Allen & Unwin and Humanities Press, Inc., New York.

thought and things are conceived as related only externally, then knowledge is luck; there is no necessity whatever that what satisfies intelligence should coincide with what really is. It may do so, or it may not; on the principle that there are many misses to one bull's-eye, it more probably does not. But if we get rid of the misleading analogies through which this relation has been conceived, of copy and original, stimulus and organism, lantern and screen, and go on to thought itself with the question what reference to an object means, we get a different and more hopeful answer. To think of a thing is to get that thing itself in some degree within the mind. To think of a color or an emotion is to have that within us which if it *were developed and completed,* would identify itself with the object. In short, if we accept its own report, thought is related to reality as the partial to the perfect fulfilment of a purpose. The more adequate its grasp the more nearly does it approximate, the more fully does it realize in itself, the nature and relations of its objects.

Thought thus appears to have two ends, one immanent, one transcendent. On the one hand it seeks fulfilment in a special kind of satisfaction, the satisfaction of systematic vision. On the other hand, it seeks fulfilment in its object. Now it was the chief contention of our second book that these ends are one. Indeed unless they are accepted as one, we could see no alternative to skepticism. If the pursuit of thought's own ideal were merely an elaborate self-indulgence that brought us no nearer to reality, or if the apprehension of reality did not lie in the line of thought's interest, or still more if both of these held at once, the hope of knowledge would be vain. Of course it may really be vain. If anyone cares to doubt whether the framework of human logic has any bearing on the nature of things, he may be silenced perhaps, but he cannot be conclusively answered. One may point out to him that the doubt itself is framed in accordance with that logic, but he can reply that thus we are taking advantage of his logico-centric predicament; further, that any argument we can offer accords equally well with his hypothesis and with ours, with the view that we are merely flies caught in a logical net and the view that knowledge reveals reality. And what accords equally well with both hypotheses does not support either to the exclusion of the other. But while doubt is beyond reach by argument, neither is there anything in its favor. It is a mere suspicion which is, and by its nature must remain, without any positive ground; and as such it can hardly be discussed. Such suspicions aside, we can throw into the scale for our theory the impressive fact of the advance of knowledge. It has been the steadfast assumption of science whenever it came to an unsolved problem that there was a key to it to be found, that if things happened thus, rather than otherwise, they did so for a cause or reason, and that, if this were not forthcoming, it was never because it was lacking, but always because of a passing blindness in ourselves. Reflection has assumed that pursuit of its own immanent end is not only satisfying but revealing, that so far as the immanent end is achieved we are making progress toward the transcendent end as well. Indeed, that these ends coincide is the assumption of every act of thinking whatever. To think is to raise a question; to raise a question is to seek an explanation; to seek an explanation is to assume that one may be had; so to assume is to take for granted that nature in that region is intelligible. Certainly the story of advancing knowledge unwinds as if self-realization in thought meant also a coming nearer to reality.

That these processes are really one is the metaphysical base on which our belief in coherence is founded. If one admits that the pursuit of a coherent system has actually carried us to what everyone would agree to call knowledge, why not take this ideal as a guide that will conduct us farther? What better key can one ask to the structure of the real? Our own conviction is that we should take this immanent end of thought in all seriousness as the clue to the nature of things. We admit that it may prove deceptive, that somewhere thought may end its pilgrimage in frustration and futility before some blank wall of the unintelligible. There are even those who evince their superior insight by taking this as a foregone conclusion and regarding the faith that the real is rational as the wishful thinking of the "tender-minded." Their attitude appears to us a compound made up of one part timidity, in the form of a refusal to hope lest they be disillusioned; one part muddled persuasion that to be skeptical is to be sophisticated; one part honest dullness in failing to estimate rightly the weight of the combined postulate and success of knowledge; one part genuine insight into the possibility of surds in nature. But whatever its motives, it is a view that goes less well with the evidence than the opposite and brighter view. That view is that reality is a system, completely ordered and fully intelligible, with which thought in its advance is more and more identifying itself. We may look at the growth of knowledge, individual or social, either as an attempt by our own minds to return to union with things as they are in their ordered wholeness, or the affirmation through our minds of the ordered whole itself. And if we take this view, our notion of truth is marked out for us. Truth is the approximation of thought to reality. It is thought on its way home. Its measure is the distance thought has travelled, under the guidance of its inner compass, toward that intelligible system which unites its ultimate object with its ultimate end. Hence, at any given time, the degree of truth in our experience as a whole is the degree of system it has achieved. The degree of truth of a particular proposition is to be judged in the first instance by its coherence with experience as a whole, ultimately by its coherence with that further whole, all-comprehensive and fully articulated, in which thought can come to rest.

But it is time we defined more explicitly what coherence means. To be sure, no fully satisfactory definition can be given; and as Dr. Ewing says, "it is wrong to tie down the advocates of the coherence theory to a precise definition. What they are doing is to describe an ideal that has never yet been completely clarified but is none the less immanent in all our thinking."* Certainly this ideal goes far beyond mere consistency. Fully coherent knowledge would be knowledge in which every judgment entailed, and was entailed by, the rest of the system. Probably we never find in fact a system where there is so much of interdependence. What it means may be clearer if we take a number of familiar systems and arrange them in a series tending to such coherence as a limit. At the bottom would be a junk-heap, where we could know every item but one and still be without any clue as to what that remaining item was. Above this would come a stone-pile, for here you could at least infer that what you would find next would be a stone. A machine would be higher again, since from the remaining parts one could deduce not only the general character of a missing part, but also its special form and function. This is a high degree of coherence, but it is very far short of the highest. You could remove the engine from a motor-car leaving the other parts intact, and replace it with any one of thousands of other engines, but the thought of such an interchange among human heads or hearts shows at once that the interdependence in a machine is far below that of the body. Do we find then in organic bodies the highest conceivable coherence? Clearly not. Though a human hand, as Aristotle said, would hardly be a hand when detached from the body, still it would be something definite enough; and we can conceive systems in which even this something would be gone. Abstract a number from the number series and it would be a mere unrecognizable x; similarly, the very thought of a straight line involves the thought of the Euclidean space in which it falls. It is perhaps in such systems as Euclidean geometry that we get the most perfect examples of coherence that have been constructed. If any proposi-

tion were lacking, it could be supplied from the rest; if any were altered, the repercussions would be felt through the length and breadth of the system. Yet even such a system as this falls short of ideal system. Its postulates are unproved; they are independent of each other, in the sense that none of them could be derived from any other; or even from all the others together; its clear necessity is bought by an abstractness as extreme as to have left out nearly everything that belongs to the character of actual things. A completely satisfactory system would have none of these defects. No proposition would be arbitrary; every proposition would be entailed by the others jointly and even singly;** no proposition would stand outside the system. The integration would be so complete that no part could be seen for what it was without seeing its relation to the whole, and the whole itself could be understood only through the contribution of every part.

It may be granted at once that in common life we are satisfied with far less than this. We accept the demonstrations of the geometer as complete, and do not think of reproaching him because he begins with postulates and leaves us at the end with a system that is a skeleton at the best. In physics, in biology, above all in the social sciences, we are satisfied with less still. We test judgments by the amount of coherence which in that particular subject-matter it seems reasonable to expect. We apply, perhaps unconsciously, the advice of Aristotle, and refrain from asking demonstration in the physical sciences, while in mathematics we refuse to accept less. And

---

*A. C. Ewing, *Idealism: A Critical Survey.* New York: Humanities Press, 1934 (p. 231).

**Coherence can be defined without this point, which, as Dr. Ewing remarks (*Idealism*, p. 231), makes the case harder to establish. In no mathematical system, for example, would anyone dream of trying to deduce all the other propositions from any proposition taken singly. But when we are describing an ideal, such a fact is not decisive, and I follow Joachim in holding that in a perfectly coherent system every proposition would entail all others, if only for the reason that its meaning could never be fully understood without apprehension of the system in its entirety.

such facts may be thought to show that we make no actual use of the ideal standard just described. But however much this standard may be relaxed within the limits of a particular science, its influence is evident in the grading of the sciences generally. It is precisely in those sciences that approach most nearly to system as here defined that we achieve the greatest certainty, and precisely in those that are most remote from such system that our doubt is greatest whether we have achieved scientific truth at all. Our immediate exactions shift with the subject-matter; our ultimate standard is unvarying.

Now if we accept coherence as the test of truth, does that commit us to any conclusions about the *nature* of truth or reality? I think it does, though more clearly about reality than about truth. It is past belief that the fidelity of our thought to reality should be rightly measured by coherence if reality itself were not coherent. To say that the nature of things may be *in*coherent, but we shall approach the truth about it precisely so far as our thoughts become coherent, sounds very much like nonsense. And providing we retained coherence as the test, it would still be nonsense even if truth were conceived as correspondence. On this supposition we should have truth when, our thought having achieved coherence, the correspondence was complete between that thought and its object. But complete correspondence between a coherent thought and an incoherent object seems meaningless. It is hard to see, then, how anyone could consistently take coherence as the test of truth unless he took it also as a character of reality.

Does acceptance of coherence as a test commit us not only to a view about the structure of reality but also to a view about the nature of truth? This is a more difficult question. As we saw at the beginning of the chapter, there have been some highly reputable philosophers who have held that the answer to "What is the test of truth?" is "Coherence," while the answer to "What is the nature or meaning of truth?" is "Correspondence."

These questions are plainly distinct.

Nor does there seem to be any direct path from the acceptance of coherence as the test of truth to its acceptance of the nature of truth. Nevertheless, there is an indirect path. If we accept coherence as our test, we must use it everywhere. We must therefore use it to test the suggestion that truth *is* other than coherence. But if we do, we shall find that we must reject the suggestion as leading to *in*coherence. Coherence is a pertinacious concept and, like the well-known camel, if one lets it get its nose under the edge of the tent, it will shortly walk off with the whole.

Suppose that, accepting coherence as the test, one rejects it as the nature of truth in favor of some alternative; and let us assume, for example, that this alternative is correspondence. This, we have said, is incoherent; why? Because if one holds that truth is correspondence, one cannot intelligibly hold either that it is tested by coherence or that there is any dependable test at all. Consider the first point. Suppose that we construe experience into the most coherent picture possible, remembering that among the elements included will be such secondary qualities as colors, odors, and sounds. Would the mere fact that such elements as these are coherently arranged prove that anything precisely corresponding to them exists "out there"? I cannot see that it would, even if we knew that the arrangements had closely corresponding patterns. If on one side you have a series of elements, a, b, c . . . and on the other a series of elements α, β, γ . . ., arranged in patterns that correspond, you have no proof as yet that the *natures* of these elements correspond. It is therefore impossible to argue from a high degree of coherence within experience to its correspondence in the same degree with anything outside. And this difficulty is typical. If you place the nature of truth in one sort of character and its test in something quite different, you are pretty certain, sooner or later, to find the two falling apart. In the end, the only test of truth that is not misleading is the special nature or character that is itself constitutive of truth.

Feeling that this is so, the adherents of

correspondence sometimes insist that correspondence shall be its own test. But then the second difficulty arises. If truth does consist in correspondence, no test can be sufficient. For in order to know that experience corresponds to fact, we must be able to get at that fact, unadulterated with idea, and compare the two sides with each other. And we have seen in the last chapter that such fact is not accessible. When we try to lay hold of it, what we find in our hands is a judgment which is obviously not itself the indubitable fact we are seeking, and which must be checked by some fact beyond it. To this process there is no end. And even if we did get at the fact directly, rather than through the veil of our ideas, that would be no less fatal to correspondence. This direct seizure of fact presumably gives us truth, but since that truth no longer consists in correspondence of idea with fact, the main theory has been abandoned. In short, if we can know fact only through the medium of our own ideas, the original forever eludes us; if we can get at the facts directly, we have knowledge whose truth is not correspondence. The theory is forced to choose between skepticism and self-contradiction.

Thus the attempt to combine coherence as the test of truth with correspondence as the nature of truth will not pass muster by its own test. The result is *incoherence*. We believe that an application of the test to other theories of truth would lead to a like result. The argument is: assume coherence as the test, and you will be driven by the incoherence of your alternatives to the conclusion that it is also the nature of truth.

STUDY QUESTIONS

1. Do you agree with Blanshard about the purposes of thought? Explain.
2. What does Blanshard mean when he says "To think of a thing is to get that thing itself in some degree within the mind." In what sense could you get the star Betelgeuse within your mind by thinking about it?
3. What, according to Blanshard, is the relationship between thought and reality? How is this view related to his theory of truth?
4. What does Blanshard mean when he says that coherence is (1) the test of truth? and (2) the nature of truth?

For Further Reading

Bradley, F. H. *Essays on Truth and Reality.* Oxford: Clarendon Press, 1914 (Chapter 7).

Ewing, A. C. *Idealism: A Critical Survey.* New York: Humanities Press, 1934 (Chapter 5).

Joachim, H. H. *The Nature of Truth.* Oxford: Clarendon Press, 1906 (Chapter 3).

Khatchadourian, H. *The Coherence Theory of Truth: A Critical Evaluation.* Beirut: American University, 1961.

Rescher, N. *The Coherence Theory of Truth.* Oxford: Clarendon Press, 1973 (esp. Chapters 2, 7, 8, and 13).

Russell, B. *Philosophical Essays.* New York: Simon & Schuster, 1966 (Chapter 6).

JAMES: TRUTH AS CONSEQUENCES

To appreciate adequately the pragmatic theory of truth, one must first grasp its theory of meaning. To have any meaning, according to William James, a statement must make some difference in the world. If the world would be the same whichever of two different statements were true, then, no matter how much the statements might appear to differ from each other, their meaning would be the same. Next, according to the pragmatists, the difference to the world that gives meaning to statements is a practical difference. To be meaningful, the statement must, if accepted and acted upon, lead to consequences that affect human welfare. From here it is an easy step to distinguish between truth and falsity. For the pragmatists, those statements which when accepted and acted upon lead to consequences that are good are accounted true; those, on the contrary, that lead to consequences that are bad are false.

For a biographical sketch of William James, see page 135.

❧ *Pragmatism*

What Pragmatism Means

Some years ago, being with a camping party in the mountains, I returned from a solitary ramble to find everyone engaged in a ferocious metaphysical dispute. The *corpus* of the dispute was a squirrel—a live squirrel supposed to be clinging to one side of a tree-trunk; while over against the tree's opposite side a human being was imagined to stand. This human witness tries to get sight of the squirrel by moving rapidly round the tree, but no matter how fast he goes, the squirrel moves as fast in the opposite direction, and always keeps the tree between himself and the man, so that never a glimpse of him is caught. The resultant metaphysical problem now is this: *Does the man go round the squirrel or not?* He goes round the tree, sure enough, and the squirrel is on the tree; but does he go round the squirrel? In the unlimited leisure of the wilderness, discussion had been worn threadbare. Everyone had taken sides, and was obstinate; and the numbers on both sides were even. Each side, when I appeared, therefore appealed to me to make it a majority. Mindful of the scholastic adage that whenever you meet a contradiction you must make a distinction, I immediately sought and found one, as follows: "Which party is right," I said, "depends on what you *practically mean* by 'going round' the squirrel. If you mean passing from the north of him to the east then to the south, then to the west, and then to the north of him again, obviously the man does go round him, for he occupies these successive positions. But if on the contrary

you mean being first in front of him, then on the right of him, then behind him, then on his left, and finally in front again, it is quite as obvious that the man fails to go round him, for by the compensating movements the squirrel makes, he keeps his belly turned towards the man all the time, and his back turned away. Make the distinction, and there is no occasion for any farther dispute. You are both right and both wrong according as you conceive the verb 'to go round' in one practical fashion or the other."

Although one or two of the hotter disputants called my speech a shuffling evasion, saying they wanted no quibbling or scholastic hair-splitting, but meant just plain honest English "round," the majority seemed to think that the distinction had assuaged the dispute.

I tell this trivial anecdote because it is a peculiarly simple example of what I wish now to speak of as *the pragmatic method*. The pragmatic method is primarily a method of settling metaphysical disputes that otherwise might be interminable. Is the world one or many?—fated or free?—material or spiritual?—here are notions either of which may or may not hold good of the world; and disputes over such notions are unending. The pragmatic method in such cases is to try to interpret each notion by tracing its respective practical consequences. What difference would it practically make to anyone if this notion, rather than that notion, were true? If no practical difference whatever can be traced, then the alternatives mean practically the same thing, and all dispute is idle. Whenever a dispute is serious, we ought to be able to

First published in 1907.

show some practical difference that must follow from one side or the other's being right.

A glance at the history of the idea will show you still better what pragmatism means. The term is derived from the same Greek word πράγμα, meaning "action," from which our words "practice" and "practical" come. It was first introduced into philosophy by Mr. Charles Peirce in 1878. In an article entitled "How to Make Our Ideas Clear," in the *Popular Science Monthly* for January of that year, Mr. Peirce, after pointing out that our beliefs are really rules for action, said that, to develop a thought's meaning, we need only determine what conduct it is fitted to produce: that conduct is for us its sole significance. And the tangible fact at the root of all our thought-distinctions, however subtle, is that there is no one of them so fine as to consist in anything but a possible difference of practice. To attain perfect clearness in our thoughts of an object, then, we need only consider what conceivable effects of a practical kind the object may involve—what sensations we are to expect from it, and what reactions we must prepare. Our conception of these effects, whether immediate or remote, is then for us the whole of our conception of the object, so far as that conception has positive significance at all.

This is the principle of Peirce, the principle of pragmatism. It lay entirely unnoticed by anyone for twenty years, until I, in an address before Professor Howison's philosophical union at the University of California, brought it forward again and made a special application of it to religion. By that date (1898), the times seemed ripe for its reception. The word "pragmatism" spread, and at present it fairly spots the pages of the philosophic journals. On all hands we find the "pragmatic movement" spoken of, sometimes with respect, sometimes with contumely, seldom with clear understanding. It is evident that the term applies itself conveniently to a number of tendencies that hitherto have lacked a collective name, and that it has "come to stay."

To take in the importance of Peirce's

principle, one must get accustomed to applying it to concrete cases. I found a few years ago that Ostwald, the illustrious Leipzig chemist, had been making perfectly distinct use of the principle of pragmatism in his lectures on the philosophy of science, though he had not called it by that name.

"All realities influence our practice," he wrote me, "and that influence is their meaning for us. I am accustomed to put questions to my classes in this way: In what respects would the world be different if this alternative or that were true? If I can find nothing that would become different, then the alternative has no sense."

That is, the rival views mean practically the same thing, and meaning, other than practical, there is for us none. Ostwald in a published lecture gives this example of what he means. Chemists have long wrangled over the inner constitution of certain bodies called "tautomerous." Their properties seemed equally consistent with the notion that an instable hydrogen atom oscillates inside of them, or that they are instable mixtures of two bodies. Controversy raged, but never was decided. "It would never have begun," says Ostwald, "if the combatants had asked themselves what particular experimental fact could have been made different by one or the other view being correct. For it would then have appeared that no difference of fact could possibly ensue; and the quarrel was as unreal as if, theorizing in primitive times about the raising of dough by yeast, one party should have invoked a 'brownie,' while another insisted on an 'elf' as the true cause of the phenomenon."

It is astonishing to see how many philosophical disputes collapse into insignificance the moment you subject them to this simple test of tracing a concrete consequence. There can *be* no difference anywhere that doesn't *make* a difference elsewhere—no difference in abstract truth that doesn't express itself in a difference in concrete fact and in conduct consequent upon that fact, imposed on somebody, somehow, somewhere, and somewhen. The whole function of philosophy ought to be to find out what definite difference it will make to you and me, at definite instants of our life, if this world-formula or that world-formula be the true one.

There is absolutely nothing new in the pragmatic method. Socrates was an adept at it. Aristotle used it methodically. Locke, Berkeley, and Hume made momentous contributions to truth by its means. Shadworth Hodgson keeps insisting that realities are only what they are "known as." But these forerunners of pragmatism used it in fragments: they were preluders only. Not until in our time has it generalized itself, become conscious of a universal mission, pretended to a conquering destiny. I believe in that destiny, and I hope I may end by inspiring you with my belief.

Pragmatism represents a perfectly familiar attitude in philosophy, the empiricist attitude, but it represents it, as it seems to me, both in a more radical and in a less objectionable form than it has ever yet assumed. A pragmatist turns his back resolutely and once for all upon a lot of inveterate habits dear to professional philosophers. He turns away from abstraction and insufficiency, from verbal solutions, from bad *a priori* reasons, from fixed principles, closed systems, and pretended absolutes and origins. He turns towards concreteness and adequacy, towards facts, towards action, and towards power. That means empiricist temper regnant and the rationalist temper sincerely given up. It means the open air and possibilities of nature, as against dogma, artificiality, and the pretense of finality in truth.

At the same time it does not stand for any special results. It is a method only. But the general triumph of that method would mean an enormous change in what I called in my last lecture the "temperament" of philosophy. Teachers of the ultrarationalistic type would be frozen out, much as the courtier type is frozen out in republics, as the ultramontane type of priest is frozen out in Protestant lands. Science and metaphysics would come much nearer together, would in fact work absolutely hand in hand.

Metaphysics has usually followed a very primitive kind of quest. You know how men have always hankered after unlawful magic, and you know what a great part in magic *words* have always played. If you have his name, or the formula of incantation that binds him, you can control the spirit, genie, afrite, or whatever the power may be. Solomon knew the names of all the spirits, and having their names, he held them subject to his will. So the universe has always appeared to the natural mind as a kind of enigma, of which the key must be sought in the shape of some illuminating or power-bringing word or name. That word names the universe's *principle*, and to possess it is after a fashion to possess the universe itself. "God," "Matter," "Reason," "the Absolute," "Energy," are so many solving names. You can rest when you have them. You are at the end of your metaphysical quest.

But if you follow the pragmatic method, you cannot look on any such word as closing your quest. You must bring out of each word its practical cash-value, set it at work within the stream of your experience. It appears less as a solution, then, than as a program for more work, and more particularly as an indication of the ways in which existing realities may be *changed*.

Theories thus become instruments, not answers to enigmas, in which we can rest. We don't lie back upon them, we move forward, and, on occasion, make nature over again by their aid. Pragmatism unstiffens all our theories, limbers them up and sets each one at work. Being nothing essentially new, it harmonizes with many ancient philosophic tendencies. It agrees with nominalism, for instance, in always appealing to particulars; with utilitarianism, in emphasizing practical aspects; with positivism, in its disdain for verbal solutions, useless questions and metaphysical abstractions.

All these, you see, are *anti-intellectualist* tendencies. Against rationalism as a pretension and a method pragmatism is fully armed and militant. But, at the outset, at least, it stands for no particular results. It has no dogma, and no doctrines save its method. As the young Italian pragmatist Papini has well said, it lies in the midst of our theories, like a corridor in a hotel. Innumerable chambers open out of it. In one, you may find a man writing an atheistic volume; in the next, some one on his knees praying for faith and strength; in a third, a chemist investigating a body's properties. In a fourth, a system of idealistic metaphysics is being excogitated; in a fifth, the impossibility of metaphysics is being shown. But they all own the corridor, and all must pass through it if they want a practicable way of getting into or out of their respective rooms.

No particular results then, so far, but only an attitude of orientation, is what the pragmatic method means. *The attitude of looking away from first things, principles, "categories," supposed necessities, and of looking towards last things, fruits, consequences, facts.*

So much for the pragmatic method! You may say that I have been praising it rather than explaining it to you, but I shall presently explain it abundantly enough by showing how it works on some familiar problems. Meanwhile the word pragmatism has come to be used in a still wider sense, as meaning also a certain *theory of truth*. I mean to give a whole lecture to the statement of that theory, after first paving the way, so I can be very brief now. But brevity is hard to follow, so I ask for your redoubled attention for a quarter of an hour. If much remains obscure, I hope to make it clearer in the later lectures.

One of the most successfully cultivated branches of philosophy in our time is called inductive logic, the study of the conditions under which our sciences have evolved. Writers on this subject have begun to show a singular unanimity as to what the laws of nature and elements of fact mean, when formulated by mathematicians, physicists, and chemists. When the first mathematical, logical, and natural uniformities, the first *laws*, were discovered, men were so carried away by the clearness, beauty, and simplification that resulted, that they believed themselves to have deciphered authentically the eternal thoughts of the Almighty.

His mind also thundered and reverberated in syllogisms. He also thought in conic sections, squares and roots and ratios, and geometrized like Euclid. He made Kepler's laws for the planets to follow; he made velocity increase proportionally to the time in falling bodies; he made the law of the sines for light to obey when refracted; he established the classes, orders, families, and genera of plants and animals, and fixed the distances between them. He thought the archetypes of all things, and devised their variations; and when we rediscover any one of these his wondrous institutions, we seize his mind in its very literal intention.

But as the sciences have developed further, the notion has gained ground that most, perhaps all, of our laws are only approximations. The laws themselves, moreover, have grown so numerous that there is no counting them; and so many rival formulations are proposed in all the branches of science that investigators have become accustomed to the notion that no theory is absolutely a transcript of reality, but that any one of them may from some point of view be useful. Their great use is to summarize old facts and to lead to new ones. They are only a man-made language, a conceptual shorthand, as some one calls them, in which we write our reports of nature; and languages, as is well known, tolerate much choice of expression and many dialects.

Thus human arbitrariness has driven divine necessity from scientific logic. If I mention the names of Sigwart, Mach, Ostwald, Pearson, Milhaud, Poincaré, Duhem, Ruyssen, those of you who are students will easily identify the tendency I speak of, and will think of additional names.

Riding now on the front of this wave of scientific logic Messrs. Schiller and Dewey appear with their pragmatistic account of what truth everywhere signifies. Everywhere, these teachers say, "truth" in our ideas and beliefs means the same thing that it means in science. It means, they say, nothing but this, *that ideas (which themselves are but parts of our experience) become true just in so far as they help us to get into satisfactory relation with other parts of our experience,* to summarize them and get about among them by conceptual short-cuts instead of following the interminable succession of particular phenomena. Any idea upon which we can ride, so to speak; any idea that will carry us prosperously from any one part of our experience to any other part, linking things satisfactorily, working securely, simplifying, saving labor; is true for just so much, true in so far forth, true *instrumentally*. This is the "instrumental" view of truth taught so successfully at Chicago, the view that truth in our ideas means their power to "work," promulgated so brilliantly at Oxford.

Messrs. Dewey, Schiller and their allies, in reaching this general conception of all truth, have only followed the example of geologists, biologists, and philologists. In the establishment of these other sciences, the successful stroke was always to take simple process actually observable in operation—as denudation by weather, say, or variation from parental type, or change of dialect by incorporation of new words and pronunciations—and then to generalize it, making it apply to all times, and produce great results by summating its effects through the ages.

The observable process which Schiller and Dewey particularly singled out for generalization is the familiar one by which any individual settles into *new opinions*. The process here is always the same. The individual has a stock of old opinions already, but he meets a new experience that puts them to a strain. Somebody contradicts them; or in a reflective moment he discovers that they contradict each other; or he hears of facts with which they are incompatible; or desires arise in him which they cease to satisfy. The result is an inward trouble to which his mind till then had been a stranger, and from which he seeks to escape by modifying his previous mass of opinions. He saves as much of it as he can, for in this matter of belief we are all extreme conservatives. So he tries to change first this opinion, and then that (for they resist change very variously), until at last some new idea comes up which he can graft upon the ancient stock with a minimum of disturbance of the latter, some idea that mediates between the stock and the new experience and runs them into one another most felicitously and expediently.

This new idea is then adopted as the true one. It preserves the older stock of truths with a minimum of modification, stretching them just enough to make them admit the novelty, but conceiving that in ways as familiar as the case leaves possible. An *outrée* explanation, violating all our preconceptions, would never pass for a true account of a novelty. We should scratch round industriously till we found something less eccentric. The most violent revolutions in an individual's beliefs leave most of his old order standing. Time and space, cause and effect, nature and history, and one's own biography remain untouched. New truth is always a go-between, a smoother-over of transitions. It marries old opinion to new fact so as ever to show a minimum of jolt, a maximum of continuity. We hold a theory true just in proportion to its success in solving this "problem of maxima and minima." But success in solving this problem is eminently a matter of approximation. We say this theory solves it on the whole more satisfactorily than that theory; but that means more satisfactorily to ourselves, and individuals will emphasize their points of satisfaction differently. To a certain degree, therefore, everything here is plastic.

The point I now urge you to observe particularly is the part played by the older truths. Failure to take account of it is the source of much of the unjust criticism levelled against pragmatism. Their influence is absolutely controlling. Loyalty to them is the first principle—in most cases it is the only principle; for by far the most usual way of handling phenomena so novel that they would make for a serious rearrangement of our preconception is to ignore them altogether, or to abuse those who bear witness for them.

You doubtless wish examples of this

process of truth's growth, and the only trouble is their superabundance. The simplest case of new truth is of course the mere numerical addition of new kinds of facts, or of new single facts of old kinds, to our experience—an addition that involves no alteration in the old beliefs. Day follows day, and its contents are simply added. The new contents themselves are not true, they simply *come* and *are*. Truth is *what we say about* them, and when we say that they have come, truth is satisfied by the plain additive formula.

But often the day's contents oblige a re-arrangement. If I should now utter piercing shrieks and act like a maniac on this platform, it would make many of you revise your ideas as to the probable worth of my philosophy. "Radium" came the other day as part of the day's content, and seemed for a moment to contradict our ideas of the whole order of nature, that order having come to be identified with what is called the conservation of energy. The mere sight of radium paying heat away indefinitely out of its own pocket seemed to violate that conservation. What to think? If the radiations from it were nothing but an escape of unsuspected "potential" energy, pre-existent inside of the atoms, the principle of conservation would be saved. The discovery of "helium" as the radiation's outcome, opened a way to this belief. So Ramsay's view is generally held to be true, because, although it extends our old ideas of energy, it causes a minimum of alteration in their nature.

I need not multiply instances. A new opinion counts as "true" just in proportion as it gratifies the individual's desire to assimilate the novel in his experience to his beliefs in stock. It must both lean on old truth and grasp new fact; and its success (as I said a moment ago) in doing this, is a matter for the individual's appreciation. When old truth grows, then, by new truth's addition, it is for subjective reasons. We are in the process and obey the reasons. That new idea is truest which performs most felicitously its function of satisfying our double urgency. It makes itself true, gets itself classed as true, by the way it works; grafting itself then upon the ancient body of truth, which thus grows much as a tree grows by the activity of a new layer of cambium.

Now Dewey and Schiller proceed to generalize this observation and to apply it to the most ancient parts of truth. They also once were plastic. They also were called true for human reasons. They also mediated between still earlier truths and what in those days were novel observations. Purely objective truth, truth in whose establishment the function of giving human satisfaction in marrying previous parts of experience with newer parts played no role whatever, is nowhere to be found. The reason why we call things true is the reason why they *are* true, for "to be true" *means* only to perform this marriage-function.

The trail of the human serpent is thus over everything. Truth independent; truth that we *find* merely; truth no longer malleable to human need; truth incorrigible, in a word; such truth exists indeed superabundantly—or is supposed to exist by rationalistically minded, thinkers; but then it means only the dead heart of the living tree; and its being there means only that truth also has its paleontology, and its "prescription," and may grow stiff with years of veteran service and petrified in men's regard by sheer antiquity. But how plastic even the oldest truths nevertheless really are has been vividly shown in our day by the transformation of logical and mathematical ideas, a transformation which seems even to be invading physics. The ancient formulas are reinterpreted as special expressions of much wider principles, principles that our ancestors never got a glimpse of in their present shape and formulation.

• • •

I am well aware how odd it must seem to some of you to hear me say that an idea is "true" so long as to believe it is profitable to our lives. That it is *good*, for as much as it profits, you will gladly admit. If what we do by its aid is good, you will allow the idea itself to be good in so far forth, for we are the better for possessing it. But is it not a strange misuse of the word "truth," you will say, to call ideas also "true" for this reason?

To answer this difficulty fully is impossible at this stage of my account. You touch here upon the very central point of Messrs. Schiller's, Dewey's, and my own doctrine of truth, which I can not discuss with detail until my sixth lecture. Let me now say only this, that truth is *one species of good,* and not, as is usually supposed, a category distinct from good, and coordinate with it. *The true is the name of whatever proves itself to be good in the way of belief, and good, too, for definite assignable reasons.* Surely you must admit this, that if there were no good for life in true ideas, or if the knowledge of them were positively disadvantageous and false ideas the only useful ones, then the current notion that truth is divine and precious, and its pursuit a duty, could never have grown up or become a dogma. In a world like that, our duty would be to *shun* truth, rather. But in this world, just as certain foods are not only agreeable to our taste, but good for our teeth, our stomach, and our tissues; so certain ideas are not only agreeable to think about, or agreeable as supporting other ideas that we are fond of, but they are also helpful in life's practical struggles. If there be any life that it is really better we should lead, and if there be any idea which, if believed in, would help us to lead that life, then it would be really *better for us* to believe in that idea, *unless, indeed, belief in it incidentally clashed with other greater vital benefits.*

"What would be better for us to believe!" This sounds very like a definition of truth. It comes very near to saying "what we *ought* to believe": and in *that* definition none of you would find any oddity. Ought we ever not to believe what it is *better for us* to believe? And can we then keep the notion of what is better for us, and what is true for us, permanently apart?

Pragmatism says no, and I fully agree with her. Probably you also agree, so far as the abstract statement goes, but with a suspicion that if we practically did believe everything that made for good in our own personal lives, we should be found indulging all kinds of fancies about this world's affairs, and all kinds of sentimental superstitions about a world hereafter. Your suspicion here is undoubtedly well founded, and it is evident that something happens when you pass from the abstract to the concrete that complicates the situation.

I said just now that what is better for us to believe is true *unless the belief incidentally clashes with some other vital benefit.* Now in real life what vital benefits is any particular belief of ours most liable to clash with? What indeed except the vital benefits yielded by *other beliefs* when these prove incompatible with the first ones? In other words, the greatest enemy of any one of our truths may be the rest of our truths. Truths have once for all this desperate instinct of self-preservation and of desire to extinguish whatever contradicts them. My belief in the Absolute, based on the good it does me, must run the gauntlet of all my other beliefs. Grant that it may be true in giving me a moral holiday. Nevertheless, as I conceive it,—and let me speak now confidentially, as it were, and merely in my own private person,—it clashes with other truths of mine whose benefits I hate to give up on its account. It happens to be associated with a kind of logic of which I am the enemy, I find that it entangles me in metaphysical paradoxes that are inacceptable, etc., etc. But as I have enough trouble in life already without adding the trouble of carrying these intellectual inconsistencies, I personally just give up the Absolute. I just *take* my moral holidays; or else as a professional philosopher, I try to justify them by some other principle.

If I could restrict my notion of the Absolute to its bare holiday-giving value, it wouldn't clash with my other truths. But we can not easily thus restrict our hypotheses. They carry supernumerary features, and these it is that clash so. My disbelief in the Absolute means then disbelief in those other supernumerary features, for I fully believe in the legitimacy of taking moral holidays.

You see by this what I meant when I

called pragmatism a mediator and reconciler and said, borrowing the word from Papini, that she "unstiffens" our theories. She has in fact no prejudices whatever, no obstructive dogmas, no rigid canons of what shall count as proof. She is completely genial. She will entertain any hypothesis, she will consider any evidence. It follows that in the religious field she is at a great advantage both over positivistic empiricism, with its anti-theological bias, and over religious rationalism, with its exclusive interest in the remote, the noble, the simple, and the abstract in the way of conception.

In short, she widens the field of search for God. Rationalism sticks to logic and the empyrean. Empiricism sticks to the external senses. Pragmatism is willing to take anything, to follow either logic or the senses, and to count the humblest and most personal experiences. She will count mystical experiences if they have practical consequences. She will take a God who lives in the very dirt of private fact—if that should seem a likely place to find him.

Her only test of probable truth is what works best in the way of leading us, what fits every part of life best and combines with the collectivity of experience's demands, nothing being omitted. If theological ideas should do this, if the notion of God, in particular, should prove to do it, how could pragmatism possibly deny God's existence? She could see no meaning in treating as "not true" a notion that was pragmatically so successful. What other kind of truth could there be, for her, than all this agreement with concrete reality?

STUDY QUESTIONS

1. What does James mean by "the pragmatic method"? Do you think it is a satisfactory method for resolving disputes? Explain.
2. What does James mean by saying that theories become instruments? Instruments to accomplish what?
3. What, according to James, does "truth" mean? Do you think that his theory of truth is true? In answering this question do you adopt his conception of truth or rely on another one? If the latter, what is the conception of truth on which you rely?
4. Can you accept James' pragmatic justification for a belief in God? Why or why not?
5. Is a belief true because it works, or does it work because it is true? Do you think this is an important question? If so, what conclusions would you draw about the pragmatic theory of truth?

For Further Reading

Blanshard, B. *The Nature of Thought*. London: Allen and Unwin, 1939 (Vol. I, Chapter 10).

Dewey, J. *The Quest for Certainty*. New York: Minton, Balch, 1929.

———. *Reconstruction in Philosophy*. New York: Henry Holt, 1920.

James. W. "The Will to Believe."

Lovejoy, A. O. *The Thirteen Pragmatisms and Other Essays*. Baltimore: The Johns Hopkins Press, 1963 (esp. Chapters 1 and 4).

Moore, G. E. "William James' 'Pragmatism.' " In *Philosophical Studies*. London: Kegan & Paul, 1922 (Chapter 3).

Russell, B. *Philosophical Essays*. New York: Simon and Schuster, 1966 (Chapters 4 and 5).

INDEX